"These wonderful volumes on the Psalms place the whole church of Christ in their author's debt. To have carried to completion the vision of such a project is a breathtaking accomplishment. And to have done it with the author's characteristically loving and careful approach to the text of Scripture, coupled with richness of exposition, humility of spirit, and wise personal and pastoral application, stimulates our admiration and gratitude. In an era when the evangelical church in the West has, by and large, turned its back on the wisdom of two millennia of Christian praise dominated by the Psalms, these four magnificent volumes provide both the equipment and the inspiration needed to discover what our Lord and Savior himself experienced. They deserve to become—indeed, are surely destined to be—the go-to resource for multitudes of preachers, teachers, and students for decades to come. We are richer because of their publication."

Sinclair B. Ferguson, Chancellor's Professor of Systematic Theology, Reformed Theological Seminary; Teaching Fellow, Ligonier Ministries

"Since the Enlightenment, it has become fashionable to hypercontextualize the Psalms, thereby repudiating eighteen centuries of Christ-centered preaching, teaching, and scholarship. In this magisterial commentary, Christopher Ash returns to the old paths by displaying Christ and his glory in all 150 psalms. The Reformers and the Puritans would have loved this warm, devotional, and accessible work, for herein Ash provides the kind of experiential, practical, and Christ-saturated exegesis that they so dearly treasured. With careful historical-theological reflection and a tender pastoral heart, Ash guides the people of God as they seek to better read, sing, meditate on, study, and preach the Psalms. This commentary will no doubt become a staple in the pastor's library for many years to come."

Joel R. Beeke, Chancellor and Professor of Homiletics and Systematic Theology, Puritan Reformed Theological Seminary

"Modern readers often gravitate toward the Psalms because in them they see a mirror for themselves and their own emotions. This is not wrong, but as Christopher Ash reminds us, it is insufficient. The writers of the New Testament and many throughout church history read the Psalms because in them they found Christ. Ash provides a comprehensive help to the church to read the Psalms afresh from that Christ-centered perspective, in a way that not only exercises our minds but feeds our souls."

Iain M. Duguid, Professor of Old Testament, Westminster Theological Seminary

"How easy it is to quickly read ourselves into the center of the Psalms, and yet how important it is *not* to do this. Christopher Ash can be counted on to see a psalm in its real setting, grasp its proper culmination in Christ, and tell its rich implications to us. Few writers think with as much faithfulness or illumination as Ash does, and these volumes will be the new treasure chest in learning and psalmody."

Simon Manchester, Former Rector, St. Thomas' Anglican Church, North Sydney, Australia

"In this four-volume work, Christopher Ash casts a vision of the Psalter that is theologically centered on Christ, typologically related to Christ, and ultimately fulfilled in Christ—a book of the Old Testament that reveals, in type and shadow, through image of king and priest, prophet and teacher, supplicant and sufferer, the divinity and humanity of Christ, who in his humanity perfectly expressed the full range of human emotions and affections in the vicissitudes of his earthly humiliation as he awaited his heavenly exaltation. Therefore, he is the true and better singer of the Psalter, the one through whom and in union with whom the Christian and the church today can sing 'the Psalms of Jesus' with eyes unveiled. Encyclopedic in scope, enlightening in content, enthusing in purpose—this magnum opus ought to find a place in every pastor's library, in every student's book budget, and on every Christian's bedside table. These volumes will hopefully change the way we read—and sing!—the Psalms for years to come."

Jonathan Gibson, Associate Professor of Old Testament, Westminster Theological Seminary

"This is a landmark commentary that belongs in the library of every Bible teacher and scholar. Grounded in wide-ranging research, warmed by sincere devotion, and crafted with unusual elegance, this work offers the reader an exegetical and theological feast for both heart and mind. Any believer who has studied and taught the Psalms knows the challenge of handling them in faithfulness as truly Christian Scripture. In these pages Ash has pursued the compelling thesis that the Psalms are emphatically Christ centered from beginning to end, having Christ as their true subject and object. For those who wish to understand how and why this is so, this study is both a treasure and a delight."

Jonathan Griffiths, Lead Pastor, The Metropolitan Bible Church, Ottawa, Canada

"How pleasing it is to find a modern, scholarly commentary that unashamedly leads us to Jesus the Messiah! The case for this Christ-centered work is carefully argued and applied to each psalm without ignoring original contexts or their relevance to believers. More controversially, Christopher Ash provides the most compelling defense to date for accepting every penitential and imprecatory line in the Psalter as appropriate on the lips of the sinless Savior, the Christian's covenant head. Helpful quotations from early Christian writers, the Reformers, and contemporary authors add to the commentary's appeal. I warmly recommend it."

Philip H. Eveson, Former Principal and Old Testament Tutor, London Seminary; author, *Psalms: From Suffering to Glory*

"To simply call this resource a commentary seems too mundane. What Christopher Ash presents us with here is an extensive and detailed exploration of the verdant theological landscape of the Psalter, with Jesus the Messiah as the lodestar. These remarkable volumes are weighty but not burdensome, erudite but not arid. Ash's pastoral insights into the Psalms reflect a maturity and wisdom that can be cultivated only over a lifetime spent in the full counsel of Scripture and ministry in the church. What a tremendous achievement this is, what a blessing it is sure to be to the church, and what a testament to the beauty and transforming power of the true and final King, Jesus Christ."

William A. Ross, Associate Professor of Old Testament, Reformed Theological Seminary, Charlotte

"With historical breadth, exegetical finesse, rhetorical care, and a deeply doxological thrust, Christopher Ash's commentary brings the Psalms closer to the center of Christian devotion—and Jesus Christ to the very center of the Psalter. These wonderful volumes have helped me grasp, more deeply than ever before, just why Dietrich Bonhoeffer called the Psalms an 'incomparable treasure.' More than that, they have revealed the incomparable treasure himself who sings in every psalm yet whose voice we so often fail to hear."

Scott Hubbard, Editor, Desiring God; Pastor, All Peoples Church, Minneapolis, Minnesota

"This new commentary—in which 'the person of Christ is central to the meaning and force of every psalm'—is theologically rich, spiritually refreshing, and carefully assembled to understand Old and New Testament themes in the light of Christ. Here is a commentary that will be rewarding in the study as the minister prepares to teach the Psalms or, indeed, the many New Testament passages that reference them. This is also great material for personal devotions. Thank you, Christopher Ash, for such a rich resource to help us know Christ."

Nat Schluter, Principal, Johannesburg Bible College

"A masterful balance of being thoughtfully Christ centered and warmly devotional at the same time. A blessing for my personal quiet time and my sermon preparation."

Denesh Divyanathan, Senior Pastor, The Crossing Church, Singapore; Chairman, Evangelical Theological College of Asia; President, Project Timothy Singapore

The Psalms

A Christ-Centered Commentary

Other Crossway Books by Christopher Ash

The Heart of Anger: How the Bible Transforms Anger in Our Understanding and Experience, coauthored with Steve Midgley (2021)

Job: The Wisdom of the Cross (2014)

Married for God: Making Your Marriage the Best It Can Be (2016)

Trusting God in the Darkness: A Guide to Understanding the Book of Job (2021)

The Psalms

A Christ-Centered Commentary

VOLUME 3
PSALMS 51–100

Christopher Ash

WHEATON, ILLINOIS

The Psalms: A Christ-Centered Commentary, Volume 3, *Psalms 51–100*

© 2024 by Christopher Brian Garton Ash

Published by Crossway
        1300 Crescent Street
        Wheaton, Illinois 60187

Portions of this work are adapted from Christopher Ash, *Bible Delight: Heartbeat of the Word of God; Psalm 119 for the Bible Teacher and Bible Hearer* (Fearn, Ross-shire, Scotland: Christian Focus, 2008); Ash, *Psalms for You: How to Pray, How to Feel, and How to Sing* (Epsom, UK: Good Book, 2020); and Ash, *Teaching Psalms: From Text to Message*, 2 vols. (Fearn, Ross-shire, Scotland: Christian Focus, 2017–2018). Used by permission of the publishers.

Cover design: Jordan Singer

First printing 2024

Printed in the United States of America

All emphases in Scripture quotations have been added by the author.

Hardcover ISBN (vol. 3): 978-1-4335-6393-5
ePub ISBN (vol. 3): 978-1-4335-6396-6
PDF ISBN (vol. 3): 978-1-4335-6394-2
Hardcover ISBN (4-vol. set): 978-1-4335-6388-1
ePub ISBN (4-vol. set): 978-1-4335-8843-3
PDF ISBN (4-vol. set): 978-1-4335-8841-9

Library of Congress Control Number: 2023938846

Crossway is a publishing ministry of Good News Publishers.

SH			33	32	31	30	29	28	27	26	25	24
15	14	13	12	11	10	9	8	7	6	5	4	3	2	1

To Tyndale House, Cambridge,
a fellowship of delight
in the Scriptures (Ps. 1:2).

Jesus, my shepherd, brother, friend,
my prophet, priest, and king,
my Lord, my life, my way, my end,
accept the praise I bring.

JOHN NEWTON
"How Sweet the Name of Jesus Sounds"

Contents

PREFACE

The Nature and Purpose of This Commentary

I am persuaded that the Psalms belong to Jesus Christ. I believe that the Psalms themselves point to a fulfillment only possible in the divine-human person of Christ. Through its quotations and echoes of the Psalms, the New Testament bears witness to a textured understanding in which Christ is central. For the larger part of church history, this has broadly been the way Christians have read the Psalms. This commentary is therefore a Christ-centered commentary, in which I seek to see Christ front and center when reading the Psalms. I have attempted to explain and argue my case in volume 1, *Introduction: Christ and the Psalms*.

Since the so-called "Enlightenment" in the eighteenth century, Christ has been eclipsed in much Psalms scholarship and preaching. With a few notable exceptions, recent commentaries tend either to omit Christ from many or all of the Psalms or mention him as little more than an afterthought. But I have become persuaded that Jesus Christ is the subject and object of the Psalms, that his majestic divine-human person is woven into the warp and woof of the Psalter, and that he is the preeminent singer of psalms, the focus of the Psalter, and the one without whom the Psalms cannot be understood aright. I therefore want to place Christ in the foreground of our reading of every psalm and to do so in ways that are shaped by the New Testament. I want to set before us what the Psalms might look and feel like if in truth they do belong to Christ.

There is much you will not find in this commentary. My background is that of a preacher and pastor rather than a trained biblical scholar. I have sought to interact with a representative sample of writers across the centuries (surveyed in volume 1, *Introduction: Christ and the Psalms*) but have not, for the most part, attempted to interact with the voluminous and ever-growing secondary literature. I hope I am sufficiently aware of the more significant debates, but for a full study of these things, readers should consult one or more of the recent technical commentaries. I have worked from the Hebrew text but have no particular expertise in the language, especially as regards Hebrew poetry, translation of tense forms, and poetic parallelism. Much scholarly debate surrounds theories of the dating, possible contexts of origins, and putative redaction histories of various psalms. Too often it seems to me that scholars construct theories on the basis of inadequate evidence; furthermore, I am not persuaded that these debates are always useful to Christian disciples seeking to weave the Psalms into their lives of prayer and praise.

This commentary is not, therefore, a substitute for technical, scholarly commentaries. What you will find here, I hope, is the Psalms read with the breadth of a whole-Bible perspective allied with the depth of a clear focus on Christ, the center of history and the fulcrum of the Bible story. I thus hope to do four things:

1. To help you understand the lyrics of these songs, what the words mean and what the poetry signifies
2. To assist us in feeling the "tune," that is, the affectional and emotional dimensions of these songs
3. To point to the volitional commitment that is asked of disciples when we join in the Psalms—for to say the Psalms means moving from the audience, where we listen without commitment, to the choir, where commitment is expected
4. To motivate you to take that step and actively to make the Psalms a part of your lives of prayer and praise

I hope this commentary will prove useful to all kinds of Christian people—and especially to those who preach, teach, or lead studies on the Psalms.

How Each Psalm Is Treated

After one or more chapter epigraphs of quotations from other writers, each psalm is considered in three sections.

The *orientation* section involves consideration of how we ought to view the psalm in the light of Jesus Christ. This includes reference to New Testament quotations and echoes and to the context of the psalm in history (if known) and in its canonical context, especially with reference to nearby psalms. I hope that setting this section first helps the reader engage in a manner that places Christ at the center, rather than on the periphery.

The *text* section begins with consideration of the structure. Since there is an extraordinarily wide variation in perceived structures, I have sought to be cautious and tentative except where the structure seems very clear. The *text* section continues with verse-by-verse commentary, taking into account the *orientation* section and seeking to make clear the meaning of the words and lines as well as the flow of the poetry.

The *reflection and response* section points to what a Christian response might look like when appropriating this psalm.

Three Questions in Psalms Interpretation

Three questions are often asked when reading the Psalms that merit even concise mention at the outset of this commentary. For a fuller discussion, please see volume 1, *Introduction: Christ and the Psalms*. These questions, with my very brief conclusions, are listed below.

1. Who are "the righteous"? A careful analysis of the Psalms gives us a portrait of those who delight in the covenant God and find assurance of final vindication in him. This assurance is rooted in the righteousness of their covenant head. Because neither David nor his successors lived with perfect righteousness, they clearly foreshadow another covenant head who will. "The righteous" in the Psalms, then, are righteous by faith in the covenant God.

2. Can Jesus Christ be considered to be praying the Psalms when the psalmists confess their sins and plead for forgiveness? My conclusion is that he does so as the covenant head of a sinful people, just as he submitted to John the Baptist's baptism of repentance. The shadow of the cross fell on him, who had no sin, as he prayed these psalms and our sin was imputed to him.

3. How are we to understand the prayers for God to punish the wicked in the Psalms? A study of the New Testament supports the

conclusion that Jesus Christ prays these prayers from a pure heart, and so we pray them—cautiously and with trembling—in him. Every time we pray, "Your kingdom come," in the Lord's Prayer, we pray for this punishment on the *finally* impenitent, even as we pray for many to repent before it is too late.

The Superscriptions and the Shape of the Psalter

Much scholarly attention has focused in recent years on the canonical order of the Psalms and the ways in which the five books of the Psalms and the superscriptions may help us understand the significance of this order. I am persuaded that the canonical order is as much the fruit of the Holy Spirit's direction as is the composition of the Psalms themselves. But I have sought to be cautious in making claims about discerning the meaning of this structure in detail. At the start of each book of the Psalter, I have included a very brief introduction to that book.

I accept the reliability of the superscriptions, while recognizing that we do not understand all the terms used in them. I have commented briefly on these terms (and the word *Selah*) the first time each appears. In particular, I accept that "of David" and similar expressions indicate authorship, and I have sought to argue this position (a minority among scholars) in volume 1, *Introduction: Christ and the Psalms.*

Texts and Translations

I have followed the normal Jewish and Christian understanding that the Masoretic Text is the most reliable witness to the original form of the texts. Some modern translations give considerable weight to the Greek translations (and sometimes also to the Dead Sea Scrolls and the ancient Versions), but I have erred on the side of caution, except where there are overwhelming reasons for rejecting the Masoretic Text. I have indicated where there is significant uncertainty.

When quoting Hebrew or Greek, I provide both the original forms and the transliteration in the main text. In footnotes I provide only the original Hebrew or Greek.

I have used the English Standard Version (ESV) as my base text (though I have at times taken liberty to break stanzas differently from the ESV). I have found this an admirable translation for the purposes of detailed study. Where there are significant differences, I have sometimes referred to the Christian Standard Bible (CSB), the King James Version (KJV), the New American Standard Bible (NASB), the New International Version (NIV), the New Revised Standard Version (NRSV), and the Revised English Bible (REB).

Hebrew Tense Forms

Scholars vary in the terminology they use for the two tense forms in Hebrew. One form may be called the perfect, the perfective, the suffix conjugation, or the *qatal*. The other may be called the imperfect, the imperfective, the prefix conjugation, or the *yiqtol*. For simplicity I use the traditional terminology *perfect* and *imperfect*, even though these do not translate simply into English perfect or imperfect tenses, especially in poetry. In general, it may be true that an imperfect form conveys an action that is continuing (typically but not always future), while a perfect form indicates an action that is completed (typically but not always past). But there are many exceptions (especially when following the *vav consecutive*).

The Divine Name "the LORD"

The Hebrew name יהוה, or *YHWH*, often written *Yahweh* and sometimes called the tetragrammaton (after its four consonants), is written "LORD" in quotations from the biblical text (in line with the usual convention for English translations). Outside quotations, I prefer to use the phrases *covenant Lord* or *covenant God*, rather than the word *Yahweh*, partly because we do not know for sure how it was pronounced but mainly because it captures the strong Old Testament context of covenantal lordship.

The Davidic King

When speaking of the Davidic king/King, I have generally capitalized *King* to encourage the reader to think toward the fulfillment of Davidic kingship in Christ, the final King. I have typically used the lowercase *king* when referring exclusively to an old covenant king, whether David or one of his successors.

Psalm Numbering

I have numbered the Psalms according to the Masoretic Text and all English translations throughout. Most patristic writers followed the Psalm chapter numbering in, or derived from, the Greek translations. This numbering differs from the Hebrew numbering as shown in table 1. So, for example, when commenting on what our English Bibles call Psalm 107, Augustine of Hippo (354–430) refers to it as Psalm 106. But even when referring to the Septuagint or Vulgate, I have translated into the Masoretic Text numbering.

Table 1 Psalm Numbering in English and Greek Versions

Psalm Number in English Versions	Psalm Number in Greek Versions
Pss. 1–8	Unchanged: Pss. 1–8
Pss. 9–10	Combined into Ps. 9
Pss. 11–113	One less: Pss. 10–112
Pss. 114–115	Combined into Ps. 113
Ps. 116	Split into Pss. 114 and 115
Pss. 117–146	One less: Pss. 116–145
Ps. 147	Split into Pss. 146 and 147
Pss. 148–150	Unchanged: Pss. 148–150

Verse Numbering

I have used English verse numbering throughout, with superscriptions labeled *S*. Where a psalm has more than a very short superscription, the Masoretic Text usually designates the superscription verse 1, increasing all subsequent verse numbers by one. Otherwise, the superscription forms the start of verse 1. I have noted this feature when commenting on each superscription.

ABBREVIATIONS

AB	Anchor Bible
ACCS	*Ancient Christian Commentary on Scripture*. Edited by Thomas C. Oden. Downers Grove, IL: InterVarsity Press, 1998–2010.
ACW	Ancient Christian Writers
AD	*anno Domini*, "in the year of the Lord," often called the Common Era, CE
BC	before Christ, sometimes called before the Common Era, BCE
BCOTWP	Baker Commentary on the Old Testament Wisdom and Psalms
BDB	Brown, Francis, S. R. Driver, and Charles A. Briggs. *A Hebrew Lexicon of the Old Testament*. Oxford: Clarendon Press, 1906.
BECNT	Baker Exegetical Commentary on the New Testament
BHS	*Biblia Hebraica Stuttgartensia*. Edited by Karl Elliger and Wilhelm Rudolph. Stuttgart: Deutsche Bibelgesellschaft, 1983.
ca.	*circa*, "approximately"
CBSC	Cambridge Bible for Schools and Colleges
CC	Continental Commentaries
CFTL	Clark's Foreign Theological Library
chap(s).	chapter(s)
CNTOT	*Commentary on the New Testament Use of the Old Testament*. Edited by G. K. Beale and D. A. Carson. Grand Rapids, MI: Baker Academic, 2007.
CSC	Crossway Short Classics
DSS	Dead Sea Scrolls
EBTC	Evangelical Biblical Theology Commentary
e.g.	*exempli gratia*, "for example"

esp.	especially
etc.	*et cetera*, "and so forth"
FC	Fathers of the Church
HALOT	*The Hebrew and Aramaic Lexicon of the Old Testament.* Ludwig Koehler, Walter Baumgartner, and Johann J. Stamm. Translated and edited under the supervision of Mervyn E. J. Richardson. 4 vols. Leiden: Brill, 1994–1999.
IBC	Interpretation: A Bible Commentary for Teaching and Preaching
i.e.	*id est*, "that is"
JBL	*Journal of Biblical Literature*
JSOTSup	Journal for the Study of the Old Testament Supplement Series
KEL	Kregel Exegetical Library
lit.	literally
LXX	Septuagint (Greek translation of the Hebrew Scriptures)
MC	A Mentor Commentary
MT	Masoretic Text
NCB	New Century Bible
NIVAC	NIV Application Commentary
NSBT	New Studies in Biblical Theology
NT	New Testament
OT	Old Testament
RCS	*Reformation Commentary on Scripture.* Edited by Timothy George and Scott M. Manetsch. Downers Grove, IL: IVP Academic, 2011–.
SBLDS	Society of Biblical Literature Dissertation Series
SBT	Studies in Biblical Theology
SJT	*Scottish Journal of Theology*
SSBT	Short Studies in Biblical Theology
SSLL	Studies in Semitic Languages and Linguistics
s.v.	*sub verbo*, "under the word"
THOTC	Two Horizons Old Testament Commentary
TOTC	Tyndale Old Testament Commentaries
trans.	translator, translated by
Vg.	Vulgate (Jerome's Latin translation of the Bible)
WBC	Word Biblical Commentary
WCS	Welwyn Commentary Series

Commentary on

PSALMS 51–100

BOOK 2 (*CONTINUED*)

———

BOOK 2 OF THE PSALTER runs from Psalm 42 to Psalm 72. Unlike almost all of book 1, Psalms 42–50 do not have David's name in the superscription. Psalms 42–49 are "of the sons of Korah" (except Ps. 43; see vol. 2), and Psalm 50 is "of Asaph." From Psalm 51 onward, "of David" is usually present again. At the end of the book, we read, "The prayers of David, the son of Jesse, are ended" (Ps. 72:20), signaling (it is usually thought) the end of the earliest "David collection." This may mean that Psalms 42–49 were also composed by David and performed by the sons of Korah and by Asaph; this was the most common view among the ancient writers but is less popular today.

Book 2 also begins a group of psalms (Pss. 42–83) with a marked preference for the general word "God" (אֵל, *El*, or אֱלֹהִים, *Elohim*) rather than "the LORD."[1] The most obvious example of this phenomenon is the virtual repetition of Psalm 14 in Psalm 53 but with the change of divine name. We do not know the reason for the preference for "God" in these psalms.[2]

---

1 Pss. 42–83 are sometimes referred to as the so-called Elohistic Psalter. The difference in divine names is quite striking. In these psalms, יהוה appears 45 times and the general terms 210 times. In the rest of the Psalter, יהוה appears 584 times and the general terms only 94 times. Mitchell Dahood (1922–1982), *Psalms*, 3 vols., AB (New York: Doubleday, 1965), 1:256.

2 For further discussion, see Bruce K. Waltke, James M. Houston, and Erika Moore, *The Psalms as Christian Lament: A Historical Commentary* (Grand Rapids, MI: Eerdmans, 2014), 185n62.

Listen to [David] crying out, and cry with him; listen to him groaning, and groan too; listen to him weeping, and add your tears to his; listen to him corrected, and share his joy. . . . The prophet Nathan was sent to that man; and notice how humble the king was. He did not brush his mentor's words aside, nor did he demand, "How dare you speak to me like this? I am the king!" King in his majesty though he was, he listened to the prophet; now let Christ's lowly people listen to Christ.

AUGUSTINE
Expositions of the Psalms

This is the most deeply affecting of all the Psalms, and I am sure the one most applicable to me.

THOMAS CHALMERS
In Charles H. Spurgeon, *The Treasury of David*

Each solitary sin, the more it is perceived in its fundamental character, and, as it were, microscopically discerned, all the more does it appear as a manifold and entangled skein of sins, and stands forth in a still more intimate and terrible relation, as of cause and effect, to the whole corrupt and degenerated condition of which the sinner finds himself.

FRANZ DELITZSCH
Biblical Commentary on the Psalms

PSALM 51

ORIENTATION

Jesus teaches that we ought to confess our sins in the manner of Psalm 51. When the prodigal son addresses his father with the words, "Father, I have sinned against heaven. . . . I am no longer worthy" (Luke 15:21), he follows the pattern of the psalm: he acknowledges his guilt fully, he confesses his sin clearly, he is forgiven and cleansed completely, and the story ends with a meal that restores to him the joy of his salvation.[1] When the tax collector beats his breast and says, "God, be merciful to me, a sinner!" (Luke 18:13), his prayer is "in effect the opening words of Psalm 51."[2]

Jesus is the glorious solution to the desperate predicament of this psalm. He is the sacrifice whose propitiation makes forgiveness assured for each believer who prays these words. Paul quotes Psalm 51:4b in Romans 3:4. Just as Psalm 51:4b expresses David's admission that he fully deserves whatever punishment he may receive, so in Romans 3:4 Paul teaches that humankind fully deserves God's punishment. Only the propitiatory death of Christ, which he goes on to expound (Rom. 3:21–26), can give us hope.

Further, we observe that in its first praying, this is a prayer of the king. The prayer for Zion (the people of God) in Psalm 51:18–19 suggests that this is important.[3] The singer is not any old individual sinner but the king; this is why his restoration is the key to the rebuilding of the walls of

---

1 Frank Lothar Hossfeld (1942–2015) and Erich Zenger (1939–2010), *Psalms*, trans. Linda M. Maloney, ed. Klaus Baltzer, 3 vols., Hermeneia (Minneapolis: Fortress, 2005–2011), 2:24–25.
2 J. L. Mays (1921–2015), *Psalms*, IBC (Louisville: John Knox, 1994), 199.
3 This is rightly noted by John Goldingay, *Psalms*, 3 vols., BCOTWP (Grand Rapids, MI: Baker Academic, 2006–2008), 2:125.

Jerusalem, for "the people stood and fell with [the king]."[4] This may point to a connection at a deeper level between David the sinful king and Jesus our sinless King. What if Jesus Christ actually prays Psalm 51?

I have argued that this is the most plausible reading of Psalms 6, 32, and 38, all of them psalms of repentance.[5] But Psalm 51 is a peculiarly intense case, including as it does repentance from original sin (51:5); this leads many to feel that Jesus cannot possibly pray this psalm of repentance, even if he may pray the others.[6] But we need to ponder the very depths of his atoning sacrifice, in which he was made sin for us (2 Cor. 5:21). Every facet and character of our sin (and David's sin) was taken by Jesus on himself, including original sin (our sin in our sinful origins). All this he made his own for us; had it not been so, his atoning death would have been insufficient for our righteousness. Jesus Christ, who was himself without sin (Heb. 4:15), took on himself even David's cry "I was brought forth in iniquity." It may be, therefore, that we should read even Psalm 51 as a prayer of Jesus as he enters into the misery of our sins for us.

Not all will be persuaded that this is so. If we are, it is important to be clear that Jesus does not repent in our place,[7] for we must repent and pray the psalm for ourselves. Nevertheless, in Psalm 51 Jesus demonstrates a horror at sin and a resolute turning from sin that together constitute a perfect repentance. Neither we nor David repents perfectly. The turning of the sinless Jesus from our sin as it envelops him is a most wonderful facet of the active obedience of Jesus Christ in his earthly life. We are saved by his sin-bearing death; we are not saved by his repentance.

---

4   E. W. Hengstenberg (1802–1869), *Commentary on the Psalms*, trans. P. Fairbairn and J. Thomson, 3 vols., CFTL 1–2, 12 (Edinburgh: T&T Clark, 1845), 2:183.

5   In this paragraph and the next I am indebted to Garry Williams and Philip Eveson (through personal correspondence), whose different perspectives have helped me clarify in my mind the theological issues involved here.

6   E.g., Andrew A. Bonar (1810–1892), *Christ and His Church in the Book of Psalms* (London: J. Nisbet, 1859), 160.

7   It seems that Richard Belcher comes close to saying this when he writes, "Christ vicariously confessed and repented in our behalf." Richard P. Belcher Jr., *The Messiah and the Psalms: Preaching Christ from All the Psalms* (Fearn, Ross-Shire, Scotland: Mentor, 2006), 87. Ferguson rightly states that "the NT knows no such category as the perfect vicarious repentance of Christ." Sinclair B. Ferguson, "'Blessèd Assurance, Jesus Is Mine'? Definite Atonement and the Cure of Souls," in *From Heaven He Came and Sought Her: Definite Atonement in Historical, Biblical, Theological, and Pastoral Perspective*, ed. David Gibson and Jonathan Gibson (Wheaton, IL: Crossway, 2013), 621.

Nevertheless, he does not simply instruct us to pray Psalm 51; perhaps he leads us in praying it.

Psalm 51 is linked to Psalm 50 by the motif of sacrifice and the question of what sacrifices are acceptable to God (50:9–14; 51:16–19).[8] Psalm 50:23 mentions both sacrifice and the right ordering of one's moral way; both of these lead naturally to Psalm 51.[9] The theme of instruction (51:13–15) links back to Psalm 49.

This is the fourth of the seven traditional penitential psalms.[10] The connection between Psalms 32 and 51 may be that Psalm 51 is David's first (heartfelt) confession and that Psalm 32 later fulfills the pledge of Psalm 51:13 to teach transgressors his ways.

In the Davidic psalms of book 2 (most of those from Pss. 51 to 71), there is perhaps a deliberate and suggestive inclusio. Psalm 51 is David's repentance after going in to Bathsheba. Psalm 72 celebrates the peaceful messianic reign connected to Bathsheba's son Solomon.[11] Here is a cameo of amazing grace.

THE TEXT

Structure

Several structures have been suggested, each with some justification.[12] To my mind, the most persuasive may be as follows: Psalm 51:1–9 focuses mainly on prayer for forgiveness (bracketed by "blot out");[13] 51:10–17 shifts the focus toward prayer for personal renewal (bracketed by a clean heart and right spirit and by a broken spirit and broken and contrite heart),

---

8   "It is as though the warning of judgment in Psalm 50 prompts the sincere repentance in Psalm 51. Psalm 50:18 denounced adulterers, and the wider context of Psalm 50 presents the Lord coming in judgment (cf. 50:1–6). The terrible prospect of judgment crushes David's rebellion and puts him on his knees in Psalm 51, crying out for mercy from the one whose righteousness his sin offended." James M. Hamilton Jr., *Psalms*, 2 vols., EBTC (Bellingham, WA: Lexham, 2021), 1:506.

9   Sidney Greidanus, *Preaching Christ from Psalms: Foundations for Expository Sermons in the Christian Year* (Grand Rapids, MI: Eerdmans, 2016), 241.

10   The traditional penitential psalms are Pss. 6, 32, 38, 51, 102, 130, 143.

11   Hossfeld and Zenger, *Psalms*, 2:18.

12   See the useful discussions of structure in Greidanus, *Preaching Christ from Psalms*, 248–50; Belcher, *Messiah and the Psalms*, 252n62. The many repetitions of words are noted in Goldingay, *Psalms*, 2:124.

13   Goldingay suggests a chiastic structure within Ps. 51:1–9. Goldingay, *Psalms*, 2:130–31.

leading naturally in to 51:18–19, which is a prayer for the renewal of the people of God.

Within this structure we may also note that (1) 51:13–15 has a theme of the King speaking to others; (2) 51:16–19 shares a theme of sacrifice; and (3) some of 51:1–9 anticipates renewal (e.g., 51:6, 8), while some of 51:10–17 returns to the motif of forgiveness (esp. 51:14a).

Superscription

^S   To the choirmaster.[14] A Psalm of David, when Nathan the prophet went to him, after he had gone in to Bathsheba.[15]

Although this psalm is suitable "for the loneliness of individual penitence," the designation **To the choirmaster** suggests that "this matchless Psalm is equally well adapted for the assembly of the poor in spirit."[16] It is a remarkable testimony to God's grace in David that he should make his intensely personal repentance so public, for true repentance is a deeply humbling work of grace; it both instructs us and provokes us to a like repentance.[17]

If, as has been suggested, Psalm 51:18–19 refers to the rebuilding of Jerusalem after the exile,[18] then these verses may be a later Spirit-inspired editorial addition. But there is no reason why David himself, as a prophet, should not have prayed them, and it is better to suppose that he did.

The drama **when Nathan the prophet went to him, after he had gone in to Bathsheba,** is recorded in 2 Samuel 12:1–15. The Hebrew for **went to** and **gone in to** is identical:[19] David went in to Bathsheba (he lay with her), and as a result, the prophet Nathan went in to David (with words of rebuke), the sinful pleasure of the one balanced by the painful mercy of the

---

14   See on Ps. 4.

15   The other historical superscriptions are for Pss. 3, 7, 18, 34, 52, 54, 56, 57, 59, 60, 63, 142. In Hebrew the superscription is verses 1–2; subsequent verse numbers are increased by two.

16   Charles H. Spurgeon (1834–1892), *The Treasury of David*, 3 vols. (Peabody, MA: Hendrickson, 2016), 1.2:401.

17   Hengstenberg, *Psalms*, 2:189.

18   E.g., A. F. Kirkpatrick (1849–1940), *The Book of Psalms: With Introduction and Notes*, 3 vols., CBSC 20 (Cambridge: Cambridge University Press, 1892), 2:285.

19   בּוֹא אֶל.

other. There are verbal connections between this incident and the psalm, including the phrase "evil in [God's] sight" (2 Sam. 12:9; Ps. 51:4) and the language of sin against God (2 Sam. 12:13; Ps. 51:4).[20] David's response to Nathan is remarkable, for "no other king of his time would have felt any compunction for having acted as he did."[21]

51:1–9 Prayer for Forgiveness

¹ Have mercy on me, O God,
        according to your steadfast love;
    according to your abundant mercy
        blot out my transgressions.
² Wash me thoroughly from my iniquity,
        and cleanse me from my sin!

Three words for comprehensive sin and three words for abundant cleansing begin David's passionate prayer. **Transgression** means active rebellion against God;[22] **iniquity** indicates a twisting, perversion, or depravity from the straight and right way; and **sin** denotes a wandering or missing of the moral mark.[23] Together they speak of sin in all its ugly fullness, for "the pollution of sin goes through the whole powers of the soul and body, . . . through mind, will, affections, senses, bodily and all."[24] The verbs for cleansing are **blot out** (also Ps. 51:9), the erasure or cancellation of a debt in God's book (e.g., Isa. 43:25; 44:22; cf. Acts 3:19; Col. 2:14) or the removal of dirt (e.g., from a bowl, 2 Kings 21:13); **wash**, used of the vigorous washing of very dirty clothes (cf. Isa. 1:16; Jer. 2:22; 4:14)[25] and often of ritual

---

20 These and others are noted in Greidanus, *Preaching Christ from Psalms*, 242.

21 Spurgeon, *Treasury*, 1.2:401.

22 Dahood, *Psalms*, 2:2–3. Eveson has "wilful defiance." Philip Eveson, *Psalms: From Suffering to Glory*, 2 vols., WCS (Darlington, UK: EP Books, 2014–2015), 1:324.

23 Kirkpatrick, *Psalms*, 2:288; Allen P. Ross, *A Commentary on the Psalms*, 3 vols., KEL (Grand Rapids, MI: Kregel, 2011), 2:187n25. These three nouns appear in Ex. 34:7 in the context of covenant mercy (cf. Ps. 32:1–2).

24 David Dickson (1583–1663), *A Commentary on the Psalms* (London: Banner of Truth, 1959), 1:304.

25 Franz Delitzsch (1813–1890) suggests "deeply ingrained dirt." F. Delitzsch, *Biblical Commentary on the Psalms*, trans. Francis Bolton, CFTL, 4th ser., vols. 29–31 (Edinburgh: T&T Clark, 1892), 2:135.

purification (e.g., Ex. 19:10); and **cleanse**, also associated with ritual cleansing, particularly of lepers (e.g., Lev. 13:6).[26] A comparably deep cleansing is prophesied in Isaiah 4:4.

In Psalm 51:1b the word translated **mercy** conveys compassion (used of Joseph in Gen. 43:30, fulfilled when Jesus is moved with compassion). There is a play on abundance: **abundant** and **thoroughly** have the same root. We might translate it "According to your abundant kindness . . . wash me abundantly." The focus is on God (**O God . . . your steadfast love . . . your abundant mercy**) before it is on David and his sin. He begins with God, in the fullness of his covenantal attributes, before speaking of his sin. Martin Luther (1483–1546) vividly contrasts "God in general or absolute terms," from whom we must flee, with God here "as He is dressed and clothed in His Word and promises, so that from the name 'God' we cannot exclude Christ."[27]

> 3   For I know my transgressions,
>   and my sin is ever before me.

To **know** here means not simply "to be cognizant of" or even "to acknowledge" but to be deeply aware. There is a connection here with Romans 3, which quotes Psalm 51:4b, for true knowledge begins with "knowledge of sin" (Rom. 3:20), as this psalm demonstrates.[28] Here is a man who knows in experience "the intolerable burden of the wrath of God," for he "is oppressed by his conscience and tossed to and fro, not knowing where to turn."[29] Psalm 32:3–4 is almost a commentary on this verse. The second line intensifies the first with the phrase **before me** (both "in my consciousness" and "opposite me, against me" as my accuser)[30] and the word **ever**, for until he is cleansed, he cannot put these sins behind him.

---

26 Kirkpatrick, *Psalms*, 2:288; Ross, *Psalms*, 2:188n26.

27 Martin Luther, *Luther's Works*, ed. Jaroslav Pelikan (Saint Louis, MO: Concordia, 1958), 12:312; 14:166.

28 The profound connection between Ps. 51 and Rom. 1:18–3:31 is persuasively argued in Hossfeld and Zenger, *Psalms*, 2:25; Richard B. Hays, *Echoes of Scripture in the Letters of Paul* (New Haven, CT: Yale University Press, 1989), 46–51.

29 Luther, *Luther's Works*, 12:310.

30 Hossfeld and Zenger, *Psalms*, 2:12. Linking this phrase to Nathan's parable (2 Sam. 12:1–4), Augustine says that the prophet "brought the sin out from behind David's back and held it before

4   Against you, you only, have I sinned
      and done what is evil in your sight,
    so that[31] you may be justified in your words
      and blameless in your judgment.

The emphasis of 51:4a is in the words **you, you only**, and **in your sight**. Far from denying that David has committed an offense against Bathsheba and Uriah, the point is that sin is, in its essence, an offense against God. A classic expression of this is in Leviticus 6:2, in which an offense against a neighbor is described as a "sin" and "a breach of faith against the Lord." It is this that renders injustice and immorality so serious. Far from minimizing the harm done to others, this confession admits that it matters more than the unbeliever can ever grasp. The phrase **in your sight** presses this home to the conscience, for "where there is grace in the soul it reflects a fearful guilt upon every evil act, when we remember that the God whom we offend was present when the trespass was committed."[32] There is no light relief from "an accusing conscience and an offended God."[33]

Paul quotes Psalm 51:4b in Romans 3:4. Psalm 51:4a sets up 51:4b. Precisely because David admits his sin (51:4a), he can go on to place himself in the hands of God, admitting in advance that whatever God chooses to say and do (his **words**, that is, any verdict he passes, his **judgment**) will be right (**justified**).[34] The verb "prevail" in Greek (Rom. 3:4; "be . . . blameless" in Ps. 51:4) translates a Hebrew verb that means "to be clean in a moral sense"[35] and therefore to prevail if tried in court. God is entirely justified when he judges.[36] To admit this, with no claim of extenuating circumstances, is a mark of true

---

his eyes." Augustine, *Expositions of the Psalms*, trans. Maria Boulding, ed. John E. Rotelle and Boniface Ramsey, 6 vols. (New York: New City Press, 2000), 2:415.

31 Most take ὅπως in the LXX to indicate purpose, although some have argued that it conveys simply consequence. E.g., Ben Witherington III, *Psalms Old and New: Exegesis, Intertextuality, and Hermeneutics* (Minneapolis: Fortress, 2017), 141; Goldingay, *Psalms*, 2:122.

32 Spurgeon, *Treasury*, 1.2:403.

33 John Calvin (1509–1564), *Commentary on the Book of Psalms*, trans. James Anderson, in *Calvin's Commentaries* (Grand Rapids, MI: Baker, 1993), 2:285–86.

34 This is what the penitent thief did (Luke 23:41). Derek Kidner (1913–2008), *Psalms*, 2 vols., TOTC (London: Inter-Varsity Press, 1973), 1:190.

35 See BDB, s.v. זכה; *HALOT*, s.v. זכה.

36 For a persuasive discussion of this quotation and its use in Romans, see the clear arguments of Thomas R. Schreiner, *Romans*, BECNT (Grand Rapids, MI: Baker Academic, 1998), 147–52.

repentance. As Luther puts it, "Judgment of self is in substance justification of God; . . . justification of self is in substance judgment of God."[37]

5   Behold, I was brought forth in iniquity,
         and in sin did my mother conceive me.[38]

Behold emphasizes what follows. David speaks of his birth[39] and then, pressing back to the roots of his existence, of his conception.[40] The parallelism makes clear that his sinfulness is not related to a supposed sinfulness in his parents' act of conception[41] since it is he who is a sinner (51:5a). Rather, he says that even in his earliest moments of existence he is shaped by **iniquity** and **sin**. Taken alongside Romans 5:12, this verse presents to us the doctrine of original sin, or sin in our human origins.[42] David

wraps up all of human nature in one bundle and says, "I was conceived in sin." . . . I am a sinner, not because I have committed adultery, nor because I have had Uriah murdered. But I have committed adultery and murder because I was born, indeed conceived and formed in the womb, as a sinner.[43]

David "is not saying he is a sinner because he sinned; rather, he is saying he sinned because he is a sinner."[44] As Derek Kidner notes, "This crime, David now sees, was no freak event: it was in character; an extreme expression of the warped creature he had always been, and of the faulty stock he sprang from."[45]

---

37 Luther, *Luther's Works*, 10:238.
38 Witherington suggests that the abuse directed at the man born blind in John 9:34 may echo this verse. Witherington, *Psalms Old and New*, 139. If so, the particular application to one man misses the point that it applies to all people.
39 The verb "brought forth," from the root "to twist, writhe," speaks vividly of the labor of childbirth.
40 For a similar reference to these two roots of human existence, see Job 3:3.
41 Theodoret of Cyrus (393–ca. 466) robustly says that some have "stupidly maintained" this idea. Theodoret of Cyrus, *Commentary on the Psalms*, trans. Robert C. Hill, 2 vols., FC 101–102 (Washington, DC: Catholic University of America Press, 2000), 1:297.
42 See Calvin, *Psalms*, 2:290–91.
43 Luther, *Luther's Works*, 12:347–48.
44 Ross, *Psalms*, 2:190.
45 Kidner, *Psalms*, 1:190.

There is also a corporate sense in which this is true of the people of God, for right back at Mount Sinai, in the episode of the golden calf, their sinfulness was apparent (cf. the similar theme in Ezek. 16; 20; 23). But the fundamental meaning of the confession is individual. Each man and woman inherits the sin of Adam; Israel's corporate sinfulness is the expression of this universal human sinfulness.

> ⁶   Behold, you delight in truth in the inward being,
>   and you teach me wisdom in the secret heart.

Behold (emphatic) builds on the "behold" in the previous verse: if a person is deeply sinful, then God must work deeply in the heart to do his work of grace. In the midst of a passionate prayer for forgiveness, this verse anticipates the renewal that dominates from Psalm 51:10 onward. Although there are uncertainties in the words translated **inward being**[46] and **secret heart**,[47] together they clearly indicate the depths of human personhood, the roots of our desires, affections, imaginations, and decisions. There is a movement from God's **delight** (which is the counterpoint to God's righteous anger) to God's gracious action (**You teach me**); **truth** (perfect sincerity, utter purity, and genuineness) is parallel to **wisdom**, of which the fear of the Lord is the root.

> ⁷   Purge me with hyssop, and I shall be clean;
>   wash me, and I shall be whiter than snow.

To **purge** means to purify from uncleanness.[48] **Hyssop**, a plant that can grow out of a wall (1 Kings 4:33), was used for ritual sprinkling, with the blood of the Passover lamb (Ex. 12:22) and with the blood of a sacrificed bird in the ceremony for the cleansing of a leper (Lev. 14:4–6). It was also used with water for ceremonial cleansing after contact with death

---

46 The only other use is in Job 38:36. Gerald H. Wilson (1945–2005), *Psalms*, NIVAC (Grand Rapids, MI: Zondervan, 2002), 1:778n15. Probably this indicates "the human internal organs (kidneys, entrails), which were regarded as the seat of feelings and decisions ('conscience')." Hossfeld and Zenger, *Psalms*, 2:13.

47 BDB: "the closed (chamber of the breast)"; s.v. סָתַם. Wilson argues that the "secret heart" suggests a willful hiding of parts of our lives from God. Wilson, *Psalms*, 1:778–79.

48 "Unsin me." Dahood, *Psalms*, 2:5. The root is חטא.

(Num. 19:16–19). The dominant use is with sacrificial blood. David "appeals to God Himself to perform the office of the priest and cleanse him from his defilement"[49]—finally by the blood of Christ (Heb. 9:25–28). Indeed, writes John Calvin, "It is the peculiar work of the Holy Spirit to sprinkle our consciences inwardly with the blood of Christ, and, by removing the sense of guilt, to secure our access into the presence of God."[50] Only when God himself washes us with the blood of Christ will we **be whiter than snow** (cf. Isa. 1:18) and walk before God with white garments to symbolize cleansed hearts (e.g., Rev. 3:4–5; 4:4). Considering what this meant for David and old covenant believers, Luther writes that David "asks to be sprinkled with the Word of faith in the coming Christ, who will sprinkle His church with His blood"; what matters is that "you believe in the validity of no satisfaction, no work, no Law, no righteousness in the sight of God except this single sprinkling."[51]

8   Let me hear joy and gladness;
       let the bones that you have broken rejoice.

The outcast returns to **hear** audible songs of **joy and gladness** (cf. in the sanctuary, Ps. 42:4), for there is joy in heaven (Luke 15:7, 10, 23–25) and joy in the heart of God (Zeph. 3:17) over every sinner who repents. He himself shares this joy as the **bones that you have broken** (lit., "crushed"; cf. the dry bones of Ezek. 37:1–14) in righteous judgment **rejoice**. Writing from his own vivid experience, Luther says,

In spite of all efforts and good works the timid, frightened, and terrified conscience remains until Thou sprinklest and washest me with grace and thus createst in me a good conscience, so that I hear that mysterious prompting, "Your sins are forgiven" (Matt. 9:2). No one notices, sees, or understands this except him who hears it. It can be heard, and the hearing produces a calm and joyful conscience, and confidence in God.[52]

49 Kirkpatrick, *Psalms*, 2:291.
50 Calvin, *Psalms*, 2:295.
51 Luther, *Luther's Works*, 12:363–64.
52 Luther, *Luther's Works*, 14:170.

9   Hide your face from my sins,
        and blot out all my iniquities.

Usually the hiding of God's face is a sign of his displeasure (e.g., Ps. 44:24). But when our sins are uncovered in his sight (90:8; cf. 32:1), nothing matters more than that they be hidden from him. Linking this perceptively with 51:3, Augustine says, "Switch your sin to a position before your face, if you want God to turn his face away from it."[53] Either I see and confess my sin so that God will not look on it, or I cover up my sin and it is ever before God's holy face in anger. The verb **blot out** ties this verse to 51:1, perhaps bookending 51:1–9.

51:10–17 Prayer for Renewal

The emphasis now begins to shift from the removal of sins to the renewal of the sinner. Luther suggests that the next section "seems to me to pertain to the gifts of the Spirit that follow the forgiveness of sins."[54]

10   Create in me a clean heart, O God,
        and renew a right spirit within me.

A **clean heart** (in which God delights, Ps. 51:6) can happen only by a work of God that is deeper than the furthest depths of sin. The verb **create** (בָּרָא, *bara*) always has God as its subject and indicates "bringing into being what did not exist before,"[55] for "nothing less than a miracle could effect his reformation."[56] Here is a work "which borroweth nothing from the creature,"[57] for it must be a new and sovereign work of God, creating a clean heart not by a measure of assistance in cleaning up an indifferent heart (which just needs a little bit of divine help for its self-improvement) but by a work of sovereign grace *ex nihilo*.

Although the verb **renew** can refer to the restoration of something existing (e.g., "repair," Isa. 61:4), here the parallel with **create** necessitates that it

53 Augustine, *Psalms*, 2:423.
54 Luther, *Luther's Works*, 12:376.
55 Kirkpatrick, *Psalms*, 2:292.
56 Calvin, *Psalms*, 2:298.
57 Dickson, *Psalms*, 1:309.

carry its meaning of "make new." The **right**[58] **spirit** means a human spirit that is morally fixed, steadfast, and resolute in its loyalty to God.[59]

This prayer anticipates—and believes—the promised new covenant (e.g., Jer. 24:7; 32:39; Ezek. 11:19; 36:26), for it involves a new creation, a "new self" (cf. 2 Cor. 5:17; Gal. 6:15; Eph. 4:24).

11   Cast me not away from your presence,
        and take not your Holy Spirit from me.

Cast me not is emphatic: "Do not fling me."[60] God removed his **Holy Spirit** from King Saul (1 Sam. 16:14); David fears this more than anything else. This language was used later about the whole people (the verb "cast out" in, e.g., 2 Kings 17:20; 24:20); the two are connected, for if this happens to the Davidic king, it will happen to his people. Only a Messiah-King with the Holy Spirit can bring his people into the presence of God.

12   Restore to me the joy of your salvation,
        and uphold me with a willing spirit.

The **joy** of God's **salvation** is found only in Christ. David "is pointing to Christ, in the contemplation of whom he was joyful even in his very tears."[61] The adjective **willing** speaks of a new human **spirit** to whom doing right is free, glad, generous, even spontaneous (cf. Ex. 35:22). Such a God-given spirit, possible only by the indwelling Holy Spirit (Ps. 51:11), is a miracle of grace.

13   Then I will teach transgressors your ways,
        and sinners will return to you.

---

58 This word (niphal participle of כון) "is often associated with God's creative activity" (e.g., "established," Ps. 24:2). Allan Harman, *Psalms*, 2 vols., MC (Fearn, Ross-Shire, Scotland: Mentor, 2011), 1:402.

59 Here, as elsewhere, Luther speaks of the natural human spirit as *incurvatus in se*. Luther, *Luther's Works*, 10:241; 25:291, etc.

60 Robert Alter, *The Book of Psalms: A Translation with Commentary* (New York: Norton, 2007), 182.

61 Cassiodorus (ca. 485–ca. 585), *Explanation of the Psalms*, trans. and ed. P. G. Walsh, 3 vols., ACW 51–53 (New York: Paulist, 1990–1991), 1:504.

The forgiven transgressor-king (51:1, 3) turns to **teach transgressors** the moral **ways** of God, for these ways can be walked only by those who **return** in the repentance of this psalm and experience the new covenant renewal in Christ to which this psalm points. This psalm, together with Psalm 32, does precisely this. In them our King teaches us that we must repent and shows us how to repent.

> 14   Deliver me from bloodguiltiness, O God,
>> O God of my salvation,
>> and my tongue will sing aloud of your righteousness.

Bloodguiltiness usually means guilt from shedding human blood[62] (as David has done to Uriah), although it can mean guilt more generally, as it is often used for Israel corporately (e.g., Isa. 4:4; Hos. 12:14).[63] In this verse the movement is from deliverance and **salvation** to a singing aloud of God's covenant **righteousness**, by which he righteously pardons his penitent people (cf. 1 John 1:9), even as he righteously punishes the impenitent.

> 15   O Lord, open my lips,
>> and my mouth will declare your praise.

Psalm 51:13–15 is summed up by this prayer, that the **lips** of the forgiven penitent will be opened, that his **mouth** can **declare** the **praise** of the God of salvation in Christ.

> 16   For you will not delight in sacrifice, or I would give it;[64]
>> you will not be pleased with a burnt offering.

For hints at a logical development from what precedes; perhaps the logic is that David offers his penitent heart *because* this is what God wants. The verb **delight** (here and in 51:6, 19) gives a window into the heart of God. This is not an absolute rejection of the sacrificial system, given by God

---

62 Hossfeld and Zenger, *Psalms*, 2:13nq.

63 Eveson follows John Stott (1921–2011) in suggesting that here it refers to being guilty of the blood of sinners he has failed to warn about judgment (e.g., Ezek. 33:1–9). Eveson, *Psalms*, 1:329.

64 Alternative translations have been suggested for the phrase "or I would give it." See Goldingay, *Psalms*, 2:123.

under the old covenant; rather, it speaks against the shallow abuse of that system (as 51:19 confirms). The context makes this clear, with its radical emphasis on heart repentance and a work of God's sovereign grace deep in the human spirit. There is a strikingly similar sentiment in Psalm 40:6, which we know to be fulfilled in the sacrifice of Christ, for, as Augustine says, "Those former sacrifices were symbolic; they prefigured the one saving sacrifice."[65] Calvin writes memorably that the old covenant sacrifices were "borrowing from Christ the necessary purchase-money of redemption."[66]

> [17]   The sacrifices of God are a broken spirit;
>   a broken and contrite heart, O God, you will not despise.

Psalm 51:17 is the counterpart to 51:16. **The sacrifices of God**[67] means those with which God is pleased. As in 51:10, the **heart** and the **spirit** are combined to convey the whole human person. The words **broken** ("shattered") and **contrite** (lit., "crushed," as in "broken," 51:8) both convey the effect of deep repentance on a person; when we see our sins in anything approaching their true horror, we are utterly crushed and devastated by the sight.[68]

51:18–19 Prayer for the Renewal of the People of God

> [18]   Do good to Zion in your good pleasure;
>   build up the walls of Jerusalem;

Zion now comes into focus, for the right standing of the King before God is the sine qua non of the prosperity of God's people. J. Alec Motyer (1924–2016) explains, "David, as king, could not sin simply as a private individual: his sin threatened the fabric of public life. Consequently, he would be as anxious for the building up of Jerusalem (Ps. 51:18) as for his own restoration."[69]

---

65 Augustine, *Psalms*, 2:427.
66 Calvin, *Psalms*, 2:305.
67 There is no manuscript evidence to support the emended vocalization behind "My sacrifice, O God" in the NIV. Hossfeld and Zenger, *Psalms*, 2:13; Harman, *Psalms*, 1:404.
68 Luther speaks (from his own experience) of "one that almost dies of despair." Luther, *Luther's Works*, 12:405.
69 J. A. Motyer, *The Psalms*, in *New Bible Commentary*, 21st century ed., ed. G. J. Wenham, J. A. Motyer, D. A. Carson, and R. T. France (Leicester, UK: Inter-Varsity Press, 1994), 518.

As David considers the city that lies at the heart of the people, and as a later generation will use these words in prayer for restoration from exile (cf. 102:13, 16), so this is also "a further prophecy [of] the new Sion . . . the heavenly Jerusalem to be built on earth" (cf. Gal. 4:26; Rev. 21).[70] Here is a prayer "that the Lord might build His church."[71] David prays for God to "hasten Zion's final glory, and then shall there be no more scandals to give the enemy cause to blaspheme, no more backslidings, no more falls; then shalt thou be fully honoured as the God of atonement."[72]

It may be that the **walls** suggest a clear distinction between the church and the world, so that the church is in the world but the world is not in the church.[73]

> [19]   then will you delight in right sacrifices,
>   in burnt offerings and whole burnt offerings;
>   then bulls will be offered on your altar.

The phrase **right sacrifices** (cf. Deut. 33:19; Ps. 4:5) indicates, in this context, sacrifices offered in a right spirit, the spirit of penitence exemplified by this psalm. **Burnt offerings** translates the usual word focusing on their ascending in smoke and flame.[74] **Whole burnt offerings** translates an adjective that emphasizes the entirety of what is offered. Together they speak of "the entire self-dedication of the worshipper."[75]

REFLECTION AND RESPONSE

1. Our major response ought, very simply, to be to make the psalm our own, both in heartfelt individual repentance and also as we join in congregational repentance.

2. David's repentance took place a year or so after his sin (evidenced by the birth and death of the son then conceived). By David's response to Nathan's rebuke, we too learn to comply humbly "with the calls to repentance,

---

70 Theodoret of Cyrus, *Psalms*, 1:302.
71 Luther, *Luther's Works*, 12:410.
72 Bonar, *Psalms*, 162–63.
73 So Thomas Alexander (fl. 1850–1865), in Spurgeon, *Treasury*, 1.2:423.
74 עוֹלָה. Kirkpatrick, *Psalms*, 2:295.
75 Kirkpatrick, *Psalms*, 2:295.

which may be addressed to [us] by his servants, instead of remaining under sin till [we] be surprised by the final vengeance of Heaven."[76] David Dickson notes "how faithful ministers ought to be in their proper charges, reproving sin, even in the greatest personages, when God calleth them unto it, and how acceptable their reproof should be to the honest heart."[77]

3. Augustine writes, "We have read about what we must shun [i.e., in the superscription]; now let us listen to what we must imitate if we have slipped into sin, for there are many who are very willing to fall with David, but unwilling to rise again with him." Cautioning against the glee with which we may watch the fall of a great saint, he goes on to say that these falls should cause us to tremble: "Let all who have not fallen listen, to ensure they do not fall; and let all who have fallen listen, so that they may learn to get up again." He preaches especially to those who "have fallen already, and study the words of this psalm with some evil thing on their consciences," and he exhorts them that "they must indeed be aware of the gravity of their wounds, but not despair of our noble physician."[78]

4. Commenting on Psalm 51:3, Luther observes that "sham saints . . . pervert this psalm and say: 'I perceive the sins of others, and the sins of others are always before me.'"[79]

5. It is worth meditating on the fact that pardon itself (pledged to us in Christ) may precede by some time our experiential grasp of it. As Dickson observes, "The dividing of the grant of pardon from the effectual intimation thereof unto the conscience, is done in God's wisdom and mercy towards his child for good; for here it ripeneth repentance, and bringeth forth this deep confession."[80]

6. Luther writes with eloquent and passionate conviction about this psalm. He scorns the "fine and pleasing theologians!" who offer life and joy without conviction of sin. Rather, he notes,

God is the kind of God who does nothing for any other purpose than to regard and love the contrite, vexed, and troubled, and . . . He is a God of

76 Calvin, *Psalms*, 2:281–82.
77 Dickson, *Psalms*, 1:302.
78 Augustine, *Psalms*, 2:411, 413.
79 Luther, *Luther's Works*, 14:167.
80 Dickson, *Psalms*, 1:304–5.

the humble and the troubled. If anyone could grasp this definition with his heart, he would be a theologian. . . .

We have to learn that a Christian should walk in the midst of death, in the remorse and trembling of his conscience, in the midst of the devil's teeth and of hell, and yet should keep the Word of grace, so that in such trembling we say, "Thou, O Lord, dost look on me with favor."[81]

7. While the instruction of others (51:13–15) is the particular responsibility of Christian leaders, it is a wholesome discipline for each Christian to share with others the joy of cleansing and the health of repentance.

8. Although the prayer for the upbuilding of the church (51:18–19) is primarily the prayer of the King, it is good for us also to conclude our penitence with the prayer that the repentance God has granted to us will also be vouchsafed to his whole church.

---

81 Luther, *Luther's Works*, 12:403, 405.

And even if you suffer calumny from a wicked ruler,
and you see the slanderer boasting, withdraw from
that place and say also the things in [Psalm 52].

ATHANASIUS
Letter to Marcellinus

A prayer of Jesus, who is attacked by wicked spiritual and
human agents, but nevertheless puts his hope in God, and
although he suffers death, is ultimately victorious.

TREMPER LONGMAN III
Psalms

King Saul along with associates like Doeg are manifestations
of the snake's offspring, the "brood of vipers" (Genesis 3:15;
Matthew 3:7; Revelation 12:9), influenced by Satan.

PHILIP EVESON
Psalms

PSALM 52

ORIENTATION

In Psalm 52 there is a speaker, a context, an individual adversary, and a congregation. The speaker is David, who here foreshadows the Messiah.

The context (in 1 Sam. 21–22, especially 21:7; 22:9–10) is during that time when David has been anointed king (1 Sam. 16) but is not yet acclaimed and acknowledged as king (2 Sam. 2:4; 5:1–5). Several psalms in this part of the Psalter come from this general period (Pss. 52; 54; 56; 57; 59; note also Pss. 34 and 142 and perhaps Ps. 7).[1] It prefigures eloquently and vividly the present age, in which Jesus has been given all authority in heaven and on earth (Matt. 28:18) but has not yet returned for every knee to bow (Phil. 2:10–11). In this age Jesus, in the body of his church, suffers hostility and persecution (cf. Acts 9:4). Closely associated with David is the house (temple/tabernacle) of the priest Ahimelech, who is slain in this terrible episode. Christ is both king and priest, and his church, which is both royal and priestly in Christ, suffers with him.[2]

The adversary is usually thought to be Doeg, although some have suggested that Saul himself is in mind.[3] Perhaps it doesn't much matter, for Doeg is clearly Saul's man. This individual has been seen as foreshadowing Judas Iscariot[4]

---

1 It is possible that others, such as Ps. 55, with its motif of betrayal, come from this period.

2 Argued persuasively in Augustine, *Psalms*, 3:13–15. Identifying the adversary as Doeg, he writes, "Let us recognize Doeg still with us today," as the world opposes the church.

3 E.g., Hengstenberg, *Psalms*, 2:211–13; Harman, *Psalms*, 1:407. While this is a minority view, it makes much sense.

4 E.g., the Venerable Bede (673–735), in J. M. Neale (1818–1866) and R. F. Littledale (1833–1890), *A Commentary on the Psalms from Primitive and Medieval Writers and from the Various Office-Books and Hymns of the Roman, Mozarabic, Ambrosian, Gallican, Greek, Coptic, Armenian, and Syriac Rites*, 2nd ed., 4 vols. (London: Joseph Masters, 1869–1874), 2:181.

and ultimately the antichrist.[5] He represents hostility against Christ and his church today.

The congregation (Ps. 52:6–7, 9b) is Christ's church. It has also been suggested that Ahimelech and his fellow priests foreshadow the church, both in their priestly calling and in their unjust sufferings.

This is one of many psalms in which words are used against the godly (e.g., Pss. 4; 12; 120; cf. the power of the tongue in James 3:1–12).

Psalm 52 shares with Psalm 51 the "steadfast love" (חֶסֶד, *khesed*) of God (51:1; 52:1, 8) and the tongue being used well (51:14; 52:9) or badly (52:2–4). After repentance in Psalm 51, much of Psalms 52–64 takes us into a world in which God's King is under great pressure.[6]

THE TEXT

Structure

One way of structuring the psalm is in terms of the address:[7] Psalm 52:1–5 is addressed in the second person to the adversary; 52:6–7 speaks in the third person about the righteous and what they will say; in 52:8–9 the psalmist speaks of himself in the first person.

It also makes sense, however, to set off 52:2–4 as a description of hostility against the King; to group 52:5–7 together as a prophecy of judgment; and to follow that with 52:8–9, the response of the righteous to that judgment. It is beneficial as well to understand 52:1, in its two halves, as setting the theme of the whole psalm; indeed, "steadfast love" (52:1) is picked up in 52:8 (and the same root in "the godly" in 52:9).[8] (We will pause for reflection at the two occurrences of *Selah*, but they do not seem here to be structural markers.)[9]

Imagery of an uprooted tree (52:5) is balanced by a fruitful tree (52:8). Trust in riches (52:7) is contrasted with trust in God (52:8).

---

5   Cassiodorus, *Psalms*, 2:1.
6   Hamilton, *Psalms*, 1:514–15.
7   Hossfeld and Zenger, *Psalms*, 2:27; Wilson, *Psalms*, 1:785.
8   Together with the bracketing of self-congratulatory speech (Ps. 52:1) with thanksgiving speech (52:9), this "great parenthesis" around the psalm is noted in Hossfeld and Zenger, *Psalms*, 2:27.
9   The word for "God" is אֵל in Ps. 52:1, 5, and אֱלֹהִים in 52:7–8. There does not seem to be any significance in this change.

Superscription

^S   To the choirmaster.[10] A Maskil[11] of David, when Doeg, the Edomite, came and told Saul, "David has come to the house of Ahimelech."[12]

Psalms 52–55 are all described by the word **Maskil**, which may suggest that we ought to read them as a minicollection.

There may be an ironic comparison between **Doeg . . . came** and **David has come**, one coming of the enemy to the antiking, the other the true King to the house of God.[13]

It is sometimes objected that Doeg did not strictly lie when he told Saul where David had been (1 Sam. 22:9), and this is used as an argument against the historical connection between the superscription and the psalm.[14] But "although the facts he reported were true, he helped to confirm Saul in a false and cruel suspicion."[15] By telling only a part of the truth, he deliberately deceived Saul and brought about a great injustice.

52:1 The Theme: Evil Boasting versus Steadfast Love

¹   Why do you boast of evil, O mighty man?
    The steadfast love of God endures all the day.

Whether or not the adversary is listening, Psalm 52:1–5, like the prophetic oracles to foreign nations, is a vivid way of conveying what he needs to hear. Psalm 52:1 sets before us "the essential matter of the whole Psalm, in brief, striking features."[16] The question **Why?** expresses both astonished horror (that he not only does evil but boasts about it; cf. Rom. 1:32) and bewilderment at the stupidity[17] of what he is doing. The form of the verb **boast** expresses an

---

10 See on Ps. 4.
11 See on Ps. 32.
12 The other historical superscriptions are for Pss. 3, 7, 18, 34, 51, 54, 56, 57, 59, 60, 63, 142. In Hebrew the superscription is verses 1–2; subsequent verse numbers are increased by two.
13 Cf. the two uses of the same verb (בוא) in the superscription to Ps. 51.
14 E.g., Alter, *Psalms*, 184.
15 Kirkpatrick, *Psalms*, 2:295.
16 Hengstenberg, *Psalms*, 2:211.
17 Goldingay, *Psalms*, 2:143.

autonomous or self-glorifying boasting, as contrasted with boasting in God.[18] **O mighty man** (mighty warrior, hero) is ironic since, whether this man exerts much power in the world (like Saul) or not (perhaps like Doeg), we will see in Psalm 52:5 that his power will come to nothing. Augustine eloquently points out that it takes very little real power to do a work of destruction (such as demolishing a house, setting fire to a crop, killing a child), but it requires real might to build a house, sow and cultivate a crop, beget and nurture a child. Even a poisonous toadstool can kill, so, Augustine asks, "Is all your power reduced to this—equality with a poisonous toadstool?"[19]

In his *First Lectures on the Psalms*, Martin Luther applies this first line directly to Christ, as if Christ said, "Do not think that you have it of yourself that you are mighty in iniquity over Me. I am only weak because I wish it, and you would have no power over Me unless it were given you from above (John 19:11)."[20]

The second line (translated literally from the MT by the ESV and CSB) is sometimes emended because it is thought to be abrupt.[21] But there is no need to do this. Indeed, "it is virtually the answer to the question of the first" line[22] and sets the theme for the psalm. As we join Christ in exposing the devil's ploys, we do so utterly confident, as was he in his earthly life, of the covenant love of his Father, which is for **all the day**, whatever that day may bring.

52:2–4 Personified Hostility to Christ and His Church

2   Your tongue plots destruction,
           like a sharp razor, you worker of deceit.

---

18 Hithpael of הלל. Willem A. VanGemeren, *Psalms*, vol. 5 of *The Expositor's Bible Commentary*, ed. Tremper Longman III and David E. Garland , rev. ed. (Grand Rapids, MI: Zondervan, 2008), 441; A. A. Anderson (1924–2021), *The Book of Psalms*, 2 vols., NCB (London: Oliphants, 1972), 1:403.

19 Augustine, *Psalms*, 3:19.

20 Luther, *Luther's Works*, 10:244.

21 Three changes are sometimes made: (1) the MT חֶסֶד אֵל (the steadfast love of God) is transposed and altered to אֶל חָסִיד (to/against the godly); (2) the LXX (ἀνομία) appears to read the Hebrew as חָמָס (violence) in place of חֶסֶד; and (3) the words "all the day" are placed differently. Some or all of these lie behind the REB, "You mighty man, why do you boast all the day / of your infamy against God's loyal servant?"; the NRSV, "Why do you boast, O mighty one, / of mischief done against the godly?"; and—most loosely of all—the NIV, "Why do you boast of evil, you mighty hero? / Why do you boast all day long, / you who are a disgrace in the eyes of God?" But the MT, represented by the CSB and ESV, is powerful, appropriate, and more likely to be original.

22 Kirkpatrick, *Psalms*, 2:296.

³ You love evil more than good,
    and lying more than speaking what is right.   *Selah*
⁴ You love all words that devour,
    O deceitful tongue.

Psalm 52:2–4 confronts and exposes the one who opposes God's King and people and makes himself an instrument of the devil, the father of lies. There is a double focus, mainly on speaking (the **tongue** as the agent of 52:2 and the whole person being addressed as a **deceitful tongue** in 52:4, the **lying** and **speaking** of 52:3, and the **words** of 52:4) but also on motivation (the repeated **You love** in 52:3, 4), for the tongue that deceives speaks from the abundance of the heart that loves evil.[23] The word **destruction** (fronted for emphasis in Hebrew) may have the sense of "threats."[24] The simile of a **sharp razor** (cf. 57:4; 64:3) reminds us that "death and life are in the power of the tongue" (Prov. 18:21).[25] Psalm 101:7 picks up **worker of deceit** ("who practices deceit"), where David says this person will not dwell in the King's house. The man being spoken about does not deceive just from time to time, as if it's an aberration; he loves evil, and "evil never forsakes the man known to love the sin which he commits."[26] **Words that devour** are words that swallow people up[27] and cause confusion.[28]

Commenting on *Selah*, Charles H. Spurgeon writes, "Let us pause and look at the proud, blustering liar. Doeg is gone, but other dogs bark at the Lord's people."[29] The people of Christ ought to expect that, as they walk in their King's footsteps, they will be subject to lies.

52:5–7 The Adversary Is Judged, and the Righteous Respond

⁵ But God will break you down forever;
    he will snatch and tear you from your tent;
    he will uproot you from the land of the living.   *Selah*

---

23 Mic. 3:2 illuminates the damage this does to God's people.
24 *HALOT*, s.v. הַוָּה.
25 Kirkpatrick quotes from William Shakespeare's *Cymbeline* 3.4 "'Tis slander, / Whose edge is sharper than the sword."
26 Cassiodorus, *Psalms*, 2:3.
27 See BDB, s.v. בלע.
28 See *HALOT*, s.v. בלע.
29 Spurgeon, *Treasury*, 1.2:426.

But probably has an emphatic sense here (cf. NIV: "Surely"). The four verbs are "a pounding prediction of utter destruction."[30] **Break you down** uses the image of the demolition of a building (cf. Judg. 8:9; Job 19:10; Ezek. 26:9); all he built ends in ruins. **Snatch** is a verb used of snatching away a coal from a fire (e.g., Prov. 6:27; 25:22; Isa. 30:14), being taken away from a place of warmth and belonging. **Tear you from your tent** suggests being torn from your home, your land, your family, so that you live "like a cast-away and vagabond" (cf. Deut. 28:63; Job 18:14).[31] **Uproot** means the final removal of a tree, so that not even its roots give hope of future restoration; **the land of the living**, in the new creation, will have no room for such a one, finally impenitent and hostile to Christ and his church.[32] This is not malice but sober prophecy, as Augustine points out:

> In this psalm . . . there is neither prayer for the wicked nor prayer against the wicked; there is simply a prophecy of what will happen to the wicked. You must not think that the psalm is saying anything out of spite; what is said is uttered in the spirit of prophecy.[33]

6   The righteous shall see and fear,
        and shall laugh at him, saying,

The response of **the righteous** (plural)—the church of Christ, when it sees this final judgment of antichrist and all antichrists—will be to **see and fear** (two verbs sounding very similar in Hebrew) **and . . . laugh at him**. When judgment afflicts a wicked person in this life, the proper response of the righteous is awe and reverence as we realize with fresh intensity that God really does act in his world (cf. what happens after the deaths of Ananias and Sapphira, Acts 5:11). Luther mentions the proper fear of Gentile believers when they see the (temporary) rejection of the Jews (Rom. 11:20–21).[34] On the last day, that fear will be infinite in its depth of reverent wonder. Augustine points us to Psalm 2:11;

30 Ross, *Psalms*, 2:214. "Violent verbs jostle one another in verse 5 with increasingly radical effect." Kidner, *Psalms*, 1:195.
31 VanGemeren, *Psalms*, 442.
32 Augustine refers to Eph. 3:14–19 to contrast this uprooting with the sure rootedness of the true believer in the love of God. Augustine, *Psalms*, 3:23.
33 Augustine, *Psalms*, 3:20.
34 Luther, *Luther's Works*, 10:245.

1 Corinthians 10:12; Galatians 6:1; and Philippians 2:12 for similar responses.[35] The verb **laugh** is not vindictive (forbidden in Prov. 24:17; cf. Job 31:29) but—akin to the laughter of God in Psalms 2:4 and 37:13—the delight that rightly greets the triumph of the justice of God (cf. Rev. 18:20; 19:1–5).

> 7   "See the man who would not make
>   God his refuge,
>   but trusted in the abundance of his riches
>   and sought refuge in his own destruction!"

See (Behold!) points to this man for emphasis,[36] that we may learn from his condemnation, be warned not to follow him, and be comforted that we need not be frightened of him. Spurgeon calls it "the divine *in memoriam*."[37] The word translated **man** is similar to that used for "mighty man" in Psalm 52:1.[38] However strong he thought he was—and pretended to be—this is his destiny. He is described by what he chose not to do (**make / God his refuge**, flee to God in faith) and by what he did (**trusted in the abundance of his riches**; cf. Ps. 49:6; Prov. 11:28; 1 Tim. 6:17–18).[39] It is not easy to know whether **sought refuge** in the final line ought to be translated "was strong." There is a play on the words **refuge** (or fortress, מָעוֹז, *maoz*) and "be strong" (יָעֹז, *yaoz*).[40] Most likely he thinks his destructive behavior will make him strong (CSB: "taking refuge in his destructive behavior").[41]

52:8–9 The Confidence of the Godly King in the Presence of His Godly People

> 8   But I am like a green olive tree
>   in the house of God.

---

35 Augustine, *Psalms*, 3:24.

36 "When *Behold* is said with hand extended, the unspeakable lot of the sinner is indicated." Cassiodorus, *Psalms*, 2:5.

37 Spurgeon, *Treasury*, 1.2:427.

38 In Ps. 52:1, גִּבּוֹר; in 52:7, גֶּבֶר.

39 Augustine perceptively includes the covetous poor, whose values are the same and who think, "If only I were rich, then I would be safe." Augustine, *Psalms*, 3:25–26.

40 Alter, *Psalms*, 185.

41 The NIV, "and grew strong by destroying others," is less likely, not least because the Hebrew gives no indication of "others."

> I trust in the steadfast love of God
>> forever and ever.

The move to an emphatic singular, **but I**, signals a finale in which the King expresses his **trust** in God's covenant **steadfast love** (חֶסֶד, *khesed*; cf. Ps. 52:1), in contrast to the false faith of his enemy. In so doing, he is the forerunner of all who will share his faith and walk in his footsteps.

The image of the **green olive tree / in the house of God** evocatively combines garden imagery, perhaps Edenic, with the temple. This may allude to the idea that the temple is a "garden of Eden" and that it will one day grow to encompass the whole new creation, with Christ at its center.[42] The image of a deeply rooted and ever-fruitful tree (contrast "uproot," 52:5) is used of the godly individual and of the whole people of God (e.g., Pss. 1:3; 92:12–15; Prov. 11:28, 30; Jer. 11:16; 17:7–8; Hos. 14:8).[43]

> 9   I will thank you forever,
>> because you have done it.
> I will wait for your name, for it is good,
>> in the presence of the godly.

The verb **thank** means a public, audible thanksgiving, a declaration or confession about God, not very different from praise. The clause **because you have done it** is emphatic (cf. "that he has done it," Ps. 22:31, and "he will act," 37:5). In context it means he has acted in judgment on the one who opposes his King and acted to vindicate his King and his people.

That the King **will wait for** the **name** (the public revelation, here in judgment) of God means he trusts that judgment will come. Jesus did this in his earthly life, waiting and weeping in prayer (cf. 1 Pet. 2:23); we are to wait in Christ as we cry day and night to God the Judge (Luke 18:7), waiting for Jesus to come (Rev. 22:20), because "faith maketh a man as sure of what is

---

42 For this wonderful Bible theme, see G. K. Beale, *The Temple and the Church's Mission: A Biblical Theology of the Dwelling Place of God*, NSBT 17 (Downers Grove, IL: InterVarsity Press, 2004).

43 See on Ps. 1 for the argument that this image focuses most especially on Christ. Here in Ps. 52, Cassiodorus takes the same approach, for "this most blessed olive contributed such fruit as could make the whole human race, which was dried out with sins, grow fat with the generosity of His mercy." Cassiodorus, *Psalms*, 2:6.

to come, as if it were perfected, and filleth him with praise for the certain hope of the performance of promises."[44]

To say that God's **name . . . is good** is profound; only those who know in experience a taste of God's sweet goodness will wait patiently for that name to be revealed in all its fullness when Jesus returns. Only the Holy Spirit can teach us this truth. Speaking of how the taste of God's goodness gave courage to the martyrs, Augustine writes,

> You may commend honey with all your might, you may exaggerate its delicious sweetness with the most expressive words you can find, but if you are talking to someone who does not know what honey is and has never tasted it, he will not know what you are talking about.[45]

REFLECTION AND RESPONSE

1. It is good quietly to read 1 Samuel 21–22 and to reflect both on the evident malice of Doeg and Saul and on the terror of the story for Ahimelech and his party—and no doubt for the fugitive David. There is a sense in which the church of Christ is like the fugitive David or the slaughtered priests in every age until Jesus returns, assailed by venom and malice allied with power.

2. As we ponder the deceit and malice laid bare in Psalm 52:2–4, we train ourselves to keep in mind at all times the truth of 52:1b. It is healthy to do this in the experienced realities of deceit and hatred today, both from outside the visible church and also, most distressingly, from within.

3. It is no malice but rather a necessary comfort to dwell on the four verbs of Psalm 52:5 and to join the righteous in seeing (by faith), fearing (with awe and reverence), and even with anticipation looking forward to that godly laughter that will accompany the judgment of God (52:6–7). For these things are sure.

4. Nevertheless, even as we do this, we heed the pastoral words of Augustine, who wisely guards against the misunderstanding of this laughter. For now, when we see someone living a bad life, we

---

44 Dickson, *Psalms*, 1:317.
45 Augustine, *Psalms*, 3:29.

have the urge to work with him and set him on a better course. At this present stage an unrighteous person may turn round and become righteous, just as a righteous one may go wrong and become unrighteous. This is why you must neither be presumptuous about your own case nor despair of his.[46]

5. As we make Psalm 52:8 our own individually, we do so in Christ, having before us in our hearts and minds the Lord Jesus as the King in David's line who most fully prayed these words before us. In him we too may be like green olive trees in the house of God, rooted, trusting in steadfast love, confident no matter what trials are sent to us.

6. Perhaps the verb "wait" in Psalm 52:9 comes as a surprise. It reminds us that this psalm is to be appropriated not only at the end of time, when Jesus returns, but when we most need it, which is now, in the time of patient waiting.

---

46 Augustine, *Psalms*, 3:24–25.

Should you hear people blaspheming against God's providence, do not share with them in their irreligion, but say [Psalms 14 and 53].

ATHANASIUS
Letter to Marcellinus

These are the sort of people in whose company Christ's body suffers and groans.

AUGUSTINE
Expositions of the Psalms

Because . . . this doctrine of our corrupt human nature is badly needed in the congregation of God, that it might be maintained forever, that we would recognize ourselves for what we are, . . . [that we] might not become proud or overconfident or trust in any merit or work of our own but live solely on the mere grace and mercy of God which he has shown us in his Son, therefore David, with diligence and at the suggestion and inspiration of the Holy Spirit, recorded this psalm twice, so that he might hammer this doctrine into us who are otherwise proud, who coddle, adorn and enhance ourselves and do not want to be nothing but rather be something before God.

NICOLAUS SELNECKER
The Whole Psalter

PSALM 53

ORIENTATION

In his commentary, John Calvin comments on Psalm 53 that "this psalm being almost identical with the *fourteenth*, it has not been considered necessary to subjoin any distinct commentary."[1] But it may be that Calvin went too far. For Psalm 53, though similar, is not identical with Psalm 14, and also it appears here as Psalm 53, in this particular place in the canonical Psalter. Charles Spurgeon observes, rightly, "It is not a copy of the fourteenth Psalm, emended and revised by a foreign hand; it is another edition by the same author, emphasized in certain parts, and re-written for another purpose."[2]

PSALM 14 AND PSALM 53

For most of the text of Psalm 53, see the commentary on Psalm 14. Here I summarize the differences and seek to comment on the significance of the psalm in book 2.

The differences may be stated simply. First, the superscription adds to that of Psalm 14 the following words:

1. "According to Mahalath." The phrase "according to" may indicate instrumental accompaniment (as we might say, "with flutes") or a musical setting, "Mahalath," now unknown to us.[3] The word "Mahalath" appears also in the superscription of Psalm 88.

---

1   Calvin, *Psalms*, 2:320.
2   Spurgeon, *Treasury*, 1.2:433.
3   It has been suggested that "Mahalath" may be the first word of a well-known song of the period, implying that the psalm be sung to that tune. Hossfeld and Zenger, *Psalms*, 2:35.

2. "A Maskil."[4] The designation "Maskil" is shared with Psalms 52, 54, and 55, suggesting that these four form a minicollection, to be read together.[5] This is significant, for it encourages us to consider how Psalm 53 functions within this collection.

Second, the covenant name, "the Lord," appears four times in Psalm 14 (14:2, 4, 6, 7). Three of these are changed to "God" (53:2, 4, 6), while the fourth disappears from Psalm 53 (see below on 53:5). This preference for *Elohim* is in line with much of Psalms 42–83 (the so-called Elohistic Psalter). No one knows why this was preferred here. It has been suggested that it may represent a conscious desire to communicate truth with a wider audience, who might not be so familiar with the covenant name; we cannot be sure.[6]

Third, there is a significant change from 14:5–6 to 53:5.

Psalm 14:5–6	Psalm 53:5
[5] There they are in great terror,	[5] There they are, in great terror, where there is no terror!
for God is with the generation of the righteous.	For God scatters the bones of him who encamps against you;
[6] You would shame the plans of the poor,	you put them to shame,
but the Lord is his refuge.	for God has rejected them.

After a shared first line (**There they are in great terror**), Psalm 14 emphasizes God's protection (**refuge**) for **the generation of the righteous**, who are the oppressed **poor** (a distinctive emphasis in Pss. 9–14). But the emphasis in Psalm 53 is on God's judgment of the oppressor (replacing **For God is with . . .** with **For God scatters the bones . . .**). We shift our gaze from those whom God accompanies to those whom God opposes.

The clause **where there is no terror** refers either to their becoming frightened even when there is no good reason to be frightened or, more likely, to the suddenness with which terror will come on them (i.e., there was no terror, and then suddenly there is). "The more secure a sinner is, and in

---

4 See on Ps. 32.
5 The word "Maskil" appears also in Ps. 53:2, "who understand" (hiphil participle of שׂכל, "be wise").
6 O. Palmer Robertson, *The Flow of the Psalms: Discovering Their Structure and Theology* (Phillipsburg, NJ: P&R, 2015), 95–102.

special a persecutor of God's people, the more terrible shall his wakening be, when God's judgment cometh on him."[7]

The remainder of 53:5 spells out vividly that while these have **en-camp**ed **against** the people of God (besieged them), their **bones** will be **scatter**ed, and they are the ones who will be **put . . . to shame** because **God has rejected them.**

Finally, there are three minor changes that do not appear to have much significance:

1. The word **deeds** (14:1) is intensified to **iniquity** (53:1), perhaps in harmony with the emphasis of Psalm 53 on judgment.
2. The verb **turned aside** (14:3) is changed to **fallen away** (53:3).
3. The word **all** in 14:4 (**all the evildoers**) is omitted from 53:4.

In common with Psalm 51, Psalm 53 focuses on "Zion" as the place of messianic promise, built up around God's penitent people (51:18–19) and from which Messiah will come (53:6).

Psalm 52 laments deceitful words "that devour" (52:4); this leads naturally into the words "who eat up my people as they eat bread" (53:4). In both psalms the hostility that threatens to gobble up the people of God is described.

In Psalm 52 the focus is on David the messianic king under pressure from such relentless and deceitful hostility. In Psalm 53 the emphasis is on the whole people ("my people," 53:4).[8]

In each psalm there is a vigorous affirmation that judgment is coming on those who oppose both the Messiah (52:5–7) and his people (53:5). In expounding and appropriating Psalm 53, we ought to give due weight to this emphatic confidence in God's judgment on the enemies of God's Christ and his people. While this serves as a comfort to the persecuted church, it functions also as a warning to us all not to become, or to be, those who devour God's precious people.[9]

---

7   Dickson, *Psalms*, 1:320.
8   There is perhaps a parallel with the individual lament of Pss. 42–43 and the ensuing corporate lament of Ps. 44.
9   Abusive pastors need to take careful note of this warning.

When someone sings [Psalms 54, 56, 57, and 142], he considers not how someone else is persecuted, but how he, being the one who suffers, is affected. And these words, as his own, he chants to the Lord. And so, on the whole, each psalm is both spoken and composed by the Spirit so that in these same words . . . the stirrings of our souls might be grasped, and all of them be said concerning us, and the same issue from us as our own words, for a remembrance of the emotions in us, and a chastening of our life.

ATHANASIUS
Letter to Marcellinus

[Psalm 54] is seen with greatest effect as a simple prophecy of Christ. Read thus, it is very plain and intelligible; requiring little more than the first idea to exhibit a perfect correspondence with the life and feelings of the Messiah.

WILLIAM HILL TUCKER
In Charles H. Spurgeon, *The Treasury of David*

PSALM 54

ORIENTATION

Psalm 54 is one of a number of psalms arising from the time when David had been anointed king but was yet hated and hunted by Saul. The psalm speaks for Christ in the days of his flesh, the true Messiah and yet despised and rejected. And in Christ it speaks for the whole church of Christ in this age of sharing in his sufferings so that we may come into his glory. It is a song of Christ and a song to be sung by the church of Christ, both corporately and individually.[1]

Psalms 52–55 are to be read together, as suggested by the common designation "A Maskil of David." Psalm 54 shares a number of similarities with Psalm 52: both assert that the "name" of God is "good" (52:9; 54:6); in both David resolves to give thanks (52:9; 54:6); the "might" of God (54:1) is similar to the word for "mighty man" (52:1); both 52:7 ("make God") and 54:3 ("set God") use the same Hebrew verb;[2] both refer to "good" and "evil" (52:1, 3, 9; 54:5–6); and in both the righteous will "see" or "look" (the same verb) on their enemies (52:7; 54:7).[3] Links with Psalm 53 are fewer: one is the verb "return" or "restore" (53:6; 54:5); another is the theme of seeking after God (53:2), similar to setting God before themselves (54:3). All four psalms share the general background of God's Christ and his people under pressure from a hostile world.

THE TEXT

Structure

The *Selah* at the end of Psalm 54:3 breaks up the psalm naturally enough. Psalm 54:1–3 includes a prayer (54:1–2) followed by the plight that

---

1 "David prefigured Christ, or the body of Christ." Augustine, *Psalms*, 3:41.

2 שׂים.

3 For more on these connections, see Hossfeld and Zenger, *Psalms*, 2:48.

necessitates the prayer (54:3). Psalm 54:4–5 is a declaration of confidence that God will help and act in judgment. Psalm 54:6–7 promises joyful thanksgiving. The "name" of God brackets the psalm and helps set its theme (54:1, 6).

Superscription

S   To the choirmaster:[4] with stringed instruments.[5] A Maskil[6] of David, when the Ziphites went and told Saul, "Is not David hiding among us?"[7]

This psalm arises from the terrifying situation of David in 1 Samuel 23:19–29 and quotes verbatim[8] from the words of the Ziphites in 1 Samuel 23:19 (something very similar is recorded in 1 Sam. 26:1). The phrase "to seek his life" in 1 Samuel 23:15 is echoed in Psalm 54:3 ("seek my life"). The trust expressed in the psalm aligns with the trust that Jonathan shares with David in 1 Samuel 23:16–17. Whereas 1 Samuel tells us how God rescued the king, Psalm 54 enables us to grasp the heart of David—and hence the heart of Christ—as he cries to the one who can save him from death (Heb. 5:7).

Far from ignoring this historical superscription (as modern commentators are sometimes wont to do), Augustine says that "from this title every verse that is sung derives its meaning"—that is, the historical context makes sense of the whole psalm. He plays on the word **hiding** and speaks of the Ziphites as representing the kind of people who are "hostile to the hidden one" (i.e., Christ) and to his people, whose lives are "hidden with Christ in God" (Col. 3:3). He says that these Ziphites, along with Doeg of Psalm 52, are "the flourishing children of this world," and he challenges his hearers to "choose which you want to be."[9] This psalm, he says, "must be the prayer of the Church hiding among the Ziphites. Let the body of Christians say

---

4 See on Ps. 4.
5 See on Ps. 4; cf. Pss. 6; 55; 61; 67; 76; Hab. 3:19.
6 See on Ps. 32.
7 The other historical superscriptions are for Pss. 3, 7, 18, 34, 51, 52, 56, 57, 59, 60, 63, 142. In Hebrew the superscription is verses 1–2; subsequent verse numbers are increased by two.
8 The only difference is between a *holem* and a *holem vav*.
9 Augustine, *Psalms*, 3:41–43.

it, the body whose good way of life is cherished in secret."[10] Although this may seem fanciful to us, his meditation on the hiddenness of Christ and his church is profound.

54:1–3 Pray the Prayer and Feel the Plight
of God's Messiah and His People

Psalm 54:1–2 invites us to join with God's Messiah in urgent prayer for rescue.

> [1]   O God, save me by your name,
>   and vindicate me by your might.

The address **O God** is fronted for emphasis in 54:1 and again in 54:2. The **name** of God means God himself as he has revealed himself by covenant in all the glory of his attributes. David sets this in parallel with his **might** (a word that echoes the ironic "mighty man" of 52:1), for God is "a mighty one who will save" (Zeph. 3:17); God's power is finally a power directed at salvation.[11] That **save** means to **vindicate** is a reminder that without justification there is no hope; God the Judge decides for Jesus his righteous King on the basis of his intrinsic righteousness and gives judgment for us only in him, as his righteousness is imputed to us.

> [2]   O God, hear my prayer;
>   give ear to the words of my mouth.

Psalm 54:2 adds urgency to the petition of 54:1.

> [3]   For strangers have risen against me;
>   ruthless men seek my life;
>   they do not set God before themselves.   *Selah*

Psalm 54:3 gives the reason for the Messiah's prayer, that we too may feel his plight even as we suffer with him in this age (e.g., Rom. 8:17; cf.

---

10 Augustine, *Psalms*, 3:45.

11 God's "might" and "name" are linked also in Ps. 20:6–7; Jer. 10:6 ("Your name is great in might"); 16:21 ("I will make them know my power and my might, and they shall know that my name is the LORD").

Col. 1:24). The three lines of this tricolon build to a climax. First, the word **strangers**[12] (in the first line) speaks, in its original context, of these Ziphites, who were Israelite in ethnicity but foreign in their values. Not only have they **risen against me**, they are (in the second line) **ruthless men** (violent, terrifying) who—like Saul in 1 Samuel 23:15—**seek my life**. But the worst thing about them (in the third line) is the one that digs deepest into their motivation: **They do not set God before themselves**. That is, they neither follow God's ways (as their guide) nor show any awareness of God's watchful eye over their words and deeds (for their consciences are seared).

Selah invites us to pause and reflect that, as this was the condition of Christ among his foes, so it is the state of his church in the midst of a hostile world. If Christ needed urgently to pray "with loud cries and tears" (Heb. 5:7), so do we.

54:4–5 Share the Confidence of God's Messiah with His People

4   Behold, God is my helper;
       the Lord is the upholder of my life.

Behold signals a new section as the Messiah turns to any who will listen and declares his confidence in God his Father. It is as if he points with a finger toward heaven. Not only is God **my helper**, he is **the upholder of my life**, for it is **my life** (my soul) that is under threat.

Martin Luther comments,

On the basis of the fact that David was much persecuted and yet never captured by Saul, but always escaped, it is understood figuratively that Christ and the Christians, though they might suffer and be killed after the flesh, yet always escape with their soul unharmed and are never captured, as the Lord promised (Matt. 10:28).[13]

---

12 Because the Ziphites were not literally foreigners and because Ps. 86:14 is very similar and uses the word "insolent" (זדים) in place of "strangers" (זרים), some manuscripts and the Targum replace "strangers" (foreigners) with "insolent men" here (e.g., NIV: "arrogant foes"; cf. Hossfeld and Zenger, *Psalms*, 2:45). This makes for easier parallelism with the following line, but as Ross points out, it is hard to see how a scribe would change the easier "insolent men" to the harder "strangers" (and the LXX has ἀλλότριος). Ross, *Psalms*, 2:233n2. It is better to stay with the MT (as do the CSB and ESV main text).

13 Luther, *Luther's Works*, 10:251.

5   He will return the evil to my enemies;
       in your faithfulness put an end to them.

He will return[14] **the evil** speaks of evil as having a boomerang quality: once it is let loose, it must find a resting place somewhere, and in the justice of God, it will come back to rest on those who sent it out.[15] The reference to **the evil** makes the evil definite, this particular evil of seeking the life of God's Messiah and his people. The word translated **my enemies** often has the sense of those who watch with hostile intent or lie in wait (cf. Ps. 56:2; Jer. 5:26; Hos. 13:7 ["lurk"]; Mark 3:2).[16]

The prayer of the second line (cf. Ps. 143:12) arises from the truth of the first line (it is prayed in accordance with the will of God) and from the **faithfulness** (lit., "truth") of God to his covenant promises to his King and people. This is an integral part of what his "name" (54:1) means, that he keeps every promise. This prayer to **put an end to them**, to do to them just what they had planned to do to David (so that their evil will "return" to them), expresses not a personal malice or revenge but a longing that God will do what he has promised to do, to vindicate his King and rescue all the King's people from those who are finally impenitent (cf. 2:12).

54:6–7 Join in the Thanks of God's Messiah with His People

6   With a freewill offering I will sacrifice to you;
       I will give thanks to your name, O LORD, for it is good.

The verb **I will sacrifice** is emphatic as (probably) is **I will give thanks.**[17] The point about the **freewill offering** is, as the phrase indicates, that it is given voluntarily; it arises not from a desire to look pious or even to fulfill

---

14   The kere of the verb is the hiphil of שוב, implying that God is the active agent, as he is. Ross, *Psalms*, 2:234n6. The kethib (what is written in the MT) has evil as the subject and can be read as a jussive: "Let evil return." While this is possible and makes for easier parallelism (so NIV), the kere "has the more common idiom" and is probably to be preferred. Goldingay, *Psalms*, 2:158.

15   Goldingay, *Psalms*, 2:160.

16   Kirkpatrick, *Psalms*, 2:306; Ross, *Psalms*, 2:240.

17   The first is explicitly cohortative; the second has no distinctly cohortative form but likely also bears this force. So Ross, *Psalms*, 2:241.

a vow but simply from a heart that is thankful. The verb **give thanks** indicates a public acknowledgment of what God has done (cf. Ps. 52:9). This is testimony to God's **name**, tying the psalm back to the prayer of 54:1: Christ prayed, and now his people pray, that God will work by his revealed promises and nature, and that is what he does. In the shadow of the cross, Jesus prays, "Holy Father, keep them in your name, which you have given me" (John 17:11). The use here of the covenant name, Lord, is unusual in Psalms 42–83 (the so-called Elohistic Psalter) and emphasizes the covenant context of the whole psalm.

The word **good** overflows with rich meaning, encompassing God's covenantal goodness in himself and all the blessings of that goodness poured out on the Messiah and all who are his. Martin Luther writes, "The name of the Lord does not give the saints anything good beyond what it is in itself, but it is in itself their good thing. And so He gives Himself, and He . . . is Himself the good and complete blessing of the saints." This "name of God is Christ Himself, the Son of God, the Word by which He verbalizes Himself and the name by which He calls Himself in eternity."[18]

> 7   For he has delivered me from every trouble,
>   and my eye has looked in triumph on my enemies.

The two verbs **has delivered**[19] and **has looked** (which have been called "perfects of confidence")[20] convey what only the Spirit of God and the eye of faith can give to a believer: the assurance that what God has promised he will perform. Even in the midst of troubles, these may be spoken. The phrase **from every trouble** and the phrase **on my enemies** are fronted for emphasis in each line. **Looked in triumph** is literally just "looked," but the sense here is of a godly satisfaction in seeing God's enemies vanquished.[21] Guarding against the abuse of this kind of look, John Calvin writes, "If their satisfaction proceed in any measure from the gratification of a depraved

---

18 Luther, *Luther's Works*, 10:252–53.
19 The subject of "He has delivered" is either "the Lord" or the "name," that is, God as he has made himself known. The NIV—"You have delivered"—makes for smoother reading (avoiding the switch from the second person in 54:6) but is unnecessary and not supported by the MT.
20 Ross, *Psalms*, 2:242.
21 Goldingay points to "they stare" in Ps. 22:17 for a similar use of the verb "to see." Goldingay, *Psalms*, 2:158.

feeling, it must be condemned; but there is certainly a pure and unblame-able delight which we may feel in looking upon such illustrations of the divine justice."[22]

REFLECTION AND RESPONSE

1. We should ponder the circumstances that gave rise to this psalm. Calvin emphasizes the terrifying situation in which David found himself. The psalm is here "to teach us that we should never despair of divine help even in the worst situation. . . . It might have appeared just as credible that God could bring the dead out of the grave, as that he could preserve [David] in such circumstances."[23]

2. We must never forget that, however deep our distress, we may pray for rescue using the words of this psalm, for "the godly can never be so surprised with trouble, but they may fly to God for delivery, as David doth here; and it is a rare virtue not to forget this relief in depth of distress."[24]

3. Psalm 54:1 reminds us to pray not simply out of our distress but on the basis of the mighty covenantal revelation that the triune God has given us in Christ.

4. When pondering what it might mean for God to act for us by his "might" (54:1), we do well to heed Luther's theology of the cross. "What is the strength of God by which he saves us?" he asks, and he answers, "It is that which is a stumbling block to the Jews and folly to the Gentiles. It is weak-ness, suffering, cross, persecution, etc. These are the weapons of God, these the strengths and powers by which He saves."[25]

5. The third line of Psalm 54:3 prompts us never to forget that at the heart and root of all hostility to God's people is a hostility to God, just as it was in the earthly days of Christ (e.g., John 15:18–19, 23).

6. Commenting on the word "faithfulness" in Psalm 54:5, Calvin writes that "nothing can support us in the hour of temptation, when the Divine deliverance may be long delayed, but a firm persuasion that God is true,

---

22 Calvin, *Psalms*, 2:327.
23 Calvin, *Psalms*, 2:321.
24 Dickson, *Psalms*, 1:322.
25 Luther, *Luther's Works*, 10:250.

and that he cannot deceive us by his divine promises." For "God could no more deny his word than deny himself."[26]

7. Meditating on the love and beauty of God, Augustine (commenting on the freely offered thanks of 54:6 and the word "good") emphasizes that our thanksgiving is freely given because it delights in freely given goodness. We thank him not because of what we hope he will give us but "for his own sake."[27]

8. A good commentary on the response of Psalm 54:6–7 is Romans 12:1: "I appeal to you therefore, brothers, by the mercies of God, to present your bodies as a living sacrifice, holy and acceptable to God, which is your spiritual worship."

26 Calvin, *Psalms*, 2:325–26.
27 Augustine, *Psalms*, 3:50.

Though blessed David spoke this psalm when pursued by
Saul, . . . at the same time he also forecasts the . . . plots
against the Savior, and in himself foreshadows the Lord's
sufferings, . . . and with the eyes of the Spirit he foresaw the
Lord suffering the same thing, betrayed . . . and crucified.

THEODORET OF CYRUS
Commentary on the Psalms

We may read these strains as expressing David's feelings in some
peculiar seasons of distress, and as the experience of Christ's
Church in every age. . . . Yet still it is in Jesus, the Man of Sorrows,
that the Psalm finds its fullest illustration. His was the soul that
was stirred to its lowest depth by scenes such as are described here.

ANDREW BONAR
Christ and His Church in the Book of Psalms

The spiritual eye ever and anon sees the Son of
David and Judas, and the chief priests appearing and
disappearing upon the glowing canvas of the Psalm.

CHARLES H. SPURGEON
The Treasury of David

PSALM 55

It is hard to exaggerate the pain of betrayal. How did Jesus feel when Judas Iscariot betrayed him? The Gospels offer hints (e.g., John 13:21); Psalm 55 opens
wide a window into Jesus's soul. The horror that the disciples felt over Judas's
betrayal is evidenced by the remembrance of his treachery almost every time
his name is mentioned (e.g., Matt. 10:4; 26:25; 27:3; Mark 14:44; John 6:71;
12:4; 18:2). No doubt Judas did many things; he is remembered for this alone.

Betrayal is the most striking feature of Psalm 55 (cf. 41:9). Many oppose
King David, but one stands out, a traitor, and David speaks of him twice
(55:12–15, 20–21). Perhaps this was Ahithophel during Absalom's rebellion (2 Sam. 15–17). But the psalm is the last of four designated "A Maskil"
(Pss. 52–55), two of which are explicitly linked to the time when David was
being hunted by Saul (Pss. 52, 54). So it may arise from some unknown
episode during that period; we cannot be sure.

As so often, David the anointed king is a type of Jesus the Messiah. What
David experienced is fulfilled in Jesus. When Jesus sang this psalm, he did
so with an intensity of feeling we can scarcely imagine.

This fulfillment in Jesus was recognized early in Christian history.
A manuscript of Jerome's (ca. 347–ca. 420) Latin version gives this psalm
the title *Vox Christi adversus magnatos Judaeorum et Judam traditorem* (The
voice of Christ against the leaders of the Jews and the betrayer Judas).[1] Just
as Paul bore in his body the marks of Jesus (Gal. 6:17), so, says Theodoret of
Cyrus, did David in an earlier age.[2] Christians today must expect the same,

---

1   Kirkpatrick, *Psalms*, 2:308; Ross, *Psalms*, 2:251.
2   Theodoret of Cyrus, *Psalms*, 1:314.

for the Lord warns us that "brother will deliver brother over to death, and the father his child, and children will rise against parents and have them put to death. . . . And a person's enemies will be those of his own household" (Matt. 10:21, 36; cf. 24:10). We need to sing this psalm not only because we may expect, in some measure, to experience this betrayal but also so that we will know how to respond with the faith of Psalm 55:22–23. It is no accident that 55:22 is clearly echoed by Peter when writing to Christians under great pressure (1 Pet. 5:7).[3]

There are several verbal and thematic links with Psalms 52, 53, and 54, including urgent prayer (54:1–2; 55:1), issues of life and death (54:3; 55:15), a feeling of terror or horror (53:5; 55:4–5), the judgment of God (52:5; 53:5; 54:5; 55:23), and trust in God (52:7–8; 55:23).

THE TEXT

Structure
The most natural divisions emerge when we note that Psalm 55:1–8 expresses sorrow, 55:9–15 indignation, and 55:16–23 assurance.[4]

Superscription

S   To the choirmaster:[5] with stringed instruments.[6] A Maskil[7] of David.[8]

These words are shared with part of the superscription to Psalm 54, suggesting that the psalms should be read each in the light of the other.

55:1–8 The Deep Sorrow of Christ and His Church
Christ here leads us, as he led David by his Spirit, in an urgent prayer (Ps. 55:1–2), explained by a reason (55:3), followed by a vivid description of

---

3   1 Pet. 5:7 and the LXX of Ps. 55:22 are the only occasions when the verb ἐπιρίπτω occurs with the noun μέριμνα in the Greek Bible.
4   E.g., Delitzsch, *Psalms*, 2:156–61; Kirkpatrick, *Psalms*, 2:308; Hamilton, *Psalms*, 1:526.
5   See on Ps. 4.
6   See on Ps. 4; cf. Pss. 6; 54; 61; 67; 76; Hab. 3:19.
7   See on Ps. 32.
8   In Hebrew the superscription is verse 1; subsequent verse numbers are increased by one.

his and our misery (55:4–5) and of the depth of his and our longing to escape (55:6–8).

1   Give ear to my prayer, O God,
         and hide not yourself from my plea for mercy!
2   Attend to me, and answer me;
         I am restless in my complaint and I moan,

The **plea for mercy** means an urgent "pleading for compassionate attention."[9] **Hide not yourself** asks God not to do what he tells us not to do when we see someone in need (e.g., Deut. 22:1–4 ["ignore"]; Isa. 58:7). We pray for God to be like the good Samaritan to us (Luke 10:30–35), to **attend to** (pay attention to) us and **answer** our prayer. The **complaint** is not grumbling but rather a passionate "lament."[10] The verbs translated **I am restless** and **I moan** are rare, and their meaning is contested. Restlessness is the most likely meaning of the first, although it may have the sense of being beaten down or brought low.[11] To **moan**[12] "similarly suggests wandering about in confusion"[13] with "the dull murmuring sounds of pain."[14] Psalm 55:2 conveys intense distress.

3   because of the noise of the enemy,
         because of the oppression of the wicked.
     For they drop trouble upon me,
         and in anger they bear a grudge against me.

In four lines of increasing intensity, the King describes the reason for his distress.[15] First, **the noise** (lit., "voice," either the sounds of their

---

9   *HALOT*, s.v. תְּחִנָּה.

10 *HALOT*, s.v. שִׂיחַ; Goldingay, *Psalms*, 2:163. The NIV—"my thoughts"—is too weak.

11 The probable root is רוד ("to move oneself backwards and forwards, to be inwardly uneasy"; Delitzsch, *Psalms*, 2:157), although it may be רדד (to beat down) or even ירד (to descend). See the discussions in, e.g., Goldingay, *Psalms*, 2:167; Wilson, *Psalms*, 1:808n10; VanGemeren, *Psalms*, 451; Ross, *Psalms*, 2:246n3.

12 Hiphil of הום. This is cohortative, perhaps expressive of a wholehearted giving of himself to distressed prayer.

13 Goldingay, *Psalms*, 2:167.

14 Delitzsch, *Psalms*, 2:157.

15 Alter translates vividly: "From the sound of the enemy, / from the crushing force of the wicked / when they bring mischief down upon me / and in fury harass me." He describes Ps. 55:3–5

hostility or their actual words, probably the latter in the light of 55:21) **of the enemy** grates on him. Next comes their **oppression**, with the sense of "pressure" and the distress they cause; the noise presses close against the King. Third, as their pressure affects the King, they **drop trouble** (evil, harm) on him. "These are people who push [harm] to the edge of the roof so that it falls down on us as we stand below."[16] And behind it all, making it so desperately grievous, is the **anger** with which they do this, not lashing out in occasional fury but plotting deliberately and continuously because **they bear a grudge against me** (cf. the long resentment of Esau, Gen. 27:41, and the evil fury experienced by Job, Job 16:9).[17] Such was the pressure on David, reaching its climax in the hostility to Jesus, overflowing in distress for his church.

> 4   My heart is in anguish within me;
>   the terrors of death have fallen upon me.
> 5   Fear and trembling come upon me,
>   and horror overwhelms me.

To be **in anguish** is used of a woman in labor. The book of Job is a study in **terror** (Job 9:34; 13:21; 41:14). **The terrors of death** horrify the King as the darkness descends. **Fear and trembling** intensify this sense, and the word **horror**, a rare strong word that makes us shudder (cf. Ezek. 7:18 in its context), together with the verb **overwhelms** only begins to convey what the Lord Jesus felt as he entered the shadow of the cross.

> 6   And I say, "Oh, that I had wings like a dove!
>   I would fly away and be at rest;
> 7   yes, I would wander far away;
>   I would lodge in the wilderness;   *Selah*
> 8   I would hurry to find a shelter
>   from the raging wind and tempest."

---

entirely as a "riveting expression of terror . . . made all the more powerful by the fact that, in an unusual syntactic pattern, the catalog of disasters rolls on in a crescendo that is essentially one long sentence." Alter, *Psalms*, 191.

16 Goldingay, *Psalms*, 2:168.

17 The verb is שׁמם in all three places.

No wonder the Lord Jesus, like David before him and many believers since, longed deeply to be anywhere but here. The **wings** of **a dove** (cf. Jer. 48:9, 28) suggest a bird that can nest in safety in a rocky crag.[18] To **lodge** (a temporary stay) **in the wilderness** suggests desperate flight. It is striking that here (as in Ps. 55:19) *Selah* comes in the middle of the sentence. We are encouraged to pause even in the middle of the description. The desperate yearning for any kind of **shelter** in a **raging** storm helps us feel the intensity of the King's distress and the anguish we may expect sometimes to experience as we follow him. Only the deep conviction that "it must be so" could nerve Jesus to refrain from calling on his Father to send legions of angels (Matt. 26:53–54). Only the knowledge of his grace in times of trial will nerve us to stay at our posts, wherever our King may place us.

55:9–15 The Righteous Indignation of Christ and His Church

Psalm 55:9 and 15 bracket this section with a prayer for God to act in judgment on the enemies of the Messiah. This is not inconsistent with the prayer of the Lord Jesus for God to forgive those who crucified him (Luke 23:34) or with our prayers that our enemies will be converted. It expresses what "Your kingdom come" means in the end for those who ultimately refuse to submit to God.

> 9   Destroy, O Lord, divide their tongues;
>   for I see violence and strife in the city.
> 10   Day and night they go around it
>   on its walls,
>   and iniquity and trouble are within it;
> 11   ruin is in its midst;
>   oppression and fraud
>   do not depart from its marketplace.

Psalm 55:9–11 refers to an unnamed **city**. The allusion (**Divide their tongues**) is to Babel (Gen. 11:1–9), the epitome of godlessness (Babylon

---

18 Eveson, *Psalms*, 1:347. Eveson wisely cautions against being misled by the very different tone of Felix Mendelssohn's (1809–1847) famous "O, for the Wings of a Dove!"

in the symbolic language of Revelation).[19] So the prayer to **destroy** (defeat, render futile; cf. "confound," Isa. 19:3) is that God will do to the cultures that oppose the Messiah what he did to Babel. "It is thus that to this day he weakens the enemies of the Church, and splits them into factions, through the force of mutual animosities, rivalries, and disagreements in opinion."[20]

The **city** has strange watchmen going **around it / on its walls**, characterized as **violence** (חָמָס, *khamas*) and **strife**;[21] these "guardians," far from keeping the city safe, ensure that it is miserable. What John will call "the world" is a murderous place (cf. John 8:44).

If **violence and strife** "guard" the city, **iniquity and trouble** are within it, with the resulting **ruin, oppression**, and **fraud** that **do not depart from its marketplace**, so that every transaction (commercial and relational) is tainted by endemic deceit (**fraud**) and the abuse of power (**oppression**). This is the world in which Christ and his church in every age must live.

12   For it is not an enemy who taunts me—
          then I could bear it;
       it is not an adversary who deals insolently with me—
          then I could hide from him.
13   But it is you, a man, my equal,
          my companion, my familiar friend.
14   We used to take sweet counsel together;
          within God's house we walked in the throng.

Suddenly and unexpectedly the King's focus narrows to one man. He will return to the plural in Psalm 55:15, for this one is in league with many. But for the moment he alone is in focus. He is not **an enemy** or **an adversary**, that is, an open foe (e.g., the chief priests, scribes, Sadducees, Pharisees, Herodians). Now he **taunts** and **deals insolently** (lit., "makes great," acts

19 Augustine, *Psalms*, 3:65. Augustine includes here a brilliant riff on Babel and Pentecost: "If there are still pagans on the rampage today, it is just as well that they speak different languages. If they aspire to one common language, let them come to the Church, for here, though we differ in our natural tongues, there is but one language spoken by the faith of our hearts."

20 Calvin, *Psalms*, 2:333.

21 This seems the most natural reading for the subject of the verb "go around." See, e.g., Marvin E. Tate, *Psalms 51–100*, WBC 20 (Grand Rapids, MI: Zondervan Academic, 2018), 52; Alter, *Psalms*, 192.

big, throws his weight around), but the time was when he did not. Had he been a known enemy, the King could **bear it** because he **could hide from him**; he could take defensive measures.

But—and here the King speaks to him in the pathos of second-person rebuke—**it is you!** In 55:13 he describes him in four ways, as a **man** (the word—אֱנוֹשׁ, enosh—indicating an ordinary person), **my equal** (i.e., someone treated as an equal in the fellowship of the disciple band in which not even their Master will lord it over them),[22] **my companion** (a warm word,[23] the very opposite of hard-edged hostility—they used to greet one another with joyful hugs), and **my familiar friend**.

With this friend there have been treasured memories. **We used to take** rightly conveys the sense of habitual **sweet counsel**, the sharing of thoughts, hopes, and fears. This friendship was not only treasured; it was enjoyed in the context of joyful piety, **within God's house** as we **walked in the throng** (probably the happy pilgrim gatherings for the exuberant festivals of the covenant, similar in feel to Ps. 42:4).

15   Let death steal over them;
          let them go down to Sheol alive;
          for evil is in their dwelling place and in their heart.

Since the betrayer is an agent of Satan (Luke 22:3), he is aligned with all the Messiah's enemies. It is therefore natural for David, and for Jesus, to move back to the plural **them**. The verb **steal over** probably has the sense of taking them by surprise;[24] they have plotted to take the Messiah's life, but unless they repent, they will discover to their horror that it is their lives that are forfeit. Like Korah and those with him (who rebelled against God's leader in their day, Num. 16), they will **go down to Sheol alive**, that is, in a sudden and fatal judgment.[25] Whether or not this happens in this life, it will

22 "What heart-piercing significance this word ['my equal'] obtains when found in the mouth of the second David, who, although the Son of God and peerless King, nevertheless entered into the most intimate human relationship as the Son of man to His disciples, and among them to that Iscariot!" Delitzsch, *Psalms*, 2:160.

23 Meaning "docile" and hence "familiar friend, trusted, intimate friend." Ross, *Psalms*, 2:247n18, 257.

24 Ross, *Psalms*, 2:248n20.

25 Here is the tragic end of Judas Iscariot's life. This "sudden destruction" is alluded to here "as the grand representation of the manner in which the bottomless pit shall one day shut her mouth for ever

happen. The final line makes clear that these are not occasional enemies, people who are good at heart; no, **evil is in their dwelling place and in their heart**. "Such as give entertainment and lodging unto wickedness, shall have hell for their lodging, where wickedness lodgeth."[26]

55:16–23 The Steadfast Confidence of Christ and His Church

> [16] But I call to God,
>   and the LORD will save me.
> [17] Evening and morning and at noon
>   I utter my complaint and moan,
>   and he hears my voice.
> [18] He redeems my soul in safety
>   from the battle that I wage,
>   for many are arrayed against me.

While Psalm 55:16–23 reprises some themes already voiced (notably, urgent prayer and painful betrayal), we have here a window into the life of faith and how assurance can rise from lament (55:1–8) and prayer (55:9–15). **But I** is emphatic;[27] assurance of answered prayer is the birthright of Christ (John 11:42) and is given, in his name, to David and all the church.[28] The use of the covenant name, **the LORD** (rare in this part of the Psalter), emphasizes the covenantal nature of this the King's confidence.

The intense persistence (**evening and morning and at noon**) and the passion of his prayer are reiterated in the first two lines of Psalm 55:17. The verb **utter my complaint** is cognate with the noun "complaint" in 55:2. The verb **moan**, while different from that translated "moan" in 55:2, means much the same.

He redeems my soul, my whole life, **in safety**. The Messiah is in the midst of **battle**, spiritual warfare of a most intense form, with **many** . . .

---

upon all the impenitent enemies of the true King of Israel, and great High Priest of our profession." George Horne, *A Commentary on the Book of Psalms* (London: Longman, Brown, 1843), 212.

26 Dickson, *Psalms*, 1:330.

27 אֲנִי without even a linking *vav*.

28 With characteristic emphasis on Christ as the head of the church, Augustine writes of the singular here, that "the body of Christ . . . is crying out in its anguish, its weariness, its affliction, in the distress of its ordeal. It is . . . a unity grounded in an individual body, and in the distress of its soul it cries from the bounds of the earth." Augustine, *Psalms*, 3:70.

arrayed against him (cf. 3:1–2, 6). Facing overwhelming odds (cf. Acts 4:27), both the Messiah and his church may be confident that the covenant God will redeem them. God has redeemed the incarnate Son, and in him, he will redeem all his people (cf. Rom. 8:23).

19 God will give ear and humble them,
   he who is enthroned from of old,   *Selah*
   because they do not change
   and do not fear God.

In Psalm 55:19 the focus begins to shift from the confidence of the Messiah to the just judgment on which this confidence is based. **God will give ear** to the prayers of his Messiah, and therefore he will **humble** the adversaries.[29] As in 55:7, *Selah* comes in the middle of the sentence, inviting us to pause and meditate on what God will do, before the second part of the verse shows us why he will do it—**because they do not change**. Because of the parallel with **and do not fear God**, it seems that their not changing has the sense of being fixed in their godless ways, settled in their hostility to Christ and his people.[30]

20 My companion stretched out his hand against his friends;
   he violated his covenant.
21 His speech was smooth as butter,
   yet war was in his heart;
   his words were softer than oil,
   yet they were drawn swords.

In 55:20–21 the Messiah speaks again, with pain in his voice, about his betrayal. **My companion** (unexpressed in Hebrew) is added by most translators to make clear that the subject of the verb must be the betrayer of 55:12–14. The word **friends** means those who were at peace with him

---

29 The verb may be understood to mean "will answer (i.e., with the paradoxical answer of judgment)" or "will humble." The general sense is much the same.

30 The NIV radically reorders the Hebrew to put "who does not change" as a description of "God, who is enthroned from of old." This makes for an easier reading but involves some violence to the Hebrew word order.

(so there was no possible justification for his treachery). To **violate a covenant** means to treat it as profane rather than sacred in the sight of God. A covenant of friendship bound the traitor to the King; he violated it.

What makes it worse—and this is so with any betrayal of trust—is that his words contradict his heart and actions. Deceit is a companion to malice, for words are often weaponized (cf. Ps. 52; John 8:44). Twice we are told about his language—**his speech** being **smooth as butter** and **his words** being **softer than oil**. What a smooth, soft, sweet talker he is, how persuasive, how seemingly gentle, nice, friendly, and warm! And yet because **in his heart** there is the deep hostility of **war** (he is opposed in principle to God's Messiah and his people), therefore his words, in their effect, are **drawn swords**, sharp, piercing, ready to harm. How frightening are smooth words from a hostile heart.

²²   Cast your burden on the LORD,
  and he will sustain you;
 he will never permit
  the righteous to be moved.

The sufferings of the King have bequeathed this precious promise to his church.[31] **Burden** means something allotted to someone, here with the sense of "the care, anxiety, etc. which are thy portion."[32] And yet our Messiah here promises, as he himself experienced, not that the Father will simply remove the burden but that **he will sustain you** under it. The reason, a cause that reaches deep into the heart of God, is that **he will never**—never!—**permit / the righteous** (those who are righteous by faith) **to be moved**, to be shaken, to slip, to slide into destruction. This is true of the King and the individual believer (cf. Pss. 15:5; 21:7), and it is true of the Messiah's church as a whole (e.g., 46:5). The enduring reliability of this glorious promise, given to new covenant believers afresh in 1 Peter 5:7, rests on the unchangeable rock that the Father was as willing as he was able to sustain his Son and that the triune God is today as willing as God is able to hold fast every man and woman in Christ.

---

31 Kidner, *Psalms*, 1:202.
32 BDB, s.v. יְהָב.

23   But you, O God, will cast them down
             into the pit of destruction;
       men of blood and treachery
             shall not live out half their days.
       But I will trust in you.

While we might prefer the psalm to end with Psalm 55:22, the final verse (55:23) is necessary. **But you, O God** is emphatic, just as "I" was emphatic at the start of 55:16. The necessary counterpart to God's upholding of his Messiah and his church is that he must and **will cast . . . down** his finally impenitent foes. The **pit of destruction** ("the pit of the abyss") means not simply death but ultimately hell. These are **men of blood** (cf. "violence," 55:9), who live by harming others, and they are **men of . . . treachery**, who operate by deceit, with a desperate discord between their words and hearts. They are children of the original liar and murderer (John 8:44). On some, like Saul of Tarsus, God had mercy. But some will never repent. These, in the vivid language of the verse, **shall not live out half their days**. While this may be true of some evildoers because they die an early death (cf. Acts 5:1–11), it is not true of all. Many of the righteous do not live out half the earthly life they might expect; Jesus himself died young. The verse teaches not that all evildoers literally die young but that an untimely death in this life is a picture and warning of the terrible eternal judgment that will come to all who do not repent (cf. Luke 13:1–5).

It is only because of the assurance of this final judgment that we may pray, as Jesus prayed, the final words with confidence: **But I** (emphatic) **will trust in you**.

REFLECTION AND RESPONSE

1. Before making these words our prayer, both individually and corporately in Christ, it is seemly for us to meditate on what they must have meant for Jesus in his earthly trials and especially in the sharp pain of his betrayal. For even though he knew that he must be betrayed and that Judas would be the traitor (John 13:21–30), the pain to his sinless heart must have been every bit as intense as this psalm conveys.

2. As we pray Psalm 55:1–5 as men and women in Christ, we must allow ourselves to feel the misery of sharing in the sufferings of Christ. Meditating on the intense distress of 55:1–2, David Dickson writes, "Though a child of God were ever so stout-hearted naturally, yet when God exerciseth his spirit with trouble, he shall be made to weep before God as a child, and must not be ashamed to be thus humbled before him." Commenting on 55:4–5, he writes, "It is not a thing inconsistent with godliness to be much moved with fear in time of danger; natural affections are not taken away in conversion, but sanctified and moderated."[33]

3. Psalm 55:6–8 helps us vocalize our natural and sometimes desperate longings to escape the miseries of this age. We express them; we feel them; and then, with Christ the Savior, who prayed in Gethsemane, we resolve afresh that we will walk in Jesus's footsteps and not succumb to them.

4. Psalm 55:9–11 assists us in gaining a true perspective on Babylon, "the world," and to see behind its deceptive facade (cf. 1 John 2:15–17). For the cultures in which we must live are deeply marked by violence (people harming people), strife (people fighting people), iniquity and trouble (people causing misery for people), ruin (people destroying beauty and goodness), oppression (people using power for their own ends), and fraud (people deceiving people).

5. When we sing of the enemies of our King and his people, we remember that we do not know the future. Some, like Saul of Tarsus, will prove to be brothers or sisters in Christ in days to come. We pray for our enemies even as we pray for the victory of God's Messiah.

6. Commenting on the description of the betrayer in Psalm 55:12–14, Derek Kidner astutely observes that such a betrayal is exactly what David himself had done to "one of his staunchest friends," Uriah the Hittite (cf. 2 Sam. 23:39).[34] Before the psalm helps nerve us to face the pain of being betrayed by a professing brother or sister in the visible church, we need first to repent of our own unfaithfulness and resolve not to prove traitors ourselves.

7. "In driving God's servant to prayer," writes Kidner perceptively, "the enemy has already overreached himself; a fact worth remembering."[35] By

33 Dickson, *Psalms*, 1:326–27.
34 Kidner, *Psalms*, 1:200.
35 Kidner, *Psalms*, 1:201.

the time we finish praying Psalm 55:16–23, we hope that the Holy Spirit will work in us to feel and know afresh this covenantal confidence of our King as we face whatever trials are given us as our "lot." Psalm 55:22 is a precious promise. Picking up the idea of an allotted burden, Charles Spurgeon writes, "He cast thy lot for thee, cast thy lot on him. He gives thee thy portion of suffering, accept it with cheerful resignation, and then take it back to him by thine assured confidence."[36]

36 Spurgeon, *Treasury*, 1.2:451.

When you are being pursued and certain ones are perpetrating slander . . . do not succumb to weariness, but being confident in the Lord and hymning him, recite the things in [Psalms 54 and 56].

ATHANASIUS
Letter to Marcellinus

Whatever pressure the saints may endure, let them turn their thoughts to this psalm and recognize themselves in it.

AUGUSTINE
Expositions of the Psalms

[Jesus's] every tear was precious, his every step was marked; the book of remembrance has a record of these so vast, and ample and full, that, were it published here, "I suppose the world itself could not contain the volumes that could be written."

ANDREW BONAR
Christ and His Church in the Book of Psalms

PSALM 56

ORIENTATION

The sorrows and faith of the Messiah are precious to God. In him and in him alone, the tears of each believer are counted, one by one, under the loving eye of God. This is the dominant thought of Psalm 56. King David, as so often in the Psalms, foreshadows the greater David, the true Messiah, and includes in him all his spiritual body, the church of Christ.[1]

Preaching Psalm 56 in Carthage in about 412 BC, Augustine insisted that his hearers must move from David to Christ, whom David foreshadowed. For "as long as you have not yet reached Christ, the divine word has only one piece of advice for you: 'Come nearer; you are not yet in a place of security.'"[2] If Augustine is right—and I think he is—then it is important for us not to stop with David in this psalm.

Psalms 52–55 are linked by the designation "A Maskil." Psalms 56–60 are tied together by the designation "A Miktam" (Ps. 16 being the only other such psalm). Psalms 56–60 are all still marked "To the choirmaster" and "of David," and all except Psalm 58 have historical notes in the superscription. All include the heading "according to" followed by what may be a tune (that for Pss. 57–59 being the same). Gerald Wilson rightly comments, "The constellation of so many common elements leaves a strong impression that these psalms constitute a purposeful collection and arrangement."[3]

---

1 Hamilton, *Psalms*, 1:537.
2 Augustine, *Psalms*, 3:81.
3 Wilson, *Psalms*, 1:820n4.

There is, however, no very sharp disjunction from Psalm 52 to 55, since the dominant context is still the King who has been anointed (1 Sam. 16) but is still persecuted, before the day of his acclamation as King. Indeed, James Hamilton is right that all the psalms from Psalm 52 to 71 "seem tinged with that tale" of Saul's persecutions.[4]

THE TEXT

Structure

The most obvious structural feature is the refrain in Psalm 56:3–4 and 56:10–11. There is also, however, a change of subject in 56:8, from the guilt of the enemies to the sorrows of the King. It may be best to consider the psalm in two sections (56:1–7 and 56:8–13) with a refrain in the middle of each.

David Dickson sees an oscillation between conflicts and victories by faith, as follows:[5]

56:1–2	First conflict in prayer	
56:3–4		First victory by faith
56:5–6	Second conflict against his enemies	
56:7		Second victory by faith
56:8	Third conflict, setting forth "his mournful condition"	
56:9–11		Third and greatest victory by faith
56:12–13	Response of thankfulness	

Superscription

S   To the choirmaster:[6] according to The Dove on Far-off Terebinths. A Miktam[7] of David, when the Philistines seized him in Gath.[8]

---

4   Hamilton, *Psalms*, 1:534.
5   Dickson, *Psalms*, 1:333.
6   See on Ps. 4.
7   The word "Miktam" may indicate "something inscribed in an enduring way," following the LXX; see Ross, *Psalms*, 2:266n3. For other psalms marked Miktam, see Pss. 16, 57, 58, 59, 60.
8   The other historical superscriptions are for Pss. 3, 7, 18, 34, 51, 52, 54, 57, 59, 60, 63, 142. In Hebrew the superscription is verse 1; subsequent verse numbers are increased by one.

According to (shared by all of Pss. 56–60) probably designates a tune. But the meaning of the Hebrew phrase translated **The Dove on Far-off Terebinths** is uncertain.[9] The **dove** may suggest a link with Psalm 55:7; some (e.g., LXX) have taken the dove as a symbol of Israel.[10] If the early identification of the dove with the people of God is correct, it may be that just as David is identified with the dove in 55:6–7, so here the Messiah speaks for all his far-off people, whether they are "silent" in sorrow or perched on faraway trees. Perhaps the combination of "dove" and "far-off" suggests a mournful or plaintive tune, as would be appropriate.

The historical note **when the Philistines seized him in Gath** refers to the terrifying incident recorded in 1 Samuel 21:10–22:1, shortly after the incident of Doeg that heads Psalm 52. That the slayer of Goliath of Gath (1 Sam. 17), who is even now carrying Goliath's sword (1 Sam. 21:8–9), should flee to Gath, of all places, is indeed to walk straight into the lion's mouth! Although 1 Samuel does not explicitly say that David was **seized**, it does say that he "escaped" (1 Sam. 22:1) and that he "pretended to be insane *in their hands*" (1 Sam. 21:13), both of which suggest that they did indeed seize him; in the light of 1 Samuel 21:11, they would have been foolish not to. The narrative also contains the only time we are told that David was afraid ("was much afraid," 1 Sam. 21:12), a motif that links strongly with this psalm (Ps. 56:3–4, 11).[11] Psalm 34 meditates on this same episode.

56:1–7 In Christ We May Trust and Pray under Pressure
The first refrain is bracketed by sections that focus on the hostile pressures on the King. The refrain itself—which sounds the keynote of the psalm— expresses his trust under pressure.

---

9   The word אלם is pointed אֵלֶם in the MT, meaning "silence" (hence CSB: "according to 'A Silent Dove Far Away'"), although the singular noun is puzzling with the plural adjective רְחֹקִים (far away). It is sometimes repointed אֵלֶם, either a (defective) plural of אֵלָה (terebinths or oaks) or the plural of אֵל (gods or an intensive plural for God). There is much discussion of this in the commentaries, all inconclusive; see Goldingay, *Psalms*, 2:181; Hossfeld and Zenger, *Psalms*, 2:58; Dahood, *Psalms*, 2:40–41; Tate, *Psalms 51–100*, 65–66; Ross, *Psalms*, 2:265–66. Zenger comments that in some of these discussions, "the fantasies of exegetes seem unlimited."

10 As early as Theodoret we find an association both with David and with the Jews in exile in Babylon. Theodoret of Cyrus, *Psalms*, 1:323.

11 Goldingay, *Psalms*, 2:183. Goldingay notes other word links between the narrative and the psalm.

56:1–2 Pressure

¹   Be gracious to me, O God, for man tramples on me;
            all day long an attacker oppresses me;
²   my enemies trample on me all day long,
            for many attack me proudly.

The urgent plea **Be gracious to me** echoes the starts of Psalms 51 (ESV mg.) and 57. The intensity of the unrelenting pressure is felt through the repeated verb **trample**[12] and the repeated **all day long** (cf. 56:5). There is some debate about the meaning of the verb translated **trample**, but this is the most likely meaning (so CSB, ESV, NASB, NRSV): people are threatening to crush the King into submission (cf. 57:3; Ezek. 36:3; Amos 2:7).[13] The verb **oppresses** has a similar sense; they press in on him, squeeze him. The subject of the attack is **man** (the same word, אֱנוֹשׁ, *enosh*, used of his betrayer in Ps. 55:13)[14]—which means man in his ordinariness, man in contrast to God[15]—and then **an attacker**—one who fights against me. In 56:2 this becomes plural: **enemies** (with the sense of those who watch or lie in wait, the same word as in 54:5) and **many** of them (cf. 3:1, 2, 6). The word **proudly** is literally the noun "height," that is, their imagined superiority or more powerful position.[16] David, and finally the true Messiah, is under great and unceasing pressure (e.g., Luke 11:53–54); his persecuted church will feel the overflow of this pressure until he returns.

56:3–4 Refrain

³   When I am afraid,
            I put my trust in you.

---

12 In Ps. 56:1 the perfective form may suggest that this is what they repeatedly do; in 56:2 the participle likewise suggests that this is a continuous activity.
13 Ross, *Psalms*, 2:271. The phrases "in hot pursuit" and "pursue" in the NIV alter the imagery unnecessarily.
14 Although the singular here is presumably generic (humankind), perhaps there is a deliberate allusion to the betrayer of Ps. 55:13.
15 Delitzsch writes vividly of "these pigmies that behave as though they were giants." Delitzsch, *Psalms*, 2:167.
16 The suggestion that it is to be taken as a vocative (NRSV: "O Most High"; Tate, *Psalms 51–100*, 66) leading into Ps. 56:3 is very unlikely, since this noun is never elsewhere used in this way. Goldingay, *Psalms*, 2:184.

4   In God, whose word I praise,
           in God I trust; I shall not be afraid.
       What can flesh do to me?

There is a chiastic pattern in the first four lines, placing the emphasis on the **word** of God.

a Fear: **when I am afraid** is literally "the day I am afraid," tying the fear to the incessant "all the day" pressure.

   b Faith: I [emphatic] **put my trust in you**. This picks up from the final words of Psalm 55:23: "But I will trust in you."

      c Word: **In God, whose word I praise** is literally "In God, I praise his word," where "praise" means publicly to boast about, for "he who can trust will soon sing."[17] While the content of the **word** is not spelled out, it must hinge on God's covenant promise to his Messiah (cf. 2:7–9), for it is only this that can provide a sure foundation for the King's trust. When the Messiah's church praises this word, we do so as those who know in Christ the assurances given in the gospel. Although we are not bibliolaters (we do not worship the Scriptures), we may praise his word, for it is intimately connected to God himself.

   b' Faith: **In God I trust**.

a' Fear: **I shall not be afraid**.

This striking chiasm moves, in apparent contradiction, from "I am afraid" to "I shall not be afraid." Only the word of promise to God's Son, given to him and to us in him, can accomplish this remarkable reversal, in the midst of pressure.

The concluding rhetorical question **What can flesh do to me?** contrasts **God** with **flesh**, for the latter can never threaten God's divine-human Messiah or those whom the Messiah promises to raise up on the last day (John 6:39). We must remember "that the contest is in reality between [our] enemies and God, and that it were blasphemous in this case to doubt the issue."[18]

17 Spurgeon, *Treasury*, 1.2:465.
18 Calvin, *Psalms*, 2:351.

56:5–7 Pressure (continued)

⁵   All day long they injure my cause;
        all their thoughts are against me for evil.
⁶   They stir up strife, they lurk;
        they watch my steps,
        as they have waited for my life.
⁷   For their crime will they escape?
        In wrath cast down the peoples, O God!

Psalm 56:5–7 makes clear that the faith of Christ, and of all who are in him, is lived out in the midst of ongoing trials. The repeated **all day long** keeps us in the terrible world of 56:1–2. **They injure my cause** may mean "They twist my words" (CSB, NIV), but the general sense is frightening, whichever way it is understood.[19] Commenting on this clause, Dickson writes, "Let the godly say or do whatsoever they can, how justly, how innocently soever they carry themselves, yet their adversaries will put another face upon their words and deeds than what is right."[20]

The second line of 56:5 intensifies from what they do to what they purpose (**all their thoughts**, in the sense of plans); they not only harm Christ and his church, but they have always intended to harm them.

The concatenation of verbs in 56:6 intensifies the pressure still further. **They stir up strife**—that is, they ignite and fuel quarrels that will set the world against Christ and his people; **they lurk**, with the sinister sense of attacking from hiding (an ambush), in a manner we have seen in Psalm 55 with the betrayer; **they watch** the **steps** (lit., "my heels")[21] of the King, lying in wait for him to stumble (cf. Mark 3:2; Luke 11:54); and they **wait** with the resolute intention of depriving him of his **life**. There is a deadly hostility at work against Christ and all his people.

The first line of Psalm 56:7 is not easy to translate. Literally, it reads, "For iniquity—escape [imperative]—for them." It makes good sense to read it

19 For discussion of the technical issues, see Hossfeld and Zenger, *Psalms*, 2:59nh; Ross, *Psalms*, 2:274.
20 Dickson, *Psalms*, 1:336.
21 There may be an allusion here to the first preaching of the gospel in Gen. 3:15, to the bruised heel of the messianic seed of the woman; see Hamilton, *Psalms*, 1:353.

as a rhetorical question (as in the CSB, ESV), asking, in an astonished tone of voice, "What? Escape? Them?!"[22] The second line follows from this and is a godly petition that God will act in righteous **wrath** to **cast** them **down** (cf. the language of going "down" in the judgments prayed for in 55:15, 23) so that they do not escape.

Reference to **the peoples** suggests a horizon wider than just the Philistines, who are David's immediate foes.[23] This wider horizon strengthens our conviction that David is not asking for personal revenge but praying, as the king, for victory on behalf of his people over the enemies of the Messiah and his God; in the end, this is a prayer that only the King can pray.[24] In lifting our eyes to a more distant horizon, it reminds us that the smallest-scale hostility to God's Messiah (here, the Philistines in Gath) always points to a worldwide rebellion against God (cf. Ps. 2).

56:8–13 In Christ We May Weep with Confidence
56:8–9 Sorrow
There is a theological connection between Psalm 56:8 and 9, that goes to the heart of the psalm.

> 8   You have kept count of my wanderings;[25]
>   put my tears in your bottle.
>   Are they not in your book?

In three poignant lines, the King affirms that his sorrows are precious to God. First, **you have kept count**[26] (i.e., kept a careful count so that you may "take account") **of my wanderings**. The word translated "tossings" in the ESV main text means the "wandering of an aimless fugitive"[27] and echoes the sad wandering of Cain in Genesis 4:14 and 16 (from which the place Nod

---

22 Ross, *Psalms*, 2:267; Hossfeld and Zenger, *Psalms*, 2:59–60. The NIV adds in "do not" to make a tidy parallel with the second line, but this is neither necessary nor justified.
23 Harman's suggestion that "the peoples" means simply "the Philistine peoples" has not proved persuasive. Harman, *Psalms*, 1:430.
24 Eveson, *Psalms*, 1:353.
25 ESV mg.
26 Unlike the CSB, ESV, NASB, NRSV, and REB, the NIV uses the imperative ("Record"), presumably to make a tidier parallel with the second and third lines, but it does so without justification from the Hebrew.
27 BDB, s.v. נוד.

takes its name) or the erratic "flitting" of a small bird in Proverbs 26:2. As seen vividly in David's desperate wanderings, the anointed King is pursued, as we might say, "from pillar to post"; he has nowhere to lay his head but is constantly on the move. Like Cain in his punishment but unlike Cain in his deservings, the Messiah wanders in a weary world. God watches and keeps loving count of each such fugitive movement.

Second, the King pleads, **Put my tears in your bottle**. The word translated **bottle** means a skin bottle such as might be used to store precious water or wine in the wilderness.[28] The tears of the anointed King have great efficacy with God (cf. Ps. 6; Isa. 38:5). They are precious in his sight.

Building on lines 1 and 2, line 3 implies that every fugitive movement and each sorrowing tear of the Messiah is recorded—one by one, with careful love—in God's **book**.[29]

The wanderings and the tears of Christ (cf. Heb. 5:7) are of infinite value to the loving heart of the Father. In Christ each experience of not belonging in this age and every sorrow in the heart of a believer is of priceless value to the heart of the triune God. As Dickson explains,

> God hath so great compassion on his servants in trouble that he reckoneth even the steps of their wanderings and pilgrimage, and numbereth all their tears, and keepeth the count thereof, as it were in a register; and therefore every troubled servant of God, when he looks upon his sufferings, should look upon God also taking as particular notice of his troubles as he himself can do.[30]

> 9   Then my enemies will turn back
>   in the day when I call.
>   This I know, that God is for me.

Psalm 56:9 follows theologically from 56:8. The sin-bearing sufferings of the Messiah win for his people a great victory. The phrase **in the day**

---

28 The NIV rendering—"List my tears on your scroll"—follows the suggestion of Dahood that "skin" here means a parchment for writing rather than a water bottle. Dahood, *Psalms*, 2:48. This makes for an easier parallelism with the third line but "flies in the face of tradition and interpretively renders a Hebrew word that means 'wineskin/waterbag' in all its other occurrences." Wilson, *Psalms*, 1:823.

29 Cf. Ex. 32:32–33; Ps. 69:28; Isa. 34:16; Dan. 7:10; 12:1; Phil. 4:3; Rev. 3:5; 13:8; 20:12, 15; 21:27.

30 Dickson, *Psalms*, 1:337.

picks up the repeated theme of "the day" from earlier in the psalm (56:1, 2, 3 ["when"], 5). The Messiah is pursued and pressured "all the day," but in whatever "day" he **calls** out to God in prayer, he is heard (cf. John 11:41–42), as will his people be. His **enemies will turn back** from their attack defeated because of the sin-bearing sorrows of the Messiah. He knows, as each man and woman in Christ may know today, **that God is for me**, words that fly like an arrow into a Christ-filled future; because God was for his Christ, all who belong to Christ may know that God is for them (Rom. 8:31).

56:10–11 Refrain

¹⁰   In God, whose word I praise,
        in the LORD, whose word I praise,
¹¹   in God I trust; I shall not be afraid.
        What can man do to me?

The refrain intensifies the theme of God's **word** by repeating the line **whose word I praise**[31] with the covenant name, **the LORD** (rare in this section of the Psalter and therefore marking particular emphasis). Again, **trust** in the **word** of covenant promise to the Messiah leads the King out of his natural fears, just as it does today for all who belong to him. The final line replaces "flesh" (Ps. 56:4) with **man** (אָדָם, *adam*), the word that hints at earthy frailty (cf. Gen. 2:7); the effect is much the same whichever word is used.

56:12–13 Thanksgiving

¹²   I must perform my vows to you, O God;
        I will render thank offerings to you.
¹³   For you have delivered my soul from death,
            yes, my feet from falling,
        that I may walk before God
            in the light of life.

---

31 There is a very small difference. Ps. 56:4 ends, "I praise *his* word [דְּבָרוֹ]"; here both lines read, "I praise the word [דָּבָר]." This is unlikely to be significant.

The two lines of Psalm 56:12 are emphatic parallelism. The first line is literally "upon me, O God, your vows," where the sense must be that **my vows to you** (the sense of "your vows") are an obligation on me to perform (as in the ESV). This is much the same as the resolution **I will render** (make good on) **thank offerings to you**. Although David is still in dire straits, he knows that he will be rescued, and so he resolves even now to offer a sacrifice of praise.

Psalm 56:13 anticipates by faith the content of his thanksgiving. **For you have delivered** (perhaps in the sense of a prophetic perfect) **my soul** (my life) **from death**. In the end, this is the deliverance of Easter Day and—for David and all who belong to Christ—of the day of resurrection. The second line develops this theme, placing the focus not on life per se but on **feet** (i.e., a life lived) kept **from falling**, whether stumbling into sin or irretrievable disaster. His enemies watch for him to stumble, but God will keep him from stumbling. In the end (for David himself did stumble badly; cf. Ps. 51), this is true for Jesus Christ, who lived and died without sin, but it is also true in the sense of Proverbs 24:16, that all who are righteous by faith in God's Messiah will not finally fall. **That I may walk before God / in the light of life** is the glorious punchline, for David in the final day of resurrection as for us in Christ on that day—all and only because the vindicated Messiah walks with the Father in the light of resurrection life.

REFLECTION AND RESPONSE

1. Meditate on the life of faith in the earthly trials of the Lord Jesus as he cries out in the words of this psalm. Walk first with him through the pressure, and watch him replace fear with faith—no doubt again and again—as he rests his destiny on the word of the Father. Wonder at his trials; marvel yet more at his faith.

2. Be realistic about how our trials will cause us to fear. And yet take heart, for the word of promise "settleth a troubled mind, strengtheneth weak courage, and relieveth the oppressed heart."[32]

3. Do not aspire to faith as a human quality; focus on the word of God, his solemn covenant promise to his Christ and, in Christ, to us. John Cal-

---

32 Dickson, *Psalms*, 1:335.

vin comments, "How prone we are to fret and to murmur when it has not pleased God immediately to grant our requests" and we have "to depend upon his naked promises."[33]

4. With the heart of a pastor, Charles Spurgeon reflects on faith and fear in the believer's experience:

> The condition of the Psalmist's mind was complex—he feared, but that fear did not fill the whole area of his mind. . . . It is possible, then, for fear and faith to occupy the mind at the same moment. We are strange beings, and our experience in the divine life is stranger still. We are often in a twilight, where light and darkness are both present and it is hard to tell which predominates. It is a blessed fear which drives us to trust. Unregenerate fear drives from God, gracious fear drives to him.[34]

5. Ponder the words "in the day when I call" (Ps. 56:9), and consider, in Christ, what a wonderful assurance there is in our prayers. Whatever the day of distress, God always hears; he always will.

6. In sorrow do not hesitate to pray, "Put my tears in your bottle," for our heavenly Father will catch every one before ever it reaches the ground. He treasures the sorrows of Christ's people, every one, as he treasured every tear of Christ on earth. Not one will be lost; not one will fail in its divine purpose.

33 Calvin, *Psalms*, 2:350.
34 Spurgeon, *Treasury*, 1.2:465.

*Who can worthily describe the power and benevolence
of this psalm? Christ prays to teach us, rises again
to raise us, praises the Father to instruct us.*

CASSIODORUS
Explanation of the Psalms

*The psalmist, foreseeing in his spirit that the gift of this promise
would come and desiring that it come quickly, said, "Be exalted,
O God, above the heavens, and let your glory be over all the earth!"
Here he . . . means that . . . when the God-man arose from the dead
and penetrated the heights of heaven, then the glory of his name
was proclaimed and believed throughout the whole wide world.*

THE VENERABLE BEDE
Homilies on the Gospels

*The Son of God himself used this psalm against his persecutors
and praised God his Father, that he freed him from their
accusations and lifted him up to a place of honor.*

NICOLAUS SELNECKER
The Whole Psalter

*Christ is the chief Speaker, entering into his own
difficulties and those of his Church. . . . But his
people can use every word of [the psalm].*

ANDREW BONAR
Christ and His Church in the Book of Psalms

PSALM 57

ORIENTATION

ORIENTATION

In Psalm 57, often sung on Easter Sunday, the Lord Jesus Christ's experience of humiliation and longing for exaltation are set together, that his people may learn how to suffer, how to pray, and how to hope.

As with several psalms in this section of the Psalter, we are in the company of David the anointed king as he endures trials before coming into his kingdom. He is a type of Christ in his sufferings and of Christ's church in our trials.[1] The connection with Christ is strengthened because 57:9 is very similar to 18:49, quoted of Christ and the worldwide mission of the church by Paul in Romans 15:9. When David declares that he will sing God's praises in the world, he foreshadows Christ, who does this today in the mission of his church.

The refrain (Ps. 57:5, 11) is pregnant with Christological meaning. In his days on earth, Jesus could and did pray that the Father would be exalted. But since Christ is both God and man, the prayer for God to be exalted is inseparable from the desire that Christ be exalted. We now pray this refrain both in acclamation that Christ is exalted (in his resurrection and ascension) and in longing for his return in glory.

Psalms 56–60 form a subgroup (see on Ps. 56). Psalm 57 especially is closely linked with Psalm 56: the general context is similar, each has a refrain, each opens with an appeal for grace ("Be gracious to me"), each closes with thanksgiving, each uses the verb "trample" (56:1–2; 57:3), and each mentions "the peoples" (56:7; 57:9).

---

1   Hamilton, *Psalms*, 1:541–42.

There are several verbal links right back to the beginning of book 1. These include God as refuge (57:1; cf. 2:12; 7:1), God as "Most High" (57:2; cf. 7:17), the verb "trample" (57:3; cf. 7:5), references to lions and teeth (57:4; cf. 3:7; 7:2), the wicked falling into their own pit (57:6; cf. 7:15), and the word "my glory" to describe David's kingly being (57:8; cf. 3:3; 4:2 [the same Hebrew word, though translated "my honor" in the ESV]).

Stylistically, the psalm includes several immediate repetitions of words or phrases for emphasis (e.g., "be merciful," 57:1; "will send," 57:3; "my heart is steadfast," 57:7; "awake," 57:8).[2]

Psalm 57:7–11 is very similar to Psalm 108:1–5, which also incorporates part of Psalm 60; see on Psalm 108 for discussion of these parallels. There are two links with Psalm 36: Psalm 57:1 is similar to 36:7, and 57:10 mirrors 36:5 almost verbatim.

THE TEXT

Structure
The simplest way to view the structure of the psalm is as two sections: Psalm 57:1–4, prayer in suffering, with the refrain in 57:5, and then 57:6–10, the confidence of faith, with the refrain in 57:11. (While the two occurrences of *Selah* may be pauses for reflection, they do not here seem to be structural markers.)

Superscription

> [S]   To the choirmaster:[3] according to Do Not Destroy. A Miktam[4] of David, when he fled from Saul, in the cave.[5]

Two questions are prompted by this superscription. First, what is the meaning of **Do Not Destroy**, which is shared with Psalms 58, 59, and 75? While this may be a tune or musical setting, the phrase **according to** has to

---

2   Ross, *Psalms*, 2:287. For a longer list, see Goldingay, *Psalms*, 2:193. Zenger suggests that Ps. 57 represents something of an intensification of Ps. 56. Hossfeld and Zenger, *Psalms*, 2:75.
3   See on Ps. 4.
4   For other psalms marked Miktam, see Pss. 16, 56, 58, 59, 60.
5   The other historical superscriptions are for Pss. 3, 7, 18, 34, 51, 52, 54, 56, 59, 60, 63, 142. In Hebrew the superscription is verse 1; subsequent verse numbers are increased by one.

be added by the translators. (The usual word used in the Psalter to signal a melody is lacking.)[6] And it seems likely that the language of the wish "Please do not destroy" has some significance, perhaps as "a kind of subheading that states the Psalm's theme and sets its tone."[7] It has been suggested that this clause alludes to 1 Samuel 26:9 ("Do not destroy him");[8] while this is possible, it would not fit so well with Psalms 58, 59, or 75. More likely, it alludes to a motif found in Deuteronomy 9:26 (where the identical phrase appears when Moses prays, "Do not destroy your people") and Isaiah 65:8, in which God promises that he will not destroy his troubled people.[9] It seems likely that, whether or not this was a tune, the plea **Do Not Destroy** is a prayer that God would preserve his Messiah and his Messiah's people.

The second question—or pair of related questions—concerns **when he fled from Saul, in the cave:**[10] To what episode in David's life does this refer? And what light does it shed on the psalm? We do not know for certain the answer to the first of these. Immediately after David flees from Gath (the context of Ps. 56), David escapes "to the cave of Adullam" (1 Sam. 22:1), where he is joined by a bitter and disillusioned rabble. The links between Psalms 56 and 57 may suggest that this is the context here.[11] Alternatively, there is the episode of 1 Samuel 24, in another cave "in the wilderness of Engedi." Some verbal links may suggest this to be the context here.[12] We cannot be sure which of these it was or if it refers to some unrecorded refuge in another cave. What is clear—and it is this, above all, that sheds light on the psalm—is that he was fleeing from Saul and was in a cave. He was a fugitive hidden from sight. The cave was for David "the symbol of his whole condition" (cf. "and in dens and caves of the earth," Heb. 11:38).[13] Charles

---

6 עַל.

7 Hamilton, *Psalms*, 1:539; cf. Hengstenberg, *Psalms*, 2:247.

8 This suggestion was made by David Kimchi (ca. 1160–ca. 1235), as noted by Alter, *Psalms*, 198, and is echoed, for example, by Theodoret of Cyrus, *Psalms*, 1:327. Saul himself pleads for his name not to be destroyed in 1 Sam. 24:21.

9 Tate, *Psalms 51–100*, 77.

10 The words "in the cave" reappear in the superscription to Ps. 142, another Davidic psalm.

11 Hengstenberg, *Psalms*, 2:248.

12 The most significant links are the word "wing" or "corner [of a garment]" (1 Sam. 24:4; Ps. 57:1; etc.), David being defended against false words (1 Sam. 24:10), the word "my soul," and—perhaps most striking—that Saul symbolically "falls" into the "pit" (the cave) into which David has been cast! Hossfeld and Zenger, *Psalms*, 2:70; cf. Wilson, *Psalms*, 1:830.

13 Hengstenberg, *Psalms*, 2:248.

Spurgeon calls this "a song from the bowels of the earth," like Jonah's from the bowels of the sea (Jonah 2), and, like Jonah's, "it has a taste of the place."[14]

Christ is the glorious anointed King, but on earth his identity was hidden. Older writers saw in the hiddenness of David a foreshadowing of the hiddenness of the Lord Jesus's divine nature during his life on earth.[15] Augustine developed this thought at some length, even speaking of the cave as a picture of the tomb.[16] Although these thoughts seem fanciful to our post-"Enlightenment" eyes, they are evocative and theologically suggestive. The Puritan David Dickson comments, "The cave was as a grave, and the army of Saul at the mouth of the grave, was as the grave-stone."[17]

57:1–4 The Messiah and His Church Lament in Time of Trial

1   Be merciful to me, O God, be merciful to me,
         for in you my soul takes refuge;
     in the shadow of your wings I will take refuge,
         till the storms of destruction pass by.

The plea **Be merciful to me** ("Be gracious to me") echoes the openings of Psalms 51 and 56, repeated here for intensity.[18] The verb **takes refuge** is common, especially in the psalms of David (including Ps. 16, the only Miktam outside this group); it moves from a perfect form (**takes refuge**, or "has taken refuge," 57:1a, suggesting a pattern of past reliance) to an imperfect form (**I will take refuge**, 57:1b), expressing continuing dependence: "that which has once taken place . . . and still, because it is a living fact, is ever, and now in particular, renewed."[19] The phrase **in the shadow of your wings** (cf. 17:8; 36:7; 61:4; 63:7; 91:4) may allude to the covenantal protection symbolized by the wings of the cherubim overshadowing the mercy seat (e.g., Ex. 25:20; 37:9;

---

14   Spurgeon, *Treasury*, 1.2:475.
15   Cassiodorus writes of the Lord's divinity, "hidden within the temple of his body." Cassiodorus, *Psalms*, 2:38.
16   Augustine, *Psalms*, 3:106.
17   Dickson, *Psalms*, 1:340.
18   "Grant me grace, grant me grace." Alter, *Psalms*, 198. Cassiodorus comments that Christ "repeatedly demanded the miracle of the resurrection since He was to undergo the dangers of the passion." Cassiodorus, *Psalms*, 2:39.
19   Delitzsch, *Psalms*, 2:174.

1 Kings 6:24; cf. Ezek. 1 [5x]; 10:8–21; 11:22).[20] The other Old Testament use of "wings" is for the corner of a garment, used as the symbol of protection (e.g., Ruth 2:12; 3:9; Ezek. 16:8).[21] This prayer—from David, from Jesus, from Christians—recognizes that **the storms of destruction** (the time of danger) will **pass by** but that, until then, he and we urgently need God's protection.

2   I cry out to God Most High,
            to God who fulfills his purpose for me.

The cry **to God Most High** introduces a motif of God's supreme height (cf. the "heavens" in Ps. 57:3, 5, 10, 11) and a contrast with the "cave" (57:S) and the "pit" (57:6). The phrase **who fulfills his purpose for me** translates a rare verb (cf. 138:8) and conveys a confidence later expressed by Paul in Philippians 1:6.[22]

3   He will send from heaven and save me;
            he will put to shame him who tramples on me.   *Selah*
        God will send out his steadfast love and his faithfulness!

The high origin (**from heaven**; cf. "God Most High," Ps. 57:2) and the repeated **will send** express the confidence of the Messiah—and now the Messiah's people—in God's covenant promises. The verb **tramples** is repeated from Psalm 56:1–2. As Augustine declares, "The Father did send from heaven and save [Christ]; the Father sent from heaven and saved him from the dead."[23]

Perhaps *Selah* (in the middle of the verse) prompts us to pause and increases our anticipation for the final, conclusive line, in which we learn what **God will send** to rescue his King and the King's people, namely, **his**

---

20 This is the most common use of "wings" in the Old Testament. There is a useful summary of the case for this symbolism in Tate, *Psalms 51–100*, 77–78.

21 Scripture also employs the image of a hen guarding her young in her "shadow" (Isa. 34:15) or under her wings (Matt. 23:37; Luke 13:34), although this image is not used with "wings" in the Old Testament.

22 This is the meaning assumed by the NRSV and REB. It is possible, however, that the verb means "to avenge" (CSB: "who avenges me"; cf. NIV: "who vindicates me"). For discussion, see Ross, *Psalms*, 2:284; Harman, *Psalms*, 1:434.

23 Augustine, *Psalms*, 3:109.

steadfast love (חֶסֶד, *khesed*, covenant love) **and his faithfulness** (to his covenant promises). This is echoed in John 1:14, where "grace" (covenant steadfast love) and "truth" (covenant faithfulness) echo this pair of attributes. In Christ, and in Christ alone, we too may receive that grace (John 1:16). When the Father sends us Christ, he sends us, with Christ, all the riches of covenant love and faithfulness (cf. 2 Cor. 1:20).

4   My soul is in the midst of lions;
         I lie down amid fiery beasts—
      the children of man, whose teeth are spears and arrows,
         whose tongues are sharp swords.

The clause **I lie down** (cohortative) probably indicates "a strong resolution" ("because of my faith I decide to lie down" in trust; cf. Pss. 3:3; 4:8).[24] The phrase **fiery beasts** has the sense of a burning that devours its prey.[25] The references to **teeth** and **tongues** as being like **spears**, **arrows**, and **sharp swords** echoes what was said of the betrayer in Psalm 55:21 (cf. 59:7). Truly, "death and life are in the power of the tongue" (Prov. 18:21). Cassiodorus observes, "Those words which they uttered: *Crucify, crucify*, are compared to a sharp sword. Just as a sharp blade brings death more speedily, so these words effected a swift death-sentence."[26]

57:5 A Confident Refrain in Time of Trial

5   Be exalted, O God, above the heavens!
         Let your glory be over all the earth!

The theme of great height ("God Most High") continues with the verb **be exalted** and the phrase **above the heavens**. The merism (a way of including everything) **heavens** and **earth** vividly encompasses the whole created order (cf. Gen. 1:1). **Glory** indicates visible, experienced majesty, the sheer weighti-

---

24 Kirkpatrick, *Psalms*, 2:332.
25 Ross, *Psalms*, 2:285. There is a full discussion in Hossfeld and Zenger, *Psalms*, 2:68nf. Some take "the sons of men" at the start of line 3 to be the end of line 2, that is, the object of their devouring (hence NRSV: "that greedily devour human prey").
26 Cassiodorus, *Psalms*, 2:42.

ness of God pressing on humankind. The crucial link between the suffering King in the body of the psalm and the exalted God in the refrain is this: God is exalted when his Christ is lifted high. For David, God will in some measure be exalted when David, God's anointed, comes into the kingdom and is given victories over surrounding peoples. But in the end it is when Jesus Christ, the God-man, is lifted high in resurrection and ascension that the triune God will be exalted and his glory be over the earth. This is so because in the incarnate Son of God, the glory of God is seen (John 1:14). Augustine explains,

> Moved by the Spirit, this prophet beheld the Lord humiliated, buffeted, scourged, punched, slapped, spat on, crowned with thorns and hung on the tree. He beheld the executioners behaving savagely and Christ enduring it; he saw in the Spirit them triumphing and him apparently defeated. He saw too that after all his humiliation and their savagery Christ rose again. . . . The prophet was transported with joy, as though he saw it all happening, and he cried, *Be lifted up above the heavens, O God.* A man you were on the cross, but God above the heavens. Let them remain on earth to rant, but you be in heaven to judge.[27]

As we wait for the Lord Jesus to return in glory, this refrain—like the prayers "Your kingdom come" and "Come, Lord Jesus!"—expresses the confident longing of Christian hearts that the cave experience of Christ's church will not last forever.

57:6–10 The Messiah and His Church Declare Confident Faith in Time of Trial

6   They set a net for my steps;
         my soul was bowed down.
     They dug a pit in my way,
         but they have fallen into it themselves.   *Selah*

Psalm 57:6 takes us straight back to the sufferings of the Messiah and his people. The parallel images of a hunter's **net** for the King's **steps** (lit., "feet") and

27 Augustine, *Psalms*, 3:113–14.

a hunter's **pit** in the path of the King's **way** use common psalmic language to express both the hidden dangers that beset the anointed King and the shadowy threats that surround his people. As a result, **my soul** (my life) **was bowed down**, unsurprisingly, since the **pit** becomes an image of the grave and Sheol. The surprise comes in the final line: **They have fallen into it themselves** (cf. 7:14–15). The sense is that of a prophetic perfect, for the eye of faith can see this before it happens. Hostility to Christ and his church is ultimately self-defeating.

The Spirit of Christ enabled David to see this in the midst of his trials, as Christ entrusted himself to the one who judges justly and now schools his people to do the same. And so the music turns to confidence. (Psalm 57:7–11 is incorporated into 108:1–5.)

> 7   My heart is steadfast, O God,
>   my heart is steadfast!
>   I will sing and make melody!

My heart is steadfast (emphatically repeated) speaks of the core of the King's being as having "enduring stability and reliability,"[28] rooted as it is in the covenant promises of the Father. Because the Messiah had this steadfast heart, he could grant it by his Spirit both to his "type," King David (the word "steadfast" is the same word translated "right" in the phrase "a right spirit" in Ps. 51:10), and now to all his disciples (cf. "stable," Col. 1:23).[29] The glad resolutions **I will sing** and **[I will] make melody** (both cohortatives) are the overflow of a heart made steadfast by the covenant promises to the Messiah, now enjoyed by us in him.

> 8   Awake, my glory!
>   Awake, O harp and lyre!
>   I will awake the dawn!

The word **my glory**[30] speaks of the kingly honor given to the anointed one as Son of God (see on Ps. 3:3), a glory now promised to his undeserv-

---

28 Wilson says that this is the sense of the niphal of כון here. The hiphil of the same verb is used in Ps. 57:6 ("they set"). Wilson, *Psalms*, 1:832.

29 Kirkpatrick points out that ἑδραῖος is used by Symmachus in his translation of this verse in the psalm. Kirkpatrick, *Psalms*, 2:324.

30 כְּבוֹדִי. "My soul" in the CSB and NIV perhaps misses the specific nuance of this word.

ing people, who may join with Christ in saying this verse. The **harp and lyre** express the glad, victorious dignity of the Messiah and of his people as they celebrate all that is theirs in Christ. The clause **I will awake the dawn** (perhaps suggesting that this was an evening psalm; cf. "lie down," 57:4), is usually thought to be a poetic device to express eager determination ("I am so keen to praise my God that I will wake up before dawn, and the sound of my singing will wake the dawn"). Augustine may be right to suggest that this finds its fulfillment in the resurrection of Christ, which awakes the dawn of a new age.[31]

> 9   I will give thanks to you, O Lord, among the peoples;
>   I will sing praises to you among the nations.

If we were in any doubt that David is a type of Christ in this psalm, this verse ought to settle the matter for us. As Dickson explains, "David was a type of Christ in sufferings, spiritual exercises, and in receiving deliveries; for this promise is fulfilled in Christ, and this undertaking is applied to Christ."[32] And John Calvin says, "As the *nations* and *peoples* are here said to be auditors of the praise which he offered, we must infer that David, in the sufferings spoken of throughout the psalm, represented Christ."[33]

In speaking of **peoples** and **nations**,[34] David shows that he grasps the worldwide breadth of the covenant with Abraham as it applies to the anointed King. We should not be surprised that this determination to praise God around the whole world should be echoed in the context of the worldwide proclamation of Christ in Romans 15:9 (quoting the very similar words in Ps. 18:49). In its context here in Psalm 57, this praise is to the God who has raised his Messiah from the grave (cf. the cave) and exalted him as God on high (57:5, 11). This declaration that "Jesus is Lord!" now echoes around the world. This verse, says Cassiodorus, "points to the heavenly activity of the universal Church, which

---

31 Augustine writes, "You do not need to be told that this is a reference to our Lord's resurrection." Augustine, *Psalms*, 3:117.

32 Dickson, *Psalms*, 1:344–45.

33 Calvin, *Psalms*, 2:366.

34 The former perhaps focusing on political entities, the latter on ethnicity—so Wilson, *Psalms*, 1:834.

in varied tongues through all the nations sings a psalmody to the Lord with devoted heart."[35]

10   For your steadfast love is great to the heavens,
          your faithfulness to the clouds.

The **steadfast love** (*khesed*) and **faithfulness** sent out by God in Christ (see on 57:3) is the highest of God's greatness, **great to the heavens** and **to the clouds**. It is not God as some abstract "god of the philosophers" but God as he is known in Christ, who is "God Most High" and who acts in covenant kindness for his people.[36]

57:11 A Confident Refrain in Time of Trial (Repeated)

11   Be exalted, O God, above the heavens!
          Let your glory be over all the earth!

Augustine closes his sermon by quoting this verse and adding, "The prophet said that to God many, many years ago; we see now that it has come true, so let us say it with him."[37]

REFLECTION AND RESPONSE

1. As we sing this psalm, we remember that none of us is the King, but we are invited to be among the unimpressive group that surrounds the King (unimpressive then, e.g., 1 Sam. 22:2, and unimpressive now, 1 Cor. 1:26–27). For to be in Christ is to be the King's friend, sharing with him the "cave" that we may share with him the exaltation. To be his friend is our only hope.

---

35 Cassiodorus, *Psalms*, 2:44.
36 Nikolaus Selnecker (1530–1592) writes of "God clothed in his kindness and goodness" and of "how [God] has manifested himself to us through his beloved Son and how he has had compassion on us." Selnecker, *The Whole Psalter*, in *Reformation Commentary on Scripture* (hereafter cited as *RCS*), ed. Timothy George and Scott M. Manetsch (Downers Grove, IL: IVP Academic, 2011–), 7:417.
37 Augustine, *Psalms*, 3:119.

2. As we ponder Psalm 57:1, we remember that those who persevere to the end (Matt. 24:13) and endure through "the storms of destruction" do so only because they belong to Christ, who first walked this way, and "have learned from the body's head the long-suffering that perseveres."[38] In him we may pray, with Charles Wesley (1707–1788), "Hide me, O my Savior, hide, till the storms of life be passed."[39]

3. From Psalm 57:2 with Philippians 1:6 and 2:12–13, "the consideration of the Lord's constant going on [continuing] in the perfecting of the work of grace . . . serveth much to strengthen our faith in prayer."[40]

4. Meditating on Psalm 57:4, we remember that unfair attacks on the righteousness of Christians are particularly painful and difficult to refute. We ought not to be surprised.

5. Commenting on the glory of God in the refrain, Calvin notes that it is no small comfort "to consider that God, in appearing for the help of his people, at the same time advances his own glory."[41]

6. When facing hidden or covert attacks (Ps. 57:6), the people of Christ may take comfort both that such attacks were made on Jesus Christ and—as the end of the verse assures us—that such attacks will always fail in the end.

7. The joy of Psalm 57:7–8 is the gladness of Christ's resurrection and of our future resurrection guaranteed in him.

8. Psalm 57:9 (with Rom. 1:1–17; 15:8–33) spurs us to be a part of the worldwide mission of the church, led by Christ in declaring the praises of the triune God in the world.

---

38 Augustine, *Psalms*, 3:108.

39 Charles Wesley, "Jesus, Lover of My Soul" (1740). Public domain. Quoted in Eveson, *Psalms*, 1:346.

40 Dickson, *Psalms*, 1:341.

41 Calvin, *Psalms*, 2:364.

[The voice of Psalm 58] is sweet and familiar to the Church's ears,
for it is the voice of our Lord Jesus Christ, and the voice of his body,
the voice of the Church as it struggles along its pilgrim way on
earth, living in peril among those who curse and those who flatter.

AUGUSTINE
Expositions of the Psalms

[In Psalm 58 we hear] the Righteous One reasoning with
the ungodly in prospect of the day of vengeance.

ANDREW BONAR
Christ and His Church in the Book of Psalms

PSALM 58

ORIENTATION

Psalm 58 is a reality check, both about the world in which the church must live and—at the same time—about the world that all too often lives within the church. It is a psalm about power. As David, hunted by Saul, knew what it was to be on the wrong side of power, so his greater son, the Lord Jesus, lived in weakness surrounded by unjust power. His church must walk in the same world. David himself sometimes used his power abusively, just as evil power infiltrates the church of Christ today in many ways.

This psalm is an exposé of the misuse of power and a declaration of judgment on it. It shares features with Psalms 14 and 53 and also Psalms 12, 82, and 101.

We may think of Jesus singing Psalm 58 in his earthly life and now leading his church in singing it. For us, as for Jesus on earth, it voices realism about evil and the encouragement of faith. For us it is also a warning, lest we misuse our power.

Connections with the preceding psalms include the following: evil going back to birth (51:5; 58:3), the power of the tongue (52:2–4; 58:3–5), the judgment of God (52:5; 53:5; 58:6–9), the "righteous" (52:6–7; 58:10–11), corruption in the heart (53:1; 58:2), violence (55:9; 58:2), the origin of evil in human planning (56:5; 58:2), and the wicked like lions (57:4; 58:6). The judgment of God on his enemies and the resulting joy of God's people echo the same themes in the Song of Moses (Deut. 32:34–43).

THE TEXT

Structure

Psalm 58:10–11 both echoes and contrasts 58:1–2 ("right"/"righteousness"; judgment; the word אָדָם, adam, in 58:1, "children of אָדָם, adam," and in

58:11, "mankind" = אָדָם, *adam*).[1] There are those who judge wrongly and a God who judges rightly. These pairs of verses bracket the psalm and give it its theme. Psalm 58:3–5 expands on the challenge to the wicked in 58:1–2 with a penetrating diagnosis. Psalm 58:6–9 voices a sustained and vividly illustrated prayer for God to act in judgment, a prayer that is greeted with joy and assurance in 58:10–11. The uncertainties surrounding 58:9 account for most of the paragraphing differences in translations.

Superscription

S   To the choirmaster:[2] according to Do Not Destroy.[3] A Miktam[4] of David.[5]

The fact that all the elements in this superscription are shared with Psalms 57 and 59, and all except "Do Not Destroy" with Psalms 56 and 60, suggests that this psalm should be read alongside them. It probably also indicates that it arose from that same period of Sauline persecution that is explicitly said to be associated with Psalms 52, 54, 56, 57, and 59.

58:1–5 The Church of Christ Walks in an Unjust World
58:1–2 A Challenge

1   Do you indeed decree what is right, you gods?
     Do you judge the children of man uprightly?

Indeed (surely, really) comes from the same root as "amen." The tone here expresses disbelief (like Sarah in Gen. 18:13: "Shall I *indeed* bear a child?"): "Do you indeed? I know you don't!" The phrases **decree what is right** and **judge . . . uprightly** signal that the subject is the use and misuse of power.[6] **Right** translates the Hebrew word for "righteousness," and **uprightly** means "in fairness"; the sense of the two terms here

---

1   Note also "the wicked" at the start of Ps. 58:3 and in 58:10.
2   See on Ps. 4.
3   See on Ps. 57.
4   For other psalms marked Miktam, see Pss. 16, 56, 57, 59, 60.
5   In Hebrew the superscription is verse 1; subsequent verse numbers are increased by one.
6   To "judge" means not only to give a decision in court but to govern (as in the book of Judges).

is much the same. **The children of man** ("the sons of *adam*") means "humankind."

We cannot be certain of the word translated **you gods**. As pointed in the Masoretic Text, the word means "silence" or "in silence."[7] This would most likely have the sense "Can you really speak righteousness in silence?" (CSB mg.)—that is, you can't do your job of governing rightly if you keep silent when you ought to speak. They are silent when they ought to speak out, just as they are deaf when they ought to listen (Ps. 58:4).[8]

A small revocalization yields "O gods" or "O mighty ones."[9] If the former, the remainder of the psalm (in which human beings abuse their power) suggests that "gods" must have an ironic sense, speaking to those who behaved like gods. Further, Scripture teaches that there is an intimate connection between supernatural powers ("gods") and human beings exercising power (see on Ps. 82), so the two senses are closer than we might think (cf. "the host of heaven, in heaven, and the kings of the earth, on the earth," Isa. 24:21).[10]

2   No, in your hearts you devise wrongs;
      your hands deal out violence on earth.

No[11] is the emphatic answer to the rhetorical question of Psalm 58:1. No! You do not use the power entrusted to you to work righteousness. On the contrary, beginning in the hiddenness of **your hearts** (cf. Gen. 8:21) and evidenced by the works of **your hands**, you do the opposite. The first verb (**devise**) just means to do; it is in imperfective form, perhaps suggesting habitual activity in the heart. The second verb (**deal out**) is ironic, for its normal use is for weighing things out on fair scales. Instead, they weigh out **violence** (חָמָס, *khamas*; cf. Ps. 55:9) **on earth**.

---

7   אֵלֶם. The same word appears in the superscription to Ps. 56 (see discussion there). The translation "silence" considers this to be the noun from one meaning of the root אָלַם (to be quiet). Another meaning of the root is "to bind," which lies behind "congregation" in the KJV (i.e., a group bound together), but no noun is otherwise attested with this meaning from this root, and this should be rejected.

8   Ross, *Psalms*, 2:299, 306.

9   The emendation is to אֵלִים and either comes from אֵל (god) or possibly אַיִל (a ram, i.e., a powerful one). Alter has "chieftains." Alter, *Psalms*, 202.

10 This verse—as noted by Kidner—uses different Hebrew words, but it is still helpful to make the connection. Kidner, *Psalms*, 1:207.

11 אַף.

This is the world in which Jesus lived, knowing as he did all that is in the human heart (John 2:25). It is the world in which his disciples must live. But as Derek Kidner points out, David himself once had to hear his own rebuke, and so do we.[12]

58:3–5 The Diagnosis

Psalm 58:2 has begun the diagnosis of the abuse of power; 58:3–5 develops this.

> 3   The wicked are estranged from the womb;
>   they go astray from birth, speaking lies.

The wicked, so prominent in the Psalter since Psalm 1:1, are character- ized first by being **estranged.** This has the double sense of "going astray" and, as a result, being "estranged" from God and people (for sin is divisive). The verb **go astray** (morally) focuses on the first of these. While this is the natural condition of all people and "an unrenewed man is a born stranger to God, to good men, and all goodness"[13] (cf. Eph. 4:18; Col. 1:21), John Calvin rightly observes that in some this wickedness is restrained by the common grace of God, but others become "monsters of iniquity."[14]

Just as Psalm 58:2 moved from the "heart" to the "hands," so 58:3 moves from the origin of estrangement (**from the womb . . . from birth**) to the evidence (**speaking lies;** cf. 4:2; 5:6; and often).[15] The origin of sin in human nature, passed down to us in Adam, is here presupposed (cf. 51:5), as is the doctrine of total depravity.

The reference to lies leads naturally, via Genesis 3, to the thought of a snake.[16]

---

12   Kidner goes on to warn us that the similarity between Ps. 58:3–5 and the scriptures quoted in Rom. 3:10–18 "is close enough . . . to warn the reader that he faces a mirror, not only a portrait. If he, unlike these as yet, has been 'granted repentance unto life' (cf. Acts 11:18), he has only God to thank." Kidner, *Psalms*, 1:208–9.

13   Dickson, *Psalms*, 1:346–47. "We all come into the world stained with sin, possessed, as Adam's posterity, of a nature essentially depraved, and incapable, in ourselves, of aiming at anything which is good." Calvin, *Psalms*, 2:371.

14   Calvin, *Psalms*, 2:371.

15   The verb "speaking" is the qal of דבר, the piel of which is used in Ps. 58:1 ("decree"). Their speaking is the very opposite of what it ought to be. The NIV—"spreading lies"—is perhaps a little periphrastic. The CSB—"liars wander about from birth"—takes those who speak lies as the subject, which is possible.

16   For this imagery used of human beings, see also Deut. 32:33; Ps. 140:3.

⁴   They have venom like the venom of a serpent,
          like the deaf adder that stops its ear,
⁵   so that it does not hear the voice of charmers
          or of the cunning enchanter.

The **serpent** is the normal generic word for a snake (or dragon monster). It does not matter if the **adder** is identified as some other snake, perhaps a cobra[17] or viper.[18] The point is that it is deadly poisonous ("a murderer," John 8:44) and resolutely deaf. Through its own decision, it **stops its ear** so effectively that not even the most **cunning** (lit., "wise," i.e., skillful) snake charmer[19] can make it listen and dissuade it from its evil.[20] Such is the power of self-deception ("deceiving and being deceived," 2 Tim. 3:13).

Unrestrained wickedness is **like** this. The word translated **like** in Psalm 58:4a ("in the likeness of") is used in Genesis 1:26 of human beings made in the "likeness" of God; perhaps there is irony here, as one made in the "likeness" of God is turned by sin into the "likeness" of the serpent. There is a terrible exposé of this horrific transformation in John 8:39–47, where Jesus traces the fact that his opponents are not able to hear him ("You cannot bear to hear my word," John 8:43) to their spiritual roots in the father of lies. Augustine notes a vivid and visible demonstration of this hard-heartedness when Stephen's hearers "stopped their ears" (Acts 7:57): "They were not deaf, but they made themselves deaf."[21]

This theme is echoed in the "plausibility structures" of human cultures that make it impossible for people to hear the word of God unless God unstops their ears, as Jesus literally and wonderfully did with the deaf. As Gregory of Nazianzus (ca. 329–390) observes, "We hide away our sin, cloaking it over in the depth of our soul, like some festering and malignant disease, as if by escaping human notice we could escape the mighty eye of God and justice. Or else we make excuses for our sin . . . by tightly closing our ears."[22]

Here is a terrible portrait of unrestrained evil, with roots in the heart (Ps. 58:2), origins going back to the womb (58:3), methods deceptive (58:3),

17 BDB, s.v. חָנָשׁ.
18 *HALOT*, s.v. חָנָשׁ.
19 For other references to snakes being charmed, see Eccl. 10:11; Jer. 8:17.
20 It doesn't matter if, in fact, snakes are deaf! The point of the metaphor is clear.
21 Augustine, *Psalms*, 3:130.
22 Gregory of Nazianzus, *Oration 2.20*, in *Ancient Christian Commentary on Scripture* (hereafter cited as *ACCS*), ed. Thomas C. Oden (Downers Grove, IL: InterVarsity Press, 1998–2010), 8:35.

consequences deadly (58:4), and remedy nonexistent (58:4–5). The church that is realistic about this condition—both in the world outside and within its own borders—will necessarily turn to prayer, as we now do, for only a supernatural work of God can change matters.

58:6–9 The Church of Christ Prays for Injustice to Be Defeated

As we move into this passionate prayer for injustice to be defeated, we meet a number of tricky textual problems. But it is worth remembering that "of the drift and scope of the words in general, which concerns the suddenness of wicked people's destruction, of this there is no question at all."[23] David foreshadows Christ leading his people in prayer that God will do what he has promised to do. Psalm 58:6–9 is an ancient form of the cry "Your kingdom come, your will be done, on earth as it is in heaven."

> 6   O God, break the teeth in their mouths;
>   tear out the fangs of the young lions, O LORD!

Psalm 58:6 is the headline prayer. Its first word (in Hebrew as here) is **O God** and its last the covenant name (rare in this part of the Psalter), **O LORD!** The wicked, like powerful predators (**young lions**), threaten the peace and order of the world and the church. The anointed King prays, and teaches us to pray, that even if "they have no capacity for good, at least deprive them of their ability for evil."[24] If the snake represents deceitful deadliness, in the lion our enemy shows himself in his true ferocious hostility (cf. 1 Pet. 5:8).[25] The strong verbs (**break** and **tear out**) together with the fierce **teeth** and **fangs** show what a power of God in judgment is necessary to defend his helpless people.[26]

> 7   Let them vanish like water that runs away;
>   when he aims his arrows, let them be blunted.

The second image (Ps. 58:7a) is clear and evocative. **Water** that so often threatens the people of God can be turned by God into a harmless stream melting away into the ground (cf. 46:3–4).

23 *The English Annotations*, in *RCS* 7:420.
24 Spurgeon, *Treasury*, 2.1:2.
25 For the association of lions and snakes, see also Ps. 91:13 and Isa. 11:7–8.
26 For "break the teeth," see on Ps. 3:7.

The third image (58:7b) speaks of hostility in terms of **arrows** (a common metaphor in Scripture). The verb **be blunted** comes either from the idea of "cutting off" or from that of "withering, fading," and therefore proving ineffective. Either way, we pray that no weapon that is fashioned against the people of God will prove effective (Isa. 54:17).

> 8   Let them be like the snail that dissolves into slime,
>   like the stillborn child who never sees the sun.

The fourth image (Ps. 58:8a) is of a snail **that dissolves into slime** and disappears. It is a prayer that wickedness, never mind how slimy it may be (and is), will dissolve into its own slime.

The fifth image (58:8b) is the most horrifying. **The stillborn child** (lit., "the miscarriage that falls from a woman") is one of the most poignant of griefs. Conception promises so much and attaches to itself such hopes, and here it is all dashed, with many tears, as young life is turned to death. Here, however, it is morally right and necessary that these destructive and evil people be removed from the earth (unless they repent). In James 1:14–15 the image is used of a wicked desire conceived in a heart, giving birth to sin and bringing death into the world. We rejoice when a sinful desire dies before it becomes a monster of violence.

> 9   Sooner than your pots can feel the heat of thorns,
>   whether green or ablaze, may he sweep them away!

Psalm 58:9 is replete with difficulties.[27] But the general sense is clear from the closing words: **May he sweep them away!** This is a prayer that the wicked will be swept away quickly and completely.

58:10–11 The Church of Christ Perseveres Because of the Joy Set before Her

> 10   The righteous will rejoice when he sees the vengeance;
>   he will bathe his feet in the blood of the wicked.

---

27 These may be studied in the technical commentaries, e.g., Ross, *Psalms*, 2:301–2; Goldingay, *Psalms*, 2:202; Delitzsch, *Psalms*, 2:183–84; Tate, *Psalms 51–100*, 82–84.

The righteous is singular (CSB: "the righteous one"), presumably generic but also perhaps hinting, as elsewhere,[28] at the true "Righteous One" (Acts 3:14; 7:52; 22:14), who leads all those who are righteous by faith in this strange rejoicing. The joy is prompted by **the vengeance**. As in Romans 12:19 (quoting Deut. 32:35), this is not a personal revenge (whether of David or of any other believer) but the utterly just, necessary, holy, and pure vengeance of the God who says, "Vengeance is mine; I will repay." All the Messiah's people rejoice when a world overrun with violence and the abuse of power is finally restored and renewed, in the new heavens and new earth.

This joy is widely attested in both the Old and New Testament,[29] for it is a gladness that rises from believing hearts when at last the will of God is done on earth in the same way that it is done in heaven.

Charles Spurgeon writes pastorally of this joy:

> [The Christian] will have no hand in meting it out, neither will he rejoice in the spirit of revenge, but his righteous soul shall acquiesce in the judgments of God, and he shall rejoice to see justice triumphant. There is nothing in Scripture of that sympathy with God's enemies which modern traitors are so fond of parading as the finest species of benevolence.[30]

We are horrified by the clause **He will bathe his feet in the blood of the wicked,** for it seems gruesome and vicious. As with other Bible imagery (e.g., see on Ps. 137:9), we need to train ourselves to enter into the stories from which this imagery arose. This is battle language. When a battle has been completely won, those who are victorious will inevitably walk through the blood of the slain; it is precisely that horrible blood—and only that blood—that demonstrates that their enemies are no more. The image of "bathing" feet may heighten this sense by implying so much blood as will prove without doubt that all the enemies are defeated, never to fight again. Rather as "steps . . . washed with butter" (Job 29:6) is an idiom for great wealth, so feet bathed in blood is an idiom for total victory.[31]

28 See on Ps. 1.
29 E.g., Isa. 63:2–3; Jer. 51:48; Ezek. 28:23; Rev. 14:19–20; 18:20; 19:15.
30 Spurgeon, *Treasury*, 2.1:3–4.
31 Eveson, *Psalms*, 1:361.

¹¹   Mankind will say, "Surely there is a reward for the righteous;
surely there is a God who judges on earth."

Here are the two great conclusions, each prefaced by **surely** for emphasis.[32] First, **there is a reward** (lit., "fruit") **for the righteous** (singular, both
generic and supremely true of the Righteous One). Just as the heart root
of wickedness grows a poisonous fruit, so the good root of faith grows a
tree with fruit that ends with joy. This, supremely, was true of Jesus Christ,
who, out of the travail and anguish of his soul, has entered into the joy that
was set before him (Isa. 53:11; Heb. 12:2).

Here is the definitive answer to the faith-sapping envy of Psalm 73:3
("I was envious of . . . the wicked") and the faithless question of Malachi 2:17
("Where is the God of justice?"); here is the assurance that what we sow
in patient faith we reap in final joy (Gal. 6:7–10) and that our labor in the
Lord is not in vain (1 Cor. 15:58). The life of wickedness may begin with
fun, but it ends in tears; the life of faith sheds many tears but ends in joy
(Ps. 126:5–6).

The final word focuses, as it must, not on the believer's life of faith but
on the **God who judges on earth**.[33] "You don't use power aright, but there
is a judgment."

REFLECTION AND RESPONSE

1. It is instructive for us to hear Jesus Christ issuing the rebuke of
Psalm 58:1–2 and giving the diagnosis of 58:3–5. Like David, we must
hear these words as rebuke and warning before we can begin to hear
them as comfort.

2. It is salutary to consider the use and abuse of power within a Christian
church by pastors, counselors, and others in positions of influence. This
psalm has much to say to them and us.

---

32 The REB rendering "there is after all" (repeated) is periphrastic but catches the sense well.

33 The word for "God" is the usual אֱלֹהִים, grammatically plural but functionally singular when it
refers to the true God. The participle "who judges" (שֹׁפְטִים), however, is also plural, which poses
a problem. Is this meant to read, "Surely there are gods who judge the earth"—as suggested by,
e.g., Alter, *Psalms*, 204; Goldingay, *Psalms*, 2:202? If so, it must be in the loose sense "Oh, yes,
there really are supernatural powers who judge the world (i.e., under the sovereignty of the
true God)." This kind of rendering is implied by Eveson, *Psalms*, 1:362.

3. We must remember that Jesus Christ alone has borne the judgment in all its fullness for his people at the cross. His atoning death is our only hope, and the working of his Holy Spirit is the only gracious ministry that can work the ugliness of Psalm 58:1–5 out of us, out of our pastors, and out of our churches.

4. As with all the prayers for God's judgment on the wicked, it is only Jesus Christ the Righteous One who can pray them with perfect purity of heart. He alone can lead us in praying Psalm 58:6–9 with a proper humility of heart (knowing our own sins) and a proper purity of motive (longing for the glory of God).

5. We see in the resurrection of Jesus the assurance that Psalm 58:10–11 is not wishful thinking. Psalm 58:11 in particular should move us not to grow weary in doing good but to persevere to the end.

6. We may close with this prayer from the sixteenth-century Lutheran Nikolaus Selnecker:

> May the eternal, good and merciful God help us graciously, so that we might recognize his sentences and his judgments, fear him, set our hope on him, persevere in patience and gentleness, as he demands of us, and that we might be saved through his Son, our Lord Christ Jesus. Amen.[34]

---

34 Selnecker, *Whole Psalter*, in *RCS* 7:420.

These prayers and sufferings of Christ . . .
have taken place especially for us.

MARTIN LUTHER
First Lectures on the Psalms

Because such histories about David's crossbearing, suffering
and deliverance are figures and images which signify the
Lord Christ and his church, . . . this psalm can and should be
understood about and spoken in the person of the Lord Christ.

NICOLAUS SELNECKER
The Whole Psalter

[Psalm 59 is] a Psalm for David himself—a Psalm for David's
Son, when he too should be rejected of his own—a Psalm
for all his followers when they should, in after ages, feel
that the disciple is not greater than the Master.

ANDREW BONAR
Christ and His Church in the Book of Psalms

David speaks as the true representative of his people against the
evil intentions of Saul who was out to kill him and endanger
the well-being of the nation. In this he reflects Christ and his
Church while Saul is a type of all anti-Christian forces.

PHILIP EVESON
Psalms

PSALM 59

ORIENTATION

Psalm 59 conveys the pressure of threat. The lurking presence of enemies fills the air. It is not so much about actual harm as about the very real threat of harm. As with other psalms from the days of Sauline persecution, the most natural way to read Psalm 59 is to see the anointed but not yet acclaimed King David to be a type of Jesus in his days on earth, as the true but not yet resurrected Messiah. As Jesus sings this psalm, he opens for us a window into the pressure of threats on his innocent heart.

But as we have done with other such psalms, we must extend the application from Christ the head to Christ's church the body,[1] for this psalm graphically expresses the plight and the prayers of Christ's church in every age when surrounded by the lurking presence of evil.

The phrase "bloodthirsty men" (59:2) appears also in 55:23 ("men of blood" but the same Hebrew), a link between the pressure here and the betrayal there.

Links with Psalm 3, another psalm of pressure on the anointed King, include "rise" / "rising up" (3:1; 59:1), "shield" (3:3; 59:11), evening and morning (59:6, 14, 16) or sleeping and waking (3:5), and the overflow of God's salvation of the King to the blessing of his people (3:8; see also on 59:5, 11, 13).

THE TEXT

Structure

Psalm 59 appears to divide into 59:1–10 and 59:11–17. Each section comprises a prayer (59:1–5, 11–13, each ending with *Selah*), a refrain (59:6–7, 14–15), and an expression of confidence (59:8–10, 16–17).[2]

---

1   E.g., Augustine, *Psalms*, 3:149–50.
2   Hengstenberg, *Psalms*, 2:262.

Superscription

^S   To the choirmaster:[3] according to Do Not Destroy.[4] A Miktam
of David,

Do Not Destroy is shared with Psalms 57 and 58. The designation
A Miktam is shared with Psalms 56–60 (and also Ps. 16). Psalms 56–60
are a subcollection within the "Second Davidic Collection" of psalms
(Pss. 51–72), and Psalms 57–59 a subset of that.

when Saul sent men to watch his house in order to kill him.[5]

This note refers to the episode recorded in 1 Samuel 19:11–17. Several features of the psalm arouse skepticism among commentators about this historical background. The psalm refers to enemies prowling around the streets and
sinning with their words, neither of which feature in the 1 Samuel narrative.
Perhaps most significant are the references to "the nations" (Ps. 59:5, 8), which
are thought to indicate a later (perhaps postexilic)[6] period in Israel's history.

The skepticism is unjustified for at least two reasons. First, the 1 Samuel
narrative is brief; there is much we are not told. It is not at all unlikely that
Saul's men prowled around the streets, sinned with their words, and matched
the portrait of the enemies in the psalm.[7] Second, as elsewhere in psalms
of David, it is entirely reasonable to suppose that David understood, from
the terms of God's covenant (cf. Ps. 2), that what happened to him in this
very personal crisis was a microcosm of the trials and destiny of the whole
people of God, over whom he was anointed as the typical messiah. So the
grand scope of the psalm's language about "the nations" is not inconsistent
with this crisis for the anointed King.[8]

---

3   See on Ps. 4.

4   See on Ps. 57.

5   The other historical superscriptions are for Pss. 3, 7, 18, 34, 51, 52, 54, 56, 57, 60, 63, 142. In
Hebrew the superscription is verse 1; subsequent verse numbers are increased by one.

6   E.g., Wilson, *Psalms*, 1:849.

7   "The Psalms and the Prophets are often the medium through which we gain a deeper insight
into events which are only sketched in the historical books after their most prominent outward
features." Delitzsch, *Psalms*, 2:187.

8   There is a list of verbal and thematic links between 1 Sam. 19 and 24 and Ps. 59 in Tate,
Psalms 51–100, 95. These include David's innocence (1 Sam. 19:4; 24:10–12; Ps. 59:3–4), the
shedding of blood (1 Sam. 19:5; Ps. 59:2), and morning (1 Sam. 19:11–12; Ps. 59:16).

This makes even clearer sense when understood as a foreshadowing of Christ and his church. Some of the older writers saw in the drama of David confined in his house a suggestion of the body of Christ in the tomb, guarded—but unsuccessfully!—by his opponents.[9]

59:1–10 Christ and His Church under Undeserved Pressure
59:1–5 Christ and His Church Pray under Pressure

¹ Deliver me from my enemies, O my God;
> protect me from those who rise up against me;
² deliver me from those who work evil,
> and save me from bloodthirsty men.

The address **O my God** signals a covenant relationship.[10] The repeated verb **deliver** (snatch away out of danger), together with **protect** (lit., "set me on high," i.e., make me inaccessibly high and therefore out of danger)[11] and **save**, conveys a fullness of rescue. The danger comes from **enemies**, whose threat becomes more intense when they actively **rise up against me** (cf. Job 27:7; Ps. 3:1); they "rise up," and so I need to be "set on high" beyond their reach. In their actions they **work evil** and are **bloodthirsty men** (lit., "men of bloods";[12] cf. 55:23 and the singular "man of blood" in 5:6), who count human life cheap (cf. Gen. 9:5–6). Later they will take the blood of God's innocent Son and seek the blood of his followers throughout the history of the church. But Augustine notes, "From these men of blood Christ is rescued: not the head only, but the body too. Christ is delivered from men of blood, from those of former days, those of today, and those who will persecute in the future."[13]

---

9   E.g., "When Saul sent and watched his house that he might slay him: when the Chief Priests sent and watched the sepulchre of Christ, unto the end that they might, as it were, keep Him in death, having closed every door to His Resurrection." The Venerable Bede, in Neale and Littledale, *Psalms*, 2:239.

10 It is a pity that "my" is omitted in the NIV.

11 Wilson, *Psalms*, 1:849. The root (שׂגב) is the same as that of the cognate noun מִשְׂגָּב, "fortress" or "high tower," in Ps. 59:16–17, providing an inclusio between the beginning and end of this psalm.

12 The NIV rendering, "those who are after my blood," narrows the meaning.

13 Augustine, *Psalms*, 3:151.

3   For behold, they lie in wait for my life;
      fierce men stir up strife against me.

For behold! Look and see! The mention of blood (Ps. 59:2) leads naturally to those who **lie in wait** (as in an ambush) **for my life.** These are **fierce men** (where the noun means strong and fierce, anticipating God our "Strength" in 59:9, 16–17). The verb rendered **stir up strife** "is particularly difficult"[14] to translate; it may mean "to conspire" (NIV) or simply "to attack."[15] But the overall picture is clear: David and supremely Jesus Christ and now his church expect to be under life-threatening pressure (cf. Mark 3:2).

      For no transgression or sin of mine, O LORD,
4   no fault of mine, they run and make ready.

These two lines emphatically affirm innocence and use the covenant name, the LORD, to appeal from covenant righteousness to the God of the covenant. David affirmed his innocence vis-à-vis Saul (e.g., 1 Sam. 20:1; 24:11), but, as was noted as early as Theodoret of Cyrus, in an absolute sense "these words apply not to David but to David's son and David's lord: he alone 'committed no sin, nor was any sin found in his mouth' (1 Pet. 2:22)."[16] The Christian disciple, like David, can affirm a covenantal righteousness that is given by grace and lived out in integrity of life. The verbs **they run** and **they . . . make ready** suggest both eagerness ("run"; cf. Ps. 18:29) and a dynamic preparation for war ("make ready"; CSB: "they run and take up a position"). The picture, for Christ as for his church today, is very frightening.

      Awake, come to meet me, and see!

The urgent plea **Awake!** (or "Arouse yourself," e.g., Ps. 3:7 and often) uses an anthropomorphism: God never slumbers or sleeps (121:3–4) and is constantly watching over his King and the King's people, but to our eyes it seems as though God is sleeping. Likewise, **Come to meet me** uses another anthropomorphism, as if God the Father runs to meet his Son, the King

---

14   Wilson, *Psalms*, 1:850n9.
15   *HALOT*, s.v. גור.
16   Theodoret of Cyrus, *Psalms*, 1:337.

(cf. 21:3), and all the King's people. Then he will **see** (a third anthropomorphism; cf. Gen. 11:5) what is happening.

5   You, LORD God of hosts, are God of Israel.
      Rouse yourself to punish all the nations;
            spare none of those who treacherously plot evil.   *Selah*

You (an emphatic adversative, "But you") is followed by an unusual piling up of titles (cf. 2 Sam. 7:27).

LORD God of hosts (cf. Pss. 80:4, 14; 84:8) combines the covenant name, **LORD**, with the assurance of his invincible power (i.e., the God of all the heavenly armies, utterly impossible to defeat and able to achieve whatever he purposes). This is the God who can so easily send "twelve legions of angels" to rescue his Son, were he to ask (Matt. 26:53).

God of Israel focuses covenant power on covenant commitment to a particular people, ultimately to Christ the anointed King and all Christ's church, Jew and Gentile. That David's enemies were part of outward Israel reminds us that hostility to God's Christ and true church may arise within the visible church.

Rouse yourself uses a verb that is synonymous with "Awake" (Ps. 59:4). To **punish** is literally "to visit," that is, to visit with a view to appropriate action (in this case to punish). As in 59:8, the reference to **all the nations**, that is, all the world outside the true people of God, first implies that Saul and his men represent this counterfeit people, just as "counterfeit professors [that is, people who profess to be Christian] and professed pagans [open non-Christians] are in effect one before God."[17] But it also hints that this prayer expands (in the manner of Ps. 2) to involve judgment on all the world.

The prayer **Spare** (be gracious to) **none of those who treacherously plot evil** speaks of those who will finally prove unfaithful to the covenant[18] that will be fulfilled in Christ. This "prayer is not motivated by personal animosity but sees his enemies as part of [the] worldwide conspiracy against God and his anointed (see Ps. 2)."[19] The *Selah* may prompt us to reflect that this

17 Dickson, *Psalms*, 1:351.
18 The verb "treacherously plot" means here to be unfaithful to the covenant. Wilson, *Psalms*, 1:850.
19 Eveson, *Psalms*, 1:364.

characterizes us all by nature. Augustine observes, "This certainly strikes fear into us. . . . Is there anyone who does not tremble on looking into his or her own conscience?"[20] Only by grace are we grafted into Christ, as David in anticipation was grafted into Christ.

59:6–7 Refrain: The Pressure Is Unrelenting

6   Each evening they come back,
      howling like dogs
      and prowling about the city.
7   There they are, bellowing with their mouths
      with swords in their lips—
      for "Who," they think, "will hear us?"

Each evening they come back conveys an atmosphere of repeated threat, with overtones of approaching gloom (cf. "And it was night," John 13:30). This is their hour and the power of darkness (Luke 22:53). The enemies of Christ and his church take on the character of the beast, **like dogs** (cf. Dan. 7), rather than the one who is truly human ("the son of man," Dan. 7:13–14). They lose the proper use of truthful, logical, reasonable language and are reduced to **howling** (growling, barking, snarling) **like dogs**, the wild dogs of the ancient Near East, "despised, unowned, loathsome, degraded, lean, and hungry."[21] When Goliath asks imperiously, "Am I a dog?" (1 Sam. 17:43), the sad answer of Psalm 59 is "Yes, you are!" That they are **prowling about the city** is reminiscent of 55:10, where violence and strife go around the city walls. This was true in Saul's day, and their heirs and successors troubled the history of Israel for many centuries (e.g., "Her judges are evening wolves," Zeph. 3:3)[22] and reached their nadir at the cross of Christ. They are with us today, wherever Christ and his church are vilified and opposed.

There they are ("Behold! Look at them!"), **bellowing** (belching, spewing out) **with their mouths,** and yet not simply incoherent drivel, for their **lips**

20 Augustine, *Psalms*, 3:159.
21 Spurgeon, *Treasury*, 2.1:15. Dogs have consistently negative associations in the Old Testament (e.g., Deut. 23:18; 1 Sam. 17:43; 2 Sam. 3:8; 2 Kings 8:13; Ps. 22:16, 20) and New (e.g., Matt. 15:26–27; Phil. 3:2; Rev. 22:15).
22 Eveson, *Psalms*, 1:365.

are **swords** (cf. Pss. 52:2; 55:21; 57:4), causing terrible damage to God's King and the King's people. The climax is the contemptuous rhetorical question they pose: **Who will hear us?**[23] This is the thought of the practical atheist; it surfaces again and again (e.g., 10:4, 11, 13; 64:5; 73:11; 94:7) and is the spirit of the fool of Psalms 14 and 53. When men or women become deaf to God (cf. the snake of 58:4–5), they assume that God must be deaf to them; he is not.

59:8–10 Christ and His Church Trust under Pressure

⁸   But you, O LORD, laugh at them;
    you hold all the nations in derision.

David believes his own Spirit-inspired words in Psalm 2, in which the verbs **laugh** and **hold . . . in derision** and also a reference to **the nations** appear (2:1, 4; cf. 37:13; 52:6; Prov. 1:26). Psalm 59:7 ends with the question "Who will hear us?" Here is the answer to that question: "The God and Father of Jesus Christ will hear you, and he is not impressed with your bravado!"

⁹   O my Strength, I will watch for you,
    for you, O God, are my fortress.
¹⁰   My God in his steadfast love will meet me;
    God will let me look in triumph on my enemies.

O my Strength may be "his strength," in which case it is presumably a reference to the strength of the enemies (NASB: "*Because of* his strength").[24] Whichever reading is adopted, the force of the verse is clear: David voices his faith in God. The verb **I will watch** (cohortative to express a strong resolve) may give an ironic twist to the hostile watching of Saul's men (in the superscription); you can watch for me, but I will watch for the covenant

---

23 The words "they think" are not in Hebrew but are inserted by most translations to make the verse read clearly.

24 The MT has עֻזּוֹ, "his strength." The LXX and Targums make a revocalization to עֻזִּי, "my strength," mirroring Ps. 59:17. Following the MT, Hamilton writes, "I take this to be David's brief contemplation of the strength of his enemies." Hamilton, *Psalms*, 1:551. There is a useful discussion in Ross, *Psalms*, 2:319n18.

God.[25] **My fortress**—my mighty tower, my high place—echoes the verb "protect" (see on Ps. 59:1). Psalm 59:10 (like 59:16–17) celebrates **steadfast love**,[26] the covenant love on which Christ relies, as do all his people today. The verb **will meet me** "has the same ambiguity as the English word 'prevent,' either to go before or act to forestall."[27] Note the similar use in 21:3 (also of the King). The conviction that **God will let me look** (the words **in triumph** have been added to clarify the sense of victory, although there is no gloating and no vindictive triumphalism) **on my enemies** (here, as in 54:5, with the sense of those who watch with hostile intent—or lurk, lie in wait, e.g., 56:2; Jer. 5:26; Hos. 13:7; cf. Mark 3:2).

59:11–17 Christ and His Church Cry for and Look Forward to Deserved Judgment

As we turn now to one of the strong prayers in the Psalms for God to judge the wicked, we remember that this is the anointed King praying that God's impenitent enemies will be punished. This is very far from personal vengefulness.[28]

59:11–13 Christ and His Church Pray for God's Just Judgment

> 11 Kill them not, lest my people forget;
>   make them totter by your power and bring them down,
>   O Lord, our shield!

The reference to **my people** reminds us that this is the anointed King praying on behalf of his church.[29]

The puzzling request of Psalm 59:11 seems to be contradicted by that of 59:13. The contradiction is only apparent. The goal of 59:11 (**lest my people forget**) is the key. A sudden and complete disappearance of the enemies would allow God's people all too quickly to forget this great act of God's judgment. Just as the pharaoh of the exodus (Ex. 7–14) and Haman (Esther) had to be defeated slowly and with many dramas so that these redemptions

25 Alter, *Psalms*, 206.
26 There is a difference between the MT as written (kethib), "My God, his steadfast love," and as read (kere), "My steadfast love God" (CSB: "my faithful God"), but the sense is much the same.
27 Ross, *Psalms*, 2:329.
28 Dickson, *Psalms*, 1:352–53.
29 Eveson, *Psalms*, 1:365.

might never be forgotten, so the defeat of God's enemies at any time in the history of the church may be delayed in order that we learn the lessons of God's slow but certain providence. So the King prays that they will be made to **totter** (or, perhaps better, "made to wander," made unstable, like Cain in Gen. 4), so that their judgment is slow and visible to the people of God. Only then can the church learn that "the Lord knows how to rescue the godly from trials" (2 Pet. 2:9).

The enemies will surely be brought **down** to Sheol. The **Lord** (sovereign one) is called **our shield** because, in protecting his King, he guarantees to guard his church. John Calvin notes,

> [The king] was now pleading the cause of the whole Church. . . . Having been chosen king by divine appointment, the safety of the Church stood connected with his person. The assault made upon him by his enemies was not an assault upon himself merely as a private individual, but upon the whole people, whose common welfare God had consulted in making choice of him.[30]

The word **shield** (cf. Pss. 3:3; 5:12) connects the singer with the God of Abraham (Gen. 15:1). Calvin speaks eloquently of our being "brought daily into that theatre where we are compelled to perceive the divine hand" of judgment.[31]

<blockquote>

12   For the sin of their mouths, the words of their lips,
     let them be trapped in their pride.
For the cursing and lies that they utter,
13   consume them in wrath;
     consume them till they are no more,
that they may know that God rules over Jacob
     to the ends of the earth.   *Selah*

</blockquote>

Psalm 59:12–13 leaves us in no doubt that the prayer of 59:11 ("Kill them not") is a plea not for pardon but for a stay of execution. In the

---

30 Calvin, *Psalms*, 2:390.
31 Calvin, *Psalms*, 2:389.

end, these grievous sins **of their mouths** and **their lips**, which stem from
their pride (lit., "height"), must lead to their complete removal from
the world of the age to come, **till they are no more**. Then all people
(**to the ends of the earth**) will **know that God rules over Jacob** (the
people of Christ).

59:14–15 Refrain: The Pressure Is Unrelenting

¹⁴   Each evening they come back,
         howling like dogs
         and prowling about the city.
¹⁵   They wander about for food
         and growl if they do not get their fill.

Psalm 59:14 repeats 59:6, probably to signify a recurrent and terrifying
threat to the people of Christ. But 59:15 varies the second part of the refrain.
In 59:7 they were confident and dangerous. Now **they** (emphatic) **wander
about** (cf. "totter" in 59:11), desperate for **food**. The verb **growl** may mean
"lodge, pass the night"[32]—that is, they stay and wait but remain hungry all
night. Or it may mean something like a hungry whimpering.[33] Probably
there is a sense of frustration, for, as Franz Delitzsch points out, the King
is the only food they really desire, and they are not going to get him![34] This
leads naturally into the glad conclusion.

59:16–17 Christ and His Church Rejoice in God's Judgment

¹⁶   But I will sing of your strength;
         I will sing aloud of your steadfast love in the morning.
     For you have been to me a fortress
         and a refuge in the day of my distress.
¹⁷   O my Strength, I will sing praises to you,
         for you, O God, are my fortress,
         the God who shows me steadfast love.

32 BDB, s.v. לִין.
33 Ross, *Psalms*, 2:320; Harman, *Psalms*, 1:445–46.
34 Delitzsch, *Psalms*, 2:192.

The verbs of glad singing (**sing . . . sing aloud . . . sing praises**) together with the repetition of God's **strength** and **steadfast love** and the words **fortress** and **refuge** (place of escape) signal that now at last **the morning** has come. Here is the song of the anointed King as he celebrates on earth the certainty of his future resurrection and the song of his church as we too celebrate in the midst of our **distress** the assurance of our future resurrection morning. The "evening" of threat and lurking danger, the nighttime of betrayal and sorrow, is past, and the morning has come.

REFLECTION AND RESPONSE

1. Charles Spurgeon nicely notes how suffering "is the tuner of the harps of sanctified songsters,"[35] for without trials we would lack so many beautiful psalms.

2. Psalm 59:1–2 is, as Augustine puts it,

> the experience of Christ in his flesh, and our experience too. Our enemies are the devil and his angels who constantly, daily, rise up against us and try to dupe us in our weakness and fragility. They are relentless in their attempts to ensnare us by their tricks, promptings, temptations, and any traps they can devise, as long as we live on earth.[36]

3. The phrases "for no transgression or sin of mine" and "for no fault of mine" (59:3–4) cause us to search our consciences, so that we walk in the light as we are covered by the righteousness of Christ.

4. The repetition of lurking threat in the refrain warns us to expect that the ending of one trial is no safeguard against the onset of another.

5. When praying for God to judge, we must take great care to avoid the twisted desires for personal revenge. Only as our pure-hearted King leads us can we hope to pray Psalm 59:11–13 with our affections set solely on the glory of God.

6. The unexpected prayer of Psalm 59:11 teaches us not to expect an immediate defeat of God's enemies, for God has his purposes of grace in delaying our rescue.

35 Spurgeon, *Treasury*, 2.1:13.
36 Augustine, *Psalms*, 3:151.

7. It is fruitful to meditate on the contrasts in the psalm between "evening" and "morning," between our weakness and God's repeated "strength" for us in Christ, and between our opponents' "pride" (i.e., pretended "height") and the high "fortress" to which God takes us as he "protects" us—for our life is hidden with Christ in God (Col. 3:3).

*The children of God must not think it strange to be put to
wrestling, striving, and fighting for a promised kingdom,
before they be settled in possession, as David was; yea,
the church of Christ must expect such like exercises.*

DAVID DICKSON
A Commentary on the Psalms

*Reading this Psalm invites us to reflect on what it would
be like to re-enter the moments of crisis in our own lives
having been shown our final outcome. . . . That seems
to be the perspective Psalm 60 intends to give.*

JAMES M. HAMILTON
Psalms

PSALM 60

Psalm 60 schools the church of Christ to fight through failures and meet challenges confident of final success. It teaches us to tie prayer to gospel promises. As the head of his church, Jesus Christ, in his life on earth, will have learned this wisdom from the psalm. Today he teaches and leads us in praying its wisdom and feeling its passion.

The two great puzzles of the psalm are also its two great contributions to the life of faith. The first is the seeming contradiction between the successes signaled in the superscription and the failures lamented in the body of the psalm. The superscription is about a victory (the historical questions are discussed below). Yet 60:1–3 and 60:10 lament what sound like terrible defeats. The psalm takes us behind the scene of final victory to open up the struggles that paved the way. This gives us insight into what it is to suffer with Christ in order that we may be glorified with him (Rom. 8:17).

The second puzzle concerns the inner dynamics of the body of the psalm, in which prayer and promise are interwoven. There is urgent prayer in Psalm 60:1–5, gospel promise in 60:6–8, and then renewed and reassured prayer in 60:9–12. The impact of gospel promise on the life of prayer is vividly illustrated by the change from 60:1–5 to 60:9–12.

Psalms 56–60 are a subgroup within book 2 (linked by the designation "A Miktam").

Psalms 56–59 (with the possible exception of Ps. 58) arise from David's persecution by Saul. Psalm 60 comes from a later period, when David is becoming established in the kingdom. It picks up several hints about the international significance of David's kingship for "the nations," "the peoples," and "the earth" (56:7; 57:9; 58:11; 59:5, 8, 13) and applies this to particular nations surrounding David's kingdom. It focuses on the implications for the people of the battles of the King. This anticipates how the victories of Christ affect the church of Christ.

There are striking echoes from Psalm 44, notably the verb "rejected," the clause "you . . . have not gone out with our armies" (44:9; cf. 60:1, 10), and the expectation of treading down our foes (44:5; 60:12). This encourages us to remember that Psalm 60, like Psalm 44, is spoken by the righteous remnant, who are the true church of Christ.

Psalm 108 is formed from parts of Psalms 57 and 60 (57:7–11 = 108:1–5; 60:5–12 = 108:6–13). This is discussed under Psalm 108.

THE TEXT

Structure
The clearest sections are Psalm 60:6–8 (God's promise) and 60:9–12 (responsive prayer). The only significant question is whether to take 60:5 with 60:6–8 and consider 60:1–4 as the first section (ending in *Selah*), or to take all of 60:1–5 as the first section (lament and prayer). Because 60:5–12 is incorporated as the second section of Psalm 108, it may be best to take 60:1–4 as the first section of our psalm. The interpretation of 60:4 (see below) also affects this decision.

Superscription

S   To the choirmaster:[1] according to Shushan Eduth. A Miktam[2] of David; for instruction; when he strove with Aram-naharaim and with Aram-zobah, and when Joab on his return struck down twelve thousand of Edom in the Valley of Salt.[3]

The Hebrew word **Shushan** means a lily-like flower. The word has both romantic associations (notably in the Song of Songs, e.g., Song 2:2, and the

---

1 See on Ps. 4.
2 For other psalms marked Miktam, see Pss. 16, 56, 57, 58, 59.
3 The other historical superscriptions are for Pss. 3, 7, 18, 34, 51, 52, 54, 56, 57, 59, 63, 142. This, the longest superscription in the Psalter, is counted as verses 1 and 2 in Hebrew. Subsequent verse numbers are increased by two.

superscription to Ps. 45) and temple connections (e.g., the decoration of the capitals of the bronze pillars and the "sea," 1 Kings 7:19, 22; 2 Chron. 4:5). It also appears (in the plural) in the superscriptions to Psalms 69 and 80, neither of which is romantic or temple related. The word **Eduth** means "testimony," one of the words used for the law. "The Lily of Testimony" (CSB) is a literal translation. The phrase[4] is generally supposed to refer to a tune or musical accompaniment.

The word **instruction** recalls 2 Samuel 1:18, where David says that his lament over Saul and Jonathan "should be taught" to the people, presumably because it will shape their convictions and affections in godly ways.[5] The word reminds us to listen carefully to its message. "Such poetry is meant to move us emotionally and motivate us to seek God when similar crisis situations arise."[6]

Aram-naharaim means Mesopotamia.[7] **Aram-zobah** was a significant Aramean state in the days of David, probably between the Euphrates and the Orontes northeast of Damascus.[8] The **Valley of Salt** was probably to the south of the Dead Sea, a region that spanned the boundary of Judah and **Edom**.[9] David's campaigns in these northern regions, in Edom (specifically in the Valley of Salt), and also against Moab and the Philistines (also mentioned in the psalm) are recorded in 2 Samuel 8:1–14;[10] 10:19; and 1 Chronicles 18:1–13.

Three historical questions arise.[11] The first is the number of Edomites struck down. The psalm superscription mentions twelve thousand, while

---

4 Goldingay says that עֵדוּת can be absolute, in which case "Lily" may be the tune, and "A Testimony" a separate part of the heading. Goldingay, *Psalms*, 2:224.
5 In both places the Hebrew is לְלַמֵּד.
6 Eveson, *Psalms*, 1:368.
7 *HALOT*, s.v. אֲרַם נַהֲרַיִם; Tate, *Psalms 51–100*, 104; cf. 1 Chron. 19:6.
8 Hengstenberg, *Psalms*, 2:277; Delitzsch, *Psalms*, 2:193; Tate, *Psalms 51–100*, 104–5.
9 Delitzsch, *Psalms*, 2:193; Hengstenberg, *Psalms*, 2:278; Tate, *Psalms 51–100*, 105.
10 There are several verbal links between 2 Sam. 8 and Ps. 60. The piel of מדד ("divide up, measure") appears only in 2 Sam. 8:2; Job 7:4; and Ps. 60:6. Hossfeld and Zenger, *Psalms*, 2:98. The verb נכה ("strike down") appears in 2 Sam. 8:5, 13, and the psalm superscription.
11 It is sometimes suggested that the Edomites invaded in the south while David's army was occupied in the north; e.g., Delitzsch, *Psalms*, 2:194; Kirkpatrick, *Psalms*, 2:338; Kidner, *Psalms*, 1:215. This is possible, but we have no evidence for it. Tate calls it "pure speculation." Tate, *Psalms 51–100*, 104. The suggestion of Motyer that God was displeased by David's northern campaign lacks support in the narratives, which portray the victories as entirely God-given and positive. Motyer, *Psalms*, 523.

the narratives (2 Sam. 8:13; 1 Chron. 18:12) say eighteen thousand. Given that the records in 2 Samuel and 1 Chronicles are very brief summaries of what were presumably sustained campaigns, it is not at all unlikely that the twelve thousand reflects one stage of a longer campaign.[12]

The second puzzle is which military commander struck them down, David (2 Sam. 8:13), Abishai (1 Chron. 18:12), or Joab (Ps. 60:S). This is easily resolved. Abishai served under Joab (2 Sam. 10:10), so his victories can be credited equally to Joab, his superior officer, or to David, his commander-in-chief.

The third puzzle is the relationship between a victory recorded in the superscription and a prayer for victory over the same enemy in Psalm 60:9. These are easily reconciled if the psalm was spoken at the time of crisis and the superscription written after the victory. Indeed, this may be part of the point: that the psalm takes us behind the scenes to see the crisis that preceded the victory and that we should learn from it ("for instruction").

60:1–4 The Church of Christ Laments with Hope[13]

1   O God, you have rejected us, broken our defenses;
       you have been angry; oh, restore us.

The first response of faith to defeat is not to be mired in misery but to speak to **God** (the first word in Hebrew). Three verbs follow in staccato succession with no softening connectives, literally, "You have rejected us, you have broken us, you have been angry." God has done these things. The experience of being **rejected** by God comes on unbelievers as judgment because they deserve it (cf. Luke 13:1–4) and on believers as a foreshadowing (and now overflow, Col. 1:24) of the sufferings of Christ (cf. Pss. 43:2; 44:9, 23; 77:7 ["spurn"]; 88:14 ["cast . . . away"]). The verb translated **broken our defenses** means, primarily, that God had, as it were, "broken out upon them" (cf. 2 Sam. 5:20) and that, as a consequence, he had broken the people as the wall of a besieged city is broken by the besiegers—it is a poignant and evocative picture. Behind all this is God's righteous anger (cf. Pss. 2:12;

---

12 Cf. Eveson, *Psalms*, 1:368. Calvin suggests that some fell in the main engagement, while others were slain subsequently while fleeing. Calvin, *Psalms*, 2:397.

13 The words "with hope" depend on a positive reading of Ps. 60:4 (see below).

79:5; 85:5). As in Psalm 44 (with which this psalm has similarities), this is the experience of the church of Christ. The prayer **Restore us** may focus on turning our fortunes back to better days, or it may mean "Turn back to us," that is, a prayer that the God who has turned his back will turn his face to us in mercy.[14]

> 2 You have made the land to quake; you have torn it open;
>   repair its breaches, for it totters.

James Hamilton rightly notes how the **land** language of this verse hints at the cosmic consequences of what happens to the people of God, for "the fate of the world hangs in the balance of what happens with Israel."[15] The earthquake language suggests a profound shaking of the moral order of creation. On **made . . . to quake**, note both the earthquake at the cross of Christ and the prophecy of Haggai 2:6–7 and 21 with its fulfillment in Hebrews 12:26–29. Every shaking of the old covenant people of God is a pointer to the cross and to the final shaking of judgment. The verb **torn . . . open** and the noun **breaches** (fractures) develop the earthquake language, opening up chasms into the abyss of hell (cf. Korah in Num. 16:30–35). The verb **totters** (often in Psalms, e.g., Pss. 10:6; 13:4; 15:5; 16:8; 17:5; 21:7— translated "moved," "shaken," "slipped") hints at the effect of this judgment on the people, who are staggering around in confusion and dismay. The cry **Repair!** ("Heal!"—with all the warmth of that word) is a call for God to do what only God can do for Christ's troubled church.

> 3 You have made your people see hard things;
>   you have given us wine to drink that made us stagger.

That all this concerns the church is clear from the phrase **your people**. **You have made . . . see** means to cause to experience rather than just to be spectators of disaster. **Hard things** reminds us of the hard service and harsh slavery in Egypt under the pharaohs (Ex. 1:14; 6:9; Deut. 26:6).[16] The image of **wine . . . that made us stagger** is a metaphor for the cup of God's

---

14 Ross, *Psalms*, 2:336.
15 Hamilton, *Psalms*, 1:556.
16 The adjective קָשֶׁה is used in all these passages.

judgment, rendering people unable to think with clarity or act with strength (cf. Ps. 75:8; Isa. 51:17, 22). This overflow of the sufferings of Christ must be drunk by his church as we walk in his footsteps.

> 4   You have set up a banner for those who fear you,
>   that they may flee to it from the bow.   *Selah*

Much debate surrounds the meaning of this verse. The key question is whether it is to be read in a negative or positive sense. The first line is straightforward, literally, "You have given for those who fear you a banner."[17] The clause **that they may flee to it** may mean "that it may be displayed" (ESV mg.).[18] The words **from the bow** may mean "in the presence of truth."[19] The two main suggested translations are along the following lines:

1. "You have given a banner to those who fear You, / That it may be displayed because of the truth" (NASB). On this reading Psalm 60:4 is a sign of hope that concludes 60:1–4 with the vision of a banner of God's truth under which the troubled people of God can assemble. This prepares us for the oracle of 60:6–8, in which this gospel truth is proclaimed.

2. "You have given a banner to those who fear you, / that they may flee to it from the bow." On this reading, the verse may speak with sarcasm of a banner that gathers them only that they may flee (cf. Jer. 4:6), "a signal for *flight* instead of *fight*."[20] As a variation of this, it may be only partly negative, a banner that may offer some hope of escape from, if no hope of victory over, the enemy archers.

The (often positive) verb "to give" (in **you have set up**) together with the application to **those who fear you** encourages me to think that the first is the more likely reading (and also because it needs no consonantal emendation

---

17 נֵס, a standard, ensign, signal, or sign.

18 לְהִתְנוֹסֵס is the preposition -לְ with a hithpael infinitive construct, either from the root נסס (to unfurl or wave a banner) or from the root נוס (to flee). For discussion, see Ross, *Psalms*, 2:336.

19 The noun is קֹשֶׁט, which means "truth, what is right." Cf. the very similar קֹשְׁטְ, "what is right," in Prov. 22:21. It is often assumed that קֹשֶׁט is here an alternative form of קֶשֶׁת, "bow."

20 Harman, *Psalms*, 1:448–49.

of the word "truth" so that it reads "bow"). If so, the banner may remind us both of Exodus 17:15 ("The LORD Is My Banner") and the messianic Isaiah 11:10, in which "the root of Jesse" will "stand as a signal (banner) for the peoples,"[21] and even to the "pole" ("banner") on which the bronze serpent was displayed in Numbers 21:8.[22] If this positive reading is correct, then the *Selah* pause for thought is very appropriate.

60:5–8 The Church of Christ Prays and Trusts the Gospel Promise

⁵   That your beloved ones may be delivered,
     give salvation by your right hand and answer us!

In order **that your beloved ones** (the language of covenantal love poetry; cf. Deut. 33:12; 2 Sam. 12:25; Jer. 11:15) **may be delivered**, the King prays—perhaps stirred by the Spirit on the basis of a hopeful truth banner (Ps. 60:4)—that God will **give salvation** by his **right hand** (his power). The answer follows immediately in Psalm 60:6–8.

⁶   God has spoken in his holiness:
     "With exultation I will divide up Shechem
     and portion out the Vale of Succoth.

The announcement that **God has spoken** need not mean that these words were given to David, newly minted, at the time, for in their substance they express the gospel promise of the covenant with Abraham as "reissued" to David. Philip Eveson rightly comments that this "was a promise fulfilled first under Joshua . . . , then under David (2 Samuel 8:1–14; 10:1–19) and ultimately by David's greater son, Jesus the Messiah (Micah 5:2–5a; Isaiah 11:1–9; Revelation 21:24, 26)."[23]

The words **in his holiness** are unlikely here to mean "from his sanctuary" (although they can mean that in other contexts), for in the context of an oath, it means "by his holiness," that is, with the guarantee that comes from the one who is not a mortal man that he might lie (Num. 23:19; Ps. 89:35;

---

21 Eveson, *Psalms*, 1:370.
22 Hengstenberg, *Psalms*, 2:281.
23 Eveson, *Psalms*, 1:371.

Amos 4:2; Titus 1:2).[24] This promise is unbreakable, for "God's 'holiness' includes His whole essential nature in its moral aspect, and that nature makes it impossible for Him to break His promise."[25]

The declaration begins **with exultation**. God is glad to promise the gospel and perform what he promises.[26] **Shechem** (at the heart of the promised land west of the Jordan) and **the Vale of Succoth**[27] (at the heart of the Transjordan part of the promised land; cf. Josh. 13:27) appear in Genesis 33:17–18 as places visited by the patriarch Jacob, his visits being like anticipatory pledges of ownership of the land promised to Abraham and his seed. Ernst Wilhelm Hengstenberg calls it "a type and a pledge of the occupancy of the land by his posterity."[28] We may legitimately extend this, as the New Testament does, to the cosmic inheritance of the people of God in the new heavens and new earth or link it, as Paul does in Romans 4:13, to the promise that Abraham will "be heir of the world." The verbs **divide up** and **portion out** remind us of Joshua apportioning the land to the tribes but—even more—to the gospel determination of God to apportion the promised land of the new creation to "all those who are sanctified" (Acts 20:32).

> 7   Gilead is mine; Manasseh is mine;
>
>   Ephraim is my helmet;
>
>   Judah is my scepter.

Psalm 60:7 repeats 60:6 in tribal language to emphasize that the whole land belongs to God (the repeated **mine . . . mine . . . my . . . my**). **Gilead** is the hill country east of the Jordan where the Transjordan tribes settled, as did the half-tribe of **Manasseh**. Between them, **Gilead** and **Manasseh** designate all the Transjordan region. **Ephraim** (shorthand for what was later the northern kingdom, to the west of the Jordan)[29] **is my helmet** (lit., "a stronghold for my head") in the sense that it was the buffer against invasion

---

24 Goldingay, *Psalms*, 2:229.

25 Kirkpatrick, *Psalms*, 2:341.

26 Hamilton, *Psalms*, 1:557.

27 The word means "booths" or "tents."

28 Hengstenberg, *Psalms*, 2:284.

29 Ephraim and Manasseh are the Joseph tribes. Four of the five times Joseph is mentioned in the Psalms are Asaph psalms (Pss. 77:15; 78:67; 80:1; 81:5). The other is 105:17 (of the patriarch rather than the tribes). The Joseph tribes, Ephraim and Manasseh, appear in 78:9, 67 (Ephraim); and 80:2 (both). They also appear here and in 108:8.

from the north.[30] **Judah**, the tribe of David, **is my scepter** (as prophesied in Gen. 49:10), for this royal tribe (as Bible symbolism unfolds) will be "the people who are called to dominion of the world."[31] Out of this tribe "Christ came, towards whom the church of old [under the old covenant] was to direct its eye" through their leaders who were his types.[32]

For this land, fulfilled in the new creation in Christ, to be secure means that all impenitent hostility must be removed and conquered. This, under the small-scale image of David's wars, is the true subject matter of this psalm.

8   Moab is my washbasin;
            upon Edom I cast my shoe;
            over Philistia I shout in triumph."

Moab (to the east), **Edom** (farther southeast), and **Philistia** (to the west) were the most prominent of the ancient enemies against whom David had to war; together they stand for hostility on every side. The **washbasin** is clearly a degrading image for a nation, including perhaps an allusion to the smelly Dead Sea, at best a place for dirty water.[33] Moab will no longer be a threat. **I cast my shoe** is either a simple metaphor for throwing a dirty shoe at a slave before dipping one's filthy feet in the washbasin or an idiom for claiming possession (cf. Ruth 4:7–10);[34] either way, Edom is no longer a threat, nor is Philistia.[35]

Although the language is unfamiliar to us, Psalm 60:6–8 is a confident declaration of the gospel.

60:9–12 The Church of Christ Fights the Good Fight of Faith with Confidence

In Psalm 60:9–12 we see the effect of this gospel promise on the King and his people.

---

30 Ross, *Psalms*, 2:348.
31 Delitzsch, *Psalms*, 2:198.
32 Dickson, *Psalms*, 1:359.
33 Delitzsch, *Psalms*, 2:199; Kirkpatrick, *Psalms*, 2:342; Ross, *Psalms*, 2:349.
34 There is no agreement about the meaning of this metaphor. See, e.g., Delitzsch, *Psalms*, 2:199; Hengstenberg, *Psalms*, 2:286; Kirkpatrick, *Psalms*, 2:342; Goldingay, *Psalms*, 2:231; Wilson, *Psalms*, 1:862n15.
35 The MT suggests that Philistia will shout, in which case it is either a shout of homage or an ironic challenge ("You can shout triumph all you like, but it won't do any good"). In the parallel Ps. 108:9, it reads, "I will shout in triumph," which is simpler. See Ross, *Psalms*, 2:337n19.

⁹   Who will bring me to the fortified city?
     Who will lead me to Edom?

We do not know exactly what historical circumstances caused **Edom** to be the particular challenge for David at this time, although 2 Samuel 8:13–14 gives a strong hint. We do not need to know. For "Edom, as in the prophetic books such as Obadiah, comes to represent, like Babylon does in other Bible books, the ungodly powers of this world that threaten the people of God."[36] **The fortified city** (cf. "besieged city," Ps. 31:21) is probably Sela (i.e., Petra), a city famously inaccessible (2 Kings 14:7; cf. Obad. 3), rather like Helm's Deep in J. R. R. Tolkien's (1892–1973) *The Lord of the Rings*.[37]

The image of our King venturing forth to Edom conjures up the vision of our Jesus going forth "conquering, and to conquer," on our behalf (Rev. 6:2). Eveson catches the feel of the victory when he speaks of

> that dramatic and awesome passage of the lone figure of Messiah, the Lord's Servant, approaching from Edom, again symbolic of all God's and his people's enemies. It is a picture of the final defeat of opposition to God. The one who will punish and "tread down" all his enemies on that final day of the Lamb's wrath is the same Lamb who was slain and himself experienced that wrath when he was crushed and punished on account of God's righteous judgment on human rebellion (Isaiah 63:1–6; 53:5–6, 10; Revelation 15–17).[38]

¹⁰   Have you not rejected us, O God?
     You do not go forth, O God, with our armies.

The lament of Psalm 60:10 takes us straight back both to 60:1–3 (note the repetition of **rejected** from 60:1) and to Psalm 44 (esp. 44:9). What has changed from the beginning of the psalm is not the church's circumstances but the church's zeal for prayer, prompted by the reiterated gospel promise of 60:6–8.

---

36 Eveson, *Psalms*, 1:372.
37 It may be some other Edomite city or "a general reference to the fortified cities of Edom." Ross, *Psalms*, 2:350.
38 Eveson, *Psalms*, 1:372–73.

¹¹   Oh, grant us help against the foe,
        for vain is the salvation of man!

The reference to **armies** (60:10) reminds us that the truly invincible armies ("hosts") belong to the Lord of hosts (cf. 59:5). All human aid (**the salvation of man**) is **vain**, ineffective.

¹²   With God we shall do valiantly;
        it is he who will tread down our foes.

The words **do valiantly** (lit., "do strength") evoke the oracle of Balaam in Numbers 24:18—on the edge of the promised land, in the context of Edom being dispossessed and Moab being defeated—that "Israel is doing valiantly."[39] The words **tread down our foes** are very similar to Psalm 44:5. Whatever trials the covenant God sends on the people of Christ, he is for them and will tread down all their enemies that they may **do valiantly** and enter the promised land of the new creation.

REFLECTION AND RESPONSE

1. The superscription placards victory as the headline that stands over all our trials, as it stands over all the sufferings of Christ. As we live in the tensions of the psalm, we remember the triumph that is as sure, on a cosmic scale, as David's was on a regional level.

2. If the positive reading of Psalm 60:4 is correct, we may rejoice that, in the gospel promises, God has set up for us a banner of truth, which we may unfurl with joy no matter how great the tribulations of the church.

3. We meditate on the grand declaration of Psalm 60:6–8. We understand that it points to the sure gift of the new creation to Christ and all his people. We remember that it all depends on the Lion of the tribe of Judah, who holds the scepter. We rejoice that no hostility or threat will lurk in the shadows in the new heavens and new earth, as they lurk around us today (cf. Ps. 59).

4. In the mission of the church, Psalm 60:9–12 calls us to pledge ourselves to go with our King in a venture of faith to the very heartlands of evil, with

39 "A manifest allusion." Hengstenberg, *Psalms*, 2:287.

spiritual gospel weapons that "have divine power to destroy strongholds. We destroy arguments and every lofty opinion raised against the knowledge of God, and take every thought captive to obey Christ" (2 Cor. 10:4–5).

5. Psalm 60:11–12 stirs us never to use our weakness as an excuse for gospel timidity. On our own we must fail, but "with God we shall do valiantly."[40]

---

40 Basil the Great, *Homilies on the Psalms*, 20.1, in *ACCS* 8:43.

David . . . is comforted in the Lord, and persuaded
of his present and future happiness . . . and of the
perpetuity of the kingdom of Christ, represented by him,
to the comfort of all Christ's subjects in all ages.

DAVID DICKSON
A Commentary on the Psalms

God promised David that his unfailing love would not depart
from him (2 Samuel 7:15) and King Jesus is the true and final
realization of David's dynasty as the angel's message to Mary
reveals (Luke 1:32–33; see Romans 1:3–4). He experienced
an exile far worse than that of David as his words from the
cross reveal (see Psalm 22:1) but God heard him because
of his godly fear and enabled him to become the author of
eternal salvation to all who obey him (Hebrews 5:7–9).

PHILIP EVESON
Psalms

PSALM 61

ORIENTATION

Confident longing and assured joy mingle in Psalm 61, as they do in the life of faith for those who are in Christ. This sure yearning and praise-filled certainty were Christ's before they are ours, and they are ours in him.[1] Psalm 61 is a short psalm but rich in imagery to stimulate the godly imagination and energize the life of faith.

This is a psalm of the anointed King, anticipating Jesus the Messiah. The background to this psalm is the covenant that God has made with him, as declared and celebrated in Psalm 2.

We do not know when in David's life he composed this psalm, although 61:6–7 strongly suggests that it was after he had been recognized as king. The suggestion that it may have been at Manahaim during Absalom's revolt makes much sense.[2]

One question that arises is the place of 61:6–7: Is this a new voice—the congregation or some individual psalmist praying for the king—or is this the king praying for himself (but using the third person)? While we cannot be sure, the superscription "Of David" may suggest the latter; David prays for himself, and by calling himself "the king," he focuses on the covenant promises to his seed, the greater son of David.

Psalms 52–55 (Maskil) and 56–60 (Miktam) were mostly set in the context of the Sauline persecutions. But Psalm 60 moves us to the days of

---

1 Augustine preaches the psalm as the prayer of Christ and his church, who "in Christ . . . all form one human person, whose head is in heaven and whose limbs are toiling on earth." Augustine, *Psalms*, 3:193.
2 Delitzsch, *Psalms*, 2:202; Hengstenberg, *Psalms*, 2:288.

the kingdom, and Psalm 61 continues this movement. There are links both backward and forward.

Psalm 61 shares with Psalm 60 the motifs of God providing safety (60:4, 12; 61:3), of God's people being those who fear God (60:4; 61:5), and of the threat from enemies.

Looking forward, we see that Psalms 61–64 may be a "subcomposition," in which Psalms 61 and 64 are linked by the words "O God, hear" (the first two words of both psalms in Hebrew), by the theme of seeking refuge in God (61:3; 64:10),[3] and by a shared longing for the presence of God.

There is a striking link with 27:4–6, which shares the theme of God's dwelling place, the use of the word "tent/tabernacle," and the imagery of a rock.[4]

THE TEXT

Structure
It is probably simplest to let the *Selah* divide the psalm into two stanzas of four verses each (Ps. 61:1–4, 5–8).[5]

Superscription

S   To the choirmaster:[6] with stringed instruments.[7] Of David.[8]

61:1–4 The Church of Christ Prays with Confident Longing in Christ

1   Hear my cry, O God,
        listen to my prayer;

---

3 Zenger suggests that there is a sequence, from the beginnings of enemy attack (Ps. 61) through the enemies' preparation for the decisive blow (Ps. 62) and the crucial reversal in the struggle (Ps. 63) to the final destruction of the foes (Ps. 64). Hossfeld and Zenger, *Psalms*, 2:109.

4 Wilson, *Psalms*, 1:869.

5 Delitzsch, *Psalms*, 2:202; Hengstenberg, *Psalms*, 2:288. Hamilton has a simple a-b-a' chiasm (Ps. 61:1–3, 4–5, 6–8). Hamilton, *Psalms*, 1:558–59.

6 See on Ps. 4.

7 See on Ps. 4. Unlike the other occurrences (Pss. 4; 6; 54; 55; 67; 76), in Hebrew this noun is singular. This difference does not appear to be significant. Cf. Hab. 3:19.

8 In Hebrew the superscription is verse 1; subsequent verse numbers are increased by one.

The first two words in Hebrew are "Hear, O God!" The word **cry** conveys intensity, while the word **prayer** points also to the content of the cry. These set the tone: the King is in urgent need, as will his church be in ages to come. This cry of the King on earth becomes the prayer of each member of his body.

2   from the end of the earth I call to you
          when my heart is faint.

The words **from the end of the earth**[9] probably point to some physical separation of David from God's tabernacle. But more deeply, they evoke the terrible spiritual experience[10] of distance from God that was the vocation of Jesus under the shadow of human sin. As they walk through this age bearing "the body of sin" and feeling the overflow of the sufferings of Christ, his people too may cry as though they were at the farthest extremity of the world. The feeling is not so very different from Psalm 42. In history this was the experience of David (perhaps when he had fled during Absalom's revolt); it had a "continued resonance" centuries later in the terrors and sadnesses of the Babylonian exile.[11] The **heart** that **is faint** means a heart so wearied by pressures, so bowed low by the sadness of sins, feeling so empty and close to death that it does not know how it can go on.

This phrase should remind us of Psalm 2:8, in which "the ends of the earth" are promised by covenant to David and ultimately to Christ. In order to win "the ends of the earth," our King had first to go to the earth in the misery of exile from his Father's presence, which he felt especially on the cross.

          Lead me to the rock
             that is higher than I,

Lead me is the prayer of the King as he trusts in the kind leading of the covenant shepherd-God (23:3; cf. 31:3). The **rock** is a strong place of safety,

---

9   Cf. Pss. 59:13; 65:5; 67:7; 72:8.
10 Hamilton describes it as "more a description of his spiritual sense of separation from God than a geographical statement of his physical location." Hamilton, *Psalms*, 1:560.
11 Wilson, *Psalms*, 1:868.

higher than I, in the sense of being far above my place of danger, beyond the threats of sin, the world, and the devil. Jesus longed for the Father to be to him this rock of safety, and by going through sufferings for us, he became that rock for us (cf. the stone or rock imagery in Rom. 9:33; 1 Cor. 10:4; 1 Pet. 2:6).

David Dickson writes, "There is a rock of refuge for safety and comfort to the exiled and perplexed saint, which is able to supply all wants, and to sweeten all sorrows; and this is the rock of God's felt friendship in Christ from heaven."[12]

> 3   for you have been my refuge,
>   a strong tower against the enemy.

The imagery of the **refuge** and **strong tower** (literally in Judg. 9:51 and metaphorically in Prov. 18:10) develops this confident longing, the yearning Christ felt and we now have in him. "The tower is there," preaches Augustine, "in front of you. Remember Christ, and enter the tower."[13]

> 4   Let me dwell in your tent forever!
>   Let me take refuge under the shelter of your wings!   *Selah*

Usually to **dwell** means to sojourn only for a time, but here the yearning is **forever**. The reference to **your tent** (i.e., the tabernacle)[14] focuses on the covenantal presence of God, given to the incarnate Son of God by eternal covenant with the Father, given to us in Christ. In parallel with this is the longing to **take refuge under the shelter of your wings**. In the context of the tabernacle, this may well suggest a covenantal safety under the wings of the cherubim over the ark of the covenant. Adopting this view, Dickson writes,

> The ground of all spiritual consolations is in the mercy and grace of God offered to us in Christ, represented by the wings of the cherubim stretched out over the mercy seat; there faith findeth a rest and solid ground able to furnish comfort abundantly.[15]

---

12 Dickson, *Psalms*, 1:361–62.
13 Augustine, *Psalms*, 3:196.
14 That the word "tent" here means the tabernacle becomes clear in the light of the "vows" (Ps. 61:5, 8). Ps. 36:7 makes a useful parallel, linking this term also with covenantal חֶסֶד.
15 Dickson, *Psalms*, 1:363.

Lying behind Psalm 61:3–4 is the assurance that the church of Christ will dwell in the presence of God in Christ forever. Augustine writes, "The Church will not be overcome; it will not be rooted out, nor will it give way, whatever the trials may be, until this world comes to an end, and we are welcomed into that eternal home to which Christ will lead us."[16]

61:5–8 The Church of Christ Prays with Joyful Praise in Christ

From Psalm 61:5 to the end, the tone of assurance is maintained, grounded in the covenantal confidence of David in the promises of 2 Samuel 7 and now to us in Christ. Psalm 61:5 and 8 are linked by both the term "vows" and God's "name"; they bracket 61:6–7, in which the King is spoken of, or speaks of himself, in the third person.

> 5   For you, O God, have heard my vows;
>   you have given me the heritage of those who fear your name.

The **vows** are probably commitments made by the King at the time of his passionate prayers, in which he promises God the Father that he will praise him when his prayers are answered (see 61:8).[17] In the end these are the prayers and the vows of Christ. **The heritage of those who fear your name**, given to the anointed King, is the inheritance pledged in Psalm 2. Ultimately, it is the whole of the new creation, given to Christ and—in Christ—to the whole church of Christ (cf. Matt. 5:5; Rom. 4:13). The King who honors the Father's name receives, on behalf of his people who will be drawn by the Spirit to fear that name, the inheritance of the nations.[18] For the promised land was, as Theodoret of Cyrus explains,

> a foreshadowing of the real inheritance; the real inheritance is eternal life, of which Christ the Lord said to the lambs on his right hand, "Come you that are blessed by my Father, inherit the kingdom prepared for you before the foundation of the world" [Matt. 25:34]. The Lord promised to give this inheritance to those who fear him.[19]

---

16 Augustine, *Psalms*, 3:197.
17 Ross, *Psalms*, 2:362; Hengstenberg, *Psalms*, 2:290.
18 "Land lost to the enemy within or without would be regained and ultimately through Christ, David's greater son, the meek shall inherit the earth (Matthew 5:5)." Eveson, *Psalms*, 1:376.
19 Theodoret of Cyrus, *Psalms*, 1:350.

The New Testament celebrates our hope in Christ of obtaining this inheritance with our King (e.g., Acts 20:32; Eph. 1:13–14; 1 Pet. 1:3–5).

> 6   Prolong[20] the life of the king;
>   may his years endure to all generations!
> 7   May he be enthroned forever before God;
>   appoint steadfast love and faithfulness to watch over him!

Psalm 61:6–7 is probably David's prayer, not simply for himself or his dynasty but ultimately for the fulfillment of his "seed" in the Messiah. For whether he was conscious of this or not, he speaks of a destiny that will be fulfilled only in the divine-human Messiah. This is not only **life** but life for **all generations, enthroned**[21] **forever before God**, in that fellowship found only in its completion in the eternal fellowship of the Father and the Son.[22] It is to this eternal government of Christ that the Davidic covenant always pointed (e.g., 2 Sam. 7:16, 26, 29; Pss. 21:6; 89:36).[23]

Covenantal **steadfast love** (חֶסֶד, *khesed*) and **faithfulness** are often combined, especially in reference to the covenant with the Davidic king (e.g., Pss. 40:11; 57:3; Prov. 20:28). "It would take a mighty sermon," says Augustine, "to expound the Lord's steadfast love and truth."[24] It would indeed. But they find their fulfillment in Christ (John 1:14).

> 8   So will I ever sing praises to your name,
>   as I perform my vows day after day.

Here is the response of great David's greater son and of all who have his Spirit in their hearts. For the **name** of the covenant God is given to us in Jesus Christ. In him, **day after day** ("from this temporal day unto that eternal day")[25] we gladly **perform** our **vows** to give him all the praise he so richly deserves.

---

20 Lit., "Days to the days of the king you will add," where the imperfect "you will add" has the sense of a prayer, not least because of the parallel imperative "appoint" in Ps. 61:7.
21 The verb (lit., "sit") must in this context refer to enthronement.
22 Theodoret of Cyrus notes that the Son is "always coexisting with the Father." Theodoret of Cyrus, *Psalms*, 1:351.
23 Kirkpatrick, *Psalms*, 2:347.
24 Augustine, *Psalms*, 3:200.
25 Augustine, *Psalms*, 3:201.

REFLECTION AND RESPONSE

1. We begin, as so often, by meditating on what each line of the psalm might have meant to David. From there we move to its fulfillment in the prayers and praises of Jesus Christ and thence gladly to make this our prayer in Christ.

2. Reflecting on the words "from the end of the earth" and the misery of persecuted Christians (or indeed the sick and housebound) being excluded from the gatherings of God's people and the ministry of word and sacraments, Dickson comments, "Albeit a man were ever so far banished from the free society of the church, and communion with God's people in ordinances, yet he is still within cry unto God."[26]

3. The images of the faint heart and then of the rock, the refuge, the strong tower, the tabernacle-tent, and the wings of refuge fuel the life of faith with rich God-given images, to strengthen faith and sweeten care.

4. The Christian will draw much from this psalm to meditate on the inheritance (Ps. 61:5) given us in Christ. John Calvin comments, as he considers the way those without faith enjoy so many of the gifts of God in this life, that "the wicked, having no possession by faith of the divine benefits which they may happen to share, live on from day to day, as it were, upon plunder. It is only such as fear the Lord who have the true and legitimate enjoyment of their blessings."[27]

5. The eternal reign of Christ (Ps. 61:6–7) has wonderful implications for the church of Christ. Augustine notes, "Not only does Christ reign in his Church during the fleeting days of this present world, but the saints will reign with him through days that will know no end."[28] Similarly, Calvin (in Augustinian style) insists that David must be speaking of the coming of Christ, and "the same succession still subsists in reference to ourselves. Christ must be viewed as living in his members to the end of the world."[29]

---

26 Dickson, *Psalms*, 1:361.
27 Calvin, *Psalms*, 2:415.
28 Augustine, *Psalms*, 3:199.
29 Calvin, *Psalms*, 2:415.

And as we are ever prone to be drawn away from God by the influence which worldly objects exert over our senses, perishing and evanescent as these are, occasion is taken to show the folly of this, and bring us to a single and entire dependence upon God.

JOHN CALVIN
Commentary on the Psalms

Jesus Christ would have found great comfort and encouragement in this psalm.

PHILIP EVESON
Psalms

PSALM 62

ORIENTATION

Under terrifying pressure, the King in Psalm 62 declares his unswerving faith in God, models that faith for us, and teaches us why and how we may walk in his footsteps. The Messiah knows that only God can be trusted. His security rests in this, as does ours in him.[1]

Although here, as in many psalms, few commentators take "of David" seriously as an indicator of Davidic authorship,[2] there are at least three reasons why this makes excellent sense of Psalm 62.

The first is contextual. Psalms 61, 62, and 63 have several links, verbal and thematic.[3] Psalms 61 and 63 include an explicit focus on the king (61:6–7; 63:S, 11), and it is natural to suppose that Psalm 62 shares this kingly theme.

Second, Psalm 62 speaks of attacks on a man of "high position" (62:4) and possessing "glory" (62:7); it makes excellent sense if he is the king.[4]

Third, after declaring his own faith in 62:1–7, the psalmist instructs "the people" about following his example (62:8–12); this too is natural and

---

1 "One clear message stands out and is emphasized in each section: the contrast between God and humans as objects of trust." Eveson, *Psalms*, 1:379.

2 For an outline of some of the common scholarly positions, see Hossfeld and Zenger, *Psalms*, 2:111.

3 These include God as rock and refuge (Pss. 61:2, 3, 4; 62:2, 6, 7, 8), the steadfast love of God (61:7; 62:12), a focus on what we do ("perform," 61:8; "his work," 62:12), and the motif of God's "wings" (61:4; 63:7).

4 The vulnerability of David ("a leaning wall, a tottering fence," Ps. 62:3) together with reference to his "high position" (62:4) and "glory" (62:7) and some similarities with Pss. 3 and 4 may suggest that the psalm comes from the days of Absalom's rebellion. But as Spurgeon says, "When this Psalm was composed it was not necessary for us to know, since true faith is always in season, and is usually under trial." Spurgeon, *Treasury*, 2.1:48.

appropriate for the king. What David does in this psalm prefigures the day when Jesus Christ, the true and final anointed King, prays this psalm and now instructs his people through its words.

There is also a pointer to the divine nature of Jesus Christ. The motif of God rendering to each "according to his work" (62:12; cf. 28:4 and elsewhere in the Old Testament) is echoed in several places in the New Testament. That God will do this is echoed in Romans 2:6 and Revelation 20:12–13 (and specifically God the Father in 1 Pet. 1:17). That Jesus is the divine Lord to whom this judgment is entrusted (cf. John 5:22) appears from the echo in 2 Timothy 4:14 and from Jesus's own lips in Matthew 16:27 and Revelation 2:23 and 22:12. Jesus Christ is both the flawless man who prayed this psalm in the days of his life on earth and also God the Son whom we fear and trust in the words of this psalm.

The Hebrew word אַךְ, *ak*, appears as the first word in the Hebrew of six verses in the psalm.[5] This very striking repetition gives the psalm a particular character. Franz Delitzsch calls it here "the language of faith, with which, in the face of all assault, established truths are confessed and confirmed."[6] Depending on context, the word can indicate a strong emphasis (the asseverative use, "truly," "surely," "yes!") or an exclusive emphasis (the restrictive use, "alone," "only"). Scholars differ as to whether to translate using exclusive words or asseverative words.[7] The context suggests something that includes but goes beyond a simple emphasis and includes here the restrictive use perhaps best conveyed by "only" or "alone." Charles Spurgeon calls it "the ONLY Psalm," and Ernst Wilhelm Hengstenberg (who calls this word "the soul of the psalm") says it models "faith alone," one of the *solas* of the Reformation.[8] Geoffrey Grogan (1925–2011) calls it "an emphatic particle that here indicates exclusiveness."[9]

There are several links to Psalm 39, including the word אַךְ, *ak* (4x); the name "Jeduthun" in the superscriptions; and the word "breath" or "vanity" (הֶבֶל, *hebel*, 39:5, 11; 62:9).

5 In the ESV translated "alone" in Ps. 62:1, 2, 5; "only" in 62:4, 6; and "but" in 62:9.

6 Delitzsch, *Psalms*, 2:206.

7 For discussion, see Goldingay, *Psalms*, 2:245; Eveson, *Psalms*, 1:379; Kirkpatrick, *Psalms*, 2:348; Ross, *Psalms*, 2:367.

8 Spurgeon, *Treasury*, 2.1:48; Hengstenberg, *Psalms*, 2:293.

9 Geoffrey W. Grogan, *Psalms*, THOTC (Grand Rapids, MI: Eerdmans, 2008), 118.

THE TEXT

Structure

Selah appears at the end of Psalm 62:4 and 8, and it probably suggests three sections of four verses each (62:1–4, 5–8, 9–12). Psalm 62:1–2 is similar to 62:5–7 at the start of the first and second sections. Although David's testimony in 62:1–7 moves into David's exhortation in 62:8–12, the word "refuge" links 62:7 with 62:8, and the shift from testimony to exhortation must not be overplayed since David is speaking to his people throughout.[10] Although 62:12 includes the only explicit address to God ("to you, O Lord"), the whole psalm is spoken in the conscious presence of God.

Superscription

S   To the choirmaster:[11] according to Jeduthun. A Psalm of David.[12]

Jeduthun (cf. Pss. 39; 77) is associated with Asaph, Heman, and others as a man to whom David entrusted the responsibilities of temple music (1 Chron. 16:38–42; 25:1–6; 2 Chron. 5:12; 29:14; 35:15; cf. Neh. 11:17).[13]

62:1–4 Christ and His Church Live by Faith Alone When Facing the Attacks of Evil

1   For God alone my soul waits in silence;
        from him comes my salvation.

Literally, Psalm 62:1a reads, "*Only* to God—silence—my soul." Behind the word "only" lies the struggle of faith, against which are arrayed all the rivals for our trust. His whole being is characterized by **silence** (the noun דּוּמִיָּה, *dumiyah*),[14] a word that appears also in Psalms 22:2 ("rest"); 39:2; and 65:1 (lit., "to you in silence is praise"). This is not so much an absence of

---

10 Hengstenberg, *Psalms*, 2:292.
11 See on Ps. 4.
12 In Hebrew the superscription is verse 1; subsequent verse numbers are increased by one.
13 The words "according to" translate the preposition עַל rather than לְ. This may suggest a tune, melody, or style associated with Jeduthun. Wilson, *Psalms*, 1:877; Goldingay, *Psalms*, 2:245.
14 Cognate with the verb דּוֹמִי in Ps. 62:5.

sound as a quiet restfulness of soul, which is the fruit of faith. It "denotes the opposite of that state of tumultuous agitation which prevails in the soul as long as it looks anywhere else for help ... than to God."[15] John Calvin expresses it with characteristic pastoral insight:

> The word implies a meek and submissive endurance of the cross. It expresses the opposite of that heat of spirit which would put us into a posture of resistance to God. The silence intended is, in short, that composed submission of the believer, in the exercise of which he acquiesces in the promises of God, gives place to his word, bows to his sovereignty, and suppresses every inward murmur of dissatisfaction.[16]

This posture of faith is illustrated by Exodus 14:13–14; Psalm 37:7; and Lamentations 3:26.

The conviction that **my salvation** (on every level from the immediate to the final) **comes** only **from him** undergirds this restful heart in the midst of tumultuous pressures (cf. Ps. 62:3–4); this was the faith of Jesus on earth and can be our trust today.

2   He alone is my rock and my salvation,
       my fortress; I shall not be greatly shaken.

Psalm 62:2 again begins with אַךְ, *ak*: "*Only* he [is] my rock and my salvation, / my fortress." The verse picks up **salvation** from 62:1 and adds **rock** and **fortress**[17] to emphasize the security that is Christ's in God and ours in Christ. **I shall not be ... shaken** expresses not wishful thinking but the sober truth of the security of Christ, who trusted the Father, and the security of Christ's people, whose life is hidden with God in Christ (Col. 3:3); the verb is sometimes translated "slip" (as in the foot slipping) or "move" (as in "be moved from a secure position") (cf. Deut. 32:35; Pss. 10:6 and often).[18] The addition of the word **greatly** probably indicates that while he may fall in the battle, he will not stay fallen or be excluded from

---

15 Hengstenberg, *Psalms*, 2:294.
16 Calvin, *Psalms*, 2:418.
17 Cf. Pss. 18:2; 59:9, 17; 144:1–2 (all "of David").
18 For the meaning of the verb, see Ross, *Psalms*, 2:374n24.

the promised land (cf. Ps. 37:24; Prov. 24:16); like a boxer, he will not be down for the count.

3   How long will all of you attack a man
          to batter him,
          like a leaning wall, a tottering fence?

If Psalm 62:1–2 expresses trust in God, 62:3–4 shows why this trust is badly needed, for the King and for his people. The **man** here would appear to be David. He asks **How long?** not only because suffering seems interminable but also because he wants it to have an end (as it did for Jesus and will for us). The King is heavily outnumbered (**all of you** against **a man**; cf. Ps. 3). The word **attack** probably has the sense of "threaten from a position of strength."[19] **To batter him** uses a verb that means "to commit murder frequently or repeatedly"[20] (cf. 2 Kings 6:32; Ps. 94:6; Isa. 1:21); this is a sustained attack by enemies for whom such violence is characteristic and determined (cf. John 8:39–44).[21]

The image of the **leaning wall** or **tottering fence** pictures one on the point of collapse—as David during Absalom's rebellion, as Jesus on the cross, and as his church in a hostile world. Derek Kidner notes that "evil, being ruthlessly competitive, is attracted to weakness, to give a last push to whatever is *leaning* or *tottering*."[22] And evil is cowardly too; Martin Luther speaks of "yanking the beard of the dead lion, which they would be afraid to touch if he were alive,"[23] which reminds us of the death of Aslan in *The Lion, the Witch, and the Wardrobe*.

4   They only plan to thrust him down from his high position.
          They take pleasure in falsehood.
          They bless with their mouths,
             but inwardly they curse.   *Selah*

19 Polel of הות, an Old Testament hapax legomenon.
20 *HALOT*, s.v. רצח.
21 If we follow the MT vocalization and read the verb as a pual rather than a piel, the sense may be that the enemies will be battered, this being the punishment they deserve; e.g., Calvin, *Psalms*, 2:420–21; Hamilton, *Psalms*, 1:565. For discussion, see Ross, *Psalms*, 2:368n7.
22 Kidner, *Psalms*, 1:221.
23 Luther, *Luther's Works*, 14:235.

Psalm 62:4 begins with the emphatic **only** (אַךְ, *ak*) to make a contrasting point to 62:1–2. Here **only** means "single-mindedly." The verb **plan** indicates a deliberate and premeditated hatred (cf. 2:2). **High position** is a noun used of the "majesty" of God (e.g., Job 13:11; 31:23), of the "dignity" of the firstborn son (Gen. 49:3), and here of David the anointed king. What unites these enemies, as in Psalm 2, is that they will not have God's King to rule over them. Christ's church is given dignity by his grace (cf. James 2:5); Satan desires nothing more than to deprive them of this.[24]

Far from taking **pleasure** in the law of the Lord (Ps. 1:2), their delight is in **falsehood** (cf. Gen. 3; John 8:44). This deceit is masked by the veneer of piety, for **they bless with their mouths**. But what is going on **inwardly**, in their hearts, is a **curse**, a desire to harm God's Messiah and church. What makes them so dangerous to the church is that they have "the appearance of godliness" and are members, indeed sometimes leaders, of churches (2 Tim. 3:1–5).

Selah gives us pause for thought as we set the restfulness of faith (Ps. 62:1–2) alongside the tumult of evil attack (62:3–4).

62:5–8 Christ's Church Walks in the Footsteps of Christ, Who Walked by Faith Alone on Earth

5   For God alone, O my soul, wait in silence,
        for my hope is from him.

Psalm 62:5a is literally "*Only* [אַךְ, *ak*] to God be silent, my soul." Psalm 62:5 differs subtly from 62:1. In place of a statement ("Silence [is] my soul"), there is an exhortation to live in the faith he professes: **Wait in silence**.[25] There is no contradiction, for a believer with a living faith needs constant encouragement to be what he is. Even Jesus needed this on earth, and this verse would have encouraged him as he exhorted himself to continue in perfect faith, without sin. The second change is the substitution of **hope**[26] for "salvation" in 62:1. This reminds us that the salvation for which Jesus yearned, which he has received in resurrection, is a salvation for which we yet hope (cf. Rom. 8:24–25).

---

24 Augustine compares Christians to Joseph elevated to greatness in Egypt. Augustine, *Psalms*, 3:206.
25 Imperative of the verb that is cognate with the noun "silence" in Ps. 62:1.
26 The word תִּקְוָה is a wisdom word often used in Job and Proverbs.

6   He only is my rock and my salvation,
         my fortress; I shall not be shaken.

Psalm 62:6 is very similar to 62:2. "*Only* he [is] my rock and my salvation." The omission of "greatly" (62:1) may represent a strengthened conviction: "I am confident not simply that I will not be greatly shaken but that I will not be shaken at all!"

7   On God rests my salvation and my glory;
         my mighty rock, my refuge is God.

Literally, this reads, "On God [is] my salvation and my glory; / a mighty rock, my salvation is (in)[27] God." The verse is bracketed with God (in Hebrew as in the ESV). The words **on God** indicate that the King's **salvation** and **glory** (his "exaltation to the throne and ongoing rule";[28] cf. 3:3–4) rest on God's power and promises.

Just as the "high position" (62:4) of Christ overflows to his people, so does his **glory**. As Augustine expresses it, citing Romans 8:30,

I shall be saved in God, and I shall be glorious in God. It is not a case of being saved and no more, of being barely saved. I shall be glorious too: saved, because . . . I have been justified by him; but glorious too, because I am not merely justified, but also honored.[29]

8   Trust in him at all times, O people;
         pour out your heart before him;
         God is a refuge for us.   *Selah*

Picking up "my refuge" from Psalm 62:7, the anointed King now speaks explicitly to his **people**. What he has modeled he now exhorts: **Trust in him**. The phrase **at all times** is functionally equivalent to "only," excluding any other times; this is faith alone. It is natural for the loyal followers of

---

27 Hebrew בֵּאלֹהִים. Either the *bet* (ב) indicates "*in* God," or it is a "*bet* of essence" and simply indicates "God." There is very little difference.

28 Hamilton, *Psalms*, 1:566.

29 Augustine, *Psalms*, 3:215.

the suffering King to wonder if they are backing a loser. All the appearance of power is on the side of those about to give the final push to the tottering wall of Christ and his people. We, the church of Christ, need to hear 62:8–12 as those who, like David's original loyal followers, will find our loyalty to Christ tested.

It is not enough—and it is not necessarily helpful—simply to be told to **trust**. We need to be told how and why. The second line opens up the "how" of trust in God: to **pour out your heart before him** is to spread out all the troubles, anxieties, sadnesses, hopes, and fears of the heart in the presence of the God who is rock, fortress, and refuge. This Jesus did on earth before the Father. We will do this only before one whom we trust. Calvin notes that "we are all too apt . . . to shut up our affliction in our own breast, . . . which can only aggravate the trouble and embitter the mind against God."[30] Luther waxed eloquent about this:

> Regardless of what it is, just throw it in a pile before Him, as you open your heart completely to a good friend. . . . Come right out with it, even if all you have is bags full of need. Out with everything; God is greater and more able and more willing than all our transgressions. Do not dribble your requests before Him; God is not a man whom you can overburden with your begging and asking. The more you ask, the happier He is to hear you.[31]

This we do because **God is a refuge for us**, our utterly safe space— at which point a *Selah* pause is very timely.

62:9–12 Christ Teaches His Church Why We Should Trust in God Alone, as He Did on Earth

9   Those of low estate are but a breath;
          those of high estate are a delusion;
      in the balances they go up;
          they are together lighter than a breath.

30 Calvin, *Psalms*, 2:425.
31 Luther, *Luther's Works*, 14:237.

The hortatory appeal of Psalm 62:8 shifts into a didactic tone in 62:9. The final "only" begins the verse in Hebrew (ESV: "but"): "Only a breath . . ." The word **breath** is the characteristic Ecclesiastes word "vanity" (הֶבֶל, *hebel*; cf. "a mist that . . . vanishes," James 4:14). Only a **breath** characterizes both **those of low estate** and **those of high estate**.[32] The word **delusion** is literally "a lie" (the same as "falsehood," Ps. 62:4),[33] something that cannot perform what it promises. **In the balances** (an old-fashioned pair of scales) **they go up** because, for all their sense of weightiness, of being people who matter (especially if they are **of high estate**), they are **lighter than a breath**. The point of the verse (following 62:8) is that we are foolish to trust in lightweights, who cannot perform on their promises. This is especially true (in this context) of the so-called heavyweights who oppose our King. We will be tempted to go over to their side as they seem to hold all the cards; we will be foolish if we do. For as Luther put it, "The favor of men is inconstant. Friend today, foe tomorrow; or as the saying goes about princes in particular, 'The favor of a prince is as fickle as April weather!'" (cf. 146:3–4).[34]

10   Put no trust in extortion;
        set no vain hopes on robbery;
        if riches increase, set not your heart on them.

The phrase **put no trust in** picks up the theme of trust from Psalm 62:8. Although the subject is possessions, the trust against which we are warned is the same as in 62:9, for trust in money is essentially trust in what people can get for themselves. **Extortion** means property gained by oppression, the misuse of their power (cf. the same word in Lev. 6:4; Ps. 73:8—"oppression"). The verb to **set . . . vain hopes** comes from the same root as "breath" (הֶבֶל, *hebel*) in 62:9. To paraphrase, "Trust in God, for he is a rock; don't trust in people or what powerful people can accumulate because people are lightweights, and your hope will be a lightweight hope" (cf. 52:7). To **set . . . your heart** is to trust. The point is that **riches** do have a tendency to **increase** (lit., "bear fruit") and therefore appeal to us as objects of our trust.

32 For the latter, see on Ps. 4:2; for both idioms, see on Ps. 49:2.
33 כָּזָב.
34 Luther, *Luther's Works*, 14:232.

But all such trust, whether in possessions (62:10) or the powerful people who get those possessions (62:9), is misplaced.

> [11]   Once God has spoken;
>   twice have I heard this:
>   that power belongs to God,
> [12]   and that to you, O Lord, belongs steadfast love.
>   For you will render to a man
>   according to his work.

The warning of 62:9–10 (balancing the rebuke of 62:3–4) is followed by a closing note that sets before the church of Christ two great reasons to trust in God. The movement begins with **God has spoken** and moves to the response of faith **I have heard**. The formula **once . . . twice . . .** is emphatic rather than numerical (cf. Job 40:5) since—as it happens—three declarations are recorded.[35] The first is **that power belongs to God** and not to the King's powerful enemies. The second is **that to you, O Lord** (the only explicit address to God, perhaps for emphasis), **belongs steadfast love** (חֶסֶד, *khesed*, covenant love, given primarily in this context to the anointed King). "Almost all scripture is summed up in these," writes Augustine, so we should "stand in awe of his power, and love his mercy."[36] We need both of these "to induce a soul to trust in God only," for "faith hath need of both, as of two wings, . . . as props whereon to settle and fix itself."[37] God's power means he is able to frustrate the wicked and save his Messiah and church, and his covenant love means he has pledged to do so. Together they make our salvation certain and induce us to place all our trust in God.

Only in the light of Christ can the third declaration be understood as supporting what David has said (**for**). That God **will render to a man according to his work** means that he will reward covenant faith and obedience and punish covenant disobedience. This truth, consistently taught in both Old Testament and New, is only good news when the King is a better king than David, when Jesus comes to be the perfect covenant-keeping King who demonstrates the flawless faith in God alone that this psalm attests to.

---

35 "Once . . . twice" is better than the NIV "one thing . . . two things." Harman, *Psalms*, 1:461.

36 Augustine, *Psalms*, 3:222.

37 Dickson, *Psalms*, 1:369.

This Jesus both keeps the covenant for us and bears the covenant curse in our place (Gal. 3:10–14), that on the last day, when he exercises this judgment according to works, all who are in his book of life will find salvation.

REFLECTION AND RESPONSE

1. Let us first meditate on the reality that Jesus lived by faith alone, spurning all rivals for his trust. Hear him speaking this psalm to the Father in his mornings of prayer. Meditate also on his seemingly fragile position (the leaning wall, the tottering fence), surrounded by enemies determined to destroy him (cf. Mark 3:6). Ponder how, even when a few rich or powerful people stood with him, he refused to place his trust in them but persevered with faith in God alone.

2. Then let us listen to the exhortation and teaching of our King in Psalm 62:8–12, considering what it means to learn the disciplines of pouring out our hearts in prayer, meditating on the empty "breathiness" that lies behind the deceitfulness of the seemingly powerful, glamorous, seductive "heavyweights" of our cultures, pondering above all the power and steadfast love of God shown to us in Christ our exalted King.

3. Let us pray Psalm 62:1–7 again, not simply as the words of our King but now as our words, shaping for us what faith in God alone can mean under pressure.

4. Consider how safe you are in Jesus, even as Jesus was utterly safe in the hands of the Father, to whom he entrusted himself at the cross. Let the words of the psalm so sink into your heart that the Holy Spirit works in your soul a quiet waiting for God to save you.

5. Let the "only" motif help the exclusivity of the psalm sink into your heart. Take each "only" in turn, the positives (62:1, 2, 5, 6) and the negatives (62:4, 9), and feel how they warn you against a false faith and stir in you a refreshment of true faith in God alone.

And if, when persecuted, you go out into the desert,
do not be afraid, as though alone, but having God
there and rising before dawn, sing [Psalm 63].

ATHANASIUS
Letter to Marcellinus

The Fathers of the Church appointed [Psalm 63] to be said
every morning, as a spiritual song and a medicine to blot
out our sins; to kindle in us a desire of God; to raise our
souls, and inflame them with a mighty fire of devotion; to
make us overflow with goodness and love, and send us with
such preparation to approach and appear before God.

JOHN CHRYSOSTOM
In Alexander Francis Kirkpatrick, *The Book of Psalms*

A Psalm for David—a Psalm for David's Son—a Psalm
for the Church in every age—a Psalm for every
member of the Church in the weary land!

ANDREW BONAR
Christ and His Church in the Book of Psalms

PSALM 63

ORIENTATION

In Psalm 63, this most beautiful song, Jesus Christ our King invites us to "go to him outside the camp" (Heb. 13:13) and to learn from him how to live the life of faith "in the wilderness" (Ps. 63:S). The psalm is first a psalm of David and then—in fulfillment—a psalm of Jesus for us to speak in Christ.

It speaks of a most attractive desire for God, of delight in God, and of joy and assurance in God. All these David exemplified only in part. At some times he contradicted them, and at all times he fell short of this ideal. For David is a type of Christ; he is not Christ. As James Hamilton observes,

> David . . . was not fully consistent in blessing God with his life (see 2 Sam 11). No one, however, could convict his greater son of sin (John 8:46). Jesus lived the words of Ps 63 more perfectly than David himself, modeling for us a life of steadfast love and satisfaction in God.[1]

If we seek simply to imitate David (i.e., David did these wonderful things, and we should try to do the same), the psalm will become law without gospel and lead us down a path of discouragement, even despair, as we fail to live up to these ideals. Franz Delitzsch exclaims how difficult it is "to adopt this choice spiritual love-song as one's own prayer! For this we need a soul that loves after the same manner."[2] This, by nature, we do not have,

---

1   Hamilton, *Psalms*, 1:574.
2   Delitzsch, *Psalms*, 2:214. Delitzsch goes on to quote Saint Bernard of Clairvaux (1090–1153), who says that to those who do not love, even the language of love is a despicable foreign tongue (*lingua amoris non amanti barbara est*).

nor did David. Only by the Spirit of Christ did David even approximate this lovely faith; only in Christ and by the Spirit of Christ may we rejoice in walking in the footsteps of David—and supremely of Jesus.

Psalm 63 exhibits significant links to Psalms 42–43 (especially the thirsty longing for the presence of God in a distant place, 42:2; cf. 143:6) and Psalm 84 (rejoicing in the lovely dwelling place of God). But the strongest links are to Psalms 61 and 62. With Psalm 62 is shared the power and glory of God (62:7, 11; 63:2), the steadfast love of God (62:12; 63:3), the frequent use of the word "soul" (62:1, 5; 63:1, 5, 8, 9 ["life"]), and the word "lie" (62:4 ["falsehood"]; 62:9 ["delusion"]; 63:11). Psalm 61 is linked to Psalm 63 by the motif of alienation ("the end of the earth," 61:2; "wilderness," 63:S), by the experience of faintness (61:2; 63:1), by the presence of God on earth ("your tent," 61:4; "sanctuary," 63:2), by the "name" of God (61:5, 8; 63:4), by a commitment to praise God (61:8; 63:3–4), by the shadow of God's "wings" (61:4; 63:7), and by the King speaking of himself in the third person (61:6–7; 63:11). There are also links to Psalm 64 (see comments there), which shares with Psalm 63 a closing note of jubilation for God's King and his church.

In Isaiah 55:1–5 we find a significant echo of the theme of God's provision for the thirsty, also in the context of God's covenant with David.

Psalm 63 includes an abundance of personal pronouns ("I" and "you"). They emphasize the intensely relational nature of the psalm.[3]

THE TEXT

Structure

Although Alexander Francis Kirkpatrick says that there is no clear division because, as he puts it, "thought follows thought out of the fulness of a loving heart,"[4] there are some structural markers. In Psalm 63:11 the King speaks of himself in the third person, marking this verse as a conclusion. The most natural way to structure 63:1–10 may be to take 63:1–5 and 63:6–10 as two sections, each beginning with the King's union with God.[5] Psalm 63:1–5

---

3   Harman, *Psalms*, 1:464.
4   Kirkpatrick, *Psalms*, 2:352.
5   There is no indication in Hebrew that Ps. 63:6 is a continuation of 63:5 (as indicated by the comma in the ESV). I have structured the psalm following the CSB, NASB, NIV, and REB, which close 63:5 with a period and begin a new sentence with 63:6.

may be subdivided into 63:1–3, David's union with God, and 63:4–5, his satisfaction in God. Similarly, 63:6–10 breaks into 63:6–8, David's union with God, and 63:9–10, his assurance of his enemies' defeat.[6]

Superscription

s   A Psalm of David, when he was in the wilderness of Judah.[7]

The superscription raises a historical question and a spiritual question. The historical question is, When was David **in the wilderness of Judah?** When persecuted by Saul, he experienced many wilderness times (e.g., 1 Sam. 23:14–15, 24; 24:1; 25:4, 21; 26:2). Nevertheless, there are several reasons to suppose that this psalm arose when fleeing Absalom. David terms himself "the king" (Ps. 63:11), which is perhaps more natural after his reign began (and indeed constitutes a believing affirmation that he is still the king, despite what Absalom has done). His flight involved passing through "the wilderness" (2 Sam. 15:23, 28; 17:16). The rare word "weary" (עָיֵף, *ayeph*, Ps. 63:1) is echoed in 2 Samuel 16:14[8] and 17:29. Fainting of thirst in the wilderness features in 2 Samuel 16:2 (cf. Ps. 63:1). David has sent the ark back to Jerusalem (2 Sam. 15:25), which would make his yearning for the presence of God all the stronger.[9] If, as I think, Psalm 62 stems from this period, the strong links between the two psalms would support this conclusion, although our appropriation of the psalm does not depend on this specific background.[10]

The spiritual question is more important. The wilderness is "a dry and thirsty land" (cf. Ezek. 19:13), away from water, food, and human company. **Wilderness** is replete with biblical associations and sets the tone for this psalm. These associations include Hagar with Ishmael, for whom God provides a well of water (Gen. 21), and the pit in which

---

6 In this I largely follow Hengstenberg, *Psalms*, 2:300. Hengstenberg sees Ps. 63:11 as a conclusion that balances the superscription.

7 The other historical superscriptions are for Pss. 3, 7, 18, 34, 51, 52, 54, 56, 57, 59, 60, 142. In Hebrew the superscription is verse 1; subsequent verse numbers are increased by one.

8 In this verse David is styled "the king," as in Ps. 63:11.

9 Ross, *Psalms*, 2:386.

10 I agree with Delitzsch that Pss. 61–63 all probably come from this period. Delitzsch, *Psalms*, 2:213.

Joseph was cast (Gen. 37), but supremely it links to that immensely formative wilderness experience between the exodus and the conquest of the promised land. The "wilderness" appears in the Old Testament most frequently in this connection (supremely in Exodus, Leviticus, Numbers, and Deuteronomy but also in Ps. 78 and often in the Prophets as they look back to that time, e.g., Jer. 2:2). It is also the place of Elijah's journey to Horeb/Sinai (1 Kings 19:4), which mirrors in many ways the experiences of David and later the Lord Jesus. The Prophets include a number of oracles speaking of God's restoration of the wilderness and provision for his people in the wilderness (e.g., Isa. 32:15–20; 35:1–10;[11] Ezek. 34:25). The herald announces the coming of Messiah in the wilderness (Isa. 40:3; Matt. 3:1).

63:1–5 In Christ the Church Is Brought into Loving Union with God and Given a Promise to Sustain It in a Wilderness World

1   O God, you are my God; earnestly I seek you;
         my soul thirsts for you;
     my flesh faints for you,
         as in a dry and weary land where there is no water.

The psalm begins with God, literally, "O God, my God *you*"—emphatic personal, covenantal address. The verb translated **earnestly I seek you** (cf. Prov. 8:17; Isa. 26:9; Hos. 5:15) may derive from the root indicating "early" (linked to the word "dawn");[12] this was how the Septuagint understood it and how many older writers read it, as they stressed the priority that "first thing in the morning" gives to urgent prayer.[13] Nowadays it is thought to mean

---

11 This includes "Then the eyes of the blind shall be opened" (Isa. 35:5), fulfilled in the ministry of Christ.

12 E.g., BDB: "look early, diligently for"; s.v. שׁחר.

13 E.g., Augustine connects it with Eph. 5:14, "Awake, O sleeper . . ." Augustine, *Psalms*, 3:232. John Chrysostom (ca. 347–407), like many writers, builds on the interpretation of Ps. 63:1 that "earnestly" means "early." Discussed in Kirkpatrick, *Psalms*, 2:353. Dietrich Bonhoeffer (1906–1945) likewise includes it in his exhortation to morning worship: "The profound silence of morning is first broken by the prayer and song of the community of faith," for "the first thought and the first word of the day belong to God." Dietrich Bonhoeffer, *Life Together*, in *Life Together; Prayerbook of the Bible,* ed. Geffrey B. Kelly, trans. Daniel W. Bloesch and James H. Burtness, vol. 5 of *Dietrich Bonhoeffer Works* (Minneapolis: Fortress, 2005), 51.

"seek earnestly" or "seek eagerly," rather than necessarily having a nuance of "early."[14] The meanings are related, for an earnest seeking of God will be an early seeking of God, since the wise align their priorities with their values.

David writes **in** (CSB, NASB, NIV; contra ESV, NRSV—"as in"—for he is actually in the wilderness) **a dry**[15] **and weary land where there is no water**. Thirst envelops everything. The wilderness shapes the language of **thirst** and **faint**ing, from the **soul** (better than just "I" since it highlights the longing of his inner being)[16] and **flesh** (the longing of an embodied being), together expressing the yearning of the whole person.[17] The verb **faints** indicates "ardent longing which consumes the last energies of a man."[18] Thirst, which is literal in the wilderness and can be assuaged only by the provision of God (e.g., Ex. 17:3; Isa. 48:21), becomes a powerful image of the desperate need for the presence of the God who alone gives life (Pss. 42:2–3 ["the *living* God"]; 143:6). Jesus yearned for this as he walked through a wilderness world (supremely in his temptations), promised this to all who "hunger and thirst for righteousness" (Matt. 5:6), and offers this, by the Holy Spirit, to all who will come to him as the fruit of his being "glorified" in his sin-bearing death (John 4:13–14; 7:37–39). Augustine perceptively notes that the word **flesh** (with all its physicality) points to a longing not just for some immaterial provision for the heart in this life but for bodily resurrection;[19] the context of the invitation to "the one who is thirsty" in Revelation 22:17 supports this.

"Think," says Augustine,

how powerful are the desires in human hearts. One person covets gold, another silver, another possessions, another ancestral lands, another plenty of ready money, another vast herds, another a spacious house, another a wife, another high rank, and another children. You are familiar with these desires, and you know how powerful they can be in the hearts of men and women. Everyone burns with desire,

---

14 See *HALOT* on the various meanings of the root שׁחר.
15 The word "dry" (צִיָּה) is sometimes translated "desert" (e.g., Pss. 78:17; 105:41; 107:35).
16 Ross, *Psalms*, 2:383.
17 For "soul" with "flesh" and "heart," see Ps. 84:2. Kirkpatrick speaks of "the emotions, the reason and the will, the physical organism in and through which they act." Kirkpatrick, *Psalms*, 2:353.
18 Delitzsch, *Psalms*, 2:215.
19 Augustine, *Psalms*, 2:234.

but there are precious few who can say to God, *My soul is athirst for you*. People thirst for the world . . . where their souls are meant to be thirsting for God.[20]

Indeed, this desire in distress is a litmus test that can reveal the true believer. For some, the desire for God evaporates in troubled times; for others, it grows, and this is a sign of spiritual life, for a living faith turns to God in trouble as a magnet does to iron.[21]

> 2   So I have looked upon you in the sanctuary,
>   beholding your power and glory.

The verb **looked upon** suggests "an intent and discerning contemplation."[22] Here, alongside the usual word for "seeing" (**beholding**), it suggests a literal and thoughtful looking at the symbols of the covenant in **the sanctuary** (the tabernacle and later the temple), which symbolized God's **power and glory** (cf. Ps. 78:60–61). The words **power** and **glory** are strongly associated with the ark of the covenant[23] (e.g., Ps. 132:8 for "power"; 1 Sam. 4:21–22 for "glory"), which would be especially appropriate if this is the time described in 2 Samuel 15:25–26.

There is some discussion about how Psalm 63:2 is related to 63:1. This focuses on the meaning of the word translated **so** (כֵּן, *ken*) and about the appropriate tense for the verb translated **I have looked upon**. Probably it means that David has delighted in the covenant God in the sanctuary in the past (63:2) and longs to do so again (63:1). The symbols of the covenant nourish his faith.

The New Testament teaches that the covenant power and revealed glory of God are to be seen finally and fully in Christ, to whom the old covenant signs pointed. It is to Christ we must look today.

> 3   Because your steadfast love is better than life,
>   my lips will praise you.

20 Augustine, *Psalms*, 3:233.
21 Hengstenberg, *Psalms*, 2:303.
22 Kirkpatrick, *Psalms*, 2:354.
23 Harman, *Psalms*, 1:465.

The reference to God's "power" leads naturally to his **steadfast love** (חֶסֶד, *khesed*, covenant love); these were linked in Psalm 62:11–12. God's power is used to fulfill his covenant promises to David. To say that his **steadfast love is better than life** is extraordinary, for **life** includes all that I am and all that I possess (cf. Mark 8:35–37). This, the "central theological idea of the psalm,"[24] makes sense only if the covenant promises—made to David and ultimately to Christ and in Christ to all Christ's church—include bodily resurrection and the new creation (cf. Ps. 16). No wonder Christ **praises** the Father for his covenant love, and no wonder we, like David, are moved to do the same by the Spirit of Christ!

As we move into the next verse there is a slight shift from delight in God to satisfaction in God.

4   So I will bless you as long as I live;
       in your name I will lift up my hands.

So builds on Psalm 63:3. The words **as long as I live** (lit., "in my life") contain a nice irony in the light of 63:3: because of your covenant love, given me in Christ, "as long as I live" means eternal life! The second line expands the first: **in your name** (i.e., as you have revealed yourself in the covenant and now in Christ) **I will lift up my hands** (cf. 28:2; 141:2; 1 Tim. 2:8), the hands being "the outward symbol of an uplifted heart" (cf. Lam. 3:41).[25]

5   My soul will be satisfied as with fat and rich food,
       and my mouth will praise you with joyful lips,

The image of a banquet moves from thirst (Ps. 63:1) to satisfaction. The words **fat and rich food** are more or less synonymous and emphatically suggest the satisfying meal to end all meals. Similar imagery is found in Psalm 23:5; Isaiah 25:6 (the messianic banquet); and Zechariah 9:15. This satisfaction, enjoyed in anticipation through the Holy Spirit, will be devoured with new creation bodily delight at the wedding reception of the Lamb (Rev. 19:9). No wonder Christ **will**

---

24 Ross, *Psalms*, 2:390.
25 Kirkpatrick, *Psalms*, 2:355.

praise the Father **with joyful lips,** as his church praises the triune God in anticipation today.

63:6–10 In Christ the Church Is Given Great Assurance

If there is a shift of emphasis from Psalm 63:1–5 to 63:6–10, it may be from delight in God to assurance from God.

> 6   when I remember you upon my bed,
>   and meditate on you in the watches of the night;

If 63:6 begins a new sentence, it will read, "When I remember you upon my bed, I meditate on you in the watches of the night." The meaning is not so very different, however it is punctuated. The two lines are parallel, the verb **remember** (indicating recall with a view to response) being developed to **meditate,** the verb used in Psalm 1:2.[26] Similarly, the static reference to **my bed** develops to the existential and dynamic time reference of **the watches of the night.** The significance of the night is partly that I am alone with my thoughts, the true "me" (cf. 17:3), and partly that what I ponder by night reveals what matters most to me. David Dickson speaks of "spiritual exercises in secret"[27] that are the mark of a deep believer, as they were the mark of Jesus. (Psalm 119:148 draws attention to the truth that God is known only through his word and not by a mere mystical experience.)

> 7   for you have been my help,
>   and in the shadow of your wings I will sing for joy.

This meditation is stirred by the past experience of God as **my help** and the assurance that, even in the wilderness, Jesus on earth and his church today can dwell **in the shadow of your wings** (see on 17:8; 36:7; 57:1; 61:4) with great **joy.**

> 8   My soul clings to you;
>   your right hand upholds me.

---

26 A similar development—from "remember" through "meditate" to "ponder"—is found in Ps. 143:5.

27 Dickson, *Psalms,* 1:373.

There is a beautiful and evocative balance in these two lines. First, **my soul** (my inner being) **clings to you**, a strong covenantal word (e.g., Deut. 11:22; 13:4; 30:20), beautifully epitomized when Ruth clings to Naomi (Ruth 1:14) and famous for its covenantal use within marriage (Gen. 2:24). **To you** is literally "after you"[28] and suggests not so much a static embrace as a dynamic and successful pursuit.

The second line moves beyond the first to show what lies behind the clinging of faith in the first place. I cling to you only because **your right hand upholds me**. Were the second line to become untrue for an instant, the first line would evaporate.

The verb **upholds** brings to mind the reason the King needs to be upheld. His enemies, so prominent in Psalm 62:3–4 (and perhaps evident in the concrete realities of Absalom's rebellion), come now into focus.

When reading 63:9–10, we need to correct our natural aversion to this declaration of destruction for enemies. Kirkpatrick is right that the King expects his enemies to be defeated "as a manifest token that God had not withdrawn from the government of the world, and was surely, if slowly, establishing His Kingdom among men."[29] These will and must be defeated, not as a matter of personal revenge, but in order that God's Messiah shall reign and restore a broken world.

9   But those who seek to destroy my life
        shall go down into the depths of the earth;
10   they shall be given over to the power of the sword;
        they shall be a portion for jackals.

Here is a vivid contrast between the King (and his church) being "*up-held*" (cf. 63:8) and the enemies who will **go down**. The first line of 63:9 reads literally, "But they [emphatic]—to destruction—they seek my soul."[30] Clearly, they **seek . . . my life**. But to whom does **destroy** refer? It could refer to the King (as the CSB, ESV, NASB, i.e., "They seek the destruction of my [i.e., the King's] life"), or it could refer to the enemies (i.e., "But those

---

28 אַחֲרֶיךָ. The recent translation of Augustine has "my soul is glued behind you." Augustine, *Psalms*, 3:243.

29 Kirkpatrick, *Psalms*, 2:352.

30 "My life" is נַפְשִׁי, "my soul," as in Ps. 63:1, 5, 8.

who—to their own destruction—seek my life . . .", cf. NIV, REB). Either is possible. Perhaps the parallelism with the second line suggests the latter.[31] The word **destroy** is associated with the desert, a wasteland, in Job 30:3.

To **go down into the depths of the earth** recalls Korah's rebellion (Num. 16:31–34) or the judgment on Tyre (Ezek. 26:20–21) and vividly pictures complete removal from this created order. The sinless Jesus descended into these depths to pay the penalty for sins (Eph. 4:9) and to rescue a people "from the depths of Sheol" (Ps. 86:13); those who are finally hostile to God's King and refuse to find refuge in his sacrifice have no alternative but to descend there eternally.

Psalm 63:10 reiterates the judgment of 63:9. As a judge hands over a prisoner to the jailer for capital sentence, so he will, in perfect righteousness, **be given over to the power of the sword** (for this idiom, see Jer. 18:21; Ezek. 35:5). The final line both reassures and horrifies in equal measure. To be the **portion for jackals** is to have one's unburied corpse on the battlefield picked over by scavengers. Here is a terrible wasteland scene (cf. the aftermath of Absalom's rebellion in 2 Sam. 18:8; Lam. 5:18; Ezek. 13:4).

63:11 Conclusion

> [11]   But the king shall rejoice in God;
>   all who swear by him shall exult,
>   for the mouths of liars will be stopped.

But the king—David here almost certainly speaks of himself in the third person (cf. Ps. 61:6); his joy is the logical response to the defeat of his enemies in 63:9–10.[32] By calling himself **the king** (especially in the context of Absalom's rebellion), he stakes by faith a claim to that kingdom given him by God through covenant that, though it is wildly contested (cf. 2:1–3), can never be removed. It is as though he says, "I, . . . having received kingship from you,"[33] **shall rejoice in** you, and no enemy can stop me.

31 So Delitzsch, *Psalms*, 2:218; Hengstenberg, *Psalms*, 2:306; Ross, *Psalms*, 2:384n8.
32 "The connexion is unintelligible unless the king is identified with the Psalmist, whose enemies are destroyed." Kirkpatrick, *Psalms*, 2:356. Cf. Tate, *Psalms 51–100*, 125; Ross, *Psalms*, 2:394.
33 Theodoret of Cyrus, *Psalms*, 1:359.

Who is indicated in the words **who swear by him** in the second line? Usually this language refers to swearing by God or the covenant Lord, that is, to true worship.[34] Commentators have differing views; some note that it is possible to swear by a king, in the sense of swearing allegiance to that king (e.g., 1 Sam. 17:55; 2 Sam. 15:21).[35] It may be that the ambiguity, as James Hamilton notes, "highlights the close connection between Israel's king and Israel's God."[36] In the end, those who pledge loyalty to God's Messiah are the same people who truly worship God, for no one can honor the Father who does not honor the Son (John 5:23).

These people are Christ's church. As John Calvin says,

> The deliverance which David received had not been extended to him as a private person, but the welfare of the whole Church was concerned in it, as that of the body in the safety of the head. . . . [T]he safety of God's chosen people, at that time, was inseparably connected with the reign of David and its prosperity—a figure by which it was the divine intention to teach us, that our happiness and glory depend entirely upon Christ.[37]

Dietrich Bonhoeffer comments on this and similar truths in other psalms and says, "We pray in these psalms for the victory of Jesus Christ in the world, we give thanks for the victory already won, and we pray for the establishment of the kingdom of justice and of peace under the king Jesus Christ."[38]

In the final line, **the mouths of liars will be stopped**. To be a "liar" is to be a spiritual heir of the first liar, the seed of the serpent of Genesis 3 (cf. John 8:44). Paul may have had this phrase, **the mouths of liars will be stopped**, in mind in Romans 3:19.[39] The law will stop every mouth speaking in self-justification. Only the atoning death of Christ can unstop mouths in praise. One of the rich contrasts in the psalm is between these "stopped" mouths and the emphatically opened mouth of the King and his people

---

34 The NIV paraphrases and assumes this, thus closing down what may be a fruitful ambiguity.
35 Goldingay, *Psalms*, 2:262; Eveson, *Psalms*, 1:387.
36 Hamilton, *Psalms*, 1:573.
37 Calvin, *Psalms*, 2:442–43.
38 Bonhoeffer, *Prayerbook of the Bible*, 167.
39 This is suggested by Kirkpatrick, *Psalms*, 2:356. LXX: ἐμφράσσω ; Romans 3:19: φράσσω . Also noted by Mark A. Seifrid, "Romans," in *CNTOT* 618.

in the repeated verbs of praise and exultation. There is a neat consonance linking Psalm 63:1 ("seek," אֲשַׁחֲרֶךָּ, *ashakhareka*) to 63:11 ("liars," שָׁקֶר, *shaqer*; "stopped," יִסָּכֵר, *yissaker*): one can seek the Lord, or one can be a stopped liar.[40]

REFLECTION AND RESPONSE

1. Ponder first what it meant for David "in the wilderness" to sing these words, and wonder at the richness and depths of his love for God and his confidence in the God who had entered into covenant with him. But then let David the type lead you, in heart and mind, to Jesus Christ the antitype, and wonder yet more at the intimacy with the Father evidenced here. For in an absolute, perfect, and eternal sense, only he knows the Father, and only he trusted the Father during his days on earth with this perfection.

2. We make the psalm our own as men and women in Christ. We ponder the desire for God evidenced in Psalm 63:1 and expressed in 63:2 in terms of the sacraments of the old covenant, and we pray for the Spirit of Christ to work this desire in our own souls so that we will seek God earnestly and early, thirst for God above all others, and long for him and ultimately for the resurrection of the body. We allow the word of God and the gospel sacraments of the new covenant (baptism and the Lord's Supper) to be both nourishment for and expressions of our love for God in Christ.[41]

3. We should reflect much on Psalm 63:3 as we make these wonderful words our own. "See how greatly," writes Martin Luther, "he esteems and magnifies the mercy [i.e., steadfast love] of God. For in the judgment of all there is nothing more precious than life. . . . From this it is clear how precious we should consider the grace of God."[42] Bonhoeffer perceptively notes that we can still desire the good things of this life (and it would be strange and inhuman not to) so long as "we recognize all these [i.e., good things] as evidences of God's gracious community with us and thereby hold fast to the knowledge that God's goodness is better than life."[43]

---

40 This consonance is noted in, e.g., Tate, *Psalms 51–100*, 125; Goldingay, *Psalms*, 2:262.

41 "Because the power and glory of God are nowhere so clearly seen as in public ordinances, therefore should the ordinances be loved and earnestly sought after; that we may find communion with God in them." Dickson, *Psalms*, 1:371.

42 Luther, *Luther's Works*, 10:305.

43 Bonhoeffer, *Prayerbook of the Bible*, 168–69.

4. Pray with Psalm 63:5 that the Holy Spirit will give you, even now, some anticipatory satisfaction in God as you look forward to that final banquet on the wedding day of Jesus.

5. Pray that Psalm 63:6–8 will stir in you, by the Spirit, a yearning for such meditation on God's goodness on your own in secret as will bring joy to your heart. Do not despise the felt experience of grace, for "the felt kindness of God, and shedding abroad of his love in the heart of a believer [Rom. 5:5], is joy unspeakable and glorious, able to supply all wants unto him, and to sweeten all troubles unto him, and to give him more comfort than what is most comfortable in this world."[44]

6. Take heart—and be sobered and warned—by the certainty of Psalm 63:9–10. Pray that many will have time for repentance and will avail themselves of the opportunity before it is too late (2 Pet. 3:9).

7. Hamilton sums up the themes of the psalm well:

Contemplate the Scriptures and your mouth will be full of praise for God. Contemplate how you will overthrow the God of the Bible and rebel against his king and your mouth will be stopped. . . . Know the Lord as God, look to him to meet your needs, and you will experience his love, which is better than life, satisfying your soul and sheltering you from harm, upholding you with a righteous right arm. Put some idol in his place and look to it for satisfaction, and you will be left empty and alone, with the wrath of God remaining upon you.[45]

44 Dickson, *Psalms*, 1:372.
45 Hamilton, *Psalms*, 1:573.

It is primarily the Lord's passion that is called to mind in this psalm, but we should recognize in it not his voice only, but ours too.

AUGUSTINE
Expositions of the Psalms

God vouchsafe to grant us, that we, freed from the arrows of the enemy, delivered from the bow of falsehood, may be guarded by Him Who giveth to all His Saints the glory of immortality for their hope of salvation.

JEROME
In Neale and Littledale, *Psalms*

The more they whetted their tongues like a deadly sword, the more their wickedness was nullified, so that the evils which they devised against the blood of the innocent One they directed instead upon themselves. This is the tendency of sinners, to harm themselves first when they hasten to oppress their neighbour.

CASSIODORUS
Explanation of the Psalms

We cannot but be reminded of the "bitter words," the plotting and scheming and underhand methods employed against our Lord. Under a cloak of piety and loyalty to Caesar they drew together a mob to have Jesus destroyed, using false witnesses and other deceitful practices.

PHILIP EVESON
Psalms

PSALM 64

ORIENTATION

In Psalm 64 God's anointed King experiences a great reversal. For the joy set before him, the founder and perfecter of our faith endures the cross and is now seated at the right hand of the throne of God (Heb. 12:2). This dramatic turnaround overflows to his people and leads to great rejoicing, for the joy set before Christ is the joy set before us.

Reversals abound in this beautifully crafted psalm. The enemies are "doers" of evil (Ps. 64:2), but in the end all eyes will be on what God has "done" and "brought about" (64:9).[1] They think they are hidden ("from ambush," 64:4), but it is the Messiah who will be hidden from their plots (64:2). They are "shooting" "bitter words like arrows" (64:3–4), but "God shoots his arrows at them" (64:7). They attack "suddenly" (64:4) but are wounded "suddenly" (64:7). They think no one will "see" them (64:5), and yet everyone will "see" their downfall (64:8–9). They have no "fear" (64:4), but the story will end with everyone fearing God (64:9). They think they have "accomplished" (תַּמְנוּ, *tamnu*, 64:6) their plot against the blameless (תָּם, *tam*, 64:4), but it is the blameless who come out on top. They use their "tongues" (64:3) as weapons, but those same "tongues" will turn against them (64:8). Their "heart" may be deep (64:6), but it is the "upright in heart" who will exult (64:10). Although they recount their plans (64:5) with wicked confidence, the final proclamation will be very different (64:9). Dread (64:1) is replaced by joy (64:10).

While there is no indication of the historical context that prompted the psalm, there are many links with nearby psalms,[2] especially with Psalm 52

---

1 In Ps. 64:2 "evildoers" is פֹּעֲלֵי אָוֶן. In 64:9 "what God has brought about" is פֹּעַל אֱלֹהִים.

2 Wilson says Ps. 64 is part of "the larger complex of Pss. 56–68, in which God's mighty acts demonstrate his power over *all* the earth so that an increasingly expansive group joins in praising him." Wilson, *Psalms*, 1:898.

(explicitly in the context of David's Sauline persecutions)[3] and with Psalms 61–63, including the theme of hostility (e.g., 61:3; 62:3–4; 63:9; and often), the motif of refuge,[4] and the verb "to watch, preserve" (61:7; 64:1).[5] There is also the destructive use of the tongue, lips, or words (e.g., 52:2; 57:4; 59:7).

In particular, the final line of Psalm 63 rejoices that "the mouths of liars will be stopped." Psalm 64 revisits the misery that is caused to the King and his people by these cutting tongues and reaffirms the certainty that they will indeed be silenced.

There are several echoes in Psalm 140 (also "of David"), including the sharp tongue (140:3; cf. "the slanderer," 140:11), evil plots (140:8), and the gladness of "the righteous" and "the upright" (140:13).

While the psalm has often been read as a general reassurance to opposed believers, there are three reasons to refer it first to the King. The first, as in so many psalms, is the ascription "of David." The second is the strong kingly context in some of the nearby psalms. The third is the striking parallel between the final verse of this psalm and the close of Psalm 63. Psalm 64:10 moves from "the righteous one" (singular) in the first line to "all the upright" in the third line. At one level this is simply a rhetorical move from a generic "any one" to "every one" of God's people. But James Hamilton has pointed out that the verse shares with Psalm 63:11 the verbs translated "rejoice" and "exult" and that in Psalm 63 the move is explicitly from the joy of "the king" to the exultation of those who "swear by him," as shown below:[6]

Psalm 63:11	Psalm 64:10
"The king shall *rejoice*."	"Let the righteous one *rejoice*."
"All who swear by him shall *exult*."	"Let all the upright in heart *exult*!"

A number of early Christian writers read the psalm as speaking of Christ's passion and exaltation and then of the sufferings and hope of his church.[7]

---

3   Zenger claims that Pss. 52 and 64 "agree so exactly in the profile they sketch of the evildoers and in the reaction of the righteous to God's judgment on those evil ones that one can read Psalm 64 as a kind of generalization of Psalm 52." Hossfeld and Zenger, *Psalms*, 2:131.
4   Pss. 61, 62, and 64 use the verb "to take refuge" (חָסָה, 61:4; 64:10) or the cognate noun "refuge" (מַחְסֶה, 61:3; 62:7–8).
5   נָצַר.
6   Hamilton, *Psalms*, 1:577–78.
7   E.g., Cassiodorus, *Psalms*, 2:90.

The theme of reversal is also echoed strikingly in both Haman (who is executed on the pole he has prepared for Mordecai, the unrecognized righteous one who is then exalted in the kingdom, Est. 4:14; 6:10; 8:2, 15) and Daniel (whose enemies are cast into the den of lions they had intended for God's righteous one, Dan. 6:23–24).[8]

As not infrequently with Hebrew poetry, there are questions about what English tenses best correspond to the Hebrew verb forms. For example, does Psalm 64:7–9 express a past rescue that David has already experienced or a future rescue that he confidently expects? Seeing fulfillment in Christ and his church may suggest that not as much hinges on these questions as might be thought. For what is already true in Christ (because his resurrection has happened) will certainly be true of his people (because their resurrection will happen).

The theme of just divine retribution is shared with, for example, Psalms 7:14–16; 37:14–15; and 54:5.

THE TEXT

Structure
The clearest break comes with the "but" at the start of Psalm 64:7.[9] Psalm 64:1–6 consists of an appeal (64:2) and a sustained exposé of the enemies (beginning with "who"). Psalm 64:7–9 tells of God's judgment (64:7–8) and humankind's response (64:9). Like 63:11, Psalm 64:10 functions as the conclusion.

Superscription

S   To the choirmaster.[10] A Psalm of David.[11]

64:1–6 Christ and His People Pray for Protection against Deep Evil

1   Hear my voice, O God, in my complaint;
      preserve my life from dread of the enemy.

---

8   See Ross, *Psalms*, 2:401.
9   Although this is simply a *vav*, it functions here as a strong adversative.
10 See on Ps. 4.
11 In Hebrew the superscription is verse 1; subsequent verse numbers are increased by one.

²   Hide me from the secret plots of the wicked,
        from the throng of evildoers,

Hear ... O God (the first two words in Hebrew) focuses this intense petition on the God who must hear (which means "hear and answer"). The next words in Hebrew, **my voice . . . in my complaint**, specify what God is to hear as a **complaint**,[12] which combines distress with thoughtful meditation (cf. Ps. 55:2). The second line intensifies this: **the enemy** (unspecified) causes **dread**, a strong word associated with trembling and paralyzing fear.[13] **Preserve**[14] **my life** shows how high the stakes are, a matter not simply of reputation (damaged by words) but of life and death. This is how it was for Jesus, and this is how it is for his followers, opposed by Satan the murderer and all his minions. The deaths of Jesus and of many of his martyred followers demonstrate that the answer to this prayer is ultimately by resurrection (cf. Matt. 10:28). Jesus was preserved from paralyzing fear (e.g., Luke 13:31–33) and given the power of an indestructible life (Heb. 7:16).

In Psalm 64:2 the camera begins to pull back (in preparation for 64:3–6) to see the "enemy," now called **the wicked** and **evildoers**, described in two contrasting terms. First, they have **secret plots** (סוֹד, *sod*), where the word conveys the feel of "a club or clique,"[15] in which there is confidential "scheming" (CSB). But then, secretive as they are, they metamorphose into a **throng**, here an angry "mob" (CSB; cf. 2:1–3).[16] Both the plotting and the mob loom large in the Gospel accounts of the crucifixion and the persecutions of the church in Acts (e.g., Acts 19:23–41). It will always be so.

³   who whet their tongues like swords,
        who aim bitter words like arrows,

---

12 The word (שִׂיחַ) has frequent wisdom associations, "referring to meditation and reflection, but ... in a desperate, painful context." Hossfeld and Zenger, *Psalms*, 2:132. Cf. Delitzsch, *Psalms*, 2:220; Ross, *Psalms*, 2:403.

13 *HALOT*, s.v. פַּחַד.

14 Although the verbs "preserve" (Ps. 64:1) and "hide" (64:2) are in imperfect form, English translations and almost all commentators take them as conveying imperatives, as signaled by the initial imperative "hear."

15 Delitzsch, *Psalms*, 2:221.

16 The rare word "throng" (רִגְשָׁה) is cognate with the word "to rage" (רָגַשׁ) in Ps. 2:1. In other contexts it may have more of a neutral feel (e.g., Ps. 68:27).

4   shooting from ambush at the blameless,
            shooting at him suddenly and without fear.

The word **who** leads to a sustained and terrifying portrait of the "enemy."
Now we discover what they are plotting and how this shows itself in the
mob that they inspire. In two closely parallel lines, Psalm 64:3 describes
their preparations with the imagery of **swords** and **arrows** (weapons of close
combat and distant attack). To **whet** means to sharpen (as in our old word
"a whetstone" to sharpen knives). They take care with their words; their
words are the fruit of careful preparation, calculated to do maximum harm.
When the crowd cries, "Crucify him! Crucify him!" it is because the leaders
have carefully primed them to say this, targeting Christ's life. Vilification of
Christians under persecution may be carefully sharpened to have maximum
impact, perhaps playing on racial prejudices (e.g., "a Samaritan," John 8:48)
or political feelings (e.g., "who have turned the world upside down," i.e.,
caused instability, Acts 17:6).

The verb **aim** is literally "to tread (i.e., bend the bow),"[17] treading on one
end of a longbow in order to bend it, fix the string, and then fire the arrow
(cf. Ps. 7:12).[18] The phrase **bitter words** tells us what the arrows signify:
words like poisoned arrows (cf. the "deadly poison" of James 3:8 or the
"harsh things" that sinners speak against the Lord in Jude 15).

They shoot **from ambush** (lit., "in, or from, secret places," using a word
that is cognate with the verb "hide" in Ps. 64:2), for they assume they are
well hidden (cf. 11:2). They shoot **at the blameless** (cf. Gen. 6:9; Job 1:1, 8;
2:3), one with integrity. This is "a name applicable to Christ in its fullest
significancy, but applied also to his members"[19] by the gracious work of the
Holy Spirit in them. Cassiodorus points out that the word applies truly to
Christ, "for He contracted no stain of sins" and is given to believers "when
they are cleansed by the Lord's mercy and made . . . pure" by grace.[20] The
enemies seek, as it were, to pierce this integrity with their arrows of falsehood, so to damage his reputation that he will never recover—but they will
fail. They plan to do this **suddenly**, in an attack that is premeditated but

17 *HALOT*, s.v. דרך.
18 Hossfeld and Zenger, *Psalms*, 2:129, 133 (plate 1).
19 Bonar, *Psalms*, 191.
20 Cassiodorus, *Psalms*, 2:92.

unexpected by the victim. They do this **without fear**, for they are supremely confident of their success. Their confidence sets the tone for Psalm 64:5–6.

> 5   They hold fast to their evil purpose;
>   they talk of laying snares secretly,
>   thinking, "Who can see them?"
> 6   They search out injustice,
>   saying, "We have accomplished a diligent search."
>   For the inward mind and heart of a man are deep.

They hold fast translates a rare form of a verb; it probably means "they grasp firmly, hold strongly onto" with determination.[21] Their **evil purpose**, literally, "their word of wickedness," echoes the "word of bitterness" in 64:3. Although they hold strongly to this "word," John Goldingay notes the irony that "it will eventually transpire that the plotters are taking hold of an evil word for themselves in a different sense from the one they think,"[22] for evil words have a boomerang quality. Not only do these evildoers hold determinedly to their purpose to assault God's Christ and his church (as they purposed to kill David), **they talk** about it. In their words they are **laying snares** (cf. Mark 12:13) and doing so **secretly**, that is, disguising their true purpose; as then, so now, words that trap the people of Christ may be wrapped in respectable, even pious, clothes. The third line of Psalm 64:5 tells us what they are **thinking** (lit., "they say," i.e., to themselves). Confident that they can cloak their deceit in the appearance of truth, they are sure that no one—let alone, God—can **see** them or their plots (cf. 10:11; 59:7). They are determined ("hold fast"), confident ("they talk," i.e., recount), and proud ("Who can see?").

And they pay great attention to detail. **They search out**, which means carefully to devise and shape, their **injustice** (an unusual plural with the sense of "violent deeds of injustice" or "[acts of] wickedness").[23] The verb

---

21 The piel of חקק is otherwise unknown. But the piel often means the same as the hiphil, and the hiphil of חקק has the well-established meaning of "grasp." The NIV—"they encourage each other"—is possible but less likely. Goldingay, *Psalms*, 2:264n5. Delitzsch says that they "make firm to themselves . . . by securing, in every possible way, its effective execution." Delitzsch, *Psalms*, 2:221.

22 Goldingay, *Psalms*, 2:268.

23 Ross, *Psalms*, 2:407; Goldingay, *Psalms*, 2:265.

we have accomplished (תַּמְנוּ, *tamnu*) echoes the word "blameless" (תָּם, *tam*); in our plots there is a perverse "integrity," a completeness—we are sure there are no weaknesses in our plans.[24] The phrase **a diligent search** suggests a plot that has been carefully researched (NASB: "We are ready with a well-conceived plot").

Referring this to Saul's persecutions of David but moving from there to the world's persecutions of Christians, Theodoret of Cyrus paraphrases like this:

> They racked their brains . . . , they came up with every stratagem against me, they left no stone unturned, assailing me openly, undermining me secretly, employing spies, patrolling desert regions, searching rocky places, on mountains and in caves and crevices hunting out the practitioners of piety.[25]

How careful, how determined, how confident they were—and how stupid: "What stubbornness of heart this was, to seek to kill a man who was wont to raise the dead!" says Augustine, referring to Christ.[26]

In the final line of Psalm 64:6, we need to ask, Who is saying, **The inward mind and heart of a man are deep**, and in what tone of voice? The **inward mind** (cf. "inmost self," 5:9) and **heart** speak of what cannot be easily detected or observed in a person (cf. Prov. 20:5). In this context what is hidden is wickedness (cf. Jer. 17:9, a close parallel of thought).[27] If, as seems likely, this line expresses the thoughts or words of the enemies of Christ and his church, the tone is one of overconfidence: "Our plans are so well hidden that no one will be able to fathom them until it is too late." And yet David records them with an eye for the deep irony they contain, almost as if he wants to add, "or so you think!"[28] But God sees, just as what lies deep inside a man was laid wide open to the gaze of Jesus (John 2:25). If so, this irony prepares us for the striking contrasts of Psalm 64:8.

---

24 Goldingay, *Psalms*, 2:267.

25 Theodoret of Cyrus, *Psalms*, 1:362.

26 Augustine, *Psalms*, 3:252.

27 Although some older writers, including Augustine and Luther, read this line in a positive sense—both of the depths of Christ's divine-human person and the depths of a mature believer—the context strongly suggests a negative meaning here.

28 Goldingay, *Psalms*, 2:268; Wilson, *Psalms*, 1:899–900; Eveson, *Psalms*, 1:389.

64:7–9 God Will Turn Such Deep Evil against Itself and Bring Joy to His Christ and His People

⁷ But God shoots his arrow at them;
    they are wounded suddenly.
⁸ They are brought to ruin, with their own tongues turned against
    them;
    all who see them will wag their heads.

Derek Kidner shrewdly observes, "It is all over in a verse and a half (Ps. 64:7, 8a), in contrast to the long, laborious scheming which it frustrates."[29] Everything is turned upside down (see the reversals noted in the *orientation* section). Here is the answer to the question "Who will see us?" As Charles Spurgeon puts it, "A greater archer than they are shall take sure aim at their hearts. One of his arrows shall be enough, for he never misses his aim."[30] God is very patient, but when Jesus does return in judgment, it will be a "sudden destruction" with no further chance to repent and nowhere to hide (1 Thess. 5:3; see also on the word "quickly" in Ps. 2:12).

Whatever decision is taken about the translation of the verbal forms (present, past, or future),[31] John Calvin is right that "the Psalmist now congratulates himself in the confident persuasion that his prayers have not been without effect, but already answered."[32] Jesus knows that his prayers are heard (John 11:42). Such confidence may be ours by the Spirit of Christ. It is demonstrated in the resurrection of Christ and guaranteed to us by his word and Spirit.

That **their own tongues** are **turned against them** reinforces the common picture of evil destroying itself. They themselves become a contradiction.

All who see them nicely reminds us that what they have plotted in secret will now be in plain view, together with the outcome of their lives (cf. Luke 12:3). To **wag** the **head**[33] is an idiom expressing horrified derision

---

29 Kidner, *Psalms*, 1:229.
30 Spurgeon, *Treasury*, 2.1:84.
31 See discussion in Ross, *Psalms*, 2:399n16; Hamilton, *Psalms*, 1:577.
32 Calvin, *Psalms*, 2:448.
33 This takes the verb as hithpael from the root נוד. The translation "will flee away" comes from taking the verb as the (otherwise unknown) hithpael from the root נדד. See Wilson, *Psalms*, 1:900n9; Harman, *Psalms*, 1:472.

(cf. Ps. 44:14; Jer. 18:16; 48:27): how unutterably stupid they have been, these confident, clever, careful plotters against Christ and his church!

9   Then all mankind fears;
          they tell what God has brought about
          and ponder what he has done.

What this verse describes will eventually be a universal response (**all mankind**) to the vindication of God's Christ and the resurrection of Christ's church. For now, the future glory of the people of Christ is still hidden under the sign of the cross. As David Dickson puts it, "Not every spectator of God's work giveth glory to God, but they only who compare his word with his works."[34] But one day all will see this.

The response will be threefold. First, they **fear**, in contradiction to the proud fearlessness of the brazen persecutor (Ps. 64:4). We see this fear in the terror of David's enemies when he comes into or is restored to the kingdom; we view it dramatically on the Day of Pentecost, when the Spirit convicts people of their guilt in crucifying the Righteous One (Acts 2:37); we see it when God acts in history to bring about his judgments (e.g., Acts 5:11); the finally impenitent will feel this when it is too late at the end of time (Rev. 6:15–17).

Then, second, **they tell**, they declare publicly the righteous judgments of God on behalf of his anointed King and his people and against his impenitent enemies. In this age this is gospel preaching, in the age to come, the theme of our songs. The clause **what God has brought about** contains an inexhaustible richness of grace.

The third verb, **ponder**, moves from public declaration to the response of thoughtful consideration, enjoyed by believers in this age and then for eternity.

64:10 The Joy of Christ Overflows to Christ's People

10   Let the righteous one rejoice in the Lord
          and take refuge in him!
      Let all the upright in heart exult!

---

34 Dickson, *Psalms*, 1:378.

I have commented in the *orientation* section on the move from the singular **the righteous one** to the plural **all the upright in heart** and the parallel with the King and his people in Psalm 63:11. The note of joyful exultation matches that at the end of Psalm 63. Even now, in the age of the church, the time of persecution, the assurance that 64:7–9 is true will encourage us to **take refuge** in the covenant God. (The use of the covenant name, **the LORD**, is unique in Pss. 60–67 and emphatically highlights the covenantal nature of David's confidence, pointing to its fulfillment in Christ.) The three verbs (**rejoice . . . take refuge . . . exult**) may be jussives (as the ESV, expressing a glad exhortation) or simple indicatives (whether present or future); we ought to do it, we do well to do it, and we will do it.[35]

REFLECTION AND RESPONSE

1. It is a sober discipline to look carefully at the sketch of the enemies and consider how their confident, careful, proud hostility to Christ may infect our own hearts because it is endemic in our cultures.

2. We should meditate on how Psalm 64:2–6 was fulfilled both in the persecutions of David (under Saul and then in Absalom's rebellion) and ultimately in the sufferings of Jesus Christ. This will lead naturally to a glad pondering on how the resurrection of Christ contradicted every lie that was spoken against him, as he who was maligned as unrighteous is seen to be the Righteous One, and he who came in weakness is raised in power.

3. In the history of the church, there are partial reversals like this, when God turns our fortunes. Pondering such times of favor will encourage our hearts.

4. We can take refuge in such a God (Ps. 64:10), knowing what we have seen him do for Jesus Christ, pondering what he has done in history, confident that he will do the same for us.

5. As Ernst Wilhelm Hengstenberg says, "The fundamental thought of the Psalm is, that the . . . wickedness of the enemies is no ground for despair, but rather for *joyous hope*:—the nearer they are to gaining their end, the nearer they are to their own destruction."[36]

---

35 See the discussions in Ross, *Psalms*, 2:400; Kidner, *Psalms*, 1:229; Goldingay, *Psalms*, 2:265.
36 Hengstenberg, *Psalms*, 2:307–8.

[Psalm 65] is a Song of the Lamb, while he leads his glorified ones to fountains of living water, and shews their old world presenting at length a counterpart to heaven, all paradise again, and better than paradise.

ANDREW BONAR
Christ and His Church in the Book of Psalms

PSALM 65

ORIENTATION

Psalm 65 celebrates the work of Christ with a richness that encompasses the whole created order. The psalm may be unlocked by asking how its three parts correlate. What links the work of atonement (65:1–4), the subjugation of a rebellious creation (65:5–8), and the joy of a rich harvest (65:9–13)? The beautiful harvest hymn (65:9–13) does not stand alone; it follows two sections that speak of salvation, confession of sin, atonement, access to God, and God's victory over evil. What unites these three parts is the work of Christ, for in Christ creation itself will be restored.

Psalm 65:1–4 is fulfilled in Christ. In Christ our prayers are heard (Ps. 65:2a; John 11:42; 14:13–14). In Christ all kinds of people come to God ("all flesh," Ps. 65:2b; "all people," John 12:32). Sin is atoned for by Christ, and in him we are chosen and brought near to God (Ps. 65:3–4a; 1 Pet. 3:18). In Christ we are satisfied (Ps. 65:4b; cf. John 4:13–14; 6:48–51; 7:37–39). In the church of Christ we belong to God's holy temple (Ps. 65:4b; 1 Cor. 3:17).[1]

The victory of God over rebellious forces of creation (Ps. 65:5–8) is demonstrated when Christ stills the roaring sea (Ps. 65:7; Matt. 8:23–27), is achieved through Christ at the cross (Col. 2:15), and is consummated when Christ returns in glory (Luke 21:25–27).[2]

---

1   "The holiness of your temple" (Ps. 65:4b) is echoed in 1 Cor. 3:17 ("God's temple is holy"), in which the temple is fulfilled in a Christian church, noted in Hossfeld and Zenger, *Psalms*, 2:142.
2   The thematic echo of Ps. 65:7 in Luke 21:25 ("the roaring of the sea") is noted by Hossfeld and Zenger, *Psalms*, 2:142; Tremper Longman III, *Psalms*, TOTC (Downers Grove, IL: InterVarsity Press, 2014), 252. Cf. Ps. 46.

In the light of these fulfillments, it is natural to understand the super-abundant harvest of Psalm 65:9–13 to point beyond a good harvest in this age to the abundance of the new creation in Christ.[3]

Psalm 65 may have been written at the time when "God responded to the plea for the land" after three years of famine "in the days of David" (2 Sam. 21:1–14).[4] It may later have been associated with the Feast of Tabernacles because of the connection with harvest. This feast was a time "when Israel's happy land . . . furnished a scene that naturally suggested the future days of a renewed earth."[5]

Psalms 65–68 appear to form a subunit.[6] There is an almost audible change of tone from the immediately preceding psalms. These psalms are overwhelmingly communal, whereas Psalms 61–64 were mainly individual. "After the yearning for God in Psalms 61–64, Psalms 65–68 joyfully shout his triumphant worldwide conquest."[7] They develop and emphasize previous indicators (e.g., 59:13) of God's work through all the world (65:2, 5; 66:1, 4, 8; 67:3–5; 68:28–32). O. Palmer Robertson notes that "four psalms represent the cry of the messianic king (Pss. 61–64). Then four psalms respond by affirming the undisturbed reign of the Divine King (Pss. 65–68)."[8] This may suggest a shift of Christological focus from the humanity of Christ as the King in David's line to the divinity of Christ as the eternal Son of God. So it may be fruitful to focus our attention on this as a psalm sung to and concerning Jesus Christ in his divine power.

Psalm 65 has other links, including that of awe or fear of God (64:9; 65:8). The theme of paying vows (65:1) is shared with 56:12; 61:8; and 66:13–14.[9]

James Hamilton comments,

> The movement of thought from Psalm 64 to Psalm 65 exactly matches the movement from the end of Revelation 20 to the beginning of Revelation 21. [So the defeat of God's enemies in Psalm 64] is followed by a comprehensive celebration of God's salvation and the way that God's people enjoy God's

---

3 Cf. the fulfillment of the prosperity of Amos 9:13–15 through worldwide mission (cf. the quotation of Amos 9:11–12 in Acts 15:15–18).

4 Eveson, *Psalms*, 1:392.

5 Bonar, *Psalms*, 194. Cf. the eschatological Zech. 14, likewise associated with the Feast of Tabernacles.

6 Grogan, *Psalms*, 121; Hossfeld and Zenger, *Psalms*, 2:141; Harman, *Psalms*, 1:475. The shared designation "A Song" may hint at this. See Gerald Henry Wilson, *The Editing of the Hebrew Psalter*, SBLDS 76 (Chico, CA: Scholars Press, 1985), 163–64, 190–91.

7 Hamilton, *Psalms*, 1:581.

8 Robertson, *Flow of the Psalms*, 111.

9 Half the references to vows in the Psalter come in Pss. 56–66. Wilson, *Psalms*, 1:905n1.

presence in a renewed creation because the chosen one has been drawn near to God in Psalm 65. . . . These things will be fulfilled when God takes his seat on the great white throne of judgment, as described in Revelation 20:11–15, then brings about the new creation in 21:1–4.[10]

The new creation in Isaiah 66:18–24 strikingly parallels the anticipation of the new heavens and new earth in Psalm 65. The two passages share the themes of (1) the hope or regathering of humankind (Ps. 65:5, 8; Isa. 66:18); (2) people from all over the world coming to Zion, God's holy mountain (Ps. 65:2, 4; Isa. 66:23); (3) "grain" given by and offered to God (Ps. 65:9; Isa. 66:20); (4) the phrase "all flesh shall come" (Ps. 65:2; Isa. 66:23); and (5) the word "sign" (Ps. 65:8; Isa. 66:19).[11]

THE TEXT

Structure
Psalm 65:9–13 is a climactic section of harvest rejoicing. Psalm 65:1–8 divides naturally into 65:1–4 (atonement and its fruits) and 65:5–8 (victory over creation). Each section ends with satisfaction (65:4) or joy (65:8, 13).

Superscription

S   To the choirmaster.[12] A Psalm of David. A Song.[13]

Psalm 65 shares the designation **A Psalm** in the immediate context with Psalms 62–64 and 66–68 and the designation **A Song** with Psalms 66–68.

65:1–4 Christ's Atoning Work Brings Us Near to God and Satisfies Us with His Goodness
Psalm 65:1–4 begins with praise and ends with rich satisfaction. The theme is access to God ("to you shall all flesh come," 65:2; "you . . . bring near, / to dwell," 65:4) through atonement (65:3).

---

10 Hamilton, *Psalms*, 1:584.
11 Wilson, *Psalms*, 1:907. Wilson calls the Isaiah passage the "closest parallel" with the psalm.
12 See on Ps. 4.
13 In Hebrew the superscription is verse 1; subsequent verse numbers are increased by one.

1   Praise is due to you, O God, in Zion,
       and to you shall vows be performed.

Praise is due to you translates the Septuagint,[14] whose translators "were trying to make more obvious sense"[15] of a verse for which the Masoretic Text literally reads, "To you in silence, praise, O God, in Zion" (see ESV mg.). The Masoretic Text should probably be preferred because it is the harder reading and because the word "silence" (דֻּמִיָּה, *dumiyah*) is used in Psalm 62:1 and 5, where it means "wait quietly" in an attitude of trust and restfulness (see on 62:1). The line appears either to mean that there is a restful quiet that issues in praise or that the praise itself is characterized by a quiet restfulness and trustfulness of heart.[16] **Zion** is named for the first time since Psalm 53:6, focusing our attention on the covenant with David, fulfilled in Christ. The performing of **vows** probably refers to the giving of public praise to God, especially for what is described in 65:2–4. Augustine extrapolates from this and says that, ultimately, to fulfill our vows means to persevere with Christ to the end; for to dwell in Zion means to live now as citizens of heaven (Phil. 3:20) with our anchor "cast . . . ahead of us . . . into that country (Heb. 6:19), to safeguard us from shipwreck when the weather here is rough."[17]

2   O you who hear prayer,
       to you shall all flesh come.

O you who hear translates a participle, "the hearing one," in a way that follows closely from Psalm 65:1 and suggests that it is the "inalienable attribute"[18] of God to hear prayer,[19] for this is "an abiding part of his glory, so that he might as soon deny himself as shut his ear to our petitions."[20]

---

14 Σοὶ πρέπει ὕμνος. The LXX seems to have translated from a repointed Hebrew term, דֻּמָּה, instead of the MT, דֻּמִיָּה, from דָּמָה, "to be like."
15 Longman, *Psalms*, 251.
16 See the discussion of options in Ross, *Psalms*, 2:411n1; Longman, *Psalms*, 251.
17 Augustine, *Psalms*, 3:268.
18 Kirkpatrick, *Psalms*, 2:361.
19 For other examples of God hearing the prayers of his King and people, see, e.g., Pss. 4:3; 6:8–9; 22:24; 34:6; 61:1; 64:1.
20 Calvin, *Psalms*, 2:452. Jonathan Edwards preached a sermon on Psalm 65:2 that strikingly echoes this idea. In it his doctrine is "It is the character of the Most High, that he is a God who hears

"This," says Charles Spurgeon, "is thy name, thy nature, thy glory. God not only has heard, but is now hearing prayer, and always must hear prayer, since he is an immutable being, and never changes in his attributes. What a delightful title for the God and Father of our Lord Jesus Christ!"[21]

With the perspective of the New Testament, we understand that all prayer is heard fully—and only—on the basis of Christ, the one man whose prayers deserve to be heard. Because of Christ, **all flesh** (all kinds of people from all over the world) can and will **come** to God. The imperfect tense, **shall . . . come**, most naturally stands as a prediction of what will happen in the future, for this "is a prediction of Christ's future kingdom."[22] "We come," writes Spurgeon, "weeping in conversion, hoping in supplication, rejoicing in praise, and delighting in service."[23] All this is the fruit of Christ's atoning work (see on 22:27).

> 3   When iniquities prevail against me,
>   you atone for our transgressions.

It is our sins that prevent our prayers from being heard (cf. Isa. 59:1). This is why David moves from answered prayer to atonement. The verb **atone**, closely associated with the sacrifices of "Zion" fulfilled by Christ, goes to the heart of Psalm 65:1–4. Prayer cannot be heard and men and women can have no access to God without atonement. **Iniquities** (the word "when" is not in the Hebrew; cf. CSB: "Iniquities overwhelm me") is literally "matters of iniquities,"[24] the unusual plural phrase perhaps suggesting a multiplicity of various kinds of iniquity. The verb **prevail** means to overwhelm,[25] for human sin is an unbearable burden (38:4) and a foe we fail to resist (cf. Gen. 4:7). The phrase **our transgressions** appears in a similar context in Psalm

---

prayer." Jonathan Edwards, "The Most High a Prayer-Hearing God," in *The Works of President Edwards*, vol. 6 (New York: G. & C. & H. Carvill, 1830), 314.

21 Spurgeon, *Treasury*, 2.1:90.
22 Calvin, *Psalms*, 2:453. Cf. the gospel promises for "all flesh" in the Old Testament quotations of Luke 3:6 and Acts 2:17.
23 Spurgeon, *Treasury*, 2.1:90.
24 דִּבְרֵי עֲוֹנֹת. The LXX translates דִּבְרֵי by λόγοι, which led older writers (e.g., Augustine, Theodoret) to refer this to the words of sinners. But the parallelism with the second line suggests that here דָּבָר has the meaning of "matters" or "affairs."
25 The verb גָּבַר is cognate with גִּבּוֹר, "warrior." It appears in Gen. 7:24 of the flood waters prevailing over the earth (perhaps a link with the imagery of Ps. 65:7).

103:12 (cf. 25:7; 32:5; 39:8; 51:1). The move from **me** to **our** is consistent with other examples of a leader associating his own sins with those of his people (e.g., Dan. 9:20; Isa. 6:5; Heb. 7:27).

4   Blessed is the one you choose and bring near,
         to dwell in your courts!
     We shall be satisfied with the goodness of your house,
         the holiness of your temple!

Blessed is the only use of the word (אַשְׁרֵי, *ashre*) in book 2 (cf. Pss. 1:1; 2:12);[26] here is the blessedness of Christ, the man of Psalm 1 and the King of Psalm 2, given to all covered by his atoning work. The **courts** are the courtyards of God's **house** or **temple**, the presence of God in Zion, fulfilled in Christ, who is the one "greater than the temple" (Matt. 12:6) and whose atoning and resurrected body fulfills all that the temple foreshadowed (John 2:19–22). To **dwell** there means to be "raised with Christ," so that "your life is hidden with Christ in God" (Col. 3:1–3). The verbs **you choose** and **you . . . bring near**, with God as subject in his sovereign grace, take language used of priests (Num. 16:5) and highlight the right of access to God (cf. Zech. 3:7), fulfilled in Christ our great high priest (the original **one**) and given to us in him. Spurgeon rightly says that Psalm 65:4a "comprehends both election, effectual calling, access, acceptance, and sonship."[27] Philip Eveson adds, "It is in Christ Jesus, the specially chosen one who came near with his own precious blood, that true believers are chosen and brought near and given access to the Father to live and dine at his table."[28]

The correlation of **goodness** (cf. 27:13; especially associated with covenant blessings in all their rich abundance) with **the holiness of your temple** is striking, for whenever earthly pleasures are divorced from true morality, they become corrupted; lasting goodness is found only with the purity of **holiness**. Our desires for the good things of life need to be reshaped by the psalm into "the appetite for God"[29] that alone leads to true satisfaction (cf. 17:15; 22:26; 37:19 ["*abundance*"]; 59:15 ["their *fill*"]; 63:5). All this—

---

26 See on Ps. 1:1.
27 Spurgeon, *Treasury*, 2.1:90–91.
28 Eveson, *Psalms*, 1:395.
29 C. S. Lewis (1898–1963), *Reflections on the Psalms* (London: Fount, 1977), 47.

prayer heard, access granted, satisfaction guaranteed—is given on the basis of Christ's atoning work.

65:5–8 Christ's Atoning Work Subdues the Rebellious Creation

5   By awesome deeds you answer us with righteousness,
        O God of our salvation,
    the hope of all the ends of the earth
        and of the farthest seas;

The clause **You answer us** may suggest that what follows is, in some way, the answer to the deepest longings of those who delight in the God who answers prayer (Ps. 65:2). The content of the answer will become apparent. But David begins with the effect, which is **awesome** (i.e., causing fear, either terror or reverent fear, depending on who experiences it),[30] and the nature of the answer, which is **righteousness**, God's work of putting a broken world to rights by fulfilling his covenant promises. This comes from the **God of our salvation** because the final rescue of the church of Christ is inseparable from the final redemption of the created order (cf. Rom. 8:18–21). There is an unbreakable connection between the salvation of Christ's church and **the hope** (i.e., the only possible solid foundation of trust) of the entire cosmos; **the ends of the earth** together with **the farthest seas** is a merism encompassing the whole world. Everything depends on God putting this prayer onto the groaning lips of Christ's church and then answering it.

6   the one who by his strength established the mountains,
        being girded with might;
7   who stills the roaring of the seas,
        the roaring of their waves,
        the tumult of the peoples,

Only a God of great **strength** and **girded with might** (his power being, as it were, his clothing) can **establish the mountains**, that is, secure the

---

30 "Awesome deeds" (niphal participle of the verb "to fear") occurs in Pss. 45:4 (of the King's victories) and 106:22 (of the exodus).

immovable stability of the cosmos, both in its physical and in its moral order. For this order is challenged by **the peoples** (as in the riot of Ps. 2:1–3), pictured here as **the roaring of the seas** and **waves**.[31] The power to still the storm (cf. Mark 4:39) comes not from a greater intensity of the world's kind of force but from the power to overcome evil with good by Christ's atoning work on the cross (cf. Col. 2:15). The victory of Christ is a fruit of the atoning work of Christ (Ps. 65:3). The storms of human tumult are stilled whenever the gospel of Christ is heard in the power of the Holy Spirit.[32]

8   so that those who dwell at the ends of the earth are in awe at your
         signs.
     You make the going out of the morning and the evening to shout
         for joy.

Just as 65:1–4 concludes with deep satisfaction in Christ, so 65:5–8 climaxes with universal **joy** in the victory of Christ. The **ends of the earth** (lit., "the ends"; cf. CSB: "those who live far away") **are in awe** (here reverent fear) **at your signs**, where the word **signs** may allude to the miracles of the exodus (cf. "his signs in Egypt," 78:43; 105:27; 135:9), fulfilled in the new exodus brought about by the cross of Christ. It is a wonderful and a fearful thing to watch Christ conquer evil at the cross and to anticipate his final victory when he returns. The **going out of the morning and the evening** is one entity (hence the singular verb "shout for joy"), encompassing the "going out of the morning," that is, the east, where it dawns, and the "going out of the evening," that is, the west, where the sun sets; it means—in a beautiful poetic idiom—the entire created order. It encompasses "every place, from east to west," and "all times, from morning to evening."[33] The whole space-time universe groans with longing for the atoning work of Christ to reach its consummation (Rom. 8:18–30). The lines of that consummation are painted in beautiful colors in the harvest scene that concludes the psalm.

---

31 The ugly word "roaring" is used of the Babylonians in Ps. 74:23 (cf. similar imagery in Isa. 17:12; Dan. 7:2–17; Luke 21:25).
32 Theodoret of Cyrus, *Psalms*, 1:366.
33 Ross, *Psalms*, 2:426.

65:9–13 Christ's Atoning Work Will Renew the Whole Creation

9   You visit the earth and water it;
        you greatly enrich it;
     the river of God is full of water;
        you provide their grain,
        for so you have prepared it.

You visit uses a verb that can refer to a visitation of judgment (e.g., "punish," Pss. 59:5; 89:32) but here to a visitation of grace (cf. "have regard for," Ps. 80:14). One of the paradoxes of the created order is that **water** may be dangerous yet is also necessary for life (cf. Job 38:3–11, 22–23, 25–27; Ps. 46:3–4). The word **greatly** sets the tone of superabundance that runs through the passage. God "is represented here as going round the earth, as a gardener surveys his garden, and as giving water to every plant that requires it, and that not in small quantities, but until the earth is drenched and soaked with a rich supply of refreshment."[34] If the promised land was "a land . . . which drinks water by the rain from heaven" (Deut. 11:11), here is the land that that land foreshadowed. The **river of God** (cf. Pss. 1:3; 46:4) directs this life-giving water wherever it is needed. **Grain** is associated with covenant blessings (e.g., Deut. 7:13; 11:14; 12:17; 14:23; 18:4) and points to a joy in God that cannot be confined to the blessings of this age (e.g., Ps. 4:7), for "every provision of water for life reminded the people that in the new earth there would be an abundant provision of life from God (see Ps. 46:4; Ezek. 47:1–12; Isa. 33:20–21; Joel 3:18; and Zech. 14:18)."[35]

10   You water its furrows abundantly,
         settling its ridges,
      softening it with showers,
         and blessing its growth.

The verb **water . . . abundantly** means to drench or saturate. The words translated **furrows** and **ridges** are probably synonymous,[36] each indicating

---

34 Spurgeon, *Treasury*, 2.1:93.

35 Ross, *Psalms*, 2:428.

36 *HALOT* translates both תֶּלֶם and גְּדוּד with "furrow."

the furrows of a plowed field. When a field is plowed, water ensures that the crop will germinate and grow, here richly and abundantly. The word **blessing** emphasizes that all this is the covenant blessing of God; it is given to us through Christ, in whom all the promises of the covenant are "Yes!" (2 Cor. 1:20).

> 11   You crown the year with your bounty;
>   your wagon tracks overflow with abundance.

Your bounty is cognate with the word "good"; the association of the word with the temple—and hence the covenant—in Psalm 65:4 ("the goodness of your house") suggests that this blessing is more than the common grace of a good harvest; it is the bounty of the new creation given in Christ. The term **wagon tracks** probably suggests harvest wagons full to bursting with grain. **Abundance** is literally "fat" (cf. 63:5).

> 12   The pastures of the wilderness overflow,
>   the hills gird themselves with joy,
> 13   the meadows clothe themselves with flocks,
>   the valleys deck themselves with grain,
>   they shout and sing together for joy.

Here is an utterly delightful picture.[37] The word **wilderness** is evocative in the light of Psalm 63 ("in the wilderness of Judah") and the broken land of 60:1–3; if God's King and his church are called to walk by faith through a wilderness world on the way to the promised land, Psalm 65 begins to open up a vision of what that wilderness will one day become. The picture of the promised land, soaking up the blessing of God in Christ and now clothing itself **with flocks** and **grain**, conjures up a scene of unsurpassed **joy** (note how joy closes 65:12 and then again 65:13, as it closed 65:8). The contrast with the groaning of Romans 8:22 could not be more astonishing. All this is because of Christ. This is Christ's living water and heavenly food.[38] As Derek Kidner says, "it is no far cry" from this harvest scene to

37   We have here "the very feel of weather—weather seen with a real countryman's eyes, enjoyed almost as a vegetable might be supposed to enjoy it." Lewis, *Reflections on the Psalms*, 67.
38   Cassiodorus, *Psalms*, 2:103.

the "welcome from the whole creation" that will greet the return of the victorious Jesus.[39] Sin brought death and decay into the world; the atoning work of Christ remakes that groaning world. Here, in vision, is "that new earth which shall stand when the old is passed away."[40]

Reflecting on the broken land of Psalm 60 and the wilderness of Psalm 63, Andrew Bonar says of Psalm 65,

> What a changed world! And every season we see something of this exhibited. But the yearly return of spring and summer after winter is an emblem of Earth's summer day, when it shall be renewed. . . . Who does not seem, in reading this majestic Psalm, to hear the very melody that issues from the happy people of that New Earth?[41]

REFLECTION AND RESPONSE

1. Psalm 65:1 shows that praise of the God and Father of our Lord Jesus Christ and praise of Christ, given in the Holy Spirit, ought to be the outflow from a deep meditation on this psalm.

2. Psalm 65:2–4 prompts us to ponder the atoning work of Christ, how iniquities overwhelm us, and how only the sovereign kindness of God in Christ means our prayers are heard as we are brought near to God. Such meditation leads to deep satisfaction in God and joy in his holiness, rejoicing not simply in the good things he promises us but in the moral order he has bequeathed to us in his covenant. We will love God more, love holiness more, love prayer more.

3. The word "hope" (65:5) encourages us to rest our hopes for the world on the creation-taming and chaos-conquering work of Christ on the cross. While we are called to be good stewards of the created order in this age, our hopes will always rest on what Christ has done and what this guarantees for a broken world.

4. A first response to Psalm 65:9–13 is simply to revel in the loveliness of God's world and the delight of this Spirit-given poetry. But then we lament that, even in the best of harvests, the reality falls short of this portrait. No

39 Kidner, *Psalms*, 1:233.
40 Denys (or Dionysius) the Carthusian (1402–1471), in Neale and Littledale, *Psalms*, 2:308.
41 Bonar, *Psalms*, 194.

harvest festival can exhaust the meaning of these words, for such celebra-tions point beyond the joys of reaping to the delights of the new creation. For all this we hope with confidence because we understand the cross of Christ. That ugly day guarantees this beautiful vision.

As all the people of God are one body, and that which is done in one age to one generation concerneth all and every one to make use of it in their generation; so every one in after ages should reckon themselves one body with the Lord's people in former ages, and make use of God's dealing with them, as if they had been present then with them.

DAVID DICKSON
A Commentary on the Psalms

[The psalmist] seems to speak of the way God brought his people into the land of promise after the exodus from Egypt and the wilderness wandering, anticipating also a restoration to the land of blessing after the yet future new exodus.

JAMES M. HAMILTON
Psalms

PSALM 66

ORIENTATION

In Psalm 66, a cheerful psalm, Christ appeals to his people (66:16), and his people summon the world (66:1–3, 5, 8) to praise the God of the gospel, whose saving power is known by what he has done for us in Christ. The appeal to the world is rooted in the testimony of one particular believer (66:13–20), whose story is the story of exodus, wilderness, and entry into the promised land. In the final analysis, this is the story of Jesus Christ, who leads his people out of the Egypt of slavery to sin, through the wilderness of testing, and into the promised land of the new creation.

We do not know the historical context of the psalm. The literary context is that Psalm 66 belongs with Psalms 65–68 (see on Ps. 65), bracketed by "of David" psalms (Pss. 65; 68). Although Psalms 66 and 67 lack "of David," the context encourages us to read them with the Davidic covenant in mind (and therefore with reference to Christ).[1]

A significant feature of Psalm 66 is the move from the corporate (66:1–12) to the individual (66:13–20). While this may simply model the great value of any believer giving a testimony in the presence of the church,[2] the strongly Davidic literary context suggests that this individual may be the King.[3] The extraordinary expense of the sacrifices this individual pledges to offer (66:13–15) is beyond what an ordinary believer could hope

---

1 Eveson, *Psalms*, 1:399.
2 Kidner, *Psalms*, 1:233; Dickson, *Psalms*, 1:390; Spurgeon, *Treasury*, 2.1:112; Calvin, *Psalms*, 2:474.
3 Kirkpatrick, *Psalms*, 2:366–67; Ross, *Psalms*, 2:436; Tate, *Psalms 51–100*, 150; Harman, *Psalms*, 1:481; Eveson, *Psalms*, 1:403.

to possess.[4] I am persuaded that the most natural way to read the psalm is—ultimately—that Christ leads his people in the praises of 66:1–12 and then gives his testimony in 66:13–20.

John 9:31 is a thematic echo of Psalm 66:18,[5] chiming with the idea that this man whose prayers are heard in Psalm 66 is, in the end, Jesus Christ, as in John 9. In Psalm 66 the people of God are tested but saved because the prayers of their leader are heard by God.

This makes for a rich gospel reading of the psalm. If this is Christ's testimony, we are not simply invited to follow his example (although we should). For his testimony, that God heard his prayer, is the ground of all our hope and praise. We are saved because God heard Christ's prayers as the sinless one who atoned for our sins.

There are many links with nearby psalms, especially Psalm 65.[6] The theme of the whole world continues (e.g., 66:1, 4, 7–8; cf. 65:5, 8; and emphatic in Ps. 67). Awe/fear is shared (66:3, 5; cf. 65:5). The unruly peoples quelled in Psalm 65:7 are the rebellious enemies of Psalm 66:3 and 7. Abundance or satisfaction is a shared motif (66:12; cf. 65:4, 9–13). The paying of vows (65:1) is developed (66:13–15). The God who hears Christ's prayers (66:20) is therefore the God who hears all prayer in Christ (65:2).

THE TEXT

Structure
The transition from plural to singular sets off two larger sections (Ps. 66:1–12, 13–20), while the three occurrences of *Selah* mark natural breaks between subsections of those larger sections, giving us "five stanzas of nearly equal length, marked off (except where the division is obvious at the end of the first part and of the whole) by *Selah*."[7] The five smaller sections are 66:1–4, 5–7, 8–12, 13–15, and 16–20.

---

4 "These are not the offerings of a private individual. The sacrifices are costly ones, ones that only someone like a king was capable of bringing on behalf of the nation." Eveson, *Psalms*, 1:403; cf. Grogan, *Psalms*, 123.

5 Hossfeld and Zenger, *Psalms*, 2:148.

6 Wilson, *Psalms*, 1:920–21; VanGemeren, *Psalms*, 501; Hossfeld and Zenger, *Psalms*, 2:147–48.

7 Kirkpatrick, *Psalms*, 2:365. Most commentators adopt this structure.

Superscription

S   To the choirmaster.[8] A Song. A Psalm.[9]

See on Psalm 65.

66:1–12 Christ Leads His People in Praise to the God of the Gospel

The three sections in Psalm 66:1–12 each begin with at least one plural imperative and describe something of God's work. The first two stanzas both end with *Selah*.[10]

66:1–4 Christ Leads His People in Calling the Whole World to Praise God

1   Shout for joy to God, all the earth;
2   sing the glory of his name;
        give to him glorious praise!
3   Say to God, "How awesome are your deeds!
        So great is your power that your enemies come cringing to you.
4   All the earth worships you
        and sings praises to you;
        they sing praises to your name."   *Selah*

The succession of plural imperatives (**shout . . . sing . . . give . . . say**—and continued in Psalm 66:5, "Come and see," and 66:8, "Bless") together with the universal scope (66:1–4 is bookended by **all the earth**) makes 66:1–12 an emphatic call to the whole world to praise the God and Father of our Lord Jesus Christ.[11] John Calvin observes that the psalmist "predicts the extent to which the kingdom of God should reach at the coming of Christ."[12] The tone of **joy**, which fills this psalm as it filled Psalm 65, demonstrates that joy truly does come to the world only when the world bows gladly to God and his Christ.

---

8   See on Ps. 4.
9   In Hebrew the superscription is the start of verse 1.
10 Tate, *Psalms 51–100*, 147.
11 Ps. 66:1 is very similar to Pss. 98:4; 100:1.
12 Calvin, *Psalms*, 2:466.

In 66:2 the words **glory** (God's nature made visible, becoming known, ultimately in Christ, John 1:14) and **name** (God's covenant self-revelation in the Scriptures; cf. Ps. 66:4) give focus to the praise. Psalm 66:2 literally reads, "Set glory his praise," and may mean "Set forth his praise in a glorious manner,"[13] "Make his praise glorious" (CSB, NASB, NIV), or **Give to him glorious praise**. The effect is much the same.

The nature of God's **deeds** will be expounded in 66:5–12. To acknowledge (**say to God**) that they are **awesome** (also in 66:5) is the proper posture of a believer before God and not inconsistent with the joy of salvation (cf. "rejoice with trembling," Ps. 2:11; "with fear and trembling," Phil. 2:12–13). The verb **cringing** probably has the sense of an obedience that is forced rather than voluntary and therefore feigned rather than heartfelt.[14]

Since **all the earth** does not yet **worship** God (which is why we pray, "Your will be done on earth as it is in heaven"), Psalm 66:4 must look to a future day when it will, when the finally impenitent enemies bow, as bow they must (1 Cor. 15:25). Even hell will praise him, albeit through clenched teeth and with bitter regrets.

66:5–7 Christ Leads His People in Calling the World to Submit to the God of Exodus Redemption

5   Come and see what God has done:
      he is awesome in his deeds toward the children of man.
6   He turned the sea into dry land;
      they passed through the river on foot.
   There did we rejoice in him,
7   who rules by his might forever,
   whose eyes keep watch on the nations—
      let not the rebellious exalt themselves.   *Selah*

The invitation **Come and see**[15] (echoed in Ps. 66:16, "Come and hear") invites all the world to join the church of Christ to see **what God has done**.

---

13 Tate, *Psalms 51–100*, 145.
14 Piel of כחש. BDB: "cringe," s.v. כחש; *HALOT*: "feign obedience, fawn," s.v. כחש; NASB: "give feigned obedience." Cf. Deut. 33:29; Ps. 18:44.
15 Cf. "Come, behold," Ps. 46:8.

This affects **the children of man**, for it is significant for all humanity. God's deeds are revealed by the crossing of the Red Sea at the exodus and the crossing of the Jordan at the entry to the promised land (66:6).[16] Those great water crossings parallel the ordering of the waters of creation in 65:5–8.[17]

There begins the final line of 66:6.[18] Whether the verb is translated **we did rejoice** or "let us rejoice" (either of which is possible), the idea seems to be that "there" at the place of exodus redemption and Jordan entrance, **we** were all present; the joy of the people then and there is the joy of the church of Christ here and now, for "the church of all ages is a unity, the separate parts being jointly involved in the whole."[19] The sin-bearing death of Christ, his resurrection, and his ascension are reckoned to have happened to us (e.g., Col. 2:20; 3:1).[20] So the redemption of a particular people (the exodus multitude) is good news for any man or woman all over the world who is grafted into this people by faith (cf. Rom. 11:13–24; Eph. 2:11–13).

That the mighty works of God are exodus shaped is of enormous significance. Baptism and new birth symbolize passing through the waters of death on the way to life.

Psalm 66:7 draws the conclusion (cf. Ex. 9:16) that the exodus redemption demonstrates the world-beating **might** of God. It teaches us that his **eyes keep watch on the nations**, so that nothing escapes his gaze. When any people becomes proud, like the pharaoh of the exodus, they need to heed the warning **Let not the rebellious exalt themselves**. Jesus Christ leads his people through the waters of the Red Sea and the Jordan. He becomes for us the fulfillment of all that the exodus prefigured. His death and resurrection become ours through faith in him; it demonstrates the victory of

---

16 Since this word for "river" is not used of the Jordan elsewhere, Tate suggests that both halves of Ps. 66:6 refer to the crossing of the Red Sea. Tate, *Psalms 51–100*, 149. But his other uses of the word נָהָר are not entirely persuasive. Given the way 114:5 sets the two crossings in parallel, it seems likely that this is the meaning here, although we cannot be certain. Alter calls it "the miraculous crossing of the Sea of Reeds, telescoped with the crossing of the Jordan." Alter, *Psalms*, 224.

17 Hossfeld and Zenger, *Psalms*, 2:145; Grogan, *Psalms*, 123.

18 This is the usual and most natural translation of שָׁם. The NIV—"Come, let us rejoice in him"—follows a less likely suggestion by Dahood, *Psalms*, 2:121.

19 Delitzsch, *Psalms*, 2:235. For this same sense of identifying the whole people of God with past generations, see Deut. 6:20–22; 26:5–9.

20 Eveson, *Psalms*, 1:401.

God over all the rebellious powers on earth. It is a joy to all who will bow to him and will prove a terror to all who will not.

66:8–12 Christ Leads His People in Calling the World
to Praise the God Who Has Tested and Saved Us

8   Bless our God, O peoples;
         let the sound of his praise be heard,
9   who has kept our soul among the living
         and has not let our feet slip.
10   For you, O God, have tested us;
         you have tried us as silver is tried.
11   You brought us into the net;
         you laid a crushing burden on our backs;
12   you let men ride over our heads;
         we went through fire and through water;
       yet you have brought us out to a place of abundance.

As Psalm 66:5–7, so 66:8–12 begins with plural exhortation to the whole world: **Bless our God, O peoples**. The reason for the call now moves from exodus redemption to a time of trial. The reference to **the living** "may point beyond the sustenance of physical life to a restoration of the souls of God's people to spiritual life."[21] The language of **feet** not **slip**ping (cf. 17:5; 18:36; 121:3) speaks not simply of physical protection but of moral protection, the guarding of the hearts of God's people in time of trial.

The testing (66:10–12b) is severe, a fiery refining (66:10; cf. 26:2 ["prove me"]; Isa. 1:25; Jer. 9:7; Zech. 13:9; James 1:2–3; 1 Pet. 1:7), for "an untempted person is a person unproved."[22] In Psalm 66:11 God brings his people into a hunter's **net**[23] and loads them with a **crushing burden** (an unusual word that conveys a sense of being pressed with agonizing weight). The word **backs** is literally the "loins" (i.e., they felt it in their inner being). The pic-

---

21 Hamilton, *Psalms*, 1:588.
22 Tertullian, *On Baptism*, 20, quoted by Cyril of Jerusalem (ca. 315–386), in *ACCS* 8:61. That God tests, refines, and proves us is also a significant theme in Job and 1 Peter (see 1 Pet. 1:7).
23 The CSB rendering "lured" is perhaps a little strong for the hiphil.

ture of **men rid**[ing] **over our heads** is terrifying, as are the trials of **fire** and **water** (cf. Isa. 43:2).

Coming as it does after the remembrance of exodus, this trial echoes the testing of God's people in the wilderness.[24] It is fulfilled in the trials of Jesus Christ and overflows to his new covenant people.

The final line, **Yet you have brought us out to a place of abundance**, points to an overflow of life after a time of desperate need. This is the promise of Christ (cf. 2 Cor. 4:17–18).[25]

Psalm 66:5–12 gives us a picture of the sufferings and resurrection of Christ, for "our Saviour himself experienced the greatest affliction of all for the sake of others and came through via the resurrection to be the first of that new creation of glory and blessing."[26] This is the shape of the life of faith. In the life of the church of Christ, these sufferings are necessary, and the outcome is sure (cf. Acts 14:22). Preaching pastorally about this, Augustine says,

> You threw us into the fire, but like silver, not like straw, for you did not reduce us to ashes but purged us of dross. Think how fiercely God tries those whose souls he has established in life. . . . All these things the whole Church suffered throughout many and varied persecutions; individual churches have also had to endure them, and still do today. . . . God seems to be acting very severely when he does these things; but do not be afraid. He is our Father, and his severity never destroys us.[27]

66:13–20 Christ Gives His Testimony of Praise to God[28]
66:13–15 Christ Pledges a Costly Sacrifice of Love to God

> [13]   I will come into your house with burnt offerings;
>   I will perform my vows to you,
> [14]   that which my lips uttered
>   and my mouth promised when I was in trouble.

---

24 Wilson, *Psalms*, 1:918; Grogan, *Psalms*, 123.
25 The same root lies behind "overflows" in Ps. 23:5.
26 Eveson, *Psalms*, 1:402.
27 Augustine, *Psalms*, 3:299–300.
28 Eveson titles this section "The King's testimony." Eveson, *Psalms*, 1:403.

> 15   I will offer to you burnt offerings of fattened animals,
>   with the smoke of the sacrifice of rams;
>   I will make an offering of bulls and goats.   *Selah*

The King (probably), speaking by the Spirit of Christ, pledges to do what David had said in Psalm 65:1, to offer the sacrifices sworn in time of **trouble**. The **burnt offerings**, "the gifts of adoring homage,"[29] are hugely costly. The only other time in the Psalms when they are offered in such a positive context is when the King offers them in 20:3.[30] Psalm 66:15 continues with a most extravagant offering. Other occasions when comparable sacrifices are offered are few; they include Numbers 7; 1 Kings 8:62–64; 1 Chronicles 29:20–22; 2 Chronicles 29:32–33; and 35:7–9.[31] The extravagance of this kingly offering pales by comparison with the day when the Lord Jesus Christ offers himself as a sacrifice for sins. The vow that this psalmist fulfills reaches its climax when the Lord Jesus fulfills the vow he has made by covenant with the Father that he will offer himself to save his people from their sins. All the offerings now given by his people are placed before God as "a fragrant offering and sacrifice" (Eph. 5:2) on the basis of what Jesus has done for us.

66:16–20 Christ Calls His People to Hear What the Father Has Done for Him

> 16   Come and hear, all you who fear God,
>   and I will tell what he has done for my soul.
> 17   I cried to him with my mouth,
>   and high praise was on my tongue.
> 18   If I had cherished iniquity in my heart,
>   the Lord would not have listened.
> 19   But truly God has listened;
>   he has attended to the voice of my prayer.
> 20   Blessed be God,
>   because he has not rejected my prayer
>   or removed his steadfast love from me!

---

29 Delitzsch, *Psalms*, 2:236.
30 Hossfeld and Zenger, *Psalms*, 2:146.
31 Cf. Hossfeld and Zenger, *Psalms*, 2:147.

The joy of Christ throbs through this conclusion. In some ways Psalm 66:16 is the key verse of the psalm, for it contains Christ's invitation to **all you who fear God**, now narrowed from the whole world (66:1, 4, 8), to **come and hear** what his God and Father **has done for** his **soul**. That is, we will hear his sufferings for sinners, his trials, his passion, the exodus he accomplished (Luke 9:31), and his resurrection. All this, Christ testifies, God has done for his soul. And this is "how much he will do for yours as well, if you are willing."[32] In sum, Christ testifies that the God of the exodus, the wilderness, and the entry into the promised land is his God, and this story is his story. It can be ours in him, for we died with him, we were raised with him, and our lives are hidden in God with him.

In Psalm 66:17 he speaks of his prayer and praise. The word **high praise** means "exaltation";[33] he lifted the Father high in his words and his deeds, in his loving obedience and his teaching. In 66:18 the Lord enters a vital caveat: **If I had cherished iniquity in my heart, / the Lord** (the sovereign one) **would not have listened** to my voice. The word **iniquity** is fronted for emphasis. The verb is literally "if I had seen," the sense being, "If, having seen [iniquity] there [in my heart], I continue to gaze upon it without aversion; if I cherish it, have a side glance of love towards it, excuse it, and palliate it."[34] This is the opposite of walking with a clear conscience before God (cf. Pss. 17:1–5; 18:20–24; John 9:31; 1 John 3:21–22). Only those who depart from iniquity (2 Tim. 2:19) are heard by God.

But truly God has listened. Most wonderfully, the condition of Psalm 66:18 is completely fulfilled by Jesus Christ our righteous King. In him and only in him, by his atoning death and now by the sanctifying work of his Spirit in our hearts, is it possible for us to walk this way.

Psalm 66:20 is a fitting conclusion, giving exuberant **blessing to God, because he has not rejected** the **prayer** of our Messiah. Nor has he **removed his steadfast love** (covenant love, חֶסֶד, *khesed*) **from** him. As he blesses God his Father for hearing his prayers and being faithful to his covenant, so we too, in Christ, may join with him in blessing the triune God—Father, Son, and Holy Spirit—for all he has done for us in Christ, that he hears our prayers in Jesus's name, and that he keeps his covenant toward us in Jesus.

---

32 Rightly understood by Augustine, *Psalms*, 3:303.
33 *HALOT*: "exaltation, praise," s.v. רוֹמֵם.
34 Spurgeon, *Treasury*, 2.1:114. Cf. Ross, *Psalms*, 2:434n20.

REFLECTION AND RESPONSE

1. Two exhortations shape our response to Psalm 66. The first is given repeatedly by the church of Christ to the whole world (66:1–3, 5, 8) and is joyfully evangelistic. We sing this psalm to call on all people everywhere to repent and bow before the God of exodus redemption, wilderness sustaining, and promised-land fulfillment—all offered to them in Christ.

2. The second exhortation is given by Christ to all who fear God (66:16), and it is to come in our hearts, with full attentiveness, and to hear what the Father has done for Christ—and therefore what the Father will do for us if we are in Christ. To hear this call properly, we must have a true fear of God in our hearts; otherwise, Christ will not cast his pearls before swine. For, as Augustine so vividly puts it, "'If you do not fear God,' he implies, 'I shall not tell my story. If no fear of God is present, there is no one to listen. Let the fear of God open ears, so that something may find its way in, and there may be a pathway for what I am about to relate.'"[35]

3. The word "awesome" (66:3, 5) should make us search our hearts to ask if we feel something of this holy *fear* in the presence of God and most especially as we meditate on the death and resurrection of Christ (which fulfills the exodus).

4. Theodoret of Cyrus comments perceptively on the picture of people giving feigned worship in Psalm 66:3 that when surrounded by a majority Christian culture, "those who are in the grip of the darkness of unbelief will give an impression of piety." "This," he says, "we witness constantly."[36] This is a wholesome warning for any church to heed, especially a thriving church.

5. The church of Christ needs to ponder the deep truth that God's entire rescue—prefigured in the exodus, the wilderness, and the promised land—becomes our story as we belong to Christ. The answer to the question "Were you there at the exodus?" is a joyful "Yes!" in Christ.

6. In times of testing, and especially of severe testing, Psalm 66:8–12 provides both sober realism and—at the end of 66:12—glorious hope. There is realism, for "when God bringeth his church into trial there is no escaping,"[37] but there is also hope, for it is the purpose of God to make

---

35 Augustine, *Psalms*, 3:303.
36 Theodoret of Cyrus, *Psalms*, 1:371.
37 Dickson, *Psalms*, 1:389.

us like Jesus.[38] In a letter commenting on the close of 66:12, Athanasius (ca. 296–373) says that although the entrance to a time of testing is very narrow, squeezed, and tight, "once inside we see a vast and limitless space."[39]

7. Psalm 66:18 leads us to search our hearts. For although we are covered by the sacrifice of Christ, our prayers will only be heard as we walk in the light. Augustine challenges his hearers not to use this verse as a springboard to look smugly at the iniquities of others; rather, he says,

> Return to yourself, and be your own judge within. In your private, secret room, in your inmost heart of hearts, where you are alone with God who sees you, let that iniquity be unacceptable to you, so that you may be acceptable to God. Do not eye it with affection; no, look down on it, despise it, turn away from it.[40]

---

38 "The oppressing nations may have had their own purpose—to destroy the people of God; but God in his sovereignty was using their oppression to make Israel pure." Ross, *Psalms*, 2:441.

39 Athanasius, *Festal Letters*, 9, in ACCS 8:61.

40 Augustine, *Psalms*, 3:304.

This psalm has a clear meaning, and does not require many words
in comment: it announces in advance the Incarnation of God the
Word, the saving manifestation, and the salvation of all the nations.

THEODORET OF CYRUS
Commentary on the Psalms

The prophet begged the Lord Christ to deign to bless us with
abundance of love by His coming, so that the salvation of
the world awaited by the nations might become manifest to
them, and they might experience the fruit of His mercy with
the greatest depth of religious feeling. So this psalm should
be both sweetest by its brevity, and preeminent through the
worth of its prophecy, since all those generations earlier it
foretold what the world now acknowledges as its salvation.

CASSIODORUS
Explanation of the Psalms

[Psalm 67] contains a prayer for a blessing upon the Church, that
besides being preserved in a state of safety in Judea, it might be
enlarged to a new and unprecedented extent. It touches shortly
[i.e., briefly] upon the kingdom of God, which was to be erected
in the world upon the coming of Christ. . . . The psalm contains
a prediction of Christ's kingdom, under which the whole world
was to be adopted into a privileged relationship with God.

JOHN CALVIN
Commentary on the Psalms

PSALM 67

ORIENTATION

At the heart of Psalm 67 is the revelation that God is good and that his goodness is known and experienced in Jesus Christ. Ignorance of this glorious truth lies behind so much of the world's unbelief (and indeed the unbelief rampant in the church).

Although the surface meaning of this psalm concerns a harvest, a careful study shows that it points beyond this theme to the covenant blessings brought by Christ to the church and, through the church, to the world. There is an echo of the words "your saving power among all nations" (67:2) in Paul's words "this salvation of God . . . to the Gentiles [i.e., nations]" (Acts 28:28).[1] This echo is pregnant with gospel significance, for it connects the goodness of God celebrated in the psalm with the goodness of God in the gospel of Christ brought to the nations in the context of Acts 28. Another New Testament theme anticipated in the psalm is the gospel dynamic of Romans 11, in which God's blessing on some evokes jealousy in others who see it, moving them also to seek this blessing by faith.[2] It is also useful to bear in mind that seed growing to harvest is a metaphor rich in gospel significance in the teaching of Jesus and the New Testament (e.g., John 4:35–42).[3]

Much debate focuses on the translation of the moods and tenses of the verbs in the psalm, especially on the perfect tense in Psalm 67:6a and whether the other tenses (imperfects) are to be translated as indicatives

---

1   Eveson, *Psalms*, 1:408.
2   Harman, *Psalms*, 1:490.
3   Eveson, *Psalms*, 1:405.

(whether present or future) or jussives (expressing a desire or prayer).[4] However they are translated, the key point is that when God blesses his church, his blessing spreads to a watching world. The most important Old Testament themes developed in the psalm are the worldwide blessing promised in the covenant to Abraham[5] and the priestly blessing of Numbers 6 (echoed in Ps. 67:1).[6] Since the covenant with Abraham is the gospel of Christ preached in advance (cf. Gal. 3:8) and since Christ is the great high priest who brings us the new covenant benefits anticipated in the Aaronic priesthood, the echoes of both the Abrahamic covenant and the Numbers 6 blessing connect Psalm 67 with Christ.

Under the old covenant, God promised an overflow of blessing to a watching world. Franz Delitzsch writes, "Each plentiful harvest is to Israel a fulfilment of the promise given in Lev. xxvi. 4, and a pledge that God is with His people, and that its mission to the whole world (of peoples) shall not remain unaccomplished."[7]

But the failure of Israel to keep that covenant meant that those promises needed to wait for the day when the Messiah, who was Israel personified, would keep the covenant and win those blessings for his people, as that people blossoms into a worldwide church.

Blessing is a critical concept for this psalm. It is important to note that true blessing is at its heart relational and moral. Blessing speaks not simply of a harvest but of a people in relationship with the covenant God, who upholds his moral order in creation.[8] Ernst Wilhelm Hengstenberg notes,

> In the fullest sense . . . the fulfilment [i.e., of the covenant blessings] is only in Christ. It is after God has procured all the blessings of grace and salvation in him to his own people, that there follows really and comprehensively the effect upon the heathen world which is the object of the Psalmist's wishes and hopes.[9]

---

4   See the discussions in Tate, *Psalms 51–100*, 154; Hossfeld and Zenger, *Psalms*, 2:149.

5   E.g., Gen. 12:3; 22:18; 26:4. Cf. Isa. 60:3; Jer. 33:9. Kidner notes, "If a psalm was ever written round the promises to Abraham, that he would be both blessed and made a blessing, it could well have been such as this." Kidner, *Psalms*, 1:236.

6   "If the spirit of the psalm . . . is that of the Abrahamic hope, its text is the Aaronic Blessing." Kidner, *Psalms*, 1:236.

7   Delitzsch, *Psalms*, 2:239.

8   Hossfeld and Zenger, *Psalms*, 2:153.

9   Hengstenberg, *Psalms*, 2:332.

Psalm 67 belongs in the subgroup Psalms 65–68 (see on Ps. 65). It shares numerous links with nearby psalms, especially Psalms 65 and 66. (Links with Ps. 68 are discussed under the treatment of that psalm.) The most significant are (1) the continued emphasis on the whole world ("the nations," "the peoples," "the ends of the earth," etc.), (2) the fruitfulness of the earth (65:9–13), and (3) the whole world coming to praise God (65:8; 66:8).

THE TEXT

Structure
Psalm 67:3 and 5 (identical) bracket 67:4 (the only three-line verse), suggesting a chiastic structure:

  a 67:1–2: prayer
    b 67:3: refrain
      c 67:4: center
    b' 67:5: refrain
  a' 67:6–7: prayer

Selah, which appears at the end of 67:1 and 4, does not seem here to have structural significance.

Superscription

   s   To the choirmaster:[10] with stringed instruments.[11] A Psalm. A Song.[12]

The designations **Psalm** and **Song** are shared with Psalms 65, 66, and 68 (see on Ps. 65).

67:1–2 Oh God, Bless Your People in Christ
That the World May Be Blessed

   1   May God be gracious to us and bless us
       and make his face to shine upon us,   *Selah*

---

10 See on Ps. 4.
11 See on Ps. 4; cf. Pss. 6; 54; 55; 61; 76; Hab. 3:19.
12 In Hebrew the superscription is verse 1; subsequent verse numbers are increased by one.

Three elements of the Aaronic blessing of Numbers 6:24–26 are turned here from the form of a blessing (spoken by the priest in the second person) into a prayer (spoken by the people in the third person): **be gracious, bless,** and **make his face to shine**.[13] All blessing comes from God alone; we deserve none.[14] The shining of God's face (here and often in the Psalms and elsewhere) is a vivid image of warm, personal relationship.

The covenant blessing, pronounced by the Aaronic priest, reaches its fulfillment when spoken to his people by Christ our great high priest, for, as Theodoret of Cyrus rightly notes, this prayer is answered by the incarnation.[15] It is expressed also whenever God pours out through Christ a fresh blessing on his church, and it is consummated when Jesus returns. The members of Christ's church here "pray for the outpouring of the full blessing which their high priest, Jesus, is to bestow by their means on all the earth."[16]

> 2   that your way may be known on earth,
>   your saving power among all nations.

The goal toward which the church ought to pray Psalm 67:1 is that God's **way** and **saving power** (lit., "salvation") **may be known**[17] throughout the world (echoing Gen. 12:3). To "know" here means personally to acknowledge and experience.[18] The **way** of God, set here in parallel with his "salvation," means "how God acts, what are those treasures of salvation which are laid up with him for his people."[19] People all over the world will know in their own experience the covenant of God, in which he reveals himself through Christ as our Father and gives us the Spirit of adoption.[20]

---

13 Cf. Pss. 4:6; 31:16; 80:3, 7, 19; 119:135.
14 Augustine, *Psalms*, 3:309; Calvin, *Psalms*, 3:2.
15 Theodoret of Cyrus, *Psalms*, 1:377.
16 Bonar, *Psalms*, 198.
17 The qal infinitive construct is literally "to know." Here it has the sense "that *one* may know," which is equivalent to the passive ("may be known"). Delitzsch, *Psalms*, 2:240.
18 For a summary of the verb ידע, see Ross, *Psalms*, 2:453n17.
19 Hengstenberg, *Psalms*, 2:332.
20 Calvin, *Psalms*, 3:3.

67:3 May All the World Praise God for His Goodness in Christ!

3   Let the peoples praise you, O God;
    let all the peoples praise you!

The verb used in both lines for **praise** indicates a public acknowledgment of who God is, of his goodness and grace. The final word in the second line (in Hebrew) gives the joyful emphasis, "Let the peoples praise you, *all of them!*" All this is focused on Christ.

67:4 World Gladness Rests on God's Good World Government

4   Let the nations be glad and sing for joy,
    for you judge the peoples with equity
    and guide the nations upon earth.   *Selah*

The emphatic gladness of the first line makes clear that what is longed for here is no forced obedience but rather the glad submission to God that comes from men and women being converted all over the world. This transformation, which happens soul by soul in the worldwide mission of the church, will come to fruition only when Christ's church is completed and the Lord returns.

The reason (**for**) is given in two parallel lines. The verb **judge** has the sense here not so much of giving judicial verdicts but of government, indeed, the kind of "righteous and mild government" that evokes glad submission and that is found only when Christ comes to bring the kingdom of God to earth.[21] While it is true that God does govern the nations at the present time, whether they know it or not (e.g., Deut. 32:8; Dan. 2:20–23; Acts 17:26), it is only when Jesus returns that the sheer goodness of his government will become evident to all. The noun **equity** (cf. Ps. 45:6; Isa. 11:4—both of the Messiah) is related to the adjective "upright"; it derives from the idea of "level ground" and means—as we say—governing with a level playing field, in complete fairness.

---

21 Delitzsch, *Psalms*, 2:240. The messianic parallels, such as Pss. 45:4–6; 72:12–14; and Isa. 11:3–5, picture the beauty of this "judgment."

The parallel line uses the gentle verb to **guide** or lead, familiar from Psalms 23:3 and 31:3 and also used of Israel coming out of Egypt in Psalm 78:14. There is—or ought to be—a present-tense gladness in grasping by faith that God is governing his world in goodness and also in anticipation of that final exultation when God's will is done on earth as it is in heaven and Christ hands over the kingdom to the Father, having destroyed every rebel power (1 Cor. 15:24).

67:5 May All the World Praise God for His Goodness in Christ!

⁵   Let the peoples praise you, O God;
      let all the peoples praise you!

This refrain is repeated word for word from Psalm 67:3. It expresses the emphatic goal the psalmist prays for.

67:6–7 Oh God, Bless Your People in Christ
That the World May Be Blessed!

⁶   The earth has yielded its increase;
      God, our God, shall bless us.
⁷   God shall bless us;
      let all the ends of the earth fear him!

Psalm 67:6a contains the only perfect-tense form in the psalm. While this may refer to a harvest gladly gathered in (i.e., a past-tense reference), it is very close in wording to the covenant promise of Leviticus 26:4 ("Then . . . the land shall yield its increase"), in which the same perfect-tense form is used with the same noun (land/earth) and the same object (increase/harvest) to speak of a future blessing.[22] Whether or not this was originally a harvest thanksgiving, it points forward to the final blessings of God's kind government in Christ.

The repeated **God shall bless us**[23] together with the covenant designation **our God** reinforces this confidence.

---

22 This lies behind the NIV rendering, "yields," taking the perfect as characteristic. The parallel is noted, e.g., by VanGemeren, *Psalms*, 513; Harman, *Psalms*, 1:489.
23 These imperfect tenses may legitimately be translated as futures (ESV), as a present followed by a future (CSB), or as a present followed by a jussive (NIV). There is little difference in the overall meaning. See the useful discussion in Ross, *Psalms*, 2:459.

Jerome shows rich biblical imagination when he connects the harvest yield to the grain of wheat falling into the ground and dying in John 12:24, and thence to Jesus and the harvest that grows from his sacrifice.[24] His suggestion is thought-provoking and profound. Augustine relates these blessings to the day of Pentecost, when many "opened themselves to the divine shower" of blessing, which issued in "a magnificent yield" of church growth.[25]

The final line sums up the glorious goal of the psalm,[26] when a countless multitude from all over the world will bow in glad and reverent fear before the covenant God who has poured out his blessings on them in Christ.

REFLECTION AND RESPONSE

1. The way that Psalm 67:1 uses the promised priestly blessing in Numbers 6 shows us that "it is safe to turn God's offers, promises, and forms of blessing his people into prayers."[27] We may pray for the blessing in Christ that God has promised.

2. We pray that God will bless us, the church of Christ. But we do not confine our prayers to this narrow horizon. Always our eyes should be on the wider world. Charles Spurgeon says that "our love must make long marches, and our prayers must have a wide sweep, we must embrace the whole world in our intercessions."[28] Philip Eveson helpfully observes that, in church history, "when God has blessed his people with a spiritual awakening it has led to renewed missionary interest."[29]

3. The depth with which this psalm understands blessing presses us to meditate on how true blessing can never be confined to the material but is fulfilled only in a joyful relationship to God in Christ, a relationship in which we gladly submit to God's kind and wise government of his world (Ps. 67:4).

---

24 Jerome, *Homilies on the Psalms*, 6, in *ACCS* 8:63.

25 Augustine, *Psalms*, 3:320.

26 Again, the verb may be taken as a jussive (ESV), expressing desire, or as a simple future (CSB: "And all the ends of the earth will fear him"), for God has promised what this prayer desires.

27 Dickson, *Psalms*, 1:392.

28 Spurgeon, *Treasury*, 2.1:128.

29 Eveson, *Psalms*, 1:409.

It was predicted that, after his Ascension into heaven, Christ would free us from the captivity of error and endow us with gifts. Here [in Psalm 68] are the words of the prophecy.

JUSTIN MARTYR
Dialogue with Trypho

Now that [David] had been made king, he infers that the Church was brought to a settled condition, and that God, who seemed to have departed, would now at length erect his throne, as it were, in the midst of it, and reign. In this it would evidently appear, that he designed, typically, to represent the glory of God afterwards to be manifested in Christ.

JOHN CALVIN
Commentary on the Psalms

PSALM 68

ORIENTATION

The energy of Psalm 68 is extraordinary. Images tumble over one another, and echoes reverberate. Derek Kidner calls it "this rushing cataract of a psalm—one of the most boisterous and exhilarating in the Psalter."[1] And yet it is famously difficult to understand.[2] The puzzles are almost all in the details, with many rare words or hapax legomena.[3] But the big picture is clear: God wins a great victory on behalf of his people. The psalm "traces God's triumphant march through the desert, his conquest over the kings of Canaan, and finally his ascension to the holy mount to reign in majesty."[4] The New Testament teaches that God wins that victory through Christ. Christ leads his people out of slavery through the wilderness into the promised land and ascends in triumph to the Father's right hand, that we may be confident of his power and love and may rejoice in the assurance of what he has achieved for us. The language is rich and vivid, with a plethora of names and epithets for God,[5] as his saving power in Christ is celebrated.

The psalm helps us grasp that our individual stories are part of a much bigger drama. Only when we understand the dynamics—and the outcome— of that greater narrative will we make sense of our individual stories.

1   Kidner, *Psalms*, 1:238.
2   E.g., "Widely admitted as textually and exegetically the most difficult and obscure of all the psalms." Dahood, *Psalms*, 2:133. Nevertheless, these difficulties have been perceived only "since the dawning of modernity." Before then, neither patristic writers nor Luther nor Calvin found it any harder than any other psalm. Goldingay, *Psalms*, 2:311. Perhaps the difficulties tell us more about our post-"Enlightenment" mindset than about the psalm.
3   Delitzsch, *Psalms*, 2:244; Tate, *Psalms 51–100*, 15.
4   Ross, *Psalms*, 2:470.
5   For a useful summary of these names and titles, see, e.g., Harman, *Psalms*, 1:491; Delitzsch, *Psalms*, 2:244; Tate, *Psalms 51–100*, 184.

The most likely original context is that climactic day when David brought the ark of the covenant up to Mount Zion at the end of centuries of wandering, completing the journey of the symbolic presence of God from Sinai to Zion (2 Sam. 6).[6] Whatever the original context, one New Testament quotation and two likely echoes shape our reading in the light of Jesus Christ. Paul adapts and quotes from Psalm 68:18 in Ephesians 4:8 to connect the drama of the psalm with the victorious ascension of Christ. The "history and prophecy of salvation," Kidner explains, "is presented in Ephesians 4:7–16 as a miniature of a far greater ascension, in which Christ led captivity captive, to share out better spoils of victory than these, in the gift (and gifts) of the Spirit."[7]

In addition, it is likely that "the earth quaked" (Ps. 68:8) is echoed in the words "I will shake . . . the earth" in Hebrews 12:26, in connection with the final shaking of the earth to bring in the kingdom that cannot be shaken, the kingdom of Christ.[8] Also, when Paul writes of the Lord Jesus coming "to be glorified in his saints" (2 Thess. 1:10), this may well echo the clause "Awesome is God from his sanctuary" (Ps. 68:35) as it is rendered in the Septuagint ("Admirable is God among his saints," NETS);[9] this strengthens the connection with the triumph of Christ. Together, these echoes encourage us to understand that the God so vividly portrayed in Psalm 68 is God as he is known to us in the triumph of Christ.

We will keep before our eyes the vision of Jesus Christ raised from the dead, ascended to the Father's right hand, triumphant over every rebel power, with all things under his feet, and given to the church; this is the immeasurable greatness of God's power "toward us who believe" (Eph. 1:19–23; cf. 1 Cor. 15:20–28). This is not simply the story of the victory of Christ; it is the wonderful news that God "gives us the victory through our Lord Jesus Christ" (1 Cor. 15:57).

Although it focuses more on redemption than creation, Psalm 68 belongs with Psalms 65–67 (see on Ps. 65). Links include (1) the exodus (cf. 66:6), (2) the wilderness journey of the people of God (cf. the Aaronic blessing in

6   Ross, *Psalms*, 2:470–71.
7   Kidner, *Psalms*, 1:238.
8   Hossfeld and Zenger, *Psalms*, 2:169.
9   Weima notes that "we see how Paul takes an Old Testament text that originally refers to God and applies it to Christ." Jeffrey A. D. Weima, "1–2 Thessalonians," in *CNTOT* 885–86. Hossfeld and Zenger add that "2 Thess 1:10 follows the LXX text of Ps 68:36 ('God is wonderful among his saints') in depicting the coming of Jesus for judgment." Hossfeld and Zenger, *Psalms*, 2:169.

67:1), (3) the universal scope of what God does (68:31–32), (4) the sanctuary (e.g., 65:4; 66:13; 68:5), and (5) the defeat of God's enemies (65:7; 66:3).

Psalm 68 retells the story of redemption in vivid poetic cameos. Three passages stand out as background for the echoes.[10] At least two of them are songs, which may explain why they are so well remembered in a psalm.

The first is the Song of Moses and the people of Israel in Exodus 15. Apart from celebrating victory over enemies, the song rejoices, in anticipation, that the covenant Lord will lead his people to his "holy abode" (Ex. 15:13), where they will be "plant[ed]" on his "own mountain . . . your abode, the sanctuary" (Ex. 15:17); that is, it celebrates not just the exodus but the whole drama of salvation up to its climax in Zion. In addition, the declaration of the victory by Miriam with all the women (Ex. 15:20–21) finds an echo in the psalm (Ps. 68:11–12).

The second background passage is the song of Deborah and Barak after the victory over Sisera, in Judges 5. In this song the earth trembles in a storm of rain (Judg. 5:5; cf. Ps. 68:8), Sinai is referenced (Judg. 5:5; cf. Ps. 68:8, 17), captives are recaptured to be released (Judg. 5:12; cf. Ps. 68:18), Benjamin is prominent (Judg. 5:14; cf. Ps. 68:27), Zebulun and Naphtali feature (Judg. 5:18; cf. Ps. 68:27), and women wait in expectation of spoil (Judg. 5:28–30; cf. Ps. 68:12). Judges 4–5 is a reenactment of exodus redemption, for the church of God is spiritually back in slavery to an oppressive power; God arises to lead them again out of this slavery and into the "rest" that is the promise of the land (Judg. 5:31).

The third passage sets the scene for the psalm. This is Numbers 10:35, echoed in Psalm 68:1,[11] as the ark sets out on its journey. The psalm retells this story as the rising up of God in Christ to lead his people out of slavery through the wilderness and finally to the heights of Zion, the heavenly temple, at the Father's right hand.

THE TEXT

Structure

The simplest divisions are probably as follows. Psalm 68:1–6 functions as an introduction, consisting of a brief summary (68:1–3) followed by an

---

10 Cf. also Num. 22–25; Deut. 32–33; 1 Sam. 2:1–10. Delitzsch, *Psalms*, 2:243.

11 In addition, the reference to "the ten thousand thousands of Israel" in Num. 10:36 may be echoed in the many thousands of Ps. 68:17.

exhortation to praise (68:4–6). Psalm 68:7–18 is a poetic dramatization of the journey of the ark from Sinai to Zion. Psalm 68:19–27 responds to that victory (68:19–23) and visualizes a victory procession (68:24–27). Psalm 68:28–35 continues the response to the victory (68:28–31) and extends it to a call to the kingdoms of the earth to respond as they ought (68:32–35). The *Selah*, appearing after 68:7 and 32, does not seem to function as a structural marker.

Superscription

S   To the choirmaster.[12] A Psalm of David. A Song.[13]

See on Psalm 65.

68:1–6 Introduction: Prepare to Rejoice in the Drama of Christ, Who Leads His Church through the Wilderness into Its Eternal Home

1   God shall arise, his enemies shall be scattered;
      and those who hate him shall flee before him!
2   As smoke is driven away, so you shall drive them away;
      as wax melts before fire,
      so the wicked shall perish before God!
3   But the righteous shall be glad;
      they shall exult before God;
      they shall be jubilant with joy!

The opening line takes us back to Numbers 10:35, as the ark of the covenant leads the church of God from Sinai to the land. The verbs **arise, be scattered,** and **flee** may be translated by simple futures (as the ESV), by a present tense to highlight that this is what God characteristically does (as the CSB), or by jussives ("Let God arise . . ."; as the NASB, NIV, NRSV, REB). The verb in Numbers 10:35 clearly expresses a desire. It matters little

---

12 See on Ps. 4.
13 In Hebrew the superscription is verse 1; subsequent verse numbers are increased by one.

whether we express desire or confidence that God will do what we desire because it is what he has promised.

The ark represented the God of the covenant among his people. David Dickson explains, "As the ark was among the Israelites, so is Christ among his people; and what ground of confidence the church had, because of that pledge of God's presence at the ark, we have the same, and a more sure ground of confidence in Christ's incarnation."[14] To "arise" here means for God, as it were, to get up from the appearance of sleep, ready to fight for his people. Christ did this in the incarnation, when he left heaven to be God with us. He arose in his victorious resurrection, after his sin-bearing death for his people. He arose in his ascension to the Father's right hand. There is a sense in which he "arises" in the heart of each one who is born from above (cf. Eph. 5:14). He arises whenever he acts to save or restore his church and carry it on through the wilderness of this age. On the last day, he will arise in judgment.[15]

Four verbs and two vivid images headline the defeat of the wicked. They are **scattered** (in contrast to God's church, which will be gathered in triumphal procession, Ps. 68:24–27); they will **flee** (cf. 68:12) in terror **before him** (before his face, the awesome face of the Lamb in his wrath); they will be **driven away**, as smoke that rises so proudly but is blown away by the wind of God's fiery judgment;[16] and they will **perish before** (lit., the face of) **God**. The images of wind blowing away smoke and fire melting wax are suggestive of God's Spirit (e.g., Luke 3:16–17).

The contrast with **the righteous** (plural, the church of Christ, righteous by faith) could hardly be more complete, with four expressions for joy (**be glad, exult, be jubilant, with joy**). All this is **before** (lit., "the face of") **God,** for the face of Christ that is as terrifying as the wrath of the Lamb is wonderful for those who are justified by his grace. When Christ our God arises from the dead, the sorrow of the disciples is turned into joy, as the rejoicing of the world is turned into lament (John 16:20). As the church walks with Christ our ark through the wilderness, we rejoice in him.

4   Sing to God, sing praises to his name;
         lift up a song to him who rides through the deserts;

---

14 Dickson, *Psalms*, 1:396. Cf. Eveson, *Psalms*, 1:417.

15 Luther, *Luther's Works*, 10:324.

16 Unlike God's church, which is taken through fire but survives (e.g., Ps. 66:12).

his name is the LORD;

exult before him!

5   Father of the fatherless and protector of widows

is God in his holy habitation.

6   God settles the solitary in a home;

he leads out the prisoners to prosperity,

but the rebellious dwell in a parched land.

Psalm 68:4–6 develops the theme introduced in 68:1–3 by focusing on God's nature and attributes (with two references to his **name** in 68:4). Who is this God, this Christ, this one represented by the ark? He is the one **who rides through the deserts**,[17] leading his people through the wilderness to the promised land. He is given (unusually in this section of the Psalter) the covenant name, **the LORD** (in the shortened form יָהּ, *Yah*).

Psalm 68:5–6 fills out something of the meaning of **his name**. The very nature of this covenant God, this God made known to us in Christ, is that he is **father of the fatherless** (cf. 27:10) **and protector**, that is, the "champion" (CSB), who acts on behalf **of widows** (cf. Luke 18:1–8). We to whom God gives salvation are weak but walk with the Christ who brings us the protection we lack. The **holy habitation**, or dwelling place, of God is the place to which Christ will bring us, as he "bring[s] us to God" (1 Pet. 3:18), signified by Zion, to which we go (cf. Ps. 68:17b); indeed, we become that temple. Augustine comments, "It is out of these orphans and widows, who no longer have any hope in the secular society that has abandoned them, that the Lord fashions a temple for himself."[18] Those related to Christ by faith are brought into the family of God (e.g., Mark 3:33–35).

God settles (a participle indicating that this is what he characteristically does) **the solitary**, the one who is alone, **in a home**, a household. Put another way, **he leads out** (in exodus rescue again and again) **the prisoners**

---

17 Sometimes the phrase בָּעֲרָבוֹת is translated "through/on the clouds" to yield the picture of God riding through the clouds, as a polemic against the Canaanite god Baal, who was supposed to do this. But the usual meaning of the word is "desert," and both the overall theme of the ark traveling from Sinai to Zion and the use of another word for "wilderness" (יְשִׁימוֹן) in Ps. 68:7 strongly suggest that "through the deserts" is the correct translation. In Isa. 43:19–20 the two words are used in parallel. Harman, *Psalms*, 1:493.

18 Augustine, *Psalms*, 3:328.

(the word often refers to prisoners in a foreign land)[19] **to prosperity**. There is a link between loneliness and imprisonment because sin separates and isolates. In the final line of Psalm 68:6, **the rebellious** probably alludes to the Israelites who rebelled in the wilderness and died in that **parched land**.[20]

In all this the church of Christ is "the great theatre where [God's] fatherly care" is manifested.[21]

Summing up 68:1–6 and looking forward to the drama that begins in 68:7, Martin Luther writes,

> Thus far we have been informed in the preface about the theme which the psalmist contemplates celebrating in song, namely, Christ and His Gospel. . . . O Christ, at the time when Thou didst go before the Israelites in their exodus from Egypt, Thou didst presage and symbolize Thy resurrection, by means of which Thou didst really precede Thy people out of the Egypt of this world to Thy Father. Thus by Thine example and Thy Word Thou dost now also lead them through the desert of faith after Thee to the Father.[22]

68:7–18 Revel in the Drama of Christ's Victory for His People

It is probably best to read these verses as a fluid and poetic celebration of what is foundationally understood by the journey of the ark from Sinai to Zion but also as what is reenacted in every act of God's redemption and culminates in the "journey" of Christ from the descent of incarnation to the cross and thence to the ascent of resurrection, ascension, and session at the Father's right hand.

7   O God, when you went out before your people,
        when you marched through the wilderness,   *Selah*
8   the earth quaked, the heavens poured down rain,
        before God, the One of Sinai,
        before God, the God of Israel.
9   Rain in abundance, O God, you shed abroad;
        you restored your inheritance as it languished;

19 Ross, *Psalms*, 2:476–77; Harman, *Psalms*, 1:493. Cf. Ps. 69:33; Isa. 14:17; Zech. 9:11.
20 Ross, *Psalms*, 2:477.
21 Calvin, *Psalms*, 3:12.
22 Luther, *Luther's Works*, 13:8.

¹⁰   your flock found a dwelling in it;
        in your goodness, O God, you provided for the needy.

Psalm 68:7–10 teaches us that the greater story we are a part of in Christ is an earth-shaking drama. Psalm 68:7 takes us back to the evocation of Numbers 10:35 in Psalm 68:1. **God,** known finally in Christ and symbolized by the ark, **went out before** his **people** as he **marched through the wilderness.** Perhaps *Selah* encourages us to bring before our hearts that scene and to remember that we are those people today, being led by Christ through the wilderness.

The references in 68:8 to **the earth quak**ing, to **Sinai,** and to a stormy downpour of **rain** dramatically help us feel the earth-shaking significance of the redemption of Christ's people: from the shaking earth at Mount Sinai (Ex. 19:18) through the storms of rescue, such as for Deborah and Barak (Judg. 5:4), to the earthquake at the cross of Christ (Matt. 27:51), then onward to the application of that victory to the church in every age (e.g., Acts 4:31) right through to the final shaking that brings in the new heavens and new earth (see above for the likely echo in Heb. 12:26). What God did then in anticipation, and what God did definitively in Christ, is a deed that reshapes the very order of creation.

In Psalm 68:9 the restoration of God's **inheritance** most likely refers to the promised land (the usual meaning of נַחֲלָה, *nakhalah*) and may hint at repeated restorations of God's church, from the return from Babylonian exile to Pentecost and on through every time of revival until the end of time. In 68:10 the **flock** is literally "living ones," a term usually used for animals but here for the people of God. The gifts of **a dwelling** in the land and the blessings of God's **goodness** (a covenant term), all given as provision **for the needy** (a common word for the poor; cf. the fatherless and widows of 68:5), paint a vivid picture of the gospel shape of redemption.

¹¹   The Lord gives the word;
        the women who announce the news are a great host:
¹²   "The kings of the armies—they flee, they flee!"
        The women at home divide the spoil—
¹³   though you men lie among the sheepfolds—
        the wings of a dove covered with silver,

its pinions with shimmering gold.
14   When the Almighty scatters kings there,
let snow fall on Zalmon.

If Psalm 68:7–10 focuses on an earth-shaking drama, 68:11–14 celebrates a great victory. The sovereign **Lord gives the word**, an announcement of stupendous victory over all the forces of wickedness. The victory is so great that **a great host** of **women . . . announce the news**, reminding us of Miriam and the women singing of God's victory at the Red Sea (Ex. 15), of the song of Deborah (Judg. 5:1–12), and of the women singing and dancing with news of David's victories (1 Sam. 18:6). A great victory calls for a great host of heralds to proclaim it. Psalm 68:12 expresses astonishment: **The kings of the armies—they flee, they flee!** This is a remarkable triumph (perhaps redolent of Abraham's victory over the kings in Gen. 14 or Joshua's in Josh. 10:16). Who would have thought that Pharaoh's horses and chariots would be defeated, that Sisera's mighty army could be routed, and, above all, that all the powers of evil would be disarmed and put to open shame at the cross of Christ (Col. 2:15)?

Psalm 68:12b–14 completes the picture. In 68:12b **the women at home—** that is, the mistresses of the houses of the victorious warriors (cf. the hopes of Sisera's mother in Judg. 5:28–30)—**divide the spoil**. This **spoil** reminds us of the Hebrews at the exodus taking the treasures of Egypt with them. It is fulfilled when Christ receives and distributes gifts to his people (see on Ps. 68:18). For by the cross, Christ plunders the "strong man" (Matt. 12:29), the devil and all his demons; despoils his house; and rescues his captives.

Psalm 68:13–14 is puzzling. While the first line of 68:13 may be a rebuke to those who had not fought (as in Judg. 5:16), the context here is the celebration of victory spoils, and it seems more likely that we should translate the term not "though" (suggesting a contrast) but "while" (CSB, NIV), so that alongside the mistress of the house distributing the spoils, the victorious warriors are now relaxing **among the sheepfolds**, that is, settled in the promised "rest," "a quiet country life"[23] (like the Shire of Tolkien's *The Lord of the Rings*). If so, then the description of the shining and decorative **dove** may speak either of the wonderful spoil or, perhaps more likely, of the

23 Ross, *Psalms*, 2:465.

redeemed church of Christ after victory is won, a precious dove decorated with the victory gifts of Christ. In Psalm 68:14 it is clear that **the Almighty**[24] **scatters kings**. We are not sure of the significance of **snow** falling on **Zalmon** (Judg. 9:48); it may be that the snow scattered over this hillside is a picture of the scattered kings. Even if we cannot be sure of all the symbolism, the overall picture of Psalm 68:12–14 is of a glorious victory.

> 15   O mountain of God, mountain of Bashan;
>   O many-peaked mountain, mountain of Bashan!
> 16   Why do you look with hatred, O many-peaked mountain,
>   at the mount that God desired for his abode,
>   yes, where the LORD will dwell forever?
> 17   The chariots of God are twice ten thousand,
>   thousands upon thousands;
>   the Lord is among them; Sinai is now in the sanctuary.

Psalm 68:15–16 sets before us a striking contrast shaped by the gospel. Here is a **mountain** in **Bashan** (the area of one of the great victories on the way to the promised land, when Israel defeated Og, king of Bashan), described as a **mountain of God**, which is either ironic or perhaps means "a majestic mountain," and as a **many-peaked mountain**. It is impressive in the eyes of the world. And yet this powerful mountain looks with envious **hatred** at the far less impressive hill of Zion. For this unimpressive hill is **the mount that God desired for his abode**, where the covenant **LORD will dwell forever**. Here is Christ, the unimpressive one on earth and yet the chosen one of the Father and the one in whom unimpressive people (1 Cor. 1:26) find themselves as the dwelling place of God (cf. John 14:23).

In Psalm 68:17 **the chariots of God** indicate his vast armies, perhaps linked with the many thousands of Israel in Numbers 10:36; these heavenly hosts (cf. 2 Kings 6:17; Hab. 3:8–15; Zech. 6:1–8) are the birthright of the Son of Man (cf. Matt. 26:53), who is their commander in chief (cf. Dan. 7:9–10). The sovereign **Lord is among them**. In a brief phrase pregnant with meaning, **Sinai is now in the sanctuary**, the place of holiness in the

---

24 For discussion of the title Shaddai, see Ross, *Psalms*, 2:480n65.

temple on Mount Zion. The ark has completed its long journey. The "place" where God entered into covenant and gave the blessings of his law (Sinai) is now the "place" from which that blessed law goes out to all the world (Zion; cf. Isa. 2:2–3). And as the letter to the Hebrews will teach, in Christ that "place" becomes the place of the new covenant in which we hear a better word (Heb. 12:18–24).

18   You ascended on high,
        leading a host of captives in your train
        and receiving gifts among men,
            even among the rebellious, that the LORD God may dwell there.

Psalm 68:18 is "the cardinal verse of the entire psalm"[25] and the climax of the drama; it would be so even had Paul not quoted it in Ephesians 4:8. The second-person address, **you**, is picked up again from Psalm 68:7–10, as the God who arose for holy war in 68:1 now completes his triumph. He **ascended on high**, which in this context indicates Mount Zion, the mountain that has been celebrated in 68:17 as the final destination of the ark from Sinai. The second line pictures a victorious warrior **leading** behind him **a host of captives**. These are those who had been captured by his enemy, whom Christ has now captured in order that he should set them free in his glad service.[26] The third line pictures him **receiving gifts among men**, that is, the victory spoils of his war. The fourth line is not entirely clear but probably means (as the CSB, ESV, NIV) that **even among the rebellious** these gifts are now given, as they surrender to the King. The goal is **that the LORD God may dwell there** in Zion in the midst of his people.

Paul quotes, and slightly adapts, the first two lines in Ephesians 4:8. He changes from the second person to the third person: "he ascended . . . he led . . . he gave . . ." This is of no semantic significance. But he also changes from "he received from" to "he gave to." Much ink has been spilled over this

---

25 Luther, *Luther's Works*, 13:20.

26 "As great conquerors of old led whole nations into captivity, so Jesus leads forth from the territory of his foe a vast company as the trophies of his mighty grace. From the gracious character of his reign it comes to pass that to be led into captivity by him is for our captivity to cease." Spurgeon, *Treasury*, 2.1:142.

modification.[27] It is usually suggested that Paul derives this rendering from the Targum and the Syriac,[28] although this has been contested.[29] The critical point is that the conqueror receives these spoils not for himself (for he has no need of them) but for the benefit of the people for whom he fought the war. He gives because he has first taken.[30]

When Christ receives a gift, that gift is necessarily received by the church because it is Christ's body;[31] all that Christ receives, he receives for us.[32]

Here is a great ascension after a stupendous victory. Dickson describes it as follows:

> Christ did not enter into his glory without a battle going before, and that with strong and many enemies; and in his fighting he carried the victory, and after his victory he triumphed, first in the cross and then in his ascension, over sin, Satan, the world, hell, grave, and all.[33]

Andrew Bonar likewise states,

> Ascended to Zion, no more wandering from place to place, *the Ark* is the centre of blessing to Israel. . . . And in this was typified the Saviour, no more a wanderer on earth from place to place, seated at the Father's right hand, and showering down his gifts on man.[34]

68:19–27 Celebrate Christ's Victory with His Gathered People over His Enemies

Before the final focus on the wider world, Psalm 68:19–27 invites us to gather with the church of Christ in celebrating his victory. The remainder of the psalm consists entirely of celebration and prayer arising from Christ's victory.

---

27 For detailed discussion of the issues surrounding this complex quotation or adaptation, see Frank S. Thielman, "Ephesians," in *CNTOT* 819–25. See also the clear discussion in Belcher, *Messiah and the Psalms*, 181–85.
28 E.g., Kirkpatrick, *Psalms*, 2:388–89; Ross, *Psalms*, 2:482.
29 Hamilton, *Psalms*, 1:603n226.
30 Hengstenberg, *Psalms*, 2:354.
31 Augustine, *Psalms*, 3:348.
32 Similarly, Luther, *Luther's Works*, 13:21; Calvin, *Psalms*, 3:26–27.
33 Dickson, *Psalms*, 1:402.
34 Bonar, *Psalms*, 203.

68:19–23 We Celebrate His Victory over His Enemies

19   Blessed be the Lord,
         who daily bears us up;
         God is our salvation.   *Selah*
20   Our God is a God of salvation,
         and to GOD, the Lord, belong deliverances from death.

Blessed be together with *Selah* invites us to meditate on and to bless God for the wonder of Christ's descent and ascent for us (Eph. 4:8). Only on the basis of this reality can we be confident that **the Lord . . . daily bears us up** (cf. 1 Pet. 5:7), because he liberates us from bondage to God's law (Matt. 11:30) and shows himself strong and willing to carry us all the way to the promised land. In the fullest sense of the word, God in Christ **is our salvation**, with salvation understood not just in its beginnings (regeneration, justification, conversion) but in its continuing and to its completion (Rom. 13:11; Phil. 1:6). In Psalm 68:20 he is literally "a God of salvations" (plural, the many rescues that contribute to the great rescue), in whom we have "deliverances" (many escapes and one final escape) from death itself. This is true in Christ, for only Christ holds the keys to death and Hades (Rev. 1:18).

21   But God will strike the heads of his enemies,
         the hairy crown of him who walks in his guilty ways.
22   The Lord said,
         "I will bring them back from Bashan,
         I will bring them back from the depths of the sea,
23   that you may strike your feet in their blood,
         that the tongues of your dogs may have their portion from
            the foe."

The **hairy crown** probably suggests the youthful arrogance that sports an impressive head of hair (cf. Absalom, 2 Sam. 14:25–26). The one **who walks in his guilty ways** is the one who deliberately and impenitently continues in those ways, rather than the one who slips and falls and repents (cf. Matt. 12:32; 1 John 1:9; 5:16). The context of Psalm 68:21–23 shows that those brought back **from Bashan** (cf. the proud mountain of 68:15) are not returned exiles but rebels who had hoped to escape, now marched back for punishment. Even death, **the depths of the sea**, will not protect them from the wrath of God. The repeated **I will bring them back** makes clear that there is no escape. The idiom to **strike your feet in their blood** uses a verb of uncertain meaning,[35] but what is clear is that they have been utterly and visibly defeated. The horrifying deaths of Ahab and Jezebel illustrate the shame of deaths under the judgment of God, in which dogs lick their blood and feast on their corpses (1 Kings 21:19; 22:38; 2 Kings 9:36). Although this imagery seems gruesome to us, it is necessary and unavoidable that the finally impenitent enemies of Christ will come to a terrible end. This destiny is placarded before us to warn us before it is too late.

The main point of Psalm 68:19–23 is that the church of Christ may rejoice in anticipation that every form of wickedness—the world, the flesh, the devil and all his hosts—will be removed from the promised land in which they can rest secure. The petition "Your kingdom come" prays for this.

68:24–27 We Celebrate His Victory with His Gathered People

24 Your procession is seen,[36] O God,
       the procession of my God, my King, into the sanctuary—
25 the singers in front, the musicians last,
       between them virgins playing tambourines:
26 "Bless God in the great congregation,
       the Lord, O you who are of Israel's fountain!"
27 There is Benjamin, the least of them, in the lead,
       the princes of Judah in their throng,
       the princes of Zebulun, the princes of Naphtali.

Psalm 68:24–27 pictures a joyful **procession** in **the sanctuary** (cf. 68:17), in which the gathered church blesses God in Christ for all he has done for us; in its original context this may have been the jubilant procession taking the ark of the covenant to Jerusalem in 2 Samuel 6. Psalm 68:25 displays an exultant assembly, full of youth, life, and song. The **great congregation** is

---

35 See the discussion in Ross, *Psalms*, 2:467n36.
36 Lit., "they have seen" with no expressed subject—hence the translation with the passive, "is seen."

literally "the congregations" (CSB: "the assemblies"), where the plural may be a plural of majesty (hence ESV). Psalm 68:26 shows that their songs are filled with the blessing of God, of Christ, of the covenant LORD, who has won this stupendous victory for us. The words **you who are of Israel's fountain** may look back to the patriarchal promises as the source of all this blessing or to God, who is the fountain of the people of Israel.

Four tribes are mentioned in 68:27 to indicate a united and gathered people. **Benjamin** is **least** both in the sense that Benjamin was Jacob's youngest son and in the sense that Benjamin was the smallest tribe (1 Sam. 9:21). That they are **in the lead** accords with the "first shall be last, and last shall be first" gospel motif that we have seen in the Zion-Bashan contrast in Psalm 68:15–17. We are not surprised that **Judah**, the tribe of David, is given prominence, although the word translated **throng** is of uncertain meaning. We do not know why just **Zebulun** and **Naphtali** are mentioned of the other tribes. While they served nobly in the war against Sisera (Judg. 5:18–20), more significantly they became the tribes to whom the messianic promise of Isaiah 9:1–7 would be given, and from their region almost all the apostles of Jesus were drawn (cf. Matt. 4:14–16).[37] Here in picture is a united church of Christ with whom we celebrate the victory of Christ. Revelation 14:1–5 develops the glad scene here celebrated.

68:28–35 Celebrate Christ's Victory as It Spreads throughout the World

The distinctive theme of the final section is the impact that Christ's ascension has on the whole world.

68:28–31 *Watch the Impact of Christ's Victory on a Rebellious World*

28 Summon your power, O God,
   the power, O God, by which you have worked for us.
29 Because of your temple at Jerusalem
   kings shall bear gifts to you.
30 Rebuke the beasts that dwell among the reeds,
   the herd of bulls with the calves of the peoples.

---

37 Eveson, *Psalms*, 1:417.

> Trample underfoot those who lust after tribute;
>
> > scatter the peoples who delight in war.
>
> [31] Nobles shall come from Egypt;
>
> > Cush shall hasten to stretch out her hands to God.

Although there are uncertainties in these verses, the overall picture is clear, as the eyes of the church of Christ are lifted from Zion's mountain to see the effect of Christ's victory on a rebellious world. In the background here, as so often, is the tumultuous rebellion seen in Psalm 2:1–3.

The thought of 68:28 is similar to Paul's prayer in Ephesians 1:19–23, in which he asks that the great power that God has worked for us in Christ when he raised him from the dead will now work in us as we know that power in our experience.

Psalm 68:29 and 31 are the positive counterpart to 68:30. **Because of your temple at Jerusalem**, that is, because the ark has made the journey, because Christ is now that temple, **kings** from all over the world **shall bear gifts to you.** Here is the "wealth of the nations" coming in to the new creation when the earth is shaken (68:8; cf. Isa. 45:14; 60:16; Hag. 2:7–9), an ingathering foreshadowed when the magi brought gifts to the infant Christ.

In Psalm 68:30 **the beasts that dwell among the reeds** probably alludes to the Behemoth or "super-beast" of Job 40:15–24;[38] this was sometimes used as a symbol for the oppressive power of Egypt.[39] In the second line **the herd of bulls** probably refers to strong nations or powerful leaders, and **the calves of the peoples** either to smaller nations or to less powerful people who follow the lead of the "bulls." In the third line, **those who lust after tribute** is literally "those with bars of silver"[40] and seems to indicate a wealth they want for themselves, which makes their giving of gifts to God's temple all the more ironic as a reversal of what they had wanted. The end result of Psalm 68:30 is the humbling of all rebellious powers.

Psalm 68:31 picks up the theme of 68:29. These rebellious powers, represented here by **Egypt** and **Cush**, send **nobles** (most likely "ambassadors")[41]

---

38 Goldingay, *Psalms*, 2:331.

39 Ross, *Psalms*, 2:485.

40 The NIV rendering, "Humbled, may the beast bring bars of silver," is quite a loose paraphrase.

41 The word is a hapax legomenon that may derive from "bronze" or a colored cloth that signifies an ambassador. Ross, *Psalms*, 2:486.

and **hasten to stretch out** their **hands**, bringing gifts **to God**. All the glory and riches of the rebellious world will be brought into the church of Christ in the new creation (cf. Isa. 19:21–25; 45:14; Zeph. 3:10; Zech. 2:10–13; Rev. 21:24),[42] beginning with some wonderful conversions (e.g., the Cushite/Ethiopian eunuch in Acts 8:26–40).[43] Augustine rightly says that Egypt and Cush are "a part to signify the whole" and that this verse refers to "the faith of all the Gentiles."[44]

The victory of Christ culminates not simply in the removal of his enemies but supremely in the enrichment of his church.

68:32–35 God Calls the Kingdoms of Earth to Respond to the Victory of Christ

> 32 O kingdoms of the earth, sing to God;
>   sing praises to the Lord,   *Selah*
> 33 to him who rides in the heavens, the ancient heavens;
>   behold, he sends out his voice, his mighty voice.
> 34 Ascribe power to God,
>   whose majesty is over Israel,
>   and whose power is in the skies.
> 35 Awesome is God from his sanctuary;
>   the God of Israel—he is the one who gives power and strength
>   to his people.
>   Blessed be God!

Psalm 68:32 begins with an appeal to the **kingdoms of the earth** (cf. 2:10–12) to **sing to God** in glad submission. The *Selah* perhaps encourages us to meditate on this worldwide missionary summons.

The God to whom they (we) are to sing is described in 68:33 as the one **who rides in the heavens**, just as he has led his people riding through the deserts (68:4). The expression **ancient heavens** emphasizes that these have been above the earth since the beginning; the one who rides as governor through these primordial heavens does indeed govern the world. **His voice,**

---

42 Hossfeld and Zenger, *Psalms*, 2:169; Longman, *Psalms*, 261.
43 Theodoret of Cyrus, *Psalms*, 1:392.
44 Augustine, *Psalms*, 3:359.

his mighty voice reinforces that this is a gospel proclamation, as the authoritative voice of God rings throughout the earth. The appeal continues in 68:34: **Ascribe power to God,** that is, acknowledge that it belongs to him, to the God known in Christ who has triumphed over sin, death, the devil, and all rebellion. The **majesty** of this God is not only **over Israel**, since he protects Christ's church, but also **in the skies,** making his people utterly safe from threat. This God (68:35) is indeed **awesome** (to be revered and feared;[45] cf. 65:5; 66:3, 5) as he rules the world **from his sanctuary** (cf. 68:17, 24), from the place to which Christ has ascended, to be given all authority in heaven and on earth (Matt. 28:18). That **he is the one who gives power and strength to his people** reminds us that the grand purpose for which Christ arose and conquered was so that he could pour out the Holy Spirit on his recaptured people. There is a tremendous emphasis on might, power, and strength in Psalm 68:33–35; all this is for Christ's church.

REFLECTION AND RESPONSE

1. Psalm 68:1–3 sets our agenda as we join in this psalm. If we enter rightly into its teaching and its affections, our hearts will be both confident in the final defeat of evil and deeply glad to belong to Jesus Christ.

2. Psalm 68:4–6 ought both to encourage and to challenge us. This section encourages us that the powerful God here celebrated shows himself in Christ to be the God who cares for those in desperate need because of sin and its terrible entailments of loneliness, unbearable burdens, and the shadow of death. The challenge is this: if God in Christ cares for the least, the lost, and the last, then so should we. John Calvin notes, "Generally we distribute our attentions where we expect some return. We give the preference to rank and splendour, and despise or neglect the poor."[46]

3. The best way to enter into the drama of Psalm 68:7–18 is probably to read slowly through these verses, allowing the vivid imagery to sink into our imaginations—all the while remembering that this is about Christ and about us as his people. The commentary may help us pick up the most important biblical echoes and alert us to the uncertainties, but there is no

---

45 The LXX term θαυμαστός is probably echoed in 2 Thess. 1:10, which describes the day when the Lord Jesus is "marveled at" (θαυμασθῆναι) by his church.
46 Calvin, *Psalms*, 3:10–11.

substitute for a slow pondering of this drama. Our aim is that when we reach 68:18, we gasp with wonder and astonishment at the ascension of Jesus Christ for us.

4. Psalm 68:19–27 can help us rejoice in response to the victory of Christ both at the sure destruction of every power of evil in the universe and at the glad gathering of the whole church of Christ. The vision of Revelation 14:1–5 reinforces the glad scene of this passage.

5. Psalm 68:28–35 encourages us in the church's task of proclamatory evangelism as we seek to declare to each needy sinner and every rebellious power the triumph of Christ and to proclaim that this triumph counts either against them, in the certainty of final failure, or—most wonderfully—for them, as they gladly join his church and sing his praises.

6. As we read the psalm, let us keep before our eyes the vision of Jesus Christ raised from the dead, ascended to the Father's right hand, triumphant over every rebel power, with all things under his feet, and given to the church; for this is the immeasurable greatness of God's power "toward us who believe" (Eph. 1:19–23; cf. 1 Cor. 15:20–28). This is not simply the story of the victory of Christ; it is the wonderful news that God "gives *us* the victory through our Lord Jesus Christ" (1 Cor. 15:57).

There are [Psalms 22 and 69], which foretell about the divine
cross and what great treachery [the Savior] submitted to
on our behalf, and the number of things he suffered.

ATHANASIUS
Letter to Marcellinus

This psalm speaks literally about the suffering of the Lord
in His own person. At the same time all the sufferings
and weaknesses of the church are also told here.

MARTIN LUTHER
First Lectures on the Psalms

His [the crucified's] footprints all through this sorrowful
song have been pointed out by the Holy Spirit in the New
Testament, and therefore we believe, and are sure, that the
Son of man is here. . . . We commence our exposition of this
Psalm with much trembling, for we feel that we are entering
with our Great High Priest into the most holy place.

CHARLES H. SPURGEON
The Treasury of David

PSALM 69

ORIENTATION

Psalm 69 gives a precious window into the soul of Jesus Christ. Jesus echoes "who hate me without cause" (69:4; cf. 35:19) of himself in John 15:25. After the cleansing of the temple, the disciples remembered the words "Zeal for your house will consume me" (Ps. 69:9a) and understood that they spoke of Christ (John 2:17). In Romans 15:3 Paul quotes "The reproaches of those who reproached you fell on me" (Ps. 69:9b) as referring to Christ. The references to thirst, to poison or gall, and to sour wine (69:21) are echoed in the crucifixion accounts.[1] The mockery of the psalmist (69:12) is fulfilled at the cross (e.g., Matt. 27:29). In Acts 1:16 and 20 Peter expresses the words of Psalm 69:25 in the singular to make the point that the supreme fulfillment of hostility to the psalmist is in Judas Iscariot's betrayal of Christ. The judgment on these enemies in 69:22–23 is applied in Romans 11:9–10 to the hardened enemies of Christ and his gospel.[2] The pouring out of God's wrath (Ps. 69:24) is echoed in Revelation 16:1 in the wider context of those who are enemies of Christ. The blotting out of names from the book of the living (Ps. 69:28; cf. Ex. 32:32–33) is echoed in Philippians 4:3 and Revelation 3:5; 13:8; 17:8; 20:12 and 15. The book of life is the Lamb's book of life (Rev. 13:8; 21:27), and those blotted out are enemies of Christ. Again and again, therefore, the New Testament declares that what David experiences is fulfilled in Christ and that the enemies are the enemies of Christ. After citing some of these New Testament references, Cassiodorus comments, "These verses, watchful reader, you will find written

---

1 Matt. 27:34 (poison or gall), 48; Mark 15:36; Luke 23:36 (sour wine); John 19:28–29 (thirst and sour wine).
2 For discussion of the unusual text form, see Seifrid, "Romans," in *CNTOT* 670.

in this psalm. So who could doubt that this psalm squares with the Lord's passion, when it is lent such notable and great authority for the expression of this meaning?"[3] Whatever else it is, Psalm 69 is above all about Christ.

Two questions arise in the psalm in connection with Christ as the singer: the admission of guilt in 69:5 and the ethics of the prayer for God's judgment on the enemies in 69:22–28. These are discussed below.

The New Testament also points us to the overflow of meaning, from Christ our head to Christ's church as his body: "David is a type of Christ but he also speaks for all God's people in their sufferings."[4] When Jesus speaks of those who hate him without cause (John 15:25), it is in the context of warning his church that they too will be hated without cause (see John 15:18–16:4). The hardened Jewish enemies of Christ in Romans 11 are also the hardened enemies of Christ's church. So while Christ speaks in the psalm, he does so not as a solitary individual but as our representative head. In so doing, he teaches us how to pray the psalm as his church.

In the concluding section of book 2, Psalms 69–71 are linked by the theme of disgrace (69:6; 70:2; 71:1, 13). This group sounds a note of suffering after the triumphant, universal tones of Psalms 65–68 and prepares the way for the perfect kingdom of Psalm 72. The sufferings of Jesus in his church continue until then (cf. Acts 9:4).[5]

There are important ties to Psalms 22 and 40 in book 1. Psalms 22 and 69 close with praise after deep suffering (22:22–31; 69:30–36). Echoes of Psalm 40 (part of which will be quoted almost verbatim in Ps. 70) include (1) sinking into mire (40:2; 69:2), (2) "more [in number] than the hairs of my head" (40:12; 69:4), and (3) sacrifices (40:6; 69:31).[6] The imagery of drowning (69:1–2) is similar to what Jonah voices in Jonah 2.

THE TEXT

Structure
There are significant parallels between Psalm 69:1–12 and 69:13–21, not least the echoing of language about waters and mud (69:1–3, 14–15). Since

---

3   Cassiodorus, *Psalms*, 2:141.
4   Eveson, *Psalms*, 1:420.
5   See Eveson, *Psalms*, 1:419; Robertson, *Flow of the Psalms*, 115.
6   Delitzsch calls Pss. 40 and 69 "twin psalms." Delitzsch, *Psalms*, 1:275.

69:21 ("*They* gave me . . .") leads in to the prayer for God to judge *them* in 69:22–28, it makes sense to take 69:1–12 and then 69:13–28 as the two main lament and prayer sections. Psalm 69:29 may be included as the conclusion of 69:13–28, but it also functions as a natural bridge into the praise section in 69:30–36.

Superscription

S   To the choirmaster:[7] according to Lilies.[8] Of David.[9]

The attribution **Of David** is echoed in Acts 1:16 and 20 and in Romans 11:9. There is much we do not know about David's troubles, and Psalm 69 seems to reflect some unknown distress for Zion and the cities of Judah (69:35). The psalm will have found striking echoes in the later trials of Hezekiah (in the Assyrian crisis), Jeremiah (e.g., the "mire" of 69:2; Jer. 38:6), and other faithful servants of God.

69:1–12 Christ Prays for His Resurrection and Therefore for the Resurrection of His Church

1   Save me, O God!
     For the waters have come up to my neck.
2   I sink in deep mire,
        where there is no foothold;
     I have come into deep waters,
        and the flood sweeps over me.
3   I am weary with my crying out;
        my throat is parched.
     My eyes grow dim
        with waiting for my God.

Psalm 69:1–3 draws us in to an experience like drowning (cf. 18:4–5, 16). The start of the first line (**Save me, O God!**) and the close of the last

7 See on Ps. 4.
8 See also on Pss. 45, 60, 80.
9 In Hebrew the superscription is verse 1; subsequent verse numbers are increased by one.

(with waiting for my God) bracket this section and are the most important parts. Jesus prays to the Father, as we now do in his name. The experience is terrifying, for "the bodily danger of a drowning man is but a shadow"[10] of what a man faces when he confronts death as the judgment of God. For the waters have come up to my neck (lit., "to soul").[11] The deep mire (slimy, disgusting)[12] is a place with no foothold, no chance of regaining control of my destiny. I am utterly helpless. As in Noah's flood, here is a man under the judgment of God.[13] His throat is parched, burning dry, with crying out in unanswered prayer; this goes on so long that his eyes—the symbol of life, energy, desire, and hope—grow dim as he waits and waits for God. Christ, like Jonah who typified him, sinks down into the depths of hell. This is what it felt like for him to walk on earth and supremely what it felt like to die on the cross for us. And yet, in the darkest moments, he cries out to the one who can save him from death (Heb. 5:7). In the overflow of his sufferings (Col. 1:24), his church must expect to feel echoes of his agony.

> 4   More in number than the hairs of my head
>   are those who hate me without cause;
>   mighty are those who would destroy me,
>   those who attack me with lies.
>   What I did not steal
>   must I now restore?

Psalm 69:4 spells out what the symbolism of the floodwaters meant for Christ. There are countless[14] and powerful enemies who are determined to destroy him (cf. Mark 3:6) and who use the weapons of the father of lies to do so (John 8:44). Their hatred is without cause, devoid of any justification (John 15:25); an entirely unjustified hatred of Christ is the essence

---

10 Dickson, *Psalms*, 1:411.

11 The word נֶפֶשׁ can mean "soul" (i.e., being) or "neck, throat." When the waters come up to my throat, my very being is under threat.

12 Mire may hint at the loathing Jesus felt for all sin and how truly disgusting it is. Bonar, *Psalms*, 207.

13 For the use of flood imagery for the judgment of God, including baptism, see Hamilton, *Psalms*, 1:616–17.

14 Although the enemies of Jesus in history could perhaps be counted, the head count of all who oppose Christ extends through history from Cain to the end of time.

of sin (e.g., John 15:22–24).[15] Christ drowns in floodwaters of deceit and hostility. The final line derives from the law in Leviticus 6:1–7; it has no explicit interrogative marker in Hebrew and may be translated either as a dismayed question (ESV) or a shocked statement (e.g., CSB: "Though I did not steal, I must repay"); the sense is much the same. It may refer to some specific false accusation against David, or it may perhaps be a shorthand for any false accusation.[16] As Augustine expresses it, "I committed no robbery, yet I was making restitution; I committed no sin, yet I was paying the penalty. Christ alone could make that claim, for only he had not robbed at all."[17] Indeed, he emptied himself of the riches that were rightfully his (Phil. 2:6–7). Christ's church must also expect to be falsely accused and to find itself drowning in life-threatening hatred.

5   O God, you know my folly;
     the wrongs I have done are not hidden from you.

The word **folly** means not a low IQ but sinful foolishness. It is easy to see what David means by **my folly** and **the wrongs I have done**, even though falsely accused in this one matter. But can Jesus Christ say this? Some say not and that this is one of the places where the type (sinful David) differs from his antitype (sinless Jesus).[18] More likely, this is an outworking of Christ being made sin for us (2 Cor. 5:21), as in other psalms expressing penitence (e.g., see on Pss. 6; 32; 38; 51). In Psalm 69:1–5 he bears the judgment of God against sinners, becoming the sinner for us.[19] When we pray 69:5 in Christ, we do so as those who are, in Martin Luther's words, *simul iustus et peccator*, confessing our sins yet recognizing that our sufferings can no longer be the punishment for our sins but are rather the overflow of the sufferings of Christ.

15 Hans-Joachim Kraus (1918–2000), *Theology of the Psalms*, trans. Keith Crim (Minneapolis: Augsburg, 1986), 191–92.
16 Ross, *Psalms*, 2:490.
17 Augustine, *Psalms*, 3:375.
18 E.g., Spurgeon, *Treasury*, 2.1:177. Calvin's suggestion that this is ironic (i.e., "You know 'my folly'—that there isn't any!") feels forced. Calvin, *Psalms*, 3:50–51.
19 Those who adopt this "imputational" view include Athanasius, *The Life of Antony and the Letter to Marcellinus*, trans. Robert C. Gregg, Classics of Western Spirituality (London: SPCK, 1980), 7; Luther, *Luther's Works*, 10:354; Dickson, *Psalms*, 1:413; Bonar, *Psalms*, 207; Bonhoeffer, *Prayerbook of the Bible*, 166. As Luther puts it, Christ "was stuck in our mud."

6   Let not those who hope in you be put to shame through me,
           O Lord God of hosts;
       let not those who seek you be brought to dishonor through me,
           O God of Israel.

Psalm 69:6 is arguably the most important verse in 69:1–12. For the first
time the church of Christ comes explicitly into view, described as **those who
hope in** God and **those who seek** God (the latter reappearing in 69:32).
The God we seek is described as **Lord** (sovereign over all), **God** (the covenant Lord), commander **of hosts** (invincible heavenly armies), and the
God of Israel, committed to his church. What can Christ mean by praying
that they will not be **put to shame** (i.e., come to objective disgrace, rather
than experience a subjective feeling of shame) or **be brought to dishonor**
because of him (**through me**)? The logic that accords with the rest of the
psalm is this: If God proves unfaithful to David, what hope can there be
for his people? If those who hate Christ, our covenant head, without valid
cause triumph in the end and destroy him, what hope can there be for his
church? In a similar vein, in the book of Esther, if Mordecai is destroyed,
will not all the Jews perish?[20] If it ends badly for him, it must end badly for
us.[21] In the end this is Christ praying for his resurrection, for only when
he is raised can we be sure that we will be raised with him. If Christ is not
raised, we of all people are most to be pitied (1 Cor. 15:12–19).

7   For it is for your sake that I have borne reproach,
           that dishonor has covered my face.

The term **reproach** means a scornful insult, public and scathing;[22] the
word reappears in Psalm 69:9–10 and 19–20.[23] It has the effect of "covering
the face" with dishonor, as though someone's dignity is covered up with

---

20 Wilson, *Psalms*, 1:951–52.
21 There are clear expressions of this logic in Eveson, *Psalms*, 1:421; Dickson, *Psalms*, 1:413; Calvin,
    Psalms, 3:53.
22 Wilson, *Psalms*, 1:952.
23 The phrase "the reproach of Christ" borne by Moses in Heb. 11:26 suggests that the overflow
    of these reproaches extends backward to the people of God before Christ as well as forward to
    the church of Christ in new covenant days. This echo is noted in Kraus, *Theology of the Psalms*,
    192.

scandal, besmirched with mud. They have thrown mud at Christ, and it has stuck. But—and this is the critical phrase—this is **for your sake**, that is, because of his loyalty to his Father. His church will have to learn to suffer dishonor "for the sake of the name" (3 John 7; cf. on Ps. 40:15–16 and the quotation in Rom. 8:36).

8   I have become a stranger to my brothers,
         an alien to my mother's sons.
9   For zeal for your house has consumed me,
         and the reproaches of those who reproach you have fallen
         on me.

Psalm 69:8 focuses on the loneliness of the Savior (cf. 31:11 and the loneliness of Job),[24] experienced by Jesus through the unbelief of his brothers and, more deeply still, by his betrayal and his disciples' desertion (e.g., John 6:66).

Psalm 69:9 goes to the heart of Christ's motivation, **zeal for your house**, for your honor, for your presence on earth, for "he burned with a holy zeal to maintain the Church, and at the same time the glory of God, with which it is inseparably connected."[25] David felt this zeal intensely (e.g., 2 Sam. 6), Jesus completely. This **has consumed me**, where the word has the double sense that (1) it is my consuming passion, the desire of my heart, and (2) it will, in the end, consume my life and lead me to death.[26] The **reproaches** of those who hate God will fall on God's Messiah, for their attitude toward Christ is inseparable from their attitude toward God (e.g., John 15:23). Christ's church also must learn to expect to walk the lonely road of faithfulness (Ps. 69:8) and pray to be consumed by a passionate zeal for Christ, his gospel, and his church, which is the house of God on earth. Christ's people must not be surprised when the world hates them.

10   When I wept and humbled my soul with fasting,
          it became my reproach.
11   When I made sackcloth my clothing,
          I became a byword to them.

24 See in Job 30 echoes of the loneliness, mockery, mire, and mud.
25 Calvin, *Psalms*, 3:54.
26 See Kraus, *Theology of the Psalms*, 192.

12   I am the talk of those who sit in the gate,
        and the drunkards make songs about me.

The ESV notes that the words **and humbled** in the first line are not in the Hebrew (lit., "And I wept with fasting, my soul"). It may be that **my soul** is a second nominative, "I, even I, wept in fasting" (cf. CSB: "I mourned and fasted"). The effect is much the same.

The first part of Psalm 69:10–11 describes weeping, **fasting**, and **sackcloth**, all signs of a heart that repents and leads a people in repentance. This was necessary for David as the head of his people, and it has been a characteristic of godly leaders ever since (e.g., Neh. 9; Dan. 9). It was a mark of John the Baptist. Although the earthly ministry of Jesus was marked by the joyful presence of the bridegroom, the heart of Jesus knew deep grief for sins and for sinners. In this psalm this godly sorrow is turned into **a reproach** (a reason for an insult) and **a byword** (CSB: a scathing "joke"). This **talk** (i.e., loud mockery)[27] extends (Ps. 69:12) from **those who sit in the gate** (i.e., the important people)[28] to **the drunkards** (i.e., the dregs of society);[29] nothing unites the world more than a shared scorn for Christ and his church. "Do you suppose, brothers and sisters," asks Augustine, "that this happened only to Christ? By no means. It happens to him every day in the persons of his members."[30]

In 69:1–12 Christ prays for his own resurrection in the face of death (69:1–5) as he endures the judgment of God against sinners, and he prays for his church (69:6) that by his resurrection they will experience resurrection and know that his sufferings were because of his guiltless zeal for the Father, as theirs ought to be today.

69:13–29 Christ Prays for the Final Judgment on His Impenitent Enemies

As Psalm 69:1–12 began with a vivid description of Christ's sufferings, 69:13–29 also begins with a description that rather closely echoes this theme (69:13–21).

---

27 Ross, *Psalms*, 2:501.
28 E.g., Ruth 4:1–2; for other examples, see Wilson, *Psalms*, 1:953n15.
29 In Hebrew there is an alliteration between "those who sit in the gate" and "those who drink strong drink."
30 Augustine, *Psalms*, 3:380.

13   But as for me, my prayer is to you, O Lord.
  At an acceptable time, O God,
   in the abundance of your steadfast love answer me in your
    saving faithfulness.

But as for me marks an emphatic contrast to the mockers of 69:9–12. As at
the start of 69:1, so here he begins with prayer (**My prayer is to you, O Lord**).
The **acceptable time** may refer to the time of the prayer ("I pray at an acceptable time," i.e., the time of my sufferings) or to a future time of answer. The
overwhelming focus on covenant love (**steadfast love**) and **saving faithfulness**
will continue through this section, as words of covenant love are piled one
on another. The prayer **Answer me** (69:13, 16–17) will be followed by one
petition after another in 69:14–18, which together press home the urgency
of Christ's need and now the need of his persecuted church.

14   Deliver me
  from sinking in the mire;
 let me be delivered from my enemies
  and from the deep waters.
15   Let not the flood sweep over me,
  or the deep swallow me up,
  or the pit close its mouth over me.

Psalm 69:14–15 closely echoes the imagery of drowning from 69:1–3,[31]
with the addition of **the pit** that might **close its mouth over me** if I die and
stay dead. Only resurrection will answer this cry, for Christ and now for
his church.

16   Answer me, O Lord, for your steadfast love is good;
  according to your abundant mercy, turn to me.
17   Hide not your face from your servant,
  for I am in distress; make haste to answer me.
18   Draw near to my soul, redeem me;
  ransom me because of my enemies!

---

31 The words for "mire" are synonyms; both appear together in Ps. 40:2: "miry bog."

The Father shows **steadfast love** that is **good** (unfailingly good) and **abundant mercy** to Christ in his distress (like a mother's tender compassion for the baby in her womb). The face of Christ is besmirched with the mud of sins (69:7b), and yet the Father's face will shine on him in his **distress** when he raises him from the dead. The **soul** (= "neck") that is threatened with drowning will know that the Father will draw near in redemption and ransom. Christ will be saved! And in that is the hope of his church.

> 19 You know my reproach,
>   and my shame and my dishonor;
>   my foes are all known to you.
> 20 Reproaches have broken my heart,
>   so that I am in despair.
>   I looked for pity, but there was none,
>   and for comforters, but I found none.
> 21 They gave me poison for food,
>   and for my thirst they gave me sour wine to drink.

In Psalm 69:19–21 Christ returns to a poignant description of his sin-bearing misery. Again, there is **reproach** (cf. 69:7, 9–10, 19–20) with **shame** (the shame he prays that his people will not endure at the end of their story, 69:6) and **dishonor**. We feel here the **broken . . . heart** of Christ, the intense loneliness as not even his three closest friends will stay awake with him in his trials (e.g., Mark 14:37). Instead of **comforters**, he is surrounded by those who give him **poison** (or "gall") and **sour wine** to intensify his sufferings with the agonies of poisoning. Nothing, but nothing, can be worse than what Christ endured on the cross. Psalm 69 helps us begin to feel this.

The reference in 69:21 to those who gave him poison leads to a sustained and strong prayer for God's judgment on them (69:22–28). (For general discussion of how we understand such prayers, see volume 1, *Introduction: Christ and the Psalms*.) Like the cry of the martyrs in Revelation 6:9–10, this prayer is against "those who have persistently shown themselves to be implacable opponents of God's anointed and therefore of God himself."[32]

---

32 Eveson, *Psalms*, 1:424.

Either the wrath of God for our sins falls on Christ, who alone can pray this prayer with purity, or it must fall on us.

One feature in this prayer is that the punishment fits the crime; there is a correspondence between what they have done to Christ and his church and what God will do to them if they remain in hardened impenitence.

22   Let their own table before them become a snare;
       and when they are at peace, let it become a trap.

The reference to **their own table before them** (cf. Ps. 23:5) is probably a way of speaking of the food they enjoy, as a metaphor for what they get in life to satisfy their appetites. As they have given poison and sour wine to Christ, so they will find **a snare** and **a trap** in all that they have desired. There is some uncertainty about the words **and when they are at peace**. It has been suggested that this may be linked to sacrificial meals over peace offerings (hence the parallel to **their own table before them**), or it may refer to those with whom they are at peace (CSB: "And let it be a trap for their allies").[33]

23   Let their eyes be darkened, so that they cannot see,
       and make their loins tremble continually.

As their persecution has caused the **eyes** of Christ to grow dim (Ps. 69:3), so theirs will **be darkened** as they lose appetite, desire, and life itself. The trembling of **their loins** corresponds to the misery they have caused to Christ. Psalm 69:22–23 is quoted in Romans 11:9–10 of hardened, unbelieving Israel, of those who are enemies (Rom. 11:28) of Christ and his church.

24   Pour out your indignation upon them,
       and let your burning anger overtake them.

The hot **indignation** and **burning anger** of God, which falls on God himself in Christ at the cross on behalf of all his people, will and must fall on all who refuse the atonement he has won.

33 For discussion, see Ross, *Psalms*, 2:492; VanGemeren, *Psalms*, 534; Goldingay, *Psalms*, 2:337; Hossfeld and Zenger, *Psalms*, 2:172nd.

25   May their camp be a desolation;
       let no one dwell in their tents.

Their camp and **their tents** are ways of speaking of their life in this age, fragile and dependent on God, even though they refuse to acknowledge this reality. The picture of a deserted campsite is eloquent of a failed life. Peter puts this in the singular in Acts 1:20 when speaking of Judas Iscariot as the supreme fulfillment of this prophecy and prayer.

26   For they persecute him whom you have struck down,
       and they recount the pain of those you have wounded.

The sufferings of Christ are, paradoxically, at the same time the judgment of God against sinners and the hateful expression of sinful people. Their persecution, although it is the definite plan of God (Acts 2:23), is nevertheless a culpable act for which they must be punished.

27   Add to them punishment upon punishment;
       may they have no acquittal from you.

Psalm 69:27 literally reads, "Give/add iniquity to their iniquity, so that they will not come into your righteousness" (cf. ESV mg.). God will, as it were, pile unrevealed iniquity onto their already known iniquity, that is, make it abundantly clear that they are wholly deserving of punishment and cannot hope to enter into God's righteousness, for they must reap what they sow if they will not come to Christ (Gal. 6:7). The CSB captures it well: "Charge them with crime on top of crime; / do not let them share in your righteousness."

28   Let them be blotted out of the book of the living;
       let them not be enrolled among the righteous.

The book of the living is a list of men and women who are alive. But it comes to designate a record of all who are granted the life of the age to come. In this second sense, to **be blotted out** means to be excluded from eternal life. If they do not enter into God's righteousness (Ps. 69:27), they cannot hope to **be enrolled among the righteous**. In the Psalms righteousness is always by faith. The unforgivable sin is to turn one's heart away from faith in Christ and to do so forever.

> 29   But I am afflicted and in pain;
>   let your salvation, O God, set me on high!

In 69:29 Christ returns to his affliction and pain and prays for God to **set** him **on high**.[34] This prayer is fulfilled in his resurrection and ascension (cf. 68:18; Eph. 1:20–21; Phil. 2:9).[35] For his church it will be the same.

69:30–36 Christ Leads His Church in Praise for the New Creation
Commenting on Psalm 69:30, Charles Spurgeon writes, "He who sang after the Passover, sings yet more joyously after the resurrection and ascension. He is, in very truth, 'the sweet singer of Israel.' He leads the eternal melodies, and all his saints join in chorus."[36]

> 30   I will praise the name of God with a song;
>   I will magnify him with thanksgiving.
> 31   This will please the LORD more than an ox
>   or a bull with horns and hoofs.
> 32   When the humble see it they will be glad;
>   you who seek God, let your hearts revive.
> 33   For the LORD hears the needy
>   and does not despise his own people who are prisoners.

Psalm 69:29 triggers a tremendous change of tone, from lament to praise. This comes in two parts. In the first (69:30–33) Christ praises God for his resurrection and ascension ("Set me on high!" 69:29) because he knows that **the humble** and **the needy**, those who are **prisoners** through the long entailments of sin, will **see it** (his resurrection) and **be glad**; those **who seek God** (for whom Christ prayed in 69:6) will experience the **revival** of their

---

34 The verb translated "set on high" also means "protect" (CSB, NIV) but with the sense of "setting on high, and therefore of putting in a position of safety." Harman, *Psalms*, 1:514.

35 Eveson, *Psalms*, 1:424.

36 Spurgeon, *Treasury*, 2.1:184.

hearts in their own distress, knowing from Christ's ascension that there is hope for them. As Spurgeon puts it, "Grateful hearts are always on the lookout for recruits. The standing consolation of the godly is the experience of their Lord, for as he is so are we also in this world; yea, moreover, his triumph has secured ours."[37]

This song of praise **will please the LORD more than an ox / or a bull with horns and hoofs** (i.e., in its entirety), for it is the sacrifice of thankful hearts. The exaltation of Christ guarantees that 69:33 is more than wishful thinking: Christ was a needy prisoner under the burden of our sins, and the Father heard his prayer; in Christ he will hear the prayer of Christ's church.

> [34]   Let heaven and earth praise him,
>   the seas and everything that moves in them.
> [35]   For God will save Zion
>   and build up the cities of Judah,
>   and people shall dwell there and possess it;
> [36]   the offspring of his servants shall inherit it,
>   and those who love his name shall dwell in it.

The call to **heaven and earth** to **praise** God for what he has done for Christ and what he will do for Christ's church echoes the motif of universal appeal that has been so prominent in earlier psalms (esp. Pss. 65–68). The inclusion of **the seas** perhaps hints that the terrifying waters and floods (69:1–3, 14–15) have been conquered by the victorious Christ. David Dickson rightly says of 69:34–36 that this is "a prophetical thanksgiving for the foreseen mercies which were to come to the church by Christ's procurement."[38]

The drama of Psalm 69 will lead the whole cosmos, groaning in futility (Rom. 8:19–22), to praise God for the revelation of the sons of God. The references to **Zion** and **the cities of Judah**, resonant after the exile, are symbolic in every age for the people of Christ in the new creation (see on Ps. 37).[39] This will be the inheritance of all his covenant **servants** (69:36;

---

37 Spurgeon, *Treasury*, 2.1:185.
38 Dickson, *Psalms*, 1:425.
39 The words "shall dwell there" in Ps. 69:35 echo "Your flock found a dwelling" in Ps. 68:10.

cf. Acts 20:28), described here beautifully as **those who love his name**, his revealed nature in his covenant promises. Christ loved this name and was himself this name incarnate.

REFLECTION AND RESPONSE

1. Hearing Psalm 69:1–29 as the words of Jesus Christ gives us a precious window into his suffering soul. Perhaps with a greater intensity than any except Psalm 22, this psalm fills out the "loud cries and tears" of Hebrews 5:7. As we meditate on it, our hearts are drawn to him in loving gratitude.

2. At the same time, we feel (from the logic of Ps. 69:6) how vital it is for us that Jesus Christ was raised from the dead. Had he not been, we of all people would be most to be pitied (1 Cor. 15:19). We thank God for his resurrection, knowing that this guarantees our own. After applying Psalm 69:29 to Christ, set on high, Spurgeon says this:

> O ye poor and sorrowful ones, lift up your heads, for as with your Lord so shall it be with you. You are trodden down to-day as the mire of the streets, but you shall ride upon the high places of the earth ere long; and even now ye are raised up together, and made to sit together in the heavenlies in Christ Jesus.[40]

3. In addition, albeit in a lesser manner, whenever a believer experiences a rescue from persecution, temptation, or suffering, his or her rescue encourages us all.

4. Psalm 69 helps us develop realistic expectations for the life of faith, that we should not be surprised when we feel we are drowning in the sorrows of this world, when we too are lonely in the midst of a world with very different values, and when we may be hated for his name.

5. When Psalm 69 has no resonances with us, we need especially to beware, for—as Luther put it—the church may be "assaulted by prosperity, by ease, by security, by strength,"[41] which sap our spiritual vitality. It is better to live in Psalm 69 than to view it dispassionately as a spectator.

40 Spurgeon, *Treasury*, 2.1:184.
41 Luther, *Luther's Works*, 10:351–53.

6. Let us remember to pray when we feel like drowning, for prayer is like gasping for breath above water.[42]

7. We must join our Messiah in the praises of Psalm 69:30–36, enjoying the assurance that our faithful God hears the needy and will not despise his people when they become prisoners (69:33) and that we will dwell with Christ in the new creation (69:35–36), accompanied by the praise of the whole restored cosmos (69:34).

---

42 Dickson, *Psalms*, 1:411.

Let us, then, shout these words with one voice: O God, give heed and help me; for as long as we are in this world we need his constant help. Whenever shall we not? Yet now most of all, when we are in distress, let us say it: O God, give heed and help me.

AUGUSTINE
Expositions of the Psalms

Versicle: "O God, make speed to save us."
Response: "O Lord, make haste to help us."

BOOK OF COMMON PRAYER
"Order for Evening Prayer"

Make haste, O God, my soul to bless!
My help and my deliv'rer thou;
Make haste, for I'm in deep distress,
My case is urgent; help me now.

CHARLES H. SPURGEON
The Treasury of David

PSALM 70

ORIENTATION

In Psalm 70—this crisp, lapidary psalm—Christ leads his church to cry urgently for God's help. The beauty and usefulness of the psalm lies in its concise and finely polished form. It encapsulates many of the themes of books 1 and 2 in brief and memorable compass.

The text is very close to the final section of Psalm 40 (40:13–17).[1] Unlike the other example of a psalm from book 1 repeated in the so-called Elohistic Psalter (notably Ps. 14 repeated in Ps. 53), this psalm does not consistently replace the covenant name of God (יְהוָה, *YHWH*) with the word "God" (אֱלֹהִים, *Elohim*). By comparison with Psalm 40:13–17, the covenant name is replaced in 70:1a and 70:4 but not in 70:1b. In 70:5a, though, "the Lord" (אֲדֹנָי, *Adonai*) is replaced by "God," and then in 70:5b "God" is replaced by the covenant name. So it is misleading to suggest that an editor has simply "Elohized" the verses from Psalm 40.

In four places Psalm 70 is crisper than the verses in Psalm 40. The first verb is omitted in the Hebrew of 70:1 (see below). The word "altogether" is omitted in 70:2. The verb "to snatch away" is omitted in 70:2. And the words "to me" are omitted in 70:3. None of these change the meaning, but they combine to increase the feeling of an urgent prayer.

Some think it likely that David, or a later editor, extracted and adapted the final verses of Psalm 40 to form Psalm 70,[2] others that David (or someone else) first wrote Psalm 70, which was later added as the conclusion of

---

1 In places the ESV translates the same Hebrew differently in these texts, which may give a misleading impression of changes. These are noted below.
2 E.g., Ross, *Psalms*, 2:512; Delitzsch, *Psalms*, 2:283.

Psalm 40.[3] Perhaps David—like many a poet—expressed similar sentiments in similar words at different times.[4] We cannot know.

Here I consider Psalm 70 in its context between Psalms 69 and 71.[5] So while some of the commentary repeats that on 40:13–17, I have endeavored to expound Psalm 70 as it stands and to treat it in its context near the end of book 2.

Psalm 70 picks up numerous motifs from Psalm 69. These may be summarized as follows:

1. Both psalms display a crying out to God, though while Psalm 69 voices a long and weary waiting (69:1–3), Psalm 70 calls to God with passionate urgency (70:1, 5).
2. The motif of shame in Psalm 69 (69:6, in which those who hope in God will be protected from it, and 69:19, in which the Messiah experiences it) will now be the destiny of those who reject the Messiah (70:2–3).
3. In both psalms the Messiah's life is threatened (69:4; 70:2).
4. In both psalms the Messiah is mocked (69:9–12; 70:3).
5. The people who seek God feature in both psalms (69:6, 32; 70:4).
6. Those who love God's name at the close of Psalm 69 (69:36) also love his salvation (70:4). The phrase "your salvation" appears in both psalms (69:29; 70:4).
7. The clause "But I am afflicted" (69:29) is identical in Hebrew to the clause "But I am poor" (70:5).
8. In both psalms the Messiah prays against his enemies (69:22–28; 70:2–3).

Psalm 70 gives the church a brief prayer that encapsulates the grand themes of Psalm 69.

Psalm 70 shares intriguing links with Psalm 38. These are the only two psalms with "for the memorial offering" in the superscription. The

---

3   E.g., Tate, *Psalms 51–100*, 204; Alter, *Psalms*, 242.
4   Hamilton uses his expositions to build on the theory that the psalms in books 1 and 2 track with the career of David and correspond to broadly consecutive incidents in his life; see Hamilton, *Psalms*, 1:619–20.
5   The many similarities with Ps. 71 will be considered there, together with the likelihood that Pss. 70 (with a superscription) and 71 (with no superscription) are meant to be taken together.

most evident parallels are the prayer "Make haste to help me" (38:22; 70:1; 71:12) and the references to "those who seek my life . . . my hurt" (38:12; 70:2).[6]

THE TEXT

Structure

Psalm 70:1 and 5 bracket the psalm with urgent cries for help.[7] In between, 70:2–3 focuses on the enemies and 70:4 on all the Messiah's people.

Superscription

S   To the choirmaster.[8] Of David, for the memorial offering.[9]

The word translated **for the memorial offering** (shared with Ps. 38:S) is literally "to bring to remembrance."[10] The "memorial portion" (Lev. 2:2; 24:7) was part of a sacrificial food offering, linked to incense (and hence, to prayer), crying to God to remember and act in mercy in accordance with his covenant (cf. Lev. 24:8). Whether or not the sacrificial association is intended, it is likely that the aim is to bring the penitent believer to God's remembrance.[11] This may be done in the context of confession of wrongdoing (e.g., Gen. 41:9) or of bringing the needs of his people before God (Isa. 62:6); the latter seems more likely here.

70:1 The Messiah Leads His Church in an Urgent Cry for God's Help

1   Make haste, O God, to deliver me!
       O LORD, make haste to help me!

---

6   Tate lists common language and links between Pss. 22, 35, 38, 40, 69, 70, 71, 102. Tate, *Psalms 51–100*, 204–5.
7   This is "a thematic inclusio." Wilson, *Psalms*, 1:967.
8   See on Ps. 4.
9   In Hebrew the superscription is verse 1; subsequent verse numbers are increased by one.
10 לְהַזְכִּיר, hiphil infinitive construct of זכר. The same form appears in 1 Chron. 16:4 (ESV: "to invoke"). The NIV rendering, "a petition," assumes, probably rightly, that the import of bringing to remembrance is to cry to God to help, which is what the psalm does.
11 Delitzsch, *Psalms*, 2:20; Kirkpatrick, *Psalms*, 1:198; Eveson, *Psalms*, 1:240.

The first **make haste** is supplied from the second line by the translator because there is no verb in the first line, which reads literally, "O God, to deliver me." Psalm 40:13 begins, "Be pleased ... to deliver me." The sense is much the same, but perhaps the omission of the verb "be pleased" conveys a greater urgency.[12] This is an urgent cry given on earth by the Messiah, who knew his desperate need (cf. Heb. 5:7). It teaches us to ask God for that same sense of heartfelt urgency in our prayers.

70:2–3 This Cry Focuses, First, on the Forces That Oppose Christ and His Church

2   Let them be put to shame and confusion
     who seek my life!
  Let them be turned back and brought to dishonor
     who delight in my hurt!
3   Let them turn back because of their shame
     who say, "Aha, Aha!"

Three parallel petitions are followed by three descriptions of those against whom the Messiah and his church must pray. That the whole church is prayed for in Psalm 70:4 presses home to us that when the Messiah prays for himself, he never prays for himself alone but for himself as our covenant head.[13] When they **seek my life**, they persecute all my church (cf. Acts 9:4); when they **delight in my hurt**, it is all Christ's church that they wish to damage; when they **say, "Aha, Aha!"** it is the whole church that they mock. The exclamation **Aha!** indicates a malicious triumph over the downfall of Christ and his people, thrown most cruelly in the face of Jesus on the cross (cf. Ps. 35:21; Ezek. 25:3; 26:2; Mark 15:29).[14]

Christ prays that the **shame** to which they sought to put him (cf. Ps. 69:19) and that he endured so that his people's lives will not end in shame (69:6) must and will come on his finally impenitent enemies. The verb **put to ... confusion** is the same as "disappointed" in 40:14; it means

12   Eveson, *Psalms*, 1:429.
13   Eveson, *Psalms*, 1:429.
14   For the possible etymology and the meaning of the exclamation הֶאָח, see Dahood, *Psalms*, 1:215; Ross, *Psalms*, 1:870.

that their plots will end in failure. There is also a sense in which every man and woman who is converted experiences in this life the shame and confusion of realizing that he or she has been going the wrong way; we pray that many more will experience these things in this life before it is too late, as we have.[15]

70:4 This Cry Focuses, Second, on the Overflow of Christ's Rescue to His Church

> 4   May all who seek you
>   rejoice and be glad in you!
>   May those who love your salvation
>   say evermore, "God is great!"

There is a contrast between those who **seek** the life of the Messiah (Ps. 70:2) and those here, the members of his church, who **seek you** (God; cf. 69:6, 32). The one group seeks to destroy the Messiah, the other to enter God's presence by means of the Messiah. This contrast of motivation issues in a contrast of destiny: the one dribbles away into shame; the other climaxes in gladness. This joy is **in you**, focused entirely on the God who has saved them. These, who have loved the name (the revelation of God in Christ, 69:36), also **love** his **salvation** (cf. "loved his appearing," 2 Tim. 4:8). Their song is not to chant, "We are great," but to **say evermore**,[16] "**God is great!**"[17] They have pinned all their hopes on God's faithfulness to them in Christ, and they will not be disappointed.

70:5 The Messiah Leads His Church in an Urgent Cry for God's Help

> 5   But I am poor and needy;
>   hasten to me, O God!
>   You are my help and my deliverer;
>   O LORD, do not delay!

<hr/>

15 Augustine, *Psalms*, 3:403.

16 The word "evermore" is the same in Hebrew as "continually" in Ps. 40:16 ESV.

17 If יִגְדַּל is a jussive, the meaning would be "Let God be great!" (i.e., let his greatness be seen and acknowledged). The effect is much the same.

The final verse is very personal, prayed by Jesus on earth and now by each of us. **But I** is emphatic.[18] The pairing **poor and needy** is a common way of speaking of "the oppressed righteous believers" (e.g., Pss. 9:18; 12:5; 35:10).[19] This is our normal condition; we are in great danger when we feel otherwise.[20]

REFLECTION AND RESPONSE

1. It is a healthy discipline to think of Jesus praying this psalm with all its urgency in his times of prayer with the Father. Meditate (Ps. 70:2–3) on the forces arrayed against him. Ponder the love with which he prays for his church (70:4), loving each one for whom he will die (cf. "who loved me and gave himself for me," Gal. 2:20).

2. As we identify with the church under pressure (cf. 2 Cor. 11:29) and expect pressure in our experience (cf. Acts 14:22; 2 Tim. 3:12), we pray this prayer for ourselves and all the church. Augustine vividly describes Lazarus (in the parable of Luke 16:19–31) as "a type of God's Church" because he is in such desperate need of God's salvation.[21]

3. We need to consider, from Psalm 70:2–3, what are the particular ways in which the world, the flesh, and the devil attack each one of us today. Although in principle this hostility is unchanging, its particular manifestations vary from age to age and from place to place.

4. Psalm 70:4 prompts us to ask if our hearts are filled with a deep seeking for God and warmed by a strong love for his salvation and to pray that God will work these things more deeply in our hearts by the Spirit of Christ, that we too may have this exultant joy and gladness that our Savior God is very great.

5. Above all, the cry "Help me *now*! Help us *now*!" ought to give passion to our prayers both individually and when we pray together. Psalm 70 helps us never pray halfheartedly, as though it didn't really matter.

---

18 This is the same in Hebrew as "as for me" in Ps. 40:17 ESV.
19 Harman, *Psalms*, 1:342n14.
20 Eveson quotes H. L. Ellison (1903–1983): "The Christian is never in greater peril than when he speaks as in Revelation 3:17." Eveson, *Psalms*, 1:259.
21 Augustine, *Psalms*, 3:409.

[Christ] speaks of himself . . . to the Father in this psalm [i.e.,
Psalm 71]. . . . [For] almost all the psalms that prophesy of
the person of Christ, represent the Son as conversing with the
Father—that is, represent Christ [as speaking] to God.

TERTULLIAN
Against Praxeas

The Almighty Lord, who is a most strong tower to all them
that put their trust in him, to whom all things in heaven, in
earth, and under the earth, do bow and obey, be now and
evermore thy defence; and make thee know and feel, that
there is none other Name under heaven given to man, in
whom, and through whom, thou mayest receive health and
salvation, but only the Name of our Lord Jesus Christ. Amen.

BOOK OF COMMON PRAYER
"Order for the Visitation of the Sick," said by
the minister after he reads Psalm 71

He that hath had long experience of God's mercy to himself,
and thankfully acknowledgeth the same, may assure himself
that the course of God's kindness to him shall not be broken
off. . . . And he who in trouble hath seen his own infirmity,
emptiness, and death, may look to see God's power and
life in raising him out of the grave of his trouble.

DAVID DICKSON
A Commentary on the Psalms

PSALM 71

ORIENTATION

There are seasons when we are acutely conscious of time passing and life fading. Aging is perhaps the most common of these. In such an autumn of life, the believer may feel fragile in faith and fearful for the future. In Psalm 71, a precious psalm, Jesus Christ, who knew all this in the premature aging he bore for our sins, gives to each believer passionate prayers to pray and confident praises to voice. He shows us how to ask to be kept to the end and to thank God that he has promised to keep us in covenant with him in Christ. In Christ the eternal God, the Creator of time, entered time for us. Jesus Christ alone is the same, yesterday, today, and forever (Heb. 13:8). He it is who has brought life and immortality to light by the gospel (2 Tim. 1:10).

The theme of time infuses almost every verse: time past, going right back to the believer's beginnings, "from my youth" (Ps. 71:5, 17), "from before my birth" (71:6); time present, marked by the words and phrases "never" (71:1), "continually" (71:3, 6, 14), "more and more" (71:14), "all the day" (71:8, 15), "all the day long" (71:24), and "still"[1] (71:17); and time future, looking forward in "hope" (71:5) to "the time of old age / . . . when my strength is spent" (71:9), "even to old age and gray hairs" (71:18) and, beyond that, to "another generation, / . . . all those to come" (71:18). This theme also links the blending of prayer (prominent in 71:1–13) and praise (predominant in 71:14–24); in Christ, because we pray in accordance with the will of God, we therefore praise in anticipation of the answers to our prayers. Praise and prayer blend in the presence of the eternal God.

---

1 Lit., "until now." The NIV rendering, "to this day," is a paraphrase.

The psalm has no superscription. Some consider that it was by David partly because it shares many connections with Psalms 69 and 70 and with several other Davidic psalms[2] and also because the few "orphan" psalms in books 1 and 2 are marked by close connection to the preceding psalm (Pss. 2 with 1; 10 with 9; 33 with 32; and 43 with 42). Those who see in the flow of books 1 and 2 a tracking through the life of King David comment on the appropriateness of Psalm 71 if it was spoken by David near the end of his life.[3]

Psalms 69, 70, and 71 form a subgroup within book 2. For links between Psalms 69 and 70, see on Psalm 70. Links between Psalms 70 and 71 include the following: (1) the plea "make haste to help me" (70:1, 5; 71:12), (2) the request that his enemies be shamed (70:2; 71:13, 24), (3) the word "evermore/continually" (70:4; 71:3, 6, 14),[4] (4) praise that God is great or powerful (70:4; 71:18), and (5) enemies who "seek my hurt" (70:2; 71:13, 24).

These links do not demonstrate that the author was David, but they show that he shared with David many characteristics; indeed, "the first person singular statements throughout have a Davidic feel."[5] The writer has a strong relationship with the covenant Lord (71:1), who has given a command to save him (71:3), who will not forsake him (a covenant verb), who shows him "faithfulness" and "righteousness" (71:2, 15 [lit., "your righteousness"], 16, 19, 24). He has a "greatness" that God will increase (71:21), and he has many enemies (71:4, 10–13, 24). All this was true of David the anointed king.

It is usually asserted that the writer is already an old man. He has clearly suffered "many troubles and calamities" (71:20). But we cannot be sure he was what we usually call old (relative to the life expectancy of his day); it is more accurate to say that he is aware of increasing frailty. Age is not a matter simply of numbers of years. It comes gradually or suddenly, sooner or later.

---

2 For some of the many echoes from other Davidic psalms, note Pss. 71:1–3 with 31:1–3; 71:5–6, 17, with 22:9–10; 71:12a with 22:1, 11, 19; 71:12b with 38:22 and 40:13; 71:13 with 35:4, 26; 71:18b with 22:30–31; 71:19a with 36:5 (these are adapted and corrected from Tate, *Psalms 51–100*, 211). I will not comment on these in the exposition, which will focus on the words as they now stand in Ps. 71.

3 One who follows this "tracking" consistently is James Hamilton. He thinks it likely that Ps. 71 is prompted by the troubles with Adonijah near the end of David's life (see 1 Kings 1), which makes the Solomon connection in Ps. 72 especially appropriate. Hamilton, *Psalms*, 1:625.

4 The Hebrew word תָּמִיד is translated "evermore" by the ESV in Ps. 70:4 and "continually" in 71:3, 6, 14.

5 Hamilton, *Psalms*, 1:621.

One may be young at seventy-five or old at thirty-three. As the parallelism of 71:9 indicates, "the time of old age" corresponds to "when my strength is spent." There is a sense in which Jesus, even though he died in his early thirties, knew what it was to age prematurely, to see his powers decline, for "*his* old age was ere he reached three-and-thirty years," for "in effect he did pass through that stage of our sojourning, worn out and wasted in bodily frame and feeling, by living so much in so short a time."[6]

Some argue that the "individual" psalmist is really the nation of Israel or Judah. Although this is very unlikely to be the original meaning,[7] it is true that the people of God owe their creation or birth to the covenant Lord (e.g., 95:6) and grow through time. In seasons when the church of Christ experiences a loss of strength, this psalm has a poignant appropriateness. In Christ the so-called "national" reading blends with the individual reading, for Christ here leads his church corporately, and each believer individually, in a beautiful psalm redolent of the poignancy of our failing powers.

Philip Eveson comments, "In that Psalm 71 echoes themes and phrases from Psalm 22 we can, through the troubles that afflicted David and from which he was delivered, see shadows of what Jesus experienced when he was greatly troubled even to the death of the cross."[8]

THE TEXT

Structure

There is no clear structure, as is evident in the wide variation of suggestions. For simplicity, I take Psalm 71:1–13 first, in which prayer predominates, and then 71:14–24, dominated by praise.

71:1–13 Christ Leads His Church in a Prayer to Be Kept to the End

> 1   In you, O LORD, do I take refuge;
>   let me never be put to shame!

---

6 Bonar, *Psalms*, 211. Bonar suggests that the surprising words "You are not yet *fifty* years old" (John 8:57) are spoken to a man who has aged beyond his years.

7 It is much more likely that a psalm focused on an individual's experience was later adopted for national use. Kirkpatrick, *Psalms*, 2:409.

8 Eveson, *Psalms*, 1:436.

2   In your righteousness deliver me and rescue me;
       incline your ear to me, and save me!
3   Be to me a rock of refuge,
       to which I may continually come;
    you have given the command to save me,
       for you are my rock and my fortress.

In you, O Lord (highlighting the covenant relationship with the covenant name—relatively rare in this section of the Psalter), **do I take refuge.** The verb is perfect in form and can also be translated "I take, or have taken, refuge," that is, habitually and definitively. The word **never** ("not ever") introduces the motif of time right at the start. I pray, as Christ prayed, not to **be put to shame** (objectively), not in the past, not now, not ever. **In your righteousness,** that covenant righteousness that always keeps the promises, **deliver me** (i.e., snatch me out of the jaws of my predators) **and rescue me** (bring the liberated prey safely out of danger) **and save me** (right to the end).[9] In Psalm 71:3 **a rock of refuge** ought probably to be translated "a rock of habitation," that is, a solid place where I can dwell.[10] The word **continually** keeps up the emphasis on a salvation that has begun, will be continued without pause, and will be completed without fail (cf. Phil. 1:6). The confident statement[11] **you have given the command**—perhaps to the heavenly armies—**to save me** can be made only by one who knows he is in secure covenant with God, as Jesus Christ knew he was with the Father, as David knew through his covenant of sonship that foreshadowed that between Christ and the Father, and as we may know in Christ.

4   Rescue me, O my God, from the hand of the wicked,
       from the grasp of the unjust and cruel man.

---

9 These nuances of the verbs are suggested by Wilson, *Psalms*, 1:969.

10 The MT has מָעוֹן, "dwelling place." Some Hebrew manuscripts follow the parallel in Ps. 31 and read מָעוֹז, "a place of protection," hence "a rock of refuge." It is better to follow the MT; cf. Harman, *Psalms*, 1:522; Ross, *Psalms*, 2:517n4.

11 Some, including the CSB and NIV, take the perfect tense as precative (expressing a request, "Give the command"), presumably because of the preceding and following imperatives; see also Goldingay, *Psalms*, 2:363. This smooths the reading and is possible, although it seems to me that a statement of what God has done is more likely. If it is a request, it is "in keeping with the promises God has made to David and his seed." Hamilton, *Psalms*, 1:621.

⁵   For you, O Lord, are my hope,
         my trust, O Lᴏʀᴅ, from my youth.
⁶   Upon you I have leaned from before my birth;
         you are he who took me from my mother's womb.
     My praise is continually of you.
⁷   I have been as a portent to many,
         but you are my strong refuge.
⁸   My mouth is filled with your praise,
         and with your glory all the day.

The plea continues in Psalm 71:4, in which the singular (**the wicked, the unjust and cruel man**) is presumably generic, emphasizing the oppressive and unfair nature of each instantiation of hostility to God's anointed (whether David in type or Christ in antitype) and any or all of his church. The words **hope** and **from my youth** in 71:5 point forward and back in time, the latter (with 71:6, 17) giving us "precious glimpses . . . of Messiah's childhood."[12] The words **Lord** (sovereign one) and **Lᴏʀᴅ** (covenant Lord) heighten the sense of greatness of the one to whom we turn.[13] Psalm 71:6 expands on "from my youth" in 71:5, going right back to **before my birth** (lit., "from the womb"), acknowledging that it is God **who took me** (lit., "cut me," i.e., cut my umbilical cord to launch me on a life of dependence on him)[14] **from my mother's womb**. The verb **have leaned** indicates objective dependence more than necessarily a subjective acknowledgment of this, which is problematic in utero.[15] The note of **praise—continually** and **all the day** (71:6, 8)—grows in volume near the end of the psalm.

The unusual word translated **portent** means a sign that causes wonder and amazement, sometimes because it is astonishingly good but more often because it shockingly demonstrates the judgment of God (e.g., "sign," 1 Kings 13:5; "a wonder," Deut. 28:46).[16] Here the context may suggest that the psalmist—and

---

12 Bonar, *Psalms*, 213.

13 The position of the *athnach* accent in the Masoretic pointing suggests that the titles should be read together, "Lord Gᴏᴅ," in the second line of the verse ("For you are my hope / O Lord Gᴏᴅ, my trust from my youth").

14 The NIV rendering, "brought me forth," is less likely; see the critique in Harman, *Psalms*, 1:523n2.

15 The verb is the niphal of סמך. Goldingay has "I have been upheld"; Goldingay, *Psalms*, 2:363. The NASB reads, "I have been sustained."

16 A "dreadful sign of divine punishment." Wilson, *Psalms*, 1:971. Some argue for a positive meaning, e.g., Longman, *Psalms*, 268; Alter, *Psalms*, 245.

certainly the Lord Jesus—is "a sign that is opposed" (Luke 2:34), one who bears in his body the marks of the judgment of God (cf. Gal. 6:17) and is regarded as forsaken by God (cf. Ps. 71:11). James Hamilton says that David (whom he thinks is the psalmist), like Joseph and Moses before him, "would appear to affirm that his own life is an installment in the pattern of the righteous sufferer, who is persecuted before being exalted to deliver God's people."[17] Philip Eveson perceptively raises the possibility that he may be at the same time a warning of God's judgment and an example of God's rescue.[18]

The word **glory** (71:8; תִּפְאָרֶת, *tiphereth*) means radiance or splendor;[19] the beauty of God is seen, paradoxically, most clearly in the sufferings of the Son and then in the overflow of those sufferings in his people (Col. 1:24).

> 9 Do not cast me off in the time of old age;
>   forsake me not when my strength is spent.

The verbs **cast off** and **forsake** speak of covenant curse, and there can be nothing worse than that in this age or in eternity. In **old age**,[20] when our **strength is spent**, then of all times we must rely on the grace of God in Christ, for then it is abundantly clear that we can contribute nothing. The doctrine of "grace alone" is never more needed than in a geriatric or dementia ward. Augustine asks, "Why be afraid that he may desert you, that he may toss you aside in your old age, when your strength has failed? That is precisely the time when his strength will be in you, when your own is gone."[21]

> 10 For my enemies speak concerning me;
>   those who watch for my life consult together
> 11 and say, "God has forsaken him;
>   pursue and seize him,
>   for there is none to deliver him."

---

17 Hamilton, *Psalms*, 1:626.
18 Eveson, *Psalms*, 1:433–34.
19 *HALOT*, s.v. תִּפְאָרֶת.
20 "Old age" (זִקְנָה) "points more to bodily weakness, rather than great age." Harman, *Psalms*, 1:523n3. Apart from the two occurrences in this psalm (71:9, 18), the others are Gen. 24:36 (Sarah beyond childbearing), 1 Kings 11:4 (Solomon), 1 Kings 15:23 (Asa diseased in his feet), and Isa. 46:4.
21 Augustine, *Psalms*, 3:422–23.

The **enemies** are described as **those who watch for my life** (lit., "watchers of my soul"), clearly hostile watchers (cf. Mark 3:2).[22] Their message, if true, is terrible: **God has forsaken him**. Although Jesus cries the cry of dereliction (Ps. 22:1), forsakenness is not the Father's last word. The confident claim **There is none to deliver him** is eloquently contradicted on Easter morning. Ever since then, the persecutors of the church have said the same; resurrection day will prove them wrong.

> 12   O God, be not far from me;
>   O my God, make haste to help me!
> 13   May my accusers be put to shame and consumed;
>   with scorn and disgrace may they be covered
>   who seek my hurt.

The move from **O God** to **O my God** emphasizes again the unbreakable covenant bond. **My accusers** are literally "the satans of my soul" (NASB: "those who are adversaries of my soul").

71:14–24 Christ Leads His Church in Joyful Praise That God Will Keep Us to the End

> 14   But I will hope continually
>   and will praise you yet more and more.

Hope based on the covenant promises that belong to Christ as Son and belong to us in Christ may be enjoyed **continually** and should issue in **praise** that grows with every year of the believer's life, **more and more**. For the prayers prayed in Psalm 71:1–13 are predicated on covenant promises, given by the Father to Christ and to all who belong to him.

> 15   My mouth will tell of your righteous acts,
>   of your deeds of salvation all the day,
>   for their number is past my knowledge.
> 16   With the mighty deeds of the Lord GOD I will come;
>   I will remind them of your righteousness, yours alone.

---

22 The NIV rendering, "those who wait to kill me," catches the sense, if somewhat periphrastically.

Psalm 71:15–16 expands on 71:14b. **Your righteous acts** is literally "your righteousness," and **your deeds of salvation**, "your salvation," for covenant righteousness always issues in covenant salvation for Christ the Son and all who are in him. The phrase **all the day** continues the motif of time. The word translated **number** uses a word that is probably cognate with the verb **tell** (i.e., recount); probably (as the ESV here and most English versions) it has the sense of an uncountable number of wonderful acts of covenant righteousness (NASB: "For I do not know the sum *of them*"; cf. John 21:25). The verb **I will come**[23] is explained by the parallel line **I will remind them** (lit., "I will cause to be remembered"); that is, I will come (to the people of God) to cause the righteousness of God to be remembered as it is seen in the salvation of Christ by the Father and the salvation of all who are in Christ. Peter echoes the urgency of bringing salvation to mind in 2 Peter 1:12–15.

> [17]   O God, from my youth you have taught me,
>   and I still proclaim your wondrous deeds.
> [18]   So even to old age and gray hairs,
>   O God, do not forsake me,
>   until I proclaim your might to another generation,
>   your power to all those to come.

Psalm 71:17–18 again sweeps from the past (**my youth**) to the future (**old age and gray hairs**) with a confident proclamation of **wondrous deeds** of salvation (supremely the resurrection of Christ and his people). The saving **might** of God in the gospel is proclaimed **to another generation** as the power of God to save sweeps on through the ages of human history.

> [19]   Your righteousness, O God,
>   reaches the high heavens.
>   You who have done great things,
>   O God, who is like you?
> [20]   You who have made me see many troubles and calamities
>   will revive me again;

---

23 The NIV rendering, "I will come and proclaim," adds the verb "proclaim," for which there is no textual evidence. Harman, *Psalms*, 1:525.

from the depths of the earth
   you will bring me up again.
21   You will increase my greatness
   and comfort me again.

The phrase **reaches the high heavens** (lit., "reaches the heights") suggests that the covenant righteousness of God is beyond being threatened by the vagaries of history or the opposition of persecutors. The question **Who is like you?** may echo the Song by the Sea (Ex. 15:11), for the work of sovereign grace is incomparable. The **many troubles and calamities** were much in evidence in the lives of David and Old Testament believers, reached their climax in the troubles of Jesus, and overflow into the sufferings of his church. The phrase **the depths of the earth** (the subterranean waters where Sheol is; cf. Job 26:5–6; Pss. 33:7; 63:9) points beyond the troubles of this life to death itself, from which to be **revived . . . again**[24] is nothing less than bodily resurrection.[25] The **greatness** of Jesus the covenant Son is the supreme greatness that God will **increase** as he gives to the church the promise of greatness in Christ and all the warmth bound up in the verb **comfort**.

22   I will also praise you with the harp
      for your faithfulness, O my God;
   I will sing praises to you with the lyre,
      O Holy One of Israel.
23   My lips will shout for joy,
      when I sing praises to you;
      my soul also, which you have redeemed.
24   And my tongue will talk of your righteous help all the day long,
      for they have been put to shame and disappointed
         who sought to do me hurt.

The final verses continue to pile up covenant terms (**your faithfulness . . . my God . . . Holy One of Israel . . . redeemed . . . your righteous help**

---

24 "Revive" is literally "restore . . . to life."
25 Hamilton, *Psalms*, 1:627.

[lit., "your righteousness"]) and bring the psalm to a close with a crescendo of vocal and musical praise (**the harp . . . the lyre . . . shout for joy . . . sing praises . . . my tongue**). The verb **talk** (Ps. 71:24) is the verb "to mutter, meditate" (הָגָה, *hagah*), first used in Psalms 1 and 2.

REFLECTION AND RESPONSE

1. Many of the phrases of Psalm 71 echo other psalms; it is easy to let them wash over us. But casting ourselves on God, in the emphatic words of 71:1–3, is, as Augustine notes, an acknowledgment of the sovereign grace of God. For "the message that resounds from nearly every syllable [is] that God's grace is entirely gratuitous, that it sets us free, . . . not in response to any efforts we make, but by God's own act."[26]

2. The most poignant references to frailty make this a precious psalm for all whose powers are weakening and all who sit by the bedside of one whose powers have failed. They give us words of urgent prayer and glad praise. As Augustine encouraged his hearers, "Do not be afraid of being cast aside in your time of weakness, when old age comes upon you. Was your Lord not reduced to weakness on the cross?"[27]

3. Those from Christian homes who can never remember a time when they did not love and trust Jesus can gladly speak in the words of this psalm of a dependence on God from before their birth. But those of us converted in childhood or adulthood may also make these phrases ours when we recognize that our conversion is evidence of an eternal election of God, such that all our days were written in his book before one of them came to be. We may not have been consciously depending on God until we were converted, any more than a Christian from childhood was consciously depending on God in the womb, but the God who has called us in Christ is the God who has watched over and determined all our days, before and after conversion.

4. The reference to "many troubles and calamities" (Ps. 71:20) encourages the suffering believer and the struggling church. We believe that God will revive us, whether in this age or in resurrection.

26   Augustine, *Psalms*, 3:413.
27   Augustine, *Psalms*, 3:422.

5. We determine to pass on the message to the next generation and are motivated, as parents and as churches, to keep proclaiming this gospel to all who will hear.

Jesus shall reign where'er the sun
Doth his successive journeys run;
His kingdom stretch from shore to shore,
Till moons shall wax and wane no more.

ISAAC WATTS
"Jesus Shall Reign"

Hail to the Lord's Anointed,
Great David's greater Son!
Hail, in the time appointed,
His reign on earth begun!
He comes to break oppression,
To set the captive free;
To take away transgression,
And rule in equity.

JAMES MONTGOMERY
"Hail to the Lord's Anointed"

In this psalm, under the shadow of king Solomon's
reign, Christ's gracious government is praised.

DAVID DICKSON
A Commentary on the Psalms

PSALM 72

ORIENTATION

The prayer in Psalm 72 is for desperate people and those who care for them, for those who are poor in spirit, for all who have no one to help them, for the ones who yearn for good government. It teaches us the kind of government we ought to long for. But more than that, it assures us that when we pray for this dominion, our prayers will be answered in, and only in, Jesus Christ. That the psalm is messianic was recognized in the Targum, which translates the opening words, "O God, give your judgments to the king messiah."[1]

The psalm speaks of Christ, who is the one greater than Solomon (Matt. 12:42). Many of the patristic writers emphasize its prophetic nature. The psalm speaks, they insist, not of Solomon but of Christ. In a sustained treatment of Psalm 72, Justin Martyr (ca. 100–165), writing in dialogue with a Jew, insists that while "you erroneously think" this psalm "refers to your king Solomon," the reality is that it "refers to our Christ," because "it is equally evident to all that none of the things foretold in the . . . psalm happened to him, for not all the kings adored him, nor did his power extend to the ends of the earth, nor did his enemies fall down prostrate before him and lick the ground."[2] Athanasius says that Psalm 72 prophesies that Christ "would come as judge over all" and that "Psalms 21, 50 and 72 indicate his kingdom and his power for judging as well as the advent of his incarnation for us and the calling of the gentiles."[3] Origen writes that Psalm 72 clearly "prophesies of

---

1 Hossfeld and Zenger, *Psalms*, 2:220.
2 Justin Martyr, *Dialogue with Trypho*, trans. Thomas B. Falls, rev. Thomas P. Halton, ed. Michael Slusser, FC 6 (Washington, DC: Catholic University of America Press, 2003), 34.1–7; cf. 64.5–6, 121.1.
3 Athanasius, *Marcellinus*, 8, 26.

Christ."[4] Both Augustine and Theodoret of Cyrus insist that it must point to Christ.[5] These writers stress fulfillment in Christ, and rightly so.

The psalm has much resonance with the reign of Solomon at its apogee.[6] It continued to speak to all his successors; every Davidic king would have Psalm 72 hovering like a glorious shadow over his reign, calling him higher and at the same time speaking to him of the need for a perfect Messiah. John Calvin observes that the reigns of these kings were "only a type and shadow" of "something far superior"; they were part of a "succession which had its end and its complete accomplishment in Christ." The psalm was given so that "from this typical kingdom they might be conducted to Christ."[7]

For always—sometimes scandalously, often tragically—the reality fell short of the prophecy. This was true of David, Solomon, and all their successors. It was true of the kings in the northern kingdom. It was true of the apostles and is true of their heirs as church leaders. It holds true for every human being who wields authority. Only Jesus Christ fully answers the call of this psalm. Alexander Francis Kirkpatrick thus argues that, reaching "far beyond" any human power, Psalm 72

> presents a picture of the kingdom of God upon earth in its ideal character of perfection and universality. It is . . . not only a prayer and a hope but a prophecy. As each successive king of David's line failed to realise the ideal, it became clearer and clearer that its words pointed forward to One who was to come, to the true "Prince of Peace."[8]

So it is not that Psalm 72 speaks words that, as it were, take off into the Scriptures only to land with Christ but rather that it speaks words with existential power all down the centuries before Christ and continues to speak

---

4 Origen, *Commentary on the Gospel of John*, 1.193, in *ACCS* 8:94.

5 Augustine, *Psalms*, 3:452; Theodoret of Cyrus, *Psalms*, 1:413–14.

6 Such parallels include the acclamation that he live long (Ps. 72:15; cf. 1 Kings 1:39); a king who prayed to govern wisely (1 Kings 3:6–9) and indeed executed righteousness and justice in some measure (Ps. 72:1; cf. 1 Kings 10:9); a blessed people in a large empire with tribute flowing from other nations (e.g., 1 Kings 4:20–21; 10); the wealth of the nations flowing in, including gold of Ophir (Ps. 72:10, 15; cf. 1 Kings 10:10–12); and the ascription of blessing to God (Ps. 72:18; cf. 1 Kings 10:9). These correspondences are noted in Eveson, *Psalms*, 1:438; Greidanus, *Preaching Christ from Psalms*, 95.

7 Calvin, *Psalms*, 3:100–101.

8 Kirkpatrick, *Psalms*, 2:417.

to those who exercise authority today. It spoke until Christ, it is fulfilled in Christ, and it continues to speak until Christ returns. It expresses the wholesome yearning for good government that every human being ought to feel, both in the church (for our pastors) and in the world.

The psalm is not quoted in the New Testament, but Matthew's account of the magi contains echoes, especially the bringing of gold from representatives of distant nations (cf. Ps. 72:10–11, 15).[9] Matthew at the very least hints that the boy whose birth he describes is the King of Psalm 72. The tribute of the nations of which the psalm speaks is also picked up in Revelation 21:26, in which "the glory and the honor of the nations" is brought into the city whose "temple is the Lord God the Almighty and the Lamb" (Rev. 21:22).[10] (There may also be an echo of Ps. 72:18, "Blessed be the LORD, the God of Israel," in Luke 1:68.)[11]

After the clear imperative in Psalm 72:1 ("Give"), many of the verbs from 72:2–17 may be translated by an English future tense ("he will") or as a jussive, expressing a desire ("may he"). Some are unambiguously jussive; others are uncertain. Most translations express 72:1–11 and 15–17 as desires and 72:12–14 as simple futures.[12] This matter—a technical question of Hebrew translation—may not be so critical for meaning, for when a prayer is according to God's will (as these are), we may be confident that God will do what we ask; such prayers merge with prophecies of what God will do.

Psalm 72 is the culmination of books 1 and 2 of the Psalter. The motif of the universal spread of the Messiah's kingship is prominent here (e.g., 72:8, 19), as is the cry of the oppressed, the poor, and the needy, which has been heard so agonizingly in preceding psalms (e.g., Pss. 9; 10).

There are several links between Psalms 71 and 72. These include the theme of righteousness, the vision of future generations belonging to God (71:18; 72:5), God's deliverance or salvation (71:2, 11; 72:12), the word "evermore/continually" (71:3, 6, 14; 72:15; also 70:4), the phrase "all the day long" (71:8, 15, 24; 72:15), and the "wondrous" works of God (71:17; 72:18).

---

9   Kraus, *Theology of the Psalms*, 195; Hossfeld and Zenger, *Psalms*, 2:220. The association of this psalm with the magi goes back at least to Tertullian, *Against Marcion*, 3.13, in ACCS 8:98. It has therefore been a psalm suited especially to the Feast of the Epiphany.

10 The primary allusion in Rev. 21:26 is to Isa. 60, but there is a thematic link to Ps. 72:10–11.

11 Greidanus, *Preaching Christ from Psalms*, 107n44.

12 See the ESV, NASB, NIV, NRSV. The CSB is the same except for Ps. 72:2, which is expressed as a future tense.

There is, however, a significant difference of tone here from that of Psalms 69–71. It is as if the growing confidence of Psalms 65–68 has been interrupted by the reality check of Psalms 69–71, with their reminder of the ongoing sufferings of the church of Christ, before being emphatically affirmed in Psalm 72.

Other related scriptures include Psalms 1 and 2, which combine righteousness of life (Ps. 1) with Davidic kingship (Ps. 2) at the start of the Psalter; Psalm 20, where again the church prays for her King; Psalms 65 and 67, in which the motif of creation restored in Christ is picked up with the mention of mountains, hills, rain, and harvest; Psalm 41, the final psalm of book 1, with its mention of the poor and needy (41:1); Psalm 89, the final psalm of book 3, with its sustained celebration of the Davidic covenant; 2 Samuel 7, the institution of the Davidic covenant; Isaiah 11:1–5, which describes the Branch that will rule and judge in righteousness; Isaiah 60–62, with its unparalleled picture of the future kingdom; Zechariah 9:9–13, which speaks of the righteous King's expansive rule and silencing of enemies; Genesis 1:26–28, with its description of the worldwide dominion of humankind, fulfilled in the second Adam; and the Abrahamic covenant so prominent from Genesis 12:1–3 onward, along with Paul's commentary on it, especially in Galatians 3:16 and 29.

THE TEXT

Structure

Psalm 72:18–20 forms a conclusion to book 2 (see below). The main themes of 72:1–17 are just government, especially for the most vulnerable (72:1–4, reprised in 72:12–14); unending rule (72:5–7, reiterated in 72:15–17); and a kingdom throughout the world (72:8–11). These repeated motifs probably provide the simplest structure.[13]

Superscription

S   Of Solomon.[14]

---

13 Greidanus, *Preaching Christ from Psalms*, 101–3. The same, or very similar, is suggested by Hossfeld and Zenger, *Psalms*, 2:206–7; Wilson, *Psalms*, 1:985.
14 In Hebrew the superscription is the start of verse 1.

The superscription **Of Solomon** (cf. Ps. 127) is of the same form as the very common "of David" superscriptions and may indicate that Solomon wrote it.[15] The Greek translators have "For Solomon,"[16] and, especially in view of 72:20, many have considered that David wrote it, perhaps in his old age, for Solomon, that is, as a prayer for the church to pray for Solomon and his heirs,[17] or that David gave it to Solomon and Solomon put it into poetry and promulgated it.[18]

Because the name **Solomon** is derived from *shalom*, שָׁלוֹם, "peace," there is an appropriateness both about the motif of peace in the psalm (72:3 ["prosperity" = *shalom*, שָׁלוֹם], 7) and about fulfillment in Jesus Christ, the great peacemaker (e.g., John 14:27; Rom. 5:1; Eph. 2:13–18; Col. 1:20).

72:1–4 The Blessings of Good Government:
Long for the Righteous Government of Christ

1   Give the king your justice, O God,
         and your righteousness to the royal son!

This headline verse identifies **the king, the royal son,**[19] as the grand subject of the psalm. This opening prayer is pregnant with significance. God's **justice** (here "judicial decisions") and **righteousness** are the only hope for the needy. Psalm 71 speaks repeatedly of God's righteousness (71:2, 15–16, 19, 24) as the psalmist's only hope. Here we pray that God will **give** his **justice** and **righteousness** to a man who will govern God's world. C. S. Lewis

---

15   Some insist that this is what the *lamed* prefix (לְ) always means in the titles when there is nothing to limit its application and therefore that it must indicate Solomonic authorship here; e.g., Delitzsch, *Psalms*, 2:298; Hengstenberg, *Psalms*, 2:388.

16   Using the preposition εἰς.

17   The Syriac combines this idea with an appreciation of fulfillment in Christ by heading the psalm "A Psalm of David, when he had made Solomon king, and a prophecy concerning the Advent of the Messiah and the calling of the Gentiles." Quoted in Kirkpatrick, *Psalms*, 2:416.

18   Calvin is an influential example of this idea. Calvin, *Psalms*, 3:99–100. But see also Bonar, *Psalms*, 214; Spurgeon, *Treasury*, 2.1:226. The Jewish commentator David Kimchi suggested that "this psalm was composed by David about his son Solomon." See Alter, *Psalms*, 248.

19   "Royal son" is literally "son of a king," perhaps pointing to Solomon as the legitimate heir of David or to any king who inherits the throne in the Davidic line. It may also carry the sense that the Davidic king is the son of God and therefore in a very immediate sense the son of a King. Augustine, *Psalms*, 3:453.

nicely comments that exercising justice means being a champion for the weak, "more like Jack the Giant Killer than like a modern judge in a wig."[20]

God entrusts his government to human beings—to Adam (Gen. 1:26–28), to Abraham that he will be a great nation keeping God's way "by doing righteousness and justice" (Gen. 18:19), to David (2 Sam. 7), and to Abraham's seed. This seed is both singular (Christ, Gal. 3:16) and corporate (those in Christ, Gal. 3:29) since the Messiah will govern the world with his people (e.g., 1 Cor. 6:2). In this psalm we hear echoes of Adam, of Abraham, and of David, all fulfilled in Christ and his church. God exercises his authority through his Messiah, for "the Father . . . has given all judgment to the Son" (John 5:22).

> 2   May he judge your people with righteousness,
>   and your poor with justice!

In Psalm 72:2 the focus shifts to those who benefit from righteous government, called here both **your people** and **your poor**—that is, they belong to God (the primary application is to God's church), and they are **poor**. Augustine points out that poverty does not simply indicate a subset of the people of God (i.e., "May he especially judge the poor among the people") but is a defining characteristic of all God's people (cf. Matt. 5:3; Luke 6:20), for "those who refuse to be God's poor do not belong to God's people."[21]

> 3   Let the mountains bear prosperity for the people,
>   and the hills, in righteousness!

A focus on **the people** continues from Psalm 72:2 ("your people"). **Prosperity** is "peace" (שָׁלוֹם, *shalom*; also 72:2 and the derivation of the name Solomon), that state not simply of absence from strife but of harmony in the whole created order. Although some have taken **mountains** and **hills** to symbolize important people (mountains) and more ordinary people (hills), it is more likely that these are synonyms to symbolize the created order. This harmony will come only when human beings govern the world aright; until then, the whole creation groans under the curse (Gen. 3:17–18; Rom. 8:19–22).

---

20 Lewis, *Reflections on the Psalms*, 17.
21 Augustine, *Psalms*, 3:454.

The phrase **in righteousness** means either (1) that righteousness (the right government of God's King) causes the created order to **bear prosperity** (peace) or (2) that the properly governed created order brings both **prosperity** (peace, harmony) and **righteousness** (right relationships) to the world. Both are true.

> 4   May he defend the cause of the poor of the people,
>   give deliverance to the children of the needy,
>   and crush the oppressor!

Those who need the King's justice are called **the poor of the people** (which may indicate the poor within the people or possibly "the poor, who are [your] people") and **the children of the needy**, which either means literally those who are children of needy parents (and therefore doubly vulnerable) or is another way of speaking of the needy in general (cf. "sons of" to indicate a characteristic). Power is given to some so that those who have it can protect the vulnerable (Prov. 31:1–9).

The King will **defend** and **give deliverance to** the weak. To do this, he must **crush the oppressor** (cf. Rom. 13:1–4; 1 Pet. 2:14). There is a play on the meaning of the words; oppression means crushing others. Now the crushers must be crushed: "Oppressors have been great breakers, but their time of retribution shall come, and they shall be broken themselves."[22] In God's mercy, this may be the crushed spirit of repentance (cf. Isa. 57:15); if not, they must share the fate of Satan, crushed beneath the feet of Christ and his church (cf. Gen. 3:15; Rom. 16:20).

All that follows about the extent and endurance of the King's rule is predicated on the righteousness of Psalm 72:1–4, later to be reiterated in 72:12–14. When we applaud greatness without goodness, disaster always follows.

72:5–7 The Lasting Blessings of Good Government: Yearn for the Unending Blessings of Christ's Kingdom

> 5   May they fear you while the sun endures,
>   and as long as the moon, throughout all generations!

22 Spurgeon, *Treasury*, 2.1:227. Cf. Ross, *Psalms*, 2:543.

6   May he be like rain that falls on the mown grass,
      like showers that water the earth!
7   In his days may the righteous flourish,
      and peace abound, till the moon be no more!

The motif of the created order (Ps. 72:3) continues with **the sun, the moon, rain,** and **showers**. This theme, together with **peace** (= "prosperity," 72:3), links 72:5–7 with 72:1–4. The focus in 72:5–7 is on the unending nature of the perfect kingdom and its abundant blessings. Only righteous government will last; all else will collapse under the weight of its own contradictions.

May they—that is, the people—**fear you**[23] is a prayer that a godly King will govern a God-fearing people, in contrast with so many ungodly kings who led their peoples astray into sin. Calvin notes that, from the perspective of the new covenant, such a vision "is far more truly applicable to" Christ than to any Old Testament king, "true religion being established in his kingdom and nowhere else."[24]

The picture of **rain that falls on the mown grass**[25] and **showers that water the earth** takes us back to Psalm 65:9–13. The whole created order is restored when the second Adam rules. As David said in his last words, "When one rules justly over men / . . . he [is] . . . / like rain that makes the grass to sprout from the earth" (2 Sam. 23:3–4).

In the **days** of this King, **may the righteous** (singular, presumably generic) **flourish,** and then **peace** will **abound** (in contrast with the terrible picture portrayed in, e.g., Pss. 10; 11; 12; 14). Calvin, again from the perspective of the new covenant, writes,

It was, indeed, the duty of Solomon to maintain the righteous; but it is the proper office of Christ to make men righteous. He . . . reforms their hearts through the agency of his Spirit. By this means he brings righteousness

---

23 The NIV rendering, "May he [i.e., the king] endure," derives from a consonantal emendation of the MT. There is no need for this emendation, and the MT is to be preferred.
24 Calvin, *Psalms,* 3:106.
25 Lit., "May he [the king] fall like rain . . ." The word translated "mown grass" (גֵּז) "can refer to what is ready for mowing, like a crop, or to what has been mown already and needs more water" for the next crop to grow. Ross, *Psalms,* 2:544n37.

back, as it were, from exile, which otherwise would be altogether banished from the world.[26]

72:8–11 The Worldwide Scope of Good Government:
Pray for the Worldwide Dominion of Christ

Every empire except one reaches a limit and is then forced to retreat. This is true on every scale of human relationships. Only the perfect kingdom of justice will spread to all the world.

> 8   May he have dominion from sea to sea,
>   and from the River to the ends of the earth!

The verb to **have dominion**[27] is used in the creation mandate of Genesis 1:26–28 (cf. Ps. 8 with Heb. 2:6–8). This King is an Adamic figure, the second Adam. At present the wrong people exercise dominion, but one day "the upright" will have dominion over (cf. "rule over," Ps. 49:14; Isa. 14:2) the world under the second Adam.

Scholars differ as to the precise meaning of **from sea to sea**[28] and **from the River** (probably the Euphrates)[29] **to the ends of the earth**. A very similar description of the Messiah's rule appears in Zechariah 9:10 (Zech. 9:9 is quoted of Jesus in Matt. 21:5). It uses language redolent of the promised land to indicate the new creation.[30] The significance of there being no borders is that because there is nothing beyond this land, there can be no threat.

> 9   May desert tribes bow down before him,
>   and his enemies lick the dust!

---

26 Calvin, *Psalms*, 3:108.

27 Alter notes a "punning echo" between the verb "to fall" (יֵרֵד, Ps. 72:6) and "to have dominion" (יֵרְדְּ, 72:8). Unlike exploitation, proper dominion falls like rain on creation. Robert Alter, *The Art of Biblical Poetry*, rev. ed. (New York: Basic Books, 2011), 165.

28 Perhaps most likely is "from the Dead Sea to the Mediterranean." Alter, *Psalms*, 249.

29 Note the prominence of this river in the description of Solomon's empire (1 Kings 4:21, 24). Keel suggests, however, that "the river" may mean the circular flood that surrounds the world in some ancient cosmologies, so that this means that "the king is to rule from one end of the earth to the other (from sea to sea and from the bitter flood [i.e., the river] to the edge of the round earth." Othmar Keel, *The Symbolism of the Biblical World: Ancient Near Eastern Iconography and the Book of Psalms*, trans. Timothy J. Hallett (Winona Lake, IN: Eisenbrauns, 1997), 20–21.

30 "The land of promise was itself not only symbolic of a lost garden in Eden but a picture of the new earth." Eveson, *Psalms*, 1:441.

> 10   May the kings of Tarshish and of the coastlands
>   render him tribute;
>   may the kings of Sheba and Seba
>   bring gifts!
> 11   May all kings fall down before him,
>   all nations serve him!

The **desert tribes** may indicate nomadic tribes, although their exact location is uncertain (not least because they are nomadic); here, in parallel with **his enemies**, they designate wild opponents of the King. As the seed of the serpent, they will **lick the dust** in submission (cf. Gen. 3:14).[31] **Tarshish** may be in the western Mediterranean (Spain?) or possibly in the Red Sea. **Sheba** is roughly modern-day Yemen. **Seba** (cf. "the Sabeans") may be Ethiopia or possibly a synonym for Sheba.[32] Whatever the precise locations, Psalm 72:11 makes it clear that it includes **all kings**, who will one day **fall down before him**, where the verb "fall down" can be used for obeisance to a king or the worship of God; for Jesus Christ it is both.[33] However wide was Solomon's kingdom at its apogee, this prophecy is fulfilled when Christ, the second Adam, returns (1 Cor. 15:20–28; cf. Rev. 11:15), he who is Lord of lords and King of kings (Rev. 17:14; 19:16).

72:12–14 The Wonderful Compassion of Good Government: Rejoice in the Compassionate Love of Christ's Rule

> 12   For he delivers the needy when he calls,
>   the poor and him who has no helper.
> 13   He has pity on the weak and the needy,
>   and saves the lives of the needy.
> 14   From oppression and violence he redeems their life,
>   and precious is their blood in his sight.

---

31 Hamilton, *Psalms*, 1:634.
32 Wilson, *Psalms*, 1:988; Harman, *Psalms*, 1:532n5.
33 Hamilton notes the use of the verb for the brothers of Joseph bowing before him (Gen. 37:7–10) and for the blessing of Judah (Gen. 49:8). "Joseph typifies David and Jesus in significant ways, and the king from David's line arises in fulfillment of the blessing of Judah." Hamilton, *Psalms*, 1:635.

The word **for** indicates that this section gives the fundamental reason why this King, and this King alone, will rule the world forever. The reason has everything to do with love. This King was foreshadowed by Job in his greatness (note the parallel between Psalm 72:12 and Job 29:12), as he was foreshadowed by Job in his sufferings. He is the King who brings to earth the exodus God who **redeems their life** and **delivers the needy when he calls** (cf. Ex. 2:23), especially **him who has no helper** and is cast utterly on God and his Messiah for deliverance. **He has pity**, a warm verb that indicates both feelings of compassion and the resulting actions of help and rescue.[34] So not only does he have **pity**, but—as the result of his pity—he **saves the lives of the needy. Oppression and violence**—exploitation and then the callous disregard for human life and dignity that always results from oppression[35]—dominate the poor and needy, especially in this context the "little ones" who belong to Christ, the godly poor. The Messiah delivers them out of love, for **precious is their blood in his sight** (cf. Ps. 116:15). Nothing matters more to Christ than the lives of those entrusted to him by his Father; he will seek, save, and raise them on the last day, every single one (John 6:39).

72:15–17 The Blessedness of the Good King: Pray for the Eternal Exaltation of Christ in Blessing

> [15]   Long may he live;
>   may gold of Sheba be given to him!
>   May prayer be made for him continually,
>   and blessings invoked for him all the day!

While **Long may he live!** (lit., "May he live") is a conventional wish of subjects for their ruler ("Long live the king!"; cf. 1 Sam. 10:24; 2 Sam. 16:16; 1 Kings 1:25, 34), here it expresses a genuine heartfelt yearning that this King will live and prosper, for in his prosperity is our peace and hope. **Gold of Sheba**, proverbially wonderful, was given to Solomon by the Queen of Sheba (1 Kings 10:10). Here, along with the wealth of the nations in Psalm 72:10, it speaks of

---

34 Ross, *Psalms*, 2:547n39.
35 See Wilson, *Psalms*, 1:989.

what the magi prefigured in their offerings to the infant King (Matt. 2:11) and what will be fulfilled when the wealth of the nations pours into this Messiah's new creation land (Isa. 60:5; 61:6; Rev. 21:26). Although the church does not need to pray *for* Jesus Christ, who is God the Son ascended on high, we do still long for his kingdom to come and pray for the consummation of his reign when he returns (cf. Rev. 22:20: "Amen. Come, Lord Jesus!").

16 May there be abundance of grain in the land;
    on the tops of the mountains may it wave;
    may its fruit be like Lebanon;
 and may people blossom in the cities
    like the grass of the field!

Creation imagery returns (cf. Ps. 72:3, 5–6; also, Pss. 65; 67; Amos 9:13) with a longing for and vision of a superabundance of prosperity, with stalks of **grain** like cedars of **Lebanon**—such is their grandeur. The vision includes **people** who **blossom** in glad and satisfied harmony with the created order. All this will come only when the perfect King rules.

17 May his name endure forever,
    his fame continue as long as the sun!
 May people be blessed in him,
    all nations call him blessed!

His name and **his fame** translate the same noun in Hebrew ("name"), meaning his revealed nature and reputation.[36] We yearn for a King with a lasting reputation, unsullied by scandal, untroubled by failure, and for the Abrahamic blessing to be poured out through him. The request **May people be blessed in him, / all nations call him blessed** echoes the Abrahamic covenant blessing (Gen. 12:1–3; 22:17–18; 26:4; etc.) fulfilled in Christ, who is Abraham's seed (Rom. 9:8; Gal. 3:16, 29), and in the Spirit poured out in him (Gal. 3:14). The word **blessed** in the phrase **call him blessed** is cognate with the word for blessing (אַשְׁרֵי, *ashre*) used with such programmatic

---

36 The "name" of the covenant God has been prominent in this part of the Psalms; see Pss. 61:5, 8; 63:4, 11; 66:2, 4; 68:4 (2x); 69:30, 36.

significance in Psalms 1 and 2 (see on 1:1 and 2:12). The Psalm 1 blessed man is the Psalm 72 King from David's line, seed of Abraham in whom all nations will be blessed.[37]

72:18–19 Bless God for All That He Is to Us in Christ!

18   Blessed be the LORD, the God of Israel,
         who alone does wondrous things.
19   Blessed be his glorious name forever;
         may the whole earth be filled with his glory!
      Amen and Amen!

There is some discussion about whether Psalm 72:18–19 is to be read as an integral part of the psalm or as the concluding doxology of book 2 of the Psalter. Comparison with the other doxologies (41:13; 89:52; 106:48) strongly suggests the latter.[38] It is, however, also entirely appropriate as the close of Psalm 72, which has celebrated and prayed for the **wondrous things** (the same noun as "wondrous deeds" in 71:17) achieved by God through his Messiah, the **glorious name** of God in his Messiah, and **the whole earth** being **filled with his glory** (cf. Num. 14:21). When we acclaim God as **blessed**, we do not give him anything he does not already possess; rather, we pray that his name will be hallowed and his will be done on earth as in heaven.[39]

72:20 The Closing Marker at the End of Books 1 and 2

20   The prayers of David, the son of Jesse,[40] are ended.

Some, who consider Psalm 72:19 to be an integral part of Psalm 72, have suggested that 72:20 marks simply the close of the so-called "Second Davidic Collection" of psalms (Pss. 51–72). But as we have seen, there is good reason

---

37 Hamilton, *Psalms*, 1:631.

38 Common elements, always in the same order, are "Blessed be the LORD," a reference to endurance ("forever," etc.), and a concluding "Amen" or "Amen and Amen." Three of the four book closings also include "the God of Israel." See Wilson, *Psalms*, 1:990n18.

39 There is a very helpful clarification of what it means to "bless" God and how this differs from praising him (contra the NIV) in Eveson, *Psalms*, 1:264.

40 The title "David, the son of Jesse" appears also in 2 Sam. 23:1; 1 Chron. 10:14; 29:26.

to understand 72:18–19 to be the doxology closing book 2. Since 72:20 comes after that, it is most natural to understand it to close books 1 and 2; there are other "of David" psalms in later books (Pss. 86; 101; 103; 108–110; 122; 124; 131; 133; 138–145), but books 1 and 2 alone are given the title **The prayers of David**. This means neither that every psalm in these books was written by David (notably Pss. 42–50) nor that no later psalms can be by David, but it reflects the fact that he is the main author and highlights the overwhelming importance of Davidic kingship in Psalms 1–72.

REFLECTION AND RESPONSE

1. Psalm 72 moves us to consider the longings of the vulnerable for justice. This is as true on a national and international level as it is for a business, a school, a neighborhood, or a family. We should long deeply for righteousness and not be blinded by success or charisma.

2. Our central focus will necessarily be the kingdom of Christ. We see this in the Gospels, as Jesus reaches out to the lame, the leper, the blind, the deaf, the tax collector, and the prostitute—the most painfully marginalized of his society. It will be consummated when he returns. Psalm 72 prompts us to pray for this reign to come, longing for "new heavens and a new earth in which righteousness dwells" (2 Pet. 3:13), a kingdom without borders, an empire without end.

3. Psalm 72:12–14 focuses our meditations on the love of the Lord Jesus Christ our King. This is beautifully expressed by David Dickson:

> The care Christ hath of his subjects is such, that there is not one so mean in all his kingdom, of whom, and whose necessities, and of whose particular petitions, he taketh not most particular and exact knowledge, whose petitions, being presented in the sense of their need, he granteth not. . . . There needeth no mediator between him and his subjects. . . . The man that hath nothing within him or without him to commend him to Christ, to assist, help, relieve, or comfort him, in heaven or earth, is not despised by Christ, but delivered from that which he feareth.

Christ cares lovingly for his people "by teaching his subjects to bear troubles, by strengthening them for the burden, by comforting them in their grief, by giving a delivery to their spirits by faith, and a full delivery at last."[41]

4. There is an important application of Psalm 72 to pastors and leaders in the church of Christ, especially in times of scandal when they have misused power. A church leader is an undershepherd, wielding his authority under Christ the King. The power of a pastor, supremely seen in the power of the pulpit, is to be exercised for the poor and needy, those who are poor in spirit, to heal them with the gospel and build them up in faith.

5. There is also a valid, and important, derivative application of Psalm 72 as we pray for our earthly leaders (1 Tim. 2:1–2). Again, Dickson expresses this well:

> A king may command within his kingdom many things, but he cannot command a blessing on his own government; he must make suit for this to God. He may leave a kingdom to his child; but because a kingdom is nothing without God's blessing, he must pray for this blessing, and seek the assistance of the prayers of the church for this intent: and this duty kings may crave of the church, and God's people should not refuse it.[42]

But as we pray for our rulers, the focus of our prayers will not be that their dominion should extend through space or time but rather that it will embody righteous judgments; our prayers will be moral in their focus more than they will petition for success.

41 Dickson, *Psalms*, 1:440–41.
42 Dickson, *Psalms*, 1:437.

BOOK 3

———

BOOK 3 CONSISTS OF Psalms 73–89. It has the scent of the Babylonian exile; this is most evident in Psalms 74, 79, and (probably) 80. The tone changes sharply from the emphatically Davidic themes of books 1 and 2. This is not to say that every psalm in book 3 owes its origin to the exile (for example, Ps. 86 is called "A prayer of David"), but the exile sets the tone for the book in its canonical form. Psalms "of Asaph" (Pss. 73–83)[1] and "of the sons of Korah" (Pss. 84–85; 87–88) dominate. The book includes more corporate psalms than individual.

---

1   The so-called Elohistic Psalter, psalms that prefer "God" to "the LORD," extend from Psalm 42 to 83 (all book 2 and the "Asaph" collection at the start of book 3). We do not know why.

When you perceive the godless flourishing in peace
and yet the righteous who suffer affliction living in
complete dejection, say what is in [Psalm 73], lest you
be caused to stumble and shaken to the foundation.

ATHANASIUS
Letter to Marcellinus

Satan has numberless artifices by which he dazzles our eyes
and bewilders the mind; and then the confusion of things which
prevails in the world produces so thick a mist, as to render it
difficult for us to see through it, and to come to the conclusion
that God governs and extends his care to things here below.

JOHN CALVIN
Commentary on the Psalms

In the time of adversity, a believer may prove weak in the faith of
that truth which was not questioned by him in prosperity, and be
near hand unto [i.e., close to] the quitting and renouncing of it.

DAVID DICKSON
A Commentary on the Psalms

PSALM 73

ORIENTATION

In Psalm 73, a highly emotional psalm, we watch a man dragged back from the brink of an abyss because of another man who plunged into that abyss for him. A believer tells us of an overwhelming temptation and how he pulled back from it into the arms of the God who loves him. When we step back and ask how he can resist this temptation and why he is welcomed into the arms of God, the answer to both questions is Christ, seen in this psalm under two aspects.

First, Jesus Christ faced this temptation in all its force, more so than ever Asaph did, and yet walked through it without sin (Heb. 4:15). As Philip Eveson writes,

> Asaph, as a representative of the Israel of God, points us to the Lord Jesus Christ, who is the true Israel (Isaiah 49:3), who, as the Suffering Servant, knew what it was to feel the temptation to give up (see Isaiah 49:4a), yet shook it off by reminding himself of his God and trusting that he would be vindicated by him (Isaiah 49:4b).[1]

The second aspect follows from the first: only because Jesus conquered the temptation of Psalm 73 can his atoning death draw Asaph, and any believer, into the arms of God (1 Pet. 2:24). Christ makes Psalm 73:23–28 possible because Christ resisted the temptations of 73:1–22.[2]

There are hints of fulfillment in Christ both when Asaph recognizes that, were he to fall, he would betray God's church (73:15) and when he resolves to

---

1 Eveson, *Psalms*, 2:21.
2 Belcher, *Messiah and the Psalms*, 96.

declare God's works to the world (73:28). While both are true for any believer, they are supremely true for Christ. Had Christ failed the test, he would indeed have betrayed his church and been unable to proclaim the Father to us.

Although this psalm marks a new stage of the Psalter, it is worth noting several thematic links back to Psalm 72. These include the words "peace" or "prosperity" (72:3, 7; 73:3), "violence" (72:14; 73:6), "oppression" (72:14; 73:8), and "forever" or "always" (72:17; 73:12). The way these terms are used in Psalm 73, however, contrasts sharply with the hopeful prophecy of Psalm 72 and brings us back from the visionary future into the painful present.

There are significant links with the wisdom themes in Psalm 37 (note the self-reflection; e.g., 37:25, 35–36; 73:2–3, 15–17, 21–22, 28) and Psalm 49 (note the references to being [1] "stupid" in 49:10 and "brutish" in 73:22 and [2] "beasts" in 49:12, 20; 73:22).

Further, there is a suggestive link back to the opening of book 2. For book 3 (Pss. 73 and 74), like book 2 (Pss. 42–43 and 44), begins with an individual lament followed by a corporate one.[3]

Psalm 73 shares thematic links also with Ecclesiastes, facing the realities of a topsy-turvy world and working through intense inward struggles as we do so.[4]

Although we do not know when or by which Asaphite this psalm was written, its message would resonate with believers in exile, "seeing the Babylonians living a life of impiety and lawlessness, and enjoying great prosperity and good fortune while they themselves were in difficulty and hardship,"[5] especially as they reflected on how God had punished them by sending them into exile for their sins; why did he not punish the Babylonians?[6]

THE TEXT

Structure

The first word of Psalm 73:1, 13, and 18 is the emphatic "truly" (אַךְ, *ak*);[7] it introduces three developing thoughts. Psalm 73:1–12 describes the temp-

---

3   Robertson, *Flow of the Psalms*, 123.
4   Belcher, *Messiah and the Psalms*, 93, 93n109.
5   Theodoret of Cyrus, *Psalms*, 2:3–4.
6   I am grateful to Tom Habib for this insight.
7   Ps. 73:13 renders this word "All."

tation; 73:13–17 reflects on it without God; 73:18–28 overcomes it in the presence of God.

Superscription

 S   A Psalm of Asaph.[8]

Apart from Psalms 73–83, only Psalm 50 is headed **of Asaph** (see comments there). Asaph was one of the musicians and song leaders appointed by David for the temple worship (1 Chron. 6:31–39; 15:17; 16:4–7) and used by Solomon (2 Chron. 5:12). He is called "a seer" (2 Chron. 29:30); along with all the other psalmists, he spoke words given from God by the Spirit. The "sons of Asaph" appear later in Israel's history (2 Chron. 20:14; 29:13; 35:15; Ezra 2:41; 3:10; Neh. 7:44; 11:22); whether or not "the sons of Asaph" were Asaph's biological descendants, they were certainly his spiritual heirs, seen in the themes and styles of their songs.

Since some of the Asaphite psalms speak of the destruction of Jerusalem (e.g., Pss. 74; 79),[9] either Asaph spoke prophetically, or "Asaph" is shorthand for "the sons of Asaph" and refers to an Asaphite author at the time of the exile.

73:1–12 Feel the Force of This Temptation

1   Truly God is good to Israel,
        to those who are pure in heart.

Truly is emphatic. This headline is Asaph's prior conviction as he faces temptation; it will be his triumphant conclusion. The covenant word **good** brackets the psalm (also Ps. 73:28; cf. 4:6; 23:6; 25:8; 34:8; 52:9; 69:16). The denial that **God is good** begins in the garden in Eden (Gen. 3) and undermines human existence. **God is good** not simply in his attributes but in his actions toward a people who are described both as **Israel** and as **those who are pure in heart** (cf. Ps. 24:4). **Israel** means, in biblical theology, the

8 In Hebrew the superscription is the start of verse 1.
9 "The predominant impression gained from reading the collection as a whole is that of a cry out of the Exile." Kirkpatrick, *Psalms*, 2:430.

true Israel of God, defined not by ethnicity (even under the old covenant; cf. Ruth, Rahab, the Ninevites in the time of Jonah) but by their hearts (cf. Rom. 2:28–29). To be **pure in heart** means to have a single affection for God and an undivided devotion to God. Jesus both proclaimed and lived this blessing (Matt. 5:8). Here is the testimony of a true Israelite (cf. John 1:47). The corollary is that God will be "crooked" with those who are "crooked in heart" (see on Ps. 18:25–26).

> ² But as for me, my feet had almost stumbled,
>   my steps had nearly slipped.
> ³ For I was envious of the arrogant
>   when I saw the prosperity of the wicked.

But as for me[10] signals an emphatic contrast. This man's **feet** and **steps** are in danger of losing their solid foothold in the truth of Psalm 73:1. The reason (**for**) is that **I was envious of the arrogant** (their pride will be a salient feature of their portrait), particularly **when I saw the prosperity** (lit., "peace," an ironic contrast to the "prosperity/peace" of 72:3) **of the wicked**. True, this is a peace in which there is no peace (Jer. 6:14), but **I saw** it with my eyes, and it is always easier to live by sight rather than by faith in unseen realities. Indeed, as David Dickson says, "If the prosperity of the wicked, and trouble of the godly be looked upon, in respect of their outward worldly estate only; it cannot but trouble a man's thoughts."[11]

Psalm 73:4–12 paints a vivid picture of what he **saw** (which includes what he heard them say and encompasses all the senses; cf. Job 21 and—in a context of unbelief—Mal. 2:17). The vivid description enables us to feel the force of this testing. To know that John the Baptist was in prison while Herod "ruled and rioted in luxury" would have pressed this temptation forcefully on Jesus.[12] The temptation is to see the world through the eyes of Job's comforters, who suppose that visible prosperity is evidence of God's blessing.

> ⁴ For they have no pangs until death;
>   their bodies are fat and sleek.

---

10 אַךְ. This Hebrew word appears at the start of Ps. 73:2, 22, 23, 28. In each case it means "But I."
11 Dickson, *Psalms*, 1:446.
12 Bonar, *Psalms*, 219.

The word **pangs** is probably figurative for struggles or afflictions. The phrase **no pangs until death** (lit., "no pangs to their deaths")[13] means either that they live their whole life untroubled by suffering or that they die peacefully without pain (or possibly both). The single adjective translated **fat and sleek** (בָּרִיא, *bari*; CSB: "well fed") is used of the good cows and good grain in Pharaoh's dream (Gen. 41:4–20), of well-fed sheep (Ezek. 34:3, 20), and of the healthy young men in Daniel 1:15 ("fatter").[14] These wicked are pictures of robust health.

5   They are not in trouble as others are;
         they are not stricken like the rest of mankind.

The parallel phrases **as others are** (lit., "the trouble of humankind") and **the rest of mankind** suggest that conspicuously wicked people prosper more than the generality of humankind. This is not an absolute truth (for they do get diseases, have accidents, and experience setbacks), but it is recognizably true enough, for all too often they have higher life expectancies and a better "quality of life" than most. The verb **stricken** or "afflicted" (CSB) can be used of being struck by disease or plague, although it does not always denote this. It is used of Job's troubles ("touch," Job 2:5; 4:5).

6   Therefore pride is their necklace;
         violence covers them as a garment.

Therefore, because of their evident success, they wear their **pride** (cf. "arrogant," Ps. 73:3) on brazen display, as **their necklace**. Because pride places me at the center of my world, I will—inevitably and necessarily—treat others as insignificant. It is a small step from this arrogance to **violence** toward others weaker than myself; it is this violence that they clothe themselves with, **as a garment**.

---

13 The NIV rendering, "They have no struggles; their bodies are healthy and strong," results from dividing לְמוֹתָם into לְמוֹ (concluding the first phrase, "to them") and תָם ("whole" or "sound"). Although this division is suggested in *BHS*, there is no adequate reason for departing from the MT word division. "Death" should be retained.

14 It is also used of the obese King Eglon (Judg. 3:17), but here in Ps. 73 the association is with health and vigor.

7   Their eyes swell out through fatness;
      their hearts overflow with follies.

The idiom of **eyes swelling out through fatness**[15] is an unfamiliar idiom
that probably suggests a visible excess of life. But it is not only their **eyes**;
their hearts overflow with follies, with imaginations, conceits, or delusions
about themselves (cf. the same noun, "imagination," in Prov. 18:11). They
dream big dreams in which they are at the center.

8   They scoff and speak with malice;
      loftily they threaten oppression.

The focus in Psalm 73:8–11 is on their words. In 73:8 the verb "to speak"
is used twice (the ESV's **speak** and **threaten** translate the same Hebrew verb).
Here is pride made audible, in mockery (cf. "scoffers," 1:1) and threats of
oppression ("Don't mess with us; we can squash you").

9   They set their mouths against the heavens,
      and their tongue struts through the earth.

The **heavens** and **the earth** are a merism, meaning the whole of creation.
With no fear of God, they speak grandly and walk through the world as
though it all belongs to them.

10   Therefore his people turn back to them,
      and find no fault in them.

Psalm 73:10 is difficult to translate. The subject is **his people**; this is about the
people of God.[16] Some consider that the first line is a promise that the people
of God will return to God (lit., "return to here"), although this would be contrary to the context. The first line probably means (as the ESV) that the people
of God are so dazzled by the successes of the wicked that they applaud them,
they make them their heroes, and they want to be like them (cf. Rom. 1:32).

---

15 The NIV translation, "From their callous hearts comes iniquity," follows a lead suggested by
    the LXX and Syriac. This, as Ross says, "may be too wide of the text." Ross, *Psalms*, 2:554.
16 The NIV rendering, "their people," is incorrect and misleading. Tate, *Psalms 51–100*, 229.

In the Masoretic Text the second line is literally "and full water flows for them."[17] The CSB probably catches the meaning best: "and drink in their overflowing words." This reinforces the first line and completes the picture of the magnetic appeal of the prosperous godless; the people of God not only want to be like them but drink in what they say.

> 11   And they say, "How can God know?
>   Is there knowledge in the Most High?"

What **they say** is now spelled out in two parallel lines that focus on whether **God**—even mockingly called **the Most High**—can really **know** about the world. **Knowledge** includes doing something about what one knows; they are not so worried about what cognition may be in God but about whether God will do anything about it. They are practical atheists (cf. Ps. 10:4, 11, 13).

> 12   Behold, these are the wicked;
>   always at ease, they increase in riches.

Behold![18] Look at them! Let your eyes take in the scene I have described. Here is the conclusion: **These are the wicked**, not languishing under punishment but **always at ease** and increasing in **riches**. They live on easy street; anyone can see that. This is what Jesus saw, as it has been seen by believers before and since. How did Jesus respond, and how will we? Psalm 73:13–17 takes us into the midst of the inward struggle of temptation.

73:13–17 Grapple with This Temptation

> 13   All in vain have I kept my heart clean
>   and washed my hands in innocence.

The first word of Psalm 73:13 (as of 73:18) is אַךְ, *ak*, which means "truly, certainly" and is emphatic. Truly it was **in vain** that **I kept my heart clean**,

---

17 The ESV follows the RSV, but this is misleading. For discussion, see Tate, *Psalms 51–100*, 229.
18 It is a pity that the NIV omits this word (here and in Ps. 73:27).

laboring to walk in godliness. The word translated **in vain** is used of the plotting of the wicked in 2:1 and of the covenant curses in Leviticus 26:16 and 20; here it echoes the words of the servant of the Lord in Isaiah 49:4 ("I have labored in vain"). This temptation afflicted Jesus Christ, as it afflicts all his disciples (cf. "See, we have left everything and followed you. What then will we have?" Matt. 19:27). Augustine expounds the phrase **in vain** this way: "If I serve God, and have to go without wealth, while those who do not serve him have plenty, . . .[w]hat I did is pointless. Where is the reward for my good life? What wages do I get for my service? I live virtuously, and I am in need, while a godless person has plenty."[19]

To have **washed my hands in innocence** is the symbolic equivalent (cf. Ex. 30:17–21; Deut. 21:6; Ps. 26:6) of a clean heart (cf. 24:4). All true piety is undermined by this temptation; Asaph stands on the edge of the abyss.

> [14]   For all the day long I have been stricken
>   and rebuked every morning.

The verb **stricken**, from which the wicked were exempt (73:5), perfectly describes this believer, as it characterized Jesus Christ, together with the verb **rebuked**, that is, being chastised for sin (lit., "my chastisement every morning"). **All the day** followed by **every morning** may suggest a suffering that envelops his whole life, with not even a morning of joy.[20]

> [15]   If I had said, "I will speak thus,"
>   I would have betrayed the generation of your children.

The verb **speak** in **I will speak thus** suggests a public utterance, even a proclamation.[21] If I had taken my private struggles and let them shape my

---

19 Augustine, *Psalms*, 3:483.
20 The NIV rendering, "every morning brings new punishments," catches the sense but is a rather loose translation.
21 Hengstenberg points out that his thoughts so far have been in the nature of a soliloquy. The question now is whether to broadcast his doubts in confident proclamation (as many a church leader has done since). Hengstenberg, *Psalms*, 2:408. Augustine asks, horrified, "Will this be the position you adopt: that those who live righteously do so to no purpose, that the just have wasted their service, that God either favors the wicked or does not care about anyone? Will you say this, will this be your story?" Augustine, *Psalms*, 3:484.

public preaching, then—behold!²²—**I would have betrayed the generation of your children** (lit., "the sons of your generation"). This betrayal is more than simply abandoning the church; it is to mislead the church and draw her astray. It matters for us all that this believer resists this temptation; everything in life and death hinges for us on Christ obeying flawlessly and resisting all temptation.

> ¹⁶ But when I thought how to understand this,
>   it seemed to me a wearisome task,
> ¹⁷ until I went into the sanctuary of God;
>   then I discerned their end.

The verb **to understand** has the same root as "knowledge" in Psalm 73:11. When I try to attain to the knowledge that I deny that God has (73:11), it is a **wearisome**, troublesome (using the same root as "trouble" in 73:5) **task**. It is no easy task to live by faith and to grasp that God does govern affairs on earth (cf. Eccl. 8:16–17). Such understanding is found in **the sanctuary of God**, the place where covenant love is declared and covenant blessings and curses expounded. Here, and here only, **I discerned their end**, their destiny. The Lord Jesus on earth had this understanding through the Scriptures, which is why he devoured them, delighted in them, and lived by them.

73:18–28 Overcome This Temptation

> ¹⁸ Truly you set them in slippery places;
>   you make them fall to ruin.
> ¹⁹ How they are destroyed in a moment,
>   swept away utterly by terrors!
> ²⁰ Like a dream when one awakes,
>   O Lord, when you rouse yourself, you despise them as phantoms.

With the third **truly** we begin the final part; Marvin Tate says that the word "gives this psalm its character of 'The Great Nevertheless.'"²³ Truly

---

22 The first word of the second line is הִנֵּה.
23 Tate, *Psalms 51–100*, 235.

the believer struggled with temptation (Ps. 73:13). But the first "truly" (73:1) and the last (73:18) define the psalm: truly God is good; truly God judges the proud. The slippery places that threatened the believer—and threatened Jesus—in 73:2 are slippery because the true condition of the wicked is that they are on the edge of the abyss, ready to **fall to ruin** at any moment. **In a moment** all their pomp, their pride, their ease will be **destroyed**, and they will be **swept away utterly by terrors** (a haunting image; cf. Job 18:14). The cry for God to "awake" (e.g., Ps. 44:23) calls for God to rise for judgment (cf. 3:7). On that day the wicked, who seem so solid, so immovable, such a fixed part of our world, will be **like a dream** and like **phantoms**. In the new creation they will be seen no more (cf. 37:10).

> ²¹　When my soul was embittered,
> 　　when I was pricked in heart,
> ²²　I was brutish and ignorant;
> 　　I was like a beast toward you.

Psalm 73:21 reads literally, "When my heart was embittered, / when I was pricked in my kidneys"; the former (lit., "heart") means the center of the human person, the latter (lit., "kidneys") the emotions and affections. When we cease to believe that God is good to his people, a sourness enters our hearts and gives us a sharp pain (**pricked**) like an internal injury to the soul, for the moral order of our existence is threatened.

In 73:22 (beginning emphatically "But I" in Hebrew) the believer looks back at what was happening to him as he played with this temptation. He was **brutish** (cf. the same Hebrew word translated "stupid" in 49:10) **and ignorant** (devoid of the knowledge or discernment that is such a theme of the psalm, 73:11, 17), **like a beast** (49:12, 20) **toward you.** That is, I became and behaved like one who had no true understanding of the world in which I lived.

But after he is delivered out of this temptation, Asaph celebrates in 73:23–28 the wonder, the almost unbelievable goodness, of being near God. To this Asaph came because, centuries later, Jesus Christ would pay for his sins; to this every man and woman in Christ is brought as Jesus brings us to God (1 Pet. 3:18).

23   Nevertheless, I am continually with you;
          you hold my right hand.

Nevertheless translates the same word that begins Psalm 73:22, "But as for me . . ." **I am continually with you** celebrates being in fellowship with God and being so for all time (cf. the motif of time in Ps. 71). **You hold my right hand** (cf. 63:8b) acknowledges that the only reason he did not slip into the abyss is that God held him tight. While the Lord may let his children "be brought to the very brink of misbelieving a necessary and saving truth, yet he preventeth their quitting it altogether; they may be very near the fall, and not fall altogether."[24]

24   You guide me with your counsel,
          and afterward you will receive me to glory.

Your counsel contrasts with "the counsel of the wicked" in Psalm 1:1. **You guide me** uses the same verb as in 5:8; 23:3; 27:11; and elsewhere. It is a precious thing to walk through life in fellowship with the all-wise God. This the Father did, by the Spirit, for Jesus Christ his Son, and this he does for all in Christ.

There is much discussion about the meaning of (1) **afterward** (is this later in this life or in the age to come?), (2) the verb **receive** or "take" (is this comparable to when God "took" Enoch [Gen. 5:24] and Elijah [2 Kings 2:5]?), and (3) **glory** (is this the life of the age to come or not?).[25] Given what Jesus says about resurrection in Luke 20:37–38, it seems likely that **afterward** and **glory** encompass both this age and the age to come, although it seems less likely that **receive** (a very common verb) means by translation (as for Enoch and Elijah).

25   Whom have I in heaven but you?
          And there is nothing on earth that I desire besides you.

If **heaven** and **earth** form a merism (a way of including everything), the two lines of this verse say much the same thing, the second line intensifying the first in speaking of **desire**. The living God is the highest desire a human

---

24 Dickson, *Psalms*, 1:445.
25 See the discussion in Tate, *Psalms 51–100*, 230.

being can know; the Father was the deepest desire of the Son on earth (cf. Ps. 40:8, quoted of Christ; 112:1; 119:35). If there is a distinct emphasis both on **heaven** and on **earth**, it may be that the former speaks of the age to come, the latter of this age.

> 26 My flesh and my heart may fail,
>   but God is the strength of my heart and my portion forever.

My flesh and my heart speaks of the whole person, body and soul. Even though this **may fail**, becoming weary in this life and closing with death, **God is the strength of my heart**, the one in whom my heart rejoices and to whom my heart turns, and he is **my portion forever**. The word **portion** usually denotes a family's share in the promised land (and hence the new creation) but also the special "portion" given to the Levites, for whom the covenant Lord himself was their portion (e.g., Deut. 10:9; Josh. 13:33). With God as my portion, I need no more.

> 27 For behold, those who are far from you shall perish;
>   you put an end to everyone who is unfaithful to you.

For behold—look! Psalm 73:27 is a summary truth that places the whole drama of this temptation into perspective, and does so in its negative aspect: **Those who are far from you shall perish**. The only question that matters for a man or woman is this: Are you near God, brought near by grace in Christ? Or are you far from God, children of his wrath (cf. Eph. 2:3)? The second line emphasizes this danger, first, by the verb **you put an end to**; second, by the emphatic **everyone**; and, third, by the horrible word **unfaithful** (lit., "prostitute").[26] This is the destiny of the proud wicked unless they repent and trust in Christ.

> 28 But for me it is good to be near God;
>   I have made the Lord GOD my refuge,
>   that I may tell of all your works.

---

26 Augustine speaks of the believer's "chaste love" for the bridegroom alone. "The speaker in our psalms loves the bridegroom alone, and loves him for himself." Augustine, *Psalms*, 3:491.

But for me is the same emphatic contrastive pronoun that begins Psalm 73:2, 22, and 23. The word **good** echoes 73:1. The phrase **near God** sums up 73:18–27. The second line makes clear that only those are truly **near God** who make the covenant God (**the Lord GOD**) their **refuge** (cf. "all who take refuge in him," 2:12). In the final line, **that I may tell** (declare, preach, proclaim, the same verb as "I will speak thus" in 73:15) **of all your works,** the phrase **your works** in this context means the hidden government of God in his world, by which the present prosperity of the wicked will end in judgment and the present trials of Christ on earth and now his church will end in goodness. This Christ proclaims to his church; this we preach to one another.

REFLECTION AND RESPONSE

1. It is important for us not to minimize the force and seriousness of the temptation faced in this psalm. For it rears its head again and again in the life of faith, the temptation to move from the life of faith to the life of sight.

2. In a penetrating section of his sermon on this psalm, Augustine probes into the motivation that lies behind the temptation Asaph describes. What lies at the root, Augustine says, is wanting from God, as a reward for piety, this-worldly blessings that the wicked seem to enjoy. It is as if we say, "Look, they are sinners, yet they have gained ample wealth in this world." And "so the speaker has confessed that he refrained from sin only because he hoped for riches. A carnal soul had traded in righteousness for visible, earthly things. What kind of righteousness is that, if it is preserved only for the sake of money?"[27]

3. Following on from this, Augustine expounds, with classic Augustinian clarity, how a desire for God is the only truly spiritually chaste desire. Commenting on Psalm 73:26, he writes,

His heart has become chaste, for now God is loved disinterestedly; the psalmist asks no other reward from God except God. Anyone who begs a different reward from God, and aspires to serve him in order to get it, is rating what he wants to get more highly than the God who, he hopes, will

---

27 Augustine, *Psalms*, 3:482–83.

give it. Does this mean that God gives us nothing? Nothing, save himself. God's award is simply God himself.[28]

4. Psalm 73 helps us feel the wonder of the Lord Jesus's perfect conquest of this temptation. It is wonderful, necessary, and glorious that Jesus resisted this temptation for us. Only because he did so could he die as the propitiation for our sins.

5. It is therefore wholesome and evangelical (in the old sense of being true to the gospel) to walk through this psalm with Asaph the believer, conscious that his being delivered from the temptation is only because of the Christ who was to come and that his being near to God is only because Christ brought him near. In anticipation (as so often with David and other believers in the Psalms), Asaph is a man in Christ, writing and struggling by the Spirit of Christ.

6. While Psalm 73:15 applies supremely to Christ, it is relevant for every believer. "What one believer does and says may have a profound effect upon the believing community as a whole."[29] We are wise to confide our doubts to those who can counsel and encourage us in faith, but we are irresponsible to proclaim them as if they were our paradoxically confident unbelief.

28 Augustine, *Psalms*, 3:491.
29 Harman, *Psalms*, 2:555.

The people of God in this psalm bewail the desolate
condition of the Church, which was such that the
very name of Israel was almost annihilated.

JOHN CALVIN
Commentary on the Psalms

The Head of the Church, who wept over Jerusalem on the
Mount of Olives, and lamented their too sure ruin, could
use these strains, and pour them into the Father's ear.

ANDREW BONAR
Christ and His Church in the Book of Psalms

The history of the suffering church is always edifying; when
we see how the faithful trusted and wrestled with their God
in times of dire distress, we are thereby taught how to behave
ourselves under similar circumstances: we learn moreover, that
when the fiery trial befalls us, no strange thing has happened
unto us, we are following the trail of the host of God.

CHARLES H. SPURGEON
The Treasury of David

PSALM 74

ORIENTATION

What has Christ to do with Psalm 74, a psalm of lament and hope in the light of the destruction of the temple by the Babylonians in 586 BC?[1]

There is a thematic echo of Psalm 74:1–2 in Acts 20:28. Both passages feature the twin motifs of God's people as a flock and of God's purchasing of them.[2] This suggests a parallel between the old covenant congregation and the new covenant church of Christ.

I suggest that a wider consideration of the New Testament points to the fulfillment of this psalm in Christ in at least five ways.

First, Jesus Christ felt the grief of this psalm for the broken state of God's church. He wept over Jerusalem as he prophesied that the disaster of 586 BC would be repeated, as indeed it was in AD 70 (Luke 19:41–44); this included the razing of the temple to the ground (Matt. 24:1–2). The grief so poignantly expressed in Psalm 74:1–11 was felt by Jesus more deeply than by any other human being.

The second arises out of the grief and zeal of the first. Jesus is the one "greater than the temple" (Matt. 12:6). The crucifixion is the ultimate destruction of the temple and the resurrection its final rebuilding (John 2:19–22).

---

1 The theory, once popular in some critical scholarship, that this is about the desecration of the temple under Antiochus IV Epiphanes in the second century BC fails especially because the temple was not then destroyed (as it clearly is here) but simply desecrated, with only the gates being burned (1 Macc. 4:38; 2 Macc. 1:8; 8:33). There is a careful rebuttal of this Maccabean hypothesis in Delitzsch, *Psalms*, 2:325–28. Delitzsch shows how very appropriate Ps. 74 would have been in the Maccabean sufferings but demonstrates that the psalm cannot have originated from then. See also Kirkpatrick, *Psalms*, 2:440–42.

2 This is noted by I. Howard Marshall, "Acts," in *CNTOT* 596, although the echo is thematic rather than verbal.

The New Testament develops this theme to show that the church of Christ is that rebuilding project on earth today (e.g., 1 Cor. 3:16; 1 Pet. 2:4–10).[3]

Third, the language of hope in Psalm 74:12–17 includes allusions to the exodus (see below); Jesus is the new Moses who leads his people in the new exodus, achieving by his death the exodus of his people (cf. "and spoke of his departure," a translation of the term ἔξοδος, *exodos*, Luke 9:31), crucified as our Passover lamb (1 Cor. 5:7). He who feels the griefs of his broken church will lead that church out of slavery and into the promised land of the new creation.

Fourth, together with exodus allusions, there is clear creation language in Psalm 74:12–17; the order of creation guarantees the completion of redemption. Here, not only is Jesus our exodus, he is the agent and sustainer of creation (e.g., John 1:3; Col. 1:17; Heb. 1:3) and the one who brings about the renewal of creation in the new heavens and new earth.

Fifth, Jesus prays for his church, so vulnerable in a dangerous world, and teaches us to pray with him. There are fruitful comparisons to be explored between the urgent petitions of Psalm 74:18–23 and Jesus's prayer in John 17, not least in the shared concern for the "name" of God (John 17:6, 22–23, 26).

It is possible to hold these fulfillments together only because Jesus Christ possesses, in his one undivided person, a fully human nature and a fully divine nature. Only because he is fully human can he feel these griefs and pray these prayers. Only because he is fully divine can he uphold and restore creation. Only because he is fully human and fully divine can he be the bringer of a new exodus through his sin-bearing death.

There are suggestive links between the individual lament of Psalm 73 and the corporate lament of Psalm 74. These include (1) the rare word "ruin" (73:18; 74:3), (2) the "sanctuary" (73:17; 74:3, 7), (3) scoffing (73:8; 74:10, 18, 22), (4) "violence" (73:6; 74:20), (5) "continually" (73:23; 74:23), and (6) "portion/heritage" (73:26; 74:2).

Psalms 74, 75, and 76 are linked by the motifs of God as Judge, the wrath of God, and God's "name." Psalm 74 has very close links with Psalm 79, including the question "How long?" (74:10; 79:5), the theme of how long the sufferings go

3   W. Dennis Tucker Jr. and Jamie A. Grant, *Psalms*, NIVAC (Grand Rapids, MI: Zondervan, 2018), 2:91–92.

on ("forever"), the desecration of the sanctuary, the wrath of God, the church as the sheep of God's pasture and God's inheritance, the reproaches of the enemy, and the "name" of God. The seemingly broken Davidic covenant is strongly echoed and developed in Psalm 89, the final psalm of book 3. Other significant links include Exodus 15, the prayer of Daniel 9:3–19, and the book of Lamentations (see especially Lam. 2:2, 7, 9). The accounts of the destruction of the temple are found in 2 Kings 24–25; 2 Chronicles 36:17–21; and Jeremiah 52.

THE TEXT

Structure
There are three main sections.[4] Psalm 74:1–11 is bracketed by the question "Why?" and marked by an emphasis on words or phrases including "forever," "How long?" "perpetual," and "from of old." Psalm 74:12–17 is "an obvious thematic unit," which sounds a very different, and hopeful, tone, looking back to the creation and the exodus, and includes the emphatic "you" address to God seven times. Psalm 74:18–23 is a chain of petitions, expressed as imperatives or negated jussives.[5]

Superscription

S   A Maskil[6] of Asaph.[7]

For the psalms of **Asaph**, see on Psalms 50 and 73. For the designation **Maskil**, see on Psalm 32. The other **Maskil** in this Asaphite collection is Psalm 78.

74:1–11 Feel the Grief of Christ's Broken Church

1   O God, why do you cast us off forever?
     Why does your anger smoke against the sheep of your pasture?

---

4 This structure is clearly outlined in Hossfeld and Zenger, *Psalms*, 2:241–42.
5 Within Ps. 74:1–11, 74:4–8 begins and ends with "meeting place," both 74:4–8 and 74:9–11 open with "signs," and the question "How long?" marks 74:9–11. Hamilton, *Psalms*, 2:14.
6 See on Ps. 32. Laments sharing this designation include Pss. 42, 44, 74, 88, 89.
7 In Hebrew the superscription is the start of verse 1.

2   Remember your congregation, which you have purchased of old,
which you have redeemed to be the tribe of your heritage!
Remember Mount Zion, where you have dwelt.

Psalm 74:1–11 is bracketed by address to God (74:1–3a, 10–11) and
especially by the question **Why?**[8]—the first word in Hebrew (fronted for
emphasis), here and in 74:11. This, like the question "How long?" (74:9–10),
is asked in faith: "The believer's asking *why?* is no quarrelling: nor is any
speech of the saints unto God a quarrelling, which endeth or resolveth in
petition and supplication, as this doth."[9]

The word **forever** is repeated in 74:3 ("perpetual"), 10, and 19 (see also
77:8; 79:5; 89:46; Lam. 5:20; contrast Ps. 103:9); God's judgment always has
about it the character of hell and therefore feels like unending misery. The
verb **cast off** (or "spurn," "reject") appears together with **forever** in Psalm
44:23 (cf. 43:2 ["rejected"]; 60:1, 10; 77:7; 88:14; 89:38; Lam. 2:7 ["scorned"];
3:17 ["is bereft"], 31). God's **anger** is worse by far than the sufferings themselves, for this is abandonment by God; unless this is reversed, we have no
hope, being "without God in the world" (Eph. 2:12).

Set against this misery are words pregnant with hope. For the church is
the sheep of your pasture (cf. Pss. 23:1–6; 80:1), of which Christ will be
the shepherd (John 10:11; Heb. 13:20; 1 Pet. 2:25; 5:2). It is **your congregation**, the assembly, gathering, or church of God (cf. Acts 20:28). It has been
purchased of old, redeemed at the exodus (Ex. 15:13, 16).[10] It is **the tribe**
(i.e., the people) **of your heritage**, and it is a remarkable thought not only
that God is our heritage (cf. Ps. 73:26, where the word "portion" is the same
word) but that we are his. This, as Charles Spurgeon says, is

a fact full of comfort: his valu[ing] of us, his dominion over us, his connection with us are so many lights to cheer our darkness. No man will
willingly lose his inheritance, and no prince will relinquish his dominions;
therefore we believe that the King of kings will hold his own.[11]

8 The word "why" is the first word of Ps. 74:1 and appears only once. Our translators have repeated it at the start of the second line because it clearly carries through the question of the
whole verse.
9 Dickson, *Psalms*, 1:458.
10 Both "purchase" and "redeem" appear in Ex. 15:13, 16. Harman, *Psalms*, 2:560.
11 Spurgeon, *Treasury*, 2.1:273.

Finally, we ask God to **remember** (i.e., call to mind and act for) **Mount Zion**, given its association with God's covenant with David, **where you have dwelt** (for the presence of God is as much a concern here as it was in Ps. 73; see 73:23–28). The description that follows is all predicated on this covenant bond, ultimately unbreakable in Christ. As Spurgeon preaches, "Can he desert his blood-bought and forsake his redeemed? Can election fail and eternal love cease to flow? Impossible. The woes of Calvary, and the covenant of which they are the seal, are the security of the saints."[12]

> 3   Direct your steps to the perpetual ruins;
>   the enemy has destroyed everything in the sanctuary!

Direct your steps translates an unusual phrase. Probably it means "Hurry!"[13] The **perpetual ruins**[14] are "the forever ruins," for it seems as though the church has been broken for a long time and shows no sign of being repaired. The reference to **the sanctuary** begins to direct our attention to the honor and holiness of God, which is the most important matter at stake in the health of the church, for this is God's holy place.

The description that follows has the ring of eyewitness testimony. It is peculiarly vivid and conveys not only the bare facts but the agonizing emotion of the scene. This is what it is to watch the church being broken.

> 4   Your foes have roared in the midst of your meeting place;
>   they set up their own signs for signs.

The verb **roared** is used of a lion, either literally (e.g., Judg. 14:5; Jer. 2:15) or metaphorically (e.g., Isa. 5:29; Jer. 2:15; 51:38), and in particular of the Messiah's enemies in Psalm 22:13. The word **meeting place** (מוֹעֵד, *moed*) can mean an appointed feast or season or a place of meeting; here the context indicates the place where God meets with his people (as in Lam. 2:6). The word **sign** here means something like our modern flag, a banner (as in Num. 2:2) that signifies a whole raft of convictions. When the flag of

12 Spurgeon, *Treasury*, 2.1:273.
13 Ross suggests the bold sense of "Step lively," as in, "Don't drag your feet; get on with it." Ross, *Psalms*, 2:586. The sense, though, must be reverent, even if it is urgent.
14 This rare word (מַשֻּׁאוֹת) shares the same root as the verb "fall to ruin" in Ps. 73:18.

Babylon is raised over the temple, it declares that the Babylonian gods are triumphant and that the God of Israel is defeated.

> 5   They were like those who swing axes
>   in a forest of trees.

Although the Hebrew of Psalm 74:5 is not easy to translate, the sense seems to be that as the invaders hacked away at the beautiful wood of the temple (74:6), it was as if they were woodcutters in a forest. In view of the later imagery of creation (esp. 74:15–17) and the symbolism by which the temple represented the whole created order in the presence of God, this analogy is peculiarly appropriate.[15] When people attack Christ's church, they seek to cut down the whole created order.

> 6   And all its carved wood
>   they broke down with hatchets and hammers.

And translates the Hebrew "and now" ("as though the watcher had followed the destroyers, his heart silently pleading, 'Not the panels, please, not the panels!'").[16] The **carved wood** includes the beautiful creation imagery of palm trees and flowers, together with the cherubim (1 Kings 6:29; cf. 2 Chron. 2:7, 14, in which the same Hebrew word is used).

> 7   They set your sanctuary on fire;
>   they profaned the dwelling place of your name,
>   bringing it down to the ground.

The phrase **to the ground** emphasizes the completeness of the destruction, fulfilled in the cross of Christ. The verb **profaned** and the word **sanctuary** evoke the holiness of God. The **dwelling place** (a word used elsewhere for the tabernacle) **of your name** introduces the significant theme of the **name** of God, his revealed nature and public reputation on earth. The worst thing about sin is that it dishonors God.

15 Hamilton, *Psalms*, 2:19.
16 Motyer, *Psalms*, 533.

8   They said to themselves, "We will utterly subdue them";
  they burned all the meeting places of God in the land.

The ruthlessness of the enemies of Christ and his church is expressed in
the cry **We will utterly subdue them**; this is the final refutation—or so it
would seem—of the confident claims of Psalms 1 and 2 that God's man will
prosper and that God's Christ will conquer the world. The phrase translated
all the meeting places of God in the land may be a plural of dignity, to
indicate the greatness of the one meeting place, the temple, or the various
courts and rooms within the temple. But probably it indicates the ruthless
eradication of all the places where the old covenant church used to meet to
pray and hear the Scriptures (later to become the synagogues).[17]

9   We do not see our signs;
  there is no longer any prophet,
  and there is none among us who knows how long.

Our signs (the same word as in 74:4) refers to the visible symbols of the
covenant in the temple, most especially the ark. These precious pledges
of covenant have been destroyed.

The statement that **there is no longer any prophet**[18] is explained in the
final line to mean that **there is none among us who knows how long** this
devastation for the church will endure. There are no visible signs of God's
covenant faithfulness to us, and there is no audible word to tell us how long
this God-forsaken agony will last.[19]

10   How long, O God, is the foe to scoff?
  Is the enemy to revile your name forever?
11   Why do you hold back your hand, your right hand?
  Take it from the fold of your garment and destroy them!

17 After careful discussion, this is the conclusion of Tate, *Psalms 51–100*, 249–50.
18 It would seem that Jeremiah has by this time been taken away to Egypt (Jer. 43) and perhaps has
    even died. Ezekiel (and Daniel, if he is to be considered a prophet rather than a wise man) have
    been taken to Babylon in the earlier deportations; if the psalm is written in or near Jerusalem,
    no prophet was present to speak God's word.
19 In an earlier context (for the northern kingdom) the tragedy of having no word from the Lord
    is compared to a famine (Amos 8:11–12).

After the harrowing description of 74:4–9, Asaph speaks again to God and repeats the questions **How long?** (picking up the close of 74:9) and **Why?** (both fronted for emphasis in the Hebrew). The word **forever** is repeated from 74:1 and 3 (see also 74:19). The verb **to scoff** is used often of the mockery of the enemies of Christ and his church (e.g., 42:10; 44:16; 55:12; 69:9; 79:12; 89:51; 102:8; 119:42). The **name** (reputation) of God is **reviled**. The vehemence of the final line is occasioned not by any personal vindictiveness but by a passionate concern for the honor of God.

74:12–17 Grasp the Hope for Christ's Broken Church

12   Yet God my King is from of old,
         working salvation in the midst of the earth.

Yet God signals a sharp and wonderful change of tone (cf. "But God," Eph. 2:4).[20] To call God **my King** is to reaffirm covenant relation not between God and any random individual but between God (as covenant Master or King) and a man who represents Israel. To say he is my King **from of old** (cf. Ps. 74:2) is to set this ancient (and ultimately, in Christ, eternal) covenant against what feels like unending God-forsakenness (the repeated "forever," 74:1, 10, 19). The line **working salvation in the midst of the earth** is the headline to be expounded in 74:13–17.

Seven times God is addressed with the emphatic personal pronoun "you" (74:13, 14, 15 [2x], 16, 17 [2x], italicized in the extracts below). In addition, twice in 74:16 there is an emphatic "yours."[21]

13   *You* divided the sea by your might;
         you broke the heads of the sea monsters on the waters.
14   *You* crushed the heads of Leviathan;
         you gave him as food for the creatures of the wilderness.

The **sea monsters** (תַּנִּינִים, *thanninim*) appear in Genesis 1:21 and Psalm 148:7 as "the great sea creatures." In the singular this is a "serpent" (e.g.,

---

20 The *vav* in וֵאלֹהִים is strongly adversative here.
21 לְךָ. Ps. 74:16a is literally "Yours the day, also yours the night."

Ex. 7:9–12). **Leviathan** (Job 3:8; 41:1–34; Ps. 104:26) designates the same monster. The two terms are used in parallel in Isaiah 27:1 in imagery that understands it or them (the imagery is fluid) to designate the serpent who appears in Scripture from Genesis 3 onward, both as a "snake" (to deceive) and as a "dragon" (to devour).[22] From this viewpoint the crushing of the head or heads of the serpent is an echo of Genesis 3:15; this is what the seed of the woman, the Messiah, will do.

There are two ways to understand the imagery of Psalm 74:13–14. The first is to identify **the sea** as the "Red Sea" at the exodus and **the sea monsters** and **Leviathan** as mocking nicknames for Pharaoh and his armies (cf. Isa. 51:9; Ezek. 29:3; 32:2). The triumph of Aaron's snake over the Egyptian snakes (Ex. 7:8–12) anticipated this crushing defeat. **The creatures of the wilderness** may possibly allude to the wild animals or birds that devoured the Egyptian corpses (on the sea shore, Ex. 14:30).[23]

The second approach is to understand that behind what happened at the Red Sea lies a cosmic struggle in which the **sea** and the **sea monsters / Leviathan** represent cosmic forces of evil. This is how the rest of Scripture understands this language.[24] Probably this second approach lies behind the first; both are true. Christ is the fulfillment of every exodus theme, as he is of the cosmic victory of God.

15   *You* split open springs and brooks;
       you dried up ever-flowing streams.

Psalm 74:15a probably alludes to the water that "splits" forth out of the rock (Ex. 17:6). If so, then we may have another connection with Christ, for "the rock was Christ" (1 Cor. 10:4). The adjective **ever-flowing** in Psalm 74:15b is used in Exodus 14:27 of the Red Sea returning to its "normal flow." So this may speak of the Red Sea being **dried up** when the

---

22 See the excellent study of this theme in biblical theology by Andrew David Naselli, *The Serpent and the Serpent Slayer*, SSBT (Wheaton, IL: Crossway, 2020). The LXX translates both words by "dragon" (δράκων).

23 Tate, *Psalms 51–100*, 243n14a.

24 See especially the use of "dragon" language in the book of Revelation (esp. in Rev. 12–13). See also Naselli, *The Serpent and the Serpent Slayer*. Such cosmic battle imagery is well known in other ancient Near Eastern sources. In the Old Testament, it is brought into a firmly monotheistic framework; these supernatural forces have no independent agency.

people crossed. But the verb **dried up** is used in Joshua 4:23 and 5:1 of the River Jordan, so the crossing of Jordan may be the reference.[25]

> 16   Yours is the day, yours also the night;
>   *you* have established the heavenly lights and the sun.
> 17   *You* have fixed all the boundaries of the earth;
>   *you* have made summer and winter.

We are firmly in creation language in Psalm 74:16–17 with its references to **the day, the night, the heavenly lights** (lit., "the lights"),[26] **the sun**, and **summer and winter**. The word **boundaries** usually refers to the borders of a people group or nation (e.g., of a tribe in the promised land), but in this context (of dangerous waters, 74:13–15), it would seem to refer to the life-preserving boundaries of Genesis 1:9–10, by which the waters are separated from the land on which animals and people can live (cf. Ps. 104:9).[27]

The combination of the language of creation and of redemption (the exodus) reminds us that the work of redemption is the restoration of the proper order of creation. The completion of Christ's church is as sure as the Creator is strong.

74:18–23 Pray Urgently for the Restoration of Christ's Broken Church

The proper response to the reassurance of Psalm 74:12–17 is not to relax but to pray, and that urgently, as here, with nine petitions in quick succession.

> 18   Remember this, O LORD, how the enemy scoffs,
>   and a foolish people reviles your name.

The first petition is that God will **remember** (cf. "remember" in 74:2, 22, and "do not forget" in 74:19, 23), that is, call to mind and act because of **this** (where "this" points forward to what follows). The covenant name, LORD, is used here for the first time in the psalm. The scoffing of the enemy

---

25 Harman, *Psalms*, 2:563.
26 The word מָאוֹר is used five times in Gen. 1:14–16. The LXX has "sun and moon," assuming this refers to "the greater lights" of Gen. 1 (cf. CSB, NIV: "the moon").
27 Eveson, *Psalms*, 2:26.

(cf. 74:10) is expanded in the second line to highlight the wicked folly of those who do this (**a foolish people**, lit., "a people of folly") and **the name** that is reviled, reminding us that the honor of God is the central issue for the state of Christ's church.

> 19   Do not deliver the soul of your dove to the wild beasts;
>   do not forget the life of your poor forever.

The second and third (parallel) petitions focus on the desperate need of Christ's church, described here as **the soul of your dove**. This unusual image highlights innocent vulnerability in the midst of **wild beasts** (cf. "sheep in the midst of wolves," Matt. 10:16). The church of Christ is **your poor** (cf. the "children" and "little ones" in Matthew's Gospel).

The word **forever** reminds us of the desperate scenes described in Psalm 74:1–11 (the word is used in 74:1, 3, 10). David Dickson observes,

> The church of God, in comparison of her many and strong enemies, is like a solitary, weak, desolate turtle dove, harmless, meek, lowly, patient in desolation, easing her grief by sighing, and exposed to a multitude of ravenous birds. . . . The church is the Lord's hospital, where his poor ones are sustained . . . and he will not neglect them.[28]

> 20   Have regard for the covenant,
>   for the dark places of the land are full of the habitations of
>   violence.

The covenant name (74:18) is followed, in the fourth petition, by explicit reference to **the covenant**, presumably in this context primarily the covenant with David, which encompasses all previous covenants of his grace. A land in which God's covenant has been forsaken and which is under the covenant curses of God will be a land with **dark places**, morally ugly and dangerous, **habitations** (NIV: "haunts") **of violence** (cf. 73:6). The word translated **habitations** (נְאוֹת, *neoth*) can mean "pasture" (e.g., 2 Sam. 7:8), "abode" (Ex. 15:13), or "habitation" (Ps. 79:7). Where the goodness and

---

28 Dickson, *Psalms*, 1:465.

beauty of God's covenant law and moral order is abandoned, a land will be terribly transformed from a nurturing pasture into a place of darkness and violence, in which it will always be the weak who suffer most. Only a new covenant can offer hope to such a land.

> ²¹   Let not the downtrodden turn back in shame;
>   let the poor and needy praise your name.

The fifth and sixth petitions emphasize the weakness of Christ's church (cf. 74:19), for the darkness and violence of 74:20 will make life very hard for **the downtrodden**, for **the poor and needy** (cf. 70:5), who are Christ's vulnerable "dove" people and the people whom the Messiah will save (72:13). The **name** so vilified in the world will be honored and praised in the restored church.

> ²²   Arise, O God, defend your cause;
>   remember how the foolish scoff at you all the day!
> ²³   Do not forget the clamor of your foes,
>   the uproar of those who rise against you, which goes up
>   continually!

Psalm 74:22–23 gives the final three petitions. The call for **God** to **arise** (cf. Num. 10:35) is followed by the appeal **Defend your cause**, literally, "Defend your defense" or "Strive your strife," using a word that speaks of God fighting a lawsuit against the scoffing of fools, who mock **all the day** and **continually** (picking up again the "forever" theme). The words **clamor** and **uproar** remind us of the chaotic riot of rebellion in Psalm 2:1. The point is not that they **rise against** us but that they **rise against you**, against God. And so, yet again, the honor of God is signaled as the central concern of the psalm as it laments the broken state of the church.

REFLECTION AND RESPONSE

1. As we make Psalm 74:1–11 our own, we first enter into the vivid and desperate sadness of the original scene; we see that it speaks not simply of one historical disaster for God's church but of every time of brokenness

in the church of Christ. In praying these verses, we enter into the grief of the Spirit of Jesus.

2. The particulars of a broken church will be different in different places and at various times. In the sixteenth century, Martin Luther lamented the "treachery" by which "ungodly Jewish interpreters" read the Scriptures in such a way as to deny the gospel of grace, "so that Christ could have no place, no honor . . . in them."[29] In the nineteenth century, Spurgeon bewailed (from 74:5) those so-called "higher" biblical critics and churchmen who use their weapons "to destroy the truth"; he longed "for an hour of Luther's hatchet, of Calvin's mighty axe," to destroy error.[30] In the twenty-first century, Philip Eveson applies this to "the sorry state of the professing church in the West."[31] Each of us ponders and grieves the manner in which the church of Christ is broken in our place and time.

3. The psalm calls us deeply to bewail the state of Christ's church. Like the people in the northern kingdom in the days of Amos, we are prone to seek refuge in our pleasures rather than facing, and lamenting, the broken state of God's people (Amos 6:4–6). What ought to grieve us most deeply is not our natural sadness that our churches are weak but the dishonor that is brought to God's name. Eveson states, "Above all the concerns that grieve us, what should affect us most should be the state of his church and the resulting dishonour that is brought to God's holy name."[32]

4. We must remember that the sorrows of Christ (e.g., his weeping over Jerusalem) led him to plunge into the darkness of God-forsakenness for us, that his love for his church and for his Father moved him to give himself in substitutionary atonement for us. Jesus is the temple whose destruction is so agonizingly described.

5. When making Psalm 74:12–17 our own, we must first make sure we understand the echoes of creation and the exodus. We understand from biblical theology the wonderful ways in which Jesus is both the upholder of creation and the bringer of a new exodus, so that we grasp, with John Calvin, that these things are "testimonies of [God's] electing love" for us in Christ.[33] These allusions give

29 Luther, *Luther's Works*, 10:430.
30 Spurgeon, *Treasury*, 2.1:274.
31 Eveson, *Psalms*, 2:22.
32 Eveson, *Psalms*, 2:24.
33 Calvin, *Psalms*, 3:173.

us comfort not simply because they are vivid but because they are guaranteed in Christ. We may be sure, as Spurgeon writes, that "every believer may plead at this day the ancient deeds of the Lord, the work of Calvary, the overthrow of sin, death, and hell."[34] Because of Christ, "the delivery of Israel out of Egypt, and the destruction of the Egyptians, is a pledge unto the church in every age after, that God will destroy their enemies, how strong and terrible they be, and will deliver his church," and also that "as the Lord hath set bounds to the sea, bounds and borders to every kingdom, to summer's heat and to winter's cold: so can he do, and so hath he done, and so will he do unto all the troubles of his own, to all the rage, power, plots, and purposes of their enemies."[35]

6. Psalm 74:18–23 stirs us to respond to gospel comfort (74:12–17) with renewed and urgent prayer. Let us be sure to make these petitions our own, both individually and corporately, remembering the repeated focus on the honor of God, the reminders of the weakness and frailty of Christ's church, and the miserable need of an unfaithful church for the restoration of gospel light and the love of God's holy law.

---

34 Spurgeon, *Treasury*, 2.1:276.
35 Dickson, *Psalms*, 1:463–64.

This is a psalm which applies the remedy of humility to the tumor of pride, but comforts the humble in their hope. By this double action it ensures that none shall arrogantly presume on themselves, and that no humble person shall despair of God.

AUGUSTINE
Expositions of the Psalms

King Jesus Christ Himself speaks, promising to judge justly when the time of universal resurrection comes. He also warns us against daring to do anything against God's command, so that eternal punishment may not rack us.

CASSIODORUS
Explanation of the Psalms

It affords matter of rejoicing and thanksgiving to the whole Church, to reflect that the world is governed exclusively according to the will of God, and that she herself is sustained by his grace and power alone.

JOHN CALVIN
Commentary on the Psalms

PSALM 75

Christ on earth believed Psalm 75. Christ exalted now speaks it to all who will listen. For Christ is both the forerunner of all believers and the Judge of all the earth. We speak these words with him as the members of the body of which he is the head, and we voice these convictions about him as we look to him to judge the world.

There is a suggestive ambiguity about who is speaking at different points. Psalm 75:1 begins with the whole church giving thanks.[1] Psalm 75:2–3 is the voice of God. The first-person singular continues in 75:4–5 (after the *Selah* at the end of 75:3), and it is not so clear whether this is the voice of God or the voice of the psalmist, for it continues straight on into 75:6–8, in which God is spoken of in the third person. Psalm 75:9 sounds like the voice of the psalmist, but then 75:10 seems to be the voice of God. The prophetic voice of the psalmist, speaking by the Spirit of God, who is the Spirit of Christ, blends with the voice of God.

There are many links back to Psalm 74, as also forward to Psalm 76 (commented on there). With Psalm 74 is shared (1) the verb for "rising" or "lifting up" (74:3 ["direct"], 23; 75:4–5, 7, 10); (2) the significance of "the earth" (74:12, 17; 75:3, 8) and its created stability (74:15–16; 75:3); (3) the covenant "name" of God (74:10, 18, 21; 75:1); (4) the Hebrew word מוֹעֵד, *moed* ("meeting place[s]" in 74:4, 8, and "set time" in 75:2); and (5) God as the one who must judge (74:11; 75:2).

---

1 But see the comment on Ps. 75:1c below.

Psalm 75 is the answer to the prayers of 74:18–23[2] and the assurance that God does judge justly. Jesus believed that truth and, as the true Israel, entrusted himself to the God who judges justly (1 Pet. 2:23). Now he is exalted, and to him is entrusted all judgment by the Father (John 5:27). He is both the one lifted up by the Father and the one who has the authority to lift up and to bring down.

There are also many connections with the song of Hannah (1 Sam. 2:1–10)[3] and therefore also with the song of Mary (Luke 1:46–55). What this psalmist says, Hannah focuses on the anointed King, as Mary grasps that the son conceived in her will be that King.

We do not know the circumstances that led to the psalm. It is sometimes suggested that the Assyrian crisis in the reign of Hezekiah would have been appropriate, although we cannot be sure.[4] It speaks now to every church enduring the trials spoken of at length in Psalm 74.

THE TEXT

Structure

See the second paragraph under the *orientation* section above.

Superscription

S   To the choirmaster:[5] according to Do Not Destroy.[6] A Psalm of Asaph. A Song.[7]

This superscription is similar to those of Psalms 76 and 77.

---

2   Delitzsch, *Psalms*, 2:336; Kirkpatrick, *Psalms*, 2:449.

3   These echoes are remarkable—noted in Hossfeld and Zenger, *Psalms*, 2:257. They include (1) the "horn" (1 Sam. 2:1, 10; Ps. 75:4–5, 10), (2) God as Judge (1 Sam. 2:10; Ps. 75:2), (3) the motifs of lifting up and bringing low, (4) pride (1 Sam. 2:3; Ps. 75:5), (5) the upholding of the "pillars" of the world (using synonyms, 1 Sam. 2:8; Ps. 75:3), (6) two groups of people, and (7) a very similar concluding formula (although Hannah explicitly refers to the King).

4   E.g., Kirkpatrick, *Psalms*, 2:449; Hengstenberg, *Psalms*, 2:428–29; Harman, *Psalms*, 2:567. This is sometimes argued from similarities with the prophecies of Isaiah at that time.

5   See on Ps. 4.

6   See on Ps. 57.

7   In Hebrew the superscription is verse 1; subsequent verse numbers are increased by one.

75:1 Headline: Christ Leads His Church in
Thanksgiving for Certain Judgment and Salvation

1   We give thanks to you, O God;
  we give thanks, for your name is near.
 We[8] recount your wondrous deeds.

The repeated and emphatic **We give thanks** sets the tone for a confident psalm.[9] The headline reason is expressed in two ways. First, **your name**—that is, the revelation of your nature, covenant promises, and purposes—**is near**. The "name" of God is prominent in Psalm 74 (74:7, 10, 18, 21) and begins Psalm 76 (76:1); the context here associates it closely with the public declaration of his words and deeds of salvation. Derek Kidner points out that the nearness of God's name finds its fulfillment in Christ, who declares that name to us (John 17:6, 26). Second, and in close parallel, are **your wondrous deeds**, a phrase that speaks of God's actions in both creation and redemption.[10] What exactly this means in this context is opened up in the body of the psalm.

75:2–3 The Promise: God in Christ Promises
His Church That He Will Judge the World

2   "At the set time that I appoint
  I will judge with equity.
3   When the earth totters, and all its inhabitants,
  it is I who keep steady its pillars.   *Selah*

---

8 The ESV mg. notes that the Hebrew is "They recount." Although some have suggested that the "wondrous deeds" ought to be the subject of the verb, this would be an expression that is unusual, if not unique. Goldingay, *Psalms*, 2:438; Hossfeld and Zenger, *Psalms*, 2:253. It is better to take the unexpressed subject to be something like "the people" (CSB, NASB, NIV), which here means the people of God (the same as the "we" of the first two lines).

9 Hossfeld suggests that the three verbs (all in perfect tense) refer back to some past rescue and praise God for that, while recognizing that there is no cause to praise in the present. Hossfeld and Zenger, *Psalms*, 2:252–53. This notion makes little sense of the confidence of the rest of the psalm. With Calvin we may say, "The verbs in the Hebrew are in the past tense; but the subject of the psalm requires that they should be translated into the future." Calvin, *Psalms*, 3:183.

10 The recounting, or declaration, of God's wonderful deeds appears also (with the same verb and noun) in Pss. 9:1; 26:7; 71:17; 78:4; and elsewhere.

At the set time[11] uses the same Hebrew word translated "meeting place" in Psalm 74:4 and 8. There is a powerful irony here, as if God says to the enemies of Christ's church, "You think you have destroyed the places and times in which I meet with my people (as you attack the church), but there is a meeting place and time that I have set for judgment, and you cannot destroy that." We may have to wait for this time (cf. Hab. 2:3), but it will come. The subject of **I will judge** is an emphatic "I." The verb **I appoint** suggests a thematic echo in Acts 17:31, for God has appointed a day when he will judge the world by the man whom he has raised from the dead.

The word **equity** means perfect fairness and justice. All wrongs will be put right. The picture of the **earth** tottering emphasizes **all its inhabitants**. The whole world is disordered by man's rebellion against God. But this will never destroy God's created order, for he promises, **It is I who keep steady its pillars**. The verb translated **totters** is used of people "melting away" in fear (e.g., Ex. 15:15; Josh. 2:9, 24; Isa. 14:31), although the verb also has the sense of being caused to quake or tremble. The picture is very similar to that in Psalms 11:3 and 82:5, where the "undermining of justice on earth connotes the undermining of the earth's foundations"[12] when his good moral order is subverted. The noun **pillars** is often used in Exodus and Numbers of the supporting pillars of the tabernacle; metaphorically (cf. the synonym in 1 Sam. 2:8), it speaks here of holding God's creation order secure (cf. Pss. 24:1–2; 104:5). The New Testament teaches us that Christ, the eternal Word and Son of God, upholds the universe (Col. 1:17; Heb. 1:3).

When the church is under bitter attack, it can feel as if the moral order of creation is being shaken. But God the Creator guarantees that this order cannot fall—and will be restored—in Christ.

Selah prompts a timely pause for reflection on the great promises of Psalm 75:2–3.

75:4–5 The Warning: Christ Warns the Proud to Humble Themselves under God's Mighty Hand

4   I say to the boastful, 'Do not boast,'
        and to the wicked, 'Do not lift up your horn;

---

11 The NIV's words "You say" are not in the Hebrew but are added to make it clear that what follows are the words of God.
12 Dahood, *Psalms*, 2:211.

5   do not lift up your horn on high,
        or speak with haughty neck.'"

Because Psalm 75:4–5 continues straight into 75:6–8 (each verse of which
begins with "for"), it may be more natural to see the *Selah* in 75:3 as marking the shift from the voice of God in 75:2–3, to the voice of the psalmist
as God's prophet, and therefore ultimately of Christ our prophet, in 75:4–5.
But whoever speaks it, this warning comes with the full authority of God.
The **boastful** appear also, for example, in 5:5 and 73:3 ("the arrogant"). The
verb **lift up** is a theme of the psalm, reappearing in 75:6–7 and 10. The **horn**
(also in 75:5, 10; cf. 1 Sam. 2:1, 10) symbolizes strength. For human beings
to **lift up** their **horn** against God indicates power with pride. The image
of the **haughty neck** is similar to that of being stiff-necked (e.g., Ex. 32:9;
33:3, 5; 34:9; Deut. 9:6, 13; 31:27; Acts 7:51).

75:6–8 The Reason: Only God Lifts Up
and Puts Down—and He Will

6   For not from the east or from the west
        and not from the wilderness comes lifting up,
7   but it is God who executes judgment,
        putting down one and lifting up another.
8   For in the hand of the LORD there is a cup
        with foaming wine, well mixed,
    and he pours out from it,
        and all the wicked of the earth
        shall drain it down to the dregs.

The threefold **for** (כִּי, *ki*, translated "for" in Psalm 75:6, 8, and "but" in
75:7) gives a triad of reasons why we ought to heed the strong warning of
75:4–5. The first part of the reason (75:6) is that the **lifting up** we naturally
long for cannot be found from any source on earth.[13] When we seek to live

---

13 The clause "From the wilderness comes lifting up" takes הָרִים as the hiphil infinitive of רוּם.
    Because this is such a common verb in the psalm, this is more likely to be the correct transla-
    tion than the alternative (with the same form), "of mountains." The latter, "the wilderness of
    the mountains," then leaves the verse without an object. The point is probably not the mention
    of three points of the compass (where "wilderness" may or may not indicate south) but rather

in God's world without God and hope we can find success from any other source than God, we are always disappointed.

The second part (75:7) is the counterpart of the first. If **lifting up** cannot be found from anywhere on earth, we need to grasp that **it is God who executes judgment**, which consists in the **putting down**[14] of **one** and the **lifting up** of **another**.

The third part of the reason (75:8) is an emphatic development of the "putting down," for it is this that we need to hear in our pride. The phrase **well mixed** appears only here in the Masoretic Text; it probably refers to mixing wine with spices (so CSB, NIV) to make it more potent.[15] The **cup** is **in the hand of the Lord**, then **he pours out from it**, and finally, **all the wicked of the earth shall drain it**. This vivid drama ought to arrest our attention. This imagery of a cup that makes someone drunk, incapacitated, and mad and that ultimately destroys that person appears in the Prophets (e.g., Isa. 51:17; Jer. 25:15–28; Ezek. 23:31–34; Hab. 2:15–16). It is used most movingly of the Lord Jesus concerning the wrath of God that he drinks for his people (Matt. 20:22; Mark 14:36; John 18:11). It appears again in the book of Revelation as the destiny of all the finally impenitent (e.g., Rev. 14:10;[16] 15:7; 16:19).

75:9–10 Summing Up

9   But I will declare it forever;
        I will sing praises to the God of Jacob.
10   All the horns of the wicked I will cut off,
        but the horns of the righteous shall be lifted up.

The final two verses respond and summarize the message of the psalm. Psalm 75:9 takes us back to 75:1. In the light of all that God has declared to

---

that all these are inaccessible places. "In other words, search where you will," you cannot find another source of lifting up than God. Kidner, *Psalms*, 2:272.

14 The same hiphil participle appears in 1 Sam. 2:7, "brings low." The same verb appears in Ps. 18:27 (= 2 Sam. 22:28) and often in Isaiah (e.g., 2:9, 11, 17).

15 Ross, *Psalms*, 2:610n33.

16 Commenting on Rev. 14:10, Beale and McDonough write, "The picture of pouring out wine resulting in intoxication indicates the unleashing of God's wrath at the final judgment.... This imagery is inspired especially by the wording of Ps. 75:8; Jer. 25:15; 51:7, all three of which are grouped together and applied by Jewish exegetical tradition to the wicked." G. K. Beale and Sean M. McDonough, "Revelation," in *CNTOT* 1132.

us, this representative of God's people says **But I** (emphatic) **will declare it forever** (lit., "I will declare forever," where the object of "declare" is everything we have heard in the psalm). In parallel, **I will sing praises to the God of Jacob**, for the subject matter of our praise is what God in Christ has done and will do for his people, who are the church of Christ.

Psalm 75:10 picks up the vivid language of **horns** to encapsulate the promise of the psalm and reaffirm that the message of Psalms 1 and 2 is true. On the one hand (cf. 75:8), **all** (emphatic) **the horns of the wicked I will cut off**, leaving them utterly powerless.[17] On the other, **the horns of the righteous shall be lifted up**. **The righteous** is singular in Hebrew, both generic (any man or woman righteous by faith) and perhaps also focused in Christ, the one righteous man in whom all righteousness is found.

REFLECTION AND RESPONSE

1. Our principal response must be to echo Psalm 75:1 and 9 in heartfelt praise for all God has done for us in Christ, especially that God has appointed a day when Christ will judge the world in justice.

2. The warnings of Psalm 75:4–5 are for the church as well as for the world. We too need to humble ourselves under God's mighty hand again and again (1 Pet. 5:6). So often we tend to revert to the self-righteousness and pride of the Pharisee and need to place ourselves again in the shoes of the tax collector (Luke 18:9–14).

3. It is worth pondering the image of drinking the cup. The Puritan David Dickson suggests that there is an element here of the punishment fitting the crime, that in our own sins we begin this terrible drinking, a process that culminates in the dreadful judgment imaged by inebriation.[18]

4. Augustine makes a strong pastoral and evangelistic appeal to all who are proud in view of Psalm 75:10: "Sinners do not want their horns broken, but they undoubtedly will be at the end. Do you dread that he will break yours for you on that day? Then break it yourself today" in self-humbling. He exhorts his hearers, "Now is the time of choosing."[19]

---

17 For this imagery, see Jer. 48:25; Lam. 2:3.

18 Dickson, *Psalms*, 1:470.

19 Augustine, *Psalms*, 4:52.

There is greater cause why princes should be afraid of God,
than why God's people should be afraid of princes.

DAVID DICKSON
A Commentary on the Psalms

O Lord God, whose dwelling is in heaven, and your name is great
in all the world, plant the dread and reverence of you and your
power in our hearts: let your threatenings and your judgments
which are heard from heaven and executed on disobedient and
gainsaying people, make us to tremble at the remembrance
of our sins and in the consideration of our weaknesses and
demerits: and let your mercies and the remembrance of your
infinite lovingkindness make our hearts still, full of evenness
and tranquility, that we may not fear the fierceness of human
beings, or the wrath of those whose spirits you can refrain, lest
we be disturbed in our duties toward you; but let us so fear
you that we may never offend against you, but may pass from
fear to love, from apprehensions of your wrath to the sense and
comforts of your mercies, through Jesus Christ our Lord. Amen.

JEREMY TAYLOR
"Collect for Psalm 76"

PSALM 76

ORIENTATION

Psalm 76, a triumphant psalm, celebrates a great victory, by which God utterly defeats the forces of evil and saves the humble of the earth. This victory is the cross of Christ.

It is likely the psalm was first sung to celebrate the defeat of the Assyrians in the siege of Jerusalem under King Hezekiah (2 Kings 18:13–19:37; 2 Chron. 32:1–23; Isa. 36:1–37:38). We cannot be sure, but the psalm fits very well with this dramatic rescue.[1] It has been included in book 3 by the final editor presumably because this earlier salvation will be of tremendous encouragement to the church in exile. Indeed, after the individual lament of Psalm 73, Psalms 74–76 form a trilogy[2] with a powerful movement, from lament and prayer (Ps. 74) through the hope of judgment (Ps. 75) to a grand fulfillment of judgment (Ps. 76).[3]

John Calvin writes, "The point . . . is, that the continual care of God in defending the Church, which he has chosen, is here celebrated to encourage the faithful without any doubt or hesitation to glory in his protection."[4]

But I want to suggest that more is at stake than Calvin envisages: it is not simply that every past rescue of the church encourages us to hope that there

---

1 The LXX refers to "the Assyrian" in its superscription. Others who see the background in the Assyrian crisis include Calvin, Delitzsch, Hengstenberg, and Zenger.

2 Links between these three psalms include God's "name" (Pss. 74:10, 18, 21; 75:1; 76:1); "Zion" (74:2; 76:2); the "God of Jacob" (75:9; 76:6); the anger and judgment of God (74:11, 18–23; 75:2–3, 7–8; 76:7–8); the scope of the judgment ("all the wicked of the earth," 75:8; "the earth / . . . all the humble of the earth / . . . the kings of the earth," 76:8–9, 12); and the character of those who need rescuing as poor, needy, and humble (74:19, 21; 76:9).

3 Hossfeld and Zenger, *Psalms*, 2:271. See also Harman, *Psalms*, 2:571; Delitzsch, *Psalms*, 2:313; Spurgeon, *Treasury*, 2.1:302.

4 Calvin, *Psalms*, 3:193.

will be future protection, true though that is. Every experience of salvation, from the exodus onward, is a shadow of the final victory, which is won by Christ our King at the cross. The hope of the church is not based on the rescue from the Assyrian crisis, wonderful though that was; it is not even rooted in the exodus, stupendous though that was; it is that day when Christ our champion disarmed the rulers and authorities and put them to open shame, triumphing over them at the cross (Col. 2:15; cf. John 12:31; 16:11).

Although the New Testament does not quote this psalm and evinces no clear verbal echoes, two lines of fulfillment bear on this psalm: the city of Zion and the Lion. The psalm focuses on Zion as the place from which God rescues his church and defeats his foes, and Jesus Christ is the fulfillment of all that Zion typified—the temple, the priesthood, the sacrifices, and the anointed King. The God who fights and saves from Zion is the God made known to us in Christ. The second is that Jesus Christ is called "the Lion of the tribe of Judah" (Rev. 5:5), and there is lion imagery implicit in the psalm (see on Ps. 76:2, 4, as well as the mention of Judah in 76:1). The Lion—who is also, paradoxically, the sin-bearing Lamb (Rev. 5:6)—is the one who triumphs by his atoning death.

Links with other scriptures include Psalms 46 and 48 (in which the rescue of Zion is prominent)[5] and Exodus 15 (notably the horse and rider, Ex. 15:1, 21; Ps. 76:6). The name "Israel" forms a small link with Psalm 73 (73:1; 76:1).

THE TEXT

Structure
Four equal sections of three verses are marked by *Selah* at the end of Psalm 76:3 and 9 and by the emphatic "But you" at the start of 76:7.

Superscription

S   To the choirmaster:[6] with stringed instruments.[7] A Psalm of
     Asaph. A Song.[8]

---

5   For similarities with and differences from Pss. 46 and 48, see Hossfeld and Zenger, *Psalms*, 2:261–62.
6   See on Ps. 4.
7   See on Ps. 4; cf. Pss. 6; 54; 55; 61; 67; Hab. 3:19.
8   In Hebrew the superscription is verse 1; subsequent verse numbers are increased by one.

76:1–3 God Is Powerful in Christ among His Church

Psalm 76:1–3 shows a dramatic narrowing focus: God is known (76:1), he is known in Zion (76:2), and there he ends wars (76:3). The verses speak first of God's greatness, then of the place where that greatness is focused, and finally on what he does from that place.

1   In Judah God is known;
          his name is great in Israel.

Judah is the tribe that became the southern kingdom, including Jerusalem and the anointed kings in David's line; here it focuses on God's people under God's Messiah. **Israel** is a name that, in its origins, speaks of the undivided people of God as a spiritual entity, finding its fulfillment in the true Israel of God (Gal. 6:16).[9] Here **God is known**, both in the covenant Scriptures and—perhaps in particular focus here—in his deeds of salvation. God has made himself known to his church by the rescue about to be celebrated. **His name** is another way of speaking of "God made known." This name **is great**, both intrinsically (in God's greatness of nature) and historically (in the rescue to be celebrated; cf. "God is great!" Ps. 70:4). **God is known** preeminently among his church, as David Dickson observes:

> Albeit God be in some sort known in all the world, because of the works of creation, manifesting some way the invisible excellencies of God, yet is he most of all made manifest to his visible church, where his word soundeth, and his works are best interpreted.[10]

2   His abode has been established in Salem,
          his dwelling place in Zion.

The horizon narrows to the focal point of God's old covenant church. This is called **Salem**, a name otherwise used only in Genesis 14:18 (and Heb. 7:1–2), perhaps suggesting a thematic connection with Abraham defeating the Canaanite kings, for Abraham's "seed," the Christ, will fully

---

9   This is rightly emphasized by Augustine, *Psalms*, 4:55–56.
10 Dickson, *Psalms*, 1:473.

achieve what Abraham's victory typified on a local level. The name **Salem** sounds like "peace" (שָׁלוֹם, *shalom*), which is appropriate since it is from here that God will end wars. The place is also **Zion**, which focuses on the covenant with David (2 Sam. 5:7), appropriate both if the psalm is about the salvation during Hezekiah's reign (a king in David's line) and if it refers to the Babylonian exiles as their hopes are turned toward the Messiah (see the massive focus on this covenant in Ps. 89 at the end of book 3). The true King of Salem is the priest-king in the order of Melchizedek (Heb. 5–7); the real King of Zion is the Messiah in David's line, who fulfills all that Zion foreshadows. Therefore, "the true Zion is the Christian Church."[11] The ESV rendering, **has been established**, is rather strong; the Hebrew simply reads "is" (so CSB, NASB, NIV).

The nouns translated **abode** (סֹךְ, *sok*) and **dwelling place** (מְעוֹנָה, *meonah*) are usually used of the "lair" or "thicket" where a beast of prey hides, most often a lion.[12] The nouns appear together in Job 38:40 in this context. Together with the mention of "prey" in Psalm 76:4, this suggests that God is here pictured as a Lion defending his people. This metaphor is not uncommon (e.g., Isa. 31:4; Jer. 25:38; 49:19; 50:44; Hos. 5:14; Amos 1:2; 3:8); Isaiah 31:4 and Amos 1:2 are of special relevance since God as Lion is there associated with Zion.

> 3   There he broke the flashing arrows,
>   the shield, the sword, and the weapons of war.   *Selah*

In Psalm 76:3 we learn what this leonine God will do. The word translated **there** is especially used in psalms of Zion (e.g., 48:6; 87:4, 6; 122:4–5; 132:17) and of the place where God causes his name to dwell (e.g., Deut. 12:5 and frequently); of all the places on earth, what is "there" is the most significant.[13] The **flashing arrows** (lit., "flashes[14] of bows") refer either to burning arrows or to the flashes of fast and frequent arrows. The fourth item

---

11 Augustine, *Psalms*, 4:56.

12 For the first, see, e.g., Ps. 10:9 (of the wicked being like a predator); 27:5 (of God's shelter); Jer. 25:38 (of the Lord's leonine "lair"). For the second, see Nah. 2:12.

13 Hossfeld and Zenger, *Psalms*, 2:265. There is suggestive consonance between "his name" (שְׁמוֹ, Ps. 76:1) and "there" (שָׁם, 76:3).

14 רֶשֶׁף is used of sparks in Job 5:7, of flashes of jealousy in Song 8:6, of thunderbolts in Ps. 78:48, and of a plague; cf. the damage caused in Deut. 32:24 and Hab. 3:5.

on the list (**the weapons of war**) is literally "war" or "battle," often taken to mean "weapons of war" in general; perhaps this comes last to suggest that God's victory will not simply destroy particular weapons (the **arrows**, the **shield**, the **sword**) but warfare itself (as in Ps. 46:9).

The New Testament helps us see the fulfillment of this vivid old covenant language in the power of Christ among his church, the one who is Melchizedek in Salem and David in Zion. Dickson notes, "As there are no means or instruments fit to destroy men which the enemy will not make use of against the church: so there is no weapon formed against her which shall prosper when she relieth on her Lord."[15]

76:4–6 God Wins the Victory in Christ over the Very Strongest Forces of Evil

Although there are puzzles about Psalm 76:4, the big picture of this section is very clear: God in Zion (i.e., God in Christ) utterly destroys and takes the spoil from every hostile power.

> 4   Glorious are you, more majestic
> than the mountains full of prey.

The God introduced in 76:1–3, who is God made known in Christ, is **glorious**, which means "being lit," that is "resplendent" (CSB, NASB), "radiant with light" (NIV).[16] The word translated **more . . . than**[17] can equally mean "from." Given the lion imagery implicit in 76:2, it seems likely that this is not a comparison ("more majestic than the mountains full of prey") but rather a vivid cameo of one coming in majesty "*from* **the mountains full of prey**" (CSB: "coming down from the mountains of prey") as a lion returning to his lair. The resplendence of God in Christ is seen when he returns to his "lair" (his church), having triumphed over his enemies. Perhaps there is even an echo of the motif of "taking captivity captive" (see on 68:18). Isaiah 14:25 says that God will break "the Assyrian in my land, and on my mountains trample him

---

15 Dickson, *Psalms*, 1:474.
16 Zenger suggests that lion imagery moves here into sun imagery, which is not uncommon in Egypt and Assyria when speaking of kings. Hossfeld and Zenger, *Psalms*, 2:267.
17 מִן.

underfoot."[18] Here is God in Christ resplendent, triumphant, returning in glory to his church.

5   The stouthearted were stripped of their spoil;
         they sank into sleep;
      all the men of war
         were unable to use their hands.

The stouthearted (lit., "mighty of heart"; cf. our phrase "brave heart," used in parallel with **men of war**) shows that even the strongest of the forces of evil has been defeated. They are **stripped of their spoil**, which becomes the victory gifts of the ascended Christ (cf. Ps. 68:18). The phrase **sank into sleep** indicates here death on the battlefield. They are **unable to use their hands** (lit., "They did not find their hands") because they no longer have power to do anything! After the clamor of battle (cf. the scene of 2:1–3), there is an eerie silence on the battlefield, for "albeit the church hath no strength in herself, yet the Lord can with a word of his mouth do all her work, and defeat her enemies."[19]

6   At your rebuke, O God of Jacob,
         both rider and horse lay stunned.

The **rebuke** of God is terrifying, able to rescue his King (18:15), to push back the waters of chaos (Ps. 104:7), to make the foundations of the earth tremble (Job 26:11). He is the **God of Jacob**, for all his power is used to save his church. The reference to **both rider** (i.e., chariot rider or chariot) **and horse** is an echo of Pharaoh's great army, attempting to keep men in slavery but powerless at God's rebuke (cf. Ex. 14:23, 26, 28; 15:1, 21). The verb **stunned** (like the phrase "sank into sleep" in Ps. 76:5) seems to indicate the deep sleep of death.

This awe-inspiring battlefield scene helps us grasp the majesty and the completeness of the victory of Christ on the cross, when every hostile power was subdued. This awe prepares us for the remainder of the psalm, which focuses on the proper response to such power.

---

18 Kirkpatrick, *Psalms*, 2:454.
19 Dickson, *Psalms*, 1:475.

76:7–9 The Cross Should Arouse Our Fear of God the Judge

7   But you, you are to be feared!
     Who can stand before you
       when once your anger is roused?

But you, you is very emphatic: "you—**to be feared**[20]—YOU!" The proper response to the victory of God in Christ is fear. This is, first, a terror of his judgment: **Who can stand before you** in **your anger**? As this terrible battle puts the watcher in awe of the divine victor, so the cross of Christ reveals the terrible judgment of God in all its fury (cf. Rom. 1:18); to see Christ on the cross is to see the wrath of God poured out against the one who has been "made . . . sin" for us (2 Cor. 5:21).

8   From the heavens you uttered judgment;
       the earth feared and was still,
9   when God arose to establish judgment,
       to save all the humble of the earth.   *Selah*

Psalm 76:8 contrasts **the heavens** with **the earth**.[21] The proper response to the declaration of judgment from on high is for the whole **earth** to **fear** and be **still**, in the silence of awed surrender. In 76:9 **when God arose** harks back to many prayers for God to "arise" (most recently 74:22). **To establish judgment** is literally "for judgment." What God did when he defeated the Assyrians anticipates the judgment for which the exiles prayed in Psalm 74, which was promised in Psalm 75 and which happened at the cross of Christ. The second line of 76:9 shifts the focus from the defeated foes to the grand purpose of this judgment, **to save all the humble of the earth**, all of them, the "humble poor" who trust in God and cast themselves on his mercy in Christ. To watch God do this in the Assyrian crisis is an encouragement to wait for the day he will do that in Christ and for the times he will continue to do it throughout church history: "When the Lord ariseth

---

20 The participle translated "to be feared" (נוֹרָא) sounds rather like "glorious/radiant with light" (נָאוֹר, Ps. 76:4).
21 The NIV rendering, "the land," misses this important contrast. See Tucker and Grant, *Psalms*, 2:114; Goldingay, *Psalms*, 2:454.

to save the meek in one place and of one generation, it is an evidence and earnest that he shall arise to save at length all and every one of the meek in every place, in all times after."[22]

76:10–12 The Cross Should Move Us to Glad Self-Giving to Christ Our Champion

Twice more the note of fearing God is sounded (Ps. 76:11–12). This sets the theme of the conclusion of the psalm.

> [10]   Surely the wrath of man shall praise you;
>   the remnant of wrath you will put on like a belt.

Psalm 76:10 is the most difficult verse of the psalm to understand.[23] The first line is the simpler of the two: **Surely** (כִּי, *ki*, usually "for" but sometimes emphatic, as here) **the wrath of man**, human wrath, **shall praise you**. In the context, the most natural meaning of **the wrath of man** is the angry hostility of people against God, his Christ, and his church (as in 2:1–3); by nature people are very angry against God. The paradoxical **shall praise you** is, in this context, because the end result is a great victory that resounds to the praise of God. "You can be as angry as you like, but you cannot avoid ending up causing events and outcomes that praise God." This supremely is what happened when men were furious at the Lord Jesus; the result was Christ's decisive victory over the powers of evil and the salvation of many people: "There we see human fury in all its ugliness directed toward the Son of God. But in God's gracious purposes that atrocious act brought honour to his name in the salvation of sinners."[24] This also is what happened when they ground their teeth in anger against Stephen, the first Christian martyr; the end result was an explosion of growth in the church (Acts 7:54; 8:4).

In the second line **the remnant of wrath** most naturally still refers to the wrath of people, in parallel with the first line, rather than changing to a reference to God's wrath; probably it refers to "the final outburst"[25] or

---

22 Dickson, *Psalms*, 1:476.
23 There is useful discussion of alternative suggestions in Ross, *Psalms*, 2:617n16.
24 Eveson, *Psalms*, 2:38.
25 Harman, *Psalms*, 2:574.

"the last futile efforts of human wrath."[26] **You** (God) **will put on like a belt** translates a verb meaning "to gird, put on." The second line thus reinforces and emphasizes the first line: however much human beings rage against God, they simply cannot prevent themselves from causing God's victory over them and over all evil. Calvin sums it up well when he writes,

> Although at first the rage of the enemies of God and his Church may throw all things into confusion, and, as it were, envelop them in darkness, yet all will at length redound to his praise; for the issue will make it manifest, that whatever they may contrive and attempt, they cannot in any degree prevail against him.[27]

11   Make your vows to the LORD your God and perform them;
        let all around him bring gifts
        to him who is to be feared,
12   who cuts off the spirit of princes,
        who is to be feared by the kings of the earth.

The response to the victory portrayed in the psalm, the triumph fulfilled at the cross of Christ, is, first, to **make your vows . . . and perform them—** that is, in old covenant language, to keep the promises of loyalty we have made (or implicitly made) to the covenant God in our prayers. Whenever we pray, we imply covenant loyalty; whenever God answers, we are pledged to live out the loyalty we have pledged. Another way of expressing this is to say, **Let all around him bring gifts**. The phrase **all around him** suggests the covenant people rather than foreign nations.[28] To **bring gifts** is to cast our crowns at his feet (cf. Rev. 4:10), acknowledging that we have nothing that we have not been given (1 Cor. 4:7); all belongs **to him who is to be feared**. The repeated **to be feared** (cf. Ps. 76:7–8) sets the tone for the close of the psalm. Psalm 76:12 hammers home the lesson of the victory. The

26 Kirkpatrick, *Psalms*, 2:455. The NIV interprets the subject in both halves of the verse as God ("Surely your wrath . . . and the survivors of your wrath . . ."). This is most unlikely. The construct phrase חֲמַת אָדָם contains no indication that the wrath is *against* humankind, even if this kind of objective genitive is a possible translation.
27 Calvin, *Psalms*, 3:201.
28 The NIV rendering, "all the neighboring lands," gives a wrong impression here and overtranslates the Hebrew. See Harman, *Psalms*, 2:574.

verb **cuts off** has the general sense of humbling.[29] The **princes**, indeed **the kings of the earth** (even more emphatic), highlights that every power on earth must surrender to this victorious God, to whom every knee must bow and every tongue confess that Jesus Christ, the victor of this psalm, is Lord (Phil. 2:10–11).

REFLECTION AND RESPONSE

1. By nature the church of God will fear powerful people in this world, most especially when they turn hostile. For a people in exile—today, as in the Babylonian exile—this psalm gives strong encouragement to fear only God (cf. Luke 12:4–5).

2. Those of us to whom any power is entrusted—whether in the church, such as pastors, or in the world, such as in government, a business, a school, or any community—do well to heed the warning of this psalm (as of Ps. 75), that God will utterly defeat every manifestation of human pride, every single one.

3. The defeat of the Assyrians is, at the very least, an episode worthy of our meditation as we let the drama of this psalm sink into our imagination. It should help us begin to grasp the cosmic, almost unbelievable, magnitude of the victory of Christ in his cross.

---

29 It is a different verb from that used in Ps. 75:10.

A Sovereign Protector I have,
Unseen yet for ever at hand,
Unchangeably faithful to save,
Almighty to rule and command.

AUGUSTUS M. TOPLADY
"A Sovereign Protector I Have"

Asaph's harp's strings are moaning to the chill night-wind, . . .
full of unkindly fears, fears arising from clouds around his soul.
Our Lord on earth had such changes in his soul as we find in this
Psalm. One day, under the opened heavens at Jordan; another,
in the gloom of the howling wilderness; one evening, ascending
the Transfiguration-hill; another, entering Gethsemane. And
so with every member of his body. Not that the love of God
varies toward them, and not that they themselves feel that
love exhausted; but providences and trials of strange sort, and
temptations buffeting the soul, hide the sun by their dark mists.

ANDREW BONAR
Christ and His Church in the Book of Psalms

Asaph was a man of exercised mind, and often touched the
minor key; he was thoughtful, contemplative, believing, but
withal there was a dash of sadness about him. . . . To follow
him with understanding, it is needful to have done business
on the great waters, and weathered many an Atlantic gale.

CHARLES H. SPURGEON
The Treasury of David

PSALM 77

ORIENTATION

Remembering is the crux of Psalm 77—remembering "works" because God is beyond time. Unchanging in his attributes, eternal in his love, he has entered time in redemption through the Lord Jesus Christ, a cosmic event that was foreshadowed by the drama of the exodus. The reason why remembering the acts of God is so significant is that what God did in the past God continues to do in the present and will do in the future. Remembering is not to say, "Well, God did this before, so maybe he will do it again." Rather, it is to say, "What God did before expresses who God is, was, and will be and what God has done in Christ, and therefore he is sure to do this again." When we remember that the church of Christ was brought into being by a work of sovereign, evil-defeating grace, we take courage for the future.

Only those who have experienced suffering can enter into the depths of this psalm. And yet the psalm itself can help those of us who have experienced little suffering to begin to feel more deeply the sufferings of Christ and his church. Here is the testimony of a journey of faith, in which a suffering believer moves from the passionate restlessness of believing to a place of reassured trust. We may be confident that this journey, anticipated in Asaph, followed by many a believer, was supremely followed by Jesus of Nazareth— and that without sin. The life of faith, when lived with integrity, has about it this movement to and fro between trouble and rest.

Further, this psalmist is not an isolated individual. He speaks for the church and has, in a manner of speaking, the burden of the church resting on his shoulders.[1] The crisis is not simply a personal one but one that calls

---

1   Hossfeld and Zenger, *Psalms*, 2:274–75.

into question the covenant promises to the Davidic King and therefore to all his church (hence the questions of 77:7–9).

The closing verse offers a suggestive hint. The footsteps of God are invisible as he goes about his powerful work, and yet he works through a visible leader (Moses) and a visible priest (Aaron). These foreshadow the greater Moses and perfect priest who will lead his church out of slavery at last. Christ leads us in lament because Christ will lead us out of slavery.

Links back to nearby earlier psalms include (1) "remembering" (74:2, 18; 77:3, 6, 11) and forgetting (74:19, 23; 77:9); (2) the theme of time, past, present, and future (so prominent in Ps. 71); (3) the exodus with its "waters" (74:12–17; 76:6; 77:16–20); (4) the "earth" being afraid (76:8; 77:18); (5) "of old" (74:12; 77:5, 11); (6) the verb "reject/spurn" (74:1; 77:7); (7) God's "anger" (76:7; 77:9); (8) "Jacob" (76:6; 77:15); and (9) hands useless in battle (76:5) or stretched out in prayer (77:2).

We do not know what crisis first prompted the psalm, but its inclusion in book 3 suggests that it was understood to be relevant to the church in exile. James Hamilton sums up the sequence since the end of book 2 as follows: "The blessings prayed for in Psalm 72 have prompted the wrestlings in Psalms 73–74, the hope for the eschatological judgment that will establish God's kingdom in Psalms 75–76, and the return to anguished wrestling in Psalm 77."[2]

There are also links with Habakkuk 3:10–15 (especially the sea "writhing") and with the account of salvation history in Psalm 78. The description of 77:16–19 evokes a similar drama to save the Messiah in 18:8–18.

THE TEXT

Structure
Psalm 77:1–9 expresses restless faith, beginning with an introduction (77:1–3, ending with *Selah*), voicing troubled meditation (77:4–6), and moving to troubled questions (77:7–9, also ending in *Selah*).

Psalm 77:10–20 expresses reassured faith, beginning with God's remembered actions (77:10–12) and moving to God's unchanging nature (77:13–15, ending with *Selah*) before remembering the exodus (77:16–19) and concluding (77:20).

2 Hamilton, *Psalms*, 2:39–40.

Superscription

^S   To the choirmaster:[3] according to Jeduthun.[4] A Psalm of Asaph.[5]

77:1–9 The Church's Lament Begins with Restless Faith
77:1–3 The Church's Lament Begins with
Resolute Attention toward God

¹   I cry aloud to God,
        aloud to God, and he will hear me.

The psalm begins with an emphatic cry to God, literally,

        My voice to God I cry
        My voice to God . . .

This psalm is troubled but never self-centered. He wants God not for what he can get from God but because God is God.[6] Charles Spurgeon observes, "This Psalm has much sadness in it, but we may be sure it will end well, for it begins with prayer, and prayer never has an ill issue."[7]

The verb **I cry** is a strong word for an urgent cry, used (poignantly, in the light of how the psalm ends) by the people of God with Pharaoh's army behind them and the sea in front of them (Ex. 14:10; cf. Deut. 26:7; Josh. 24:7). The verb translated **and he will hear me** can be translated "in order that he may hear me,"[8] and the context suggests that this is what it means here; that is, it gives "the reason for his praying rather than the result."[9]

²   In the day of my trouble I seek the Lord;
        in the night my hand is stretched out without wearying;
        my soul refuses to be comforted.

3   See on Ps. 4.
4   See on Pss. 39, 62.
5   In Hebrew the superscription is verse 1; subsequent verse numbers are increased by one.
6   This is developed strongly by Augustine, *Psalms*, 4:74.
7   Spurgeon, *Treasury*, 2.1:312.
8   Ross, *Psalms*, 2:631; Goldingay, *Psalms*, 2:158; Hossfeld and Zenger, *Psalms*, 2:274.
9   Eveson, *Psalms*, 2:41.

The phrase **in the day of my trouble** (בְּיוֹם צָרָתִי, *beyom tsarathi*) is used by Jacob in Genesis 35:3 ("the day of my distress") and in Psalm 86:7. **I seek the Lord** (the sovereign one) continues the resolute focus on God; the response of faith to troubles is neither despair nor self-pity but prayer (cf. Matt. 7:7). **In the night** believers are alone with their thoughts and with God. **My hand is stretched out** expresses intense prayer,[10] and that **without wearying** (lit., "It does not grow numb"),[11] perhaps an echo of when Moses's hands were held up in prayer for a long time of battle (Ex. 17:12);[12] later another leader of the people of God will labor through nights of prayer for his church (cf. Luke 6:12). The refusal **to be comforted** is not obstinacy but rather a rejection of all superficial comfort[13] (cf. Jer. 6:14; 8:11); nothing will satisfy him except the restored presence of the God he loves and seeks for himself and his people.

| 3 | When I remember God, I moan; |
| | when I meditate, my spirit faints.   *Selah* |

Intentionally remembering God is the defining mark of the psalm (Ps. 77:3, 6, 11). But for now, **when I remember God, I moan**; this clause employs a strong word (הָמָה, *hamah*), used of the soul in "turmoil" (42:5; cf. 55:17); it can even mean to roar in distress. Memory makes the spirit grow weaker (**faints**; cf. Jonah 2:7) rather than stronger. Psalm 77:4–9 will show why. There is an agonizing contrast between God in his perfections and the state of his world and church in its afflictions: "The fact that the world is evil beyond cure only makes the proof that God's power and goodness could fix things more lacerating to Asaph's soul."[14] Surely the Lord Jesus felt this agony, and his followers have known something of it too.

Spurgeon writes,

He is wretched indeed whose memories of The Ever Blessed prove distressing to him; yet the best of men know the depth of this abyss. . . .

---

10 Niphal of נגר, with the basic meaning of flowing or being spilled and hence of being fully stretched out. It suggests intense prayer that pours out the heart.

11 The verb (פוג) is used in Gen. 45:26 of Jacob's heart becoming numb.

12 A different word is translated "weary" in Ex. 17:12, but the general sense is the same.

13 Hans-Joachim Kraus, *Psalms*, trans. Hilton C. Oswald, 2 vols., CC (Minneapolis: Fortress, 1993), 2:115.

14 Hamilton, *Psalms*, 2:41.

Alas, my God, the writer of this exposition well knows what thy servant Asaph meant, for his soul is familiar with the way of grief. Deep glens and lonely caves of soul depressions, my spirit knows full well your awful glooms![15]

Selah prompts us to pause and pray that we will feel something of this holy grief.

77:4–6 The Church's Lament Reaches Deep into the Believer's Heart

4   You hold my eyelids open;
        I am so troubled that I cannot speak.

Although the searchlight of the soul points inward here, it begins with God: **You hold . . .** Probably the unusual idiom **You hold my eyelids open** (lit., "You grasp the eyelids of my eyes") means that God makes him sleepless in order that he should do business with God.[16] And yet he says, **I am so troubled that I cannot speak**; only the ministry of the Holy Spirit through "groanings too deep for words" (Rom. 8:26) can suffice to pour out his pain.

5   I consider the days of old,
        the years long ago.

Perhaps **days** and **years** suggest time in its smaller brackets and larger sweeps. The word translated **long ago** (עוֹלָמִים, *olamim*) also means "forever." The move from the first line (merely **days** and **of old**)[17] to the second (**years** and "forever") intensifies the search.

6   I said,[18] "Let me remember my song in the night;
        let me meditate in my heart."
        Then my spirit made a diligent search:

---

15 Spurgeon, *Treasury*, 2.1:313.
16 Tucker and Grant, *Psalms*, 2:124.
17 Cf. Pss. 74:12; 78:2.
18 "I said" is not in the Hebrew.

Let me remember is quietly resolute ("I *will* remember"). As Martin Luther explains, "To remember the works of God is not a bare contemplation of them but always to thank Him in them, and thus through them to place one's hope in God, fear Him, love Him, seek Him, and to hate evil and flee sin."[19] The phrase **my song in the night** refers either to glad evening songs of praise in days past or to the sad songs he now sings in the nighttime of his soul, perhaps expressed in Psalm 77:7–9.[20] **My song** (affections as well as thoughts), **my heart** (will and desire), and **my spirit** (the core of my being) together indicate that this **diligent search**[21] expresses deep seriousness; his whole being is engaged with this lament and the questions that follow.

77:7–9 The Church's Lament Asks (and Implicitly Answers) the Most Important Question in the Cosmos

> 7   "Will the Lord spurn forever,
>   and never again be favorable?
> 8   Has his steadfast love forever ceased?
>   Are his promises at an end for all time?
> 9   Has God forgotten to be gracious?
>   Has he in anger shut up his compassion?"   *Selah*

These three two-line questions ask about the nature of God himself (perhaps pondering Ex. 34:6). At their heart is the covenant (in this context with David but in principle any and all of the covenants of grace). The verb **spurn** appears in Psalm 43:2 and Lamentations 3:31. **Steadfast love** (חֶסֶד, *khesed*) is covenant love. **His promises** are covenant promises. His grace (**be gracious**) is covenant grace. **His compassion** is covenant compassion.[22] The repeated language of **forever**[23] . . . **never again** . . . **forever** . . . **for all time** highlights the extraordinary and contradictory nature of these questions. For they bring unspeakable queries into the open and ask, Will the God who has promised

---

19 Luther, *Luther's Works*, 11:11–12.

20 The word "song" (נְגִינָה) usually refers to a song set to stringed instruments.

21 The verb is the piel of חפשׂ, which has the nuance of a careful search.

22 The word "compassion" is cognate with "be comforted" (Ps. 77:2).

23 For this "forever" theme in book 3, see Pss. 74:1; 79:5; 89:46; cf. 44:23; Lam. 5:20.

to be favorable forever reject us forever? Will the eternal covenant love and promises prove not to be eternal? Will the unchangeable nature of the unchangeable God prove changeable after all? Will God not be God? The verb **shut up** is used "for clenching the hand into a fist and hence for withholding."[24]

These questions show how restless faith works toward assurance through a focus on the eternal nature of God, as Spurgeon explains: "It is a blessed thing to have grace enough to look such questions in the face, for their answer is self-evident and eminently fitted to cheer the heart."[25] The questions are suggested by fear, but they are also the cure of fear.

Selah gives us a timely pause before we move on in the journey of faith from restlessness to reassurance, for it is superficial to move too quickly to our goal.

77:10–20 The Church's Lament Tends to Reassured Faith
77:10–12 The Movement to Reassured Faith Begins
with Remembering the Wonderful Works of God
Psalm 77:10–12 shows us the beginnings of the victory of faith: this is how true faith moves from turmoil to rest.[26]

> [10]   Then I said, "I will appeal to this,
>   to the years of the right hand of the Most High."

Two translation questions affect how we understand this verse. The verb translated **I will appeal to this** can also mean "This is my wound" (e.g., NASB: "It is my grief").[27] The noun translated **the years** may mean "the changing of."[28] If these alternatives are correct, the verse will read something like this: "So I say, 'I am grieved that the right hand of the Most High has changed'" (CSB); in this case the verse expresses distress that the God he thought to be unchangeably faithful seems not to be so (in line with the

---

24 Alter, *Psalms*, 269.

25 Spurgeon, *Treasury*, 2.1:314. Spurgeon speaks vividly of putting unbelief "through the catechism."

26 Dickson calls Ps. 77:10–12 "the begun victory of faith" in which the psalmist resolves "to settle his faith on God's word, confirmed by his works"; later Dickson says that "in the inward exercise of God's children, after a while's darkness cometh light; after grief, comfort; and after wrestling, cometh victory." Dickson, *Psalms*, 1:483.

27 This is how BDB and *HALOT* understand the verb; s.v. חלל. For discussion, see Ross, *Psalms*, 2:633n17; Goldingay, *Psalms*, 2:459.

28 For discussion, see Ross, *Psalms*, 2:633n18.

fears expressed in 77:7–9). In this case, 77:10 functions as the conclusion to 77:1–9.

If these alternatives are not accepted, then the verse stands as in the ESV and functions as the beginning of the movement to assurance: "Now I will rest my confidence on the proven character of the Most High God, as seen in . . . [what follows in 77:13–20]." **The Most High** emphasizes the power of God over all enemies (first found in Gen. 14:18–22 in the context of Abraham's victory over the Canaanite kings).

> ¹¹   I will remember the deeds of the LORD;
>   yes, I will remember your wonders of old.
> ¹²   I will ponder all your work,
>   and meditate on your mighty deeds.

In each of these four lines, the believer determines to **remember** (2x), **ponder**, and **meditate on** (as he has done in Ps. 77:1–9 but now at last with a better outcome) **the deeds of the LORD, your wonders** (where the word "wonders"—also used in 77:14—is often associated with the Davidic covenant, e.g., 89:5) **of old** (see 77:5), **all your work**, and **your mighty deeds**. What these are will become clear in 77:13–20, as a type of the redemption given to us in Christ.

77:13–15 The Movement to an Assured Faith Must Rest on the Unchangeable Nature of God, Revealed in His Works

> ¹³   Your way, O God, is holy.
>   What god is great like our²⁹ God?
> ¹⁴   You are the God who works wonders;
>   you have made known your might among the peoples.
> ¹⁵   You with your arm redeemed your people,
>   the children of Jacob and Joseph.   *Selah*

The **way** of God (through the sea, Ps. 77:19) and the **wonders** that he works reveal two things. First and foremost, they reveal that he is **holy**. In

---

29 "Our" is not in the Hebrew, but this must be the sense.

his holiness is bound up all his perfections. Second, they reveal that he **is great** (cf. 76:1), displaying his **might** and his strong **arm**. His power is shaped by his holiness, to exalt his name by redeeming a **people**. These people are called **the children** (lit., "sons") **of Jacob and Joseph**. This designation (also used in Obad. 18) probably highlights the unbreakable unity of the whole people—all Jacob's sons, the twelve tribes, not excluding the Joseph tribes (Ephraim and Manasseh), which dominated the northern kingdom and were taken into exile by Assyria long before the Babylonian exile.[30] God shows his holiness by giving to Christ a whole, undivided people, and Christ shows that might and holiness by promising that not one will be lost (John 6:37–39).

77:16–19 The Exodus Redemption, Fulfilled in Christ, Is the Foundation of Assured Faith in Times of Trouble

16   When the waters saw you, O God,
           when the waters saw you, they were afraid;
           indeed, the deep trembled.
17   The clouds poured out water;
           the skies gave forth thunder;
           your arrows flashed on every side.
18   The crash of your thunder was in the whirlwind;
           your lightnings lighted up the world;
           the earth trembled and shook.
19   Your way was through the sea,
           your path through the great waters;
           yet your footprints were unseen.

Cassiodorus says of these verses, "You [the psalmist] hymn Christ's miracles."[31] Hamilton titles this section "The Forward-Pointing Past" and writes,

---

30 Four of the five times Joseph is mentioned in the Psalms are Asaph psalms in this group (Pss. 77:15; 78:67; 80:1; 81:5). The other is 105:17 (of the patriarch rather than the tribes). The Joseph tribes, Ephraim and Manasseh, appear in book 3 in 78:9 and 67 (Ephraim) and in 80:2 (both). They also appear in 60:7 and 108:8.

31 Cassiodorus, *Psalms*, 2:250.

As Asaph worships God, he speaks of the exodus, the Red Sea, Sinai, and the way God brought Israel through the wilderness. That pattern of events implicitly declares hope for and faith in the one who promises a new exodus, a new covenant, a new provision for a new wilderness sojourn on the way to a new and better land of promise where the new king from David's line will reign over a renewed people.[32]

The imagery is flexible and vivid and seems to combine the crossing of the Red Sea (Ex. 14–15), the wild storm at Mount Sinai (Ex. 19), and possibly also cosmic imagery of God pushing back the forces of evil and darkness (see on Ps. 74:12–17). In 77:16 **the waters** are personified; they **saw you** and **were afraid**. This is more than poetic license; **the deep** (the place of Sheol) **trembled**. Death itself feared and fled when Christ died for sinners. The wild storm language of 77:17–18 evokes the storm at Mount Sinai (Ex. 19); the battle language of **arrows** is reminiscent of Psalm 76:3. The **whirlwind** means storm clouds wheeling round and round. Psalm 77:19 is the climax, with this redeeming God making his **way through the sea,** walking through the hostile sea, pushing back the waters, the phrase **your path through the great waters** emphasizing what a stupendous battle this was, when Christ died for sinners. The sea, writes David Dickson, is "where no man can wade, except God be before him, and where any man may walk, if God take him by the hand, and lead him through."[33]

The final line of 77:19 prepares the way for 77:20: **Yet your footprints were unseen**. The God of the exodus, the God who wins the victory in Jesus Christ, the God who redeems his church today through all her trials, is **unseen,** for his judgments are unsearchable and his ways inscrutable (Rom. 11:33).

77:20 Conclusion: The Unseen God Leads
His People by the Seen Christ

20   You led your people like a flock
     by the hand of Moses and Aaron.

---

32 Hamilton, *Psalms*, 2:43–44.
33 Dickson, *Psalms*, 1:487–88.

Although Psalm 77:20 follows directly from the "unseen footsteps" in 77:19, it functions as a conclusion. It contains two elements. First, God led his people **like a flock**. God is the shepherd. Jesus Christ will be the good shepherd who leads his people like a flock, knows each by name, makes certain that each one will be raised on the last day. Second, the invisible God led the exodus people **by the hand of Moses**, the leader, **and Aaron**, the priest; "Moses and Aaron are the figure of Christ" for us.[34]

It is often noted that the psalm comes to "an abrupt halt." Perhaps like the book of Jonah, it invites us to ask for ourselves how the story will end.

REFLECTION AND RESPONSE

1. It is important to speak Psalm 77:1–9 not as the doubting words of sinful unbelievers but as the Spirit-inspired words of a courageous believer struggling with restless faith in time of trial. It is salutary to ponder that Jesus himself, living the life of faith without sin, knew what it was to enter this darkness. We learn supremely from Christ what it is to walk through this valley in faith.

2. We learn also—perhaps especially from the transition marked in Psalm 77:10–12—how a restless faith may win through to a reassured faith. We may need to do this many times before we die.

3. Our central meditation ought to rest on the eternal excellencies of God in his holiness and how those perfections are known to us in Christ, who is the same, yesterday, today, and forever. This foundation underpins the logic of remembering. We do not remember the exodus simply because it is vaguely encouraging to see what God did in the past; we look back to that event because it foreshadowed a later, timeless, supreme, wonderful work of redemption in the death and resurrection of Jesus Christ.

4. We may lift our eyes in hope, knowing that, as Andrew Bonar puts it, "the God of Israel, . . . the God of the Passover-night, the God of the Red Sea, the God of the Pillar-cloud, the God of Sinai, the God of the wilderness, the God of Jordan,—the God, too, we may add, of Calvary, and the God of Bethany" are one and the same. Indeed, as Bonar writes, "There is

---

34 Johannes Oecolampadius (1482–1531), *Sermons*, in *RCS* 8:37.

a day coming when we shall, with Christ our Head, sing of the Church's safe guidance to her rest, in such strains as these, remembering how often by the way we were ready to ask, 'Has God forgotten to be gracious?'"[35]

---

35 Bonar, *Psalms*, 230–31.

This psalm speaks about Christ; in fact, it is Christ who speaks it.

MARTIN LUTHER
First Lectures on the Psalms

*What a God! What a people! How glorious in grace
the One! How low sunk in sin the other! How low
must mercy condescend in helping such a people!*

ANDREW BONAR
Christ and His Church in the Book of Psalms

PSALM 78

ORIENTATION

The message of Psalm 78 is that God is astonishingly gracious in the face of human sin, that Christ is desperately needed, that Christ is promised, and that Christ is precious.[1]

Fulfillment in Christ may be approached from two directions. First, we can approach it from the psalm itself, which retells significant parts of the history of God's old covenant church. As for all history, the question is for what purpose this is told. The key is 78:1–11 and 78:67–72. In the psalm's extraordinary oscillation between amazing grace and persistent sin, the question that dominates so much of the old covenant is raised: Can human sin defeat the grace of God? The answer is that it cannot and will not—but only because of Christ, whom David typified in his kingdom. The psalm laments a repeated pattern of unbelief, but the central message is the wonder of what God has done in salvation and mercy (78:4), with persistent grace in the face of persistent sin. This is why a psalm with so much negative comment concludes on such a bright note of hope. The surprise is not that Ephraim is rejected (78:67) but that all Israel is not rejected, for that is what they, and we, deserve. Ultimately, the only reason that God "passed over former sins" is because he would one day put forward Christ "as a propitiation by his blood" (Rom. 3:25).

---

1   Calvin writes of "how tenderly and graciously" God "cherished" his church and how "his inestimable goodness was clearly manifested, not only in his free adoption of them at first, but also in continuing by the uninterrupted course of his goodness to strive against the rebellion of so perfidious and stiff-necked a people." Calvin, *Psalms*, 3:225.

The surprising conclusion is that a part of the church—that designated by "Ephraim" and focused on "Shiloh"—is rejected (Ps. 78:67)[2] and a part chosen, under the leadership of David (78:68–72). "Ephraim" is condemned (78:9–11), for "not all who are descended from Israel belong to Israel" (Rom. 9:6); only those who truly belong to Christ will be saved. John Calvin writes, "The children of Ephraim are . . . here spoken of by way of comparison to warn the true children of Abraham from the example of those who cut themselves off from the church and yet boasted of the title of the church without exhibiting holy fruits in their life."[3] Having said this, Psalm 80 needs to be set alongside Psalm 78, for it affirms that while salvation will not come from Ephraim (the Shiloh sanctuary is rejected), salvation may yet come to Ephraim.

We do not know when the psalm was written.[4] A good case can be made that this was the original Asaph, writing perhaps early in David's reign. But it may have been a later member of the Asaphite guild of songwriters.[5] Whenever it was written, it stands now in book 3, in a context strongly colored by the Babylonian exile, at a time when there was neither a Davidic king nor a temple in Zion. This psalm could continue to be sung only by those who believed that one day the true King in David's line would come, who would shepherd God's flock "with upright heart" and "with . . . skillful hand" (78:72). The psalm speaks ultimately of the Messiah in David's line, in whom the true remnant of the church (those to whom faith is given) will be saved.

The second direction of approach is from the New Testament, in which Jesus Christ is the Son of David. If, Derek Kidner notes, the psalm warns Israel before the Babylonian exile to heed the warning of the rejection of "Ephraim,"

---

2   Four of the five times Joseph is mentioned in the Psalms are Asaph psalms in this group (Pss. 77:15; 78:67; 80:1; 81:5). The other is 105:17 (of the patriarch rather than the tribes). The Joseph tribes, Ephraim and Manasseh, appear in book 3 in 78:9 and 67 (Ephraim) and in 80:2 (both). They also appear in Pss. 60:7 and 108:8.

3   Calvin, *Psalms*, 3:236–37.

4   For a useful overview of opinions, see Tate, *Psalms 51–100*, 284–86.

5   Because of the motif of the failure and rejection of "Ephraim," the three main suggestions are (1) the events of 1 Sam. 1–5, (2) the defection of the northern kingdom after the death of Solomon (1 Kings 12), and (3) the destruction of the northern kingdom by the Assyrians (2 Kings 17). Of these, the first accords most closely in terms of echoes in the psalm, as will be shown in the exposition.

the Christian user of the psalm knows that history did repeat itself, and that finally the chosen tribe refused its King, and did so in the chosen city ([78:]68); but he also knows that God has more than kept the promise to David, and has established a Mount Zion that is "the mother of us all" (Gal. 4:26 AV).[6]

There are three New Testament passages worth reflecting on: Matthew 13:34–35; 1 Corinthians 10:1–5; and John 6. From these the New Testament suggests three more lines of fulfillment.

The first is when Matthew writes that the teaching of Jesus in kingdom parables "fulfill[s]" Psalm 78:2 (Matt. 13:35).[7] This must mean more than simply that Jesus teaches in a slightly similar manner to Asaph in Psalm 78 (especially since the parables of Matt. 13 are very different from the retelling of history in Ps. 78). Rather, both the manner and the subject matter of Jesus's teaching fulfills Psalm 78. Like the public teaching of Jesus, the psalm is parabolic in its manner (78:1–2). In its subject matter, it leads toward the true kingdom typified in David.[8] The psalm that culminates in the kingdom of David will reach its fulfillment in the kingdom of Christ. Jesus is the wisdom teacher of Psalm 78 and the Davidic King prophesied in Psalm 78.

The second line of fulfillment concerns Jesus as the rock from which living water flows (78:15). There is no direct echo, but 1 Corinthians 10:4 suggests that the rock from which the water flowed "was Christ."

The third line of interpretation focuses on Jesus as the true manna, to which the manna in the wilderness points. The quotation "He gave them bread from heaven to eat" in John 6:31 may come from various Old Testament sources, but Psalm 78:24 is probably the strongest. 1 Corinthians 10:3 speaks of the manna as "spiritual food" immediately before indicating that this food, alongside the miraculous water, is fulfilled in Christ, who is the Father's provision to give his people life in a wilderness world. The reference in 1 Corinthians 10:5 to some being "overthrown in the wilderness" echoes Psalm 78:31.[9] In Revelation 2:17 Jesus promises

---

6 Kidner, *Psalms*, 2:281.

7 For the text form, see Craig L. Blomberg, "Matthew," in *CNTOT* 49.

8 Blomberg, "Matthew," in *CNTOT* 49; Hamilton, *Psalms*, 2:61.

9 For this matrix of echoes, see Andreas J. Köstenberger, "John," in *CNTOT* 445; Tucker and Grant, *Psalms*, 2:163.

"the hidden manna" to the one who conquers by continuing to believe to the end.[10] Jesus is the true bread from heaven who sustains his people in the wilderness.

When reading the psalm in Christ, it is important not to default to legalism or moralism. The psalm does not just tell us that previous generations failed and thus that we must try harder. It is meant to lead us to faith in Christ, the true David, the true bread from heaven, the true rock from which living water flows, and to call us to listen to Christ, the true teacher of wisdom.

The Masoretes reckoned that a verse at the heart of Psalm 78 is the numerical center verse of the Psalter.[11] If so, then it may be no accident that this, the second longest psalm, appears here.[12] It may also suggest that the central message of the psalm is of great importance in the Psalter.

Psalm 78 shares several links with nearby psalms, especially Psalm 77. Perhaps the most significant are the recollections of the exodus (74:12–17; 76:6; 77:15–20) and the motif of the church as a flock in need of a shepherd to lead them. As Psalm 77 ends with God leading his people like a flock by the hand of Moses and Aaron (77:20), so Psalm 78 ends with God leading his people like a flock by the leadership of David (78:68–72).[13]

THE TEXT

Structure

Psalm 78:1–8 is generally accepted as the introduction, giving the nature ("a parable," 78:1–4) and purpose (to retell the law so that future generations will set their hope in God, 78:5–8) of the psalm. This is balanced

---

10 Perhaps the "hiddenness" of this manna corresponds in some way to the parabolic nature of the psalm. Both Rev. 2:17 and the reference to Ps. 78:2 in Matt. 13:35 use the perfect middle/passive participle of κρύπτω.

11 The Masoretes reckoned this was Ps. 78:36. Hossfeld and Zenger, *Psalms*, 2:285. The Babylonian Talmud reckoned it was 78:38. Witherington, *Psalms Old and New*, 168n3. The point may be less that a particular verse and more that the whole psalm is central to the Psalter.

12 Hossfeld and Zenger, *Psalms*, 2:285.

13 See also Pss. 79:13; 80:1. Other links between Pss. 77 and 78 include (1) God's might/power (עֹז, 77:14; 78:26; and a cognate word in 78:4), (2) God's right hand (77:10; 78:54), (3) God as the "Most High" (77:10; 78:17, 35, 56), (4) the wonderful deeds of God (77:12, 14; 78:4, 11, 32), (5) the theme of remembering or forgetting (77:3, 6, 9, 11; 78:7, 11, 35, 39, 42), and (6) "of old" (77:5, 11; 78:2).

by the conclusion (78:67–72), the rejection of Ephraim and the election of David. In between, the historical retrospects are bracketed by sections about Ephraim (78:9–11, 56–66). Psalm 78:12–55 appears to consist of two overlapping retellings of history (probably 78:12–39 and 40–55, although some see the break after 78:41). This yields a chiastic structure:

a 78:1–8: Introduction
   b 78:9–11: Section about Ephraim
      c 78:12–39: Retelling of history
      c' 78:40–55: Retelling of history
   b' 78:56–66: Section about Ephraim
a' 78:67–72: Conclusion

Superscription

^S   A Maskil[14] of Asaph.[15]

The designation **A Maskil**[16] probably here has the sense of a wisdom teaching to be pondered, although not all "Maskil" psalms obviously fit this characterization.

78:1–8 Introduction: The Nature and Purpose of the Psalm
78:1–4 The Nature of the Psalm: Christ Will
Speak in Parables about His Kingdom

¹   Give ear, O my people, to my teaching;
    incline your ears to the words of my mouth!
²   I will open my mouth in a parable;
    I will utter dark sayings from of old,[17]

The repeated **my**, the address to **my people**, and the repeated **my mouth** signal a voice speaking with the authority of God; this is fulfilled in the voice

---

14 See on Ps. 32.
15 In Hebrew the superscription is the start of verse 1.
16 See Pss. 32, 42, 44, 45, 52, 53, 54, 55, 74, 78, 88, 89, 142. Cf. 47:7.
17 The phrase "from of old" echoes a theme in Pss. 74:2, 12; 77:5, 11.

of Christ. The appeal (very similar to Ps. 49:1–4)[18] presupposes that within
the visible church, some will "take care . . . how [they] hear" (Luke 8:18)
and others will not. Augustine perceptively notes that those who hear do so
only because God has given them "the grace of the Spirit" and hence faith.[19]

The parallel terms **a parable** and **dark sayings** together indicate truths
that engage the hearer and call for thoughtful meditation and response,
exactly as Jesus's parables did.[20]

> 3   things that we have heard and known,
>   that our fathers have told us.
> 4   We will not hide them from their children,
>   but tell to the coming generation
>   the glorious deeds of the LORD, and his might,
>   and the wonders that he has done.

The history that functions as a "parable" or "dark saying" is—at the same
time—well known (Ps. 78:3), recounted by **our fathers** (cf. 44:1; Judg. 6:13).
The subject of the psalm is signaled in Psalm 78:4 to be **the glorious deeds**
(cf. Ex. 15:11) **of the LORD, and his might** (cf. Ps. 77:14), / **and the wonders**
(also 78:11, 32; cf. 72:18; 75:1) **that he has done.** These are his gospel acts
of salvation. This gospel must be handed on to future generations (e.g.,
Eph. 6:4; 2 Tim. 3:15).

*78:5–8 The Purpose of the Psalm: The Law Is to Lead Us
to Faith in the God Made Known to Us in Christ*

> 5   He established a testimony in Jacob
>   and appointed a law in Israel,
>   which he commanded our fathers

18 Ps. 49:4 also uses the words "parable" and "riddle/dark saying." Compare similar "wisdom" ap-
     peals in, e.g., Deut. 32:1; Prov. 5:1; 8:1–9; and frequently. For other psalms with a very strong
     "wisdom" tone, see Pss. 37 and 73.
19 Augustine, *Psalms*, 4:91.
20 The terms have a broad semantic range. Sometimes the latter refers to "riddles" (as in Samson's
     riddle in Judg. 14:12–19) but sometimes to things like the "hard questions" asked by the queen
     of Sheba (1 Kings 10:1). The essential focus is not so much on their hiddenness as on their
     depth (Tucker and Grant, *Psalms*, 2:141) and on the need to engage personally with them.

to teach to their children,

6   that the next generation might know them,
the children yet unborn,
and arise and tell them to their children,

7   so that they should set their hope in God
and not forget the works of God,
but keep his commandments;

8   and that they should not be like their fathers,
a stubborn and rebellious generation,
a generation whose heart was not steadfast,
whose spirit was not faithful to God.

The **testimony** or **law** in this context means the whole revelation or teaching of God in the old covenant, especially as it bears witness to God's acts of salvation (i.e., ultimately, the law as it testifies to the righteousness of God in Christ, Rom. 3:21). This is **appointed** by God (the same verb as "set" in Ps. 78:7) with the command that it be taught by fathers to children and by children to their children down the generations of the church (paradigmatically in Deut. 6:4–9).[21] The purpose of these Scriptures is given both positively (Ps. 78:7) and negatively (78:8).

The three lines of 78:7 characterize living faith as to **set their hope in God** (i.e., make God their "confidence," Prov. 3:26),[22] a personal trust; to **not forget the works of God,** that is, to remember God's nature and salvation and to act on what one remembers; and to **keep his commandments,** with "the obedience of faith" (Rom. 1:5; 16:26).

Psalm 78:8 gives a comparably full—but ugly—portrait of unbelief. The word **stubborn** means a refusal to submit (e.g., Deut. 21:18–20; Pss. 66:7; 68:6, 18; Isa. 1:23; 30:1), as does the verb **rebellious** (also in Ps. 78:8, 17, 40, 56). Christ was rejected by a stubborn and rebellious generation (Acts 2:40).[23] The reason for their stubbornness and rebellion lay hidden in a **heart** that was **not steadfast,** that is, not settled and firm in its trust in God.[24]

---

21 There is a wordplay between "established" (hiphil of קוּם, "caused to arise," Ps. 78:5) and "arise" (קוּם, 78:6); God causes his law to "arise" so that one generation will "arise" and tell the next.

22 The noun "hope" means the object of hope, what or whom we rest our hope on.

23 The LXX term for "stubborn" (Ps. 78:8) is σκολιός, also used in Acts 2:40 ("crooked").

24 Lit., "They did not make firm their heart." The verb is causative rather than stative. Tucker and Grant, *Psalms,* 2:145.

Or to put it another way, their **spirit was not faithful to God**. They were unbelievers within the visible church of God. The purpose of the psalm is to warn the present generation not to be like Psalm 78:8—which is the focus of most of the historical reminiscence in the body of the psalm—but to be like 78:7, to put their faith in the God who will be seen to have made his salvation known in Christ. For the wonders of salvation of 78:4 are all found, and only found, in Christ.

78:9–11 First Focus on Ephraim: Unbelief in the Church Means That Christ Is Desperately Needed

9 The Ephraimites, armed with the bow,
    turned back on the day of battle.
10 They did not keep God's covenant,
    but refused to walk according to his law.
11 They forgot his works
    and the wonders that he had shown them.

The rebellious generation (Ps. 78:8) is now portrayed. They are called **Ephraimites** ("sons of Ephraim"), and this designation is important for understanding the psalm. The story begins in Genesis 48, in which Jacob blesses Ephraim, the younger son, above Manasseh, his older brother.[25] Ephraim, thus privileged by grace (cf. Jacob over Esau), became the dominant tribe (cf. "the ten thousands of Ephraim, / . . . the thousands of Manasseh," Deut. 33:17), both among the northern tribes and arguably among all twelve tribes. They were proud and protective of their prominence (cf. Judg. 8:1–3).[26] The sanctuary at Shiloh was in their territory (1 Sam. 1). They were among the tribes who were slow to accept David as king (2 Sam. 2:8–10), and from their number came Jeroboam, the first king of the breakaway northern kingdom after the death of Solomon and the one who led them astray with golden calves (1 Kings 11:26–12:33). Their history is a sorry one of ungodliness. They were destroyed by the Assyrians

---

25 In Gen. 48:1 they are "Manasseh and Ephraim." By the end of the chapter, and thereafter in the Old Testament, they are "Ephraim and Manasseh."

26 Note also their prominence in the terrible chapters with which Judges closes (Judg. 17:1, 8; 18:2, 13; 19:1, 16, 18). I am grateful to Caleb Howard for this observation.

in 701 BC (cf. the verdict in 2 Kings 17). They were characterized by an "anti-Christ spirit that opposed the king 'after God's own heart'";[27] their history "was to make them almost a symbol of backsliding and apostasy";[28] the prophet Hosea brings this into sharp focus (see the many references to "Ephraim" in Hos. 4–12).

The phrase **armed with the bow** is echoed in the phrase "a deceitful bow" in Psalm 78:57 (tying 78:9–11 to 78:56–66). The **day of battle** may refer to 1 Samuel 4–5, which is the background to Psalm 78:56–66.[29] Whatever the battle, what matters is that they **did not keep God's covenant** (i.e., here, the Sinai covenant enshrined in the Torah; also 78:37), **refused**[30] **to walk according to his law**, and **forgot his works** and **wonders** (in direct contradiction to 78:7). They deliberately, culpably, and obstinately refused to trust the covenant God.

"Ephraim" describes the old covenant church under their dominant character of those who belonged to the covenant people by name but not by nature. In our terms, these are merely nominal believers. Augustine links them to the proud spirit that seeks to use the law as a means of works-righteousness (cf. Rom. 9:31).[31] Writing of **the day of battle**, Martin Luther says,

> This day of battle should be understood . . . as referring to the greatest and most wonderful battle of all. That was the battle of Christ against the devil in the day of His suffering. For this battle was spiritual and so great and of such a nature that all the battles of the world were hardly a figure, a shadow, a weak sign of this one.[32]

In this battle the (unbelieving) Jews "turned back . . . when they repudiated Christ."[33] Luther moves beyond the original historical reference into the deeper significance of these verses; "Ephraim" means the visible church that rejects Christ.

27 Eveson, *Psalms*, 2:50. Eveson here sums up the spiritual significance of Ephraim especially clearly.

28 Kidner, *Psalms*, 2:282.

29 Ross, *Psalms*, 2:662; Witherington, *Psalms Old and New*, 178.

30 This same verb (מֵאֵן) is used in Hos. 11:5, again of "Ephraim."

31 Augustine, *Psalms*, 4:98.

32 Luther, *Luther's Works*, 11:41.

33 Luther, *Luther's Works*, 11:41.

78:12–39 First Main Historical Remembrance:
God's Grace in Christ Will Triumph over Unbelief
78:12–16 The Story Begins with Exodus
and Wilderness Grace in Christ

> ¹² In the sight of their fathers he performed wonders
> in the land of Egypt, in the fields of Zoan.

Psalm 78:12–16 begins with the exodus. **The fields of Zoan** is another way of saying **the land of Egypt**.[34]

> ¹³ He divided the sea and let them pass through it,
> and made the waters stand like a heap.
> ¹⁴ In the daytime he led them with a cloud,
> and all the night with a fiery light.

Cloud and **fiery light** echo Exodus 13:21; **a heap** echoes Exodus 15:8 (cf. Ps. 33:7); **he led them** echoes Exodus 15:13 (cf. Ps. 77:20). With mercy writ large and dramatic, we see foreshadowed "the spiritual redemption of [God's] people from the bondage of sin and misery by Christ."[35]

> ¹⁵ He split rocks in the wilderness
> and gave them drink abundantly as from the deep.
> ¹⁶ He made streams come out of the rock
> and caused waters to flow down like rivers.

From the exodus we move into **the wilderness** and to the two episodes recorded in Exodus 17:1–7 and Numbers 20:2–13. The verb **split** is the same verb used in Psalm 78:13 ("divided"): as God divided the sea to enable his people to pass through, so he divided the hard rock to bring life-giving water. Salvation always overcomes humanly insuperable obstacles. The phrase **abundantly as from the deep** (lit., "and caused to drink as

---

34 Zoan (Gk. Τάνις) was a significant city in Egypt (cf. Num. 13:22) and stands as one part for the whole (cf. Isa. 19:11, 13; 30:4; Ezek. 30:14). The "fields of Zoan" means the region in which this city was prominent, that is, Egypt itself.
35 Dickson, *Psalms,* 2:7.

from great deeps") together with **streams** and **waters to flow down like rivers** emphasizes the overwhelming sufficiency of God's provision. This provision of life-giving water from a rock prefigures Christ (1 Cor. 10:4), by whose "glorification" in atoning death the living waters of the Spirit are given (John 4:13–14; 7:37–39).

78:17–39 By Mercy and by Judgment God Leads His People toward Faith in Christ

17	Yet they sinned still more against him,
	rebelling against the Most High in the desert.
18	They tested God in their heart
	by demanding the food they craved.
19	They spoke against God, saying,
	"Can God spread a table in the wilderness?
20	He struck the rock so that water gushed out
	and streams overflowed.
	Can he also give bread
	or provide meat for his people?"

We begin with a focus on the evil desires of the heart. **Yet they sinned still more** is repeated in Psalm 78:32, a bell tolling their doom; the pattern became a sad paradigm (e.g., Num. 20:13; 27:14; Deut. 32:51), a persistent pattern of hardened unbelief. The designation **Most High** (see Pss. 18:13; 73:11; 77:10; 83:18) emphasized the seriousness of their (and our) sin. The verbs "rebel" (מָרָה, *marah*; also 78:8) and "test" (נָסָה, *nasah*, the root of "Massah") reappear in 78:40 and 56, at the start of subsequent sections. Alexander Francis Kirkpatrick notes, "The two words sum up Israel's behaviour: they rebelled against God by constant disobedience to His revealed Will; they tempted Him, by sceptical doubts of His goodness, and insolent demands that He should prove His power."[36]

The food they craved is literally "food for their נֶפֶשׁ, *nephesh*," where *nephesh* focuses on the human being as one who has desires and needs. Here the desires are a sinful craving. Far from praying in faith and then waiting in hope, they demanded that God should satisfy their desires; this is religion

36 Kirkpatrick, *Psalms*, 2:468.

as a mask for self-centeredness. Instead of past provision (the water from the rock, 78:20a) promoting fresh faith, as it will do in a true believer, the kindness of God is presumed on, so that wrath is stored up (Rom. 2:4–5). The question **Can God spread a table in the wilderness?** is spoken in a very different spirit from the faith of Psalm 23:5 ("You prepare a table before me / in the presence of my enemies"). Psalm 78:20 begins with the word usually translated "behold"; here it has the sense "Oh, sure, God did that then, but can he give us what we want now?" There is something almost absurdly ironic about this question in the light of the water from the rock.[37]

> [21] Therefore, when the LORD heard, he was full of wrath;
>   a fire was kindled against Jacob;
>   his anger rose against Israel,
> [22] because they did not believe in God
>   and did not trust his saving power.

Psalm 78:21–22 alludes to the fiery judgment at Taberah (Num. 11:1–3). God gives "a fiery 'No' to the spirit of the demand" but then in Psalm 78:23–29 "a prodigious 'Yes' to the substance of it."[38] Numbers 14:11 is "a verse which might serve as a motto for this Psalm."[39]

> [23] Yet he commanded the skies above
>   and opened the doors of heaven,
> [24] and he rained down on them manna to eat
>   and gave them the grain of heaven.
> [25] Man ate of the bread of the angels;
>   he sent them food in abundance.

Manna is the first provision of food (Ex. 16). The opening of **the doors of heaven** speaks of provision from God himself (cf. Gen. 7:11; 28:17; 2 Kings 7:2; Mal. 3:10). The **manna** is called both **grain** and **the bread** made from

---

37 Delitzsch, *Psalms*, 2:367.
38 Kidner, *Psalms*, 2:283.
39 Kirkpatrick, *Psalms*, 2:469. Numbers 14:11 reads, "And the LORD said to Moses, 'How long will this people despise me? And how long will they not believe in me, in spite of all the signs that I have done among them?'"

these grains. **Angels** translates "mighty ones" (אַבִּירִים, *abirim*); the context indicates that they are "mighty ones" in the heavens, that is, angels.[40] Again, the **abundance** is emphasized. When Jesus's opponents allude to this psalm (John 6:31), Jesus replies that he himself, in his death, is the spiritual food typified in the manna. Paul teaches the same in 1 Corinthians 10:3 ("spiritual food"), and Jesus promises "the hidden manna" to the one who overcomes by faith (Rev. 2:17). Augustine says, "As bread from heaven [Christ] is rained down on the whole world through the clouds of the gospel."[41]

26   He caused the east wind to blow in the heavens,
       and by his power he led out the south wind;
27   he rained meat on them like dust,
       winged birds like the sand of the seas;
28   he let them fall in the midst of their camp,
       all around their dwellings.
29   And they ate and were well filled,
       for he gave them what they craved.
30   But before they had satisfied their craving,
       while the food was still in their mouths,
31   the anger of God rose against them,
       and he killed the strongest of them
       and laid low the young men of Israel.

The story continues from the manna to the quails (Num. 11) because the same sinful craving characterized the unbelieving church on both occasions. The **east wind** in parallel with the **south wind** probably means a southeasterly wind (the wind of Num. 11:31). Again, there is reference to **what they craved** and **their craving** (cf. Ps. 78:18), now using the word תַּאֲוָה, *taavah*, a strong desire, which lies behind the name "Kibroth-hattaavah" ("graves of craving") in Numbers 11:34. Psalm 78:30–31 (cf. 106:15) alludes to Numbers 11:33. Paul may refer to this in 1 Corinthians 10:5 ("They were overthrown in the wilderness"). The fact that **the strongest of them** and **the young men** are under judgment makes the point that this was not the urgent hunger

---

40 In Ps. 103:20 the word is used in parallel with "angels." Harman, *Psalms*, 2:588n10.
41 Augustine, *Psalms*, 4:106.

of the starving but the greedy passion of the discontented strong. Perhaps in their strength there is an echo of the proud self-confidence of Ephraim.

32   In spite of all this, they still sinned;
           despite his wonders, they did not believe.
33   So he made their days vanish like a breath,
           and their years in terror.

Psalm 78:32–33 indicates that this punishment had to happen again and again because the same sinful passion continued to characterize the people. The people's unbelieving response to the report of the spies may be echoed here, for Numbers 14:11 ("in spite of all the signs") is similar to 78:32b.[42] **Breath** is the word הֶבֶל, *hebel*, so characteristic of Ecclesiastes, an empty, vain, and ultimately pointless thing. What a tragedy for human lives, with all their potential and dignity, to end like this![43] Probably this refers to the deaths of the unbelieving wilderness generation (Num. 14:28–34). This is the punishment for human sin, that "the whole life of mortals speeds away" and that "even a life that seems more extended is but a mist that lasts a little longer."[44]

34   When he killed them, they sought him;
           they repented and sought God earnestly.
35   They remembered that God was their rock,
           the Most High God their redeemer.

When he killed them, they—that is, those who survived—**sought him**. This is expressed in a way that suggests a repeated pattern. Again and again, human mortality prompts some kind of seeking after God. Indeed, this may look as if it is done **earnestly**. They have heard about the covenant God being a **rock** and **redeemer**. In the face of death, they turn to him—or so it appears.

36   But they flattered him with their mouths;
           they lied to him with their tongues.

---

42 Delitzsch, *Psalms*, 2:369.
43 There is a Hebrew wordplay between "breath" (הֶבֶל) and "terror" (בֶּהָלָה). Alter, *Psalms*, 275.
44 Augustine, *Psalms*, 4:108.

³⁷   Their heart was not steadfast toward him;
           they were not faithful to his covenant.

Psalm 78:36–37 shows that this is not a genuine repentance. It is a matter of the **mouths** and **tongues**, not of the **heart**. The word **flattered** here means to "deceive." Here is the religion of words, which sounds genuine but is not (cf. Isa. 29:13; Jer. 12:2; Mark 7:6; the letter of James). A true repentance of the **heart** always issues in a **steadfast** heart toward God, that is, an ongoing faithfulness **to his covenant** (see Ps. 78:8, 10).

The phrase **not steadfast** is echoed in Peter's condemnation of Simon the magician in Acts 8:21,⁴⁵ in a very similar context of someone wanting God's gifts without desiring God.⁴⁶

³⁸   Yet he, being compassionate,
           atoned for their iniquity
           and did not destroy them;
        he restrained his anger often
           and did not stir up all his wrath.
³⁹   He remembered that they were but flesh,
           a wind that passes and comes not again.

Yet he is emphatic (וְהוּא, *vehu*). The precious adjective **compassionate** echoes Exodus 34:6 ("merciful"). The outflow of his warm compassion is atonement (cf. Pss. 65:3; 79:9), the restraining of his righteous anger, the passing over of former sins because Christ will be set forth as a propitiation for sins (Rom. 3:25). Humankind, under the judgment of God since Genesis 3, is **but flesh** (weak and frail), with our "spirits" just **a wind that passes and comes not again**. On such God shows himself compassionate in Christ.

78:40–55 Second Main Historical Remembrance:
God's Grace in Christ Will Triumph over Unbelief

⁴⁰   How often they rebelled against him in the wilderness
           and grieved him in the desert!

45 See Marshall, "Acts," in *CNTOT* 572.
46 Augustine, *Psalms*, 4:108.

41   They tested God again and again
          and provoked the Holy One of Israel.

Psalm 78:40–41 can function equally well as the conclusion to the preceding section or the introduction to the second retelling of the history.

How often recalls Numbers 14:22 ("these ten times"). Again, the verbs **rebel** and **test** (cf. Ps. 78:17–18, 56) are used, together with two verbs that direct our attention to the holiness of God, **grieved** and **provoked**. These anthropomorphic verbs are used not because the impassible God can be changed by our sin but to help us grasp the depth of his holiness (hence the designation **the Holy One of Israel**; cf. 89:18). The focus moves from what they did and where they did it (**in the wilderness, in the desert**) to the one against whom sin is always directed (**God, the Holy One of Israel**).

42   They did not remember his power
          or the day when he redeemed them from the foe,
43   when he performed his signs in Egypt
          and his marvels in the fields of Zoan.

They did not remember takes us back to the importance of godly remembering (and acting accordingly; 78:7, 11). Psalm 78:42 is the springboard that returns us to the beginning of the story **when he redeemed them from the foe** in Egypt or Zoan (see on 78:12). What follows is a poetic reminder of a selection of most of the ten plagues,[47] not in chronological order; these give an overwhelming impression of the righteous anger that God directs against the enemies of his covenant people.[48] There may be a subtext that this anger must also be directed against those who are his covenant people only in name.

44   He turned their rivers to blood,
          so that they could not drink of their streams.

---

47 The text makes no mention of the plagues of gnats, boils, or darkness. There is unlikely any significance in these particular omissions.
48 For a useful comment on the poetic license shown in the choice and conflation of plagues, see Tucker and Grant, *Psalms*, 2:154n30.

This is the first plague, the Nile turned to blood (Ex. 7:17–25; cf. Ps. 105:29 and the echo in Rev. 16:4).

45   He sent among them swarms of flies, which devoured them,
          and frogs, which destroyed them.

Psalm 78:45a is the fourth plague, the flies (Ex. 8:20–32), and Psalm 78:45b, the second, the frogs (Ex. 8:1–15).

46   He gave their crops to the destroying locust
          and the fruit of their labor to the locust.

This is the eighth plague, the locusts (Ex. 10:1–20).

47   He destroyed their vines with hail
          and their sycamores with frost.
48   He gave over their cattle to the hail
          and their flocks to thunderbolts.

Psalm 78:47–48 alludes to the seventh plague, the hail (Ex. 9:13–35). The **frost** may mean icy hailstones. The hail killed the cattle (Ex. 9:19) and was accompanied by "fire flashing continually in the midst of the hail" (Ex. 9:24), hence the **thunderbolts**. The death of the cattle may also allude to the fifth plague, the death of the livestock (Ex. 9:1–7).

49   He let loose on them his burning anger,
          wrath, indignation, and distress,
          a company of destroying angels.
50   He made a path for his anger;
          he did not spare them from death,
          but gave their lives over to the plague.
51   He struck down every firstborn in Egypt,
          the firstfruits of their strength in the tents of Ham.[49]

---

49 Ham is the father of "Egypt" (Gen. 10:6).

Psalm 78:49–51 moves to the final and climactic plague, the death of the firstborn (Ex. 11:1–10; 12:29–32). **He let loose** (lit., "he sent") **his burning anger** (cf. Job 20:23), / **wrath, indignation**, which causes deep **distress**, brought about by **a company of destroying angels**[50] (Ex. 12:13, 23; Heb. 11:28). Psalm 78:50 pictures God's judgment as a stream of fire (line 1), as an executioner (line 2), and as a **plague** (line 3)—all terrifying, each inescapable. **Their lives** is literally "their נֶפֶשׁ, *nephesh*" (cf. the sinful craving of 78:18). The tragedy of the unbelieving church is that it mimics unbelieving Pharaoh and attracts the same just judgment.

To describe **every firstborn** as **the firstfruits of their strength** (i.e., the first fruit, in conception, of the strength of manhood)[51] emphasizes that judgment on the Egypt of the pharaohs is a judgment on human pride and power, which so characterizes the unbelieving church under the title "Ephraim." The plagues are a double-edged reminder, speaking both of the powerful redeeming grace of the covenant God but hinting also at the terrible danger of the unbelieving church.

> [52]   Then he led out his people like sheep
>   and guided them in the wilderness like a flock.
> [53]   He led them in safety, so that they were not afraid,
>   but the sea overwhelmed their enemies.
> [54]   And he brought them to his holy land,
>   to the mountain which his right hand had won.
> [55]   He drove out nations before them;
>   he apportioned them for a possession
>   and settled the tribes of Israel in their tents.

The final section continues the focus on what God has done but moves from his judgment on Pharaoh to his redeeming grace toward his people. The image of being **led out . . . like sheep, like a flock**, recalls Psalm 77:20. The focus is on the kind care of the Redeemer, who **led out**, who

---

50 Lit., "angels of harm/evil." In this context this does not mean "evil angels" but rather "angels who bring harm."

51 Cf. Gen. 49:3 ("Reuben . . . the firstfruits of my strength"); Deut. 21:17. A "proud father" may be thankful to God for this gift, or he may begin to think that he, who has fathered a human being, can do anything!

guided, who **led . . . in safety**, and who **brought them to his holy land**. At every stage of redemption, the covenant Redeemer takes the initiative—and all this in spite of persistent sin. His kindness is emphasized by the absence of any need to fear (78:53a), since "terror and dread" fell on their enemies (Ex. 15:16). These verses are almost a commentary on Exodus 15:13–17. The **mountain** in Psalm 78:54 may be a reference to the land in its aspect as "hill country" rather than a specific reference to Mount Zion.[52]

78:56–66 Second Focus on Ephraim: Unbelief in the Church Means That Christ Is Desperately Needed

56   Yet they tested and rebelled against the Most High God
           and did not keep his testimonies,
57   but turned away and acted treacherously like their fathers;
           they twisted like a deceitful bow.
58   For they provoked him to anger with their high places;
           they moved him to jealousy with their idols.

In Psalm 78:56 it seems that we enter the promised land (following 78:55). What follows especially echoes the days of the judges, especially the events of 1 Samuel 4–5. The subject (**they**) now focuses on Israel in their nature as "Ephraim" in the promised land, that is, an unbelieving church. The verbs **tested** and **rebelled** echo Psalm 78:17–18 and 40, for the sin of the exodus and wilderness generation still marks the old covenant church in the land. **They . . . did not keep his testimonies** recalls Ephraim in 78:10. The **deceitful bow** reminds us of Ephraim in 78:9. The same idiom appears in Hosea 7:16 (again of Ephraim). The point of the metaphor is that this bow misses the mark; it "discharges its arrow in a wrong direction" and "makes no sure shot."[53] It is a picture of sin, defined as missing the mark. The reference to **high places** (cf. Ezek. 20:27–29) and **idols** takes us right into the promised land. All this **moved him to jealousy** (see, most significantly,

---

52 Cf. the parallelism in Isa. 11:9; 57:13. Harman, *Psalms*, 2:594n17.

53 Delitzsch, *Psalms*, 2:373. Alter suggests that "the image seems to be of a bow that flips out of the hands of the archer, shooting the arrow in the wrong direction, or not shooting at all." Alter, *Psalms*, 278. The effect is much the same.

the discussion of the sins of the northern kingdom in 2 Kings 17:9–15; cf.
Deut. 32:16, 21; Jer. 8:19).

> 59   When God heard, he was full of wrath,
>   and he utterly rejected Israel.
> 60   He forsook his dwelling at Shiloh,
>   the tent where he dwelt among mankind,
> 61   and delivered his power to captivity,
>   his glory to the hand of the foe.

Psalm 78:59–61 remembers the capture of the ark by the Philistines in
1 Samuel 4–5 and the associated defeat, although it also, no doubt, looks
ahead to the final destruction of the northern kingdom by the Assyrians.
What Psalm 78:21 said of the wilderness generation, 78:59 has to say of
the generations in the land. Psalm 78:60, with its focus on **his dwelling**
(tabernacle) **at Shiloh**, focuses again on Ephraim, in whose territory this
sanctuary lay. Here "the tent of meeting" was set up when they entered
the land (Josh. 18:1); here, later, was a more solid building (as 1 Sam. 1–3
seems to imply). The wonder of this place (the tabernacle) is that it is **where**
God himself **dwelt among mankind**, that is, the only place on earth where
a human being could have access to God. The nouns **power**[54] and **glory**[55]
refer here to the ark of the covenant. The Philistines captured the ark; it
never returned to Shiloh but was taken instead to Kiriath-Jearim (1 Sam.
7:2) and completed its long journey from Sinai when David brought it
with great rejoicing to Mount Zion (2 Sam. 6; cf. Ps. 68). The rejection of
Shiloh stands, just before the Babylonian exile, as an object lesson of the
danger of not trusting the covenant God (Jer. 7:12–15). It finds a parallel
in the threat of the risen Jesus to remove a "lampstand," that is, a church,
in Revelation 2:5 and 3:16.

> 62   He gave his people over to the sword
>   and vented his wrath on his heritage.
> 63   Fire devoured their young men,

54 Ps. 132:8 refers to "the ark of your might/power."
55 The word is תִּפְאָרֶת, "beauty," and is used in association with the ark in Lam. 2:1 ("splendor").
    Cf. the synonym in 1 Sam. 4:21 ("The glory has departed from Israel").

and their young women had no marriage song.
64   Their priests fell by the sword,
        and their widows made no lamentation.

The judgment of Psalm 78:62–64 parallels that on the wilderness generation. God **gave his people over to** (lit., "shut them up to") dying by **the
sword**, even though they are now dwelling in **his heritage**, his treasured
possession, and are themselves that possession, at least outwardly. **Fire**
(here probably a metaphor for war, as in Numbers 21:28, but reminiscent
of the literal fire at Taberah in Ps. 78:21) **devoured their young men**, the
strength and hope for the future, so that **their young women** (the word
usually means "virgin" or young woman of marriageable age) **had no marriage song**, that is, no wedding day when their beauty is praised in song (as
we praise the beauty of a bride today). If this destruction of their future is
not enough, 78:64 adds that **their priests fell by the sword** (as the sons of
Eli did literally in 1 Sam. 4:11), so that there is no more mediator between
them and God, and that **their widows** (i.e., not just the widows of the priests
but all the widows of war) **made no lamentation**, not because they do not
care but because the horrors of war overwhelm them and provide them no
opportunity to show this final honor to their husbands. What happened
to the hardened Egyptians of Pharaoh happens to the impenitent nominal
members of the church. And yet this is not the end of the story, which is
yet sweetened with a serving of grace.

65   Then the Lord awoke as from sleep,
        like a strong man shouting because of wine.
66   And he put his adversaries to rout;
        he put them to everlasting shame.

The vivid anthropomorphic images of Psalm 78:65 picture the sovereign
God (**the Lord**) like a man waking from sleep and like a warrior (**strong man**)
emboldened by **wine** to furious acts of courage. God does not actually sleep,
but he seems to his people to sleep when he does not act to save (cf. 44:23;
73:20). God does not get drunk, but his furious actions in judgment may remind us of a drunken warrior. It is a frightening picture, and it is meant to be.
In the first instance, the putting of **his adversaries to rout** and **to everlasting**

shame[56] most likely refers to the defeat of the Philistines in 1 Samuel 5,[57] but it points beyond, both to the great triumphs of King David's reign and to the extensive kingdom of King Solomon. Beyond that, it hints at a greater rout and an eternal shame for the enemies of God and his people before Christ.

If we were in any doubt as to the source from whom the extraordinary change of Psalm 78:65–66 is to come, 78:67–72 will answer us.

78:67–72 Christ Is the Only Hope for the Church

> 67   He rejected the tent of Joseph;
> he did not choose the tribe of Ephraim,

In this context, **the tent of Joseph**, in parallel with **the tribe of Ephraim**, most likely refers to the sanctuary at Shiloh, whose rejection has been sung about in Psalm 78:60–64. The rout of the enemies celebrated in 78:65–66 does not mean that Shiloh and Ephraim will be saved. This sobering verse sounds the death knell to all false assurance within the church.

> 68   but he chose the tribe of Judah,
> Mount Zion, which he loves.

Psalm 78:68–72 bursts on us as a wonderful surprise, even if those who know the story as it develops under Samuel and then David may not be so surprised. The clause **which he loves** locates the election of Christ's people solely and wonderfully in the sovereign love of the covenant God. From **the tribe of Judah** comes not only King David but Christ (Heb. 7:14). Here, writes David Dickson,

> is his mercy, with an intimation of the main means of the mercy, which is the coming of Christ in the flesh, out of the tribe of Judah. Thus God

---

56 The word "shame" (הֶרְפָּה) is the same as that translated "reproach" or "scoff" or "scorn" when inflicted on God's Messiah and his people (e.g., Pss. 69:7, 9–10, 19–20; 71:13; 74:22).

57 Ps. 78:66 "is moulded after" 1 Sam. 5:6–12 but also "embraces all the victories under Samuel, Saul, and David" from this time forward. Delitzsch, *Psalms*, 2:375. Kidner notes that "the next half-century was to see Israel brought to its zenith" and that this development in the history is "utterly unexpected" and "shows the steadfast love of God in the most robust and unsentimental colours." Kidner, *Psalms*, 2:285.

will not depart from Israel, and yet he will not be found save in the tribe of Judah, out of which came Christ, the root and fountain of mercy to all Israel who should seek God through him.[58]

69   He built his sanctuary like the high heavens,
         like the earth, which he has founded forever.

His sanctuary in Mount Zion is celebrated in cosmic (**like the high heavens, / like the earth**) and eternal (**founded forever**) terms. The temple is, symbolically, the cosmos in which God dwells among his people. Since neither Solomon's temple nor the Second Temple (destroyed in AD 70) endured, those who continue to sing this psalm must celebrate a greater temple, or, more accurately, one who is "greater than the temple" (Matt. 12:6). The temple planned by David and built by Solomon was "a pledge to show that Christ was to come."[59] In Christ the very cosmos is upheld by his word of power (Col. 1:17; Heb. 1:3).

70   He chose David his servant
         and took him from the sheepfolds;
71   from following the nursing ewes he brought him
         to shepherd Jacob his people,
         Israel his inheritance.
72   With upright heart he shepherded them
         and guided them with his skillful hand.

The words **he chose** sum up the conclusion of the psalm. We choose to sin, repeatedly, culpably, incorrigibly. God chooses to save. Only the sovereign grace of God, sending Christ to fulfill all the promises to David and effectually calling men and women into Christ, can bring any hope. This is the new covenant, so badly needed, so certainly prophesied, so wonderfully brought down to us in the death of Christ.

The humble beginnings of David are emphasized—**from the sheepfolds, from following the nursing ewes**, with all the associations of gentle, caring

58 Dickson, *Psalms*, 2:27.
59 Calvin, *Psalms*, 3:279.

leadership—in contrast to the pride of "Ephraim." David, the despised youngest brother, is the chosen shepherd of God's people (cf. 2 Sam. 5:2). This obscure shepherd (1 Sam. 16:11) becomes God's shepherd for God's flock and the foreshadowing of the great, good, and chief shepherd of God's sheep. The word **inheritance** is repeated from Psalm 78:62 ("heritage"), but now the true heritage of God consists of all those given by the Father to the Son (John 6:37–39). Jesus Christ is the despised and humble one, and all his followers are to walk in his footsteps as humble, unimpressive people (cf. 1 Cor. 1:18–2:4).

David leads **with upright heart** and **with . . . skillful hand**. If David's kingship sometimes approximated this, the good shepherd demonstrates both in perfection. All the oscillations of the old covenant people, with these turbulent alternations of mercy and judgment, can, as Dickson describes, lead to "no settled state, till they be put under the government of David, who in this is a type of Christ," for "whatever measure David had of those properties, was but a shadow of the perfections of Christ in his government."[60]

REFLECTION AND RESPONSE

1. We do well to feel horror as we read the story of the old covenant church and to dwell on each episode and the heart of unbelief that it revealed. But we must never do so in a pharisaical spirit. The psalmist "holds up before the people the history . . . as a glass in which they might see their own face."[61] And yet, even as new covenant people, the face that we see in this mirror is the face of the "old man" in each of us by nature. We are no better. This is "a 'parable' not for Israel only, but for every individual in the Christian Church."[62]

2. We must be warned by the pride of Ephraim. The contrast between Ephraim in its self-confidence and the kingdom of David in its humility speaks to us eloquently of the gospel of the Lord Jesus and of our call to eschew all human pride in our discipleship and our churches.

3. Against the background of the horrifying instability of the old covenant church, we feel what deep longings old covenant believers must have

60 Dickson, *Psalms*, 2:28–29.
61 Hengstenberg, *Psalms*, 2:451.
62 Kirkpatrick, *Psalms*, 2:465.

had for the promised new covenant in the Messiah. This can make us feel more deeply the wonder of the new covenant and the astonishing beauty of Jesus Christ, the Son of David.

4. It is good to come back to Psalm 78:5–8. We too have an obligation both to live out a life of amazed faith, humbled by the love of God in Christ, and to do all we can to pass on that wondering faith to the next generation, both in our families and in our churches.

5. Charles Spurgeon closes his comments on this psalm with these words:

Thus have we ended this lengthy parable, may we in our life-parable have less of sin, and as much of grace as are [sic] displayed in Israel's history, and may we close it under the safe guidance of "that great Shepherd of the sheep."[63]

---

63 Spurgeon, *Treasury*, 2.1:347.

Should the adversaries rush in and attack, and continuing
their aggression, pollute the house of God and slay the saints
and hurl their bodies to the winged creatures of the heaven,
in order that you not lie cowering, recoiled on yourself,
before their cruelty, you must sympathize with those who
suffer, and make your appeal to God, reciting [Psalm 79].

ATHANASIUS
Letter to Marcellinus

The church of God may be brought so low, as here we see once
it was. . . . So many of God's people as live to see such public
calamities and misery, must not despair of a recovery, but should
and may run to God and pray for the church in affliction, expecting
order after confusion, and after dissipation, to see a gathering of
God's people again; and after apparent overthrow of religion, a
restoring of God's public worship, as the example of the psalmist
in this psalm teacheth, whose courage and confidence in God for
relief of the Lord's people are wonderful, as the state of the church
at that time, seemed to be desperate. As the holy Ghost . . . giveth
warning here to all churches in all ages to beware to provoke the
Lord unto wrath, lest he deal with them as he dealt with those
Israelites, so he giveth warrant to all afflicted churches to follow the
example of this afflicted church, to run to God for help; for which
cause he hath given this psalm to be made use of by the church.

DAVID DICKSON
A Commentary on the Psalms

PSALM 79

ORIENTATION

Psalm 79 is a psalm for Good Friday and all the "Good Fridays" of the perse-cuted church. It cries with visceral pain and paints in primary colors this great question, which echoes around both Old and New Testaments: Why does the righteous anger of God burn against his faithful servants? The theological nub of the psalm is the tension between God's jealous anger burning against his covenant people (79:5) and that same righteous anger poured out on the ungodly (79:6). Almost certainly, the context that provoked the psalm was the desecration of Jerusalem by the Babylonians in 586 BC.[1] In that judg-ment the righteous remnant of the church ("your servants . . . your faithful," 79:2) suffered along with the unrighteous; the jealous anger of the covenant God burned against the whole church. But why? What the Babylonians did was—at the same time—an evil deed and the jealous anger of God against his people (cf. the Assyrians with the northern kingdom, Isa. 10:5). God used evil deeds to put into effect his righteous judgments.

But this is not the whole story. For at the heart of the psalm lies the honor of God (his "name," Ps. 79:6, 9), the covenant compassion of God (79:8), and, above all, atonement (79:8–9). The faithful remnant are not intrinsi-cally good people; they are people who receive atonement for their sins. If Psalm 74 reassures the ruined church of Christ from the truth of creation, Psalm 79 brings comfort from the springs of atonement. This atonement is

---

1   This is sometimes questioned because the psalm describes only the desecration rather than the destruction of the temple. But arguably, it is the desecration that is the crowning tragedy; noth-ing worse can happen to a holy place than to be defiled by unholiness. Hengstenberg, *Psalms*, 3:2. For a helpful discussion about the debates over dating, see Tate, *Psalms 51–100*, 298–99.

possible only because one day the perfect "Israel" will give himself to bear the wrath of God for his people's sins. He will be the ruined temple (John 2:18–22) and, in his outpoured blood (cf. Ps. 79:3, 10), will atone for their sins. He reveals his Father's name and does so supremely in his death (John 17:6, 26). Jesus Christ is the one in whom the tensions of the psalm will be resolved, as he suffers as the representative head of his people.

Jesus is also the one who wept for his ruined church (Luke 19:41–44; cf. Matt. 23:37–38), using language sometimes evocative of this psalm (e.g., Luke 21:24).[2] Jesus entered most fully into the lament of the psalm. The Savior who leads us in singing this song today is the one on whom the fire of God's jealous, righteous anger (Ps. 79:5) burned with infinite ferocity as he took on himself the sins of his people in order that this wrath might be drained to the dregs in his substitutionary sufferings. Then—and only then—the sins of his people would be atoned for (79:9) and the name of God be vindicated as his church is rescued.

Echoes in the book of Revelation confirm that this psalm continues to be the godly cry of the persecuted church.[3] The cry of the martyrs (Rev. 6:10) echoes Psalm 79:3, 10, and 12 (the righteous "avenging" of their "blood"), as does the vision of "Babylon" being repaid for the "blood" of God's "servants" (Rev. 19:2). The vision of the nations trampling the temple and holy city in Revelation 11:2 echoes Psalm 79:1, and 79:2–3 is echoed by the dead bodies of the two witnesses lying in the street of the evil city "where their Lord was crucified" (Rev. 11:8). The sufferings of their crucified Lord overflowed into the persecutions of his people in the days when Psalm 79 was written and will continue to overflow to his persecuted church until he returns. Psalm 79 speaks ultimately of the cross of Christ and of the overflow of his sufferings to his church.[4] The elect, who cry day and night to God the Judge, may use Psalm 79 to give shape to their cry (Luke 18:7). In terms reminiscent of the psalm, God has promised to "grant relief to you who are afflicted . . . when the Lord Jesus is revealed . . . in flaming fire, inflicting vengeance on those who do not know God" (2 Thess. 1:7–8; cf. "that do not know you," Ps. 79:6).

---

2 Witherington, *Psalms Old and New*, 187–88.

3 See Witherington, *Psalms Old and New*, 186–87.

4 Ker records moving stories of Huguenot martyrs using this psalm as they died. The last words of John Owen (1616–1683), at a time when the church was under great pressure in England and Scotland, are supposed to have been Ps. 79:8. See John Ker, *The Psalms in History and Biography*, Leopold Classic Library (Edinburgh: Andrew Elliot, 1886), 106–8.

There are many links with Psalms 77 and 78,[5] notably the image of the church as God's sheep, which concludes all three psalms (77:20; 78:71–72; 79:13). Links between Psalms 78 and 79 include (1) "inheritance/heritage" (78:62, 71; 79:1), (2) the sanctuary (78:68–69; 79:1), (3) "heaven . . . earth" (78:69; 79:2), (4) unlamented/unburied corpses (78:64; 79:2–3), (5) God's anger (78:58–59; 79:5) burning like a fire (78:21; 79:5), (6) God's compassion (78:38; 79:8), and (7) atonement (78:38; 79:9).

Psalms 74 and 79 share many features, including (1) God's inheritance/heritage (74:2, 7; 79:1); (2) God's church as sheep (74:1; 79:13), with the word "habitation" meaning "pasture" (74:20; 79:7); (3) the questions "Why?" (74:1; 79:10) and "How long?" (74:10; 79:5); and (4) God as Judge (74:22; 79:10–12). Distinctive emphases of Psalm 79, in contrast to Psalm 74, include (1) a focus on the terrible sufferings of the people, "particularly . . . the underlying hatred towards the LORD and his people";[6] (2) a focus on "the nations" and "the neighbors," that is, on social groups hostile to the church; (3) an explicit link with the sin of the church; and (4) a focus on the honor of God's "name."[7]

There are several links with Jeremiah. The closest are (1) the very similar wording of 79:6–7 and Jeremiah 10:25 and (2) the quotation of Micah 3:12 in Jeremiah 26:18, echoed in Psalm 79:1. Psalm 79 also shares parallels with Psalm 102 (note the similarity of 79:11 and 102:20). It is not surprising that Lamentations bewails the same event in some similar ways (e.g., 79:1; Lam. 1:10). The echoes of "nations," "burning anger," "jealousy," and "call upon the name" of God in Zephaniah 3:8–9 (cf. Ps. 79:5–6) suggest that this prophecy functions as an answer to the yearnings of the psalm. Daniel's prayer exhibits thematic similarities (Dan. 9:4–19).

THE TEXT

Structure
Perhaps the clearest division is to take Psalm 79:1–12 in three equal sections (each beginning with an address to God), with 79:13 as a conclusion. Psalm

---

5   Links with Pss. 80–82 will be discussed later. Zenger suggests that there is a "compositional arc" from the lament of Pss. 79 and 80 through God's answer in Ps. 81 to God's recapture of world government in Ps. 82. Hossfeld and Zenger, *Psalms*, 2:307.

6   Harman, *Psalms*, 2:601.

7   These are helpfully discussed in Hossfeld and Zenger, *Psalms*, 2:305.

79:1–4 and 9–12 each includes "your servants" (79:2, 10), blood poured out (79:3, 10), and mockery (79:4, 12), which may suggest that these sections balance around the central section, in which the covenant name, "the LORD," is the focus. "Nations" appears in each section (79:1, 6, 10).

Superscription

S   A Psalm of Asaph.[8]

79:1–4 The Lament of Christ's Ravaged Church

1   O God, the nations have come into your inheritance;
they have defiled your holy temple;
they have laid Jerusalem in ruins.

Psalm 79:1–4 screams with pain. But it is addressed (as is each section of the psalm) to **God** in prayerful lament from the very beginning. All the verbs ("have come," "have defiled," "have laid," "have given," "have poured out," "have become") are in the perfect-tense form; this is "a chain of 'flash pictures'"[9] of a past event.

The three lines of 79:1 form a terrible crescendo of compressed tragedy. First, they **have come into** God's place; then, **they have defiled** it; finally, **they have laid** it **in ruins**. The subject is **the nations**, the Gentiles, the outsiders to God's old covenant church; the world (in John's terminology) has come into the church (cf. Lam. 1:10). The invasion is into **your inheritance** (cf. Ps. 78:62, 71), the precious possession of God, and the desecration is of **your holy temple**, with emphasis on God's holiness. The verb **defiled** is a strong word (CSB: "desecrated"), used of the defilement of Dinah in Genesis 34 and frequently in Leviticus, Numbers, Deuteronomy, and the Prophets (especially Ezekiel) of ritual uncleanness. Defilement invading holiness turns the entire order of creation upside down.[10] And yet the Babylonian defilement was not the first dirt to come into God's holy place, for the people of Israel had themselves brought both ritual and—more importantly—moral

---

8   See on Pss. 50, 73. In Hebrew the superscription is the start of verse 1.
9   Hossfeld and Zenger, *Psalms*, 2:303.
10   Calvin, *Psalms*, 3:282.

dirt into the sanctuary (e.g., 2 Chron. 36:14; Ezek. 5:11; 23:38). When the Babylonians **laid Jerusalem in ruins**[11] (fulfilling the prophecy of Mic. 3:12, quoted in Jer. 26:18), they completed the destruction of God's church that the corrupt church had itself begun.

> 2   They have given the bodies of your servants
>   to the birds of the heavens for food,
>   the flesh of your faithful to the beasts of the earth.
> 3   They have poured out their blood like water
>   all around Jerusalem,
>   and there was no one to bury them.

Psalm 79:2–3 is heartrending.[12] "Almost every word expresses the cruelty of these enemies of the Church."[13] **Bodies** means corpses, now treated simply as meat (cf. **flesh**) for birds, picking at the bones like vultures, and wild beasts, tearing at their flesh (the word **beasts** means wild animals, rather than farm animals); here are unburied corpses, torn by jackals and vultures. The covenant curses warned of this outcome (Deut. 28:26; cf. Jer. 7:33; 16:4; 34:17–20); creation order is turned upside down as animals eat not vegetation but human beings (Gen. 1:30). This created order was symbolized by the holy temple. And yet some of these corpses were of **your servants** (i.e., covenantally faithful servants), **your faithful** (the חֲסִידִים, *khasidim*, the recipients and givers of covenant חֶסֶד, *khesed*), the believing and genuine members of the church. **Their blood**, so precious to God (Ps. 116:15), was **poured out** (cf. Rev. 16:6) like a sacrifice, but **like water**, it was counted very cheap. This happened **all around Jerusalem** because **there was no one to bury them** (cf. Ps. 78:64b). It is as though the desecration of the temple was a nuclear explosion spreading death in expanding waves **all around** and contradicting everything the temple stood for, in life and creation order.

> 4   We have become a taunt to our neighbors,
>   mocked and derided by those around us.

---

11   The word "ruins" (עִיִּים) means "a heap of stones," reminding us of what Jesus said about the destiny of a later corrupt temple (Matt. 24:2).

12   Parts of these verses are quoted freely in 1 Macc. 7:17 of a later atrocity.

13   Calvin, *Psalms*, 3:282.

Psalm 79:4 is very similar to 44:13 (see Rom. 8:36, which quotes Ps. 44:11 regarding the sufferings of the righteous; cf. Jer. 51:51; Dan. 9:16). The words **taunt, mocked,** and **derided** end the description with a torrent of abuse.[14] The **neighbors, those around us,** are probably peoples like the Edomites, Moabites, and Ammonites (cf. Ezek. 25:1–14; Obadiah). What makes this so serious, as Psalm 79:12 will demonstrate, is that to mock God's church is to taunt God. The tragedy of a ruined church is not simply the suffering of believers; it is the mockery of God's holiness.

79:5–8 The Plea of Christ's Ravaged Church for God's Anger to Be Redirected

The prayers in this and the following section alternate between the rescue of God's people and the punishment of their oppressors, the two facets of "Your kingdom come."

> 5   How long, O LORD? Will you be angry forever?
>   Will your jealousy burn like fire?

The question **How long?** (e.g., Pss. 6:3; 74:10; 90:13) and the address to the covenant **LORD** move us from lament to urgent petition. Perhaps "How long?" covers both lines of the verse: "How long, O LORD, will you be angry forever, / [how long] will your jealousy burn like fire?" While 79:1–4 expresses the cruelty of the enemies of the church, it expresses—at the same time and even more fundamentally—the righteous anger of God (cf. Deut. 32:22; Ps. 78:21), who is jealous for the faithful love of his bride, the church (cf. Ex. 20:5; 34:14; Deut. 4:24, echoed in Heb. 12:29). "When God's people fall from their matrimonial covenant with God, and their heart and eyes go a whoring after idols, no wonder the Lord be jealous, and his wrath for this be most hot."[15]

> 6   Pour out your anger on the nations
>   that do not know you,
>   and on the kingdoms
>   that do not call upon your name!

---

14 Cf. Pss. 74:22; 78:66; 89:41, 50; 123:4; Lam. 3:61; 5:1; Ezek. 23:32; 36:4.
15 Dickson, *Psalms*, 2:32.

7   For they have devoured Jacob
      and laid waste his habitation.

In Psalm 79:6–7 we pray for God's righteous anger to be poured out (cf. 79:3, 10) on **the nations** (cf. 79:1) **that do not know** God, that is, refuse to know him personally or acknowledge him as the true God (cf. Pharaoh, Ex. 5:2)—or, to put it another way, **the kingdoms** (a word that focuses not so much on their culture as on their power) **that do not call upon** his **name** (Ps. 79:9), in prayer (the mark of true faith). The irony, as the faithful will have known, is that much of nominal Israel fits this description.

Psalm 79:7 gives the reason (**for**) why justice demands that God's righteous anger be poured out on these peoples. **They have devoured Jacob**, where the root "devoured" is the same as the "food" of the vultures in 79:2, **and laid waste** (cf. "in ruins," 79:1) **his habitation**, a word that usually means "pasture" (a link with the flock imagery in 79:13).

To pray this is not incompatible with praying that people will repent; it is to pray, "Your kingdom come," in accordance with what God has promised (e.g., Deut. 30:7). Those who finally refuse to worship must be punished. To pray this aright, we must remove from our hearts all private vengefulness. Our concern, led by the Lord Jesus, is with the salvation of God's church and therefore with the restoration of justice in the universe.

John Calvin writes pastorally about this, observing that

the pious Jews here not only lay out of consideration their own particular advantage in order to consult the good of the whole Church, but also chiefly direct their eyes to Christ, beseeching him to devote to destruction his enemies whose repentance is hopeless. [And so] they do not cast aside the affection which charity requires; for, although they would desire all to be saved, they yet know that the reformation of some of the enemies of Christ is hopeless, and their perdition absolutely certain.[16]

8   Do not remember against us our former iniquities;
      let your compassion come speedily to meet us,
      for we are brought very low.

16 Calvin, *Psalms*, 3:287–88.

In Psalm 79:8 the focus returns to the need of God's church for salvation. The phrase translated **our former iniquities** can also be translated "the iniquities of former generations" (ESV mg.).[17] The confession of "our sins" in 79:9 may suggest the first,[18] although the similarity with Jeremiah 11:10 may favor the latter.[19] But whether this refers to the iniquities of their forefathers (cf. "the sins of Manasseh," 2 Kings 24:3) or their own earlier sins, what matters is that God **not remember** (i.e., remember and act on) them **against us**. They urgently need (**let . . . come speedily**) the Lord's **compassion**, his tender mercies (cf. Pss. 77:9; 78:38), **for we are brought very low**, an evocative phrase (cf. Judg. 6:6). This is the plea of Christ's ravaged church in every age.

79:9–12 The Plea of Christ's Ravaged Church for Atonement and Justice

> 9   Help us, O God of our salvation,
>   for the glory of your name;
>   deliver us, and atone for our sins,
>   for your name's sake!

In Psalm 79:9 two new notes are sounded. First, the appeal is **for the glory of your name** and **for your name's sake!** Here is the voice of believers who (in contrast with 79:6) call on God as he has revealed himself in covenant faithfulness and promise (those promises all fulfilled in Christ, 2 Cor. 1:20). This name has **glory**, for it is weighty and revelatory. God helps his church for the sake of his **name** because a saved church makes that name known in authentic witness. **Our salvation** proclaims his **name**. This is the supreme motive in our prayers for our rescue.

The second new note is the plea **Atone for our sins** (cf. Pss. 65:3; 78:38). God's "compassion" (79:8) means not that he turns a blind eye to sins (for this would contradict his holy justice) but that he sends his Son to make atonement for sins.

---

17   "Former" translates רִאשֹׁנִים. If this is an adjective, it means "former"; if it is a substantive, it means "of the former (i.e., generations)."

18   So Ross, *Psalms*, 2:674; Tate, *Psalms 51–100*, 297.

19   Hossfeld and Zenger, *Psalms*, 2:303; Delitzsch, *Psalms*, 2:379.

¹⁰   Why should the nations say,
        "Where is their God?"
      Let the avenging of the outpoured blood of your servants
        be known among the nations before our eyes!

The taunting question **Where is their God?** (cf. Ps. 42:10; Joel 2:17) is among the most painful for a believer to hear, for it calls into question the "glory" and the "name" of God, our conviction that God has made himself known on earth. God is invisible, but he has chosen to reveal himself. He has done so in creation in sufficient measure to make people without excuse (Rom. 1:18–20). He has done so in redemption, through the Scriptures in his church. The fact that **the nations** (Ps. 79:1, 6) ask this question means that they have come into contact with the church; they have within their horizon all they need to know God, if only they will.

The echoes of 79:10b in Revelation 6:10 ("avenge . . . blood") and 19:2 ("has avenged . . . the blood of his servants") mean that we cannot lightly dismiss these words as sub-Christian. The **avenging** means not our flawed vengefulness but God's perfect punishment (cf. Deut. 32:35, quoted in Rom. 12:19). The **outpoured blood** (cf. Ps. 79:3) stresses their terrible hatred for Christ and his church. That this is of **your servants** emphasizes that these are true believers, not the merely nominal church. The cry for this to **be known among the nations before our eyes** is not a bitter plea but a petition for unboundedly public justice, known both **among the nations** and **before our eyes**. This longing is of a piece with a care for the "name" and "glory" of God.

¹¹   Let the groans of the prisoners come before you;
        according to your great power, preserve those doomed to die!

Again the focus shifts, here from judgment on the impenitent to the misery of God's penitent people. **The groans** (cf. Ps. 12:5) **of the prisoners** reminds us of the Hebrew slaves under the pharaohs. When these **come before you**, the church may be confident that the righteous Judge will hear them (Ex. 2:23–25; Luke 18:1–8). **According to your great power** (lit., "arm") reminds us of exodus redemption, fulfilled in the death and resurrection of Christ; the phrase **those doomed to die** is literally "the sons of death," that is, people marked by the shadow of death in all their days (cf. "the groans of the prisoners" and "those . . . doomed to die," Ps. 102:20). The church of Christ, living under the shadow of death, and most acutely in days of persecution, groans with Spirit-given longing for the redemption of our bodies (cf. Rom. 8:18–25).

> 12   Return sevenfold into the lap of our neighbors
>   the taunts with which they have taunted you, O Lord!

Psalm 79:12 returns to **the taunts** and the **neighbors** of 79:4. What matters most is not that they have taunted us but that **they have taunted you, O Lord!** Those who mock Christ's church mock God, just as those who persecute Christians persecute Christ (Acts 9:4). The image of the **lap** is of giving something like grain into the lap of a stretched-out robe (cf. Luke 6:38). **Sevenfold** does not mean a recompense over and above what is deserved but rather a perfect, complete, and just retribution (cf. Lev. 26:18–24). This is what God promises against anyone who kills Cain (Gen. 4:15), in contrast to the vengeful "seventy-sevenfold" overkill of Lamech (Gen. 4:23–24).

79:13 Conclusion: Christ Leads His Ravaged Church in Endless Praise

> 13   But we your people, the sheep of your pasture,
>   will give thanks to you forever;
>   from generation to generation we will recount your praise.

But we marks an emphatic contrast at the start of a striking conclusion. **Your people** is a covenant phrase (cf. the covenant watchword "You will be my people, and I will be your God"). **The sheep of your pasture** (cf. the pastoral overtones of "habitation" in Ps. 79:7) is spoken by scattered lost sheep yearning for a great and good shepherd (cf. 74:1; 77:20; 78:70–72; 80:1; 100:3). The promise to **give thanks to you** and **recount your praise** means publicly to acknowledge that the God to whom the church laments and prays is the God known to us in Christ as the God of our salvation, the God who has provided atonement, the God who hears the prayers of his people. This is **from generation to generation** (cf. 78:4) because God's covenant faithfulness in Christ will never end (cf. Luke 20:37–38). As David Dickson puts it, "The troubles of the Lord's people and their mourning are but temporal and of short endurance; but their deliverance and comfort, when their troubles are ended, are everlasting."[20]

REFLECTION AND RESPONSE

1. It is worth reflecting, from Psalm 79:1, on the different ways in which "the nations" can invade and pollute Christ's church (for the emphasis is not so much on the invasion as on the pollution). Overt persecution is the most obvious parallel to the Babylonian depredations. But whenever wickedness invades the church, this psalm is relevant. This may be through false teaching or morally compromised living, especially among the leaders of the church: "It is an awful thing when wicked men are found in the church and numbered with her ministry."[21] Martin Luther reads the psalm morally, where the nations represent "vices and evil thoughts" invading the church and the soul of the individual Christian; although this is not the original meaning, it reminds us that "the passions of the flesh" do indeed "wage war against your soul" (1 Pet. 2:11).[22]

2. Although for many of us Psalm 79:2–3 describes something beyond our experience, the persecuted church knows it all too well. At the heart of "the world" lies an incurable hostility to Christ and his church (cf. John 15:18–16:3).

3. "Who can refute a sneer?" was William Paley's famous comment when speaking about a contemporary who mocked Christianity.[23] Psalm 79:4 prompts us to review the different ways in which our culture treats the Bible as absurd, irrelevant, or even evil. When we set these alongside 79:12, we discover hope since all mockery of God's church is a taunting of God, which can never be the last word.

4. The alternation between prayers for the church's redemption and petitions for the final judgment of its persecutors reminds us that the prayer

---

20 Dickson, *Psalms*, 2:36.
21 Spurgeon, *Treasury*, 2.1:36.
22 Luther, *Luther's Works*, 11:90.
23 Edward Gibbon, *The Rise and Fall of the Roman Empire*, 6 vols. (London, 1776).

"Your kingdom come" must necessarily include the yearning for the final destruction of evil. We should let this psalm both purify our desires of any selfish vengefulness and at the same time shape them into Christ-centered longings for the kingdom of God (cf. Luke 18:1–8).

5. Psalm 79 directs our attention urgently to the atonement God has given us in Christ. This is our only hope.

6. To pray Psalm 79 will always bring us, in the end, and through many tears, to the joyful gospel confidence of 79:13.

7. James Hamilton sums up the psalm like this:

> The wrath of God on people and land seen in Psalm 79:1–3 anticipates the wrath that would fall on Christ on the cross. The reproach borne by God's people in 79:4 anticipates the one on whom all the reproach would fall (Rom 15:3). The answer to the "How long?" question is: until the return of Christ. The Lord showed forth the glory of his name as Jesus was lifted up to be highly exalted (John 12:23–24, 28, 32). Atonement there was accomplished, that God's people might have their sins covered, that the Lord might remember them no more. The Lord will answer every prayer of Psalm 79, and God's people will recount his praise forever.[24]

---

24 Hamilton, *Psalms*, 2:68–69.

The psalm [i.e., Psalm 80] . . . foretells the salvation coming . . . through the Lord Christ.

THEODORET OF CYRUS
Commentary on the Psalms

Jesus . . . pointed to himself as the true vine (John 15:1). In other words, he was indicating that he was true ideal Israel and all the living branches of the vine are the people of God united to Jesus. . . . He is not only real Israel, God's firstborn son, but the son of man of Daniel 7 who represents God's people and the royal son who stands at God's right hand and whom he has made strong for himself.

PHILIP EVESON
Psalms

PSALM 80

ORIENTATION

Like Psalms 74 and 79, Psalm 80 teaches us how to pray for a ravaged church. Although the New Testament does not quote or clearly echo Psalm 80, this psalm breathes the Spirit of Christ. Christ is the one who most fully enters into the yearnings of the psalm and, at the same time, the one who fulfills those longings. The psalm shapes us to pray in the name of Christ and for the church of Christ. For Christ is the only, and all-sufficient, hope for a ravaged church.

The distinctive tenor of the psalm is its warm concern for *all* the church. The focus is on the northern tribes (see on 80:1–2 and on "Joseph" in 77:15; 78:67). We do not know whether it was written before or after the destruction of the northern kingdom by the Assyrians in 722 BC, or whether it was written by a "northerner" or a sympathetic "southerner"; in many ways it doesn't matter.[1] The spirit is that of Hezekiah, who reached out to the lost north when he "sent to all Israel and Judah, and wrote letters also to Ephraim and Manasseh" to invite them to Passover. His messengers were mocked and scorned, but "some men of Asher, of Manasseh, and of Zebulun humbled themselves and came to Jerusalem" (2 Chron. 30:1, 10–11). Through Jeremiah, God promises, "I will be the God of all the clans of Israel" (Jer. 31:1). This hope never went away (see Ezek. 37:15–28; cf. Isa. 11:11–16; Hos. 1:10–11).

---

1 For different views about the date and provenance, see, e.g., Hengstenberg, *Psalms*, 3:8–9; Kirkpatrick, *Psalms*, 2:483; Tate, *Psalms 51–100*, 309–13; Anderson, *Psalms*, 2:581; Harman, *Psalms*, 2:607n1; Kidner, *Psalms*, 2:288–89.

Psalm 80 was incorporated into book 3 as a prayer for lost sheep. Although Psalm 78 decrees that salvation will not come *from* "Ephraim" (cf. 78:56–67), it is still possible that salvation will come *to* them.

Psalm 80 cries to God to be the shepherd of these lost sheep (80:1–3), knowing that he shepherds by the hand of a human leader, priest, and King, foreshadowed by Moses, Aaron, and David (cf. 77:20; 78:70–72). His shepherd heart finds its fulfillment in the divine-human good shepherd, whose heartbeat is for the lost sheep (Matt. 18:10–14; Luke 15:1–7), the "other sheep . . . also" (John 10:16), given him by the Father (John 6:37–39, 44) and to whom he is committed in strong and passionate love. He it is who weeps tears for his people and bears mockery for them (Ps. 80:4–7).

The unity of the one people is also indicated by the image of the vine (80:8–19), for a vine is a connected organism, such that each branch is linked by ties of living nurture to the root and therefore to every other branch. It is no accident that Jesus warns unbelieving Israel using the language of a vineyard (Mark 12:1–12) and then speaks of himself as the true vine (John 15), the embodiment of all that Israel was called to be and the fulfillment of all that Psalm 80 cries for.

The strongest link with nearby psalms is that of the church of God as a flock (e.g., 74:1; 77:20; 78:70–72; 79:13). There are other links especially with Psalms 74 and 79, including (1) long-suffering (74:1, 9–10; 79:5; 80:4), (2) mockery (74:10, 18; 79:4; 80:6), and (3) calling on God's name (79:6; 80:18). The rare verb "turn back" in 80:18 echoes the same verb used of Israel's apostasy in 78:57.

THE TEXT

Structure
The clearest structural marker is the almost verbatim refrain in Psalm 80:3, 7, and 19. Psalm 80:14 has some similarities, using the same root "turn" and the same address to God as in 80:7. Psalm 80:14 is sometimes taken as the close of 80:9–14 (i.e., functioning like another refrain) or as the start of 80:14–19 (which gives a tidy division of two sections of six verses). I suggest taking three unequal sections, marked by the clear refrain, and then breaking the final section with a weaker subdivision before or after 80:14.

Superscription

S   To the choirmaster:[2] according to Lilies.[3] A Testimony. Of Asaph,
     a Psalm.[4]

In the superscription to Psalm 60, the phrase "Shushan Eduth" means "a
lily of testimony," using the same two nouns as appear here but with the first
in the singular and in construct form. Here **Lilies** is plural and both **Lilies**
and **Testimony** are in absolute form. So **Lilies** is probably a tune. It is not
clear in what sense the psalm is a **Testimony**. Perhaps it means instruction
how to pray for deliverance.[5]

80:1–3 Pray for Christ the Good Shepherd to Restore His Church

1   Give ear, O Shepherd of Israel,
         you who lead Joseph like a flock.
     You who are enthroned upon the cherubim, shine forth.
2   Before Ephraim and Benjamin and Manasseh,
     stir up your might
         and come to save us!

Ephraim and Benjamin and Manasseh represent Rachel's sons **Joseph**,
father of **Ephraim** and **Manasseh**, and **Benjamin**, Joseph's brother (Gen.
30:22–24). These two half-tribes and one tribe marched together behind
the ark (Num. 2:18–24). In a later age, to say that "Rachel is weeping for her
children" (Jer. 31:15) became a way of saying that the northern kingdom
was lost to the Assyrian invasion.

The deepest allegiance of **Benjamin** was not to the house of David. The
hostilities between Saul (of the tribe of Benjamin) and David (of the tribe
of Judah) cast a long shadow. Shimei the Benjaminite was from "the house
of Joseph" (2 Sam. 19:16, 20) and hostile to David (2 Sam. 16:5–8). The

2 See on Ps. 4.
3 See on Pss. 45, 60, 69.
4 The LXX adds ὑπὲρ τοῦ Ἀσσυρίου. While this is unlikely to be original, it shows that by that
   time some made the connection with the Assyrian invasion of the northern kingdom. In Hebrew
   the superscription is verse 1; subsequent verse numbers are increased by one.
5 Hengstenberg, *Psalms*, 3:11–12.

rebel Sheba was a Benjaminite (2 Sam. 20:1). Only Judah followed David after the death of Saul; Benjamin did not (2 Sam. 2:8–10). The prophecies both to Solomon (1 Kings 11:13) and to Jeroboam (1 Kings 11:32, 36) spoke of only "one tribe" remaining with the house of David, and this is what happened (1 Kings 12:20). Even if some of Benjamin's territory was incorporated with Judah (1 Kings 12:21; 2 Chron. 11:23; 15:8), their core loyalty was with the north, as in Psalm 80.[6]

Psalm 80 is a prayer for these lost sheep, lost in 722 BC after the Assyrian invasion. The psalm accompanies all the spiritual Rachels of the church in every age weeping for their lost children.

The imagery of God as **Shepherd of Israel** probably derives from Jacob's testimony in Genesis 48:15 (cf. Gen. 49:24). This combines strength to protect with a covenant commitment to care. The verb to **lead** or guide is used of God in Psalms 48:14; 77:20; and 78:52 and is used ironically in Lamentations 3:2 ("He has *driven* and brought me / into darkness without any light"). The image of the people of God being **like a flock** is shared with Psalms 74:1; 77:20; and 78:70–72. The address **you who are enthroned upon the cherubim**[7] is closely connected with the ark of the covenant (e.g., 1 Sam. 4:4; 2 Sam. 6:2; 2 Kings 19:15); the covenant God is the warrior who rides before his people on a chariot-throne supported by fierce cherubim, who are "guardians of holiness and agents of judgment."[8] The cry that this strong shepherd-God will **shine forth** (cf. Ps. 50:1–2, another Asaph psalm) is echoed in the refrain (80:3, 7, 19) and may well allude to the fiery-cloudy pillar in the wilderness;[9] 80:2 is a prayer that this God will "shine upon the tribes" as he leads them through the wilderness. Here it means much the same as **Stir up your might**—that is, bring your unchanging omnipotence into action for your lost sheep on earth (as in 78:65)—**and come to save us** ("to save" also appears in 80:3, 7, 19).

3   Restore us, O God;
     let your face shine, that we may be saved!

---

6   For a clear explanation, see Hengstenberg, *Psalms*, 3:9–11.
7   The Hebrew ("the one who sits the cherubim") does not specify whether God is sitting in between the cherubim (CSB, NIV) or on the cherubim (ESV, NRSV, REB). Probably the image is God riding on the chariot-throne supported by the cherubim (cf. Ps. 18:10).
8   Kidner, *Psalms*, 2:289.
9   Hengstenberg, *Psalms*, 3:13.

Restore us is literally "Cause us to (re)turn." This can mean to restore our fortunes, to bring us back into the visible church and to bring prosperity to that church (cf. God's statement to Jacob, "I . . . will bring you back," Gen. 28:15),[10] especially in return from exile (e.g., Jer. 12:15; 16:15; 30:3). But here it also means a turning of heart in repentance (e.g., Lam. 5:21):[11] "Bring us to repentance," for only when the church is penitent will they be restored, and repentance is a gift of God, not something they can stir themselves up to do (cf. 2 Tim. 2:25). This is a prayer that "God, by giving repentance, would reclaim his people from their apostasy . . . and so deliver and save them," for "their repentance and returning unto God is the first step unto their relief and delivery from procured misery of captivity or any other calamity."[12]

Let your face shine echoes the priestly blessing of Numbers 6:25. The shining face—the gracious presence and favor—of God can come only to a penitent people. This line echoes "Shine forth . . . and come to save us" in Psalm 80:1–2.

All this is, in effect, a prayer for Christ, the good shepherd who leads his lost sheep back into the fold and then leads his church like a flock. Christ is the strong covenant champion and warrior for his people, enthroned on the cherubim. Christ is the light of the world who shines forth on his people. Christ is God come to save us.

80:4–7 Pray for Christ the Atoning Mediator to Restore His Church

4   O Lord God of hosts,
      how long will you be angry with your people's prayers?
5   You have fed them with the bread of tears
      and given them tears to drink in full measure.
6   You make us an object of contention for our neighbors,
      and our enemies laugh among themselves.

The question **How long?** echoes Psalms 74:10 and 79:5. Psalm 80:4 goes to the heart of the lament, while 80:5–6 speaks of its sorrows. In 80:4 the

---

10 Jacob here, "in his exile beyond the Euphrates, and in his restoration to Canaan, typified the fate of his people." Hengstenberg, *Psalms*, 3:13.

11 Kirkpatrick, *Psalms*, 2:485; Tucker and Grant, *Psalms*, 2:186–87.

12 Dickson, *Psalms*, 2:39.

agony is that God (note the covenant name, the LORD, and the covenant phrase **your people**) is **angry** (lit., "smokes" or fumes; cf. Deut. 29:20; Ps. 74:1). This may mean that he is angry even at their **prayers** (cf. Isa. 1:12–15). Certainly it means that he is angry despite their **prayers**; although they pray, their prayers do not "get through" the smoke of God's righteous anger; they do not have access to God in prayer.[13] Since the prayer of a righteous person has great power (James 5:16), this must mean that the people who are praying are not penitent, not faithful members of the covenant. We need a man who is faithful to pray for the lost sheep who are not.

The sufferings are described in Psalm 80:5 in terms of their sorrow and in 80:6 in terms of their appearance. In themselves they weep so copiously that their **tears** are their diet—their **bread** (cf. 42:3) and their **drink**.[14] This sorrow was finally borne by Christ for his people as he wept our tears. **An object of contention** probably means that the church finds itself "at odds with" (CSB) the world, although it may have the sense of being an object of contempt. Both are often true. The phrase **among themselves** reminds us that mockery of the church of God is an enjoyable and shared cultural occupation.

> 7 Restore us, O God of hosts;
>   let your face shine, that we may be saved!

The refrain, strengthened from 80:3 by the title **of hosts**, reminds us of the central petition of the psalm.

80:8–19 Pray for Christ the True Vine to Restore His Church

> 8 You brought a vine out of Egypt;
>   you drove out the nations and planted it.
> 9 You cleared the ground for it;

---

13 Similar imagery may be suggested in Lam. 3:44 if the "cloud" with which God has wrapped himself is a cloud of anger, "so that no prayer can pass through." Kirkpatrick, *Psalms*, 2:485.

14 The phrase "in full measure" is literally "a third" (שָׁלִישׁ), that is, one-third of an unspecified measure. The other place in which this is used is Isa. 40:12, in which this "one-third" measure is a very small one to God in which to contain the dust of the earth. But here it is clearly a large measure, for tears. If it is a third of a "bath" it would represent "a huge drinking goblet." Kirkpatrick, *Psalms*, 2:486.

> it took deep root and filled the land.
> 10   The mountains were covered with its shade,
>   the mighty cedars with its branches.
> 11   It sent out its branches to the sea
>   and its shoots to the River.

The image of the church of God as **a vine** is probably adapted from the prophecy that Joseph will be "a fruitful bough" and that "his branches [will] run over the wall" (Gen. 49:22).[15] It reappears in Isaiah 5:1–7 (an oracle of judgment); Isaiah 27:2–6 (an oracle of promise);[16] Jeremiah 2:21; and Hosea 10:1 and 14:7 (cf. Ezekiel's use of vine imagery for Israel, e.g., Ezek. 17:1–10). In Psalm 128:3 a child-bearing wife whose children contribute to the flourishing of the people of God is "like a fruitful vine."

Much biblical theology is compressed in this vivid metaphor. At both ends of the exodus story there is a moral wilderness, in the **Egypt** of the pharaohs and in **the nations** of Canaan. By contrast, a vine is an organism with a life-giving order and fruitfulness. The first four verbs have God as subject: **You brought . . . out** in exodus redemption (cf. the same verb as "led out" in Ps. 78:52), and then (fast-forwarding to the settlement of the land) **you drove out the nations**, with their disgusting moral disorder (cf. Ex. 23:28; 33:2; 34:11; Ps. 78:55). In place of this **you planted** your vine, to be a place of life and joy (cf. Ex. 15:17; "And I . . . will plant them," 2 Sam. 7:10; Ps. 44:2). To emphasize all you did for it, **you cleared the ground for it,** so that you had given all needed resources (cf. Isa. 5:2).

What follows in Psalm 80:9b–11 is an amazing cameo of grace. **It took deep root** (down into God's life) **and filled the** (promised) **land.** Psalm 80:10–11 probably hints at the four points of the compass around the promised land. **The mountains** are probably the hill country of Judah in the south, while **the mighty cedars** are the cedars of Lebanon in the north. **The sea** is the Mediterranean to the west, while **the River** (probably here the Euphrates) is the eastern boundary of the ideal promised land (cf. similar imagery for the promised land in Deut. 11:24). Here in miniature is a picture of God recolonizing a wild world with order, life,

---

15 See also on the possible echo of this verse in the word "son" in Ps. 80:15.
16 Note especially Isa. 27:6, "and fill the whole world with fruit."

and joy (cf. the four points of the compass associated with the Abrahamic blessing to the world, in Gen. 28:14). What follows demonstrates that this was never more than a foreshadowing of the true vine.

> [12] Why then have you broken down its walls,
> so that all who pass along the way pluck its fruit?
> [13] The boar from the forest ravages it,
> and all that move in the field feed on it.

The force of the question **Why then?** (to which, at one level, the psalmist knows the answer, which is why he prays for restoration and repentance) is the seeming contradiction between God planting and God breaking down. It rests on the true supposition that when God acts, he will not contradict what he has done or break what he has made, for "God cannot leave off, far less destroy, a work which he has once begun" (cf. Phil. 1:6).[17] Although sin has led to this tragedy, the destruction of the church cannot be the end of the story.

The tragedy is the polar opposite of Psalm 80:8–11 (cf. 89:40–41). The protective **walls** are **broken down** by God in judgment, so that the world that has so compromised the worship of the church now runs riot within it. **All who pass along the way** adds to the picture of a ravaged church, such that anybody and everybody can mock and play havoc with it. Both the moral uncleanness and the violence are conveyed by the image of the **boar**, a wild and unclean animal. This—here presumably an image of Assyria or its king—brings uncleanness into the place that ought to be pure (cf. 79:1, of the Babylonians at a later date).[18]

> [14] Turn again, O God of hosts!
> Look down from heaven, and see;

These two lines are transitional within Psalm 80:8–19. Instead of "restore" (cause us to turn), the plea is for the very powerful God (**God of hosts**) to

---

17 Hengstenberg, *Psalms*, 3:15.
18 The noun translated "all that move in the field" (זִיז) appears also in Ps. 50:11 (another Asaph psalm). We are not sure of its precise meaning, but clearly it speaks of creatures that cause destruction among crops. (The NIV "insects" is too precise.) For discussion, see Ross, *Psalms*, 2:691n17; Harman, *Psalms*, 2:610n8; Tucker and Grant, *Psalms*, 2:190n18; Alter, *Psalms*, 286.

turn again to his people.[19] Before we turn in repentance, God must turn to us in grace.[20] He does this, finally and climactically, by sending Jesus Christ. Here he "teaches the springing up of Christ the Lord."[21] **Look down from heaven, and see** reminds us of Exodus 2:23–24.

> have regard for this vine,
> 15   the stock that your right hand planted,
>   and for the son whom you made strong for yourself.
> 16   They have burned it with fire; they have cut it down;
>   may they perish at the rebuke of your face!
> 17   But let your hand be on the man of your right hand,
>   the son of man whom you have made strong for yourself!

What will it mean for God to **have regard for this vine?** Our understanding of the whole psalm rests on the answer to this question. From very early days, Christian writers have understood that there is a failed vine and a restored vine, the latter of which stands in continuity with the former and is founded on Jesus Christ. Augustine writes,

> Let us . . . learn what became of the first vine, and what is to be expected of the second—though both are one vine, for the second is not a different vine but the selfsame. From it sprang Christ, for salvation comes from the Jews; from it came the apostles, and from it the first believers.[22]

The parallelism in Psalm 80:15 suggests that **the stock** (a rare word probably meaning the root or stock on which the vine is grown)[23] and **the son**[24] are images either of the whole people (cf. Ex. 4:22; Hos. 11:1) or of the King.[25]

---

19 The same verb (שׁוּב) is used but now in the qal.
20 Motyer, *Psalms*, 538.
21 Theodoret of Cyrus, *Psalms*, 2:49.
22 Augustine, *Psalms*, 4:146.
23 The word כַּנָּה is an Old Testament hapax legomenon. For discussion, see Ross, *Psalms*, 2:691n18. *HALOT* has "shoot," s.v. כֵּן.
24 The word "son" can also be used of a "branch." In Gen. 49:22, the word "bough" in the prophecy "Joseph is a fruitful bough" translates the same word, בֵּן. Hence Dickson says, "There was a branch to come of the stock of Israel, for whose cause the nation of the Israelites could not be utterly forsaken and destroyed, and this was the Messiah." Dickson, *Psalms*, 2:45.
25 The Targum understands this to be "the King Messiah." Delitzsch, *Psalms*, 2:383.

They (the Assyrians) **have burned it** (the vine)[26] **with fire; they have cut it down**. The most natural way to understand the second line—**May they perish**—is that **they** still represents the Assyrians: "May the Assyrians perish." This is a prayer for God to act in judgment against the enemies of the church.

In Psalm 80:17 **the man of your right hand** is a play on "Benjamin," which means "the son of the right hand" (Gen. 35:18). It means the man in whom your strength and authority is vested. **The son of man** (lit., "son of אָדָם, *adam*") means a human being. Both denote the people (the vine) or their King. The repetition of **You (have) made strong for yourself** (Ps. 80:15, 17) makes clear that the reference is the same. Although **the son of man** may simply mean a mortal human being, it is no accident that it is also the title of the greatest human being to whom is entrusted cosmic authority (Dan. 7:13). Philip Eveson notes, "The psalmist . . . looks to a future Benjamin, to the man at God's right hand (see Ps. 110:1) through whom God will bless the whole nation as God's vine."[27]

Psalm 80:14–17 is a prayer that the vine will be restored, and it suggests that this restoration is through a King or leader who embodies in himself all that Israel, the vine, was called to be. It should be no surprise, then, when a man who is "made strong" for God the Father, who is the man of the Father's right hand, who is the Son of Man, Israel personified, should call himself "the true vine" (John 15:1).

> 18   Then we shall not turn back from you;
>   give us life, and we will call upon your name!

In the light of the repeated prayer that the church be caused to return to God, Psalm 80:18 is of great importance. When God answers the prayer of 80:14–17, **we** (the church, and especially the lost sheep) **shall not turn back**[28] **from you**. The church will be restored not just outwardly but inwardly. When new life is given (**Give us life**), there will be access to God in prayer (**We will call upon your name**, the opposite of 80:4) and true worship.

---

26 "It" is feminine—thus denoting grammatically that the antecedent is the vine.

27 Eveson, *Psalms*, 2:69.

28 The verb here is not the verb שׁוּב but סוּג, "to turn back" (cf. its use in Ps. 44:18: "Our heart has not turned back"). The verb is used in 78:57 of Israel's apostasy and in 53:3 ("They have all *fallen away*").

19   Restore us, O Lᴏʀᴅ God of hosts!
        Let your face shine, that we may be saved!

The refrain, strengthened from 80:3 and 7 by adding the covenant name, Lᴏʀᴅ, reminds us of the central petition of the psalm.

REFLECTION AND RESPONSE

1. Perhaps the most important response to this psalm is to allow it to arouse in us a warm concern and heartfelt prayer for the repentance and restoration of all the lost sheep of Christ's church. This will include those who have never belonged to Christ (such as the many in Corinth who belong to Jesus from eternity but have not yet been converted, Acts 18:10; these are the lost sheep of Luke 15:1–7) and also those who have been despised, mistreated, or caused to stumble within the church (Matt. 18:10–14). Unlike the people who simply care for their own ease, we ought to be grieved by "the ruin of Joseph" (Amos 6:6) and pray for God to bring them into the good shepherd's fold.

2. Psalm 80:1–3 encourages us to pray with confidence and urgency to the God who, in Christ, is mighty to save and committed to lead as the shepherd.

3. The tears and mockery of Psalm 80:4–7 invite us to enter into the deep grief of Christ for his ravaged church, to feel that grief, and to allow that grief to drive us to prayer.

4. The image of the vine in Psalm 80:8–19 can stir us in imagination, letting the beautiful metaphor help us feel how much it matters to a wilderness world that there should be a life-giving, joyful vine, a healthy church of Christ. In old-fashioned language, Cassiodorus rejoices in this picture:

Asaph . . . beheld Christ's vineyard extended over the whole world, and its vine-leaves overshadowing mountains and cedars. It is a truly blessed vision, and reflexion on its beauty renews us. . . . The vineyard bears as its juicy grapes holy fruits; it bears martyrs, rears prophets, begets apostles, brings forth innumerable faithful. All the splendid achievements in holy Church are appropriately incorporated in this imagery.[29]

---

29 Cassiodorus, *Psalms*, 2:292.

5. The tragedy of the ravaged vine reminds us of Scripture's warning that Jesus is willing and able to remove a "lampstand" (Rev. 2:5) as judgment on the sin of a particular church or group of churches. David Dickson observes,

> The most glorious and best planted church may for its unfruitfulness, and provocation of God by its ill fruits, be plucked up again. . . . It is a wonderful and astonishing judgment, to see the Lord . . . plucking up the plantation of his church once made by him, and yet the provocation of a wicked generation may procure this evil, which hardly can be believed till it come. . . . [And yet] when the Lord's church is in the worst condition, she is not so wasted and destroyed, but a remnant is left to present by prayer her condition unto God, to deal with him for her restoration.[30]

Psalm 80 can stir us to be that praying remnant.

6. All in all, the psalm presses home to us that the only hope of a ravaged church is Christ. He is our great and good shepherd, the mighty Savior enthroned on the cherubim, the mediator in whose name we pray, the true vine, the Son of God made strong for himself, the man of God at the Father's right hand, the Son of Man. Here is Dickson again: "The refuge, rest, consolation, and confidence of a distressed church or person is Christ; and toward him must the afflicted cast their eye for relief, as here the church in her deepest desolation doth."[31]

30 Dickson, *Psalms*, 2:44.
31 Dickson, *Psalms*, 2:46.

[Psalm 81 reveals] the mind of God—the heart, the bowels of compassion, displayed in every line,—the breathing of tender love.

ANDREW BONAR
Christ and His Church in the Book of Psalms

The gracious God who is present in Christ to the congregation is the fulfillment of all thanksgiving, all joy and yearning in the Psalms. As Jesus, in whom God truly dwells, longed for community with God because he had become human like us (Lk. 2:49), so he prays with us for the fullness of God's nearness and presence with those that are his.

DIETRICH BONHOEFFER
Prayerbook of the Bible

PSALM 81

ORIENTATION

Psalm 81 is a warm and passionate appeal from Christ to trust Christ. Both dimensions ("from Christ" and "to trust Christ") are suggested by biblical theology.

In many ways the psalm is the divine answer to the laments that have preceded it in book 3. Apart from Psalm 75:2–5, there has been no clear and direct word from God; now there is. Psalm 81 is "the first psalm to provide God's perspective on the crisis of exile."[1]

But it is a word given through the psalmist, Asaph, who functions as a prophet, the spokesman of God. It is the word of one man who has listened attentively to God speaking to a church who badly needs to listen to him because, as they listen to him, they are listening to God. We have seen, especially in Psalms 37 and 78, that Christ, who is to us both wisdom and prophet, is the voice behind each prophet and wisdom teacher. Christ is our supreme instructor and, in a sense, our sole instructor (Matt. 23:10). The prophets (among whom the psalmists are numbered) spoke by the Spirit of Christ (1 Pet. 1:10–12). The exhortation to listen to God (which is so emphatic in this psalm) becomes concrete in the command on the Mount of Transfiguration: "This is my beloved Son . . . ; listen to him" (Matt. 17:5). God, who spoke through the prophets, summed up all that speaking when he spoke by his Son (Heb. 1:1–2).

But it is also an appeal to trust Christ. It is an exhortation to trust the God of exodus redemption and wilderness provision, unlike the church in the wilderness (Acts 7:38), which did not. But that grace of God (as all

---

1 Tucker and Grant, *Psalms*, 2:210.

the old covenant) was but "a shadow of the things to come," whereas "the substance belongs to Christ" (Col. 2:17). The psalm is not an appeal to trust the shadow but to rest our confidence on the substance, on Christ. Christ is our Passover, our exodus, our rock in the wilderness, our living water, our true manna; everything foreshadowed in the exodus redemption and wilderness provision finds its substance in him.

Of the other psalms that treat of the unbelief of the wilderness generation (Pss. 78; 95; 106), Psalm 95 is the closest to Psalm 81 because both contain strong appeals from God. Hebrews 3:1–4:13 preaches, mainly from Psalm 95, the need to continue to "hold fast our confidence" in Christ and "hold our original confidence [i.e., in Christ] firm to the end" (Heb. 3:6, 14). If the response to Psalm 95 is to trust in Christ, then a right hearing of Psalm 81 will lead us the same way.

The historical context of Psalm 81 is a joyful festival ("our feast day," חַג, hag, 81:3). The Feast of Tabernacles is the most likely occasion.[2] This festival season (Lev. 23:23–43; Num. 29:1–38) is given "that your generations may know that I made the people of Israel dwell in booths when I brought them out of the land of Egypt" (Lev. 23:43). This began with trumpets at new moon (the first day of the seventh month), continued with the Day of Atonement on the tenth day of the month, and concluded with the Feast of Tabernacles or Booths, starting on the fifteenth day of the month (i.e., full moon) for a week. This became a tremendously significant festival (e.g., when Solomon brought the ark into the completed temple, 1 Kings 8:1–11; when Ezra taught the returned exiles, Neh. 8:1–18) and was a prominent and emphatic part of Zechariah's prophecy of the consummation of all things (Zech. 14:16–19). Like the start of this psalm (Ps. 81:1–3), it was to be a time of great rejoicing when the joy of the Lord would be the people's strength (Neh. 8:10, 12, 17).

A few have argued for Passover as the festival,[3] although the links with the Feast of Tabernacles are stronger. What matters is not so much the precise identification of the celebration as its content, which is the saving kindness of God in the history of the old covenant church. Jesus Christ fulfills all the festivals. As James Hamilton writes,

2 VanGemeren, *Psalms*, 617; Grogan, *Psalms*, 145; Kidner, *Psalms*, 2:292; Kirkpatrick, *Psalms*, 2:489; Longman, *Psalms*, 301–2; Tate, *Psalms 51–100*, 318; Tucker and Grant, *Psalms*, 2:201; Eveson, *Psalms*, 2:72.
3 Delitzsch, *Psalms*, 2:392; Hengstenberg, *Psalms*, 3:13; Harman, *Psalms*, 2:613.

Jesus came and fulfilled the feasts: he is the Passover lamb whose death sets in motion the new exodus. He is the one who tabernacled among us (John 1:14), and he will tabernacle over his people with his presence (Rev 7:15). He provides himself as the fulfillment of manna from heaven (John 6:32–35) and water from the rock (John 7:37–39). He fulfilled Pentecost through the giving of the Spirit, and he will fulfill the Jubilee when he comes at the final trumpet call of God (1 Thess 4:16).[4]

There are strong links with Psalm 80. These include (1) "Joseph" (80:1; 81:5), (2) "out of (the land of) Egypt" (80:8; 81:10), (3) a contrast of speakers and listeners (in Ps. 80 the people speak and hope God will listen; in Ps. 81 God speaks, and his people must listen), (4) an answer in Psalm 81 to the questions "Why?" and "How long?" (80:4, 12), and (5) the replacement of a diet of tears (80:5) with a diet of plenty (81:16).

The psalm combines challenge with gospel hope that with repentance there will be a new exodus and a fresh experience of wilderness provision.[5] Philip Eveson writes that Psalm 81

is placed appropriately at this point in Book 3, for it gives an explanation as to why the people have experienced the sufferings described in the previous psalm and serves to hearten God's people with a word of hope if only they would listen and respond accordingly.[6]

There are several links with Psalm 50 (also Asaph), with the Song of Moses (Deut. 32), and with the Song by the Sea (Ex. 15:1–20).

THE TEXT

Structure
Psalm 81 naturally divides into 81:1–5b (the psalmist's introduction to the feast) and 81:6–16 (the words of God through the prophet). The placement of 81:5c is discussed below. Psalm 81:6–16 pauses briefly after the *Selah* in 81:7.

---

4   Hamilton, *Psalms*, 2:85–86.
5   Hamilton, *Psalms*, 2:81.
6   Eveson, *Psalms*, 2:72.

Superscription

S   To the choirmaster:[7] according to The Gittith. Of Asaph.[8]

The Gittith is a musical instrument, a musical setting or tune, or a cele-
bratory occasion (or perhaps a combination of these).[9] Since Psalm 81
accompanies a festival, perhaps a celebration is the most likely context.[10]

81:1–5b Rejoice in Christ Our Exodus!
Here we have imperatives (Ps. 81:1–3) followed by the reason to heed the
imperatives (81:4–5b).

81:1–3 Celebrate the Festival of Christ!

1   Sing aloud to God our strength;
        shout for joy to the God of Jacob!
2   Raise a song; sound the tambourine,
        the sweet lyre with the harp.
3   Blow the trumpet at the new moon,
        at the full moon, on our feast day.

The verbs **sing aloud** (sing joyfully) and **shout for joy** (a triumphant shout)
overflow with jubilation. The reason is **God our strength**, a word used by the
church at the exodus (Ex. 15:2), often of the Davidic king (e.g., Pss. 21:1; 28:7;
59:9, 17; 62:7; 118:14), of the Lord's servant (Isa. 49:5), and elsewhere; God is
the strength and therefore the joy of his people supremely because he is the
strength of our King Messiah. In parallel is **the God of Jacob** (also Ps. 81:4),
a strong theme in book 3 (cf. 75:9; 76:6; 77:15; 78:5, 21, 71; 79:7; 84:8; 85:1;
87:2). God promised to bring Jacob out of Egypt (Gen. 46:1–4), "for God was
Jacob's God, because God was by covenant Abraham and his children's God,
whose children also we are, who are Christ's, Gal. iii. 29."[11]

---

7   See on Ps. 4.
8   In Hebrew the superscription is verse 1; subsequent verse numbers are increased by one.
9   See on Ps. 8; cf. Ps. 84. For discussion of the three alternatives, see Tate, *Psalms 51–100*, 318.
10 Tucker and Grant, *Psalms*, 2:200.
11 Dickson, *Psalms*, 2:50.

Psalm 81:2 calls for this joy to be accompanied by instruments. The **tambourine** is associated with women celebrating (notably in Ex. 15:20 and 2 Sam. 6:5 but in many other contexts). The adjective **sweet** means pleasant or delightful; in 2 Samuel 23:1 David is called "the *sweet* psalmist of Israel." The sweetness of the music is of value only because of the overwhelming sweetness of Christ.

The **trumpet** in Psalm 81:3 is not so much a musical accompaniment (as it is in Ps. 150) but rather a call to the church to assemble[12] (not dissimilar to church bells in some cultures). As the trumpet stirs the heart, so the church needs to be stirred up to praise. The **new moon** is the first day of the (lunar) month, and the **full moon** is in the middle of the month. The Feast of Tabernacles spans both.

81:4–5b Rejoice Because of Christ Our Exodus!

4   For it is a statute for Israel,
          a rule of the God of Jacob.
5   He made it a decree in Joseph
          when he went out over the land of Egypt.

Psalm 81:4–5 gives the reason (**for**) the people of God celebrate the festival (referent of **it** in these verses). In words that are more or less synonymous, the feast is described as **a statute** (חֹק, *khoq*, something given with binding force), **a rule** (מִשְׁפָּט, *mishpat*, a decision or judgment of God), and **a decree** (עֵדוּת, *eduth*, something that bears witness to God). The feast is **for Israel**, the old covenant church. It is given by **the God of Jacob** (see on 81:1). And specifically it is **in Joseph**, either because Joseph had been the preeminent leader of the church while in Egypt or because of a special focus on the northern tribes (cf. Pss. 78; 80). This festival was instituted by God **when he went out over** (i.e., either "passed over" or "went out against") **the land of Egypt**.[13] That is, this decree is rooted in covenant grace, fulfilled to us in Christ.

---

12 See Tate, *Psalms 51–100*, 318. In other contexts this may be a call to assemble for war (e.g., at Jericho or for Gideon).

13 This refers to when God acted in judgment on Egypt (cf. the similar sense of Ex. 11:4).

81:5c–16 Listen to Christ and Trust Him for Wonderful Satisfaction!
81:5c Hear a Fresh Gospel Word from God

> I hear a language I had not known:

It is possible that this line refers to the foreignness of the tongue of the pharaohs' Egypt (as in "a people of strange language," Ps. 114:1). It would then be a relative clause appended to the previous phrase (i.e., "the land of Egypt, [where] I heard an unfamiliar language"). This would be a new thought and seems unlikely.[14]

More likely, this is the prophet's introduction to the divine speech that (on this reading) begins in 81:6. In this case the question arises as to what the clause **I had not known** might mean. What is it about God's revelation that was not previously known, and in what sense?

One possibility—and especially if **I hear** is translated "I heard"[15]—is that this looks back to the fresh revelation of the meaning of the covenant name, "the LORD," given to Israel at the time of the exodus (Ex. 3:13–14; 6:2–8, in the context of being brought out from burdens): "I heard a new revelation of God." But it is unclear what it could mean for the psalmist to say this many years later.

A second option is that the verb "to know" can refer not to cognition but to acknowledgment ("that I had not previously acknowledged"). In this case the psalmist says, "I am now going to tell you something from God that I had not previously acknowledged and felt the full force of." This would introduce a confession of sin by the psalmist in a way that does not harmonize with the rest of the psalm.

In my view the most plausible solution is that the psalmist is saying something like this: "Just as God revealed something fresh about his redeeming nature to Moses (the first approach above), so he has given me this fresh word of redemptive reminder and appeal to pass on to you. The word I am about to speak is a fresh word of gospel appeal given to me by God." Jesus supremely listens to the Father and speaks this word (cf. Isa. 50:4; John 12:49).

In Psalm 81:6–16 God himself becomes, through the prophet (and ultimately through Christ), the preacher at the festival. His sermon is gentle

---

14 See Delitzsch, *Psalms*, 2:396.

15 As in the CSB and NIV. The tense form (imperfect) may have a past reference here, as it does later in the psalm; this is argued by Goldingay, *Psalms*, 2:546n5.

and serious; it expresses in a "tender and gracious manner" the way God "allured them to himself" (cf. Hos. 2:14–15).[16]

81:6–7 Hear What God Has Done for His People in Christ

> 6   "I relieved your shoulder of the burden;
>   your hands were freed from the basket.
> 7   In distress you called, and I delivered you;
>   I answered you in the secret place of thunder;
>   I tested you at the waters of Meribah.   Selah

The background to Psalm 81:6 is Exodus 1:11–14; 5:1–9; and 6:6. The **burden** is heavy and wearisome. The **basket** in this context[17] refers to the heavy baskets the enslaved Israelites used for carrying bricks. Derek Kidner observes the vivid concreteness of **shoulder**, **hands**, **burden**, and **basket**, which convey so much more of the misery than abstract nouns.[18] This is spoken to a later generation as if they were present (**your shoulder . . . your hands**; cf. "a covenant with *us*," Deut. 5:2) because every generation of the church is present at the exodus, and every generation experiences, in the present tense, the exodus redemption of Christ.[19] In biblical theology this burden can be understood as the unbearable burden of sins (Matt. 11:28; cf. John 8:34–36) and of the law without the gospel (Acts 15:10; cf. Matt. 23:4). As John Calvin writes, "God has . . . redeemed us from the cruel and miserable tyranny of Satan, and drawn us from the depths of hell."[20]

In distress you called (cf. Ps. 50:15, which uses the same word "distress"; ESV: "trouble") recalls Exodus 2:23–25. The contrast between, on the one hand, the people calling and God answering and, on the other, God calling and the people failing to answer, as in what follows in the psalm, is poignant. **The secret place of thunder** refers to the hiddenness of a thick

---

16 Calvin, *Psalms*, 3:309.

17 This particular word (דוד) is not used in Exodus, but the allusion is clear.

18 Kidner, *Psalms*, 2:294.

19 As an example of this idea, see Isa. 10:27, where the Assyrian burden needs to be removed, as the exodus is brought into the present. "Who was this who *eased their backs of burdens?*" asks Augustine. "No other than he who cried out, *Come to me, all you who labor and are heavily burdened.*" Augustine, *Psalms*, 4:158.

20 Calvin, *Psalms*, 3:315.

thundercloud. The primary reference may be to Mount Sinai, "shrouded in smoke and terrible with the voice of God,"[21] although storm clouds are also associated with God coming on the clouds to rescue (cf. Pss. 18:7–15; 77:16–19). God is hidden, mysterious, transcendent, and sovereign. And yet, precisely in this hiddenness, he answers his people's cry; there is perhaps a richer meaning here in the hiddenness of Christ, seen by Peter, James, and John in the transfiguration but otherwise unseen unless and until he makes himself known.

The final line (I tested you . . .) is a surprise and moves the story on from the exodus and Sinai to the two occasions, near the start (Ex. 17:1–7) and near the end (Num. 20:2–13) of the wilderness wanderings, when the people had quarreled with Moses (**Meribah** is from the verb "to quarrel").[22] The irony is that while from the people's point of view they were putting God to a test (Ex. 17:2, 7), at a deeper level God was testing them to see if they would trust the exodus Redeemer later known in Jesus Christ.

81:8–10 Hear and Worship God in Christ

8   Hear, O my people, while I admonish you!
    O Israel, if you would but listen to me!
9   There shall be no strange god among you;
    you shall not bow down to a foreign god.
10 I am the LORD your God,
    who brought you up out of the land of Egypt.
    Open your mouth wide, and I will fill it.

The urgent admonition (Ps. 81:8) is given now to the generation of the church in the present (much as in the exposition of "today" in Heb. 3–4): I admonish you! The address Hear, O my people is reminiscent of Deuteronomy 6:4 (the Shema). The church is called my people and Israel, both covenant terms, here and again in Psalm 81:11 and 13. The verb admonish

---

21 Kidner, *Psalms*, 2:294.
22 The phrase "waters of Meribah" (waters of quarreling) appears also in Num. 27:14; Deut. 32:51; 33:8. These episodes are alluded to in Ps. 78:20. Hamilton makes the interesting suggestion that these two Massah/Meribah episodes, early and late in the wilderness, may be "a brief way to refer to the whole of Israel's time in the wilderness." Hamilton, *Psalms*, 2:83.

is deeply serious (cf. "I will testify against you," Ps. 50:7; "solemnly warn," Deut. 8:19). In the clause **if you would but listen to me** is encapsulated the hortatory burden of the psalm, which is fulfilled in the injunction of the Father at the transfiguration to listen to Christ.[23] This is the ironic reversal of the people's complaint that God is not listening to them; the root problem is that they are not listening to God.

Psalm 81:9 expresses crisply the first two commandments. This is "the leading article of the covenant, and almost the whole sum of it."[24] There is to be **no strange god** or **foreign god**, no other god but the covenant Lord and no man-made (idolatrous) construction of the true God. This leads straight in to 81:10a, echoing the opening of the Ten Commandments (Ex. 20:2; Deut. 5:6), the gospel foundation of all rightly understood law, a gospel foundation fulfilled in the exodus redemption of Christ.

Open your mouth wide, and I will fill it may be an exhortation to "open the mouth wide" to "eat" the words of God, by obedient, trusting listening (cf. Jer. 1:9).[25] It seems more likely, however, that it is an anticipation of the gospel promise of Psalm 81:16, a "taster" of the rich meal that is about to be offered, if only we will listen to Christ and trust in Christ.

81:11–12 Be Careful to Listen to God in Christ

11   "But my people did not listen to my voice;
        Israel would not submit to me.
12   So I gave them over to their stubborn hearts,
        to follow their own counsels.

The psalm will end with an allurement of gospel hope in Psalm 81:13–16. Before that, there is a sober warning. Psalm 81:8 ("Hear," that is, "Listen!") is followed by **But my people did not listen** (again, as in 81:8, with the parallel address **my people** and **Israel**). In parallel with **did not listen** is **would not submit** (lit., "Israel was not willing to me," that is, "was not willing to bow in trusting obedience to me"). This culpable deafness comes from **stubborn**

---

23   "That same God, in view of the greater redemption from slavery to sin and Satan, demands that we look to his beloved Son and 'hear him.'" Eveson, *Psalms*, 2:75.
24   Calvin, *Psalms*, 3:318.
25   Ross, *Psalms*, 2:716.

hearts (cf. Deut. 29:19; Jer. 7:24; and often). There is nothing lacking in God's speaking or God's grace.

The judgment (**So I gave them over**) expresses a frequent and terrifying theme of biblical teaching, from the day when Adam and Eve left the garden (cf. Prov. 1:29–31 and the haunting refrain of Rom. 1:24, 26, 28). To be given over to my own **stubborn heart**, to **follow** (lit., "walk in," the same verb as Ps. 81:13b) my **own counsels**, to do just what I want, sounds so attractive but is, in reality, so terrible (cf. 78:29–31). The alternative to listening to God's Son is not freedom (*pace* the rioters in 2:1–3) but desolation. The cause of our misery rests "nowhere but in ourselves."[26] Indeed, "if any man come short of God's blessing, he beareth the blame himself."[27]

81:13–16 Be Wooed by What God Offers Us in Christ

> [13]   Oh, that my people would listen to me,
> that Israel would walk in my ways!
> [14]   I would soon subdue their enemies
> and turn my hand against their foes.
> [15]   Those who hate the LORD would cringe toward him,
> and their fate would last forever.
> [16]   But he would feed you with the finest of the wheat,
> and with honey from the rock I would satisfy you."

As in Psalm 81:8 and 11, the church is called **my people** and **Israel**. The psalm closes not with warning but with a tender gospel invitation to be heard today, in whatever "today" the listener resides. The sequence from 81:8 ("Hear, Listen!") through 81:11 ("But my people did not listen") concludes not with judgment but with invitation: **Oh, that my people would listen to me**. In every age this is the gracious call of God. The "ultimate expression" of this "earnest desire of God" to gather sinners into the church is found in Jesus Christ (cf. Matt. 23:37–39; Luke 15:1–32).[28] This open and universal call is entirely consistent with the sovereignty of God in election

26 Calvin, *Psalms*, 3:324.
27 Dickson, *Psalms*, 2:59.
28 Harman, *Psalms*, 2:618.

(as Calvin rightly argues),[29] but it presses home to us that reprobation is God's "strange work" and not (if we may speak anthropomorphically) so close to his heart as is salvation.

With an alternation of first-person and third-person verbs (in a way that is not uncommon and need not jar us as it tends to in English), Psalm 81:14–16 places before us the two sides of gospel promise. Psalm 81:14–15 expresses the necessary negative: God in Christ will **soon** (although "soon" can seem a long time to us; cf. Luke 18:8 ["speedily"]; 2 Pet. 3:8) **subdue** the hardened and finally impenitent **enemies** of Christ and his church (**those who hate the LORD**). God's **hand** (God in action in the world) will **turn** (a key verb in Ps. 80, see 80:3, 7, 14, 19) from disciplining his people to be **against their foes**. The verb **cringe** has the sense of a forced submission, which may be feigned but cannot be avoided.[30] The line **Their fate would last forever** is literally "Let their time be forever." This can be understood in two ways. If the subject is those who hate the Lord, it implies an unending, cringing submission, always unwilling, eternally inescapable (as the ESV). If the subject is God's people, then it means that the time of blessing for God's people will last forever. Both are true, although the latter involves an awkward change of subject.

The psalm closes (Ps. 81:16) with a beautiful gospel promise. All that is ours in Christ is described in tactile, sensory language as **the finest of the wheat** and **honey from the rock,** for the spiritual blessings that are ours in Christ (Eph. 1:3) will be substantial and bodily in the new creation.[31] This is "the honey of the Gospel."[32]

REFLECTION AND RESPONSE

1. We ought to allow Psalm 81:1–5 to begin and end our meditation on this psalm, being stirred up to exuberant praise for God in Christ, our exodus Redeemer. It is worth pondering what it can mean for overflowing praise (81:1–3) to be decreed for us (81:4–5). Lest we bridle at this thought

---

29 Calvin, *Psalms*, 3:324–25.

30 See on Pss. 18:44; 66:3.

31 Note the echoes of Deut. 32:13–14. The word "spiritual" in Eph. 1:3 does not mean "immaterial" but rather "from the Holy Spirit."

32 Jerome, in *ACCS* 8:144.

and reply that praise, if it is to be authentic, must be spontaneous, we do well to remember that God knows our frailty and has given us the command and reasons to praise in order that our hard hearts be stirred up by his kindness. As we gather to celebrate his grace, we stir up one another to this praise, which can grow and rise up within our hearts until it becomes warm and tender.

2. The balance between our speaking and our listening is one we must never lose, for, as Kidner reminds us, "God looks for listeners as well as singers."[33] To speak or sing to God without an attentive ear to hear his voice in the Scriptures is the route to empty worship. The wilderness generation is a standing warning to us about this danger.

3. The vivid language of the misery of slavery (Ps. 81:6–7) helps us feel viscerally the agonies and weariness of unforgiven sins. Only then will we be deeply grateful for Christ our Passover, sacrificed for us.

4. The bracing, heartfelt appeal of Psalm 81:8–10 presses home to the church of Christ today the overwhelming call to a singleness of heart in our worshiping obedience (Matt. 6:33; James 1:8).

5. Psalm 81:11–12 invites us to consider the misery of those who are handed over to their own decisions, so that we are warned not to follow them, and resolve to do all we can to persuade them to trust in Christ.

6. The tender heart of God, revealed in Psalm 81:13–16, can move us to a glad believing in Christ and a steady perseverance with Christ. And yet there is an open-endedness about the close of the psalm: Will the people—will you, will I—listen to Christ and come to him in believing obedience?[34] This is the ultimate challenge of the psalm. Only when this question is properly answered can the joy of 81:1–3 be securely grounded.

---

33 Kidner, *Psalms*, 2:293.
34 Tucker and Grant, *Psalms*, 2:210.

[The Psalter] did not even conceal the fact that he received all the authority of judgment from the Father, but also announces that he is coming as judge of all [in Psalms 50, 72, and 82].

ATHANASIUS
Letter to Marcellinus

Asaph the seer lets them see, what the eye of flesh did not see, God, God among the gods, and brings him out to their dismay from his place of concealment.

ERNST WILHELM HENGSTENBERG
Psalms

PSALM 82

ORIENTATION

Psalm 82 makes us long for the Lord Jesus to return and assures us that he will. The psalm tells us of a dramatic confrontation between God (אֱלֹהִים, *Elohim*, a plural of dignity) and the gods (also called אֱלֹהִים, *elohim*, meaning a plurality of beings). The question that lies at the heart of the interpretation of the psalm is this:[1] Who are "the gods" over whom "God" takes his stand (82:1)? Are they spiritual beings, superhuman but subdivine (angels, evil spirits, the idol-gods of the nations), or are they powerful human beings addressed as "gods"?

Most, if not all, the older writers (including patristic, Reformation, and Puritan) considered them to be the latter.[2] God rebukes powerful people, to whom has been entrusted the delegated authority of God to exercise judgment over other human beings. Those given authority "are set apart as the representatives of God on earth."[3] This is why obedience to those in authority is an outworking of fearing God (cf. Ex. 22:28; Lev. 19:32; Rom. 13:1–7; and supremely the fifth commandment as an outworking of reverence to God). To come before the judge is to come before God (Ex. 21:6; 22:8), for God is with them when they give judgment (cf. 2 Chron. 19:5–7). Solomon sits on the throne of God (1 Chron. 29:23).

---

1 Tate comments that "this short psalm has generated an enormous amount of scholarly attention" and is "*sui generis* in the Psalter." Tate, *Psalms 51–100*, 332.

2 For older writers, see *ACCS* 8:145–48; *RCS* 8:70–73; Augustine, *Psalms*, 4:172–73; Theodoret of Cyrus, *Psalms*, 2:56; Luther, *Luther's Works*, 11:111; Calvin, *Psalms*, 3:327–28; Dickson, *Psalms*, 2:60. Among modern writers, this view is supported by Hengstenberg, *Psalms*, 3:28–32; Delitzsch, *Psalms*, 2:401–2; Kirkpatrick, *Psalms*, 2:495; Grogan, *Psalms*, 146–47; Motyer, *Psalms*, 539; Harman, *Psalms*, 2:619; Spurgeon, *Treasury*, 2.1:410.

3 Hengstenberg, *Psalms*, 3:30–32. Hengstenberg mounts a vigorous defense of the "human judges" reading of the psalm.

The rebuke of Psalm 82:2 and the exhortation of 82:3–4 make perfect sense on this reading, for this is what the Scriptures teach about human rulers under God. When they fail to do this, the moral foundations of the earth are shaken (82:5; cf. 11:1–3). It is sometimes objected that the judgment of 82:7 is tautologous if they are mortal humans, but this objection is not persuasive since powerful men often need the humbling reminder that they are mortal, for they behave as if they were not.

If this is correct, then a further question arises: Are they wicked rulers within the people of God (so that those whom they oppress are within Israel), or are they the rulers of a power like Babylon (so that those they oppress are Israel as a whole)? The canonical context (in book 3) tends toward the latter, but the dichotomy is false. The worldwide scope of 82:8 suggests that God's rebuke encompasses not only wicked rulers within Israel but all evil judges everywhere.

The mention of "the divine council" (lit., "the council or assembly of *El*") in 82:1, however, reminds us of the "sons of God" gathered in the presence of God in Job 1:6 and 2:1 and of Micaiah's vision in 1 Kings 22:19–23, Isaiah's vision (Isa. 6:1–13),[4] and the territorial "gods" implied in Deuteronomy 4:19; 29:26; and 32:8–9. Many modern writers, therefore, consider these "gods" to be spiritual beings, who have been using their power in the world for evil purposes.[5] That is, they are the Satan and his fallen angels or evil spirits or the gods of other nations. Having been created with immortality in the heavenly places, now they are cast out of heaven and must perish, so that God's will can be done on earth as it is in heaven.

Two considerations can help us decide between these alternatives. The first is the strong organic connection in the Scriptures between people exercising power and the spirits that breathe in them as they do. The spirit of the Satan breathed in the Sabeans and Chaldeans when they afflicted Job (Job 1:13–19); it lay behind the way the king of Babylon thought of himself (Isa. 14:12–20, a man who behaved as though he were divine, but was brought down to Sheol); it is explicit in the apocalyptic language of Daniel 10:12–21 and 12:1, where

---

4   Some have also suggested Isa. 40:1–8; Zech. 1:7–17; 3:1–5. See Tate, *Psalms 51–100*, 332.

5   For this view, see, e.g., Tucker and Grant, *Psalms*, 2:215; Goldingay, *Psalms*, 2:560–62; Alter, *Psalms*, 291; Mays, *Psalms*, 269–70; Dahood, *Psalms*, 2:269; VanGemeren, *Psalms*, 624; Tate, *Psalms 51–100*, 340–41; Anderson, *Psalms*, 2:592–93; Kraus, *Psalms*, 2:155–56; Longman, *Psalms*, 305; Kidner, *Psalms*, 2:296–97. Often this view is connected with Canaanite stories of a council of the gods.

Michael is clearly an angelic being (see Jude 9; Rev. 12:7); when David used his power to call a sinful census, Satan lay behind him (1 Chron. 21:1); an evil spirit tormented King Saul and drove him to wickedness (1 Sam. 16:14); the king of Tyre was a godlike creature but was brought down to destruction (Ezek. 28:11–19), as was Assyria (Ezek. 31:1–18). Those who used their power to oppose Christ were children of the devil (John 8:44); there are "cosmic powers over this present darkness" (Eph. 6:12); there is a "ruler," even a "god" "of this world" (John 12:31; 14:30; 2 Cor. 4:4), the Satan who entered into Judas Iscariot (Luke 22:3); this spirit claims to be God (cf. 2 Thess. 2:4). Whenever a human being exercises power other than by the Spirit of God, a darker spirit is at work. In their pretense to be a god, they represent spiritual and demonic powers.[6] So "the gods" may, at the same time, be spiritual beings in the heavenly places and powerful human beings on earth in whom their spirits breathe.

The second consideration reinforces the first and brings us to what Jesus means in John 10 when he quotes from Psalm 82:6. He is accused of "blasphemy, because you, being a man, make yourself God." Jesus replies,

> Is it not written in your Law, "I said, you are gods"? If he called them gods to whom the word of God came—and Scripture cannot be broken—do you say of him whom the Father consecrated[7] and sent into the world, "You are blaspheming," because I said, "I am the Son of God"? (John 10:33–36)

What kind of argument is Jesus making from the psalm? It is often suggested that he is arguing from the lesser to the greater: "If these human rulers were called gods, you can hardly complain when I, who am greater than they, call myself the Son of God."[8] There is some force in this. But James Hamilton is right to object that this kind of argument does not quite work.[9]

---

6   Writers who see either deliberate ambiguity or both human and superhuman dimensions include Hossfeld and Zenger, *Psalms*, 2:330–31; Ross, *Psalms*, 2:725; Eveson, *Psalms*, 2:78. Zenger notes, "The 'heavenly' and 'earthly' spheres overlap."

7   Delitzsch contrasts the holy, consecrated life of Jesus with the unholy life of those condemned in Ps. 82. Delitzsch, *Psalms*, 2:401–2.

8   This is the argument of Calvin, followed by many others: "By these words Christ did not mean to place himself among the order of judges; but he argues from the less to the greater, that if the name of God is applied to God's officers, it with much more propriety belongs to his only begotten Son." Calvin, *Psalms*, 3:336.

9   In this I agree with Hamilton's critique of the argument but disagree with the way he resolves the issue. See Hamilton, *Psalms*, 2:90–91. He considers that Jesus is implying, from Ps. 82, that

It leaves itself open to this objection: "Yes, Jesus, that is true. But we are not simply arguing about terminology, about who can use the designation 'god' and in what sense. For you *are* claiming more—a lot more—than human kings and judges, on whom rests the delegated authority of God to judge. And in claiming so much more, you are guilty of blasphemy."

I suggest that the organic connection between human beings exercising power and the spirit by which they do so may be the key. Human judges are "gods" not simply because they are powerful but because—although they may not realize this—they are representatives on earth of spiritual forces in the heavenly places. We can discern what sorts of spiritual forces they represent by the ways in which they exercise their power. By the same argument, we ought to be able to discern what Spirit breathes in Jesus by the works he does, which are (as in Ps. 72) precisely what he calls "many good works from the Father" and "the works of my Father," and it is by those works that we recognize that, as Jesus says, "the Father is in me and I am in my Father" (John 10:32, 37–38). Jesus is not simply playing with words; just as evil rulers represent evil spirits and share their nature, so Jesus represents the Father and shares his nature. Jesus is the perfect image of God. When Psalm 82 addresses human beings as "gods," this was, in a strange way, "a foreshadowing of the Incarnation," in which God and man are so wonderfully joined together.[10] The dark side of this is that human beings alienated from God necessarily use their power as representatives of false gods or idols.

The psalm therefore does not simply expose the culpable injustice of humans misusing power (although it eloquently does that) but also at least hints at the dark spiritual dimension that lies behind their wickedness. The true God will send a true Son of God in whose heart breathes the true Spirit of God (given "without measure," John 3:34), and he will judge the earth in righteousness so that the true God will inherit the nations (Ps. 82:8).

There is one other hint in the New Testament about this psalm. The exhortation "*Deliver* them from the *hand* of the wicked" (82:4) may be echoed when the Gospels speak of Jesus being "delivered" or "betrayed"

---

he, Jesus, is by rights one of the divine council. I entirely agree with all Hamilton says about the deity of Jesus but am not persuaded that this is what Jesus is here arguing.

10   Kirkpatrick, *Psalms*, 2:497.

into the "hands" of the wicked (e.g., Mark 9:31; 14:41).[11] By suffering under the injustice of Psalm 82, Jesus the Son of God will conquer evil and come into his kingdom.

Links with other scriptures include Psalm 81 (for in both Ps. 81 and Ps. 82 God speaks), Psalm 50 (another Asaph psalm in which God appears for judgment), Psalm 58 (in which "gods" are similarly rebuked), Psalm 95 ("a great King above all gods," 95:3), and especially Isaiah 3:13–15. The last of these is a striking parallel, including the verb "taken his place" and the noun "princes"; here there is no question that God is contending with "the elders and princes of his people."

THE TEXT

Structure

Psalm 82:1 is Asaph's introduction, and 82:8 is an urgent prayer. Psalm 82:2–7 moves from accusing question (82:2) through challenging exhortation (82:3–4) and searching assessment (82:5) to tragic verdict (82:6–7).

Some argue that because there is no explicit indication of a change of speaker, Asaph is still the speaker in 82:2–7,[12] others that this is the voice of God. But if Asaph is the speaker, he speaks with the authority of God, so the impact is much the same. There is some question about who speaks 82:5 (see below).

Superscription

S   A Psalm of Asaph.[13]

82:1 Shocking Introduction: God among the Gods

1   God has taken his place in the divine council;
         in the midst of the gods he holds judgment:

---

11 See Rikk E. Watts, "Mark," in *CNTOT* 234.
12 Goldingay, *Psalms*, 2:559; Eveson, *Psalms*, 2:78.
13 See on Pss. 50, 73. In Hebrew the superscription is the start of verse 1.

Irony abounds: **God** is portrayed as **in the midst of the gods**. The verb **has taken his place**[14] is literally "stands" (as the CSB), a verb that conveys authority[15] and purposefulness; if God has been sitting in the usual position of authority, now he stands to give **judgment** (the great theme of the psalm). It is an electric moment and a terrifying one for those misusing their authority. The **divine council** is literally "the council or the assembly of God [*El*]." The usual meaning of the noun **council** (עֵדָה, *edah*) is "assembly" or "congregation"; it may refer to Israel as the congregation of God (cf. Num. 27:17; 31:16; Josh. 22:16–17), in which case **the gods** are its leaders and judges. Some understand "of God [*El*]" to have the more general sense of "mighty" (KJV: "the congregation of the mighty") or "great" (NIV: "the great assembly"), but it is better to retain the reference to God (cf. NASB: "in his own congregation").

82:2–7 God Condemns All Un-Christlike Use of Power

> 2 "How long will you judge unjustly
>   and show partiality to the wicked?   *Selah*

The question **How long?** echoes the cry of those in lament; now God asks it not because he does not know the answer but because it expresses his grave displeasure. There is a "terrible sternness" in this question (for which the *Selah* prompts an appropriate pause).[16] To **judge unjustly** embraces any unfair use of power (e.g., Lev. 19:15, 35).[17] Such unjust exercise of power echoes down the ages but reaches its climax in the mistreatment of Jesus Christ.[18] To be unjust always involves showing **partiality** (favoritism) **to the wicked,** for whom the breakdown of justice generally works out well, since "Might is right" becomes the effective law of the land.

---

14 Niphal participle of נצב. Cf. Isa. 3:13.

15 In Gen. 37:5–8 Joseph's sheaf rises and "stands" (niphal of the same verb, נצב), while his brothers' sheaves bow to him. In 1 Sam. 19:20 Samuel stands "as head" (the verb נצב) over the prophets. For a useful discussion of the meaning of God standing here, see Tate, *Psalms 51–100*, 335.

16 Delitzsch, *Psalms*, 2:403.

17 The NIV rendering, "defend the unjust," keeps a tidy parallel with the second line but is narrower than the Hebrew demands.

18 Augustine makes this point from the parable of the tenants in the vineyard in Matt. 21:33–41. Augustine, *Psalms*, 4:174–75.

3   Give justice to the weak and the fatherless;
         maintain the right of the afflicted and the destitute.
4   Rescue the weak and the needy;
         deliver them from the hand of the wicked."

Examples abound in the Prophets of injunctions to use power rightly, as it is here described (e.g., Isa. 1:17). In the Psalms, perhaps Psalm 72 is the most eloquent expression of a King who does exactly this. God entrusts human beings with power precisely so that they will use it on behalf of those who cannot defend themselves (cf. Prov. 31:1–9). Psalm 82:3–4 clearly implies that this is what they have not been doing.

5   They have neither knowledge nor understanding,
         they walk about in darkness;
         all the foundations of the earth are shaken.

The shift from second- to third-person speech may indicate that 82:5 is the voice of the psalmist. Or it may be the voice of God turning—as it were, with an expression of pained disgust—away from direct address to speak to any who will listen. This diagnosis demonstrates that the evil behavior of these "gods" is not an occasional aberration but rather the expression of their fallen nature.

The first line has no expressed object, literally, "They do not know, and they do not understand." The implication is that they neither know nor understand that they are accountable to the true God and that he is watching and standing in judgment over them. They do not have what Solomon prayed for, "an understanding mind to govern" (1 Kings 3:9). And so **they walk about** (the verb form[19] suggests a regular to-ing and fro-ing, the normal stuff of life that ignores God, "in carnal security and self-complacency")[20] **in darkness**, the blind judging the blind (cf. Prov. 2:13), for corruption always brings the judge into a moral shadow (cf. Ex. 23:8). Because the men of power walk in moral darkness, **all the** moral as well as physical **foundations**[21] **of the earth are shaken** (cf. the similar imagery in Pss. 11:3; 75:3).

---

19 Hithpael of הָלַךְ.
20 Delitzsch, *Psalms*, 2:403.
21 For this word (מוֹסָד), see Deut. 32:22; Ps. 18:7; Prov. 8:29; Isa. 24:18; Jer. 31:37; Mic. 6:2.

Augustine relates this verse to those who crucified Christ, who did not understand the wisdom of God (1 Cor. 2:8); the earthquake at the cross is a vivid and climactic demonstration of the foundations being shaken.[22]

> 6   I said, "You are gods,
>   sons of the Most High, all of you;
> 7   nevertheless, like men you shall die,
>   and fall like any prince."

After the accusing question (Ps. 82:2), the implied catalog of failures (82:3–4), and the diagnosis of their culpable ignorance (82:5), 82:6–7 states God's sentence. The divine declaration (I—emphatic[23]—said) of 82:6 gives extraordinary dignity to these judges (see the discussion above; see also on Ps. 8). It is not simply that they like to think of themselves as divine (although they do) but rather that God himself calls them **gods, / sons of the Most High,** sharing his likeness and exercising his authority on earth. The use of **the Most High** may reinforce their accountability; they may be "high," but there is one who is "Most High."

Nevertheless introduces a sentence of death that is all the more acutely tragic in view of the dignity that precedes it. **Like men** is literally "as אָדָם, *adam*," perhaps an echo of the judgment of Genesis 3 on fallen humankind. The second line of 82:7 intensifies the first, both by its movement from **men** in general to **prince** in particular and in the development from **die** to **fall**, the latter often used of violent and untimely death (e.g., 91:7).[24] No matter how powerful a human being you are, you will die—and die badly.

82:8 Come, Lord Jesus!

> 8   Arise, O God, judge the earth;
>   for you shall inherit all the nations!

Arise, O God echoes Numbers 10:35. The cry to God to **judge the earth** is a prayer that what has been seen in vision in Psalm 82:1–7 may

---

22 Augustine, *Psalms*, 4:175–76.
23 אָנִי.
24 This is suggested by Hengstenberg, *Psalms*, 3:37.

come to pass on **earth**, with no limitation of geography, as the second line emphasizes, **for** (this is the reason why we cry to God to judge the earth) **you shall inherit all the nations**, with no exception (cf. what is said of the Messiah in 2:8). From Theodoret of Cyrus in the patristic era[25] through Martin Luther at the time of the Reformation[26] and Charles Spurgeon in the nineteenth century[27] to Derek Kidner in the twentieth,[28] Christian readers have understood that this is a prayer for Jesus to return.

REFLECTION AND RESPONSE

1. When we are strong, Psalm 82 warns us. When we are entrusted with power, whether in government, business, school, or family, we are in danger, for "men in honour and power readily forget God; . . . the splendour of their power maketh them to forget their duty to God above them, and to their subjects under them."[29] Luther paraphrases the message like this: "It is true that you are gods over all of us, but not over the God of all of us. For God, who appointed you as gods, surely wills that He Himself shall be an exception and that His Godhead shall not be subjected to your godhead."[30]

2. All who are "weak . . . fatherless . . . afflicted . . . destitute . . . needy" (Ps. 82:3–4)—and this is almost the definition of the church—may take great encouragement from Psalm 82. For God has taken his stand against these unjust "gods"; he has pronounced his verdict; God will arise to judge the earth; "he has fixed a day on which he will judge the world in righteousness by a man whom he has appointed" (Acts 17:31). Jesus will return. We cry, "Come, Lord Jesus!"; our cries are not in vain.

---

25 "This refers unmistakably to the judgment of Christ the Lord: to him in his humanity the Father said, 'Ask of me, and I shall give you nations for your inheritance, and the ends of the earth as your possession.'" Theodoret of Cyrus, *Psalms*, 2:57.

26 "He prays for another government and kingdom in which things will be better . . . ; that is the kingdom of Christ." Luther, *Luther's Works*, 13:72.

27 "There is one who is 'King by right divine,' and he is even now on his way. The last days shall see him enthroned, and all unrighteous potentates broken like potter's vessels by his potent sceptre. The second advent is still earth's brightest hope. Come quickly, even so, come, Lord Jesus." Spurgeon, *Treasury*, 2.1:413.

28 "The psalm, having traversed some of the ground which Revelation will explore, ends very much as that book ends with its 'Come, Lord Jesus!'" Kidner, *Psalms*, 2:299.

29 Dickson, *Psalms*, 2:61.

30 Luther, *Luther's Works*, 13:44.

3. Above all, Psalm 82 makes us think about the spiritual dimensions of power and helps us be realistic about the dark powers behind injustice but also moves us to wonder and praise God that Jesus Christ is the true Son of the Most High, who is God not merely in delegated title and authority but in the dignity of his being as God the eternal Son. As Hamilton sums it up,

> God entrusted all judgment to the Son (John 5:22), who announced as he went to the cross that the time had come for the world's ruler to be thrown down (John 12:31; cf. Rev 12:9). Through him God the Father disarmed the rulers and authorities, putting them to shame, triumphing over them in him (Col 2:15). As a result, all authority in heaven and on earth now belongs to the Son (Matt 28:18), who sent out his disciples to claim his inheritance, all nations, by making disciples of them (Matt 28:19–20; cf. Ps 2:8).[31]

---

31 Hamilton, *Psalms*, 2:92.

*The prophet [in Psalm 83] implores the divine aid against the
enemies of the Church. . . . To stir up himself and others to
greater earnestness and confidence in prayer, he shows, by many
examples, how mightily God had been wont to succor his servants.*

JOHN CALVIN
Commentary on the Psalms

PSALM 83

ORIENTATION

Psalm 83 helps us be realistic about the bitter hostility of the world toward Christ and his church, reassures us that this hostility is bound to fail, and shows us how to pray for Christ's name to be lifted high all over the world.

This psalm is neither well known nor much loved, partly because psalms that pray for God's judgment on the wicked are not our favorites and partly because of the bewildering number of people groups and names in 83:6–11. But it is a fitting conclusion to the Asaph collection (Pss. 73–83) and has an important message for us. The repetition of "name" is worth noting: first the "name of Israel" (83:4) and then the "name" of God (83:16, 18). These are connected, for the determination to wipe out "the name of Israel" is an outworking of desire that God not be known in the world. The name of the God of Israel will be lifted high in all the earth (83:18) only when the enemies of God's church are frustrated.

In biblical theology this leads us to Jesus Christ, who is the embodiment of Israel, the righteous remnant. The hostility toward Israel reaches its climax in enmity toward Christ. He was surrounded by enemies on every side determined to destroy him (e.g., Mark 3:6). They killed him, but in his death he defeated death and the one who holds the power of death (Heb. 2:14; cf. Col. 2:15). God did for Jesus what this psalm prays for the people of God.

Today the church of Christ is surrounded by a hostile world and prays this psalm in Christ, that the enemies of the church of Christ will be defeated or converted, so that Christ, the name above all names, will be powerful and lifted high in the earth (Eph. 1:21; Phil. 2:9–10; cf. Acts 3:15–16).

Psalm 83 shares significant links with Psalm 82. Powerful, wicked people are writ large in each. Each closes with a prayer for the kingdom of God on earth, with verbal echoes of the title "Most High" (82:6; 83:18) and of the words "the earth" and "all" ("the earth . . . all the nations," 82:8; "all the earth," 83:18). There is an ironic link with Psalm 81, where God speaks but his people will not listen; now in Psalm 83:1 they plead with him to speak! "The pastures of God" (83:12) echoes the pastoral motif of other Asaph psalms (74:1; 77:20; 78:70–72; 79:13; 80:1). The title "Most High" is prominent in Asaph psalms (50:14; 73:11; 77:10; 78:35; 82:6), as is the "name" of God (74:10, 18, 21; 75:1; 76:1; 79:6, 9; 80:18). The "whole earth" theme features also in Psalms 50:1, 4; 74:12; 76:8–9 and 12. Although the words used are different, Psalm 83 echoes Psalm 1 in "chaff" (83:13; cf. Ps. 1:4) and Psalm 2 in the "uproar" (83:2; cf. Ps. 2:1–3).

The attack on Jehoshaphat in 2 Chronicles 20:1–30 is the most likely historical context, although we cannot be sure.[1] There the enemies are Moab, Ammon, and Edom (also called "Mount Seir"; see 2 Chron. 20:1–2, 10, 22; cf. Ps. 83:6–7); Jehoshaphat relies on God's kingship over the nations (2 Chron. 20:6; cf. Ps. 83:18); the enemies are determined to drive the people of God out of their inheritance (2 Chron. 20:11; cf. Ps. 83:4, 12); and the Spirit of God comes on an Asaphite to speak to the assembly (2 Chron. 20:14). The psalm shapes the church's prayers in every time of trial (including Nehemiah's struggles and the Maccabean period).

Both the names of the enemies and the scale of the hostility in Psalm 83 appear to go beyond even 2 Chronicles 20. Given the canonical context in book 3, which suggests reading it in the context of the Babylonian exile, it is perhaps best to understand the psalm as describing, with poetic freedom but theological accuracy, the enduring hostility of the world for Christ and his church. As Philip Eveson notes,

> We must not forget that there is a war that has been operating since Eden to destroy God's "seed" but the promise of Genesis 3:15 is that it will not

---

1   For vigorous defenses of this background, see Delitzsch, *Psalms*, 2:406; Hengstenberg, *Psalms*, 3:39–41.

succeed. There is a descendant, Jesus the Messiah, who has defeated the snake and his brood and shortly the God of peace will crush Satan under our feet (Romans 16:20).[2]

THE TEXT

Structure
The *Selah* at the end of Psalm 83:8 divides the psalm into two parts. Psalm 83:1–8 mainly describes the enemies, while 83:9–18 gives the substance of the prayer.

Superscription

^S   A Song. A Psalm of Asaph.[3]

83:1–8 Feel the Pressure of the World's Hostility toward God, His Christ, and Christ's Church

¹   O God, do not keep silence;
    do not hold your peace or be still, O God!

Before looking around at "the wind and the waves" (Ps. 83:2–8), the eye of faith looks resolutely at God. The first word (אֱלֹהִים, *Elohim*) and the last (אֵל, *El*) emphasize this. With three almost synonymous urgent requests, Asaph pleads with God to speak and act—for when God speaks, God acts. **Do not keep silence** is literally "not silence with you," but the verb "to be" is implied. **Do not hold your peace** (or perhaps "Do not be deaf") is likewise a plea for God to hear prayer and speak and act in response. **Do not . . . be still** is a plea for God to be active.

Augustine notes that Jesus was silent at his trial in order to submit to God's judgment.[4] Now the church may cry to the risen and ascended Jesus to act in power.

---

2 Eveson, *Psalms*, 2:84.
3 In Hebrew the superscription is verse 1; subsequent verse numbers are increased by one.
4 Augustine, *Psalms*, 4:179.

2   For behold, your enemies make an uproar;
       those who hate you have raised their heads.

3   They lay crafty plans against your people;
       they consult together against your treasured ones.

4   They say, "Come, let us wipe them out as a nation;
       let the name of Israel be remembered no more!"

For behold is an emphatic start to 83:2–4. "Look, God, look!" The ene-mies of the church are **your enemies** and **those who hate you**, for to hate God is to hate his church.

Setting 83:2 alongside 83:3 reminds us that the hostility is both public and secret. In 83:2 they **make an uproar**, a vivid verb suggesting a thunderous turmoil (cf. "in turmoil," 39:6; "thundering," Isa. 17:12), reminding us of the united mob rioting against God and his Christ in Psalm 2:1–3. And they **have raised their heads** in prideful threat, the very opposite of humble submission.[5] In the end, as Psalm 110 teaches us, it will be the head of Christ that is raised in victory (110:7). Indeed, as David Dickson nicely remarks, "The more din the enemy makes, the more insolent he is, the higher he lifteth his head, he is the more near to be knocked down by God's appearing for his people against him."[6] James Hamilton perceptively connects the "enemies" (i.e., enmity) and their "heads" to the gospel promise of Genesis 3:15.[7]

But alongside the very public, proud cultural superiority of Psalm 83:2, there is a craftiness at work in 83:3 because they are the sons of the "crafty" serpent in the garden of Eden (Gen. 3:1).[8] **They lay crafty plans** in secret counsel as **they consult together**. There is something dark about their words, the very opposite of authentic gospel behavior (cf. 2 Cor. 4:2). Whether or not their words are secret, their true motives are hidden behind a mask of virtue.[9]

The ones against whom they plot are **your people, your treasured ones**, where the latter designation implies a people hidden safely in God (cf. the

---

5   Given the memory of the defeat of Midian in Ps. 83:9, 11, we should note that in Judg. 8:28, "Midian . . . raised their heads no more."

6   Dickson, *Psalms*, 2:64.

7   Hamilton, *Psalms*, 2:94.

8   This connection is also made by Hamilton, *Psalms*, 2:94.

9   When they "accumulate . . . teachers to suit their own passions" (2 Tim. 4:3), they don't advertise it.

KJV: "thy hidden ones").[10] These people—those of the old covenant church, Christ himself when on earth, those of the church of Christ—are precious. In Christ now their lives are "hidden with Christ in God" (Col. 3:3). They are the apple of God's eye (Zech. 2:8). But precisely because of this intimate covenantal tie, those who constitute the seed of the serpent always say to one another, **Come**—the invitation to join the world—**let us wipe them out as a nation** (lit., "from being a nation"); / **let**[11] **the name of Israel** (with all its rich covenantal associations; cf. Gen. 32:28) **be remembered no more!** That is, not only will Israel be wiped off the map, but there will be no inheritance of Israel, no memory, no impact on the history of the world. This invitation lies behind the cry "Crucify him!" at the trial of Jesus Christ (Mark 15:13–14).[12]

This aim (remembered in Ps. 83:12 from earlier in Israel's history) has behind it as "prime agent . . . Satan, who has all along from the beginning been exerting himself to extinguish the Church of God."[13] With an eye to biblical theology, Augustine rightly says, "The name *Israel* is undoubtedly to be understood here as embracing those descendants of Abraham to whom the apostle says, *You are the descendants of Abraham, his heirs according to the promise* (Gal 3:29)."[14]

5   For they conspire with one accord;
       against you they make a covenant—
6   the tents of Edom and the Ishmaelites,
       Moab and the Hagrites,
7   Gebal and Ammon and Amalek,
       Philistia with the inhabitants of Tyre;
8   Asshur also has joined them;
       they are the strong arm of the children of Lot.   *Selah*

Psalm 83:5 (beginning with **for**, as in 83:2) is the headline for 83:5–8. Who **they** are will be expanded in 83:6–8. The focus now is on their unity

---

10 The verb root is צפן. This verb is used twice in Ex. 2:2–3 of Moses's mother hiding Moses in a basket.
11 The move from the first line to the second is simply a *vav*. The CSB and NIV translate it "so that . . ." The effect is much the same.
12 Theodoret of Cyrus, *Psalms*, 2:59.
13 Calvin, *Psalms*, 3:340.
14 Augustine, *Psalms*, 4:180.

(**conspire**[15] **with one accord, make a covenant**) and their overwhelming number. In diabolical imitation of true unity in the one God, there is a paradoxical unity in opposition to God and his Christ (2:1–3; Acts 4:25–27; cf. Luke 23:12).

Several of the peoples in Psalm 83:6–8 appear as Saul's enemies (1 Sam. 14:47) and David's enemies (2 Sam. 8:12).

The tents of Edom does not mean that they were nomadic—for they were not—but is a poetic way of speaking of their dwellings. The Edomites were the descendants of (nonelect) Esau (Gen. 36:1), whose "perpetual enmity" (Ezek. 35:5) continued at least down to the Babylonian exile (Ps. 137:7) and made them a symbol of hostility to the church of God and therefore liable to the judgment of God (cf. Isa. 34:5–6; 63:1; Jer. 49:7–22).

The **Ishmaelites** were the descendants of (nonelect) Ishmael (Gen. 16:15; 17:20; 25:12–18); they "settled over against" the people of God (Gen. 25:18). Their merchants sold Joseph into slavery (Gen. 37), and they were later associated with the Midianites (Judg. 8:24; cf. Ps. 83:9).

The people of **Moab**, together with those of **Ammon**, were descended from Lot's incestuous unions with his daughters (Gen. 19:36–38). **Moab** became long-term enemies of Israel (e.g., Num. 22–25; Judg. 3:12–30; 2 Kings 3:4–5; Isa. 15–16; Jer. 48; Zeph. 2:8–11 [with Ammon]). The **Hagrites** (probably descendants of Hagar) are mentioned in 1 Chronicles 5:10 and 19–20 as those living east of Gilead who were enemies of Saul.

We do not know who the people of **Gebal** were or where it was located. At the time of settlement in the land, they are mentioned in connection with Lebanon (Josh. 13:5). In the reign of Solomon, they worked with the builders of Hiram, king of Tyre (1 Kings 5:18); the association with Tyre is also made later in Ezekiel 27:9. So they may have been in the north,[16] although the association in this verse with Ammon and Amalek has suggested to some the south.[17]

The people of **Ammon**,[18] along with those of Moab, were descended from Lot's incest with his daughters. Together with **Amalek**, they allied themselves with Moab in the days of the Judges (Judg. 3:13). Centuries later, Ammon fought with the Moabites against Jehoiakim, shortly before

---

15   "Conspire" is the niphal of the verb עוץ, used in the hithpael in Ps. 83:3 for "consult together."
16   Perhaps the Phoenician city of Byblos. See Dahood, *Psalms*, 2:274.
17   Perhaps linked to Edom. See Ross, *Psalms*, 2:734.
18   The name is linked with modern Amman, the capital of Jordan.

the Babylonian exile (2 Kings 24:2). After the murder of the Babylonian governor Gedaliah, the assassin Ishmael fled to the Ammonites (Jer. 41:15). Jeremiah declared an oracle against them (Jer. 49:1–6).

Amalek notoriously attempted to wipe Israel off the map in Exodus 17:8–16 and has been condemned by God "from generation to generation" (cf. Deut. 25:19). Even Balaam declared an oracle against them (Num. 24:20). They were allied with the Midianites in the time of Gideon (Judg. 6:3, 33; 7:12; cf. 10:12). Saul was told to devote them to destruction (1 Sam. 14:48; 15:2–3). One who bore the name of Agag, their king at the time of Saul (1 Sam. 15:8), was "Haman the Agagite," who threatened to exterminate the people of God in a later age (Est. 3:1).

Philistia was a thorn in Israel's side from the days of the Judges until David finally subdued them (cf. 1 Kings 4:21). **Tyre** did not always attack Israel but rather seduced her by her wealth (cf. Isa. 23; Ezek. 26–28).

Asshur means Assyria. Here we are told that they **joined** the other enemies and became **the strong arm**—that is, the allies and providers of reinforcements to—**the children of Lot** (i.e., the Moabites and Ammonites, regarded here perhaps as the ringleaders of this demonic alliance). In history this may refer to a time before the rise of Assyria to regional superpower status (after which they didn't offer assistance to anyone!), or it may be symbolic of powerful hostility to the people of God.

The fact that Babylon is not mentioned probably indicates that the psalm was written before the days of Babylonian threat and then exile. Although this list contains puzzles, the central point is clear: the world is united in wanting to remove "the seed of the woman," the Christ and all who are his, from the face of the earth.

83:9–18 Pray Urgently and with Confidence for the Defeat and Conversion of the Enemies of God, Christ, and His Church

9   Do to them as you did to Midian,
      as to Sisera and Jabin at the river Kishon,
10 who were destroyed at En-dor,
      who became dung for the ground.
11 Make their nobles like Oreb and Zeeb,
      all their princes like Zebah and Zalmunna,

¹²   who said, "Let us take possession for ourselves
          of the pastures of God."

Psalm 83:9–12, the first part of the prayer, remembers (and interweaves) two rescues recorded in Judges 4–8. **Midian**, together with its princes **Oreb and Zeeb** and its kings **Zebah and Zalmunna** (Judg. 7:25; 8:3, 5), was surprisingly defeated by Gideon (Judg. 6–8).[19] **Sisera** was the army commander of **Jabin**, king of Canaan (Judg. 4:2), wonderfully defeated by Deborah and Barak (Judg. 4–5) by **the river Kishon** (Judg. 4:13; 5:21). **Endor** is close to the battleground of Judges 4,[20] where the unburied corpses of the defeated foes lay as **dung for the ground**. In both cases, God rescues his people through their weakness (for the former, Gideon's tiny army; for the latter, the critical roles of Deborah and Jael, two women, who stepped up at a time of weak male leadership) and therefore has about it the shape of the gospel.

We note the parallel between the goal of the enemies today ("Come, let us wipe them out," Ps. 83:4) and then (**"Let us take possession for ourselves / of the pastures[21] of God,"** 83:12). "We know this belongs to God, but we will take it for ourselves." In every age God, who is faithful and consistent, will not allow his precious property to be stolen. Anyone who tries to destroy what is God's precious possession in Christ will themselves be destroyed (cf. 1 Cor. 3:16–17).[22]

¹³   O my God, make them like whirling dust,
          like chaff before the wind.
¹⁴   As fire consumes the forest,
          as the flame sets the mountains ablaze,
¹⁵   so may you pursue them with your tempest
          and terrify them with your hurricane!

---

19 Midian's defeat is also remembered in Isa. 9:4 and Hab. 3:7. Three identical Hebrew suffixes [מוֹ] in 83:11 give "a rhythm and sound as of rolling thunder": "make *them*, the nobles *of them*, . . . the princes *of them*." Delitzsch, *Psalms*, 2:410.

20 It is mentioned in Josh. 17:11 and later in 1 Sam. 28:7. For its location, see Delitzsch, *Psalms*, 2:410; Ross, *Psalms*, 2:743.

21 The word (נְוֵה) can mean "habitations" but has pastoral overtones (see Pss. 23:2; 65:12; 74:20; 79:7; Lam. 2:2).

22 Eveson helpfully makes this connection. Eveson, *Psalms*, 2:85.

O my God begins Psalm 83:13–15, an urgent appeal that God will do in the present crisis of the church what he did in that ancient time of trial. The zeal and the vivid imagery of the petition are driven not by a fevered and vengeful imagination but by the warm yearning that God will be honored (as becomes clear in 83:18). The first image is of **whirling dust**[23] and **chaff before the wind**. Although the noun for **chaff** is different from that in Psalm 1:4, it still reminds us of the destiny of the wicked there. Whatever legacy they might have expected to leave on earth, in the storm of God's judgment they will be blown away. This—which they had intended to do to the church—will happen to them. The second picture is a firestorm, using fire as a common image of God's hot anger (cf. Deut. 32:22). The references to **the forest** and **the mountains** cast a vision of a massive, even cosmic, storm. This **tempest**, or **hurricane**, is the personal just judgment of God that will **pursue them** so that they cannot escape and **terrify them** (the same verb as in Ps. 2:5, for the enemies of God's Christ).

16 Fill their faces with shame,
       that they may seek your name, O LORD.
17 Let them be put to shame and dismayed forever;
       let them perish in disgrace,
18 that they may know that you alone,
       whose name is the LORD,
       are the Most High over all the earth.

There is an extraordinary, even paradoxical, tension in this conclusion. On the one hand, we ask for the most terrible punishment (Ps. 83:16a, 17), filled with **shame** (using two different words),[24] **dismay**, and **disgrace**.

On the other hand, two parallel expressions of purpose take us to the heart of the prayer. The first is **that they may seek your name, O LORD**. There is no reason to suppose, with John Calvin, that this is merely "a forced and slavish submission,"[25] for the language of seeking is the vocabulary of the heart. To seek the name of God is to bow before him and long to know

23 The noun גַּלְגַּל means something like a wheel—hence rolling or whirling. Dust is probably implied by the parallel with chaff (cf. Isa. 17:13).
24 The noun קָלוֹן and the verb בוּשׁ.
25 Calvin, *Psalms*, 3:349.

him in covenant love (like those who call on the name of the Lord, Joel 2:32; Acts 2:21; Rom. 10:13). For some the shame here spoken of is the shame of conviction of sin (cf. "the things of which you are now ashamed," Rom. 6:21), for "shame has often weaned men from their idols, and set them upon seeking the Lord,"[26] and "sometimes people must be brought to nothing . . . *so that* they may be brought to God."[27] This, says Augustine, could not be prayed for "unless within the ranks of the enemies of God's people there were also certain individuals to whom this grace is to be granted before the final judgment" (cf. Acts 18:10).[28] For such people we may even say that they **perish in disgrace** as they die with Christ in conversion. Some from every one of the peoples named in Psalm 83:6–8 are now in Christ.

But if 83:16b holds before us a wonderful hope, 83:18 ends the psalm on a yet higher note. The concluding focus is not on converted individuals, brands plucked from the burning (cf. 83:14), but on the great God they now acknowledge (**know**). The combination of **you alone**, the **name**, the covenant **Lord**, and **the Most High over all the earth** is emphatic (cf. Mal. 1:11). The sovereign greatness of God is seen in Christ, to whom is given the name above all names. It is seen when he comes to judge the world, but it is seen supremely in the majestic love by which he saves some.

REFLECTION AND RESPONSE

1. Psalm 83:1 helps us identify with the persecuted church. It is good for us to be keenly aware of the world's hatred for the church.

2. Reflection on the composite picture of Psalm 83:2–3 can help us discern how the hatred of the seed of the serpent for the seed of the woman manifests itself in our culture and time. It shows itself simultaneously in the mob-like pressure of culture and in the inherent deceitfulness by which human beings naturally conceal our true motives for opposing God and his Christ and church; we will not admit that it is because we love darkness rather than light since our deeds are evil (John 3:19). Psalm 83:4 presses home to us that there can be no compromise between darkness and light

26 Spurgeon, *Psalms*, 2.1:422.
27 Motyer, *Psalms*, 540.
28 Augustine, *Psalms*, 4:183.

(cf. 2 Cor. 6:14–16). The line that begins with the hatred of Cain for Abel passes through the Amalekites in Exodus 17 and through their descendant Haman in Esther 3–7 to the cross of Christ and on to every hostility of the world for the church (John 15:18–16:4).

3. The concrete specifics of enmity in Psalm 83:6–8 (despite all their puzzles) remind us that the devil uses particular peoples and human powers at particular times to do his evil work. But the headline in 83:5 reminds us that the one thing that unites a fractured world is hostility to Christ. They may express their dislike in different ways, but it is always directed against Christ.

4. It is good to meditate on the astonishing rescues of Judges 4–5 and Judges 6–8 as we pray the prayer of Psalm 83:9–12, to remember how God used weakness to overcome strength, and to consider how this weakness reaches its apogee in the cross (cf. 1 Cor. 1:18–2:5). But mainly these verses strengthen our assurance in our prayers for the church, confident that God has always, does always, and will always protect his precious people, as he protected and raised Christ. Commenting on the designation "your people . . . your treasured ones" in Psalm 83:3, Calvin says this:

> It is worthy of notice, that those who molest the Church are called *the enemies of God*. It affords us no small ground of confidence that those who are our enemies are also God's enemies. This is one of the fruits of his free and gracious covenant, in which he has promised to be an enemy to all our enemies . . . [because] . . . the welfare of his people . . . cannot be assailed without an injury being, at the same time, done to his own majesty.[29]

5. We are challenged to enter wholeheartedly into Psalm 83:13–15, as we are schooled to care passionately for the honor of God. But 83:16–18 will help us here, as we remember that God's name is most dramatically honored in the conversion of men and women all over the world. The finally impenitent will be removed from the earth, but it is even more wonderful that the new heavens and earth will be filled with those who have been shamed and humbled into gladly acknowledging the name of the Most High God as he has rescued us in Christ.

29 Calvin, *Psalms*, 3:338–39.

*Train yourself until you have a capacity for God; long
and long for what you will possess for ever.*

AUGUSTINE
Expositions of the Psalms

*It is the office of the eternal Spirit to inspire
our hearts with holy desire.*

LANCELOT ANDREWES
"Sermon on Luke 11:2"

*That pilgrimage of Israel, to the place where the Lord had
put his name, was significant of more than met the eye. It
told of other pilgrims who should in after ages travel through
the world with their heart toward the Lord, and their hope
fixed on seeing him revealed at the end of their pilgrimage in
another manner than they knew him by the way. It included,
too, the journey of him who, as Chief of Pilgrims, was to
take the same road, share the same hardships, feel the same
longings, hope for the same resting-place, and enter on the
same full enjoyment of the Father's grace and glory.*

ANDREW BONAR
Christ and His Church in the Book of Psalms

PSALM 84

ORIENTATION

All goodness is found in God, and God may be found in Christ. Therefore, Jesus Christ is of infinite value and immeasurable goodness. Psalm 84 is a beautiful psalm that points us to Christ, for Christ is both its supreme singer and its treasured subject. The psalm breathes a warm desire for God and a rich delight in God. When Jesus sang this psalm on earth, it was, as it were, an expanded form of the words "I love the Father" (John 14:31). And yet Christ is also the subject of the psalm. For all that is typified here is fulfilled in him: the temple (for he is "greater than the temple," Matt. 12:6), the altars (for he is priest and sacrifice), and the anointed King (for he is the true Messiah).[1] As we walk through the psalm, we see how Christ as singer and Christ as subject blend and merge.

Both the individual Christian and the church of Christ[2] are dwelling places of God by the Spirit. The psalm points to each in fulfillment.

The vision of the new Jerusalem in Revelation 21:1–22:5 is a grand fulfillment of the longings of the psalm. Connections include (1) God dwelling and tabernacling with his people (Rev. 21:3; cf. Ps. 84:1), (2) the refreshing waters of life in all its fullness (Rev. 21:6; 22:1–2; cf. Ps. 84:2), (3) the insistence that the wicked must be excluded (Rev. 21:8, 27; cf. Ps. 84:10–11), and (4) the glory of God replacing the sun (Rev. 21:23; 22:5; cf. Ps. 84:11).

---

1 There is a clear and helpful paragraph on the transposition to a new covenant context in Eveson, *Psalms*, 2:88–89.
2 "This psalm speaks of Christ's church, for which . . . the prophet . . . sighs." Luther, *Luther's Works*, 11:136.

The Asaph collection closes with Psalm 83. The first Korah collection (Pss. 42–49) is now followed by a second: Psalms 84–88 (excluding Ps. 86). Each begins with longing for the house of God (Pss. 42–43; 84) and ends with a focus on death (Pss. 49; 88). There are several links between Psalm 84 and Psalms 42–43.[3]

In Psalm 84 we see a marked change of tone from Psalm 83, although there are at least two links. Gerald Wilson has pointed out that the designation "A Psalm" is shared among all the psalms in Psalms 82–85.[4] And the plea that God will hear prayer (84:8) is similar to how Psalm 83 begins (83:1).

The prayer for the anointed King in 84:9 suggests that a Davidic king was on the throne when the psalm was written.[5] It is placed here in book 3, however, as a poignant reminder of what had been lost and as a prayer—one that the exiles continued to pray—that it would be restored.[6]

THE TEXT

Structure

The appearance of *Selah* at the end of Psalm 84:4 and 8 yields three sections of four verses each (84:1–4, 5–8, 9–12, possibly paralleling 42:1–5, 6–11; 43:1–5).[7] The first and third sections close with "blessed," and the second begins with it (84:4, 5, 12). Each contains the title "Lord of hosts" or "Lord God of hosts." I adopt this division, although 84:8 and 9 are closely tied by the theme of prayer, and some prefer to take them together.

---

3 Links include the following: (1) each is an individual prayer of longing for God, in which the memory, the absence, or the presence of God is prominent (Pss. 42:3, 6, 11; 43:5; 84:7); (2) the prospect of "appearing" before God features in each (42:2; 84:7); (3) the expression "the living God" is unique to these psalms (42:2; 84:2); (4) the temple, tabernacle, or house of God appears in each (42:4; 43:3; 84:1, 4), as do the altars (43:4; 84:3); (5) in each the "soul" appears with its nuance of the seat of desire; and (6) the verb "sing for joy" in 84:2 (רָנַן) is cognate with the "glad shouts" of 42:4 (רִנָּה).

4 "The effect . . . is to soften the transition between these two author-groupings and to bind them together more closely." Wilson, *Editing of the Hebrew Psalter*, 164.

5 Some think it originated at the time of Absalom's rebellion; e.g., Delitzsch, *Psalms*, 3:2; Hengstenberg, *Psalms*, 3:50.

6 Cf. Tucker and Grant, *Psalms*, 2:244.

7 Kirkpatrick, *Psalms*, 2:505.

Superscription

S   To the choirmaster:[8] according to The Gittith.[9] A Psalm of the
     Sons of Korah.[10]

84:1–4 Blessed Are All Who Know God in Christ

1   How lovely is your dwelling place,
         O LORD of hosts!
2   My soul longs, yes, faints
         for the courts of the LORD;
     my heart and flesh sing for joy
         to the living God.

"Longing is written all over this psalm" and never more strongly than
at the start.[11] The adjective **lovely** speaks not so much of the beauty of
the temple as of the intense love that the psalmist feels for it (not so
much "How beautiful it is" but "How much I love it").[12] Or, to be more
accurate, he loves the God who is found there. **Your dwelling place** is
literally "your tabernacles" (as in Ps. 43:3), a plural of intensified wonder. The designation **LORD of hosts** (prominent in the psalm, see 84:3,
8, 12) is a source of terror to God's enemies but a foundation of security
and delight to God's people.[13] The believer is described in terms of the
soul (often designating the human person as having desires), the **heart**
(pointing to inwardness), and the **flesh** (reminding us of our embodied
being). The verb **longs** is intense (cf. the uses in Gen. 31:30; Job 14:15;
Ps. 17:12).[14] The verb **faints** means to be "spent" or grow weak with longing (e.g., Pss. 31:10; 39:10; 69:3 ["grow dim"]; 71:9; 73:26 ["may fail"]).

---

8   See on Ps. 4.
9   See on Ps. 8; cf. Ps. 81.
10 See on Ps. 42. In Hebrew the superscription is verse 1; subsequent verse numbers are increased
    by one.
11 Kidner, *Psalms*, 2:302.
12 The word (יָדִיד) may be translated "beloved" (e.g., Deut. 33:12; Pss. 60:5; 127:2; Isa. 5:1; Jer.
    11:15). The REB rendering, "How dearly loved," catches the sense well.
13 Tucker and Grant, *Psalms*, 2:245.
14 The verb (כסף) is here in the niphal, as in Gen. 31:30. Ps. 17:12 and Job 14:15 use the qal.

The verb translated **sing for joy** means to give a ringing cry, usually (although not always) with joy.[15] To call God the living God focuses our attention on God as the source (the only source) of life. This is not an abstract longing for "God" but rather a desire of God as he is known in the covenant, fulfilled in Christ. Jesus Christ knew these desires and fulfilled them himself, becoming both the perfect believer and the perfect ground of our trust.

> 3   Even the sparrow finds a home,
>   and the swallow a nest for herself,
>   where she may lay her young,
>   at your altars, O LORD of hosts,
>   my King and my God.

The **sparrow** and **swallow** may be images of the psalmist,[16] picturing himself as an insignificant person who yet finds a home with God through Christ. The word translated **sparrow** is used of birds dwelling in the shelter of Israel, pictured as a large tree (Ezek. 17:23), of frail exiles returning (Hos. 11:11), and of vulnerable loneliness (Ps. 102:7). Perhaps the reference to **where** the swallow **may lay her young** suggests the psalmist's family or simply a place where others can be nourished and have access to God. **At your altars** probably has the sense of "near your altars"; it is a reminder that what makes the temple special is the access to God made possible through sacrifice. The designations **my King and my God** emphasize covenant relationship. With the perspective of biblical theology, we have here the assurance that God may be found through Christ and that there is a place with God for the most insignificant person.

> 4   Blessed are those who dwell in your house,
>   ever singing your praise!   *Selah*

Psalm 84:4 sums up the longing and delight of 84:1–4. Here is the only truly good life. For the ascription **blessed** (אַשְׁרֵי, *ashre*; also 84:5, 12), see

---

15 *"Cry out in the night"* (Lam. 2:19) is an exception, a cry of pain.
16 So Delitzsch, *Psalms*, 3:4; Eveson, *Psalms*, 2:90. The precise identification of the two nouns is uncertain and unimportant; both designate a kind of small bird.

on Psalm 1:1. The verb to **dwell** appears also (in contrasting context) in 84:10. With the perspective of the New Testament, to **dwell in** God's **house** is to have access to the triune God through Christ. To be **ever singing your praise** is the only proper response of those who truly know God in Christ.

84:5–8 Blessed Are All Who Travel to Meet God in Christ

5   Blessed are those whose strength is in you,
       in whose heart are the highways to Zion.
6   As they go through the Valley of Baca
       they make it a place of springs;
       the early rain also covers it with pools.
7   They go from strength to strength;
       each one appears before God in Zion.

The next ascription of **blessed** moves from the delight of knowing God in Christ (Ps. 84:1–4) to the tension that there must be a pilgrimage before this knowledge is consummated in the redemption of our bodies. Psalm 84:5 begins, "Blessed is the אָדָם, *adam*," indicating any ordinary human being. This journey needs **strength**, which is found **in you**, for the God who is the end of the journey also gives strength for the road. The second line of 84:5 is literally "in whose heart are the highways" ("Zion" is not in the Hebrew). The word **highways** originally meant a track made firm with stones or infill.[17] The context of the psalm indicates that the highways in view are the pilgrimage paths that lead up to Zion. To have these in the **heart** is to have the desires of 84:1–4 in the soul (cf. Phil. 3:12–14). It is to long wholeheartedly for the presence of God as it is known in Christ. The ascription of blessing to the one who desires this indicates that this longing will always be fulfilled. There may be many obstacles, but the one who wants God will find God in Christ.[18]

---

17   *HALOT*, s.v. מְסִלָּה. For the common metaphorical uses of the word, see Prov. 16:17; Isa. 59:7; Jer. 31:21.
18   "Many hindrances must be cleared away if the poet is to get back to Zion, his true home; but his longing carries the surety within itself of its fulfilment." Delitzsch, *Psalms*, 3:5. For "nothing can withstand the longing desires of the godly." Calvin, *Psalms*, 3:351.

This highway is the way of the cross. When Jesus set his face on this strange highway, his strength was in his Father and his destination assured (cf. Luke 9:51).[19]

We do not know where or what **the Valley of Baca** was,[20] but the contrast in the rest of Psalm 84:6 strongly suggests that it was a place without water.[21] The word **Baca** sounds very similar to the Hebrew word for weeping;[22] the Septuagint understood it this way, and it has become influential in Christian tradition (e.g., "valley of tears," CSB mg.)—a valley without water will be a place of sorrow. Like the Israelites in the dry wilderness, God opens for them **a place of springs** (that is, water from the rock, who is Christ, 1 Cor. 10:4). The **early rain** may indicate the autumn rains (cf. Joel 2:23). The word translated **pools** probably ought to be translated "blessings" (the two words are very similar, and pools of water would certainly be a blessing).[23]

The idiom **from strength to strength** has entered the English language; here is persevering pilgrimage through difficult days. The verb moves from plural in the first line (**They go**) to singular in the second ("He appears"), the latter of which is usually translated **Each one appears** (as in the ESV). To **appear before God** means here to be viewed by God with favor, a favor that will be possible only because Jesus Christ appears before the Father for us.

8   O Lord God of hosts, hear my prayer;
          give ear, O God of Jacob!   *Selah*

Although the psalmist has not yet told us the content of his **prayer**, it must be related to his longings in Psalm 84:1–4 and the journey of 84:5–7. The desire of his heart is to walk in the highways to the house of God and to appear before God. That prayer will be made more specific in 84:9, but the *Selah* encourages us to pause in between the two verses. He prays and we pray for strength to get to the end of the journey and for life-giving water in dry and grief-filled valleys on the way.

---

19 Motyer, *Psalms*, 540.

20 See the useful note in Ross, *Psalms*, 2:751n15.

21 The plural means something like "balsam trees" in 2 Sam. 5:24; 1 Chron. 14:14–15. There is a theory that these trees grow in dry places, which would fit with the contrast that follows. Kirkpatrick, *Psalms*, 2:507; Hossfeld and Zenger, *Psalms*, 2:349.

22 "Baca" is בָּכָא; the root "to weep" is בכה.

23 The MT is בְּרָכוֹת (blessings), sometimes emended to בְּרֵכוֹת (pools).

84:9–12 Blessed Are Those Who Delight in and Trust God in Christ

9   Behold our shield, O God;
         look on the face of your anointed!

Our attention is now focused (using the same verb "to see") on one particular man. **Behold**—see—**our shield, O God**.[24] It becomes clear in the second line that this **shield**, the man who protects his people, is **your anointed**, the King in David's line (cf. 1 Sam. 2:10; Ps. 2:2),[25] who is finally Jesus the Messiah. To **look on the face of** the **anointed** King is to view him with favor and blessing. This man supremely appears before God in Zion; every other appearing before God rests on the Messiah standing before the Father. We pray for God's blessing on the King so that pilgrimage can happen.[26] Only Jesus the Messiah can give access to God: "For us, Jesus, with his unchanged priestly-kingship, is the eternal guarantor of our security, acceptance and blessedness."[27] It is the Messiah "through whom alone every good thing is purchased, and must be conveyed unto us."[28]

10   For a day in your courts is better
        than a thousand elsewhere.
     I would rather be a doorkeeper in the house of my God
        than dwell in the tents of wickedness.

For ties Psalm 84:10 to 84:9. We pray for God's favor on the King because access to God depends on him, on the Father's favor to the Son.

Two contrasts highlight the wonder of the presence of God. First, **a day in your courts** (see 84:2) is contrasted with **a thousand elsewhere**.[29] At one level

---

24 It is possible to take "shield" with "O God" as vocative together (cf. KJV: "O God our shield," as in Ps. 84:11, in which God is a shield), but the parallel with the second line, in which the one spoken of is the king, makes it more likely that the king is "our shield" in this verse (as in 89:18, in which "our shield" is in parallel with "our king").

25 With the striking exception of Cyrus in Isa. 45:1, "anointed" in the singular always designates the King in David's line. In 1 Chron. 16:22 and Ps. 105:15, the plural expands this anointing to the whole people of the Messiah, who share the King's anointing (cf. 1 John 2:27).

26 Eveson, *Psalms*, 2:92.

27 Motyer, *Psalms*, 540.

28 Dickson, *Psalms*, 2:74.

29 The word "elsewhere" is inserted to make it easier to read; the Hebrew simply says, "A day in your courts is better than a thousand."

this is simply saying that the presence of God is wonderful. But it prompts us to consider the nature of time, especially when we set this verse alongside 2 Peter 3:8. It is not simply that one day in God's presence is better than a thousand days of the same kind but rather that a day in God's presence is a different kind of day. As Augustine so eloquently expresses it, we aspire to "thousands of days," for we "want a long life here." But rather, he says,

> Let them make light of thousands of days and desire one day, the day that has no sunrise, no sunset, the one day that is an eternal day, the day that does not displace yesterday or find itself hard pressed by tomorrow. That one day is what we should desire. What use are thousands of days to us? We are traveling from thousands of days towards one day, just as we are proceeding from many virtues to one alone.[30]

In the second contrast, the word translated **a doorkeeper** occurs only here in the Old Testament. It is related to the word for "threshold" and is thought to mean someone who stands at the threshold, rather than the holder of an official position.[31] The point of the contrast is that it is better to be on the very outer edge of the presence of God than to be comfortably inside (i.e., to **dwell in**) **the tents**[32] **of wickedness.**

11   For the LORD God is a sun and shield;
      The LORD bestows favor and honor.
      No good thing does he withhold
          from those who walk uprightly.

For again ties this verse back to Psalm 84:10 and thence to 84:9. Psalm 84:11 is rooted and grounded in the favor of the Father to the Son. God is **a sun**, for he is "the living God" (84:2), and in him is the light of life (cf. 27:1; Isa. 60:19–20; Mal. 4:2; Rev. 21:23; 22:5). John Calvin writes,

> As the sun by his light vivifies, nourishes, and rejoices the world, so the benign countenance of God fills with joy the hearts of his people,

---

30 Augustine, *Psalms*, 4:200. See also Lewis, *Reflections on the Psalms*, 114–15.
31 See the note in Tate, *Psalms 51–100*, 355.
32 Perhaps "tents" is an ironic contrast to the tabernacle.

or rather, that they neither live nor breathe except in so far as he shines upon them.[33]

He is **a shield**, for

the godly are subject to dangers and perils from without, especially from enemies bodily and spiritual, and have need of preservation and defence from all adverse power, malice, and craftiness, and this protection only God is able to give.[34]

Both God (Ps. 84:11) and the King (84:9) are our **shield**. Together, Father and Son protect Christ's church.[35] The words **favor** (or "grace") and **honor** (or "glory") reach their fulfillment in the grace and glory that is given to the church in Jesus Christ.

The wonderful promise **No good thing does he withhold** rests on the fact that all goodness resides with God and none apart from him and on the fact that his gift of "every spiritual blessing" (i.e., every blessing from the Spirit)[36] is given to his people in Christ (Eph. 1:3; cf. Rom. 8:28–39). The phrase **those who walk uprightly**[37] (contrast "the tents of wickedness," Ps. 84:10) reminds us that only those in whom the Spirit of holiness is at work are truly members of the Messiah's people (cf. Heb. 12:14).

<blockquote>

[12]   O LORD of hosts,
    blessed is the one who trusts in you!

</blockquote>

The third **blessed** concludes the psalm on a note of faith alone, **the one** (the אָדָם, *adam*) **who trusts in you** (cf. Ps. 40:4). A blameless walk, avoidance of the tents of wickedness, joy in God, strength to travel to our home in God—all this is the mark not of the Pharisee but of the believer.

---

33 Calvin, *Psalms*, 3:365.
34 Dickson, *Psalms*, 2:75.
35 Hamilton, *Psalms*, 2:103.
36 The expression does not distinguish immaterial blessings from material but rather blessings that come from the Spirit from those that do not.
37 The word translated "uprightly" means "with integrity" or "blamelessly" (בְּתָמִים).

REFLECTION AND RESPONSE

1. We cannot make ourselves delight in God or enter into the desires of Psalm 84:1–4. This affection characterized fully the life of Jesus of Nazareth. He alone has desired the Father intensely and without wavering. It is only in him and by his Spirit that we may find our spirits welling up with an echo of 84:1–4. For this we must pray.

2. The beautiful picture of the small bird and her chicks can touch our hearts and cheer our souls when we grasp that we too are frail, lonely, and vulnerable and that there is yet a welcome and a "nest" for us in the presence of God. This is what Christ did on earth, as the most unlikely people found God in him; it is what he still does today.

3. When we set the journey of Psalm 84:5–8 alongside the desires of 84:1–4, it reminds us that no matter how much we may delight in God, the consummation only comes when we finally reach our heavenly home. Psalm 84:5–8 provides us with precious assurance for the journey, the pilgrimage through the dry and sorrowful valleys of this life. The promise of going "from strength to strength" may paradoxically be accompanied by increasing weakness of body and mind, and yet there is inward renewal by the Spirit (cf. 2 Cor. 4:16).

4. In our prayers we must not omit Psalm 84:9, knowing that it is perfectly answered in Jesus Christ. As we say, "Behold our shield, O God; / look on the face of your anointed," our petition turns to praise. For we know that the Father loves the Son. For us the burden of 84:9 is to press home to our hearts that every blessing in the triune God, every beauty and perfection in God, is ours in Jesus Christ alone.

5. The contrasts of Psalm 84:10 encourage us to meditate on the timeless wonder of the presence of the eternal God. This is the background to the precious promises of 84:11, which may be claimed by each believer in Christ. Almighty God gives us always and only what is good for us. This promise is perhaps most precious precisely at those times when it seems not to be true.

[Psalm 85] is full of Messianic hopes. The Incarnation is the true answer to the prayer of Israel; and in Christ almost every word of the second part [i.e., 85:8–13] finds its fulfilment.

ALEXANDER FRANCIS KIRKPATRICK
The Book of Psalms

PSALM 85

ORIENTATION

Psalm 85 teaches the church of Christ how to pray when in dire straits. It is far from the only psalm to do this. But it brings to bear on our troubles a grand truth: the triune God is unchanging in his covenant love, and therefore everything he has ever done, each action he is doing, and every work of salvation he will do is revealed in Jesus Christ, who is the same yesterday, today, and forever. When the psalmists look back on a past action of grace as the spur to their prayers, they do so not in the vague hope that God might see fit to do something similar again if he feels like it; rather, they are convinced that God is utterly consistent and therefore that what God has done is what God will and must do to be true to his nature.

Theodoret of Cyrus writes,

> The psalm prophesies both shadow and reality at one and the same time:
> . . . God . . . foreshadowed salvation . . . in the fortunes of Israel, freeing
> them from servitude, at one time to Egyptians, at another to Babylonians.
> . . . The psalm . . . foretells both the Jews' return from Babylon and the
> salvation of the . . . world.[1]

We do not know the historical context that lies behind the psalm. It is sometimes thought that 85:1–3 looks back to the first return of the exiles, while 85:4–7 expresses a sad disappointment at the subsequent history and

---

1   Theodoret of Cyrus, *Psalms*, 2:67.

a longing for more. This context fits well.[2] There is nothing in the psalm, however, that confines it to this time. Ernst Wilhelm Hengstenberg rightly concludes that "the description of the distress out of which the people had been delivered, is conveyed in terms which are entirely general"—and therefore, because no indications are clear or specific, "we are hence entitled to draw the conclusion that the Psalm was designed for the use of all times of protracted distress."[3]

The return from exile points forward to the final exodus given by Christ.[4] John Calvin notes that, for the Jews, "their restoration to their own country was connected with the kingdom of Christ, from which they anticipated an abundance of good things," and therefore he writes, "I cordially embrace the opinion which is held by many, that we have here a prophecy concerning the kingdom of Christ."[5]

Three motifs are noteworthy in the psalm:

1. In various forms the verb "to turn" (שׁוּב, *shub*) appears in 85:1, 3, 4, 6, and 8. Sometimes God is the subject of the turning; at other times his people turn.
2. The "land" features explicitly in 85:1, 9, and 12 and implicitly in 85:11 ("the ground . . . the sky"). A theology of creation is never far from the thought of the psalm.
3. Covenant words abound: salvation (85:4, 7, 9), steadfast love (85:7, 10), peace (85:8, 10), faithfulness (85:10, 11), and righteousness (85:10, 11, 13).

The word "good" (also a covenant blessing) links Psalm 85 with Psalm 84 (84:11; 85:12), as does the word "glory/favor" (84:11; 85:9). Psalm 84 voices an individual believer's longing for revived life; Psalm 85 does the same for the church.

2   Kirkpatrick argues persuasively for this background, citing Zech. 1:12 as a key text evidencing "the depression and despondency which were rapidly crushing the life of the feeble church of the restoration [i.e., from exile]." To these people, says Kirkpatrick, the psalm offers "the assurance that the prophetic promises of a glorious Messianic future were not a delusion." Kirkpatrick, *Psalms*, 2:510.
3   Hengstenberg, *Psalms*, 2:62; cf. Tate, *Psalms 51–100*, 368–69.
4   Hamilton, *Psalms*, 2:107–8.
5   Calvin, *Psalms*, 3:367, 375.

The voice of God is a thematic link with Psalm 81 (81:5; 85:8). It has connections with Psalms 44,[6] 80, and 126. Psalm 85 also echoes the language
of Exodus 32–34, a foundational text for the forgiveness of the covenant
Lord for his sinful church.

THE TEXT

Structure

Psalm 85:1–7 addresses God in the second person, while 85:8–13 speaks
of God in the third person.

Within this major division, the first section may be subdivided into
85:1–3 (marked by six perfect-tense verbs of the form "You did [some-
thing]") and 85:4–7. God's anger and the verb "to turn" are shared by 85:1–3
and 85:4–7. In 85:4–7 two imperatives (85:4) and an imperative and jussive
(85:7) bracket two questions (85:5–6).

The second section may be subdivided into 85:8–9, which gives what we
might call the headline answer to the preceding questions, and 85:10–13,
which gives the covenant answer.

Superscription

^S   To the choirmaster.[7] A Psalm of the Sons of Korah.[8]

85:1–3 All Past Favor of God to His Church
Has the Typical "Shape" of Jesus Christ

¹   Lord, you were favorable to your land;
          you restored the fortunes of Jacob.
²   You forgave the iniquity of your people;
          you covered all their sin.   *Selah*
³   You withdrew all your wrath;
          you turned from your hot anger.

---

6 As the first "sons of Korah" collection (Pss. 42–49) begins with an individual followed by a
   corporate lament (Pss. 42–43; 44), so it is with the second (Pss. 84; 85).
7 See on Ps. 4.
8 See on Ps. 42. In Hebrew the superscription is verse 1; subsequent verse numbers are increased
   by one.

In Psalm 85:1–3 six verbs, all in perfect-tense form, appear with no connectives (asyndetic), like the rattle of a machine gun. Some influential writers, including Augustine, Cassiodorus, and Martin Luther, have argued that these are something like the "prophetic perfect," celebrating what God will do in Christ. Augustine expresses this well: "The prophet sings of Christ who is to come, but he expresses himself in the past tense. He speaks of future events as though they were already past, because with God what to us is future is already accomplished."[9]

Nevertheless, it is much more likely that the verbs refer to some past experience of salvation.[10] Hengstenberg expresses the logic like this:

> There cannot be given any more solid foundation for a prayer in which it is desired that God should do something, than to appeal to what he *has already done*, inasmuch as, just because he is the unchangeable God, those deeds which proceed from the necessity of his being, partake of a prophetic character.[11]

In three pairs, the sequence moves back from result to cause. The use of the name the LORD sets a covenantal tone that will be celebrated later in a kaleidoscope of covenantal terms. **You were favorable** (i.e., "delightful") employs a warmly "affective"[12] word, used, for example, in Proverbs 3:12 of a father's delight in his son or in Psalm 44:3 of God's delight in his people. This delight is focused on **your land**, for the promised land—and finally the new creation—belongs to God before it belongs to his church. This early mention of **land** anticipates the restoration of the whole created order in Christ.

Much debate has surrounded the word translated **the fortunes**. The verb **you restored** is the verb "to turn" (שׁוּב, *shub*). But what did God "turn"? Either the noun "fortunes" (שְׁבוּת, *shebuth*) comes from the same root (שׁוּב, *shub*), or it derives from "a captivity" (שְׁבִית, *shebith*). The former yields the

---

9   Augustine, *Psalms*, 4:205. See also Cassiodorus, *Psalms*, 2:321–22; Luther, *Luther's Works*, 11:164. This has recently been revived by Zenger. Hossfeld and Zenger, *Psalms*, 2:360–63.

10   Goldingay, *Psalms*, 2:605; Tate, *Psalms 51–100*, 368; Delitzsch, *Psalms*, 3:9.

11   Hengstenberg, *Psalms*, 2:63. Dickson expresses a similar thought in more general terms: "As grace is the only ground of God's bounty to his people, so is it the only ground of his people's prayer for new experiences of his grace." Dickson, *Psalms*, 2:77.

12   Goldingay, *Psalms*, 2:606.

meaning "You turned the turning," that is, "You restored the fortunes"; the latter leads to "You turned the captivity" (KJV: "Thou hast brought back the captivity of Jacob"; NASB: "You restored the captivity of Jacob"), in which case the reference is probably to the return from exile. The arguments are partly technical (the meaning of the Hebrew noun)[13] and partly contextual (from the places where this phrase occurs in the Old Testament). The contextual evidence demonstrates that while the phrase sometimes refers to return from exile (esp. Ps. 126), it has a broader range of meaning; Job 42:10 and Ezekiel 16:53 are perhaps the clearest evidence for this semantic range since neither refers to return from exile. The translation "restored the fortunes" is best. Whenever this psalm is sung, the church of God looks back to some past time of God's evident delight in them, shown in the restoration of their circumstances.

Psalm 85:2 (redolent of Ex. 34:7) begins to move the thought back to what led to this favor. God smiles only on forgiven sinners. Two metaphors are given (both familiar from Ps. 32:1). First, **You forgave** (lit., "you lifted") **the iniquity** uses the image of sin as a burden (cf. "Christian" in *The Pilgrim's Progress*); second, **You covered all their sin** pictures sin as a stain on the ground that cries out for judgment (cf. Cain's in Gen. 4:10), unless it is covered by atonement (which is quite different from being covered up in pretense, as Ps. 32 makes clear). *Selah* seems here to be a pause for wonder, love, and praise rather than a structural marker.

Psalm 85:3 (with echoes of Ex. 34:6–7) drills down to the reason forgiveness is so urgent and necessary. In his holy perfection, God has, and must necessarily have, **wrath** and **hot anger** against sinners.[14] **You withdrew** means that God has taken it back; the cross of Christ shows us that he has taken back onto himself **all** the wrath formerly directed at his now-forgiven people. **You turned from** echoes the answer to the prayer of Moses in Exodus 32:12 ("Turn from your burning anger").

All this, in Psalm 85:1–3, looks back to some old covenant rescue. The echoes ring especially strongly from the episode of the golden calf

---

13 Part of the problem is that in the MT the word is pointed in three different ways (שְׁבִית, שְׁבוּת, שְׁבִית). For clear explanations, see *HALOT*, s.v. שְׁבוּת, שְׁבִית; Hossfeld and Zenger, *Psalms*, 2:360na; Goldingay, *Psalms*, 2:155; Tate, *Psalms 51–100*, 364n2b.

14 Christopher Ash and Steve Midgley, *The Heart of Anger: How the Bible Transforms Anger in Our Understanding and Experience* (Wheaton, IL: Crossway, 2021), chaps. 10–15.

(Ex. 32–34). This rescue, including the turning away of the wrath of God, the forgiveness of sins, and the delight of God in his people, typifies and has the "shape" of what God will do in Christ, the Son in whom he delights. Every subsequent season of God's favor on Christ's church has the same fundamental "shape": the turning away of anger, the fresh forgiveness of sins, the refreshment of delight.

85:4–7 The Church of Christ Prays in Harmony with This Past Christ-Shaped Favor

4	Restore us again, O God of our salvation,
	and put away your indignation toward us!
5	Will you be angry with us forever?
	Will you prolong your anger to all generations?
6	Will you not revive us again,
	that your people may rejoice in you?
7	Show us your steadfast love, O LORD,
	and grant us your salvation.

The urgent prayer of Psalm 85:4–7 builds closely on God's Christ-shaped rescue in the past. **Restore us again** echoes 85:1. The prominence of God's anger (**your indignation**, a word that has overtones of vexation and grief,[15] and **your anger**) echoes 85:3. The word **salvation** brackets the prayer (85:4, 7) and reappears in 85:9. In 85:6, **revive us again** is literally "turn [שׁוּב, *shub*] and give us life." Luther perceptively notes that this prayer is answered when God turns toward us in the incarnation and unites the divine nature with our human nature so as to give us life.[16] This answer reaches its climax when the Father gives life to the Son, who has been crucified for us. **That your people may rejoice in you** reminds us that "when God changeth the cheer of his people, their joy should not be in the gift, but in the giver."[17]

Psalm 85:7 sums up the prayer. God will **show us** his covenant **steadfast love** and give us his **salvation** when he sends his Son. Augustine says bluntly

---

15 The root (כעס) is translated "irritation," "grief," "vexation," and "provocation" in the ESV in 1 Sam. 1:6; Pss. 6:7; 10:14; Ezek. 20:28.

16 Luther, *Luther's Works*, 11:158.

17 Dickson, *Psalms*, 2:79.

that "'your salvation' means your Christ" and paraphrases this prayer, "Grant us your Christ, let us know your Christ, let us see your Christ."[18]

85:8–13 The Triune God "Speaks" Christ's Salvation to His People
85:8–9 The Headline Answer

8   Let me hear what God the LORD will speak,
        for he will speak peace to his people, to his saints;
        but let them not turn back to folly.
9   Surely his salvation is near to those who fear him,
        that glory may dwell in our land.

It is sometimes thought that **Let me hear** introduces a new speaker, but there is no need for this. For **what God the LORD**[19] **will speak** is what he has consistently spoken—certainly from Exodus 32–34 onward. Cassiodorus rightly says that the speaker "proclaims the coming of the Lord Saviour."[20] Nevertheless, as in the similar Habakkuk 2:1, the Spirit-inspired psalmist needs to quiet his heart and pay attention to what God says, just as we do.

The clause **For**[21] **he will speak peace** sums up the covenant blessing of peace (cf. Lev. 26:6; Num. 6:22–26); this is promised (cf. Isa. 57:19; Hag. 2:9) and given in Christ (cf. Luke 2:14; John 14:27; Rom. 5:1; Gal. 6:16; Eph. 2:14). It encompasses far more than the absence of strife and includes the well-being of the whole created order. This is promised **to his people, to his saints,** where the latter word (חֲסִידִים, *khasidim*) denotes the true church, to whom God gives covenant love and whose members' lives are marked by covenant love toward others. This focus on the true church is heightened by the final line of Psalm 85:8, for turning back (the verb שׁוּב, *shub*, again) to sinful **folly** is a sign of one who is a member of Christ's church in name but not in nature. **Those who fear him** (85:9) stresses that God's peace is for the true church.

---

18 Augustine, *Psalms*, 4:210–12. Similarly, Luther says that this verse "speaks of the first advent and the first showing of the Lord Christ." Luther, *Luther's Works*, 11:159.

19 "God the LORD" is an unusual word order. Some divide "God" and "the LORD" and place them in separate sections, "Let me hear what God will speak; the LORD will speak peace . . ."; the meaning is unchanged.

20 Cassiodorus, *Psalms*, 2:324.

21 The word translated "for" (כִּי) may convey emphasis here (CSB: "Surely").

Surely (אַךְ, *ak*, emphatic, "Yes!") **his salvation** (prayed for in 85:7, given in Christ) **is near,** a contrast with the fearful "forever" and "to all generations" of 85:5. This salvation came near in the kingdom of Jesus Christ (Matt. 3:2; 4:17) and is nearer now than when we first believed (Rom. 13:11). **That glory may dwell in our land** expresses a beautiful confidence that the visible presence of God, promised in the covenant (e.g., Ex. 29:43–46; Isa. 40:5; 46:13; 51:5; 56:1; 60:1–2; Hab. 2:14; Hag. 2:7–9), will be seen and will **dwell** permanently on earth through Christ (cf. Luke 2:32; John 1:14). As Augustine observes, "The prophet prays that in the very land where he himself was born a still greater glory may dwell, because from there Christ began to be preached. . . . There did Christ appear."[22]

85:10–13 The Covenant Answer

10   Steadfast love and faithfulness meet;
       righteousness and peace kiss each other.
11   Faithfulness springs up from the ground,
       and righteousness looks down from the sky.
12   Yes, the LORD will give what is good,
       and our land will yield its increase.
13   Righteousness will go before him
       and make his footsteps a way.

It is possible to overanalyze Psalm 85:10–13. **Steadfast love, faithfulness, righteousness**, and **peace** are covenantal attributes of God and exist in perfect harmony within the divine simplicity. There is no tension and has never been any conflict between them.[23] God's **steadfast love** is his eternal, covenantal loving-kindness fulfilled in Christ.[24] God's **faithfulness** is his absolute truthfulness to all his promises, which find their "Yes" in Christ (2 Cor. 1:20). God's **righteousness** is his covenantal commitment

---

22 Augustine, *Psalms*, 4:215.
23 In this I disagree with Tucker and Grant, who suggest that "steadfast love" and "peace" are covenant blessings, while "faithfulness" and "righteousness" are covenant responsibilities. Tucker and Grant, *Psalms*, 2:267. I do not think the broader uses of the words support this, for all four are both covenant attributes of God and covenantal responsibilities of his people.
24 Luther develops this harmony of the attributes of Christ at some length. Luther, *Luther's Works*, 11:169–71.

to "do the right thing" by keeping his promises and rescuing his people without compromising his holiness (see Rom. 3:21–26 for New Testament commentary on this theme in the light of the atonement). **Peace**, as we have seen from Psalm 85:8, sums up the covenant blessings that are ours in Christ.[25] Psalm 85:10 pictures four of these, like personified attributes, in a glad alliance, **meet**ing, **kiss**ing, in joyful cooperation, seen for the first time in human history embodied in Jesus Christ on earth, working together for the salvation of Christ's church.

In 85:11 the additional dimension of the created order is introduced, with the picture of **faithfulness** springing **up from the ground** and meeting **righteousness** looking **down from the sky** (cf. similar imagery in Isa. 32:16–17; 45:8). The broken creation, in which the will of God is not yet done on earth in the same way that it is done in heaven, is finally restored in Christ, who will rule all things in the new creation (Eph. 1:10). There may also be the implication that, finally, the church of Christ will be marked by the character of Christ and that these attributes will be seen in us.

Psalm 85:12 builds on the creation language of 85:11. **What is good** means covenant blessings (cf. on Ps. 4:6), as does the **land** yielding **its increase** (cf. Lev. 26:4; Ps. 67:6). This glory of a restored creation is prophesied in, for example, Hosea 2:21–23; Joel 2:18–27; and Amos 9:13–15 and will be fulfilled in Christ (see Rev. 21:1–22:5).

There is some debate about the precise imagery in Psalm 85:13, but probably it indicates **righteousness** (representing all the covenant attributes) walking before God like a herald. In some measure, John the Baptist occupied this kind of role (cf. Isa. 40:3–4). The church of Christ is to be marked by growing righteousness of life; the new creation will be a place "in which righteousness dwells" (2 Pet. 3:13).

REFLECTION AND RESPONSE

1. The move from past favor (Ps. 85:1–3) through present prayer (85:4–7) to the assurance of future salvation (85:8–13) is perhaps the most important theme to appropriate from the psalm. We can meditate on past rescues,

---

25 Further, after the order of Melchizedek, Jesus Christ is "king of righteousness" and "king of peace" (Heb. 7:2). See Bonar, *Psalms*, 254.

former times of God's blessing on the church, and it is good to do so. As we do that, our attention will be directed, by 85:1–3, to the Christ-shaped nature of those blessings, whenever they may have occurred. All genuine times of God's favor to the church have been marked by the glad assurance of the forgiveness of sins and the turning away of God's anger, given to us in Christ alone. We naturally focus our attention on our troubles; the Spirit shows us in this psalm how to concentrate on the need for restored relationship with God.[26]

2. There are times of phony prosperity for churches when all seems to be well (in terms, perhaps, of numbers, budgets, influence, or facilities), but unless the prominence of forgiveness, the turning away of God's anger, and glad assurance are present, no time in church history can be reckoned a genuine time of gospel blessing.

3. When we do look back to such genuinely Christ-shaped days, however, we may be stirred to pray Psalm 85:4–7 with a glad urgency, knowing that we always call on the triune God to do what he does in Christ when he acts to save. As we pray this psalm, we may attend quietly and joyfully to the beautiful painting of covenant fulfillment in Christ that the psalmist gives us in 85:9–13. We enter into the vivid imagery, while remembering the simplicity of God (and therefore that the words are no more than poetic personifications of his indivisible attributes). We are encouraged to rejoice in the beautiful harmony there is in Christ, the wonder of his atoning death, and the cosmic grandeur of what he will do in remaking a broken world.

---

26 This point is helpfully brought out in Eveson, *Psalms*, 2:98.

*Notice how abundantly and masterly [David in Psalm 86] praises
God and refers to his goodness, loyalty, and power in order to
warm up his faith and heat up his prayer. We should do the same.*

MARTIN LUTHER
Summaries

*It having been difficult in the judgment of carnal
reason for David to escape from the distresses with
which he was environed, he sets in opposition to its
conclusions the infinite goodness and power of God.*

JOHN CALVIN
Commentary on the Psalms

PSALM 86

ORIENTATION

Psalm 86, an intensely personal psalm, may be considered a prayer that each believer prays to Christ, through Christ, and with Christ. That it is "a prayer of David" suggests, as so often with the Davidic psalms, that Jesus Christ prayed it on earth. Indeed, it makes perfect sense to think of what it would have meant to him. That each believer then prays it through and with Christ is a pattern we are familiar with in the Psalms. But it also invites us to speak it to Christ, for he is our Lord, and what is affirmed of God is true of Christ as God.

Augustine develops this remarkable Christological theme in his introduction to Psalm 86, drawing out its implications for prayer and using this psalm as an example. Because Christ is God, we pray to Christ. Because the church is the body of Christ, Christ prays for us as our priest, and we pray in union with him. All that we pray, we pray in union with Christ.[1]

The repeated covenant term "servant" (86:2, 4, 16) is appropriate for David, who is designated "the servant of the LORD" in the superscription to Psalm 18 (cf. 2 Sam. 7:5). Together with Isaiah's "servant of the Lord," this theme finds its fulfillment in Jesus, the Lord's final servant (cf. Acts 3:13, 26), for "David [in Ps. 86] thus becomes a type of the Messiah as the Suffering Servant" (cf. Heb. 5:7).[2]

The psalm gives no indication of the historical circumstances that led to it being written, beyond the very general language of Psalm 86:14.[3] For the canonical context, the links with other psalms are of two kinds.

---

1 Augustine, *Psalms*, 4:220. Augustine's exposition of this theme, though not easy to follow, is profound.
2 Eveson, *Psalms*, 2:196.
3 For example, Calvin thinks it arises from the period of David's persecution by Saul, while Hengstenberg argues for the time of Absalom's revolt. Calvin, *Psalms*, 3:380; Hengstenberg, *Psalms*, 3:67.

First, Psalm 86 echoes the language of many other Davidic psalms.[4] Robert Alter comments, "A reader who has been going through the Book of Psalms in sequence by this point will have encountered almost every line of this poem, with minor variations, elsewhere."[5]

As Allan Harman notes, "Every verse is an echo of another part of the Old Testament. Well-known Scripture has been moulded into a new song."[6] There is no reason to suppose that David himself did not do this. John Goldingay helpfully cautions against the wooden idea that these are literary quotations stitched together by an amateur scribe; rather, he suggests, this is "more like the relationship between [the book of] Revelation and the OT," in which the writer is so soaked in the Old Testament Scriptures that he can hardly help but allude to them or quote them.[7] How much more might this be the case with David echoing his own—perhaps earlier—psalms. As Philip Eveson writes, it was not "that David looked up texts and strung different verses together to form this prayer. His mind was full of Scriptural phraseology and this fresh prayer flowed as a result of hiding God's word in his heart."[8]

Second, the psalm has significant links with the adjacent Korah psalms in book 3 (Pss. 84; 85; 87; 88). With Psalm 84 is shared (1) life/living (84:2; 86:2) and (2) "who trusts in you" (84:12; 86:2). With Psalm 85 we may note the following: (1) "life" (85:6 [lit., "turn and make live"]; 86:2), (2) godly/saints (85:8; 86:2), (3) salvation (85:7, 9; 86:2), (4) forgiveness (85:2; 86:5—though different words are used), (5) "good" (85:12; 86:5, 17 ["favor"]), (6) "steadfast love" (85:7, 10; 86:5, 13), (7) the verb "to turn" (Ps. 85 [frequent]; 86:16), and (8) the echoes of Exodus 34:6 (85:10–11; 86:5, 10, 15). Links with Psalms 87 and 88 are noted where those psalms are treated.

There are also three kinds of wider links within book 3. (1) The motif of the "gods" (86:8) is shared with Psalm 82; (2) the phrase "the day of my trouble" (86:7) echoes 77:2; and (3) the motif of the nations of the world,

---

4   These are too many to mention. In this commentary we focus on Ps. 86 as it stands. For those who wish to explore the echoes, many have been noted, for example, in Delitzsch, *Psalms*, 3:14–16; Kirkpatrick, *Psalms*, 2:514n1; Harman, *Psalms*, 2:639–44.

5   Alter, *Psalms*, 303.

6   Harman, *Psalms*, 2:630.

7   Goldingay, *Psalms*, 2:619.

8   Eveson, *Psalms*, 2:101.

so strikingly stated in 86:9, is shared in various ways with 79:1, 6; 80:8; and 82:8 and shared implicitly with Psalm 83 (in God's judgment of nations).

In addition, the psalm echoes Exodus 32–34 (the golden calf and its aftermath).

Putting these kinds of links together—especially those with psalms elsewhere in book 3 and those with other Davidic psalms—may help us discern why this one Davidic psalm has been included in book 3. While there is no general agreement about this question, I suggest that the reason may—at least partly—be to suggest to believers struggling with exile that their spiritual pain is not new. David their anointed king has been here before, and what cheered David can encourage them; they too may pray what David prayed and expect the answer for which David hoped.[9] It also reminded the believers in exile of their hope for a future Messiah in David's line.[10] This suggests to us that we may set this prayer of Jesus Christ alongside our struggles and pray it again with and through him in our later struggles, which are the overflow of his sufferings.

THE TEXT

Structure
While Allen Ross is correct that "any number of arrangements can be made because there are a number of themes that are repeated within the psalm itself,"[11] the most natural division (as in the ESV paragraphing) is probably to take the following three sections:[12] Psalm 86:1–7 (petition), 8–13 (worship of the greatness of God), and 14–17 (petition). At the center of each is a declaration about God (86:5, 10, 15).

One interesting feature is the unusual number of emphatic second-person singular pronouns.[13] While most of the second-person references are in the form of pronominal suffixes, six of them are emphatic, using

---

9   Eveson helpfully notes that this Davidic psalm prepares us for Ps. 89 with its unremitting focus on God's covenant with David. Eveson, *Psalms*, 2:102.

10 Hamilton, *Psalms*, 2:114.

11 Ross, *Psalms*, 2:784.

12 I have found the most persuasive detailed structural analysis to be that of Zenger in Hossfeld and Zenger, *Psalms*, 2:369.

13 This paragraph follows Walter Brueggemann, *The Message of the Psalms: A Theological Commentary*, Augsburg Old Testament Studies (Minneapolis: Augsburg, 1984), 60–63.

the separate pronoun "you" (אַתָּה, *atah*). These occur twice in each section (italicized below), and they may be arranged chiastically. They appear near the beginning and end (86:2, 17) and in each declarative verse about God's nature (86:5, 10, 15).

> **a** 86:2: "*You* are my God"
>> **b** 86:5: "For *you*, O Lord"
>>> **c** 86:10: "For *you* are great"
>>> **c'** 86:10: "*You* alone are God"
>> **b'** 86:15: "But *you*, O Lord"
> **a'** 86:17: "Because *you*, LORD"

Superscription

^S A Prayer of David.[14]

The designation **A Prayer** appears above Psalm 17 (David) and Psalm 90 (Moses).[15] The appropriateness of this title for Psalm 86 is clear: the psalm is replete with petition, and the noun "prayer" appears again in 86:6 (cf. the link with 84:8). There may be an allusion to 72:20, which concludes the collection termed "The prayers of David" and encourages us to link Psalm 86 with books 1 and 2; here is "a prayer of David" to set alongside the collection "The prayers of David."

86:1–7 The Passionate Prayer of Christ and Each Covenant Servant

1 Incline your ear, O LORD, and answer me,
    for I am poor and needy.
2 Preserve my life, for I am godly;
    save your servant, who trusts in you—you are my God.
3 Be gracious to me, O Lord,
    for to you do I cry all the day.
4 Gladden the soul of your servant,
    for to you, O Lord, do I lift up my soul.

---

14 In Hebrew the superscription is the start of verse 1.
15 The designation "A Prayer" also heads Pss. 102 and 142.

This passionate prayer rests on the covenant connection between the one who prays and the God to whom he prays. This connection is signaled by the covenant name (the LORD, Ps. 86:1, 6) and the covenant terms **your servant**[16] (86:2, 4, 16), the **Lord** (86:3, 4, 5, 8, 9, 12, 15), **my God** (86:2), and **steadfast love** (86:5). **Incline your ear**[17] is balanced with **Give ear** (86:1, 6). **Answer me** is bracketed by the confidence of **You answer me** (86:1, 7).

The condition of the one praying is given in two parallel phrases with an unusual word order, literally, "Poor and needy, I [am]," and "Godly, I [am]."[18] To be **poor and needy**[19] indicates spiritual dependence on God rather than (necessarily) material poverty, although the two are often associated; the phrase may include those who are materially rich so long as they are "poor in spirit" (Matt. 5:3).[20] The word **godly** (חָסִיד, *khasid*) means one who first receives the covenant love of God (חֶסֶד, *khesed*) and then demonstrates that love in human relationships. In its perfection, only Christ can claim this, but for those in Christ, the word signals loving commitment and belonging, expressed in trust (**who trusts in you**)[21] rather than boasting, and is focused on covenant grace (**You are my God**).[22]

There is perhaps a progression in the appeals in Psalm 86:1–4, from hearing and answering prayer (86:1) through much-needed rescue (86:2) and the outpouring of grace (86:3) all the way to the giving of joy (**Gladden the soul**, 86:4). The idiom to **lift up** the **soul** conveys the thought of a human being in urgent need (the word **soul** often conveys a human being in the aspect of needs or desires) raising his or her eyes in worship and trustful dependence expressed in prayer.

---

16 About half the Old Testament occurrences of the expression "your servant" occur in Ps. 119. Hossfeld and Zenger, *Psalms*, 2:372.

17 Theodoret vividly imagines "a sick person unable through weakness to speak more loudly and obliging the physician to bring his ear down to his mouth." Theodoret of Cyrus, *Psalms*, 2:72.

18 Each has the personal pronoun אֲנִי at the close of the phrase.

19 For other examples of this pairing in the Psalms, see Pss. 35:10; 37:14; 40:17; 70:5; 74:21; 109:16, 22.

20 Augustine applies this teaching thoughtfully to the rich in the light of 1 Tim. 6:17. Augustine, *Psalms*, 4:222–23.

21 The Hebrew of Ps. 86:2b has an unusual word order, lit., "Save your servant—you are my God—who trusts in you." Some (e.g., NIV, REB) put "you are my God" as the opening of 86:3, of which the first line is thought by some to be too short, but there is no good reason to depart from the MT phrasing. See Hossfeld and Zenger, *Psalms*, 2:369; Harman, *Psalms*, 2:640.

22 On this theme, see Augustine, *Psalms*, 4:223; Lewis, *Reflections on the Psalms*, 112–13; Bonhoeffer, *Prayerbook of the Bible*, 172; Ross, *Psalms*, 2:781.

⁵   For you, O Lord, are good and forgiving,
      abounding in steadfast love to all who call upon you.

In Psalm 86:1–4 the connecting word "for" has been used to ground the prayer in the poverty of the psalmist (86:1), in the covenant standing of the psalmist (86:2), and in the persistent prayers of the psalmist (86:3–4). Now in 86:5 it reaches its climax; above all, prayer rests on the nature of God, who is **good** (a frequent covenant refrain later in the Psalter, e.g., 100:5; 106:1; 107:1; 118:1, 29; 136). Commenting on finding true goodness only in God, Augustine writes, "The psalmist was disgusted by the bitterness of earthly things and longed to taste sweetness; he sought a fountain of sweetness, but did not find it on earth. Whichever way he turned, he always found scandals, terrors, troubles and temptations."[23]

Further, God is **forgiving**, the adjective (only here in the Old Testament) indicating that God is ready to forgive and that this is—in the words of the Book of Common Prayer—his "property," proper to his essential nature. Finally, God is **abounding in steadfast love** (cf. Ex. 34:6–7); it is rich and inexhaustible.

⁶   Give ear, O Lord, to my prayer;
      listen to my plea for grace.
⁷   In the day of my trouble I call upon you,
      for you answer me.

In Psalm 86:3–7 the verb "to call"[24] occurs three times (86:3 ["cry"], 5, 7). The logic is clear: you abound "in steadfast love to all who call upon you" (86:5); therefore I claim this promise, and "to you do I cry [i.e., call] all the day" (86:3), and **in the day of my trouble I call upon you** (86:7)—that is, I will trust your abundant steadfast love given also to me. Commenting on the implications of the phrase "all the day," Augustine beautifully imagines members of the church taking turns in prayer through history: "You have cried out during your days, and your days have expired; someone else took your place and cried out in his days; you here, he there, she somewhere else."[25]

---

23 Augustine, *Psalms*, 4:226.
24 קָרָא.
25 Augustine, *Psalms*, 4:225.

Give ear echoes 86:1, **my prayer** alludes to the superscription, and the **plea for grace** reflects 86:3 ("Be gracious"). The **day of my trouble** (which means distress or pressure, with the feeling of being squeezed) intensifies the spiritual poverty and need of 86:1.

86:8–13 The Wholehearted Worship of a Covenant Servant

Although Psalm 86:11 includes a petition, 86:8–13 makes no request for rescue, in sharp contrast to 86:1–7 and 86:14–17. The canvas broadens from the squeezed circumstances of the psalmist ("trouble," 86:7) to an expanse that extends vertically from the heavens above ("the gods," 86:8) to Sheol beneath and horizontally across "all the nations" (86:9).

8   There is none like you among the gods, O Lord,
      nor are there any works like yours.
9   All the nations you have made shall come
      and worship before you, O Lord,
      and shall glorify your name.
10   For you are great and do wondrous things;
      you alone are God.

In 86:8 we look up to the God who is truly God. Both lines of 86:8 begin with the word "there is/are not" (אֵין, *en*; i.e., "There is not one like you among the gods, O Lord, / and there are not works like yours"). **Gods** means the gods of the nations (who appear in 86:9, as in 89:7–14; 95:3–5; 96:4–5; and frequently),[26] those spiritual beings who have no independent existence (i.e., they are not divine) and yet have some kind of demonic existence. The root of the noun **works** is the same as that for the verbs **made** and **do** in 86:9–10. Far from the gods of the nations (and any other idols today) having an autonomous existence, **the nations** whose allegiance they claim have been **made** by the true God; they are a part of his **works**, for he is the only Creator of all that exists. Psalm 86:8 expresses forthrightly the fact

26 Part of the background is the gods of Pharaoh's Egypt, whose defeat is celebrated in the closely parallel words of Ex. 15:11. Bonar comments on Ps. 86:8, "There was a time when Israel sang verse 8 at the Red Sea; there has been a time when the Church has sung it in view of the cross; there is a time at hand when Christ and every member of his shall sing it before the throne." Bonar, *Psalms*, 258.

that informs the absolute necessity that we speak of God only in the ways he has revealed about himself. We cannot work upward by analogy from created things; as Augustine says,

> Whatever else the human mind may think of, nothing that is made is like the Maker. Everything in the universe, except God himself, was made by God. Who could conceive an adequate idea of the difference between him who made it, and what was made?[27]

Psalm 86:9, "one of the great missionary statements of the Psalter,"[28] draws a bold conclusion from the God-ness of God declared in 86:8. Because God has made **all the nations**, it is certain that they will **come** (implicitly to Zion, fulfilled in Christ) **and worship** before him,[29] and they **shall glorify his name** (cf. 96:8), that name above every name finally given to the risen Christ. Revelation 15:3–4 echoes Psalm 86:8–9, and the words "All nations will come / and worship you" are taken closely from 86:9.[30] John Calvin rightly says that David "has an eye to the kingdom of Christ, prior to whose coming God gave only the initial or dawning manifestation of his glory, which at length was diffused through the whole world by the preaching of the Gospel."[31] Theodoret of Cyrus writes, "The time after the Incarnation . . . demonstrated the truth of the prophecy: after the saving Passion the divine choir of the apostles were sent into the whole world, the Lord saying to them, 'Go, make disciples of all nations.'"[32]

Psalm 86:10 almost repeats 86:8, with two uses of the emphatic personal pronoun (**you**), with the verb **do** echoing **works like yours**, and with **you alone** pressing home the incomparable God-ness of God. The phrase **wondrous things** can be used both of creation and redemption (cf. 78:4, 11, 32 ["wonders"]). For the statement **You alone are God**, see 2 Kings 19:15 (= Isa. 37:16; cf. Neh. 9:6; Ps. 83:18).

---

27 Augustine, *Psalms*, 4:232.
28 Tucker and Grant, *Psalms*, 2:281.
29 For variations on this theme in the Old Testament, see Isa. 2:1–5 // Mic. 4:1–5; 25:6–7; 60; 66:18–19; Hag. 2:1–9; Zech. 8:20–22; 14:16–19. David himself introduced this theme, to be fulfilled as a result of the sufferings of Christ, in Ps. 22:27–31 (see on Ps. 22).
30 Beale and McDonough, "Revelation," in *CNTOT* 1134.
31 Calvin, *Psalms*, 3:386.
32 Theodoret of Cyrus, *Psalms*, 2:74.

This celebration of the sheer, objective God-ness of God would have been eloquent on the lips of the Lord Jesus and is given that we may echo it today. It leads in to Psalm 86:11–13, in which Christ prayed, and his church prays, to respond with wholehearted praise.

11   Teach me your way, O LORD,
        that I may walk in your truth;
        unite my heart to fear your name.

The petition of Psalm 86:11a–b is expressed twice in parallel. **Teach me your way** asks the Lord not simply to show the believer what is the right way but to lead him or her in it (cf. Ex. 33:13; Pss. 25:4–5, 8; 27:11; 119 [often]), **that I may walk in your truth**. The unique and striking final line (86:11c), **Unite my heart to fear your name** asks that all the affections be directed in wholehearted integrity, with an undivided heart, toward the reverent fear of the God who has revealed himself in his "name." This prayer was answered perfectly in the life of the Lord Jesus on earth; it is now poured out by his Holy Spirit on his church (cf. Jer. 32:39; Ezek. 11:19–20; 36:26–27),[33] for God "leads us to his way by leading us to his Christ; he leads us in his way by leading us in his Christ."[34] Here is true purity of heart (Matt. 5:8) and the only remedy to the "double-mindedness" that characterizes the unregenerate (James 1:5–8; 4:8).

12   I give thanks to you, O Lord my God, with my whole heart,
        and I will glorify your name forever.
13   For great is your steadfast love toward me;
        you have delivered my soul from the depths of Sheol.

The undivided heart, prayed for in Psalm 86:11, pours out thanksgiving in 86:12 and does so **forever**, adding the dimension of time to the canvas of high, low, and wide space. This, the perfection of praise, awaits the coming of the only man in history with an undivided heart, who thanks the Father with his **whole heart** (cf. Deut. 6:5; Pss. 111:1; 138:1), who makes known the

33 Hossfeld and Zenger, *Psalms*, 2:374.
34 Augustine, *Psalms*, 4:235.

Father's name and glorifies him forever (John 17:1, 4, 6, 26). Only in Christ can we echo this praise. The **steadfast love** of Psalm 86:13 is **great** (echoing the "great" in 86:10) first **toward** Christ, with whom the Father has been in an eternal covenant of love; in Christ it is great toward David and now to each member of Christ's church. Christ has been **delivered . . . from the depths of Sheol**,[35] and in him, so have David and all his church. James Hamilton is right to argue, "The deliverance from Sheol almost suggests that the restored Zion (cf. Pss. 84–85) is led by the resurrected king from David's line."[36]

86:14–17 The Passionate Prayer of a Covenant Servant

[14]   O God, insolent men have risen up against me;
  a band of ruthless men seeks my life,
  and they do not set you before them.

In Psalm 86:14 the source of "the day of my trouble" (86:7) comes into view, at least in general terms. **Insolent men** means those who are proud and presumptuous; it hints at the scoffers of Psalm 1:1.[37] For **ruthless men**, see 37:35 and 54:3. The **band** (עֵדָה, *edah*) in other contexts indicates a congregation but here something more like a criminal gang or a hunting pack. To **have risen up** means either courtroom prosecution (e.g., Deut. 19:16) or warfare (Deut. 20:12; 22:26 ["attacks" = "rises up"]; Pss. 3:1; 27:3) or both. The aim is to seek the **life** of the Messiah and his people, for this hostility brooks no negotiation. At the root of the enmity lies this: **they do not set** God **before them** (contrast the Messiah in 16:8).

[15]   But you, O Lord, are a God merciful and gracious,
  slow to anger and abounding in steadfast love and faithfulness.

Psalm 86:5 and 10 echoed parts of Exodus 34:6–7. Psalm 86:15 does so emphatically. Allan Harman notes, "No greater appeal could be made

---

35 The "depths" of Sheol (cf. Deut. 32:22) does not designate some separate area of the dead but rather the furthest extent of Sheol.

36 Hamilton, *Psalms*, 2:114.

37 The Hebrew word (זֵדִים) appears in Pss. 19:13 ("presumptuous sins"); 119:21, 51, 69, 78, 85, 122; Prov. 21:24 (with the link to scoffers).

in proclaiming the character of God than to use the very words that God used of himself."[38] God is **merciful** (moved by the sufferings of his Christ and Christ's church), **gracious** (stooping low to show undeserved favor to Christ's people in need), **slow to anger** (for judgment is his "strange work," and he is determined to save Christ's people), and **abounding in steadfast love and faithfulness**, so much so that he made these qualities incarnate in Jesus Christ (John 1:14, in which "grace" means much the same as "steadfast love," and "truth" is the same as covenant "faithfulness"). The God who persisted in love with his people after the golden calf (Ex. 32) continues in love to his exiled remnant and finally sends his Son to be the Savior of the world.

> [16]   Turn to me and be gracious to me;
>   give your strength to your servant,
>   and save the son of your maidservant.
> [17]   Show me a sign of your favor,
>   that those who hate me may see and be put to shame
>   because you, LORD, have helped me and comforted me.

Turn to me echoes the theme of turning in Psalm 85. **Be gracious to me** echoes 86:3 (see 25:16 for line 1). To **give your strength to your** covenant **servant** is what God did partially to David in victories, what God did comprehensively to Jesus Christ in resurrection, and what he now does by that resurrection power in Christ's people (cf. Eph. 1:19–23). There is debate about the significance of **the son of your maidservant**. Most likely it means a servant not bought in the slave market but born in the household, with full rights as part of the family (cf. Ex. 21:4; 23:12; Ps. 116:16).[39] Perhaps it reaches its fulfillment when Jesus is born of the Lord's "handmaid" (Luke 1:38 KJV).[40]

Show me is literally "Work for me," using the root so prominent in Psalm 86:8 ("works"), 86:9 ("made"), and 86:10 ("do"). **Favor** is literally "good" (cf. "You, O Lord, are good," 86:5). The **sign** is here a visible demonstration so that **those who hate me may see** it. This sign, fulfilled in the

---

38 Harman, *Psalms*, 2:644.
39 Hossfeld and Zenger, *Psalms*, 2:375; Tate, *Psalms 51–100*, 383. The NIV rendering—"because I serve you, just as my mother did"—goes beyond what the Hebrew warrants.
40 This is suggested by Augustine, *Psalms*, 4:241.

death and resurrection of Christ, is the preeminent work of God to **put to shame** the devil and all his hosts (cf. Col. 2:15). Supremely, the resurrection demonstrates that the covenant Lord has **helped** and **comforted** his Christ; the bodily resurrection of each believer will be the final proof of the same wonderful help and comfort.

REFLECTION AND RESPONSE

1. As with many other psalms, it is instructive to read the prayer first as the words of Jesus on earth and to meditate on what they meant for him, in fulfillment of all that David foreshadowed. But then we must make this prayer our own, individually as a man or woman in Christ.

2. The phrase "poor and needy" (Ps. 86:1) reminds us that God has given us—as he gave to Jesus on earth—"this prayer for the poor and afflicted," so that "despair . . . may not overwhelm our minds under our greatest afflictions."[41] Let us then make use of this God-given prayer. Indeed, as David Dickson argues, whereas "misbelief" seeks to turn distress "unto discouragement and desperation" for us, faith grasps from this psalm that "affliction and weakness, and want [lack] of all help and comfort from man, are the Lord's forerunners to advertise [announce to] the believer, that the Lord is coming."[42]

3. As we pray Psalm 86:1–4, the petition for a gladdened soul goes beyond a simple, almost gloomy, prayer to be rescued. "Fearing that [my soul] would wither away in bitterness and lose all sweetness of your grace," writes Augustine, "I lifted it up to you. Give it delight in your presence; you alone are delight, and the world is full of bitterness." He goes on to say that "our hearts will not go moldy, if raised up to [Christ]." Just as we move grain up from the damp basement, where it can go moldy, so, rather than allowing "your heart to molder on earth, . . . lift your heart to heaven."[43]

4. The prayers of the psalm are punctuated with wonderful affirmations of faith in 86:5, 8–10,[44] and 15. In our prayers we do well not to focus entirely

---

41 Calvin, *Psalms*, 3:380–81.

42 Dickson, *Psalms*, 2:84.

43 Augustine, *Psalms*, 4:225–26.

44 Kidner shrewdly describes the praise of Ps. 86:8–13 as "a deliberate act of praise—deliberate, because the final verses reveal no abatement of the pressure, and no sign, as yet, of an answer." Kidner, *Psalms*, 2:311.

on our need but to lift our hearts to what we know of the powerful and gracious character of God in Christ, as revealed in Exodus 34:6–7 and all through the Scriptures. It is not a waste of time to rehearse these declarations in prayer. In some ways, the most important petition is that of Psalm 86:11, to be taught God's ways in Christ and given an undivided heart by the Spirit of Christ. If God gives me such a heart, I will give thanks gladly, praise wholeheartedly, and then pray with assured passion.

5. Psalm 86:11 also presses home to us with unrelenting realism that by nature our hearts are divided. Calvin writes of

a tacit contrast, which has not been sufficiently attended to, between the unwavering purpose with which the heart of man cleaves to God when it is under the guidance of the Holy Spirit, and the disquietude with which it is distracted and tossed so long as it fluctuates amidst its own affections.

Therefore, he goes on, "in the word *unite*, there is a very beautiful metaphor, conveying the idea, that the heart of man is full of tumult drawn asunder, and, as it were, scattered about in fragments, until God has gathered it to himself, and holds it together in a state of stedfast and persevering obedience." David affirms that free will cannot do this but that "uprightness of heart is entirely the gift of God."[45]

6. Dickson builds on this idea, noting "the natural disease of sinful men's hearts, to be loosed from God, and scattered and distracted about a variety of vain objects, which are offered unto them to follow; and this disease God alone can cure." But he continues,

It is not sufficient for a man once to resign over his heart to God in his conversion, but this resignation of the heart must be renewed upon all occasions into God's hand, that he may tie the affections to himself and to his holy law, and reclaim the heart from ranging and going a-whoring from him after sinful objects; for this prayer for uniting the heart is David's prayer, who long before was converted.[46]

---

45 Calvin, *Psalms*, 3:388.
46 Dickson, *Psalms*, 2:89.

In this psalm a city is sung about and celebrated, a city
of which we are citizens by virtue of being Christians,
a city from which we are absent abroad as long as we
are mortal, and towards which we are travelling.

AUGUSTINE
Expositions of the Psalms

The miserable and distressing condition in which the Church
was placed after the Babylonish captivity, might be apt to sink
the minds of the godly into despondency; and, accordingly, the
Holy Spirit here promises her restoration in a wonderful and
incredible manner, so that nothing would be more desirable
than to be reckoned among the number of her members.

JOHN CALVIN
Commentary on the Psalms

What Mount Zion and the temple were for the Israelites
is for us the church of God in all the world.

DIETRICH BONHOEFFER
Prayerbook of the Bible

Saviour, since of Zion's city
I through grace a member am,
Let the world deride or pity,
I will glory in your name.
Fading are the world's vain pleasures,
All their boasted pomp and show;
Solid joys and lasting treasures
None but Zion's children know.

JOHN NEWTON
"Glorious Things of Thee Are Spoken"

PSALM 87

ORIENTATION

In the incarnation of God the Son, the love of God came down to earth. In vivid and heartwarming poetry, Psalm 87 prophesies something of the wonder of what that means for a broken world. It is almost a commentary on the phrase "a plan for the fullness of time, to unite all things in [Christ]" (Eph. 1:10), together with the barrier-breaking vision of Ephesians 2:11–22. For the love that God settles on Zion under the old covenant is the love of the Father for the Son, a love that will overflow through Jesus Christ into a broken world to reach and rescue the lost.

In the Septuagint, Psalm 87:5 speaks of "Mother Zion," since people are "born in her." But even without the word "Mother," the imagery of this psalm may have been in Paul's mind when he wrote that "the Jerusalem above is free, and she is our mother" (Gal. 4:26).[1] The images of Zion or Jerusalem as the city of God, the bride of the Lamb, and the mother of the church of Christ are combined in the book of Revelation.[2] "Mount Zion . . . , the heavenly Jerusalem," is the church to which new covenant believers belong (Heb. 12:22).

In the light of biblical theology, the most natural way to read the psalm is as describing people from all over the world being given birthrights in Zion, the church of Christ. The prophetic theme of a worldwide church is found clearly, for example, in Isaiah 44:5 ("This one will say, 'I am the LORD's'")[3] and Zechariah 2:11 ("And many nations shall join themselves

---

1   Kidner, *Psalms*, 2:316.
2   E.g., Rev. 14:1–5; 21:1–22:5.
3   Delitzsch calls this verse "the key" to the meaning of the psalm. Delitzsch, *Psalms*, 3:17.

to the LORD in that day, and shall be my people").[4] The end point of the imagery of being "born in Zion" is to be given citizenship in heaven (Phil. 3:20) and birth from above, which is by the Holy Spirit (John 3:1–8). This wider picture helps us read the psalm in the light of Christ.

As often characterizes poetry, the language is concise and evocative. Although it has puzzled scholars, the main outlines are clear when read in the light of the rest of the Scriptures. Three kinds of imagery are mingled: a city, a people, and a book in which names are registered.[5] *The English Annotations* from the post-Reformation period says, "The argument of the psalm (a glorious argument, briefly but emphatically set out in this short psalm) is the future fullness of the church and the conversion of all nations . . . to the Christian faith."[6]

We do not know when or for what human reason the psalm was written. The mention of Babylon (Ps. 87:4) suggests a connection to the Babylonian exile. In its canonical context in book 3, it is associated with the responses of believers to the exile. The fulfillment of Psalm 87 awaits the coming of Christ and the explosive birth of the church after Pentecost.

The most significant link with Psalm 86 is the prophecy "All the nations you have made shall come / and worship before you" (86:9). This "mission thought [in Ps. 86] . . . becomes the ruling thought" in Psalm 87.[7] James Hamilton comments, "It is as though the king made his appearance in Psalm 86 [a psalm of David], and in 87 we have a wide angle statement about the result of his reign."[8] The confidence that there will be "springs" in the pilgrimage to Zion (84:6) rests on the assurance that all our "springs" arise from the presence of God in Zion (87:7). Psalm 87 is one of the beautiful promises that keeps the pilgrim persevering on the road to Zion in Psalm 84.[9] If Psalm 83 speaks of the final defeat of rebellious nations, Psalm 87 adds the glorious prospect that some from those nations will surrender gladly, before it is too late.

Psalm 87 has many connections with the first Korah collection, and especially with Psalms 46 and 48. These include (1) the holy mountain (48:2; 87:1), (2) the

---

4   Other relevant texts include Isa. 2:2–4; 11:1–10; 18:7; 19:23–25; 60:3; Mic. 4:1–2; Zeph. 2:11; 3:9–10; Zech. 8:20–23.

5   Motyer, *Psalms*, 542.

6   *The English Annotations*, on Ps. 87:1, in *RCS* 8:95.

7   Delitzsch, *Psalms*, 3:16.

8   Hamilton, *Psalms*, 2:119.

9   Cf. Hossfeld and Zenger, *Psalms*, 2:386.

city of God (46:4; 48:1, 8; 87:3), (3) knowing God (46:10; 87:4), (4) the city being established by God (48:8; 87:5), (5) the Most High (46:4; 87:5; also 47:2), and (6) water that refreshes (46:4; 87:7, using different words). The idea of Zion as fruitful mother may suggest a thematic link with the bride in Psalm 45.[10]

THE TEXT

Structure

Selah provides a natural marker at the end of Psalm 87:3 and 6 and suggests a simple chiastic structure:

> **a** 87:1–3: The glory of Zion
> > **b** 87:4–6: The children of Zion
> **a'** 87:7: The joy of Zion

There is a smaller chiasm within 87:4–6; 87:4 balances 87:6 with the repetition of "This one was born there."

Superscription

> ˢ   A Psalm of the Sons of Korah.[11] A Song.[12]

The second collection of **Korah** psalms (Pss. 84; 85; 87; 88) resumes. This superscription is repeated (in a different word order and with extra material) at the head of Psalm 88, tying the two psalms closely together.

87:1–3 In Christ Love Is the Sure Foundation of the Church

Psalm 87:1–3 speaks of a foundation, a love, and a glory. All this is given in Christ.

> ¹   On the holy mount stands the city he founded;
> ²   the LORD loves the gates of Zion
>   more than all the dwelling places of Jacob.

---

10 Hossfeld and Zenger, *Psalms*, 2:386.
11 See on Ps. 42.
12 In Hebrew the superscription is the start of verse 1.

³ Glorious things of you are spoken,

O city of God. *Selah*

Psalm 87:1 begins enigmatically—literally, "his foundation on the holy mountains." This unusual opening draws us into the poem. It rapidly becomes clear that "his" means "God's" and that what is founded on the "holy mountains"[13] is the city of Zion (as in 2:6; 3:4; 15:1; 48:1).[14] The image of a mountain speaks of impregnability and security, and the possession of holiness indicates the presence of God, who guarantees that safety.

The root of the noun "foundation" (**the city he founded**) is used of Zion in Isaiah 14:32 ("The LORD has founded Zion"), in Isaiah 54:11 ("O afflicted one . . . I will . . . lay your foundations with sapphires"), and in Psalm 24:2 ("For he has founded it upon the seas"; cf. 78:69, in which his sanctuary is built "like the earth, which [God] has founded forever"). In the exile, God "kindled a fire in Zion / that consumed its foundations" (Lam. 4:11). But here—unlike the Jerusalem destroyed by the Babylonians—is a mountain on which God dwells on earth (hence its holiness), one that is indestructible.[15] This is "the city that has foundations, whose designer and builder is God" (Heb. 11:10).

The stability of this "mountain" rests on the love of God, for **the LORD loves the gates of Zion** (cf. Ps. 78:68). The form of the word **loves** indicates an unchanging affection.[16] This love is freely chosen, undeserved, and arises in the heart of God through no merit on the part of his people. The **gates**, as the places of entry and exit and the focus of business and government, stand, as *pars pro toto*, for Zion in its entirety.[17] The comparison

---

13 The plural is probably a plural of majesty ("the supremely holy mountain"), although it may indicate that Mount Zion makes all the surrounding mountains holy.

14 This language of a holy mountain was brought, with the ark, from Sinai to Zion (cf. Ps. 68:17).

15 Some older writers link the stable foundations of the city to "the foundation of the apostles and prophets" (Eph. 2:20; cf. the imagery of Rev. 21:14), with Christ the cornerstone; e.g., Augustine, *Psalms*, 4:247; Theodoret of Cyrus, *Psalms*, 2:77; Luther, *Luther's Works*, 11:176.

16 VanGemeren, *Psalms*, 655.

17 It is striking how prominent the gates are in the vision of Ezekiel's temple (Ezek. 40–48) and in the book of Revelation (e.g., Rev. 21:12–21, closely associated with foundations). Theodoret speaks of churches on earth as being like gates of the city, "through which it is possible to enter it; in them [the churches] we are instructed and trained, and learn the way of life of that city." Theodoret of Cyrus, *Psalms*, 2:78. While attractive, this interpretation strays some way away from the original imagery.

(**more than**) indicates that God's love for Zion is the focal point of his love for all the church (**the dwelling places of Jacob**); without Zion—without Christ—there is no foundation, no city, no church. This love has been poured into our hearts by the Holy Spirit (Rom. 5:5).

Psalm 87:3 sets the scene for 87:4–6, which will fill out the content of these **glorious things**. We are about to watch the glory, the visible presence of God on earth. This glory—far from being visible in the old covenant Jerusalem,[18] in the Jerusalem where Jesus was crucified, or in the physical Jerusalem today—is **spoken** of prophetically and awaits the coming of Christ and the birth of his church (cf. Gal. 4:25–26). Indeed, what makes the church blessed is "not present possession but hope, not sight but faith."[19] "Under the type of the city of Jerusalem ... [the psalmist describes] that very church of Christ beloved in the beloved Son of God by God the Father."[20]

87:4–6 In Christ Unity Is the Glory of the Church

> 4   Among those who know me I mention Rahab and Babylon;
>   behold, Philistia and Tyre, with Cush—
>   "This one was born there," they say.
> 5   And of Zion it shall be said,
>   "This one and that one were born in her";
>   for the Most High himself will establish her.
> 6   The LORD records as he registers the peoples,
>   "This one was born there."   *Selah*

There is one God, and there ought therefore to be one united world. That there is not means we must pray for the day when the will of God is done on earth in the same way as it is done in heaven. This will happen as the love of God flows out through the worldwide mission of the church of Christ.

Some very surprising births are the theme of Psalm 87:4–6. **I mention** is perhaps a little weak, for the verb[21] indicates here a "loud and honourable

---

18 "It served as a type, but like a shadow it passed away." Augustine, *Psalms*, 4:252.
19 Dickson, *Psalms*, 2:93.
20 Johannes Bugenhagen (1485–1558), *Interpretation of the Psalms*, in RCS 8:95.
21 Hiphil of זכר.

public mention,"[22] "as it were a formal proclamation on a state occasion"[23] by "the divine king."[24] Five astonishing nations are among those declared by God to be **those who know me**, in the personal knowledge to be given in the new covenant (Jer. 31:33–34). These are "named to stand for the rest" of the world.[25]

God begins with the ancient enslaving enemy, **Rahab**, a word that means a monster and was used derisively, as a mocking nickname, of Egypt (Isa. 30:7; cf. Ps. 89:10; Isa. 51:9).[26] Then there is the recent oppressor, **Babylon** (lit., "Babel," a word that conjures up a very different city, one that has no sure foundations, Gen. 11:1–9). Indeed, Augustine explains, "By Babylon the city of this world is meant . . . one wicked city."[27] The nature of Babylon can be transformed into the character of Jerusalem only through him who justifies the ungodly (Rom. 4:5), and yet now some from these proud and powerful enemies of God are declared to know God.

As if this were not astonishing enough, **behold**, there are more: **Philistia**, the ancient, bitter, and persistent irritant, who harrowed the church in the promised land for so many years; **Tyre**, the rich northern neighbor, not so much an oppressor as a seducer; and then **Cush**, which stands in Scripture as a symbol of far-distant lands.[28] From all these—proud, hostile, rich, strong, and distant—flock men and women who come to know God (cf. Rom. 5:9–11)! John Calvin exclaims,

> What a glorious distinction of the Church, that even those who held her in contempt shall come flocking to her from every quarter, and that those who desired to see her completely cut up and destroyed, shall consider it the highest honour to have a place among the number of her citizens.[29]

22 Delitzsch, *Psalms*, 3:19.
23 Kidner, *Psalms*, 2:315.
24 Tate, *Psalms 51–100*, 386.
25 Augustine, *Psalms*, 4:252.
26 The word here (רַהַב) is different in both consonants and pointing from the name of the Jericho prostitute in Josh. 2:1 (רָחָב). Some older writers confused these; e.g., Jerome and Cyril of Jerusalem, in *ACCS* 8:157–58; Augustine, *Psalms*, 4:252; Theodoret of Cyrus, *Psalms*, 2:78.
27 Augustine, *Psalms*, 4:252.
28 Grogan calls it "the fringe of Israel's world." Grogan, *Psalms*, 153. Cush is usually thought to be somewhere south of Egypt, but we are not sure. The LXX translation Αἰθιόπων simply means "dark-skinned" rather than necessarily Ethiopian. See Tate, *Psalms 51–100*, 391.
29 Calvin, *Psalms*, 3:400.

What is more, God says of each, **This one was born there,** that is, in Zion.[30] Zion is both a place and a mother.[31] That is, these people each "experience a spiritual change which, regarded from the New Testament point of view, is the new birth out of water and the Spirit."[32] These, in belonging to the church of Christ, to use the language of Hebrews, "have come to Mount Zion and to the city of the living God, the heavenly Jerusalem, and to innumerable angels in festal gathering, and to the assembly of the firstborn who are enrolled in heaven" (Heb. 12:22–23).[33] It is as though their documentation says, "Born in Babylon. Born again in Zion."

And, at the start of Psalm 87:5 (*vav*), does not signal a new and separate fact. We might translate it "indeed,"[34] for this is an expansion and explanation of the wonder of 87:4. The declaration of God in 87:4 is now expanded: **This one and that one**—literally, "a man and a man," where the idiom means "each and every one"[35]—**were born in her,** which makes it clear that the births celebrated in 87:4 and 6 are wonderful because they are counted as births **in her,** that is, in Zion, in the church of Christ. That **the Most High himself will establish her** emphasizes the unbreakable foundation of 87:1, guaranteed by the highest power in the universe. When Christ builds his church, nothing can break it (cf. Matt. 16:18).

Psalm 87:6, returning to the phrase **This one was born there,** declares that this is what the covenant Lord (**the LORD**) solemnly **records as he registers the peoples,** like a divine registrar of births. For this image of a book in which God names those given eternal life, see Exodus 32:32; Psalm 69:28 (cf. 109:13); Isaiah 4:3; Ezekiel 13:9; Daniel 12:1; Malachi 3:16; Luke 10:20; Revelation 3:5; 13:8; 17:8; 20:12, 15; and 21:27. God notes each individual "no less particularly than if their names were all written up in a book, one by one."[36]

---

30 Eveson helpfully notes how important it was, after the exile, to be able to prove "whether they belonged to Israel" (Ezra 2:59; cf. Ezra 2:59–63; Neh. 7:5). Eveson, *Psalms,* 2:112.

31 For the imagery of Zion as mother, see, e.g., Isa. 49:19–22; 51:18; 54:1–10 (immediately followed by Zion's foundations in 54:11); 66:7–14.

32 Delitzsch, *Psalms,* 3:19.

33 This link is made by, among others, Theodoret of Cyrus, *Psalms,* 2:77.

34 So, rightly, Zenger in Hossfeld and Zenger, *Psalms,* 2:378.

35 Delitzsch, *Psalms,* 3:20; Tate, *Psalms 51–100,* 386. The identical idiom (אִישׁ וְאִישׁ) appears also in Est. 1:8 ("each man"; cf. the similar idiom in Lev. 17:10, 13).

36 Dickson, *Psalms,* 2:95.

87:7 Christ Is the Joy of the Church

7　　Singers and dancers alike say,
　　　"All my springs are in you."

The words translated **singers and dancers** may be two separate groups but more likely indicate one group of celebrating musicians.[37] Whatever the precise meaning, it is clearly jubilant; 1 Samuel 18:6 catches the atmosphere well, as does the exultation in 2 Samuel 6, when David brings the ark to Zion. The reference to **springs** or fountains of life-giving water connects with the imagery of God's mountain in Psalm 87:1–3 (cf. the waters coming out of Eden in Gen. 2:10–14; the river that makes glad the city of God in Ps. 46:4; the water flowing out of Ezekiel's temple in Ezek. 47:1–12). These are "the wells of salvation" (Isa. 12:3). They find their fulfillment in the vision of Revelation 22:1–2. The point of the word **all** is that there is no other source of life; it comes only through Christ as we belong to his church. As Augustine says, "It is as though the home of all happy people . . . were in this city."[38] To reach these springs of joy, we may, like Paul, count as rubbish all the treasures of this world (Phil. 3:7–10).

REFLECTION AND RESPONSE

1. From the child on the school playground to the would-be immigrant seeking a visa, the longing to belong grows deep in the human psyche. This psalm speaks to that longing, both to settle our hearts on the yearning to belong in the only place ultimately worthy of our affections and to encourage us that, by the grace of Jesus Christ, it is possible for us to be born from above and be given citizenship birthrights in the church of Christ, no matter how distant or hostile we may have been. As Cassiodorus exclaims, "How blessed is he who with the Lord's guidance reaches that city, where every thought is overwhelmed, and each and every desire transcended!"[39]

37　וְשָׁרִים כְּחֹלְלִים. Since there is no connecting *vav*, this may indicate one group. The word translated "dancers" may mean "musicians," although BDB and *HALOT* suggest dancing; s.v. חול.

38　Augustine, *Psalms*, 4:255.

39　Cassiodorus, *Psalms*, 2:341.

2. When the visible church of Christ is weak, troubled, and despised and has no visible glory, this psalm encourages us with a vision of firm foundations, a sure establishment, rooted and grounded in the love of God in Christ. "That the faithful may not be deceived," writes Calvin, by "this shadowy appearance of things" (viz., the proud prosperity of the world and its haughty disdain for the church), we must remember the message of this psalm, that "the Church of God far excels all the kingdoms and polities of the world, inasmuch as she is watched over, and protected by Him in all her interests."[40] We ought to allow this psalm to lift our eyes to the glorious things spoken of Christ's church, which, because they are spoken by God, who cannot lie, are most certain to be fulfilled. Above all, we should value the love of God given to us in Christ more than all worldly measures of success, for "the dignity of any place, person, or society proceedeth not from any thing in the place or society, but from the Lord's election and free love."[41]

3. The vision of Psalm 87:4–6 (anticipating Rev. 7:9) should thrill our hearts when we see barriers being broken in the fellowship of a local church. Here is the true answer to the longings of our culture for diversity and inclusion. When we look out at a Christian meeting and say to ourselves, "There is no way I would be worshiping with these men and women were it not for Christ," then joy should fill our hearts. What is more, the association of these nations with a previously persistent and bitter hostility to the church of God should cheer us that the church will "not be troubled by the multitude of their foes for the present time" but can "look to the multitude of friends and converts which they would have hereafter."[42]

4. The image of God himself recording the names of one and then another for life reminds us that this decision is his alone and that our perceptions may be mistaken. As Charles Spurgeon warns, God's "census of his chosen will differ much from ours; he will count many whom we should have disowned, and he will leave out many whom we should have reckoned. His registration is infallible."[43] We must make sure of our election in the ways that Peter expounds (2 Pet. 1:10).

---

40 Calvin, *Psalms*, 3:393. On pp. 393–96 Calvin writes eloquently and pastorally about the message of this psalm for a troubled church.

41 Dickson, *Psalms*, 2:93.

42 Dickson, *Psalms*, 2:92.

43 Spurgeon, *Treasury*, 2.1:479.

[The Psalter] says . . . through [Christ's] own lips [in
Psalm 88], Your wrath has pressed heavily upon me.

ATHANASIUS
Letter to Marcellinus

The passion of our Lord is prophesied here.

AUGUSTINE
Expositions of the Psalms

In the midst of life we are in death: of whom may we seek for
succor, but of thee, O Lord, who for our sins are justly displeased?

BOOK OF COMMON PRAYER
"Order for the Burial of the Dead"

Such as are most heartily afflicted in spirit, and flee to God
for reconciliation and consolation through Christ, have no
reason to suspect themselves, that they are not esteemed, and
loved as dear children, because they feel so much of God's
wrath: for here is a saint who hath drunken of that cup,
(as deep as any who shall read this psalm,) here is one so
much loved and honoured of God, as to be a penman of holy
Scripture, and a pattern of faith and patience unto others.

DAVID DICKSON
A Commentary on the Psalms

Psalm 88 is like Gethsemane before Golgotha.

JAMES M. HAMILTON
Psalms

PSALM 88

ORIENTATION

In Psalm 88 we walk with a man who prays in hell itself. In the Book of Common Prayer, this psalm is set for evensong on Good Friday. In this "the saddest Psalm in the whole Psalter,"[1] no light breaks through. The final word is "darkness." Human enemies, so prominent in other psalms, are nowhere in view. The gaze of the sufferer is entirely taken up—in terrifying loneliness—with the absence of God. Those who immerse themselves in the psalm are sucked, as by a terrible whirlpool, into the jaws of Gehenna. And yet we must go there.

Descriptions of hell may be of a very different kind. In Job 18 Bildad paints a bloodcurdling picture of the punishment of the wicked. But he does so as an outsider, telling—and in no loving spirit—one who is there how terrible it must be and why he deserves to be there. Psalm 88 is spoken by a man who is inside a living hell; he speaks by the Spirit of Christ as he predicts the sufferings of Christ, with only the faintest hint of the glories to follow (1 Pet. 1:11). Dietrich Bonhoeffer rightly discerns that "the one who . . . has come to such infinite depths of suffering is none other than Jesus Christ himself."[2] Each Christian walks here to try to grasp something of the sacrifice of Jesus "who loved me and gave himself for me" (Gal. 2:20). But we walk this psalm also to prepare us to take up the cross daily and suffer with Christ (Luke 9:23; Rom. 8:17). "Spread out before us here," Bonhoeffer notes, "is the anguish of the entire Christian community throughout all time, as Jesus Christ alone has wholly experienced

---

1 Kirkpatrick, *Psalms*, 2:523.
2 Bonhoeffer, *Life Together*, 54.

it."[3] As Augustine says near the start of his sermon on this psalm, "The passion of our Lord is prophesied here. But the apostle Peter reminds us, *Christ suffered for us, leaving us an example, so that we may follow in his footsteps* (1 Pt 2:21)."[4]

We do not know the historical context of the psalm.[5] The identity of Heman the Ezrahite is discussed below, but whoever he was and whenever he lived, he "must have been a man of deep experience, who had done business on the great waters of soul trouble."[6] In its canonical context in book 3, Psalm 88 has long been understood to shed light on the exile: the Syriac translation added the words, "Concerning the people in Babylon," and the Targum reads Psalm 88:6 as "You have placed me in exile, which is like the deepest pit." Now it accompanies the church in every Good Friday of her distress.

Psalm 88 shares many connections with nearby psalms, most especially with Psalm 86. These include (1) the verb "save" (86:2; 88:1), (2) the "day" (86:3; 88:1, 9), (3) "incline your ear" (86:1; 88:2), (4) "prayer" (86:S, 6; 88:2, 13), (5) troubles (86:7; 88:3, using different words in Hebrew), (6) "Sheol" (86:13; 88:3), (7) "strength" (86:16; 88:4, using different words), (8) "wonders" (86:10; 88:10, 12), (9) "steadfast love" (86:5, 13, 15; 88:11), (10) "faithfulness" (86:15; 88:11), and (11) the word for "afflicted" or "poor" (86:1; 88:15).

Suggestive thematic links connect Psalm 88 with Psalm 84, the first song of this small "Korah" collection.[7] Each is a "prayer" (84:8; 88:2, 13) of a "soul" (84:2; 88:3, 14) longing for the God who gives light ("a sun," 84:11; contrast 88:6, 12, 18). The first finds "strength" in God and "goes from strength to strength" on the journey (84:5, 7), while the second "has no strength" (88:4). One longs for "the living God" (84:2); the other endures death without him (Ps. 88). Yet both are authentic parts of the life of faith. Psalm 88 describes an unavoidable stretch of the highway to Zion (84:5), as John Bunyan's (1628–1688) *Pilgrim's Progress* so vividly portrays the journey. Paradoxically, the agony of Psalm 88 demonstrates the longing

---

3   Bonhoeffer, *Prayerbook of the Bible*, 169.
4   Augustine, *Psalms*, 4:258.
5   The psalm goes beyond the situation of someone enduring sickness—and particularly leprosy, which has been suggested; see Kirkpatrick, *Psalms*, 2:523.
6   Spurgeon, *Treasury*, 2.2:1.
7   Hossfeld and Zenger, *Psalms*, 2:396–97.

for God that is declared to be "blessed" in Psalm 84; dark though it is, it will lead to blessing.

Links with Psalm 89 are discussed under that psalm.

Significant links with other psalms include the perils of the King in Psalms 6:5 (Sheol as the place with no remembrance or praise); 18:4–6 ("cords of death," "torrents," "Sheol"); 22 (many echoes); 28:1 (the silence of the pit); and 31:11 and 22 (loneliness, "cut off" from God).

Links with the book of Job include the terrors of Sheol and Abaddon (e.g., Job 26:5–6), "Abaddon and Death" (Job 28:22), going down into the pit (Job 33:24), darkness (e.g., Job 20:26), the terrors of God (Job 6:4), and loneliness (e.g., Job 19:13–15; 30:10).[8]

The condition of the suffering believer here echoes that of Joseph cast into a pit (Gen. 37:12–36), Jonah in the depths of the sea (Jonah 1:15–2:9),[9] Uzziah with his leprosy (2 Chron. 26:16–21), Hezekiah in his illness (2 Kings 20:1–11), Jeremiah thrown into a well (Jer. 38:6; cf. the torment of his poems of Lamentations),[10] and John the Baptist cast into prison (Mark 6:17). The sufferings of Christ overflowed into the lives of believers before Christ, just as they overflow into the church today.

Finally, before we walk through the text of the psalm, it is important to acknowledge that every word of this psalm—as of all the Psalms—is given by inspiration of the Holy Spirit. Commentators commonly see in the Psalms a mixture of good words and confused or ill-advised words. But this approach is deeply problematic. It places us in the all-powerful position of deciding which words are good and which are not. This we must not do with Holy Scripture.[11] Every word is from God by the Spirit of Christ.

---

8 For detailed observations, see Delitzsch, *Psalms*, 3:23. For the fulfillment of the book of Job in the sufferings of Christ and the life of the believer, see Christopher Ash, *Job: The Wisdom of the Cross*, Preaching the Word (Wheaton, IL: Crossway, 2014).

9 Links with Jonah include "depths," "waves," "Sheol," calling out to God, going down into the depths, and a longing to come before God. For detailed observations, see Robert Luther Cole, *The Shape and Message of Book III (Psalms 73–89)*, JSOTSup 307 (Sheffield: Sheffield Academic Press, 2000), 175–76.

10 See Kirkpatrick, *Psalms*, 2:524.

11 Even Calvin falls into this trap, in my view, when he writes that the psalmist "gave utterance to *those confused conceptions* which arise in the mind of a man under affliction," and later, "Nor is it wonderful that a man endued with the Spirit of God was, as it were, so stunned and stupefied when sorrow overmastered him, as to allow *unadvised words* to escape from his lips." Calvin, *Psalms*, 3:410; italics added.

THE TEXT

Structure

The psalm probably consists of three sections (Ps. 88:1–9a, 9b–12, 13–18).[12] Each begins with lament and the covenant name (88:1–2, 9b–c, 13). The first and third describe suffering with echoes of "soul" (88:3, 14), "companions" (88:8, 18), dimness or darkness (88:9a, 18), and God's "wrath" (88:7, 16). The central section (88:9b–12) speaks of the dead in general, rather than the psalmist in particular, and consists of rhetorical questions focusing on God's covenant attributes. This is "the compositional center of the psalm, . . . the axis of meaning in the psalm."[13] The occurrences of *Selah* at the end of 88:7 and 10 do not seem to be structural markers but rather pauses for thought.

Superscription

> s   A Song. A Psalm of the Sons of Korah. To the choirmaster:[14] according to Mahalath Leannoth. A Maskil[15] of Heman the Ezrahite.[16]

The designation **A Song. A Psalm of the Sons of Korah** is shared (in mirror-image word order) with the superscription of Psalm 87, tying the two together (although Ps. 88 "is as gloomy as Psalm 87 is cheerful").[17] **To the choirmaster** reminds us, perhaps to our surprise, that this dark psalm is to be used in corporate worship. **According to Mahalath** appears in the title to Psalm 53 (see comments there). The meaning of **Leannoth** is uncertain; either it is connected with singing or with being humbled or downcast.[18] There are probably references to more than one **Heman** in the Old Testament.[19] A famously wise man of that name is mentioned along with "Ethan the Ezrahite" (see superscription to Ps. 89) in 1 Kings 4:31.

---

12 This division "is so clearly indicated in the text that this proposal recommends itself unquestionably over other divisions." Hossfeld and Zenger, *Psalms*, 2:391–93.

13 Hossfeld and Zenger, *Psalms*, 2:392.

14 See on Ps. 4.

15 See on Ps. 32. Laments sharing this designation include Pss. 42, 44, 74, 88, 89.

16 In Hebrew the superscription is verse 1; subsequent verse numbers are increased by one.

17 Delitzsch, *Psalms*, 3:23.

18 These are two meanings of the root ענה; see Hossfeld and Zenger, *Psalms*, 2:390.

19 For summaries of the evidence, see Hamilton, *Psalms*, 2:124–25; Tate, *Psalms 51–100*, 395.

The designation **Ezrahite** may be connected with Ezra after the exile or perhaps with the family of Zerah (see 1 Chron. 2:6).[20] The most likely association is with one of David's musicians (linked with Jeduthun and Asaph) whose family featured also in this capacity in the reigns of Hezekiah and Josiah (see 1 Chron. 6:33; 15:17–19; 16:41–42; 25:1–6; 2 Chron. 5:12; 29:14; 35:15).

88:1–9a An Introductory Tour of Hell on Earth

1   O LORD, God of my salvation,
        I cry out day and night before you.
2   Let my prayer come before you;
        incline your ear to my cry!

O LORD, the first word in Hebrew, sets a tone of relentless second-person address to God in the context of covenantal expectation. The addition of **God of my salvation** makes this first line the clearest ray of hope in the psalm. It shines its light throughout the darkness, for the Father to whom Jesus prayed, the God to whom Heman prayed, the God to whom the church has always prayed, is the covenant God who saves. By these words, writes John Calvin, "he restrains the excess of his sorrow, shuts the door against despair, and strengthens and prepares himself for the endurance of the cross."[21] Those in Christ may remember, as we walk in the darkness, that we have "entered into covenant with God for [our] everlasting salvation," which nothing can change.[22]

The combination of **day** with **night** and the expression **before you**[23] together mark persistent and unflagging prayer as the defining characteristic of faith in the psalm (cf. "who cry to him day and night," Luke 18:7). The addition in Psalm 88:2 of **my prayer** and **before you** (lit., "before your face") intensifies this motif, as does the appeal to **incline your ear** (see on 86:1) **to my cry** (a loud, ringing cry, here of distress).

20 Kirkpatrick, *Psalms*, 2:524.
21 Calvin, *Psalms*, 3:408.
22 Dickson, *Psalms*, 2:97.
23 נֶגְדֶּךָ. The NIV rendering, "to you," follows a suggestion of Dahood but misses the nuance of being in the presence of God. Dahood, *Psalms*, 2:302.

The description of distress in 88:3–9a moves from "I" as subject (88:3–5), to God as the one who acts (88:6–8a) before returning to "I" (88:8b–9a).

³   For my soul is full of troubles,
        and my life draws near to Sheol.
⁴   I am counted among those who go down to the pit;
        I am a man who has no strength,
⁵   like one set loose among the dead,
        like the slain that lie in the grave,
    like those whom you remember no more,
        for they are cut off from your hand.

Dark irony abounds in the terrible imagery here. **For my soul** (used in the sense of a human being with desires) **is full of troubles** (lit., "evils") uses a verb (**is full of**) that means "to satisfy," usually in a positive sense (e.g., 17:15; 22:26; 63:5; 65:4; 81:16), with an "abundance" (37:19). But here (as in Lam. 3:15, 30) it is deeply ironic: "My desires are satisfied with plenty of evils."[24] The REB rendering—"I have had my fill of woes"—catches this well. David Dickson writes that "his soul is full of troubles, replenished so that it can hold no more."[25] In Psalm 88:3b **my life draws near to** (touches) **Sheol**, the place of death: "My life is on the brink of the place of death."

In 88:4a he is reckoned as just one in a whole crowd **who go down** (are on the very point of descending) **to the pit**; we see him on the edge of the abyss. In 88:4b he says, **I am a man** (using a word that suggests a warrior or strong man, גֶּבֶר, *geber*) **who has no strength**: "I am a hero with no more heroism."

Psalm 88:5a epitomizes the paradox of freedom in the absence of God: I am **like one set loose among the dead**, where the adjective **set loose**[26] is often used of a slave being set free (e.g., Ex. 21:2, 5, 26; Deut. 15:12, 18). In Job 3:19 death is the place where "the slave is free from his master." But what a terrible freedom! "You are free to go where you want, so long as you remain among the dead." Psalm 88:5b pictures **the slain** on a battlefield,

---

24 Augustine mentions the sorrows of Jesus in Gethsemane (Matt. 26:37–38). Augustine, *Psalms*, 4:259.

25 Dickson, *Psalms*, 2:98.

26 חָפְשִׁי.

cast into the common **grave** (as in the horrifying imagery of Ezek. 32:20–32),[27] just "an unknown soldier,"[28] a casualty of war. In Psalm 88:5c–d the focus begins to shift toward God: **like those whom you remember no more**, where **remember** has the sense of watching and loving care. To be forgotten by God is the worst that can happen; even when dementia robs someone of memory, we long to know that God remembers.[29] To be **cut off from** the **hand** of God means to be finally beyond all hope (cf. 37:22). This accumulation of sad images piled one on top of another crushes the spirit; it helps us feel the horrors of hell. Psalm 88:6–8a shows that there is worse to come.

> 6   You have put me in the depths of the pit,
>   in the regions dark and deep.
> 7   Your wrath lies heavy upon me,
>   and you overwhelm me with all your waves.   *Selah*
> 8   You have caused my companions to shun me;
>   you have made me a horror to them.

One horror of hell is that only God can put someone there (Luke 12:5). **You have put me in the depths of the pit**, where **the depths** adds horror to horror: "the most profound wretchedness, deeper than any other misery" (cf. Lam. 3:5; Ps. 86:13).[30] The **regions dark** translates a word that speaks of intense darkness ("utter darkness"),[31] with **deep** added to make it clear that this is a place of utter dismay.

Psalm 88:7 moves from the fact that God has placed him there to the reason why: **your wrath** refers to God's settled, holy anger against sinners. It **lies heavy upon me**, with the sense of something pressing down, crushing me with its unbearable weight (cf. Christian's burden in *The Pilgrim's Progress*). The image of 88:7b moves from an unbearable weight to **waves**, terrible sea breakers (cf. 42:7; Jonah 2:3), as the floods

---

27 Tate, *Psalms 51–100*, 396.
28 VanGemeren, *Psalms*, 659.
29 This conviction lies behind the epitaph "Known unto God" inscribed on British Commonwealth war graves of unknown soldiers.
30 Augustine, *Psalms*, 4:262.
31 Tate, *Psalms 51–100*, 396–97.

of judgment **overwhelm**[32] him. *Selah* provides a timely reminder not to rush too fast over these images.

The focus of Psalm 88:8 is not on the attitude of the **companions** (perhaps misleadingly suggested by the word **shun**) but on the terrible state of the sufferer. The first line is literally "You have caused my companions to be distant from me." The reason they are distant is given in the second line, where the word **horror** is an almost indescribably awful word (lit., the plural of "abomination"), an intensive plural that conveys "the fullness, the essence, of horror."[33] Hell is a place of infinite loneliness because each inhabitant has become unutterably repulsive. This is what the cross of Christ looks like, when Christ became repulsive for us.

> I am shut in so that I cannot escape;
> 9   my eye grows dim through sorrow.

Finally we return to the sufferer as the subject: **I am shut in**, restrained, imprisoned, confined, **so that I cannot escape**. There is no escape from hell, and therefore, **my eye** (the organ that expresses desire and life) **grows dim through sorrow** (where the word **sorrow** indicates deep anguish).

After this "introductory tour" of hell, we long for some hope. We remember that Jesus went here for us. But the psalm will not allow us too quickly to move to a shallow cheerfulness. Psalm 88:9b–12 brings us to the heart of the psalm.

88:9b–12 Calling on the Fundamental Structure of the Universe

> Every day I call upon you, O LORD;
> I spread out my hands to you.

The second section begins, like the first, with urgent petition. In words that echo Psalm 88:1–2 (note the appeal to the covenant **LORD**, calling out to God, and the reminder that this is **every day**). **I spread out my hands to you** is similar to the familiar lifting up of the hands in prayer (e.g., 28:2; cf. 1 Tim. 2:8).

---

32 The word "overwhelm" translates the verb "to afflict" (ענה), which may be an echo of "Leannoth" in the superscription.

33 Hossfeld and Zenger, *Psalms*, 2:390.

Psalm 88:10–12 is the literary and theological heart of the psalm. The sufferer asks God three pairs of questions. On the answer hinges Christ's, Heman's, and our destiny.

> 10   Do you work wonders for the dead?
>   Do the departed rise up to praise you?   *Selah*

There are two movements in the first pair. First, it advances from **wonders** to **praise**. The word **wonders**[34] speaks of God's acts of redemption (e.g., Ex. 15:11; Pss. 77:11, 14; 78:12) and of God's judgments on his enemies (e.g., Isa. 25:1–2) and on his sinful people (e.g., Isa. 29:14; Lam. 1:9 ["terrible" = "a wonder"]). The term appears in parallel with "your faithfulness" in Psalm 89:5, for his wonders are all acts of covenant faithfulness. The promised "*Wonderful* Counselor" (Isa. 9:6) will bring these wonders to a climax. The proper response to the amazing works of God is **to praise** him.

The second movement is from **the dead** to **the departed**, where the latter translates the word רְפָאִים, *rephaim*, often rendered "the shades" or "the ghosts," the shadowy spirits of the departed (translated "shades," "dead," or "departed" in the ESV of Job 26:5; Prov. 2:18; 9:18; 21:16; Isa. 14:9; 26:14, 19). The word sometimes carries overtones of the strongest or most heroic among the dead.[35] Even they will not be able to praise the God of wonders. *Selah* invites us to pause and ponder this.

> 11   Is your steadfast love declared in the grave,
>   or your faithfulness in Abaddon?

Steadfast love and **faithfulness** are a familiar pair of covenant terms. The **grave** is intensified by the word **Abaddon**, which means "Destruction" or "Ruin" (cf. Job 26:6; 28:22; 31:12; Prov. 15:11; 27:20). In Greek this is "Apollyon," and both terms refer to the devil (as Destruction personified) in Revelation 9:11. The health of the universe depends on the covenant love and truthfulness (cf. "grace and truth" in John 1:14) being **declared** in public acclamation.

---

34 פֶּלֶא.

35 The name is also given to a pre-Israelite group in the promised land (e.g., Deut. 2:11); it is not known if there is a connection between these uses. See the helpful notes in Tate, *Psalms 51–100*, 397–98; VanGemeren, *Psalms*, 661.

¹²   Are your wonders known in the darkness,
         or your righteousness in the land of forgetfulness?

In the third pair, **wonders** (see Ps. 88:10) parallels **righteousness**, again a covenantal term. God does the right thing by keeping his promises, punishing his enemies, and rescuing his people. The place is now described as **darkness** and **forgetfulness** (CSB, NIV: "oblivion"), which takes us back to 88:5 ("those whom you remember no more"). The word **known** parallels "declared" in 88:11 and "praise" in 88:10.

The logic of all three pairs of questions is this: the harmony of the cosmos depends on the greatness and goodness of the Creator and the glad acknowledgment of his character, expressed in praise; if a man who would offer this praise (a believer) dies and stays dead, then praise is taken away from the God who deserves it. This contradicts the fundamental structure of the universe. Ultimately, if the eternal Son of God is separated from the Father and goes forever to the place of the dead, the foundations of the universe in the Holy Trinity would be torn apart. This cannot be. Although no music of joy is heard in this psalm, it is impossible to reiterate these covenant attributes (wonders, steadfast love, faithfulness, righteousness) without feeling at least a glimmer of hope.

88:13–18 The Tour of Hell Continues

¹³   But I, O LORD, cry to you;
         in the morning my prayer comes before you.

But I is emphatic. Like the first and second sections (cf. Ps. 88:1–2, 9a), the third begins with lament, including the covenant name, **LORD**, and a reference to time (**in the morning**), trusting that there will be a "morning" of joy to follow evenings of tearfulness (cf. 130:6).[36]

¹⁴   O LORD, why do you cast my soul away?
         Why do you hide your face from me?

---

36 The logic of the "morning" as a symbol of God acting to put right a broken world is similar to that of Job 38:12–15.

The covenant name, the LORD, appears here for the fourth time. The word translated **why** is oriented toward the future ("What is the purpose or goal?") and therefore is pregnant with hope.[37] As in Psalm 88:3, the sufferer speaks of his **soul** and rightly understands that it is God who has placed him in his distress (as in 88:6–8). What hurts most is not his sufferings but being sent away from the presence of God (**cast . . . away**) so that the **face** of God in blessing is hidden from him (contrast Num. 6:24–26). The distress of hell is not what it contains but what it lacks; hell is exclusion from the presence of God (cf. "The door was shut," Matt. 25:10).

> 15   Afflicted and close to death from my youth up,
>   I suffer your terrors; I am helpless.

The phrase **close to death from my youth up** need not mean a terrible disease that leads to early death or a life of constant mortal danger (although it may); fundamentally, it means that from the moment he is born, he is living under the shadow of death.[38] This is not the preserve of the especially miserable but the state of all humankind, were we but to acknowledge it. The word **terrors** is often associated with the paralyzing fear that will afflict the enemies of God (e.g., Ex. 15:16; 23:27; Josh. 2:9) but is also experienced by Job, the blameless believer (Job 9:34; 13:21; cf. 33:7), as it will be by the greater Job, the Lord Jesus Christ, and sometimes by his followers as they suffer with him. The word translated **helpless** (an Old Testament hapax legomenon) seems to mean something like being utterly paralyzed with fear or at a loss to know how to bear up under this suffering.[39]

> 16   Your wrath has swept over me;
>   your dreadful assaults destroy me.
> 17   They surround me like a flood all day long;
>   they close in on me together.

---

37 The word is לָמָה (famous from the opening of Ps. 22). For this nuance in the meaning of the word, see Hossfeld and Zenger, *Psalms*, 2:390–91nl.

38 The participle גֹּוֵעַ "emphasizes the fundamental, existential 'condition of being subject to death.'" Hossfeld and Zenger, *Psalms*, 2:390. Cf. Goldingay, who translates the word by the participle "dying," that is, moving toward death all through life. Goldingay, *Psalms*, 2:643.

39 Hossfeld and Zenger, *Psalms*, 2:391; Goldingay, *Psalms*, 2:643.

Wrath here means burning anger (a word always used of God's anger). **Your dreadful assaults** translates another word for the terrors of God (cf. Job 6:4). This believer is utterly destroyed by this burning wave of anger and onslaught of terror. The **flood** waters of judgment **surround** the believer on all sides and do so **all day long**. This is inescapable and relentless. The word **together** means "altogether" or "completely."

> ¹⁸   You have caused my beloved and my friend to shun me;
>   my companions have become darkness.

As in Psalm 88:8, **caused . . . to shun** means that God has caused them to be distant from him. Here the "companions" of 88:8 are intensified with the addition of **my beloved** (i.e., my loved one, anyone I am deeply fond of) **and my friend** or neighbor.

The profound loneliness is rammed home in the enigmatic final line, literally, "my companions—darkness!" This final (rare) word means "a dark place." The plural is translated "regions dark" in 88:6. It appears in Psalms 74:20 ("the dark places"); 143:3 ("darkness"); and Lamentations 3:6 ("darkness"). The final line may mean, "Darkness has become my companion" or "My companions are now darkness." Perhaps more likely, the word "companions" completes the thought of the first line, and the final word is dramatically disconnected:

> You have caused my beloved and my friend to be distant, my
>   companions.
> DARKNESS!

This experience of hell on earth foreshadows the agony of Gethsemane and the darkness of the cross. That darkness overflows to the lives of those who make up Christ's church.

REFLECTION AND RESPONSE

1. We may expect several blessings from immersing ourselves in the darkness of this psalm. The first is a deeper appreciation of what it cost the Lord Jesus to give himself for our sins (Gal. 1:4). It helps us "behold Jesus,

the man of sorrows and acquainted with grief."[40] The Epistles teach us why Jesus had to die. The Gospels invite us to watch as horrified spectators. Psalm 88 takes us, as far as mortals may be allowed, into the jaws of hell with Jesus our Savior, so that we feel, shudder, and tremble as the wrath of God descends on him.

2. If this is what hell feels like to a man who prays, what must the horror be for one who does not? If ever we needed incentive to flee from the wrath to come (Luke 3:7), Psalm 88 provides it with visceral immediacy. Even the faintest echo of the screams of hell will stir us so that the love of Christ controls us (2 Cor. 5:14) and our heart's desire and prayer to God will be for others to be saved from this judgment (cf. Rom. 10:1).

3. The misery of the psalm presses home to us the misery of a world in the shadow of death. This world can never be our home. The psalm helps us "groan inwardly as we wait eagerly for adoption as sons, the redemption of our bodies" (Rom. 8:23).

4. Paul speaks of a strange lack in Christ's afflictions (Col. 1:24). All-sufficient to atone for sins, Christ's sufferings yet overflow to Christ's people in the world, for "great heaps of affliction are the ordinary position of God's children in this life."[41] As Satan sifts us like wheat (Luke 22:31), we may therefore expect some echo of Psalm 88. We should not be surprised.

5. Augustine, using the image of Christ as head and the church as his members (as he often does), writes,

> It might happen to any one of them to be saddened and feel pain amid human trials, and Christ wanted to make sure that anyone in that state would not think himself or herself distant from his grace. The body would learn from its head that these experiences are not sins, but only signs of human infirmity, and so the choir would be chiming in with Christ's leading voice.[42]

6. Calvin suggests that part of the reason for the psalm is "that our distresses, however grievous, may not overwhelm us with despair," and that "we should . . . rest assured that the Spirit of God, by the mouth of Heman,

---

40 Spurgeon, *Treasury*, 2.2:7.
41 Thomas Wilcox (ca. 1549–1608), *Expositions upon the Psalms*, in *RCS* 8:100.
42 Augustine, *Psalms*, 4:260.

has here furnished us with a form of prayer for encouraging all the afflicted who are, as it were, on the brink of despair to come to himself."[43]

7. Dickson writes,

> What trouble of wounded spirit some of God's children have felt in former times, others dear to God may find the like in after ages, and all men ought to prepare for the like, and should not think the exercise strange when it cometh, but must comfort themselves in this, that other saints whose names are recorded in Scripture, have been under like affliction.[44]

8. Derek Kidner perceptively comments that this psalm witnesses "to the possibility of unrelieved suffering as a believer's earthly lot. The happy ending of most psalms of this kind is seen to be a bonus, not a due."[45] Recognizing that our sufferings are a part of the greater sufferings of Christ is a deep encouragement. For, as Cassiodorus writes,

> Let no person fear the wretchedness which makes men blessed. . . . Let none fear the sadness which bestows eternal joy. How slight a thing is momentary death when its purpose is to win enduring life! . . . Who would be ashamed of the pains which the Lord Christ deigned to bear?[46]

9. One strange encouragement from this psalm is that Heman continued to pray in the midst of his troubles[47] and that he was evidently sustained in them so that he could give this song of prophecy to the church of Christ. All psalms come at a cost to the composer (just as prophecy came with a cost to the prophet, especially perhaps Hosea and Jeremiah), and this more than most; it is to be valued all the more for that.

---

43 Calvin, *Psalms*, 3:407.
44 Dickson, *Psalms*, 2:96.
45 Kidner, *Psalms*, 2:319.
46 Cassiodorus, *Psalms*, 2:350.
47 This is perceptively noted by Kidner, *Psalms*, 2:317.

By our Lord's grace we have undertaken to speak to you
about this psalm, beloved, and you should be aware that it
deals with the hope we hold in him, Christ Jesus our Lord.

AUGUSTINE
Expositions of the Psalms

The state of Christ's, no less than of David's kingdom,
may sometimes seem to human sense in a condition
quite contrary to what is promised concerning it.

DAVID DICKSON
A Commentary on the Psalms

Though with a scornful wonder,
Men see her sore oppressed,
By schisms rent asunder,
By heresies distressed,
Yet saints their watch are keeping,
Their cry goes up, "How long?"
And soon the night of weeping
Shall be the morn of song.

S. J. STONE
"The Church's One Foundation"

PSALM 89

Jesus Christ is King and not yet King. In truth he is wonderfully, utterly, unbreakably secure, the King, "the head of the body, the church. He is the beginning, the firstborn from the dead, that in everything he might be preeminent" (Col. 1:18). And yet when he declares, "All authority in heaven and on earth has been given to me" (Matt. 28:18), an honest look at the state of the church in the world makes us grieve at the tension between promise and experience. Psalm 89 teaches us how to walk the way of the cross with our Savior, to lament with faith, and to rejoice with realism.

The larger part of the psalm (89:1–37) celebrates the eternal covenant between the Father and the Son, echoed in God's fatherly covenant with David.[1] Apart from the broad theme that all the promises of God are "Yes!" in Christ (2 Cor. 1:20) and the frequent pattern of King David being a type of Christ, several New Testament echoes suggest that Jesus Christ is the fulfillment of what is celebrated in Psalm 89:1–37. Gabriel tells Mary that her son will be "the Son of the Most High" and will be given "the throne of his father David" with a kingdom of which "there will be no end" (Luke 1:32–33); all three themes—the Son of God, the throne of David, and an unending reign—feature prominently in Psalm 89. When Mary sings that, in the birth of her son, God "has shown strength with his arm" and "has

---

1 Dickson speaks of this as "the covenant of grace, made between God and Christ, typified by David . . . the substance [of which] was to be found only in Christ." Dickson, *Psalms*, 2:107. A strong confidence that all these covenant promises are fulfilled in Christ was widespread among writers from the patristic period through the Reformation (Calvin was very robust about this) to the Puritans. Since the so-called "Enlightenment," it has been less common.

scattered the proud" (Luke 1:51), she echoes Psalm 89:10 and connects the coming of Christ with the victory of God in the world.[2] Jesus is "the offspring of David" (John 7:42; Acts 13:22–23) who will endure "forever" (John 12:34), echoing Psalm 89:3–4 and 36. When Jesus stills the storm (Mark 4:37–39), he demonstrates on earth the sovereignty of God and his King over the seas (Ps. 89:9, 25).[3] Jesus Christ is "the faithful witness, the firstborn of the dead, and the ruler of kings on earth" (Rev. 1:5, echoing Ps. 89:27, 37).[4]

Further, there is a suggestive hint that what is true of Christ overflows to the privileges of his church (cf. Ps. 89:15–18: "Blessed are the people who know the festal shout . . ."). Peter writes that Christians may "call on [God] as Father" (1 Pet. 1:17). In Psalm 89:26 it is said of the King, "He shall cry to me, 'You are my Father.'" In the Greek this verse is echoed in 1 Peter. The privilege of the King, the Son, is inherited by all who belong to the King.[5] Christians share the access to God as Father enjoyed by their King and all the blessings that flow from this.

There is also a significant echo from the later part of the psalm. In Psalm 89:50–51 the mockery or reproach of the anointed King is experienced also by his faithful people. In calling this "the reproach of Christ," Hebrews 11:26 suggests that the sufferings in the psalm are fulfilled in Christ and then in all who belong to Christ, both before Christ (as in Heb. 11) and after Christ (cf. "If you are insulted for the name of Christ . . . ," 1 Pet. 4:14).[6]

Guided by these echoes and themes from biblical theology, we understand Psalm 89:1–37 to speak of the security of Christ in the Father and the privileges of the church in Christ. We read 89:38–52 with the sufferings of Christ in mind as well as the sufferings of the church of Christ, both the Old Testament remnant who suffered "the reproach of Christ" again and again and the new covenant church today. Psalm 89 leads us to celebrate the reliability of Christ with confidence while facing the sober truth that

---

2   David W. Pao and Eckhard J. Schnabel, "Luke," in *CNTOT* 262; Kraus, *Theology of the Psalms*, 195.

3   Hossfeld and Zenger, *Psalms*, 2:414–15.

4   Elsewhere in Scripture, these three titles occur together only in Ps. 89. Beale and McDonough, "Revelation," in *CNTOT* 1089; see also Kraus, *Theology of the Psalms*, 203.

5   This psalm is the only place in the canonical LXX that the idiom "to call on . . . Father" (using ἐπικαλέω and πατήρ) appears. Kraus, *Theology of the Psalms*, 202.

6   Hossfeld and Zenger, *Psalms*, 2:414–15.

if we were to live by sight rather than by faith, we should reach a very different conclusion.[7]

We cannot be sure of the historical circumstances that led to the psalm being written.[8] Clearly, something threatened the very existence of the whole Davidic dynasty. Because the text does not mention the temple or the destruction of Jerusalem, we cannot be certain that this was the Babylonian exile, although that remains the most likely answer since the exile of Jehoiachin marked the end of David's visible dynasty (2 Kings 24:8–17; cf. Matt. 1:11). But the crises of Rehoboam with the Egyptians (2 Chron. 12:1–12), of Hezekiah with the Assyrians (2 Kings 18–19), and of Josiah's death (2 Kings 23:29–30) have all been suggested. Perhaps the lack of historical certainty makes it easier for us to transpose the psalm into a new covenant key, in which our confidence in Christ (Ps. 89:1–37) needs to be held together with our experiences of suffering with Christ (89:38–52): that Jesus is King even when he seems not to be King.

The most significant elements of the canonical context are as follows. First, Psalm 89 is closely tied to Psalm 88. Links include (1) "a Maskil" and "an Ezrahite" in the superscriptions; (2) the fear of death (Ps. 88 [often]; 89:47–48); (3) the word "Sheol" (88:3; 89:48); (4) God "remembering" (88:5; 89:47, 50); (5) the wrath of God (88:7, 16; 89:38, 46); and (6) the covenant attributes of "steadfast love," "faithfulness," and "wonders" (88:10–12; 89 [often]). The corporate lament of Psalm 89 comes from the same world in which a believer prays in the very mouth of hell (Ps. 88).

Second, we have seen that book 3 of the Psalter is pervaded by exile (see on Ps. 73). Not all the psalms in this book were written in exile. But they have been placed together because they are appropriate as the church learns to live in exile.

The third canonical context is with psalms or parts of psalms that have a strong royal theme (notably Pss. 2; 18; 72; 78:70–72; 110; 132)[9] and scriptures that speak of the covenant with David (principally 2 Sam. 7 and 1 Chron. 17 but also 2 Sam. 23:1–7; 2 Chron. 13:5; Isa. 55:1–5; Jer. 33:19–22). This is the crucial historical and theological background.

---

7 Kidner speaks of the tension between Ps. 89:1–37 and 89:38–45 as being "like an unresolved discord [that] impels us towards the New Testament, where we find that the fulfilment will altogether outstrip the expectation." Kidner, *Psalms*, 2:319.

8 For various suggestions, see Belcher, *Messiah and the Psalms*, 270n101; Tate, *Psalms 51–100*, 413–18.

9 It is notable that direct divine speech features in several of these psalms (Pss. 2:7; 110:4; 132:11–12), as in Ps. 89.

Although most of Psalm 89 is in the singular, the whole church is present in 89:17–18 ("our horn . . . our shield . . . our king") and 89:50 ("your servants").

THE TEXT

Structure

The psalm appears to fall into three main sections. Psalm 89:1–37 is gloriously upbeat and ends with *Selah*. The *Selah* after 89:4 marks off 89:1–4 as an introduction within this section. Psalm 89:5–37 divides into 89:5–18, which speaks about God's covenant with David, and 89:19–37, in which God speaks to David and his seed. Psalm 89:38–45 (again ending with *Selah*) is a strong and coherent lament. Psalm 89:46–51 closes the psalm with prayer (punctuated by *Selah* after 89:48).

Although 89:52 is the conclusion to book 3, it also functions with great appropriateness as the conclusion to this psalm.

Superscription

S   A Maskil[10] of Ethan the Ezrahite.[11]

As with Heman in Psalm 88, there may be references to more than one **Ethan** in the Old Testament. A famously wise "Ethan the Ezrahite" is mentioned along with Heman (see superscription to Ps. 88) in 1 Kings 4:31. As well as references to this name in 1 Chronicles 2:6–8, Ethan is associated with Heman and Asaph, Levites with ministries of song in the temple (1 Chron. 6:42; 15:17–19). The designation **Ezrahite** may be connected with Ezra after the exile or perhaps with the family of Zerah (see 1 Chron. 2:6).[12]

89:1–37 The Church Is Securely Blessed in Christ

89:1–4 The Covenant between the Father and the Son Is Sure

Psalm 89:1–4 is a headline for the entire psalm. It moves from what the psalmist ("I") says (89:1–2) to what God says (89:3–4). The two are connected in a nice chiasm:

---

10 See on Ps. 32. Laments sharing this designation include Pss. 42, 44, 74, 88, 89.

11 In Hebrew the superscription is verse 1; subsequent verse numbers are increased by one.

12 Kirkpatrick, *Psalms*, 2:524.

   a "forever"

     b "built up"

       c "establish"

       c' "establish"

     b' "build"

   a' "all generations"

1   I will sing of the steadfast love of the Lord, forever;
> with my mouth I will make known your faithfulness to all generations.

2   For I said, "Steadfast love will be built up forever;
> in the heavens you will establish your faithfulness."

In Hebrew the first word is "the steadfast loving deeds" (the plural of חֶסֶד, *khesed*, also in Ps. 89:49).[13] The attribute "steadfast love" appears seven times in the psalm (89:1, 2, 14, 24, 28, 33, 49; see also "the godly one(s)," חֲסִידִים, *khasidim*, 89:19). In parallel is **your faithfulness** (אֱמוּנָה, *emunah*), which also appears seven times (89:1, 2, 5, 8, 24, 33, 49), together with the cognate adjective "faithful" (89:37), the cognate verb "stand firm" (89:28), and the double "Amen"[14] in 89:52. This is the grand theme of the whole psalm, the covenant mercies of God, fulfilled in Christ.

The repeated **forever** together with **to all generations** draws attention at the start to the enduring nature of what is celebrated. The reference to **the heavens** in 89:2b has the same sense: just as the heavens are eternal, so is God's faithfulness.[15] The clauses **I will sing**, **With my mouth I will make known**, and **For I said** emphasize that the entire psalm will be a public declaration of these eternal attributes of the covenant God. The verbs **be built up**[16] and **establish**[17] indicate something built to last. This covenant is

---

13 The use of the plural is relatively rare. Other occurrences, when used of God, are 2 Chron. 6:42; Pss. 17:7; 25:6; 106:7, 45; 107:43; Isa. 55:3 (significantly in the context of "steadfast love for David" overflowing in a promise to the whole nation); 63:7; Lam. 3:22, 32). In 2 Chron. 32:32 and 35:26, it refers to the deeds of steadfast love done by Hezekiah and Josiah, respectively.

14 "Amen" comes from the same verbal root as "faithful(ness)" (אמן).

15 Hengstenberg, *Psalms*, 3:98; Tate, *Psalms 51–100*, 409. For similar imagery, see Ps. 36:5.

16 This verb (בָּנָה) is prominent in Nathan's oracle to David (2 Sam. 7:5, 7, 13, 27; 1 Chron. 17:4, 10, 12).

17 This root (כון) appears in Ps. 89:2, 4, 14 ("foundation"), 21, 37.

"like a building which hath a foundation already laid by a wise and powerful builder, and shall come up certainly to perfection, and endure for ever."[18] Similar imagery is used of the world in 24:2, for the moral order of creation is ultimately inseparable from the building of God's covenant with his Messiah.

> 3   You have said, "I have made a covenant with my chosen one;
>   I have sworn to David my servant:
> 4   'I will establish your offspring forever,
>   and build your throne for all generations.'"   *Selah*

Though not in the Hebrew, the words **you have said** are implied. The repetition of the verbs **establish** and **build** together with **forever** and **for all generations** tie these verses closely to Psalm 89:1–2. The love of God is focused on the covenant with **David**, especially his **offspring** or "seed."[19] The parallel clauses **I have made** (lit., "cut") **a covenant** and **I have sworn** reinforce the strength of this promise. The designations **my chosen one** (cf. 78:70) and **my servant** (cf. Ps. 18:S; Isa. 42:1) are covenant titles of honor. The **throne** focuses attention on the offspring of David as King.

This covenant is an echo of the eternal covenant between the Father and the Son, which is absolutely secure and eternal. This is the foundation of the psalm. This covenant concerns all who are in Christ, for "what is promised concerning Christ, concerneth all believers in him to the world's end."[20]

89:5–18 The Church of Christ Is Blessed Because of the Sure Covenant of the Father with the Son

There is no consensus about whether or how to subdivide Psalm 89:5–14. I will take this in three sections: 89:5–8, 9–12, and 13–14.

> 5   Let the heavens praise your wonders, O Lord,
>   your faithfulness in the assembly of the holy ones!

---

18 Dickson, *Psalms*, 2:109. Cf. "As surely as this promise culminates in Christ, so surely is it significant to us." Hengstenberg, *Psalms*, 3:99.

19 Both Augustine and Theodoret rightly link the idea of covenant "seed" to the "seed" of Abraham fulfilled in Christ, corporately with his church (Gal. 3:16, 29). Augustine, *Psalms*, 4:276; Theodoret of Cyrus, *Psalms*, 2:85.

20 Dickson, *Psalms*, 2:110.

6   For who in the skies can be compared to the LORD?
     Who among the heavenly beings is like the LORD,
7   a God greatly to be feared in the council of the holy ones,
     and awesome above all who are around him?
8   O LORD God of hosts,
     who is mighty as you are, O LORD,
     with your faithfulness all around you?

There is no one and nothing that can bear comparison with God (cf. Ps. 86:8). One powerful way to convey the transcendence of God is to consider that the "heavenly beings"—creatures who are supernatural and above anything we know on earth—bow in adoration before God. And if they do, everything does. Psalm 29:1–2 celebrates this reality emphatically and provides helpful background to this section.[21]

In six parallel lines 89:5–7 declares in praise God's supremacy over every power in the heavenly places. Six phrases interpret one another: **the heavens** and **the skies** (lit., "clouds")[22] speak of the region in which powers exist that are superhuman but subdivine (cf. 19:1). **The assembly of the holy ones**, **the heavenly beings** (lit., "sons of gods," or "the mighty"), **the council of the holy ones**, and **all who are around him** designate the spiritual beings in this region, sometimes termed angels or demons, sometimes gods or goddesses, and sometimes idols.[23] Every power above is summoned to **praise your wonders** and **your faithfulness**, where **wonders** means all the amazing deeds of covenant love by which God makes and sustains the world and redeems his people.[24] This is covenant faithfulness in action. Psalm 89:6–7 moves from this summons to praise God to a vigorous declaration that **the LORD**, the covenant God, is the only true God. These beings bow in awe (even terror)[25] before the sheer God-ness of the one true God.

Psalm 89:8 builds to a climax with the emphatic **LORD God of hosts**, the declaration of his incomparable **might**, and the vivid picture of his **faithfulness all around** him as an ever-present attendant, such that God

---

21 Hengstenberg, *Psalms*, 3:100.
22 For other uses of this word in the Psalms, see Pss. 18:11; 36:5; 57:10; 68:34; 108:4.
23 For similar language, see 1 Kings 22:19–21; Job 1–2; Isa. 6:1–3; Jer. 23:18. And see on Ps. 82.
24 This is a significant theme in book 3; see Pss. 75:1; 77:11; 78:4, 11, 32; 88:12.
25 The verb translated "to be feared" means to be made to tremble in terror or awe. BDB, s.v. ערץ.

is never seen or known without his faithfulness. As Franz Delitzsch puts it, "His glory would only strike one with terror; but the faithfulness which encompasses Him softens the sunlike brilliancy of His glory, and awakens trust in so majestic a Ruler."[26] The main burden of 89:5–8 is that the covenant between Father and Son is made by God, who is almighty and unfailingly faithful; he has decided to do it, and he has the power to do what he has decided. What God does in Christ is no fragile accident of history; it rests on the "structure" of deity at the heart of the universe.

> [9]   *You* rule the raging of the sea;
>   when its waves rise, *you* still them.
> [10]   *You* crushed Rahab like a carcass;
>   you scattered your enemies with your mighty arm.
> [11]   The heavens are yours; the earth also is yours;
>   the world and all that is in it, *you* have founded them.
> [12]   The north and the south, *you* have created them;
>   Tabor and Hermon joyously praise your name.

The emphatic pronoun **you** occurs five times in this section (italicized above). God is the emphatic subject (cf. Ps. 74:12–17). Psalm 89:9–12 moves from the heavenly realms to the earth, beginning with **the raging** (i.e., proud uprisings)[27] **of the sea** with **its waves** (cf. 46:3; 65:7; 93:3–4). This imagery sometimes refers to rebellious nations and sometimes to the evil powers of chaos that threaten the moral order of the world (cf. Job 38:8–11). When a man stills these waters, we ask, "Who then is this?" (Mark 4:41). **Rahab** may indicate a storybook monster (i.e., Leviathan), who embodies all the forces of hostility to God (cf. Job 9:13; 26:12; Ps. 74:12–17; Isa. 51:9–10), or the power of Egypt (either as the oppressor at the time of the exodus or as an unreliable ally in the days of Isaiah; cf. Ps. 87:4; Isa. 30:7). The phrase **like a carcass** means something that has been "pierced." The scattering of **your enemies with your mighty arm** is echoed by Mary (Luke 1:51; see the *orientation* section above), for it is Jesus Christ who wins this final victory (cf. Col. 2:15).

---

26 Delitzsch, *Psalms*, 3:36.
27 The same root is translated "arrogantly" in Ps. 17:10.

Psalm 89:11 moves from the hostile sea to **the heavens** above, **the earth** beneath, and **the world** (i.e., the inhabited world of human beings). **The world and all that is in it** echoes Psalm 24:1 (quoted in 1 Cor. 10:26). The key words are **yours**, for they are under God's almighty power, and **you have founded them**, that is, built them as a place of moral order. The reason for the covenant between the Father and the Son is that the moral order of the world should be rebuilt. There is a question about the significance of **Tabor and Hermon** in Psalm 89:12. These mountains (the modest Mount Tabor and the impressive Mount Hermon) may indicate east and west (Hermon to the east of the Jordan, Tabor to the west), to balance **the north and the south**, although they are not used in this way elsewhere.[28] They may be centers of worship, indicating the submission of false worship to the Lord.[29] Or perhaps Tabor is a reminder of the victory of Deborah and Barak (Judg. 4:6, 12, 14). Whatever the precise significance, the force of Psalm 89:12 is to support 89:9–11: the God who makes the Father-Son covenant is utterly without rival.

13 You have a mighty arm;
       strong is your hand, high your right hand.
14 Righteousness and justice are the foundation of your throne;
       steadfast love and faithfulness go before you.

Psalm 89:13–14 sums up 89:5–12. The putting together of **arm, hand,** and **right hand** (see also 89:10, 21) speaks comprehensively about God in action. The adjectives **mighty, strong,** and **high** emphasize omnipotence. But it is 89:14 that draws 89:5–14 to a climax. The four covenant words are **righteousness** (God doing the right thing by powerfully fulfilling his covenant), **justice** (God setting the world to rights), **steadfast love** (חֶסֶד, *khesed*, covenant love), and **faithfulness** (God doing unfailingly what he has promised to do). These form **the foundation**[30] **of your throne**, for all God's government of the world is based on and inseparable from these

28 Harman, *Psalms*, 2:659.
29 For a possible allusion to false worship on Tabor, see Hos. 5:1. The name "Hermon" is cognate with the solemn "ban" (חרם); the name "baal-hermon" (Judg. 3:3) may suggest false worship on Hermon.
30 The root "foundation" (כון) appears in Ps. 89:2, 4, 14, 21, 37 ("established").

covenantal attributes. They **go before** God as constant attendants (as in 89:8: "all around you").

Psalm 89:15–18 moves from covenant faithfulness to the implications of this reality for the church of Christ. The covenant with David was always intended to bring blessing to David's people (cf. 2 Sam. 7:10).

¹⁵   Blessed are the people who know the festal shout,
        who walk, O LORD, in the light of your face,
¹⁶   who exult in your name all the day
        and in your righteousness are exalted.

Blessed (אַשְׁרֵי, *ashre*) here at the end of book 3 echoes its use at the start of book 1 (see on Ps. 1:1). This blessing rests on **the people who know the festal shout**, also described as those **who walk . . . in the light of your face**. The second helps interpret the first. To walk in the light of God's face is to walk in the light (cf. 1 John 1:7). The word translated **festal shout** can mean different things in various contexts; here it must mean a glad and confident acclamation in authentic corporate worship. Psalm 89:16 expands on this. These people **exult in your name**, that is, in you as you have revealed yourself in the Scriptures, and do so consistently, **all the day**. The final line (**and in your righteousness are exalted**) probably means that God's covenant righteousness, working on them and in them, lifts them up to live the life of obedient faith.

¹⁷   For you are the glory of their strength;
        by your favor our horn is exalted.
¹⁸   For our shield belongs to the LORD,
        our king to the Holy One of Israel.

Psalm 89:17–18 gives us the reason (**for**) why the church described in 89:15–16 is blessed. The covenant God is **the glory** (the word means "beauty") **of their strength**, which means that by his **favor** or grace, **our horn** (i.e., our strength) **is exalted**. And so the focus narrows to the King (returning to the theme anticipated in 89:3–4). The one who is **our shield**, our defender on earth (cf. 84:9), **belongs** in covenant love **to the LORD** and is—now for the first time this critical word is used—**our king**. In 89:17–18 we are brought back to 89:1–4. The people who are blessed in the covenant are the church that belongs to the King, who is by covenant the Son to God the Father. This focus on the King leads directly in to the sustained celebration of this covenant in 89:19–37.

Commenting on 89:17–18, John Calvin writes,

> As the chief protection of the people was in the person of their king, it is here expressly shown, that the maintenance of the welfare of the faithful by his instrumentality is the gift of God. But it is to be noticed, that the prophet's mind was not so fixed upon this temporal and transitory kingdom as to neglect, at the same time, to consider the end of it, as we shall presently see. He knew that it was only on account of Christ that God made his favour to flow upon the head of the Church, and from thence upon the whole body. [And so] we must remember that what is said of this kingdom, which was a shadow of something greater, properly applies to the person of Christ, whom the Father has given to us to be the guardian of our welfare, that we may be maintained and defended by his power.[31]

89:19–37 In Christ the Church Is Unbreakably Secure
Again and again, what is promised to Christ is what is attributed to God earlier in the psalm: great power (Ps. 89:5–13, 21–27), a mighty arm and hand (89:13, 21–23), a raised "horn" (89:17, 24), power over the waters (89:9–10, 25), and steadfast love and faithfulness (89:1, 2, 14, 25).

> [19]   Of old you spoke in a vision to your godly one, and said:
>   "I have granted help to one who is mighty;
>   I have exalted one chosen from the people.
> [20]   I have found David, my servant;
>   with my holy oil I have anointed him,
> [21]   so that my hand shall be established with him;
>   my arm also shall strengthen him.

The first characteristic of the covenant is election. Here is one **chosen from the people** (for he had to be one of us; cf. Heb. 2:17) and **found** in

---

31 Calvin, *Psalms*, 3:430–31.

the drama of 1 Samuel 16:6–13 (cf. 1 Sam. 13:14).[32] This man is a shadow of the final man, the incarnate Son of God, whom the Father sent and then chose—after the Son became a man—to be his covenant **servant**. The phrase **to your godly one** may refer to "godly ones" since most manuscripts have the plural. If so, then **You spoke in a vision** indicates Samuel (1 Sam. 3:1–21) and Nathan (2 Sam. 7), with David included as the one about whom the visions were spoken. The main point is the content of what God said. **I have granted help to one who is mighty** (lit., "to a warrior") makes perfect sense for David (a warrior; cf. 2 Sam. 17:8) and finally for the greatest warrior the world has known. David is **anointed** with God's **holy oil** to equip him with the Spirit (1 Sam. 16:13) for his work, just as the Holy Spirit filled Jesus without measure (John 3:34) for his ministry on earth.[33] As a result of this eternal election, the powerful **hand** of God is **established** with Jesus Christ, who is **strengthen**ed on earth for all his work.

David Dickson writes,

> As David was in type, so Christ is in truth, and in all respects, more eminently than David, a strong helper, mighty to save, appointed of the Father to help us in all cases, and to whom we are directed to go, that we may find help; he is one of our kind, taken out from among the people, acquainted with the meanest condition his subjects can be in, exalted to be a Prince and Saviour, chosen and predestinated, as man, for the office before the world was, devoted to the service of the redemption, sanctification, government, and salvation of his people, and filled, as man, with the Holy Ghost above measure, that out of his fulness we may all receive grace for grace.[34]

22   The enemy shall not outwit him;
    the wicked shall not humble him.
23   I will crush his foes before him
    and strike down those who hate him.
24   My faithfulness and my steadfast love shall be with him,

---

32 For "finding" as a picture of God's gracious election, see Deut. 32:10.
33 Augustine makes the connection with the bridegroom-king being anointed with the oil of gladness in Ps. 45:7. Augustine, *Psalms*, 4:286.
34 Dickson, *Psalms*, 2:118–19.

and in my name shall his horn be exalted.
25   I will set his hand on the sea
and his right hand on the rivers.

Psalm 89:22–25 moves from election to conquest. These words echo 2 Samuel 7:10, which was a promise for the people. Here it is a promise for the King, since the King "receives everything for the community, and without [him] the community receives nothing."[35] **The enemy shall not outwit**[36] **him; / the wicked shall not humble** (afflict, oppress) **him.** His foes will be **crush**ed and struck down. Psalm 89:24 brings us back to the covenant that lies behind these victories: **my faithfulness and my steadfast love** are always **with him**, for in him "grace" (i.e., covenant love) and "truth" (i.e., covenant faithfulness) become incarnate on earth (John 1:14). His **horn**, that is, victory and strength (cf. Ps. 75:4–5), are **exalted**, lifted high. And in particular, he will **set his hand** and **right hand** (powerful agency) **on the sea** and **the rivers**. Here "sea" and "rivers" are a general way of speaking of all hostile powers, whether earthly or supernatural; he will do on earth what God is praised for doing in 89:9. Christ the chosen one is the victorious one.

26   He shall cry to me, 'You are my Father,
my God, and the Rock of my salvation.'
27   And I will make him the firstborn,
the highest of the kings of the earth.
28   My steadfast love I will keep for him forever,
and my covenant will stand firm for him.
29   I will establish his offspring forever
and his throne as the days of the heavens.

The third focus is on the relationship of the covenant Son with the Father and the consequences of this relationship. The cry **You are my Father** (cf. 2 Sam. 7:14; Ps. 2:7), heard so movingly on earth in the prayers of Jesus, accompanies **You are . . . my God** (cf. John 20:17) and **You are . . . the Rock of my salvation**, that is, the strong God who saves me (cf. Ps. 18:2). The

---

35 Hengstenberg, *Psalms*, 3:107.
36 The verb (hiphil of נשׁא) probably has the sense of "get the better of"—so NIV. See Tate, *Psalms 51–100*, 410–11n23a.

right to call God "Father" belongs to Jesus Christ by nature and is given to us in Christ. All the benefits of the covenant come to us through Christ, as John Owen explains: "The whole inheritance granted unto Christ is eternally secured for us. . . . Thus in all things infinite wisdom has provided that no second forfeiture should be made of the inheritance of grace and glory."[37]

The counterpart to this filial cry is the word of the Father: **I will make him the firstborn**, the son with all the rights of inheritance and dignity; this title, given to Israel corporately in Exodus 4:22, is given to the King as their federal head (cf. Heb. 1:6: "when [God] brings the firstborn into the world"). Or to put this another way, **I will make him . . . the highest of the kings of the earth**. The word **highest** (עֶלְיוֹן, *elyon*) echoes the title "Most High" used elsewhere of God (e.g., Ps. 87:5). Here is the promise of Psalm 2 expanded (cf. the covenant blessing of Deut. 28:1: "God will set you high above all the nations of the earth"). Psalm 89:28 takes us back to the **steadfast love** of the **covenant** that undergirds the relationship of the Son to the Father and all the blessings of the psalm. This covenant God **will keep for him forever**, and it **will stand firm**[38] **for him**. It is unbreakable: "Because of Christ the covenant is trustworthy; in him the covenant is established; he is the mediator of the covenant, he is the one who puts his seal to it, who guarantees it and witnesses it."[39] All this leads to the establishment of **his offspring forever**, that is, **his throne** (his rule) **as the days of the heavens** (with the same sense of eternity as in 89:2b).

> 30   If his children forsake my law
>   and do not walk according to my rules,
> 31   if they violate my statutes
>   and do not keep my commandments,
> 32   then I will punish their transgression with the rod
>   and their iniquity with stripes,
> 33   but I will not remove from him my steadfast love
>   or be false to my faithfulness.

---

37 John Owen, *Christologia, or, A Declaration of the Glorious Mystery of the Person of Christ*, in *The Works of John Owen*, edited by William H. Goold (1850–1855; repr., Edinburgh: Banner of Truth, 1965–1968), 1:216.

38 The verb "stand firm" has the same root as "faithfulness" (see on Ps. 89:1).

39 Augustine, *Psalms*, 4:287.

34   I will not violate my covenant
       or alter the word that went forth from my lips.

Psalm 89:30–34 addresses a central question about the covenant of God: Is it conditional or certain? If it is conditional, it cannot be certain and will fail, as Old Testament history relates all too graphically; if it is certain, then it cannot be conditional but also cannot then be just (for it is unjust for God to save a still rebellious people). The grand answer of the New Testament is that the covenant is at the same time conditional (for it must be fulfilled) and certain (for one will come who will fulfill it for his people).

Psalm 89:30–31 expresses in the strongest possible terms the worst-case rebellion.[40] The verbs **forsake, do not walk, violate** (which has the sense of "desecrate"), and **do not keep**, together with the nouns **law, rules** (i.e., covenant judgments), **statutes**, and **commandments**, envisage a near-total rejection of the covenant. And yet, even then, the covenant will not fail. There will be severe discipline (89:32) but not the removal of **steadfast love** and **faithfulness**. The church may **violate** the covenant (89:31), but God will not **violate** his **covenant** (89:34). What he has promised to David—and ultimately to Christ—he will unfailingly do.

35   Once for all I have sworn by my holiness;
       I will not lie to David.
36   His offspring shall endure forever,
       his throne as long as the sun before me.
37   Like the moon it shall be established forever,
       a faithful witness in the skies."   *Selah*

Psalm 89:35–37 presses home emphatically the message of 89:30–34. When God swears by his **holiness**, he swears by his very own being (cf. "the Holy One of Israel," 89:18); no stronger oath can be made (cf. 60:6; 105:42; Jer. 23:9; Amos 4:2; 6:8). Psalm 89:36–37 (echoing the vision of Ps. 72) concludes that everything celebrated thus far in the psalm will most

---

40 "The strongest possible descriptions of sin are designedly chosen in order to express the thought that the substance of the covenant is altogether independent of human conditions, that even the greatest unfaithfulness on the part of man does not alter the faithfulness of God." Hengstenberg, *Psalms*, 3:108–9.

assuredly come to pass. Calvin comments, "Until we come to Christ, God might seem to be unfaithful to his promises. But in the branch which sprung out of the root of Jesse, these words were fulfilled in their fullest sense."[41] "How certain," writes Augustine, "how firm, how plain, how unambiguous are all these promises concerning Christ!"[42]

There is uncertainty about whether the phrase **faithful witness** refers to **the moon**; it is more likely that God himself is the witness to undergird his promise with his own nature.[43]

89:38–45 The Church of Christ Lives under the Sign of the Cross

38   But now you have cast off and rejected;
         you are full of wrath against your anointed.
39   You have renounced the covenant with your servant;
         you have defiled his crown in the dust.
40   You have breached all his walls;
         you have laid his strongholds in ruins.
41   All who pass by plunder him;
         he has become the scorn of his neighbors.
42   You have exalted the right hand of his foes;
         you have made all his enemies rejoice.
43   You have also turned back the edge of his sword,
         and you have not made him stand in battle.
44   You have made his splendor to cease
         and cast his throne to the ground.
45   You have cut short the days of his youth;
         you have covered him with shame.   *Selah*

It is important to be clear that while the lamented destruction of David's line is an accurate description of what is experienced, it is not the last word. Here is an apparent failure of the covenant but not a final failure. Matthew 1:12–16 portrays the continuing line of David, which, as it were, went underground until the coming of the Messiah.

41 Calvin, *Psalms*, 3:446.
42 Augustine, *Psalms*, 4:294.
43 So Tate, *Psalms 51–100*, 425–27.

In sixteen staccato lines, the experienced reality of the church is described as the polar opposite of everything that has been so confidently promised and so gladly praised. God is the subject of almost every verb, beginning with the emphatic **But . . . you**[44] at the start of Psalm 89:38. These things have not happened because a well-meaning god has been overwhelmed by forces beyond his control; all this he—the all-powerful, faithful God—has actively done. He has not simply permitted these things, as though his arm had been twisted; he has done them. This is the shock. But these things are said neither in unbelief nor in final bewilderment; they are voiced in faith (cf. the spirit of Ps. 44:9–16 or Hab. 1:2) and therefore soaked in sure and certain hope.[45] Far from taking us into a cavern of despair, the psalm conducts us into a place of honesty, in which we set our experience side by side with the promises of God. We do not pretend that things are otherwise than how they are, but neither do we water down what God has promised us in Christ.

Psalm 89:38 laments that the **wrath** of God rests on the **anointed** one (i.e., the King; cf. 18:50). To all appearances, **the covenant** (89:3, 28), which God said he would not violate (89:34), has been **renounced**[46] (a word used elsewhere only in Lam. 2:7 ["disowned"]). The **crown** (contrast Ps. 132:18), which is a sign of being consecrated to God,[47] has been **defiled**, made dirty, **in the dust**, the place of death (cf. Ps. 74:7; Lam. 2:2; 5:16). Psalm 80:12 gives background to 89:40–41; the word for **walls** is used in 80:12 of the protective walls of a vineyard; there is also here a reference to **all who pass by**. This King is fulfilled in the true vine of Israel; on the cross his "walls" are broken down, and all who pass by **plunder him**. What was true for the vine-King is true of his people who walk the way of the cross. The **scorn** or taunts of the **neighbors**, those who pass by, is a theme in 44:14; 79:4, 12; and 80:7. "These reproaches," given to the King in David's line, "are really the reproach of Christ, and, at bottom, are meant for him."[48] Far from the

---

44 The first word is וְאַתָּה, which is "but you" rather than "but now."

45 "He is contending only against *appearances*, and knows in God that he is contending only against appearances." Hengstenberg, *Psalms*, 3:111. The old covenant related visibly to outward Israel, which did indeed make the covenant void and experience the covenant curses. But it also related to the true and invisible church, for whom the covenant can never be voided.

46 Piel of נאר.

47 BDB; *HALOT*, s.v. נֵזֶר.

48 Spurgeon, *Treasury*, 2.2:34.

King's **right hand** being victorious (89:25), that **of his foes** is **exalted** so that **all his enemies rejoice** (89:42). Now the King is defeated in battle (89:43).[49] Far from shining in **splendor**,[50] his **throne** is **cast . . . to the ground**. He dies young and is exposed to public **shame** (89:45).

Although this no doubt owes its origin to some historical crisis for the Davidic monarchy (and most probably the exile), it finds its climax in the cross of Christ and then describes, in some measure, every circumstance in which the church of Christ experiences suffering with Christ and the postponement of the fulfillment of the promises that are ours in Christ. That is, it speaks to the church of Christ in every age, most acutely in each time of trial.

89:46–51 Therefore the Church Prays for Christ to Return

In the movement of the psalm, we have come from a starting point of faith (Ps. 89:1–4) through a confident, believing reception of the promises of God in Christ (89:5–37) to a realistic look at the state of Christ's troubled church, in which the kingdom of Christ seems very far from being realized. Now, in response to the contrast between promise and experience, we pray. The prayer we are given is divided by *Selah* at the end of 89:48 into two parts. In each part the petition "Remember" appears (89:47, 50).

> ⁴⁶ How long, O LORD? Will you hide yourself forever?
>   How long will your wrath burn like fire?
> ⁴⁷ Remember how short my time is!
>   For what vanity you have created all the children of man!
> ⁴⁸ What man can live and never see death?
>   Who can deliver his soul from the power of Sheol?   *Selah*

The cry **How long, O LORD?** is a frequent response of faith to troubles (cf., in book 3, Pss. 74:10; 79:5; 80:4; elsewhere, 6:3; 13:1; 35:17; 90:13; 94:3; 119:84); it is not a cry of despair but a petition of faith, confident that there will be an end to the trials: "Here the psalmist turneth his complaint into prayer for remedy, to show that he did not fret, but believe, that the

---

49 For discussion about the translation "the *edge* [lit., 'stone'] of his sword," see Hengstenberg, *Psalms*, 3:113.

50 The word מֶזַח means purity, clarity, and hence, a shining luster.

Lord both could and would give relief."⁵¹ The agony of God hiding his face is echoed from Psalm 88:14. The misery of God hiding his face is deeper than any human suffering.

The plea in 89:47, **Remember how short my time is**, uses an unusual word⁵² that means something like "length of life" (it is used in this sense in Job 11:17 ["your life"]; Ps. 39:5 ["my lifetime"]). Literally meaning, "Remember my life(time)," here it must be in the sense "Remember how short is my lifetime." This is expanded in Psalm 89:48 into a deep anxiety about facing **death** or **the power** (lit., "hand") **of Sheol** (where death is thought of as a power). Psalm 89:47–48 could have come out of Psalm 49 (or even Ecclesiastes), and we need to ask what connection they have with the apparent failure of the kingdom of the Messiah. In the light of the New Testament, we may see that only a Messiah who wins the victory over the last enemy, even death, can give true hope to his suffering church. Only one man has conquered death, and he has done so for us. The victories of David, or any of David's successors in Old Testament history, are as nothing when compared with this final victory.

49   Lord, where is your steadfast love of old,
         which by your faithfulness you swore to David?
50   Remember, O Lord, how your servants are mocked,
         and how I bear in my heart the insults of all the many nations,
51   with which your enemies mock, O Lᴏʀᴅ,
         with which they mock the footsteps of your anointed.

The second prayer twice uses the word **Lord** (sovereign one) and returns to the grand theme of God's **steadfast love**⁵³ and **faithfulness**. Psalm 89:49 asks the question—to the sovereign one, in particular—that encapsulates the tension of the entire psalm. The plea to **remember**, which focused on our frail mortality in 89:47, now speaks to the pain of mockery. The second line of 89:50 is literally "I carry in my bosom⁵⁴ all

51 Dickson, *Psalms*, 2:128.
52 חֶלֶד.
53 The word is plural here, as in Ps. 89:1: "your deeds of steadfast love."
54 The noun (חֵיק) may mean one's chest, lap, or breast, depending on the context. Always it means "close to my fondest being." For other uses, see Gen. 16:5 ("embrace"); Ex. 4:6 ("your cloak");

the many nations" ("the insults of" is not in the Hebrew); in the context of 89:50a ("your servants are mocked") and 51 ("your enemies mock"), the addition of "the insults of" probably catches the sense correctly. The significance of 89:51 is that the **enemies** who **mock** the church are the enemies of the **LORD** and the enemies of his **anointed**, the Christ (cf. 74:18, 22; 79:12). When they mock his **footsteps** (an unusual expression), it means they scorn him "wherever he goes and wherever he stands."[55] Here are the unseen steps of the Christ who led his people out of slavery (77:20). Still he walks with his people; when they are mocked, so is he. The logic (like that of John 15:18–21 and 1 Pet. 4:14) is that the despised church may pray because the honor of God and of Christ depends on our vindication.

89:52 The Closing Marker at the End of Psalm 89 and Book 3

52   Blessed be the LORD forever!
      Amen and Amen.

Psalm 89:52 is the concluding blessing of book 3 of the Psalter; it is very similar to those that conclude books 1 (41:13), 2 (72:18–19), and 4 (106:48).[56] And yet it functions well as the conclusion to Psalm 89. The word **forever** has been a significant theme in the psalm (from 89:1 onward). The word **Amen** comes from the same root as "faithful" and "faithfulness." We might paraphrase and expand as follows: "In conclusion—holding together the promises (89:1–37) with our troubled experience (89:38–45), and in the light of our prayers (89:46–51)—let us ascribe blessedness to the covenant Lord forever. For we want to add our affirmation ('Amen') emphatically ('Amen and Amen') to the fact that he is unfailingly faithful." Or, more briefly, "Blessed be the covenant Lord for all time. It's all true! It's all true!" This is very similar to 2 Corinthians 1:20: "For all the promises of God find their Yes in [Christ]. That is why it is through him that we utter our Amen to God for his glory."

---

55 Num. 11:12; Ruth 4:16 ("on her lap"); 2 Sam. 12:3, 8 ("in his/your arms"); 1 Kings 1:2; 3:20 ("at her breast"); Job 19:27 ("within me"); Prov. 6:27 ("next to his chest"); Isa. 40:11.
55 Hengstenberg, *Psalms*, 3:115.
56 See on Ps. 41:13.

REFLECTION AND RESPONSE

1. The overall movement of the psalm begins with faith (Ps. 89:1–4), dwells richly on the promises of God through his covenant with and in Christ (89:5–37), sets this honestly alongside the experience of the church of walking under the sign of the cross (89:38–45), before closing with passionate prayer (89:46–51) and renewed faith (89:52). It is a healthy discipline to meditate on each of these in turn.

2. In Psalm 89:1–4 we orient our hearts toward Christ. We declare, with Ethan, that we too will make our lives a song, proclaiming with our mouths the covenant love and faithfulness of God given to us in Christ without fail, like a strong building.

3. In Psalm 89:5–8 we discipline ourselves to turn away from the pressing griefs of a troubled church and to focus on the sheer, transcendent God-ness of God in heaven. Derek Kidner writes of "the temptation to focus on the immediate scene and make God incidental to it."[57] Psalm 89:5–8 helps us resist this tendency. Psalm 89:9–14 applies this theme of the magnificent God-ness of God to this world, particularly to a troubled church dwelling in a world of raging, chaotic seas and monsters of evil. Psalm 89:15–18 focuses our hearts on the truth that all our blessings are to be found entirely in Christ (cf. Eph. 1:3), and Psalm 89:19–37 expands on this theme. Psalm 89:19–29 encourages us to ponder the victory of Jesus Christ on the cross and the implications it has for his final victory with his church on earth.

4. Psalm 89:30–34 is a strong encouragement to weak Christians and a church distressed by sins and scandals. Writing eloquently about this matter, Owen rightly concludes that although

> the Lord will be as it were compelled to deal sharply with them for their iniquities and transgressions: yet his "loving-kindness," that shall abide with Christ in reference to the preservation of his seed; his "faithfulness," that shall not fail; his covenant and his oath shall be made good to the uttermost.[58]

5. Psalm 89:32 must not be taken lightly. The word "stripes" means "flogging" and is the word used in Isaiah 53:5 ("with his stripes we are

---

57 Kidner, *Psalms*, 2:320.

58 John Owen, *The Doctrine of the Saints' Perseverance Explained and Confirmed*, in *Works*, 11:253.

healed," KJV). Together with the teachings of Proverbs 3:11–12 and Hebrews 12:3–11, this verse encourages us to take seriously the discipline of God. As Dickson puts it,

> The sharpest rods and sorest stripes wherewith God visiteth the children of Christ, may, and do, harmonize with loving-kindness to them; for they are fatherly corrections, medicinal preservatives against sinning afterward, and tokens of God's hating sin—not of rejection of their persons, but rather effects of his love to the persons corrected.[59]

Even as we—a local church corporately, the Christian church in a region or country, or individual believers—endure the Father's discipline, we may and must remember that God will never turn us away from Christ, for God "never withdraws [his mercy] from Christ's body, which is the Church."[60] Psalm 89:35–37 presses this theme home with comforting forcefulness.

6. Psalm 89:38–45 repays a slow and thoughtful meditation, in which we ask ourselves, "In what ways in my life, my church, and my world does it appear that Jesus is not truly the all-powerful King?" There will be different answers in various cultures and times. But always there will be answers, so long as we need to pray, "Your will be done on earth as it is in heaven," and on every day in which Jesus waits for all his enemies, and finally death itself, to be placed in subjection under his feet (1 Cor. 15:24–28).

7. Psalm 89:46–48 and then 89:49–51 give us prayers to pray when we set side by side the promises of Jesus the King and the experience of Jesus the crucified, of the blessed church and the church under the sign of the cross. Finally, 89:52 invites us to close as we began, with a glad affirmation of confidence and assurance in Christ: "Certain of his promises, let us believe in what has been done already, and rejoice in what is being fulfilled in the present, and hope for what is still to come."[61]

---

59 Dickson, *Psalms*, 2:123.
60 Augustine, *Psalms*, 4:290. Augustine preaches pastorally at some length about this issue to answer the concerns of "any anxious person" who fears that he or she will be cast off from Christ.
61 Augustine, *Psalms*, 4:301.

BOOK 4

BOOK 3 (PSS. 73–89) IS DOMINATED by the Babylonian exile. Not all these psalms were originally written in this context, but in their final form, exile casts a shadow over everything. We may naturally expect that book 4, which comprises Psalms 90–106, begins to answer the questions raised by exile, and we will not be disappointed. Ultimately, however, it speaks to the deeper questions that exile represents, the questions of sin and wrath, forgiveness and hope.[1]

The psalms in book 4 address, between them, the following four issues raised at the end of book 3.[2]

1. The suffering of Christ and the church's suffering under the wrath of God (Ps. 89:46: "How long?")
2. Human life in the shadow of death as a grievous experience (Ps. 89:47–48)
3. The covenant faithfulness of God to send the Messiah (Ps. 89:49)
4. The kingdom of God's Messiah (e.g., Ps. 89:27) and God's victory over those who mock his Messiah (Ps. 89:50–51)

One significant theme in Psalms 93–99 is that the covenant Lord is King. This is discussed under Psalm 93.

---

1 For one understanding of book 4, see Robertson, *Flow of the Psalms*, 147–82.
2 I have adapted these from VanGemeren, *Psalms*, 687–88.

We blossom and flourish as leaves on the tree,
And wither and perish—but nought changeth thee.

WALTER CHALMERS SMITH
"Immortal, Invisible, God Only Wise"

Our life hurries on at a great pace, and when we
least expect it, it slips away, and we die.

JEROME
Homilies on the Psalms

The very best time of life, the first, flees away from poor
mortal man; sicknesses follow, then melancholy old age and
weariness, and, finally, the cruel hand of inexorable death.

VIRGIL
Georgics

Whatever there is in the world, it fades away, it passes.
That is why Christ, that is why the new life, that is why
eternal hope, that is why the consolation of immortality has
been promised us and . . . has already been given us.

AUGUSTINE
"Sermon 359.9"

PSALM 90

Those who have stood at a graveside and—not long after declaring the precious words of Jesus, "I am the resurrection and the life"—have read Psalm 90 (as set in the Book of Common Prayer's "Order for the Burial of the Dead") will have poignant memories of this most evocative psalm.

The psalm leaves us with this question: When people stand at our grave-side and ask, "What was the point of this short life?" what answer can we hope that God will give? Can what we do ever have lasting significance?[1] Is it possible for our work to be "establish[ed]" (90:17) when it all ends in death? This psalm is given to those "who through fear of death were subject to lifelong slavery" (Heb. 2:15); perhaps no human literature expresses the sorrow of the shadow of death as poignantly as does Psalm 90. Its great theme is the pain of time-bound mortal creatures. Time is everywhere in the psalm: "all generations" (90:1), "days" or "years" (90:4, 9, 10, 12, 15), "a watch in the night" (90:4), "morning" (90:5, 6, 14), and "evening" (90:6).

The psalm is given to set before us the one who "offered up prayers and supplications, with loud cries and tears, to him who was able to save him from death" (Heb. 5:7), who experienced for us all the sadness of Psalm 90. He partook of our flesh, was "made like his brothers in every respect," so that he might "make propitiation for the sins of the people," having himself "suffered when tempted" (Heb. 2:17–18). Jesus is the answer to the anxieties of Psalm 90 because he entered into this sadness for us: "The meeker than

---

1 "The psalm addresses in various ways the question, In the sure knowledge of our death, what gives meaning to our time now and how should we understand our time from the perspective of that moment when our life is at an end?" Patrick D. Miller, *Interpreting the Psalms* (Philadelphia: Fortress, 1988), 125.

Moses, Christ on earth, could use this Psalm in sympathy with us."[2] Perhaps we may use Psalm 90 as a prayer for the church led by Jesus, expressing his lament on earth and now voicing our yearnings for eternity.

Psalm 90 expresses both our natural fear of death and the faith-filled confidence that we may now have in Christ. In the light of the resurrection of Christ, the final verse (90:17) is transposed into the new key of 1 Corinthians 15:58: "Therefore, my beloved brothers, be steadfast, immovable, always abounding in the work of the Lord, knowing that in the Lord your labor is not in vain." In this life we may have assurance that there is no condemnation (Rom. 8:1) while still groaning in mortal bodies and longing for the redemption of those bodies on the last day (Rom. 8:23).

Two contexts are to be borne in mind, the historical and the canonical. In its historical context, this psalm is titled "A Prayer of Moses." We do not know what prompted Moses to voice this beautiful psalm, but there are many possibilities. Moses no doubt felt these things personally, perhaps when the people grumbled (Num. 11:1–3) or when discouraged by the report of the spies (Num. 14:26–45) or on Mount Pisgah before his death (Deut. 34). But the psalm is plural, an expression of the laments and prayers of the whole church. So perhaps Moses prayed this prayer when the people asked him to intercede for them during the plague of snakes in Numbers 21:4–9. The intercession of Moses in Exodus 32 provides very significant background to the psalm. Note the plea for God to "turn" and "relent" (Ex. 32:12; Ps. 90:13), the only Scriptures in which both these verbs are used in petition to God.[3] Just as the Mosaic covenant was threatened by the golden calf, so the Davidic covenant is threatened by the exile.[4] Links with Deuteronomy 32–33 include (1) the imagery of God giving birth (Deut. 32:18; Ps. 90:2, using the same two verbs), (2) the Lord having "compassion" (Deut. 32:36; Ps. 90:13), and (3) Moses being called "the man of God" (Deut. 33:1; Ps. 90:S).[5] There are echoes also of Exodus 15.

In its canonical context, Psalm 90 is the first psalm in book 4 and therefore lies on the other side of a crucial "seam" in the Psalter with Psalm 89. The most significant ties to Psalm 89 are (1) the question "How long?" (89:46) and (2) the agony of living under the shadow of death (89:47–48). Given the

---

2   Bonar, *Psalms*, 273.

3   Robertson, *Flow of the Psalms*, 151–52. The two terms are identical in the Hebrew, שׁוב and נחם (in the niphal), though the ESV translates them "return" and "have pity" in Ps. 90:13.

4   Hamilton, *Psalms*, 2:154.

5   Robertson, *Flow of the Psalms*, 151.

prominence of exile in book 3, this connection prompts us to set side by side the poignancy of the wilderness wanderings (in exile for a whole generation) with the sorrows of exile; it is very remarkable to find the only psalm headed "of Moses" appearing at this point, after the reminder of the apparent destruction of the Davidic covenant at the end of Psalm 89.[6] O. Palmer Robertson observes, "Now the people have been exiled from their land once more, just as they were compelled to exist outside the land during their sojourn in Egypt and their wandering in the wilderness under Moses' leadership."[7] Lamentations 5:16–22 provides some striking parallels, spoken at the time of exile; these include an acknowledgment of sin (Lam. 5:16), the confidence that God reigns forever (Lam. 5:19), and the plea for restoration (Lam. 5:21).

Psalm 90 also shares a more general contextual link with the Wisdom Literature, especially the book of Ecclesiastes.[8]

THE TEXT

Structure

The major division is between Psalm 90:1–12 and 90:13–17. Psalm 90:1–12 is a lament over human transience. It may be subdivided into 90:1–2 (about God's eternity), 90:3–6 (lamenting human transience), 90:7–11 (grieving human sin), and 90:12 (the concluding petition).[9]

---

6   Gerald Wilson's theory has been very influential. He regards Pss. 90–106 as "the editorial 'centre' of the final form of the Hebrew Psalter," expressing "the 'answer' to the problem posed in Ps 89 as to the apparent failure of the Davidic covenant with which Books One–Three are primarily concerned." Wilson's answer is that the Lord God is King, has always been King, and will always be King, and therefore the end of the Davidic monarchy is not as disastrous as has been thought. Wilson, *Editing of the Hebrew Psalter*, 214–19. While Wilson has served us well in highlighting the significance of psalms on the "seams" between books, we need to supplement his insights with the confidence shown in the remainder of the Psalter that the Davidic monarchy is not at an end because the Messiah will come; this continued confidence in the Messiah is rightly noted by Robertson, *Flow of the Psalms*, 147–48.

7   Robertson, *Flow of the Psalms*, 152.

8   Note (1) Ps. 90:2 with Prov. 8 (see below); (2) the fragility of human life in Job; (3) the verb ידע (twice in Ps. 90:11–12), a prominent wisdom verb; (4) the fear of God (90:11); (5) the prayer for "a heart of wisdom" (90:12); and (6) the word עמל (toil), which is prominent in Ecclesiastes. On these links, see Hossfeld and Zenger, *Psalms*, 2:418. "What Ecclesiastes preaches, this psalm prays." Eveson, *Psalms*, 2:135.

9   Although Ps. 90:12 is sometimes paragraphed with what follows (e.g., ESV) because it is a petition, this petition is really the conclusion of all the thinking from 90:1–11. Ps. 90:13 marks a new beginning and a fresh tone.

Psalm 90:13–17 consists of a series of petitions. Psalm 90:17 shares with 90:1–2 (1) the name "Lord," (2) the pronoun "our" ("for us," "upon us"), (3) the verb "to be," and (4) a longing for the remedy for transience. Psalm 90:1–2 and 90:17 form something of a "frame" around the psalm.

Superscription

S   A Prayer of Moses, the man of God.[10]

The reference to **Prayer** heads Psalms 17, 86, 90, 102, and 142, and closes book 2 (72:20). Since Moses was the intercessor *par excellence* in the covenant crisis of the golden calf (Ex. 32–34), it is especially appropriate that this psalm is titled **A Prayer**.

The designation **of Moses** is unique in the Psalter.[11] Apart from Psalm 77:20 (in book 3), all the other references to Moses in the Psalms are in book 4 (99:6; 103:7; 105:26; 106:16; and note the Moses context of Ps. 95). There is a strong link between Israel in exile and Israel in the wilderness.[12]

The designation **man of God** indicates a prophet. It is used of Moses elsewhere (Deut. 33:1; Josh. 14:6; 1 Chron. 23:14; 2 Chron. 30:16) and also of Samuel as a prophet (e.g., "All that he says comes true," 1 Sam. 9:6–10), of Elijah (e.g., 1 Kings 17:18), of Elisha (e.g., 2 Kings 4:7), of David (2 Chron. 8:14), and of unnamed prophets.

90:1–12 Pray with Jesus Christ for the Wisdom to Know Our Human Condition Aright
90:1–2 Begin with a Settled Assurance of Our Home in the Eternal God

1   Lord, you have been our dwelling place
        in all generations.

10 In Hebrew, the superscription is the start of verse 1.
11 The main arguments against Mosaic authorship are (1) that Ps. 90:1 appears to look back at a long history of the people and (2) that 90:13–17 reads oddly on the edge of the promised land. E.g., Kirkpatrick, *Psalms*, 3:547. But (1) the history does go back to the age of the patriarchs, and (2) much of the wilderness period was nowhere near the edge of the promised land. Motyer comments crisply that those who cannot accept Mosaic authorship "are notably short of impressive reasons for doing so." Motyer, *Psalms*, 545.
12 The Targum hints at this link when it reads, "A prayer of Moses the prophet, when the people of Israel sinned in the desert." See Tate, *Psalms 51–100*, 438.

<blockquote>
2   Before the mountains were brought forth,

        or ever you had formed the earth and the world,

        from everlasting to everlasting you are God.
</blockquote>

The first line is astonishing; it "shines upon the psalm" "like a star from another world."[13] It addresses God as **Lord**—"the Ruler of the world,"[14] a title used twice in Psalm 89:49–50 and again in the closing verse of this psalm—saying, **you** (emphatic, you the Lord of all the world) **have been our dwelling place / in all generations**. In words that echo Moses's words in Deuteronomy 33:27 ("The eternal God is your dwelling place"), a most wonderful connection is established between time and eternity, between **you**, the eternal one, and us (**our dwelling place**). The word translated **dwelling place**[15] is used of God's "habitation," whether in heaven or on earth in Zion (e.g., Deut. 26:15; 2 Chron. 30:27; 36:15; Pss. 26:8; 68:5; 76:2). It can be used of dens of animals (e.g., Job 37:8; 38:40; Ps. 104:22; Song 4:8; Jer. 9:11) and includes the idea of a safe place or hiding place (hence the translation "refuge" in Ps. 91:9). It may also have the connotation of a place of help.[16] The phrase **in all generations** is echoed three times in Psalm 102, which also has a theme of human transience (see 102:12, 18, 24). Today the church of Christ dwells in safety with lives "hidden with Christ in God" (Col. 3:3), as the dwelling places of the Father and the Son by the Spirit (John 14:23).

Psalm 90:2 is almost a commentary on the phrase "the eternal God" in Deuteronomy 33:27, and it also hints at the "wisdom" theme of the psalm by its similarity to Proverbs 8:25, in which wisdom personified says,

<blockquote>
Before the mountains had been shaped,

    before the hills, I was brought forth.
</blockquote>

The verbs **brought forth** and **formed** are birthing verbs, used boldly of God the Creator, for the God who "gave . . . birth" to Israel (Deut. 32:18)

---

13 Artur Weiser (1893–1978), *The Psalms: A Commentary*, OTL (London: SCM, 1962), 603.

14 Kirkpatrick, *Psalms*, 3:548.

15 The MT מָעוֹן. The emendation in some manuscripts to מָעוֹז is unnecessary. Hossfeld and Zenger, *Psalms*, 2:417.

16 Cf. Isaac Watts (1674–1748), "O God, Our Help in Ages Past" (1719). Public domain. See *HALOT*, s.v. מָעוֹן; Tate, *Psalms 51–100*, 432.

also "gave birth" to the whole world.[17] **The mountains** here signify the most solid and ancient part of creation (e.g., Deut. 33:15; Prov. 8:25; Hab. 3:6). To say **before the mountains were brought forth** means "before anything came into being, before time itself." In the second line this is expanded into **the earth** (the whole cosmos) **and the world** (תֵּבֵל, *tebel*, the habitable world). Book 4 contains about half the uses of **the world** in the Psalms, mostly emphasizing its stability in times of turmoil (90:2; 93:1; 96:10–13; 97:4; 98:7–9).

The words **everlasting** and **all generations** appear repeatedly in 89:1–37; their repetition here is not coincidental, for the eternity of the covenant with David rests on the eternity of God himself. The clause **You are God** focuses on God's eternal and unchanging being; he simply is, above even time.[18]

Commenting on 90:1–2, Patrick Miller observes that "finding meaning in our life *now* in the face of death *then* depends on placing the starting point of our understanding outside ourselves."[19] The Lord Jesus consistently did this in his life of prayer to the Father, whose eternal being was his "dwelling place."

90:3–6 Pray for Realism about Human Transience

3   You return man to dust
        and say, "Return, O children of man!"
4   For a thousand years in your sight
        are but as yesterday when it is past,
        or as a watch in the night.
5   You sweep them away as with a flood; they are like a dream,
        like grass that is renewed in the morning:
6   in the morning it flourishes and is renewed;
        in the evening it fades and withers.

---

17 Similar "birthing" language is used of parts of the created order in Job 38:8, 28–29.

18 It may be better to place a comma between "from everlasting to everlasting" and "you are God" (as the KJV). The three temporal adverbial clauses ("before the mountains were brought forth," "or ever you had formed the earth," and "from everlasting to everlasting") build up to the main statement: "You are God." God simply is God! I am grateful to Travis Wright for this observation.

19 Miller, *Interpreting the Psalms*, 126.

In Psalm 90:3–6 we learn why we so desperately need a dwelling place with the eternal God. These verses paint a sober picture of our transient mortality before 90:7–11 reveals the cause. **You return man**—ordinary mortals, "the little human being"[20]—**to dust**, where the word for **dust** means matter that is crushed or pulverized;[21] although a different noun is used, the allusion to Genesis 2:7 and 3:19 seems clear.[22] It is no coincidence that the verb from this root appears in Isaiah 53:10 ("Yet it was the will of the LORD to crush him"): the Father spoke those terrible words, "Return to dust," to his Son on the cross as he was crushed for us.

The second line emphasizes the first,[23] using the phrase **children of man** ("sons of אָדָם, *adam*," i.e., humankind); the combination of the singular in the first line (any particular man or woman) and the generic plural (humankind) in the second line is frighteningly comprehensive. On any day, the Creator can decree that any man or woman or any number of men and women must return to dust. There is no appeal; on that day he, she, or they must die. None of us knows and not one of us can control the day of our death. Not only are our lives brief, they are absolutely at the Creator's disposal.[24]

The three lines of Psalm 90:4 move from **a thousand years** (a practical infinity, unimaginably long; cf. Gen. 5:27; Eccl. 6:6) through **yesterday when it is past** (a day that is past and gone so soon) right down to **a watch in the night**, just a third of a night.[25] This language conveys better than philosophical statements the grandeur of the eternity of God and the astonishing brevity of even the longest human life. Similar imagery is used in Psalm 84:10 and 2 Peter 3:8. Martin Luther expresses it vividly:

What we in point of time consider and measure as a long-drawn-out measuring tape, all of that he sees wound up in a single ball. And so both

---

20 This is the translation of אֱנוֹשׁ in Hossfeld and Zenger, *Psalms*, 2:416.

21 דָּכָא. The verb from this root is used in Ps. 89:10 ("You crushed Rahab"). The adjective appears in the sense of "crushed in spirit" in Ps. 34:18; Isa. 57:15.

22 In Gen. 2:7; 3:19, the more common noun עָפָר is used. For death as a return to dust, see Job 10:9; 34:15; Ps. 104:29.

23 The suggestion that the second "return" has a positive sense (either "Return to life" or "Return in repentance") is highly unlikely given the flow of the passage.

24 Kirkpatrick, *Psalms*, 3:549.

25 Alter, *Psalms*, 318.

the last and the first human being, death and life, are to him no more than a moment.[26]

In Psalm 90:5–6 three more images are used to show us what it means when God decrees, "Return to dust." First, **you sweep them away as with a flood.** There is some debate about the translation of the Hebrew verb.[27] It either uses the image of a rainstorm (as in Ps. 77:17; Isa. 28:2; cf. Matt. 7:25–27) or simply means to snatch or sweep away. John Calvin rightly comments that this need not be a sudden or particular disaster but refers to death itself, which "may fitly be called an invisible deluge."[28] Second, **they are like a dream** (lit., "they are sleep"), probably referring to the sleep of death (cf. Ps. 76:5; Jer. 51:39, 57); we are so fragile, and it takes as little to make us die as it does to put us to sleep. Third, we are **like grass** in a hot climate, which springs up with the dew of the morning and is withered and faded by sundown.[29] Each of these images is linear and final. A sober understanding of human mortality has no place for "the circle of life" in some of its popular cultural manifestations.

We may be confident that Jesus not only understood but deeply felt this sad realism about his own transience as a human being living under the judgment of God for us.

90:7–11 Pray for a Sober Grasp on Human Sinfulness and the Wrath of God

7   For we are brought to an end by your anger;
         by your wrath we are dismayed.
8   You have set our iniquities before you,
         our secret sins in the light of your presence.
9   For all our days pass away under your wrath;
         we bring our years to an end like a sigh.
10   The years of our life are seventy,
         or even by reason of strength eighty;
         yet their span is but toil and trouble;

---

26 Luther, *Luthers Werke*, WA 22:402, quoted in Kraus, *Psalms*, 2:216n1.
27 For the technical discussion, see Hossfeld and Zenger, *Psalms*, 2:417nd; Tate, *Psalms 51–100*, 433–34.
28 Calvin, *Psalms*, 3:466.
29 For this common image of human life, see, e.g., Pss. 37:2; 103:15–16; 129:6; Isa. 37:27; 40:6–8; 51:12.

they are soon gone, and we fly away.

11   Who considers the power of your anger,

and your wrath according to the fear of you?

Psalm 90:7–11, omitted from some lectionaries because it is not thought to be comforting,[30] is of the utmost importance. It feels hard to read these verses at the graveside through our tears. And yet without a sober acceptance that death is God's punishment for sin, there can be no dawning of gospel hope; we need to be afraid of God before we can find comfort in the gospel.[31]

Psalm 90:7–9 forms a subsection with a balanced structure: **bring to an end** (90:7a, 9b); **your wrath** (90:7b, 9a); **our iniquities** and **our secret sins** (90:8).

We are brought to an end (cf. "consumed," Job 4:9; "made [to] vanish," Ps. 78:33; "pass away," 102:3; "consumed," Lam. 4:11). **We are dismayed** conveys paralyzing terror, as with Joseph's brothers in Genesis 45:3 (cf. Pss. 30:7; 48:5; 83:17; 104:29) or an army facing a rout (Judg. 20:41). It is right to be terrified in the face of death, for death is the visible expression of the **anger** and **wrath** of a holy God;[32] death is not natural, however much we accustom ourselves to it.

Psalm 90:8, at the center of 90:7–9, places the focus on **our iniquities** and **our secret sins**, where the latter is literally "our concealed things,"[33] perhaps primarily things we try to keep hidden from God but maybe also things hidden so deep in our hearts that we deceive ourselves about their presence (cf. "deceiving and being deceived," 2 Tim. 3:13). Much as I prefer the cover of darkness (cf. John 3:19–21), I cannot prevent my sins from being **set . . . before you** and placed **in the light of your presence** (cf. Ps. 139:1–3). The Book of Common Prayer thus addresses God as "Almighty God, unto whom all hearts be open, all desires known, and from whom no secrets are hid."[34] As C. S. Lewis famously said in his sermon "The Weight of Glory," "In the end that Face which is the delight

30 Miller, *Interpreting the Psalms*, 125.
31 Luther, *Luther's Works*, 13:78–79.
32 These words for God's anger "suggest hotly burning breath" and therefore connect with the image of grass withering in Ps. 90:5. Alter, *Psalms*, 319.
33 Qal passive participle of עלם (to hide). A cognate word is used in Ps. 44:21: "the secrets of the heart."
34 Book of Common Prayer, "Collect for Purity," from the service of the Lord's Supper.

or the terror of the universe must be turned upon each of us."[35] Death is the wages of sin (Rom. 6:23).

Psalm 90:9 recapitulates the sadness of 90:7 with the addition of **all our days** followed by **our years**, both time in its small divisions and life in its longer periods. The verb **pass away** has the sense of a day declining toward evening (cf. Jer. 6:4: "Woe to us, for the day *declines,* / for the shadows of evening lengthen"); the sadness of a late afternoon is a microcosm of the sorrow of aging. A **sigh** here means something like "a moan" or a sad whimper (cf. "mourning," Ezek. 2:10), weary and forlorn. This is how it ends. Henry Francis Lyte (1793–1847) observes,

> Swift to its close ebbs out life's little day.
> Earth's joys grow dim, its glories pass away.[36]

In Psalm 90:10 **the years of our life** (lit., "the days of our years")[37] may—and even this would presumably be exceptional in Old Testament days after the flood—reach **seventy** (the famous "threescore years and ten" of the KJV), or **by reason of strength** (the word suggests great strength, a remarkable vigor)[38] **eighty**. The addition of the second phrase hints at the lengths to which we will go to gain a short extension of our lives.[39] But even then, however hard we try and however we may succeed in living a long life, when compared with God's eternity, how pathetic we are! The word translated **their span** suggests something in which one takes pride, not necessarily in the sense of sinful pride but with the sense of energy and gladness,[40] the days of eager hope and vigorous energy. And yet even this is tainted with **toil** (wearisome labor)[41] and **trouble**. For as Job observes,

---

35 Preached at Saint Mary the Virgin, Oxford, in June 1942. C. S. Lewis, *The Weight of Glory* (New York: HarperOne, 1980), 38.

36 Henry Francis Lyte, "Abide with Me" (1847). Public domain.

37 For this idiom, see Gen. 47:8–9.

38 גְּבוּרֹת is an intensive plural; see Tate, *Psalms 51–100*, 435.

39 Luther quotes Cicero: "No one is so old as not to hope that he will live yet another year." Perhaps from *De Senectute*, 19, quoted in Luther, *Luther's Works*, 13:100.

40 *HALOT*, s.v. רֹהַב; hence CSB and NIV: "the best of them."

41 The word (עָמָל) is frequent in Job (Job 3:10, 20; 4:8; 5:6, 7; 7:3; 11:16; 15:35; 16:2; 20:22); cf. Ps. 107:12 ("hard labor").

Man who is born of a woman
    is few of days and full of trouble.
He comes out like a flower and withers. (Job 14:1–2)

These days, short and spoiled as they are, **are soon gone**, which probably has behind it the idea of a weaver's shuttle or spool of yarn, unwinding fast and irreversibly.[42] That **we fly away** completes the terrible picture (cf. Job 20:8; Eccl. 6:12).

Psalm 90:11 concludes 90:7–11 by coming back to **your anger** and **your wrath**. The question **Who considers?** (lit., "Who knows?" in the wisdom sense of "Who grasps? Who gets the message of 90:3–10?") prepares us for the prayer of 90:12. The second line is literally "and as your fear, (so) is your wrath." This may mean (1) that we are right to be very frightened of you because you are very angry[43] or (2) that if we grasp the intensity of your righteous anger against sinners, then we will live in the reverent fear of you.[44] While both are true, the latter accords better with the wisdom tone of the psalm and the movement into the prayer of 90:12.

90:12 Pray for a Heart of Wisdom

[12]   So teach us to number our days
            that we may get a heart of wisdom.

Psalm 90:12 is the conclusion and response to all that has been declared in 90:3–11. The prayer **to number our days** has nothing to do with knowing how long we will live—for that we cannot know—and everything to do with grasping that every day is a gift of God, that death is God's just punishment for sinners, and that **a heart of wisdom** is found only by seeking in the eternal God "our dwelling place" (90:1). Similar sentiments are expressed in Deuteronomy 5:29 and 32:29. Derek Kidner comments, "Perhaps nowhere outside the book of Ecclesiastes is the fact of death so resolutely faced, or the fear of God so explicitly related to it."[45] The tragedy

42 See Hossfeld and Zenger, *Psalms*, 2:417. For this imagery, see Job 7:6; Isa. 38:12.
43 So Alter, *Psalms*, 319.
44 So Kirkpatrick, *Psalms*, 3:552.
45 Kidner, *Psalms*, 2:330.

of human life is that fear of death does not necessarily lead to repentance (cf. Rev. 9:20), but the Lord Jesus knew perfectly this "heart of wisdom." Those given new birth in him will learn to live wisely each day, making the most of the time given to us (cf. Eph. 5:16; Col. 4:5).

90:13–17 Pray in the Name of Jesus Christ for Restoration and Significance
90:13–16 Pray for Jesus to Return

¹³   Return, O LORD! How long?
      Have pity on your servants!
¹⁴   Satisfy us in the morning with your steadfast love,
      that we may rejoice and be glad all our days.
¹⁵   Make us glad for as many days as you have afflicted us,
      and for as many years as we have seen evil.
¹⁶   Let your work be shown to your servants,
      and your glorious power to their children.

Psalm 90:13–16 shares with 90:3–12 the verb "to turn/return" (90:3, 13) and the theme of time ("morning," "days," "years," 90:4, 5, 6, 9, 10, 12, 14, 15). And yet the focus has shifted from the general sadness of human transience to a more Israel-specific yearning for the restoration of covenant blessings to the people of God; note the use of the covenant LORD for the first time and the phrases **your servants**, **your steadfast love**, **your work**, and **your glorious power**, all of which are most naturally associated with covenant blessings. Also, the question **How long?** echoes the same question in book 3 in Psalms 74:10 and 80:4. In some ways we are taken back to 90:1–2, in which the church of God celebrates that the eternal God is "our dwelling place." It is profitable to consider the connection between the restoration of Israel from exile and the resurrection from the dead, which is the only remedy to 90:3–12. The connection is profound. Exile, like death, is a punishment for sins, and death is, in its fundamental nature, an exile from the presence of God. It follows that return from exile is like a national resurrection (cf. the valley of dry bones in Ezek. 37). Ultimately, it is only the coming of Christ to fulfill the covenant that will bring the church of God back from the dead. It is for this that we now pray in Psalm 90:13–16.

In 90:13 the verb **return** means to "relent," in the sense of Jonah 3:9–10. The verse echoes the words of Moses in Exodus 32:12 and Deuteronomy 32:36. The verb **have pity** appears in Isaiah 40:1 ("comfort"). Luther rightly observes that "this petition includes in veiled language a prophecy of the coming Christ, since eternal salvation could be achieved only by Christ."[46]

In Psalm 90:14, **satisfy** means to give the kind of satisfaction experienced after a full meal, an image of longings fulfilled (cf. Prov. 13:12). The **morning** is a commonly experienced time of fresh hope, often associated with God acting in mercy (e.g., Pss. 30:5; 46:5; 143:8); in the end it is an image of "resurrection morning." Joy and gladness **all our days** is the polar opposite of days under God's wrath (90:6, 9–10, 12). While return from exile might give some anticipation, the final experience is rightly described by Augustine:

> The day that is coming is a day without end. All those days we know now will be present together, and that is why they will satisfy us. Where there is nothing of which it could be said that this does not exist because it has not come yet, and nothing that has ceased to exist because it has come already, the days do not yield place to other days that follow. All days are present at once, because there is but a single day that stands, and does not slip away; and that is eternity.[47]

The theme of gladness continues in 90:15, with **days** of affliction or being humbled under God's wrath, even **years** of trouble (**evil** in the sense of troubles or disasters). There is a similar prophecy of abundant restoration in Isaiah 60:7, with "a double portion" that more than compensates for the troubles. In the end, "it is clear that in these sweeping words the prophet is praying for the coming of Christ into the flesh," for "the context of the passages . . . shows that Moses is praying for a remedy against God's all-embracing wrath over sin. Since only the Messiah could secure this remedy, this petition includes Christ."[48] Only then can the church of God look forward to "an eternal weight of glory beyond all comparison" (2 Cor. 4:17).

In Psalm 90:16 **your work** means especially what God does to rescue his church (cf. Deut. 32:4; Ps. 92:4; Hab. 3:2). **Your glorious power** translates a

---

46 Luther, *Luther's Works*, 13:131.
47 Augustine, *Psalms*, 4:312.
48 Luther, *Luther's Works*, 13:134.

word that means "splendor and majesty,"[49] translated "majesty" in the ESV of Psalms 45:3–4; 111:3; and Lamentations 1:6.

90:17 Conclusion: Pray to Do Something of Lasting Significance in Christ

> [17]   Let the favor of the Lord our God be upon us,
>   and establish the work of our hands upon us;
>   yes, establish the work of our hands!

The three lines of Psalm 90:17 mark an emphatic conclusion. **Favor** (נֹעַם, *noam*) is a warmly aesthetic word meaning "beauty" (cf. 27:4) or "pleasant-ness" (cf. Prov. 3:17; also used of "gracious" words in Prov. 15:26; 16:24), "as it were, a flood of grace."[50] **The Lord** brings us back to Psalm 90:1, bracket-ing the psalm with the almighty power of God. Theodoret of Cyrus rightly links the first line with the incarnation, for "then it was that the light of the knowledge of God rendered [the church] splendid and illustrious."[51]

The repetition of **upon us** in the second line helps us understand the meaning of the second and third lines. There is a connection between the beauty of God resting "upon us" in Christ and the plea to **establish the work of our hands upon us**. The verb **establish** "is the word used for keeping dynasties or buildings unshaken. Against the dismaying ephemerality of human existence, in which a life sprouts and withers like grass, God can give fleeting human experience solid substantiality."[52] And yet he does this only in and through Christ. The phrase **the work of our hands** can refer to anything that any human being does, but it has special reference to what believers do under the covenant blessing of God (e.g., Deut. 2:7; 14:29; 16:15; 24:19; 28:12; 30:9; Job 1:10).

Psalm 90:17 is answered when Jesus Christ prays it and is raised from the dead and given all authority in heaven and on earth. Because of his resurrection, it will be answered for his church, the members of which are exhorted to "be steadfast, immovable, always abounding in the work of the

---

49 *HALOT*, s.v. הָדָר.
50 Luther, *Luther's Works*, 13:137.
51 Theodoret of Cyrus, *Psalms*, 2:101.
52 Alter, *Psalms*, 320.

Lord, knowing that in the Lord"—the risen Lord Jesus—their "labor is not in vain" (1 Cor. 15:58).

REFLECTION AND RESPONSE

1. Each part of the psalm awaits our prayerful pondering. It is important to spend time on Psalm 90:1–2, for the sadness of 90:3–12 "is not given the first word or the last."[53] We do not often spend time meditating on the timeless and eternal being of God, but we ought to, for only as we do so will the preciousness of "You have been our dwelling place" become apparent. This is the privilege that we have in Christ, our lives hidden with him in God, the Father and the Son dwelling in our hearts by the Spirit. No security on earth can rival these promises.

2. Psalm 90:3–6 needs to be felt as well as understood. It should make us weep. The images of 90:5–6 are there to help us feel the sorrow of human mortality. They are a severe antidote to all shallow wishful thinking about this world. Calvin pastorally points out that so many of our errors stem from the fact that we "foolishly imagine that we shall nestle in this world for ever."[54]

3. But Psalm 90:3–6 needs always to be accompanied by 90:7–9, with its surgical probing of the sinful human heart. What Paul expresses with analytical rigor in Romans 5:12–21, Moses paints poetically in these verses. Psalm 90:10–11 forces us to look honestly at human life, even at its very best and most successful. Only when we have allowed 90:3–11 to sink into our hearts can we pray 90:12 with deep desire, longing to walk through this life with a heart of wisdom. And yet, even here, 90:1–2 shines light as we hold this hope together with a realism about human sin, the wrath of God, and the shadow of death.

4. Luther writes,

The entire human race fell so far away from God and is so thoroughly blinded by original sin that man knows neither himself nor God. Indeed, he does not even know his own sorry state, although he feels it and

53 Kidner, *Psalms*, 2:328.
54 Calvin, *Psalms*, 3:465.

languishes under it. He neither understands its origin nor does he see its final outcome. Therefore the misery which our first parents brought on themselves as a result of their sin and transmitted to their posterity is indescribably great. I ask you to consider how foolishly the wisest men have discoursed on death, the gravest and most horrible punishment of sin.[55]

5. The motif of time that runs through the psalm prompts us to think about what it is to live as time-bound beings. James L. Mays observes, "Time is the medium of our mortality and so the favorite focus of our folly. . . . The young think they are immortal, the old despair because their time is over. Time is a burden when we have to wait, a scarcity when we are busy. It is the source of anxiety, illusion, remorse."[56]

6. We need to pray Psalm 90:13–16 conscious of its covenantal background and always remembering that any prayer for covenant mercy is a petition for Christ. We thank God for Jesus; we pray for a fresh work of Jesus in our lives and our churches; we cry for Jesus to return in glory.

7. On the face of it, Psalm 90:17 is a dangerous prayer: "Lord, please make me a significant, even an important, person!" The rebuke to Baruch in Jeremiah 45:5 warns us that this cannot be the way to pray this verse. The plural ("the work of *our* hands") reminds us that this is a petition for the work of the church of Christ together and not a prayer for my personal success. And yet I can pray that, by God's grace, I will contribute something of lasting value to the work of God in building the church (cf. 1 Cor. 3:10–15).

8. Charles Spurgeon writes this on Psalm 90:17:

We come and go, but the Lord's work abides. We are content to die, so long as Jesus lives and his kingdom grows. Since the Lord abides for ever the same, we trust our work in his hands, and feel that since it is far more his work than ours he will secure it immortality. When we have withered like grass, our holy service, like gold, silver, and precious stones, will survive the fire.[57]

55 Luther, *Luther's Works*, 13:76.
56 Mays, *Psalms*, 295–96.
57 Spurgeon, *Treasury*, 2.2:66.

There is a safe and secret place,
Beneath the wings Divine,
Reserved for all the heirs of grace;
O be that refuge mine!

HENRY FRANCIS LYTE
"There Is a Safe and Secret Place"

This psalm, like so many, speaks first and foremost of Jesus
the Messiah. He is the king who was given these assurances of
God's help and the promises of deliverance, vindication and
glory. Previous psalms have presented similar assurances from
God to his king (see Psalm 21). Christ our representative head
has fully met the conditions and known the promises fulfilled
through his own ministry in this world. But all who love God
and belong to Jesus Christ can take to heart the words of this
psalm and know the life and salvation that he has obtained.

PHILIP EVESON
Psalms

PSALM 91

"In the whole collection there is not a more cheering Psalm," wrote Charles Spurgeon of Psalm 91.[1] But does it promise too much? Can it possibly be true?[2] Who, if anyone, can claim it? It is all in the singular. One person declares his or her faith, and that same person is given the promises.

We should first reject a not-uncommon approach, which sees this blessed person as being anyone who has sufficient faith. If you believe these promises enough, they will come true for you. Erich Zenger seems to come close to this when he writes that, in the face of dangers, "one prays oneself into the hope, indeed the certainty that one is protected and gifted with life by YHWH. . . . In reciting the psalm, the petitioner constitutes the saving counter-world, as projected in the psalm, against the threatening world in which he lives."[3] An extension of this thinking is the idea that the psalm can be used in a quasimagical way, as a sort of charm or amulet. This notion was embraced in the Middle Ages, and some embrace it today.[4]

These subjective readings understand "faith" as being a human "work" smuggled in through the back door; faith becomes something we need to do, and do strongly, if we are to benefit from it. This misunderstands the nature of faith and places on us an unbearable burden.

Three factors help us understand what the psalm truly means.

---

1 Spurgeon, *Treasury*, 2.2:88.
2 Belcher, *Messiah and the Psalms*, 58.
3 Hossfeld and Zenger, *Psalms*, 2:429.
4 William L. Holladay, *The Psalms through Three Thousand Years: Prayerbook of a Cloud of Witnesses* (Minneapolis: Fortress, 1993), 184, 289.

First, the promises of the psalm correspond strikingly to the covenant blessings given to Israel. These (and their opposites in covenant curses) include (1) the absence of the need to fear (Lev. 26:6; Ps. 91:5), (2) safety in the presence of "thousand[s]" of the wicked (Lev. 26:7–8; Ps. 91:7), (3) dwelling with God (Lev. 26:11; Ps. 91:1–2, 9), (4) safety from harmful beasts (Lev. 26:6, 22; Ps. 91:13), and (5) protection from disease and plague (Deut. 28:21; Ps. 91:3, 10).[5] The psalmist personifies Israel.

Second, there is a remarkable agreement between the blessings promised here and those given to the King, for example, in Psalm 21. These include (1) "salvation" (21:1, 5; 91:16), (2) answered prayer (21:2; 91:15), (3) long life (21:4; 91:16), and (4) victory over enemies (21:8–12; 91:8). So perhaps the psalmist is the King, and ultimately the Messiah, as the covenant head of Israel. Philip Eveson argues, "There are good grounds for believing that the psalm is addressed primarily to the Davidic king as the Lord's Anointed, especially in his representative role as head of his people."[6]

The third factor comes, strange as it may seem, from the devil, in the temptations of Jesus (Matt. 4:5–7; Luke 4:9–12). Before his quotation from this psalm, the devil says to Jesus, "If you are the Son of God, throw yourself down . . ." (Matt. 4:6; Luke 4:9). Here "Satan challenges Jesus to demonstrate that he is the one to whom the Psalm 91 statements were made."[7] It's as if he said, "If you are the Son of God and can therefore legitimately claim these promises for yourself, then prove it." Jesus accepts that this is so, even as he refuses to use this right.

This New Testament reflection sheds light on our first two observations. First, Jesus is the true Israel, who resists the temptations in the wilderness, as the old Israel had failed to do.[8] The promises given to Israel are given to him. Second, they are given to him as the Davidic King, the Messiah, the covenant head of his people. He receives them on their behalf, as the head for the members of his body. "Where Israel failed to keep the terms of the

---

5   Other references in Lev. 26 and Deut. 27–28 can be found. These are adapted from Belcher, *Messiah and the Psalms*, 58–61.

6   Eveson, *Psalms*, 2:142–43. Eaton writes, "The individual on whom such promises are lavished could hardly be any but the king." J. H. Eaton, *Kingship and the Psalms*, SBT, 2nd ser., vol. 32 (London: SCM, 1976), 57.

7   Hamilton, *Psalms*, 2:165.

8   Kirkpatrick, *Psalms*, 3:557; Longman, *Psalms*, 332.

covenant, Christ has succeeded so that as our representative he now offers to us the fullness of covenant blessing."[9]

The promises of Psalm 91 are given to the Messiah on behalf of the church. Christ has "the first right and title" to these promises, and we inherit them in him.[10]

Thematic echoes in the New Testament support the conviction that we inherit these blessings in Christ. In Hebrews 1:14 angels are called "ministering spirits sent out to serve for the sake of those who are to inherit salvation." This echoes the promise of Psalm 91:11 ("For he will command his angels concerning you") and applies it to "those who are to inherit salvation," that is, the church. In Luke 10:19 Jesus says to his disciples, "Behold, I have given you authority to tread on serpents and scorpions, and over all the power of the enemy, and nothing shall hurt you." This echoes parts of Psalm 91:13 and applies it to the disciples of Jesus.[11] Second Timothy 4:17 ("So I was rescued from the lion's mouth") may echo another part of Psalm 91:13. Romans 8:28–39 has been called, "in effect, a summary of Psalm 91."[12] The promises of Psalm 91 are given to Christ and to us in him.

These New Testament passages answer the question "Does Psalm 91 promise too much?" with a resounding "No!" And yet the New Testament also teaches that the fullness of these blessings awaits the resurrection and the new creation; here we have the firstfruits and down payment, by the Holy Spirit (Rom. 8:23; Eph. 1:13–14), but the end is not yet. Elisabeth Elliot (1926–2015) implicitly acknowledged this tension when she called the story of her martyred husband *The Shadow of the Almighty*, for those who live in the shadow of the Almighty may yet suffer and die.

In the immediate context in the Psalter, Psalm 91 functions as God's gracious answer to the prayer of Moses in Psalm 90:13–17. Links between Psalms 90 and 91 include (1) the similarity of 91:1–2 and 9 with 90:1 (and the repetition of the infrequent word מָעוֹן, *maon*, from 90:1 in 91:9); (2) language of time, common in Psalm 90, in 91:5–6; (3) the promise "When he

9 Belcher, *Messiah and the Psalms*, 60.
10 Dickson, *Psalms*, 2:141.
11 Pao and Schnabel, "Luke," in *CNTOT* 318; Hossfeld and Zenger, *Psalms*, 2:432.
12 Hossfeld and Zenger, *Psalms*, 2:433.

calls to me, I will answer" (91:15), which picks up the prayer and petition theme of 90:S and 13–17; (4) the verb "satisfy" (91:16; 90:14); and (5) the verb "show" (91:16; 90:16). Psalm 92, following this answer to prayer, expresses thanksgiving.

Other scriptural links include the promise of a serpent crusher in Genesis 3:15, some of the words of Eliphaz to Job in Job 5:17–26,[13] and some of the promises of Proverbs 3:21–35. As with Psalm 90, Psalm 91 echoes some of the language and thought of the Song of Moses in Deuteronomy 32.

THE TEXT

Structure

Psalm 91:1–2 declares the headline truth (91:1) and expresses faith in that truth (91:2). After this, 91:3–13 is spoken to an individual ("you" is singular throughout) to expound the covenant promises. Psalm 91:14–16 is the direct speech of God pressing home the blessings. The psalm has something of a crescendo, from the faith of 91:1–2 through the exposition of blessings in 91:3–13, climaxing in the very words of God himself in 91:14–16.

Much guesswork has accompanied the mixture of "voices" (from "I" to "you" and back again), not least the idea that the psalm was written to be spoken antiphonally in some liturgies. We simply cannot know, and Hebrew poetry knows much of varying "voices," which are common stylistic devices.

91:1–2 In Christ We Are Safe with God

1   He who dwells in the shelter of the Most High
         will abide in the shadow of the Almighty.
2   I will say to the LORD, "My refuge and my fortress,
         my God, in whom I trust."

---

13 We must ask why the unreliable Eliphaz (see Job 42:7) and the reliable psalmist say similar things. The answer is that the blameless Job prefigures the suffering Christ, who endures the very opposite of covenant blessing so that he can become the covenant curse for his people (Gal. 3:13).

Psalm 91:1 is a headline for the psalm. Since **dwells** (lives, sits, as in 1:1; 2:4) and **abide** (lodge, spend the night) are more or less synonyms, as are **shelter** (a secret, hidden, and therefore safe place)[14] and **shadow**,[15] and also **Most High** and **Almighty**,[16] the two lines logically form a tautology: "If you are safe with the all-powerful God, you are safe with the all-powerful God"; this is "a tautology of emphasis."[17] Jesus dwelt in this shelter on earth, and we are called to do the same as we abide in Christ.

Psalm 91:2 is said by one who believes 91:1 and who trusts (**in whom I trust**) this covenant God (note the covenant name, LORD, and the covenant word **my God**). Both **refuge** (also in 91:9; cf. 14:6; 62:7; 71:7; 73:28; 94:22; 142:5) and **fortress** (cf. 18:2; 31:3; 71:3; 144:2) are common words, especially on the lips of David. Supremely this is a profession of intimate faith on the lips of Jesus on earth.

91:3–13 God Promises Safety and Victory to Christ and to His People in Him

3   For he will deliver you from the snare of the fowler
        and from the deadly pestilence.
4   He will cover you with his pinions,
        and under his wings you will find refuge;
        his faithfulness is a shield and buckler.
5   You will not fear the terror of the night,
        nor the arrow that flies by day,
6   nor the pestilence that stalks in darkness,
        nor the destruction that wastes at noonday.
7   A thousand may fall at your side,
        ten thousand at your right hand,
        but it will not come near you.
8   You will only look with your eyes
        and see the recompense of the wicked.

---

14 The word is used in this sense in 1 Sam. 19:2; Job 40:21; Pss. 27:5; 31:20 ("cover"); 61:4; Song 2:14 ("crannies").
15 The word appears in the phrase "the shadow of your wings" in Pss. 17:8; 36:7; 57:1; 63:7. It is used in the sense of "protection" in Eccl. 7:12; Song 2:3; Lam. 4:20.
16 The word (שַׁדַּי) is used in the Psalms only here and in Ps. 68:14.
17 Grogan, *Psalms*, 160.

In Psalm 91:3, **for** may express emphasis ("Indeed!"). **He** is emphatic. **Deliver** means to snatch away or rescue. **The snare of the fowler** (for this metaphorical phrase, see 124:7; for "fowler," see Prov. 6:5; Jer. 5:26; Hos. 9:8) is the trapping net used by a hunter of birds. We are uncertain how to translate **the deadly pestilence**, but it denotes something (anything) terrifyingly destructive.[18] In Psalm 91:4 **pinions** (cf. Deut. 32:11; Job 39:13; Ps. 68:13) is used in parallel with **his wings** (cf. Deut. 32:11); this may allude to the wings of the cherubim to express covenant safety in God (see on Ps. 57:1; cf. Ruth 2:12). Alluding to Matthew 23:37, Augustine writes, "If a hen protects her chicks under her wings, how much safer will you be under the wings of God, safe against the devil and his angels, those powers of the air which hover like hawks, all ready to snatch the feeble hatchlings!"[19] **His faithfulness** means being true to his covenant (with Christ and therefore with Christ's people). **A shield and a buckler** may refer to two kinds of shield (as an image of comprehensive protection) or perhaps may use a hendiadys to express emphasis ("a shield that shields").[20]

Psalm 91:5–7 moves from what God does—for the king, for Christ, for the church—to our experience. **The terror** (cf. Deut. 28:67 in the context of covenant curses; Pss. 64:1; 119:120; Prov. 1:33; Song 3:8) **of the night** vividly conveys the feeling of what we still call "night terrors," when dangers take paralyzingly fearsome forms in our fevered imaginations. **The arrow that flies by day** is scarcely less frightening. Together, these phrases cover the gamut of fearful experiences. **The pestilence** (cf. Ps. 91:3) **that stalks in darkness** is frightening because you cannot see it and therefore cannot protect yourself from it (like an invisible virus). The word **destruction** may refer to an epidemic (Deut. 32:24), a disaster (Isa. 28:2), or a sharp sting (Hos. 13:14).[21] Again, the combination of **darkness** and **noonday** covers all circumstances. Psalm 91:7 may refer to the battlefield but more likely continues the image of disease or plague. **A thousand** with **ten thousand**

---

18   The first word (דֶּבֶר) means something like a bubonic plague (cf. Ex. 9:1–7; Deut. 28:21; Ps. 78:50) or a sharp sting (Hos. 13:14, perhaps alluded to in 1 Cor. 15:54–55; see Ray E. Ciampa and Brian S. Rosner, "1 Corinthians," in *CNTOT* 747–48). The second word (הַוּוֹת) means "destruction." Hence either "a sting that destroys" or "a plague that destroys."

19   Augustine, *Psalms*, 4:319.

20   See Tate, *Psalms 51–100*, 448n4d.

21   *HALOT*, s.v. קֶטֶב.

conveys a large number growing unimaginably large (cf. 144:13).[22] The picture of a plague (perhaps like the Black Death in fourteenth-century Europe) running amok,[23] with just one man untouched is extraordinary. When we ask what this means in the realities of the life of faith, Augustine writes, "To whom is this promise addressed? To the Lord Jesus Christ, brothers and sisters: who else? The Lord Jesus is present not only in himself, but in us too" (quoting Acts 9:4). He goes on to point to the promise of final victory in Christ.[24]

Psalm 91:8 brings this section to a close. Christ and all who are in Christ will, on the last day, **look with** their **eyes / and see the recompense of** (i.e., the just retribution on) **the wicked**. Linking this verse with 91:13, James Hamilton rightly notes that **the wicked** are the seed of the serpent (in the language of Gen. 3:15 or John 8:44).[25]

9   Because you have made the LORD your dwelling place—
        the Most High, who is my refuge—
10   no evil shall be allowed to befall you,
        no plague come near your tent.
11   For he will command his angels concerning you
        to guard you in all your ways.
12   On their hands they will bear you up,
        lest you strike your foot against a stone.
13   You will tread on the lion and the adder;
        the young lion and the serpent you will trample underfoot.

Psalm 91:9 echoes the profession of faith in 91:1–2.[26] In 91:10 **evil** is used in the sense of harm. The word **plague** can mean any disease, calamity, or

---

22 For other uses of "a thousand" with "ten thousand," see Judg. 20:10; 1 Sam. 18:7.
23 "In all likelihood, the setting evoked is a raging epidemic in which vast numbers of people all around are fatally stricken." Alter, *Psalms*, 322.
24 Augustine, *Psalms*, 4:323.
25 Hamilton, *Psalms*, 2:166.
26 The ESV margin draws our attention to a small question of translation. The MT is literally "for you [singular, emphatic] the LORD my refuge, the Most High you have made your dwelling place." Since the verse seems (like Ps. 91:3–8 and 10–13) to be addressed to "you," the most likely reason for the first-person suffix "my refuge" is that it is like an autobiographical aside, as in the CSB: "Because you have made the LORD—my refuge, / the Most High—your dwelling place . . ." The noun "dwelling place" is the same as in 91:1 (מָעוֹן).

disaster.[27] The **tent** is a frequent image, in both the Old and New Testaments, of fragile human life. Psalm 91:11–12 (quoted by the devil in the temptations of Jesus) promises—to the King and his people—that God **will command his angels concerning you**, those creatures who are supernatural but subdivine and whose work is to be "messengers"[28] to run errands for God. Their instructions are **to guard you in all your ways**; they are—in the proper sense—guardian angels. God exercises his providential oversight of human affairs through the intermediate agency of these creatures. Their protection is described in 91:12 in terms of preventing Christ, and his people, from stumbling (**lest you strike your foot against a stone**; cf. 119:165; Isa. 8:14). Their standing orders (cf. Ps. 34:7) are to protect Christ from harm and now to guard all Christ's people. They came to minister to Jesus in the wilderness (Matt. 4:11), and one came to strengthen him in Gethsemane (Luke 22:43), as they had protected Elisha under threat (2 Kings 6:16–17). And yet Jesus did not claim this right when he chose to be condemned to die for sinners (Matt. 26:53–54).

Psalm 91:13 is the climax of 91:9–13. The combination of two words for **lion**[29] and two words for **serpent**[30] point to open hostility and subtle seduction, for the devil is sometimes like a fierce dragon (like a lion, 1 Pet. 5:8)[31] and sometimes like a deceptive snake.[32] It was recognized early in church history that the power to trample on the serpent "the Creator conferred on his Christ, first of all, even as [Psalm 91] teaches."[33] Christ is the serpent crusher of Genesis 3:15. Christ has been victorious for us over "every enemy

---

27 In the Psalms the word (נֶגַע) appears also in Pss. 38:11 ("plague"); 39:10 ("stroke"); 89:32 ("stripes").

28 The word (מַלְאָךְ) can mean "angel" (e.g., Ex. 23:23) or "messenger" (e.g., Ezek. 17:15 ["ambassadors"]), depending on the context.

29 The first word (שַׁחַל) appears in Job 4:10; 10:16; 28:8; Prov. 26:13; Hos. 5:14; 13:7. The second word (כְּפִיר)—often translated "young lion," although our knowledge of the words for lion is incomplete—appears in Judg. 14:5 (Samson) and several times in Job, Psalms, and Proverbs.

30 The first word (פֶּתֶן) may mean an adder, cobra, or some other deadly snake. The second word (תַּנִּין) has wider resonances, being used of the great sea creatures in Gen. 1:21; of "a sea monster" in Job 7:12; of "the sea monsters" in Ps. 74:13; of "great sea creatures" in Ps. 148:7; of Leviathan in Isa. 27:1; of Rahab in Isa. 51:9; of "a monster" in Jer. 51:34. It is also used of Aaron's snake in Ex. 7 and in parallel with the word here translated "adder" in Deut. 32:33.

31 The theme of God's champion victorious over lions is seen in Samson (Judg. 14:5–6), David (1 Sam. 17:34–35), and Daniel (Dan. 6:21–23).

32 For a helpful study of this theme, see Naselli, *The Serpent and the Serpent Slayer*.

33 Tertullian, *Against Marcion*, 4.24, in ACCS 8:174.

of [our] salvation, how fierce, strong, and cruel soever he be; how crafty, malicious, and dangerous soever he be."[34] Because Christ has done this for us at the cross, we may be assured that "the God of peace will soon crush Satan under [our] feet" (Rom. 16:20).

91:14–16 God Promises to Save to the Uttermost All Who Are in Christ

14   "Because he holds fast to me in love, I will deliver him;
         I will protect him, because he knows my name.
15   When he calls to me, I will answer him;
         I will be with him in trouble;
         I will rescue him and honor him.
16   With long life I will satisfy him
         and show him my salvation."

In Psalm 91:14–16 God speaks directly. These promises are "spoken immediately by God the Father, of his Son Jesus Christ as man, and of every believer and true member of his mystical body."[35] The verb translated **holds fast . . . in love**[36] expresses a "deep and passionate attachment,"[37] used of the covenant God's love for his people (Deut. 7:7; 10:15) and—in a very different context—of Hamor's attachment to Dinah (Gen. 34:8). Here it speaks first and foremost of the intimate and unchanging love of the Son for the Father, now overflowing by the Spirit into the loyal love of every member of Christ's church, before and after the coming of Christ. This phrase stands in parallel with **he knows my name**; that is, he knows, with intimate personal loyalty, me as I have revealed myself on earth in the covenant. It is in this sense that Jesus speaks in John 17 of the Father having given him his name and Jesus then manifesting that name to his disciples, that they too may "know the name" of God (cf. John 17:6, 11–12, 26), or—to express this another way—to make the Father known (John 1:18).

---

34 Dickson, *Psalms*, 2:147.
35 Dickson, *Psalms*, 2:147. Cf. Belcher, *Messiah and the Psalms*, 60.
36 חָשַׁק.
37 Harman, *Psalms*, 2:679.

To this Christ and—in Christ—to all Christ's church are given the promises of deliverance or protection (Ps. 91:14), of answered prayer (91:15a), of his presence in troubles (91:15b), of final rescue and honor (91:15c), of satisfaction and long (finally eternal) life (91:16a), and of salvation in all its fullness (91:16b). The verb **protect**[38] means to place inaccessibly high, out of all danger. The word **trouble** or distress encompasses all the pressures and pains of the human heart (cf. 31:7 ["distress"]; 46:1; 81:7 ["distress"]; 120:1). **Long life** (lit., "length of days") is, in the end, eternal life, for, as Augustine points out, "this is what will wholly satisfy us. . . . No stretch of time, however lengthy, can satisfy us if it has an end."[39] The verb to **satisfy** means to be filled, as by a good meal (cf. Ruth 2:18; Pss. 81:16; 90:14; 104:28; 105:40 ["abundance"]; 147:14). To be shown God's **salvation** is, in the end, to experience in Christ the redemption of our bodies (Rom. 8:23), on that day that is nearer to us now than when we first believed (Rom. 13:11), the day for which we hope and wait (1 Thess. 5:8), knowing that it is ready to be revealed on that last day (1 Pet. 1:5).

REFLECTION AND RESPONSE

1. Before giving ourselves to the enjoyment of the sheer wonder of Psalm 91, it is worth reflecting that the sufferings of Jesus demonstrate his loving determination to be made poor for those he came to save. All these privileges were his by right. But he waived his rights and experienced the opposite—all for us.

2. To a world paralyzed by fear, troubled by infectious diseases, broken by wars and conflicts, Psalm 91 lays out a vision of a life of fearless confidence, based on sober realities far from the shallow make-believe that cannot combat terror when it comes.

3. What greater incentive can there be than this psalm, asks David Dickson, "to induce a soul to embrace the free offer of grace in Christ, tendered in the gospel to sinners, or to move him to entertain friendship with God, by still believing in him, and resting on him?"[40]

38 Piel of שׂגב (used of the King in Ps. 20:1; also 69:29, "Set me on high").
39 Augustine, *Psalms*, 4:343.
40 Dickson, *Psalms*, 2:148.

4. Alongside this offer of the gospel is an implicit challenge to "be all the more diligent to confirm your calling and election" (2 Pet. 1:10). Christ has first rights to all these blessings. Only those in whom the Spirit of Christ has begun to place this lively faith and passionate love can truly lay claim to these promises in Christ.

5. Hamilton expresses with comprehensive clarity the message and implications of the psalm. It is worth quoting him at length:

> No one more epitomizes Psalm 91 than Jesus. No one lived more in God's presence, more inhabited the shelter of the Most High, the shadow of the Almighty. No one took refuge in God like Jesus, was delivered like Jesus, and trampled the dragon like Jesus. No one loved God or knew God's name like Jesus. No one called on God like Jesus, experienced God's presence in distress like Jesus, or was delivered even from death like Jesus. No one will be more glorified by God than Jesus, who has received the name above every name, and no one will be more satisfied than Jesus. Jesus is the fulfillment of everything stated in Psalm 91.
>
> Because Jesus lived out the fullness of this Psalm, his people can take up their crosses and follow him. His people can inhabit the hiding place, the shadow of the Most High, entering boldly to find grace in time of need. Those who belong to Jesus can take refuge in God, experience God's deliverance, and God will soon crush Satan under their feet (Rom 16:20). When they have been delivered, they will be glorified (Rom 8:30), satisfied with long life as they behold God's salvation (Rom 8:21–25).[41]

6. After telling a moving story of how a verse from this psalm cheered him in the midst of wearisome pastoral work during a cholera epidemic, Spurgeon writes, "He who can live in its spirit [the spirit of Psalm 91] will be fearless, even if once again London should become a lazar-house [a hospital for people with infectious diseases], and the grave be gorged with carcasses."[42]

41 Hamilton, *Psalms*, 2:167.
42 Spurgeon, *Treasury*, 2.2:88.

[Psalm 92] encourages to the practice of righteousness, and preserves us from fainting under the cross of Christ, by proposing to our view a happy issue out of all our afflictions.

JOHN CALVIN
Commentary on the Psalms

[Psalm 92] reminds us that we are more than conquerors in and through Christ the head of the Church who died and rose victorious and reigns on high with God the Father.

PHILIP EVESON
Psalms

PSALM 92

Psalm 92 invites us to enter into the joy of Jesus Christ. This joy coexists with the poignant sorrow of Psalm 90. It is a gladness of anticipation.

Several factors suggest that before it overflows to the church, Psalm 92 refers especially to the King. The exalted "horn" (92:10) most often refers to the King in David's line. The psalmist's victory is the same as God's victory (92:9–11). Even the metaphor of the fruitful tree (92:12–15) is often associated with kings (see on Ps. 1; cf. this imagery in Judg. 9:7–15; Ezek. 17:22–24). Revelation 15:3–4 ("the song of Moses" and "the song of the Lamb") resonates with Psalm 92:5.[1]

It is not difficult to imagine Jesus praying this psalm in his days on earth. He lived in paradoxical joy among his disciples (e.g., Mark 2:18–19) and rejoiced in the Holy Spirit precisely when he experienced the deep and hidden wisdom of God (Ps. 92:5) in rejection and incomprehension (Luke 10:21). For the "joy" set before him, he "endured the cross" (Heb. 12:2). In the days of his deepest weakness, he was confident of final victory (e.g., Matt. 26:64). He invites his faithful servants to enter into his joy (Matt. 25:21, 23).

This background of Christ's joy suggests three ways for Christians to read the psalm. First, we hear it as the gladness of Jesus our King in his prayers on earth.

Second, we celebrate that our hope is grounded on the sure victories of Jesus our King. Just as Psalm 90:17 leads to 1 Corinthians 15:58, so Psalm 92 finds its fulfillment in 1 Corinthians 15 when the risen Jesus destroys every rebel power and hands the kingdom over to God the Father (1 Cor. 15:24).

---

1 Beale and McDonough, "Revelation," in *CNTOT* 1133–34; Hossfeld and Zenger, *Psalms*, 2:445.

Third, we enter into his joy as we too anticipate his final victory.

There are many links between Psalm 92 and Psalms 90 and 91. These links include (1) "the Most High" (91:1, 9; 92:1), (2) gladness (90:14–15; 92:1–3), (3) the "name" (91:14; 92:1), (4) "steadfast love" (90:14; 92:2; cf. many times in Ps. 89), (5) "faithfulness" (91:4; 92:2), (6) references to time (Pss. 90 [often]; 91:5–6; 92:2), (7) the "works" of God (90:16; 92:4–5), (8) the works of your/our hands (90:17; 92:4), (9) wisdom verbs of knowing and the like (90:11–12; 92:6), (10) humankind like grass (90:5–6; 92:7), (11) destruction (91:6; 92:7), (12) verbs of seeing (90:16; 91:8; 92:11), (13) old age and long life (90:10–11; 91:16; 92:14), and (14) God's house or dwelling (90:1; 92:13). If Psalm 90 laments and Psalm 91 gives promises, Psalm 92 rejoices in those promises. Although these psalms make no explicit reference to the exile, it may be that Psalms 90–92, beginning book 4 after the exile motif in book 3, speak with special relevance to the church in exile. This focus connects with the New Testament theme of exile as Christian discipleship (e.g., Heb. 11:13; 1 Pet. 1:1, 17; 2:11).

As well as looking back to Psalms 90 and 91, Psalm 92 is like an "overture"[2] to Psalms 93–100, most especially in its focus on the supreme rule of God (92:8), foreshadowing the refrain "The LORD reigns" (93:1; 96:10; 97:1; 99:1). This psalm exhibits particular links with the wisdom language of 94:8–11.

Psalm 92 also connects in significant ways to the wisdom teaching of Psalms 37 and 73, each of which grapples in different ways with the prosperity of the wicked. The tree imagery as blessing for the righteous echoes Psalm 1. The strong links between Psalms 1 and 2 then strengthen our persuasion that the blessings of Psalm 92 are given to Christ and thus given to us in Christ.

THE TEXT

Structure

Psalm 92:1–3 forms the introduction and 92:12–15 the conclusion. Each includes the verb "declare" (92:2, 15). The central section (92:4–11) begins with "for" and probably has a symmetrical structure with the short 92:8 at the center. Psalm 92:7 and 9 (three lines each) balance one another on either side of 92:8, celebrating the defeat of the wicked. Psalm 92:4–5 rejoices in

---

2   Hossfeld and Zenger, *Psalms*, 2:443.

God's works and is perhaps balanced by 92:10–11, rejoicing in the victory of the King. Depending whether "this" in 92:6 is taken to refer backward or forward, this verse may be taken with 92:4–5 or with 92:7; on balance, the latter seems more likely.

Superscription

S   A Psalm. A Song for the Sabbath.[3]

This is the only psalm headed **for the Sabbath**. It seems unlikely that this simply means "to be sung on Sabbath days" since presumably many of the other 149 psalms were sung then. Probably there is a deeper, symbolic significance. Given that the Sabbath is the sign of a completed creation (Gen. 2:1–3), there may be a creation significance (cf. Ps. 92:4–5). But given the theme of the psalm, which points to the final fruitfulness of the righteous and the final judgment of the wicked, the Sabbath rest of the new creation is more likely. Psalm 95 is interpreted in these terms in Hebrews 3–4, and this is probably the meaning here. The psalm celebrates the unending day of that final Sabbath rest. When the "salvation" with which Psalm 91 ends is completed, "then shall this Psalm have its most fitting place, sung, as it shall be, in the stillness and calm of the eternal day."[4] Mark 2:23–3:6 would also repay reading alongside the psalm, setting out as it does something of the beautiful Sabbath significance of Jesus, the Lord of the Sabbath. Jesus is the one who offers Sabbath rest to those who will take on them his yoke and learn from him, as this psalm encourages us to do (cf. Matt. 11:28–29).

92:1–3 Introduction: Declare with Gladness
God's Covenant Love to and in Christ

1   It is good to give thanks to the LORD,
         to sing praises to your name, O Most High;
2   to declare your steadfast love in the morning,
         and your faithfulness by night,

3   In Hebrew the superscription is verse 1; subsequent verse numbers are increased by one.
4   Bonar, *Psalms*, 277–78. A reference to the new creation is supported by Delitzsch, *Psalms*, 3:66.

3   to the music of the lute and the harp,
          to the melody of the lyre.

It is good signals the headline of the psalm, where **good** indicates both
that it is fitting (good in God's eyes) and also that it is to our benefit and
blessing, "pleasant to God and profitable to us and others."[5] The three verbs
give thanks, sing praises, and **declare** convey an atmosphere of shared
public rejoicing. The verb **declare** is repeated in the final verse as the punch
line: proclamation will be the lasting fruit of the psalm. The combination
of the covenant name, **the LORD,** and the title **Most High** focus on the
sovereignty and covenant identity of the God whom we praise.

At the heart of Psalm 92:1–3 is **your steadfast love** (covenant love) and
your faithfulness, the two grand themes of Psalm 89, fulfilled when a man
is born who is full of covenant love (grace) and covenant faithfulness (truth)
in John 1:14. **Morning** and **night** is a merism, meaning "all the time." But
morning is often the time of prayer and praise (e.g., Pss. 5:3; 57:8; 88:13),
of fresh hope and expectation (cf. 46:5 ["God will help her when morning
dawns"]; 130:6), anticipating the resurrection awakening (cf. 17:15), while
night is the time when the reminder of God's **faithfulness** to us in Christ is
most needed, when we need to know of the Lord who "in the night season
walks his rounds of watching care."[6] David Dickson writes, "The matter of
God's praise and our rejoicing, are chiefly the Lord's mercy and truth, in
pitying and pardoning, and lovingly entreating sinful men, and performing
the promises of the covenant to his people, contrary to their deserving."[7]

The phrase translated **to the music of** is literally "upon the . . . and upon
the . . ." The word translated **lute** is literally "ten," that is, some ten-stringed
instrument (cf. 33:2; 144:9). We do not know exactly what this or the **harp**
or the **lyre** was (as evidenced by the different translations suggested).[8] The
word translated **to the melody of** is the word *Higgaion* (הִגָּיוֹן, used perhaps
for a musical pause, along with *Selah* after 9:16). This term comes from the

5   Dickson, *Psalms*, 2:149.
6   Spurgeon, *Treasury*, 2.2:117.
7   Dickson, *Psalms*, 2:150.
8   The NIV follows the LXX and takes the first two as one instrument, "the ten-stringed lyre."
    This is possible, but the Hebrew is literally "upon the ten and upon the [second instrument],"
    which most naturally suggests two. For background and illustrations, see Hossfeld and Zenger,
    Psalms, 2:437–38.

root "to speak, or muse" (the same root used for meditation in 1:2).[9] But even if we do not know exactly what this musical form or these instruments were, the clear impression is of wholehearted, vocal, shared, and thoughtful praise. We do well, though, always to remember Charles Spurgeon's dictum that "fine music without devotion is but a splendid garment upon a corpse."[10]

92:4–11 Rejoice in the Victory of God's Christ and the Defeat of God's Enemies

4   For you, O LORD, have made me glad by your work;
        at the works of your hands I sing for joy.
5   How great are your works, O LORD!
        Your thoughts are very deep!

The tone of joy is emphasized by the verbs **made . . . glad** and **sing for joy** (i.e., give a ringing cry of joy) in Psalm 92:4. **Your work** and **the works of your hands** may look back to creation, but the context here suggests that they include the future judgment of God's enemies, which reestablishes the moral order of creation, "his justice in the government of the world."[11]

Psalm 92:5 responds in joy and gladness. The exclamation **how** may cover both lines (as the CSB, NIV, REB). The covenant name, LORD, is used in 92:4–5, emphasizing the covenant nature of what God does. What he does (**your works**) stands in parallel with **your thoughts** (meaning intentions, plans, purposes).[12] These are described as **great** and **very deep**. God's plans and God's work are deep (cf. "Your judgments are like the great deep," 36:6) because they are not obvious on the surface, as 92:6–7 will expound (cf. Isa. 55:8–9; Rom. 11:33). That God's purposes toward his people are always and only purposes of grace and that his plans toward the impenitent are

---

9   Zenger suggests "a rhythmic, meditative accompanying sound [on a stringed instrument] . . . , against which the text was sung in a kind of talking song (recitative technique or 'melodrama')." Hossfeld and Zenger, *Psalms*, 2:439. Tate proposes "soft or meditative singing or chanting to the accompaniment of a stringed instrument." Tate, *Psalms 51–100*, 461.

10 Spurgeon, *Treasury*, 2.2:117.

11 Calvin, *Psalms*, 3:496.

12 The noun מַחֲשָׁבָה is used of God's plans and purposes (e.g., Ps. 40:5 in parallel with wonderful deeds; Jer. 49:20; 50:25) and to contrast God's purposes with ours (Isa. 55:7–9). Elsewhere, it is used of human plans or schemes (e.g., Prov. 16:3; Job 21:27; Jer. 18:12).

always and only righteous anger is far from obvious when we look at the surface of affairs on earth. With pastoral realism, Augustine says, "No sea is as deep as this design of God, whereby he allows the wicked to flourish while good people labor under hardships." Only the cross of Christ enables us to grasp this truth and to persevere; so, he says, "Hold tight to Christ."[13]

> 6   The stupid man cannot know;
>   the fool cannot understand this:

Psalm 92:6 shows that although God's thoughts are indeed "deep," "the fault lies with ourselves" if we do not discern them.[14] The word **this** at the end of 92:6 may refer back to the deep thoughts and works of God in 92:5 or forward to the destiny of the wicked in 92:7—or perhaps to both. The one who does not **know** or **understand**[15] all this is described first as **the stupid man**, literally, "the brutish man"—that is, those whose sin has lowered their desires below what is truly human.[16] He is also called **the fool** (using a word that also appears in 94:8 but otherwise only in Proverbs and Ecclesiastes).[17] This person looks on the surface of things and deduces that it is better to live without the constraints of God and his laws. He thinks the one who fears God is the stupid person. But however intellectually accomplished he may be, he has failed to grasp the most fundamental moral truth of the universe. "Do not congratulate the fish," writes Augustine, "that is enjoying its tasty bait."[18]

> 7   that though the wicked sprout like grass
>   and all evildoers flourish,
>   they are doomed to destruction forever;

13 Augustine, *Psalms*, 4:352.
14 Calvin, *Psalms*, 3:498. Cf. Pss. 10:4; 14:1 (= 53:1).
15 The Hebrew is literally "does not know . . . does not understand," rather than "cannot" (so, rightly, the CSB and NIV). While it is no doubt true that his mind is darkened so that he cannot grasp this reality, the Hebrew here does not explicitly say this.
16 אִישׁ־בַּעַר. The word בַּעַר appears in Pss. 49:10 ("the stupid"); 73:22 ("brutish"); Prov. 12:1; 30:2. Kidner quotes Samuel Johnson (1709–1784) of people who simply want to be free of care: "It is sad stuff; it is brutish. If a bull could speak, he might as well exclaim,—Here am I with this cow and this grass; what being can enjoy greater felicity?" Kidner, *Psalms*, 2:335.
17 כְּסִיל (several times in Proverbs, once in Ecclesiastes).
18 Augustine, *Psalms*, 4:353.

Good and evil cannot be separated from the unbreakable givenness of the moral order of creation. Those who think morality can be shaped by our decisions need to think again. The verbs **sprout**[19] and **flourish**[20] acknowledge that this is how it appears.[21] **The wicked** is intensified to **all evildoers** to show how serious the problem is (cf. Job 22; Ps. 73:4–12; Ezek. 7:10–11). But the word **grass** spells their doom (cf. Pss. 37:1–2; 90:5–6; 102:4, 11; 103:15–16); their end is **destruction** and that **forever**, with no opportunity to sprout again.

8   but you, O Lord, are on high forever.

Psalm 92:8, unusually short, is "the pivotal verse"[22] of the psalm. **You** is emphatic. The covenant name, **Lord**, is used again. **On high** means beyond danger, above threat, invulnerable to attack, governing the world with no rival. This word anticipates "The Lord reigns" in subsequent psalms (cf. "mightier than . . . ," 93:4). And God is this **forever**.[23]

9   For behold, your enemies, O Lord,
        for behold, your enemies shall perish;
      all evildoers shall be scattered.

Psalm 92:9 emphatically presses home 92:7. The repeated **for behold** invites us to "Look! Look!" with the eyes of faith. The repeated **your enemies** calls into question the adage that God hates the sin but loves the sinner: "Those who set themselves against the Lord will find that he is personally set against them."[24] The first two lines show "staircase parallelism" of a kind we will meet in Psalm 93:3 and often in the Psalms of Ascent (Pss. 120–134). The effect is that **shall perish** hits us with particular force.[25] **All evildoers**, who so frighteningly flourished in 92:7, **shall be scattered**, broken up by their own

19 This verb (פרח) is translated "flourish" in Ps. 92:12–13 (also 72:7: "May the righteous flourish").
20 This verb (צוץ) is translated "blossom" in Ps. 72:16.
21 Cf. 1 Macc. 9:23.
22 Tate, *Psalms 51–100*, 467.
23 Although "forever" translates a different Hebrew word in Ps. 92:7 (עֲדֵי־עַד) and 92:8 (לְעֹלָם), the meaning is the same.
24 Motyer, *Psalms*, 547.
25 For the verb "perish," see Judg. 5:31; Job 4:11; Ps. 83:17.

contradictions; they may gather together in united hostility to God and his Christ (2:1–3; cf. Acts 4:24–27), but in the end, "The seemingly solid phalanx of antagonism breaks up and disperses, disintegrated from within."[26]

> [10]   But you have exalted my horn like that of the wild ox;
>   you have poured over me fresh oil.
> [11]   My eyes have seen the downfall of my enemies;
>   my ears have heard the doom of my evil assailants.

The gladness of Psalm 92:4–5 is now focused on a very specific victory, most likely that of the King, because it reminds us of the promises to the Messiah in Psalm 2.[27] The God who is "on high" (92:8) has **exalted** (lifted high) the **horn**—that is, the strength and power—preeminently of the King. To "exalt the horn" is used of the King in 1 Samuel 2:10 (Hannah's song, anticipating the Magnificat) and in Psalms 18:2; 89:17; and 132:17. In 112:9 God exalts the horn of any righteous one. In 148:14 "he has raised up a horn for his people," perhaps by the exaltation of his Messiah. The **wild ox** is a picture of tremendous power (for the animal, see Job 39:9–10; for this idiom, see Num. 23:22; 24:8; Deut. 33:17). There are translation uncertainties in the verb rendered **poured** in Psalm 92:10b, but in the context here, it probably means something like an anointing as part of a victory celebration (cf. 23:5; 45:7).[28] The word **fresh** means luxuriant and is usually used of flourishing trees; **fresh oil** may mean thick or rich oil; figuratively, it conveys a picture of great blessing, strength, and vigor (sometimes in a kingly or priestly context), naturally linked with the Messiah.[29]

In 92:11 the ESV words **the downfall of** and **the doom of** are not in the Hebrew but are inferred from the context. The Hebrew is literally, as in the CSB,

> My eyes look at my enemies,
> when evildoers rise against me,
> my ears hear them.

---

26 Kirkpatrick, *Psalms*, 3:561.
27 Eveson, *Psalms*, 2:153.
28 For the technical discussion, see the long note in Tate, *Psalms 51–100*, 462–63.
29 Hamilton, *Psalms*, 2:172–73.

The verb translated **seen** here has the sense of "looking in triumph" (cf. in this sense Goliath looking at puny David in 1 Sam. 17:42).[30] The Hebrew does not say what exactly he has seen and heard, but in the context of Psalm 92:7 and 9, it seems he anticipates seeing their defeat and hearing some sounds associated with that victory.[31] The reference to **my enemies** and **my evil assailants** as a designation of those who are God's enemies (92:9) makes sense if the singer is intimately associated with God; ultimately, he sings by the Spirit of the one who will be so closely identified with God that his enemies are God's enemies and his exaltation is God's victory. Dickson rightly says that the psalmist is "a type of Christ" and that this victory is shared with all those who have "an interest in Christ" by faith.[32]

92:12–15 Conclusion: Be Sure That Those in Christ Will Declare with Gladness God's Praises Forever

12   The righteous flourish like the palm tree
          and grow like a cedar in Lebanon.
13   They are planted in the house of the LORD;
          they flourish in the courts of our God.
14   They still bear fruit in old age;
          they are ever full of sap and green,
15   to declare that the LORD is upright;
          he is my rock, and there is no unrighteousness in him.

Psalm 92:12–14 is an expansion of and commentary on 1:3 (cf. Prov. 11:28). A work of grace in the heart grows without limit, just as wickedness always and inevitably destroys the heart of an unbeliever. The verb **planted** (or perhaps "transplanted") appears in Psalm 1:3 (also Jer. 17:8; several times in Ezek. 17; 19). Although **the righteous** is singular, as are the verbs in Psalm 92:12, the meaning is clearly generic, as 92:13 is completely in the plural. The verb **flourish** in 92:12 and 13 translates the verb "sprout" in 92:7a.[33] This

---

30 Tate, *Psalms 51–100*, 463.
31 Tucker and Grant, *Psalms*, 2:365.
32 Dickson, *Psalms*, 2:153.
33 In Ps. 92:7, 12, it is in the qal, but in 92:13, in the hiphil, possibly with intensive or elative force. Hossfeld and Zenger, *Psalms*, 2:435.

sprouting is not like ephemeral grass (92:7) but **like the palm tree** (famous for flourishing in desert places) and **like a cedar in Lebanon,** the most majestic tree of the ancient world.[34] Here is endurance, beauty, and majesty. What a contrast to the "grass" of the wicked, sprouting today so proudly but shriveled and gone tomorrow! As with Psalm 1, supremely this is true of Jesus Christ, for "Christ is a cedar that is not blooming with the flower of the world."[35] Now it can be true of all who are in Christ.

Psalm 92:13 shows that lasting beautiful growth—which is growth in godliness and virtue—can happen only **in the house of the LORD** and **in the courts of our God.** This language picks up the imagery of the temple as a re-creation of the garden in Eden.[36] Only in intimate relationship with God does this happen, and only in Jesus Christ can it happen, for only by abiding in him can anyone abide in the Father. Dickson observes,

> The Lord's children are like trees which do not grow in every soil, are not nourished with every moisture; the place of their planting, growth, and flourishing is the house of the Lord, where the word and Spirit of the Lord, joined with the holy ordinances, may be had for food.[37]

Theodoret of Cyrus writes of "the growth of virtue . . . growing up over a long time and requiring much attention, yet reaching on high, bearing fruit in season and of pleasant taste, as it is planted in the divine paradise in the house of God."[38]

Psalm 92:14 continues the image of the tree. Those who are righteous by faith **still bear fruit** (the verb is translated "increase" in 62:10 and "brings forth" in Prov. 10:31) **in old age** (lit., "gray hairs"). The adjective translated **full of sap** simply means "full" in the sense of a rich fatness. The word **green** is the word translated "fresh" in Psalm 92:10. Together these

---

34 For the associations of palm trees, see Ex. 15:27; Lev. 23:40; Num. 33:9; Deut. 34:3. The palm tree is an image of a beautiful woman in Song 7:7–8 and the cedar of Lebanon of a virile and majestic man in Song 5:15. Delitzsch waxes eloquent in praise of the palm tree: "There is no more charming and majestic sight than the palm of the oasis, this prince among the trees of the plain . . . —a picture of life in the midst of the world of death." Delitzsch, *Psalms,* 3:71.

35 Luther, *Luther's Works,* 11:232.

36 Hengstenberg, *Psalms,* 3:147. For Zion as a "planting" of righteousness, see Isa. 60:21; 61:3.

37 Dickson, *Psalms,* 2:154.

38 Theodoret of Cyrus, *Psalms,* 2:110–11.

two words mean something like "healthy and green" (CSB). Martin Bucer (1491–1551) comments nicely,

> Although this duty, to set forth the praises of God, . . . is a duty that lies on the young as well as the old, yet the performance of it becomes old people best, because of their authority and long experience in worldly affairs, in which respect they may be accounted more able and vigorous.[39]

Psalm 92:12–14 cannot mean that all the righteous live into old age, for the Lord Jesus died young, and many faithful disciples have been martyred. It means rather that once the work of grace has begun in their hearts, it continues to grow in them until the day they die. There is within each true believer a life that cannot be extinguished, for though the outward self wastes away, the inner self "is being renewed day by day" (2 Cor. 4:16). Dickson explains, "True believers shall still persevere, and the decay of the outward man shall not hinder the renewing of their inward man day by day, and their last works shall be better than their first."[40] An inward beauty grows in the believer and bears fruit to eternity (cf. 1 Pet. 3:4).

Psalm 92:15 is the climax, echoing Deuteronomy 32:4. The righteous do not endure for their own sakes. Rather, to all eternity they will **declare** (cf. Ps. 92:2) to the listening universe the truth celebrated in this psalm. This reality is expressed in three ways, all of which are true in Christ. First, God **is upright**, absolutely just, upholding the moral order of the universe (cf. 33:4–5); it will be seen on the last day, when Jesus Christ judges the world, that wickedness has not prospered and that righteousness has been vindicated. Second, God is **my rock**; as the Father was the "rock" of Jesus on earth, so the triune God is the "rock" of each believer. Third, **there is no unrighteousness in him**, not an iota, "no darkness at all" (1 John 1:5).

REFLECTION AND RESPONSE

1. It is instructive to meditate on what Psalm 92 would have meant on the lips of Jesus in his prayers, to read through line by line and feel how it

---

39 Bucer, Annotations on Ps. 92:15, in *RCS* 8:126.
40 Dickson, *Psalms*, 2:154.

might have strengthened faith and sweetened care for him in his mortal frailty and as he underwent the most acute temptations.

2. In the context of the sober and sad realism of Psalm 90, Psalm 92:1–3 reminds us that it really is good—in every way—for us to practice the disciplines of praise, alongside other believers, accompanied by music, as we focus on the covenant love of God in Christ. In the morning times of life, we may forget to do this, as we enjoy this world and begin to feel it can be our home; in the long nights, we struggle to do this as our hearts are filled with burdens and sadness. In both times, we need to stir one another up to this work of praise and thanksgiving.

3. Psalm 92:4–7 helps us never forget that the purposes of God are deep. William Cowper (1731–1800) captures this profundity well:

Deep in unfathomable mines
Of never-failing skill
He treasures up his bright designs
And works his sovereign will.[41]

We need to encourage one another to look at the world with the eyes of faith, not to the things that are seen but to the things that are unseen, which are eternal and sure (2 Cor. 4:18).

4. Psalm 92:8 is the center of the psalm and deserves to be the center of our meditation. Although it is very brief, so much hangs on this unchangeable truth, as it is expounded in both halves of the psalm. "The man who can hold fast this one truth, that God is eternally *height*, will never despond under the cross, and will laugh at the triumph of the wicked."[42]

5. We are encouraged in Psalm 92:9–11 to ponder again the victory of God's Messiah, to wonder at his awesome "horn" of strength, to marvel at the beauty of his anointing, and to be quite sure that on the last day, all will see that he has the name that is above every name.

6. Psalm 92:12–14 is precious to those growing older but can be valued by us all when we grasp the wonder of a work of grace growing without limit within our troubled hearts.

---

41 William Cowper, "God Moves in a Mysterious Way" (1774). Public domain.
42 Hengstenberg, *Psalms*, 3:145.

7. The climax is found in Psalm 92:15. We pray that, day by day, year by year, we will be part of a church that declares in word and deed that God is good.

8. Augustine speaks of the restful Sabbath of the trusting heart:

This tranquil joy, born of our hope, is our Sabbath. What this psalm has to enjoin upon us, what it has to sing about, is how Christians are to conduct themselves in the Sabbath of their hearts, in that freedom and tranquility and serenity of conscience where no disturbance touches them. The psalm speaks about situations which may often trouble people seriously, and it teaches you how, in spite of all, you are to celebrate the Sabbath in your heart.[43]

43 Augustine, *Psalms*, 4:346–47.

*Do you seek to glorify God in the day of preparation? You have
the praise written in [Psalm 93]. For at that time when the
crucifixion occurred, the house of God was built up, indeed, to
hold off the enemies that assault it. On account of this victory it
is fitting to sing to God, using the things said then in [Psalm 93].*

ATHANASIUS
Letter to Marcellinus

Messiah's kingdom stilling the uproar of the nations.

ANDREW BONAR
Christ and His Church in the Book of Psalms

PSALM 93

ORIENTATION

The will of God will be done on earth as it is done in heaven because Jesus triumphed on the cross. In Psalm 93 we celebrate the supremacy of the sovereign God over all things, most especially over all the enemies of Christ's church. Whereas some psalms speak of the human King, the Messiah, coming into his kingdom, others—and this is one—celebrate the kingship of God in heaven. There is no contradiction between the two. Indeed, in the divine-human person of Jesus Christ, the two strands merge. Jesus is the human Messiah who will rule the world; Jesus is God the Son who, with God the Father and God the Holy Spirit, will rule the world.[1]

The cry "The Lord our God / the Almighty reigns" in Revelation 19:6 (cf. Rev. 11:17) echoes the opening words of the psalm, "The LORD reigns."[2] Because of the blood of the Lamb (which is so significant in Revelation), the almighty God comes into his kingdom at last. The kingdom of God, announced by Jesus at the start of his public ministry (Mark 1:14–15) and demonstrated when he stilled the storm (Matt. 8:23–27; Luke 8:22–25), is now consummated (cf. 1 Cor. 15:24–28) because he triumphed on the cross (Col. 2:15). On the cross all the floodwaters of God's righteous judgment overflowed on Jesus; he drowned for us, and now we can go free. Now "the sea [is] no more" (Rev. 21:1), its hostility silenced forever. Because Jesus has "overcome the world" (John 16:33), his church may take heart. The psalm is thus especially appropriate at any time and in any place where the church faces terrifying threats.

---

1 Delitzsch, *Psalms*, 3:73.
2 In the Greek the words κύριος and ἐβασίλευσεν appear both in the LXX of Ps. 93:1 and in Rev. 19:6.

This psalm echoes themes in Psalm 92, including (1) exaltation (92:8, 10; 93:4); (2) the word מְאֹד (*meod*, very; 92:5; 93:5); (3) the house of God (92:13; 93:5); and (4) the trustworthiness or faithfulness of God (92:2; 93:5). Links with Psalm 94 include (1) the verb דָּכָא (*daka*, to crush) in 93:3, "roaring," and 94:5, "crush"; (2) references to God's law (93:5; 94:12); (3) exaltation (93:1; 94:2 ["the proud"]); (4) "slip/move" (93:1; 94:18); and (5) "throne" (93:2; 94:20).

Other links include the watery threats of Psalm 46, the kingship language of Psalm 47 (esp. 47:8: "God reigns over the nations"), and the victory celebration of Exodus 15. Old Testament texts that look forward to the final reign of God include Isaiah 24:23 and 52:7.

THE TEXT

Structure

The psalm is so short that it hardly needs structural analysis. Psalm 93:1–2 celebrates the rule of God. Psalm 93:3 portrays a terrifying threat before 93:4 calms the storm. Psalm 93:5 seems to stand apart, although, as we will see, its message is integral to the rest of the psalm.

93:1–2 God in Christ Rules the World

1   The LORD reigns; he is robed in majesty;
        the LORD is robed; he has put on strength as his belt.
        Yes, the world is established; it shall never be moved.
2   Your throne is established from of old;
        you are from everlasting.

The **LORD reigns**[3] (two words in Hebrew) is a headline for Psalms 93–100.[4] It reappears verbatim in 1 Chronicles 16:31; Psalms 96:10; 97:1; and

---

3   Much scholarly debate has focused on the theory of Sigmund Mowinckel (1884–1965) that this ought to be translated "The Lord has begun to reign" (thought to express "not merely a fact . . . but an act," that is, the return from exile; Kirkpatrick, *Psalms*, 3:564) and that it was used in a hypothetical ceremony for the "enthronement of Yahweh" at a hypothetical autumn festival. See Sigmund Mowinckel, *The Psalms in Israel's Worship*, trans. D. R. Ap-Thomas (New York: Abingdon, 1967), 107–9. Alter calls this "a scholarly exercise in historical fiction" since there is no evidence for such a festival. Alter, *Psalms*, 328. See also the refutations in Kidner, *Psalms*, 2:337–38; Tate, *Psalms 51–100*, 474–75; Tucker and Grant, *Psalms*, 2:374.

4   Tucker and Grant, *Psalms*, 2:373.

99:1. This is more than a mere theological statement; it is a joyful acclamation, a celebration of a profoundly wonderful truth.[5] The language of being **robed** or "girded" (**put on . . . as his belt**)[6] uses anthropomorphic language to help us grasp that the attributes of God's **majesty** and **strength** are inseparable from him; whenever he "appears" in human affairs, he comes as one who is the commander in chief of the universe.[7] Supremely, this majesty is seen in the strength with which Jesus resisted temptation and stood up to all his enemies[8] and when the Father gives the Son the glory that he had with him from the foundation of the world (John 17:5).[9]

The third line of Psalm 93:1 rejoices that **the world** (the habitable world) **is established**, secure, firmly founded. And therefore **it shall never be moved** or shaken.[10] There is a solidity about human affairs, both in their creational aspect (our place on the planet) and in their social and political aspects. They feel very insecure, but God has guaranteed that he will remake them in a new creation in which righteousness will dwell (2 Pet. 3:13). When the moral foundations of the world are under threat (see on Ps. 11), we need to remember this promise. The world has no autonomy, no stability in its own right; its only hope rests on the sovereignty of the God of the Scriptures.

Psalm 93:2 continues this theme and emphasizes that this government has not begun recently and will not end. This **throne** has been **established** (the same verb as in 93:1) **from of old**, an eternal government, because it is the rule of the Creator, who is **from everlasting**.

93:3–4 God in Christ Rules over Every Threat to Christ's Church

3   The floods have lifted up, O Lord,
        the floods have lifted up their voice;
        the floods lift up their roaring.

---

5   Although God's kingship is eternal, we catch the feel of this acclamation in the cries of 2 Sam. 15:10 (for Absalom) and 2 Kings 9:13 (for Jehu). It is almost as if to say, "Three cheers for the king! Long live the king!"

6   This verb (hithpael of אזר) is used of strapping on armor in Isa. 8:9.

7   The word "majestic" (גֵּאוּת) derives from the root "rising" (as in Ps. 89:9: "the *raging* of the sea"). It is used of human pride in Ps. 17:10 ("arrogantly") and Isa. 28:1–3 ("proud"), and of God's majesty in Isa. 12:5 ("gloriously") and 26:10 ("majesty").

8   Augustine, *Psalms*, 4:362.

9   Theodoret of Cyrus, *Psalms*, 2:113.

10   For this language of the believer, the church, or the whole world being (or not being) shaken, see Pss. 46:2; 82:5; 94:18; 96:10.

With vivid staircase parallelism (see Ps. 92:9 and often in the Psalms of Ascent), repetition and development convey an atmosphere of growing threat: "The opposition of the enemies of the church is compared to the growing flood and raging sea."[11] **The floods** (lit., "the rivers") are a vivid picture of threat as they **lift up**[12] their voices in anger. The word **roaring** comes from the root "to crush"; it indicates terrifying breakers crashing against the shore (CSB: "pounding waves").[13]

Sometimes this language of wild rivers is used metaphorically of powerful nations (e.g., of Assyria in Isa. 8:7 and of Egypt in Jer. 46:7–8). The "waters [lit., 'rivers'] of Babylon" in Psalm 137:1 are perhaps both literal and metaphorical in this sense. In 89:25 the Messiah governs the rivers. In 24:2 the world is established on the rivers.

Here is a most urgent and terrible threat to Christ and his church (both his church before he came, the old covenant church, and his church in new covenant days). The **voice** becomes a **roaring** as the cacophony of threats approaches its climax.[14]

> 4 Mightier than the thunders of many waters,
>   mightier than the waves of the sea,
>   the LORD on high is mighty!

The three-line crescendo of Psalm 93:3 is matched by the beautiful three-line diminuendo of 93:4, ending with the calm assurance that **the LORD on high is mighty**. The **thunders** are literally "voices" (the same word as in 93:3, "their voice"). The **waves** means terrifying breakers (cf. 42:7; 88:7; Jonah 2:3). The word translated **on high** is a vital link to Psalm 92:8. Although this is true for the triune God, ultimately it is in Christ that we see this great "height" of God: "Christ is wonderful on high."[15] And so the church of God lives in a world that is at the same time a place of great felt danger and a place of unbreakable real security.

---

11 Dickson, *Psalms*, 2:155.

12 While the first two verbs are perfect in form and the third is imperfect, it is unlikely that this has any significance. See VanGemeren, *Psalms*, 709.

13 Cf. the use of this root (דכה) in Ps. 44:19: "You have *broken* us."

14 For this language of water as threat to ordered creation and the people of God, see also Ps. 74:12–17.

15 Luther, *Luther's Works*, 13:236.

93:5 God in Christ Upholds His Holy Church

5   Your decrees are very trustworthy;
          holiness befits your house,
          O LORD, forevermore.

The word **decree** (עֵדוּת, *eduth*) is one of several used for the law of God in Psalm 119 (cf. the use of the word *torah* in 94:12). The word **trustworthy** comes from the same root as "faithfulness" and "amen" (a major theme in Ps. 89). **Forevermore** is literally "for length of days" (as at the close of Ps. 23). But what does the law of God have to do with God's sovereignty over all creation? The answer is that the law of God expresses the character and nature of God, which underlies the moral and physical order of creation. The stability of the world and the trustworthiness of the Scriptures are two sides of the same coin; it is not possible to have one without the other. The **house** of God, the temple, is a microcosm of creation, anticipating both Christ (the one "greater than the temple," Matt. 12:6) and the church (1 Cor. 3:16; 1 Pet. 2:5). The reason **holiness befits** this house is that only a **house** of holiness can have the stability of the creation that God will preserve and remake.[16] If this psalm was sung during or after the exile, it was a reminder that Solomon's temple was destroyed precisely because its worship did not exhibit holiness (cf. Jer. 7), which is also why the later temple was destroyed in AD 70. Only a church in which holiness is paramount can stand and last to the new creation (cf. Heb. 12:14).

REFLECTION AND RESPONSE

1. We cannot meditate too much on the simple and profound truth that in Jesus Christ God has established his kingdom, that Jesus Christ is the head over all things for the church, and that therefore we are absolutely secure in Christ, no matter what threats loom over God's church.

2. Writing pastorally, John Calvin says,

Our not investing God with the power which belongs to him, as we ought to do, and thus wickedly despoiling him of his authority, is the source of

16 For this theme of holiness, see also Pss. 96:9; 97:10–12; 99:3, 5, 9.

that fear and trembling which we very often experience. . . . [Indeed,] were we well persuaded of his invincible power, that would be to us an invincible support against all the assaults of temptation.[17]

3. When human powers favor the church, we must beware, and we must remember their instability. This warning to the church in the seventeenth century is as relevant today:

> If any king be kind to his church, his people have reason to thank God, but they must not lean to such a king, his reign shall be but short: and if any king be forward, and oppose himself to the church, we must not be too much afraid of him, because his kingdom is but lately begun, and is of short continuance.[18]

This is both a salutary warning for the church not to become identified with any one political movement or ruler and, at the same time, a comfort that we need not be frightened when culture or governments move against us.

4. The final verse (Ps. 93:5) is both a comfort and a challenge. It is a great comfort that God's word is secure and trustworthy, that the church may "wait with tranquil minds for their salvation amidst all the tempests and agitations of the world,"[19] because God has promised in his "decrees" that this salvation will come. It is a challenge to make and keep holiness paramount within each local church. Our holiness is far more important than our success by any worldly metric. Only those who both hear and do what Christ teaches will survive those floodwaters of judgment (Matt. 7:24–27).

---

17 Calvin, *Psalms*, 4:6.
18 Dickson, *Psalms*, 2:156.
19 Calvin, *Psalms*, 4:5.

*The saints do not pray for the Lord to destroy wicked teachers,
and to throw them headlong into Tartarus, but rather to
restrain them, humble them, and if they are at all amenable to
cure, to convert them. But if they are not amenable to cure, he
should punish them and destroy them. . . . As far as personal
relations are concerned, let them pray for their persecutors, but
in matters concerning God's glory, they should pray against
them and call down a terrible destiny on their heads.*

HIERONYMUS WELLER VON MOLSDORF
Interpretation of Some Psalms

Opposed we may be, but comfortless we are not.

J. ALEC MOTYER
The Psalms

PSALM 94

ORIENTATION

God has appointed a man to do everything for which Psalm 94 prays (Acts 17:31). This is the man who, in his life on earth, himself prayed this psalm and believed every word of its message. This man taught his disciples to pray, "Your kingdom come," which is a summary of the yearning of this and a number of other psalms. Now this man, the risen Jesus Christ, leads his church, by his Spirit, to pray the psalm for ourselves, confident that, because of him, it is true and will be answered.

Several possible New Testament echoes support the understanding that the risen Jesus does what is spoken of God in this psalm. Jesus "is an avenger" (1 Thess. 4:6)[1] and will be "revealed from heaven . . . in flaming fire, inflicting vengeance" (2 Thess. 1:7–8),[2] demonstrating the expectation that Jesus will act as God in the way that Psalm 94:1 prays. The "consolations" that God gives in 94:19 may be echoed in the "comfort" we experience "abundantly" "through Christ" (2 Cor. 1:5). We may be sure that "the LORD will not forsake his people" (Ps. 94:14, likely echoed in Rom. 11:1–2)[3] because he brings them salvation through Christ. So now, in and through Christ, his church cries out for the will of God to be done on earth as it is in heaven, crying day and night for "justice" (Luke 18:7–8; cf. Ps. 94:15) and calling out, "How long?" (Rev. 6:9–11; cf. Ps. 94:3).

---

1 Weima argues that this verse likely alludes to Ps. 94:1 and notes that "the apostle attributes to Jesus a role that the Old Testament attributed to God." Weima, "1–2 Thessalonians," in *CNTOT* 877–78.

2 This is mentioned in Eveson, *Psalms*, 2:161.

3 Ciampa and Rosner, "1 Corinthians," in *CNTOT* 704–5; Kraus, *Theology of the Psalms*, 200.

In the context of book 4, Psalm 93 picks up the assurance of God's almighty rule (sounded in 92:8) with the magnificent words "The LORD reigns"; this phrase (96:10; 97:1; 99:1) or the same theme in other words (e.g., "a great King above all gods," 95:3; "the King," 98:6) resounds throughout Psalms 95–99. In Psalm 94 the theme of judging the world is an emphatically kingly motif. It also shares a significant "wisdom" tone with Psalm 92 (compare 92:6–7 with 94:8–11).[4] Psalm 94 has several links with Psalm 93. These include (1) the root דָּכָא (*daka*, crush) in 93:3 ("roaring") and 94:5; (2) references to God's law (using two different words in 93:5 and 94:12); (3) a contrast between God's exaltation (93:1) and that of the proud (94:2); (4) the verb מוֹט, *mot*, to slip or move (93:1; 94:18); and (5) the word "throne" (93:2; 94:20).[5] If, as seems likely, book 4 has been compiled, following book 3, as the beginnings of a response to the exile, then this theme of God's sovereignty is especially relevant to the church living as exiles in this world (cf. 1 Pet. 1:1, 17; 2:11).

THE TEXT

Structure
There are four clear sections. Psalm 94:1–7 is a prayer (94:1–2) followed by a lament concerning the wicked (94:3–7). Psalm 94:8–11 speaks of God in the third person and is a wisdom-style rebuke to the foolish. Psalm 94:12–15 is a beatitude, mixing second-person address to God with third-person statements about God. Psalm 94:16–23 is an individual lament and prayer, bracketed by words for evil, wickedness, or iniquity.

94:1–7 Cry to God for Jesus to Return in Judgment

¹   O LORD, God of vengeance,
         O God of vengeance, shine forth!
²   Rise up, O judge of the earth;
         repay to the proud what they deserve!

---

4 Note especially the repetition of the rare word "stupid" in Pss. 92:6 and 94:8.
5 For these and other links, see Tate, *Psalms 51–100*, 489.

Psalm 94:1–2 defines the psalm.[6] The primary focus is on God himself, who is spoken of in three ways. He is the covenant LORD, for his judgment fulfills the covenant curses and blessings. Second (emphasized with staircase parallelism), he is the **God of vengeance**. This must be cleansed of its associations with arbitrary and vindictive personal revenge (e.g., Lamech in Gen. 4:24; the Babylonians in Lam. 3:60; cf. Lev. 19:18, where it is immediately contrasted with loving neighbor as self). Here it means fair legal justice (e.g., Ex. 21:20)[7] but actioned with the heat of righteous indignation.[8] The noun **vengeance** is in the plural, probably to convey intensity.[9] The most important biblical control is the quotation of Deuteronomy 32:35 ("Vengeance is mine"; cf. Deut. 32:41, 43) in Romans 12:19, in the context of the prohibition of taking revenge and also of the teaching that governments punish lawbreakers on behalf of God (Rom. 13:1–4). The third description of God is **judge of the earth**, recalling Abraham's words in Genesis 18:25 (cf. Pss. 58:11; 82:8; 96:10; 97:8–9; 98:9; 99:4).

The three verbs form a crescendo: **shine forth** means to appear in visible, incontrovertible clarity in judgment (cf. Deut. 33:2; Pss. 50:2; 80:1); **rise up** means getting up, ready for action; **repay**[10] leads to the climax, a precise plea: **Repay to the proud what they deserve!** The **proud** comes from another root meaning to "rise up."[11] For the noun translated **what they deserve**, see also Psalm 28:4 ("due reward"); 137:8 ("what you have done to us"); and Lamentations 3:64. This is a prayer not for "overkill" but for justice to be done. When Jesus prayed this psalm, the answer—given in the resurrection—is that he himself is appointed as the man who will render this

---

6   The verb שׁוּב (to turn/return) appears in three critical places: here in Ps. 94:2 ("repay"), at the end of the blessing in 94:15 ("return"), and at the very end in 94:23 ("bring back").

7   In biblical Hebrew the verb נָקַם "is used to describe action taken to correct an imbalance based on a wrong committed. In a case or two the meaning is vindictive retaliation, but the normal use is with a non-pejorative sense." Ross, *Psalms*, 1:459. Other divine examples include Gen. 4:15; Judg. 11:36; 2 Sam. 4:8; Pss. 18:47; 58:10; 79:10; 99:8; 149:7; Ezek. 25:17.

8   Alter criticizes "retribution" as being too cool a word: "The speaker is filled with rage at the dominance of injustice in the world." Alter, *Psalms*, 331.

9   "Plural of amplification," *HALOT*, s.v. נְקָמָה. Also, it is possibly "denoting the completeness of the retribution." Kirkpatrick, *Psalms*, 3:567.

10 Hiphil of שׁוּב, "cause to return (to them)."

11 The adjective גֵּאֶה, from the root גאה, is used of a rising up against God and his people in, for example, Pss. 10:2; 17:10; 31:18, 23; 36:11; 59:12; 73:6. Elsewhere, it may refer to the rising up of cosmic hostile forces (e.g., 46:3; 89:9) and even of the majesty of God (68:34; 93:1).

judgment (Acts 17:31). The New Testament teaches that it becomes for us a prayer for the Lord Jesus to return (2 Thess. 1:7–10).

> ³   O LORD, how long shall the wicked,
>   how long shall the wicked exult?
> ⁴   They pour out their arrogant words;
>   all the evildoers boast.
> ⁵   They crush your people, O LORD,
>   and afflict your heritage.
> ⁶   They kill the widow and the sojourner,
>   and murder the fatherless;
> ⁷   and they say, "The LORD does not see;
>   the God of Jacob does not perceive."

The reference to "the proud" at the end of Psalm 94:2 leads to a vigorous lament about these people. We do not know whether these were foreign invading powers or evil rulers within Israel, nor exactly when they were active; we know what we need to know, which is what they did—and still do—to Christ's church. The cry **How long?** (cf. 6:3; 74:10; 80:4; 90:13) is the call of agonized faith, which yet is certain there will be an end. This end, we now know, will come when Jesus returns.[12]

Psalm 94:4 focuses on their demeanor, which is exultant and confident. They do not speak hesitantly or apologetically; rather, **they pour out** (spew out, belch out) **their arrogant words** (lit., "they pour out, they speak arrogance," where the noun "arrogance" appears in 31:18 ["insolently"] and 75:5 ["haughty"]), and they **boast**. The phrase **evildoers** ("doers of evil") appears again in 94:16.

Psalm 94:5–6 moves from their demeanor to their actions. The verbs are terrifying: they **crush**[13] (the same verb as the "roaring" floods in 93:3) **your people**, where "your" shows how serious and foolish this is. **Your heritage** points to the promised land—and now the church—as God's precious possession.[14] To **afflict** this heritage is folly indeed. The verbs **kill** and

---

12 Longman, *Psalms*, 338.
13 For other uses of this verb (piel of דכא), see Prov. 22:22; Ps. 72:4; Isa. 3:15. Also, it is used of what Jesus endured at the cross in Isa. 53:5.
14 The word "heritage" appears alongside the "people" of God also in Deut. 9:26, 29; 1 Kings 8:51; Ps. 28:9.

murder heighten the sense of terror. The victims—**the widow . . . the sojourner . . . the fatherless**—use common Old Testament language for the most vulnerable, especially the vulnerable in the church of God (cf. Ex. 22:21–22; Pss. 10:14; 68:5; 82:3; 146:9; Mal. 3:5). To be one of these is the characteristic position of a believer (e.g., Pss. 39:12; 119:19) and was felt acutely to be so in the exile (Lam. 5:3). This strong language expresses the hatred of the world for the church in every age. This lament is not just for the church under acute persecution but for the whole church at all times.

Psalm 94:7 unlocks a critical motivation, the unshakable conviction that they can oppose Christ and his church without fear of being repaid. It is not simply that they think what they think; **they say**, they vocalize, they rationalize, they explain what they are thinking. Two verbs are used, to **see** (cf. 10:11) and to **perceive** (or understand). As we might say, "God neither sees it nor gets it, neither knows nor grasps what we are doing. So we can go on doing it without fear." As David Dickson wrote in the seventeenth century, "Oppression of the just cauterizeth the conscience, extinguisheth the sense of Deity, and maketh the oppressor secure and fearless of judgment."[15]

94:8–11 Be Warned That God Sees and Knows

8   Understand, O dullest of the people!
       Fools, when will you be wise?
9   He who planted the ear, does he not hear?
       He who formed the eye, does he not see?
10   He who disciplines the nations, does he not rebuke?
       He who teaches man knowledge—
11   the LORD—knows the thoughts of man,
       that they are but a breath.

Psalm 94:8–11 adopts the wisdom tone of Proverbs. The infant Jesus heard and believed this as he "grew . . . , filled with wisdom," and "increased in wisdom" (Luke 2:40, 52); then he taught this wisdom and

15 Dickson, *Psalms*, 2:160.

teaches it to us today through the psalm. **Understand** uses the same verb translated "perceive" at the end of Psalm 94:7.[16] You think God doesn't get it, but it is you who don't get it! The word translated **dullest** is a strong word (used in parallel with **fools**), meaning stupid or brutish (cf. 49:10; 73:22; 92:6): "you dunderheads."[17] Brutish behavior (94:5–6) comes from a brutish lack of understanding; a wrong view of God leads to evil behavior toward people. The verb translated **be wise** means to act prudently or successfully. It is not simply that the behavior of these people is wrong; it is doomed to failure.

The argument of 94:9 is simple and profound (cf. 10:11; 59:7; Prov. 20:12): it is absurd to suppose that the Creator endowed us with these faculties while lacking them himself, so if I begin to act like this, the question comes to me, "Who is the stupid one now?"

Psalm 94:10 develops this theme in a surprising way with the description of God as **he who disciplines the nations**. The word translated **disciplines** includes instruction, admonition, and chastening; this is the language of the schoolroom. That God does this for **the nations** (the whole world) has been anticipated, for example, in 2:10 ("Now therefore, O kings, be wise") and by the very public calls of wisdom (e.g., Prov. 8:1–11); it is implied by the condemnations of evil behavior in Amos 1–2 (presupposing that they ought to have known these things were wrong) and by the general revelation of God in Romans 1:19–23. God is at work in human history, and his work includes **rebuke** and **teach**ing, if only men and women will listen.

Psalm 94:11 is the climax. The covenant Lord **knows the thoughts of man** (humankind), where **thoughts** includes intentions, designs, and plans. You think he doesn't see or hear or perceive, but he knows the desires of your heart, let alone your words and secret deeds. What is more, he knows that all your wicked plans **are but a breath**, where **breath** is the frequent Ecclesiastes word הֶבֶל, *hebel*, vanity, emptiness. You make firm plans, but they are no more firm than a breath of air. There is a God, and the prayer of 94:1–2 will be answered. Jesus believed this, and now Jesus is the man appointed to give the answer.

---

16 It is a pity that the ESV disguises this important link. Contrast the CSB: "'The God of Jacob doesn't pay attention.' / Pay attention, you stupid people!" (Ps. 94:7–8).

17 Tate, *Psalms 51–100*, 482.

94:12–15 Believe the Blessing of God's Discipline until Jesus Returns

12   Blessed is the man whom you discipline, O Lord,
    and whom you teach out of your law,

13   to give him rest from days of trouble,
    until a pit is dug for the wicked.

14   For the Lord will not forsake his people;
    he will not abandon his heritage;

15   for justice will return to the righteous,
    and all the upright in heart will follow it.

For **blessed** (אַשְׁרֵי, *ashre*), see on Psalm 1:1. Jesus believed this beatitude when on earth; now he teaches it to his church. After the warning of 94:8–11, we are still wondering why the church has to wait so long for vindication and what God might be doing in the meantime. The beatitude of 94:12–15 gives a surprising answer. People think that "Christ and the Christians were being afflicted" because they deserve it, writes Martin Luther, but the psalm persuades us of "the opposite, that those who are afflicted are pleasing to God and those who are enjoying themselves are hateful."[18] **The man** (גֶּבֶר, *geber*, a warrior or strong man) **whom you discipline** was Jesus on earth and has been every believer in Christ, before and after he came; every true child of God is disciplined. For God to **teach** from his **law** (תּוֹרָה, *torah*, instruction) means far more than imparting information; it involves a lifetime of learning and includes sometimes painful discipline. Psalm 94:3–7 describes those who do not undergo this discipline, who are God's paradoxical agents to impose this discipline on the church. Psalm 94:12 declares that blessing rests on those who undergo it. "You make pain your precision tool to teach us our lesson," writes Augustine; "you arrange that the pain itself shall teach us."[19] All this is **to give him rest from days of trouble** (i.e., evil or harm), where **give him rest** includes a quiet confidence in the midst of troubles as well as the final end of troubles. Here is both "inward quietness in face of outward troubles" (cf. Isa. 7:4)[20] and the sure prospect

18 Luther, *Luther's Works*, 13:242.
19 Augustine, *Psalms*, 4:401.
20 Kidner, *Psalms*, 2:342. Cf. Tate, *Psalms 51–100*, 484.

of final rest.[21] The picture of **a pit** (a hunter's pit, as in Pss. 7:15; 35:7; 57:6) being **dug for the wicked** tells us what happens "when the burial day dawns for the wicked."[22] Eternal rest is prepared for Christ and his church, while a terrible pit is being dug for those who will not repent.

We may be sure of this promise because of the covenant, which is ours in Christ. Psalm 94:14 picks up from 94:5 the language of God's **people** and **heritage**. The verbs (**forsake, abandon**) indicate unfaithfulness to a covenant. This God will not do (cf. 1 Sam. 12:22) and cannot do: "He may cast them down, but he never can cast them off."[23] Only with Christ—the final "Yes!" to all the covenant promises (2 Cor. 1:20)—do we discover the riches of how God will do this (see the likely echo in Rom. 11:1–2).

Psalm 94:15a literally reads, "For to righteousness,[24] judgment will return."[25] This probably means that all the judgments in the land will become righteous; there will be a general restoration of righteousness. The CSB rendering, "For the administration of justice will again be righteous," expresses this notion well. Ultimately, this hope looks forward to "new heavens and a new earth in which righteousness dwells" when Jesus returns (2 Pet. 3:13).

Psalm 94:15b literally reads, "and after it all the upright in heart." Probably this means that those who are **upright in heart** will support and participate in this reestablishment of righteousness. Those who undergo God's discipline may trust God's good purposes.

94:16–23 Be Confident in the Comforts of Christ until Jesus Returns

> [16] Who rises up for me against the wicked?
>   Who stands up for me against evildoers?
> [17] If the LORD had not been my help,
>   my soul would soon have lived in the land of silence.
> [18] When I thought, "My foot slips,"
>   your steadfast love, O LORD, held me up.

---

21 The verb (hiphil of שקט) is often used in Joshua and Judges of the promised land being given rest from enemies (e.g., Josh. 11:23; Judg. 3:11).
22 Cassiodorus, *Psalms*, 2:404.
23 Spurgeon, *Treasury*, 2.2:145.
24 The MT has צֶדֶק (righteousness). The *BHS* emendation to צַדִּיק (righteous), followed by the ESV, is unnecessary.
25 The verb "return" (שׁוב) is important for this psalm, appearing also in Ps. 94:2, 23.

19   When the cares of my heart are many,
        your consolations cheer my soul.

The tone changes in Psalm 94:16 to a very personal lament (all in the first-person singular until the words "our God" in 94:23). These were life-and-death struggles for believers before Jesus, supremely for Jesus, and for his church today.

Despite the vigorous rebuke (94:8–11) and the declaration of blessing (94:12–15), the **wicked** and **evildoers** (cf. 94:3–4) are still harassing the psalmist, as they persecuted Christ and his people. The waiting question, "How long?" (94:3), becomes the survival question: **Who rises up for me . . . ? Who stands up for me . . . ?** Cassiodorus comments on the paradox that the believer conquers not by inflicting wounds but by suffering:

> It is as if he were about to fight in the battle-line and be wounded by diverse javelins; and he does not conquer by hand-to-hand conflict, but rather obtains victory by suffering. This is the kind of conflict in which he who endures is victorious, and he who wounds loses.[26]

In 94:17–18 the dangers (**the land of silence**, 94:17b; **My foot slips**, 94:18a) are bracketed by the covenant **LORD** who brings **help** (94:17a) and by the covenant **steadfast love** that upholds (**held me up**, 94:18b), as though the troubled believer is enveloped in God's love. The **land of silence** (lit., just the one word "silence") means the place of the dead (cf. the parallel in 115:17). **When I thought** is literally "when I said" (i.e., to myself). **My foot slips** uses the verb (frequent in the Psalms) often translated "moved" or "shaken."[27] Luther perceptively links this image with Peter's fears when walking on water; for us, as for Peter, the steadfast love that holds us up is the hand of Christ (Matt. 14:30).[28]

In Psalm 94:19 **cares** means troubled thoughts in the context of distress.[29] These are **of my heart** (lit., "in the midst of me") because they attack the core of the believer's being. And they are **many**. Jesus felt this on earth; his

---

26 Cassiodorus, *Psalms*, 2:405.

27 E.g., Pss. 15:5; 16:8. Examples of the idiom of the feet being (or not being) shaken or slipping (or not slipping) include 17:5; 121:3.

28 Luther, *Luther's Works*, 13:248. Kirkpatrick writes, "I gave myself up for lost, but the right hand of love had hold of me all the time." Kirkpatrick, *Psalms*, 3:570.

29 Cf. the same noun (שַׂרְעַפִּים) in Ps. 139:23.

disciples must expect it. And yet in the midst of this are **your consolations**, a warm, strong word used of comfort to mourners (Jer. 16:7) and of the comfort of a mother's breast to a troubled baby ("her consoling breast," Isa. 66:11).[30] These consolations are found in Christ (cf. 2 Cor. 1:5), only because there was a day when he "looked . . . for comforters, but . . . found none" (Ps. 69:20); the Father did comfort Jesus on earth and finally comforted him at his right hand, but on the cross he endured the terrible loneliness of the complete absence of consolation and did so for us.

> 20   Can wicked rulers be allied with you,
>   those who frame injustice by statute?
> 21   They band together against the life of the righteous
>   and condemn the innocent to death.

In Psalm 94:20–21 the focus turns again to the persecutors of Christ and his church. The phrase **wicked rulers** is literally "a throne of destruction/ corruption," perhaps a parody of the judge's seat (called "thrones for judgment" in 122:5).[31] **Those who frame** (fashion, shape) **injustice** (lit., "trouble" or "mischief" caused to others)[32] **by statute** conjures up the terrifying picture of mischief enshrined in law. The word **statute** is here a parody of God's righteous law. Not content with occasional persecution, God's enemies institutionalize hostility to Christ in law, as with Haman's edict, written, sealed, promulgated throughout the empire of the world (Est. 3:12). Psalm 94:21 continues the picture (cf. 37:32–33), with that strange "unity" of divided humankind (cf. 2:1–3; Luke 23:12; Acts 4:27), who **band together against the life** (or "soul") **of the righteous / and condemn the innocent to death** (lit., "and they condemn innocent blood").

For Christ's people, characteristically weak, it is true to say, "On the side of their oppressors there was power, and there was no one to comfort them" (Eccl. 4:1). And yet, in Christ, there is one who comforts (Ps. 94:19).

> 22   But the LORD has become my stronghold,
>   and my God the rock of my refuge.

30 For some other occurrences of the root (נחם), see Pss. 23:4; 71:21; 90:13.
31 Tate, *Psalms 51–100*, 491.
32 BDB: "trouble, mischief (done to others)," s.v. עָמָל.

²³   He will bring back on them their iniquity
         and wipe them out for their wickedness;
         the LORD our God will wipe them out.

Psalm 94:22 uses the familiar words **stronghold, rock,** and **refuge** of the covenant God, as David had often done in the psalms that bear his name. This is the testimony of David, of Jesus on earth, and of each believer. Psalm 94:23 (the only three-line verse in the psalm, for an emphatic conclusion) promises that **he will bring back on them their iniquity** (the third use of the verb "to turn"; cf. "repay," 94:2; "return," 94:15), which brings the psalm full circle. The church lives in a world of much **iniquity** and **wickedness,** but because of Jesus, we may be confident that God will do what we prayed for in 94:1–2. The staircase parallelism of the final two lines presses home this assurance: he will **wipe them out . . . wipe them out.** The final reference to **our God** reminds us that this believer speaks for the whole church. Supremely, when Jesus prays this, he leads his church in prayer.

As the psalm began with a resolute focus on God (94:1–2), so the final two words in Hebrew are translated **the LORD our God.**

REFLECTION AND RESPONSE

1. When praying Psalm 94:1–2, we exclude all thoughts of revenge. Instead, we pray for Jesus to return and judge the world with righteousness (Acts 17:31). Our longings are deepened when we pray about the world's hatred as portrayed in the psalm. We long for people either to be converted or to be frustrated and defeated.

2. The horror of Psalm 94:6 prompts us to remember that whenever practical atheism seeps into the visible church, and those with power begin to think they can act without God watching, it is the most vulnerable who suffer abuse.

3. But even as we pray, we remember that God waits in patience for others, as he once waited for us, to repent (cf. Rom. 2:4; 2 Pet. 3:9). In our longing for final judgment, we must "not hack down the bridge of God's mercy"[33] after we have crossed it but must hold open the offer of the gospel

---

33 Augustine, *Psalms,* 4:381.

to all for as long as God does. We must not be surprised at a long period of painful waiting. Since God "did not interfere" while wicked men tyrannized the church, "we need not be surprised that he should subject her now to protracted persecutions, nor should we conclude that, because he does not immediately proceed to cure existing evils, he has utterly forsaken her."[34]

4. We all need the rough warning of Psalm 94:8–11, addressed to all who play truant from God's school of discipline. It is hard to be called a fool, but that is what we need to hear whenever we slip into the practical atheism that thinks we can act, speak, or even imagine without God watching, hearing, and fully grasping what we are doing.

5. In 1 Corinthians 3:20 Paul quotes from Psalm 94:11, in a context of warning against putting our trust in human beings within the church.[35] We need this warning not to make idols of Christian leaders.

6. We badly need the surprising beatitude of Psalm 94:12–15. When we experience the painful rod of God's discipline, we are blessed. God is educating us in his school. It is a paradox that the same persecutions that render the wicked guilty are God's instrument for the good of Christ's people. Augustine writes that people who believe this blessing

bear up patiently when evildoers get all the luck, and they bear patiently, tolerantly, the hardships that fall to good people until this world comes to an end, until iniquity shall pass away. They are blessed already, for God has instructed them in his law, and made them gentle through days of misery, until a pit is dug for the sinner.[36]

Linking together unfair treatment and the discipline of God, Augustine also says that this God

uses bad people to put us through our paces, and trains us through their pestering. A good person is scourged with the malice of a bad one. . . . Thus does God fashion our pain into a lesson for us. Bad people do only as much harm as God allows them to do, in the time during which he spares them.[37]

---

34 Calvin, *Psalms*, 4:13.
35 Ciampa and Rosner, "1 Corinthians," in *CNTOT* 704–5.
36 Augustine, *Psalms*, 4:375.
37 Augustine, *Psalms*, 4:404.

7. Andrew Bonar writes, "The Church and her Head bless the Lord for those very dealings that call for vengeance, these being instructive and sanctifying chastenings to his own, though their enemies did not mean to help them to their crown."[38] Further, the assurance of Psalm 94:14, echoed in Romans 11:1–2, encourages us not to lose hope for the future of the church.

8. As we pray Psalm 94:16–23, we do so walking in the footsteps of Jesus. The Father kept him, comforted him, stood up for him, and was his stronghold, rock, and refuge. How much more, having given us his Son, will God keep, comfort, and stand up for us, and be to us a stronghold, rock, and refuge. So often it is only suffering that makes us flee to God as our fortress; in easy days we forget that this refuge is our only hope. Speaking of the experience of sometimes lonely discipline, Charles Spurgeon writes,

This . . . is a bitter trial, and a sore evil under the sun; yet it has its purpose, for it drives the heart still more completely to the Lord, compelling it to rest alone in him. If we could find friends elsewhere, it may be our God would not be so dear to us. . . . Never is the soul safer or more at rest than when, all other helpers failing, she leans upon the Lord alone.[39]

9. Above all, Psalm 94 ought to move us to pray afresh, "Come, Lord Jesus!"

38 Bonar, *Psalms*, 284.
39 Spurgeon, *Treasury*, 2.2:146.

This is a prophecy of Christ, which is extensively dealt with in the letter to the Hebrews. It foretells of the time of the New Testament and of the voice of the gospel. In sum, it teaches us Christ and draws us to him and to the Word of God as to the right way of serving him. And it warns us against the example of the unbelieving fathers in the desert, who could not enter the Promised Land because of their unbelief and disrespect.

MARTIN LUTHER
Summaries

Look back, my soul, with holy dread,
And view those ancient rebels dead;
Attend the offered grace today,
Nor lose the blessing by delay.

Seize the kind promise while it waits,
And march to Zion's heavenly gates;
Believe, and take the promised rest;
Obey, and be forever blessed.

ISAAC WATTS
"Come, Let Our Voices Join to Raise"

It is a Psalm of invitation to worship. It has about it a ring like that of the church bells, and like the bells it sounds both merrily and solemnly, at first ringing out a lively peal, and then dropping into a funeral knell as if tolling at the funeral of the generation which perished in the wilderness.

CHARLES H. SPURGEON
The Treasury of David

PSALM 95

ORIENTATION

Psalm 95 is a passionate call for a true Israel. It begins with a call to authentic worship and closes with a warning not to be like the old Israel. The critical question for a Christian church is to ask, How is this call to be heard today? The answer cannot be simply to exhort one another to try harder, to see if we can do better than they did, "to learn from the mistakes of the past,"[1] good as it is to do that. If we read this simply as exhortation, we are bound to be disappointed. It is exhortation, but—like all biblical exhortation—it is a call founded on the gospel of Christ and therefore a call to the obedience of faith, rather than simply to obedience. The sustained exposition of part of the psalm in Hebrews 3:7–4:10 shapes our new covenant reading of the psalm.[2] Hebrews gives robust exhortation in the context of the priesthood of Jesus. Jesus is faithful to God on behalf of his people (see Heb. 2:14–3:6; 4:14–5:10). Jesus is the true Israel, the true Son of God. He heard and heeded both parts of Psalm 95. He responded with true worship (95:1–7) and was—for the first time in salvation history—the complete antithesis of the unfaithful old Israel (95:8–11). He resisted temptation in the wilderness (Matt. 4:1–11; Luke 4:1–13).[3] By his atoning death, he makes propitiation for his unfaithful people (Heb. 2:14, 17), so that he can be "the source of eternal salvation to all who obey him" (Heb. 5:9).

---

1   Tucker and Grant, *Psalms*, 2:401.
2   Greidanus considers that preaching Ps. 95 in the light of Heb. 3–4 "is probably too complicated" because of the complex argumentation in Hebrews. Greidanus, *Preaching Christ from Psalms*, 325. Hebrews is complex—that's true. Nevertheless, I suggest that the priesthood of Jesus Christ provides the key to a new covenant reading of the psalm.
3   Longman, *Psalms*, 340.

The response that Hebrews enjoins is not simply to try harder but to hold our original confidence in Christ firm to the end (Heb. 3:6, 14). The gospel appeal of Acts 2:40 ("Save yourselves from this crooked generation"),[4] far from simply calling for renewed effort, is a call to "repent and be baptized . . . in the name of Jesus Christ for the forgiveness of your sins" so that we "receive the gift of the Holy Spirit" (Acts 2:38). Only by being grafted into Christ and receiving the Holy Spirit do we become members of the true Israel. All our striving to enter God's rest (Heb. 3:13; 4:11) is done by the Spirit of Christ, "the apostle and high priest of our confession" (Heb. 3:1), who first responded to Psalm 95 for us that we may now respond to its appeal in him. Jesus Christ died "that he might bring us to God" (1 Pet. 3:18). He leads us in worship. He leads us in heeding the warning at the end of the psalm. He brings us to the promised rest.[5]

While it is true that Christ is the prophet who warns us in this psalm and that Christ is God our rock and our shepherd (Ps. 95:1, 7), above all, the truth we need is that Christ is our priest.

Although there is no superscription, Hebrews speaks of the psalm being spoken "in David" (Heb. 4:7 KJV).[6] This may mean that David wrote the psalm, although it may be a way of saying "in the Psalter."[7] The psalm offers no indication of when or for what precise purpose it was written. In its canonical context in book 4, the theme of the wilderness links strongly with the pain of exile.

The designation of God as "rock" picks up the language from Psalm 94:22 (cf. 92:15). In the high praises of "a great God" and "a great King" (95:3), this word echoes the theme of the Lord's reign (anticipated in 92:8; prominent in Ps. 93)[8] and anticipates the continuation of that theme in Psalms 96–99 (note especially 96:10; 97:1; 98:6; 99:1). Psalm 95 calls for the

---

4 The word γενεά appears in the LXX of Ps. 95:10. The words γενεά and σκολιά appear in the LXX of 78:8, which is a closer echo. But the motif of the unfaithful wilderness generation is prominent in Pss. 78, 95, and 106 and is implicit in Ps. 81.

5 For detailed consideration of the text form of the quotation and the way that Hebrews appropriates Ps. 95, see George H. Guthrie, "Hebrews," in *CNTOT* 952–56.

6 ἐν Δαυίδ. The preposition is usually taken to be instrumental, "by David" or "through David." The LXX has τῷ Δαυιδ in its superscription to Ps. 95.

7 Kidner, *Psalms*, 2:344.

8 Mention of "the sea" in Ps. 95:5 echoes God's dominion over the floods, waters, and sea in 93:3–4.

proper response of faith to the God who reigns. The theme of joy in God's works (95:1–2, 9) echoes 92:1–5.

Meribah (95:8) appears in Psalms 81:7 and 106:32. There are similarities with the prophetic appeals in Psalms 50 and 81. First Corinthians 10:1–13 is a comparable appeal to a new covenant church not to be like the wilderness generation, pointing them to Christ as the "spiritual Rock" and pointing them to the provision of a "way of escape" from temptations.

Another New Testament passage that sheds light on a Christian appropriation of the psalm is Colossians 1:15–20. This passage combines Christ as agent and firstborn of creation (Col. 1:15–17; cf. Ps. 95:1–5) with Christ as the firstborn from the dead and head of the church (Col. 1:18–20; cf. Ps. 95:6–7).

THE TEXT

Structure[9]

The psalm consists of three appeals (two invitations and a warning), each followed by a reason. Psalm 95:1–5 is an invitation to worship (95:1–2) followed by a reason to do so (95:3–5). Psalm 95:6–7c is another invitation to worship (95:6) followed by a reason to do so (95:7a–c). Psalm 95:7d–11 is a warning (95:7d–9) followed by a reason to heed it (95:10–11).

95:1–5 Come with Christ the Agent of Creation to God the Creator

1   Oh come, let us sing to the LORD;
      let us make a joyful noise to the rock of our salvation!
2   Let us come into his presence with thanksgiving;
      let us make a joyful noise to him with songs of praise!

The invitation is plural, emphatic, exuberant, and focused. It is all plural (**us**), an invitation to the church—and to all humankind, if they will

---

9   There is no good reason to suppose that two separate psalms have been stitched together (and not very well), as has frequently been suggested. For a comprehensive discussion of these debates, see W. S. Prinsloo, "Psalm 95: If Only You Will Listen to His Voice!," in *The Bible in Human Society*, ed. M. Daniel Carroll R., David J. A. Clines, and Philip R. Davies (Sheffield: Sheffield Academic Press, 1995), 393–410. The verb בוא in 95:6 and 11 provides a significant thematic link between the two parts.

listen. It is emphatic, beginning with a plural imperative (**Oh come**)[10] and followed by four plural jussives (**let us sing . . . let us make a joyful noise . . . let us come**[11] **. . . let us make a joyful noise**). It is exuberant, especially in the repeated **make a joyful noise**.[12] Augustine compared it to singers overflowing with joy and letting out "wild whoops to give utterance to a gladness of spirit, since they are unable to put into words what the heart has conceived." "Well then," he continues, "if they shout for joy over earthly happiness, ought not we to shout for joy over heavenly happiness, which certainly cannot be spelled out in words?"[13] All this is focused on the covenant God (**the LORD**), who alone is **the rock of our salvation**, a title (**rock**)[14] and phrase associated with both Moses and David (e.g., Deut. 32:4, 15, 18, 30–31; 2 Sam. 22:47; Ps. 18:46). When Jesus rejoices in the Holy Spirit, he models this exuberant praise for us (Luke 10:21).

> 3 For the LORD is a great God,
>   and a great King above all gods.
> 4 In his hand are the depths of the earth;
>   the heights of the mountains are his also.
> 5 The sea is his, for he made it,
>   and his hands formed the dry land.

With the word **for**, Psalm 95:3–5 gives the reason why we ought to respond to the invitation of 95:1–2. A declaration of God's greatness (95:3) is followed by the proclamation of his work as Creator (95:4–5). **A great God** with **a great King** points to God's government of the world, rather than other attributes of his being. The contrast with **all gods** does not suggest that God is of the same kind as other **gods** (merely rather greater than them). It is clear, for example, from 47:2; 77:13; and 96:5 that the true God is the only real God.[15]

---

10 The first word in the Vulgate, *Venite*, provides the name for the use of Ps. 95 as a "call to corporate worship" canticle in many Christian traditions.

11 In Ps. 95:1 "come" is the verb הלך (to walk); in 95:2 "come" is קדם (come to meet).

12 Hiphil of רוע, "to raise a shout" (BDB), often a war cry, cheering, or a shout of triumph (*HALOT*).

13 Augustine, *Psalms*, 4:411.

14 This wording may connect with water from the rock in Ex. 17:1–7 and Num. 20:2–13, the former of which is alluded to at the end of the psalm.

15 The use of the definite article in the NIV ("the great God," "the great King"), while not in the Hebrew, conveys the sense well.

Other **gods** exist in the imaginations of their worshipers and in some sense as demonic spiritual beings, but they have no objective existence independent of the true God and the world he has created.[16]

In 95:4–5 this unique greatness is focused on God's work of creating all things, using two merisms. Psalm 95:4 speaks of **the depths of the earth**, where **depths** means something like "unexplored or unfathomable depths," beyond what human beings can control or understand.[17] The word **heights** is a rare word meaning an impressive peak.[18] **The heights of the mountains** may have an association with where human beings place idol temples,[19] just as **the depths of the earth** may suggest places inhabited by demons. No matter how grand or how impenetrable, it is all made by the true God, and it all belongs to him. Psalm 95:5 reinforces this idea by mentioning **the sea** (often associated with threats, e.g., 93:3) and **the dry land**,[20] where people can live.

When Christ brings us to this true God (1 Pet. 3:18), he does so as "the image of the invisible God, the firstborn of all creation," in whom "all things were created, in heaven and on earth, visible and invisible, whether thrones or dominions or rulers or authorities" (Col. 1:15–16). Christ, who is the divine agent of creation, brings us to the triune God of creation. In Christ, nothing, whether "height" or "depth," can separate us from the love of God (Rom. 8:39).

95:6–7c Come with Christ the Head of the Church
to the Covenant God of the Church

6   Oh come, let us worship and bow down;
       let us kneel before the LORD, our Maker!

---

16 See the carefully nuanced exposition of idols by Paul in 1 Cor. 8:4–6 (in which they have no real existence) and 10:19–22 (in which they are associated with demons). See also Witherington, *Psalms Old and New*, 222.

17 The word מְחְקְרֵי is an Old Testament hapax legomenon. It derives from the root חקר, "to search" (used, e.g., in Job 38:16 ["the *recesses* of the deep"] and Jer. 31:37 ["can be *explored*"]).

18 BDB: "eminence," s.v. תּוֹעָפוֹת; *HALOT* (after long discussion): "the heights, the peaks of the mountains," s.v. תּוֹעָפוֹת. The word appears also in Num. 23:22 ("horns"); 24:8 ("horns").

19 "His are the tops of the mountains, even should the demons times beyond counting persuade the fools among men to build on them temples dedicated to them." Theodoret of Cyrus, *Psalms*, 2:124.

20 The word יַבָּשֶׁת appears only here and in Ex. 4:9 ("dry ground").

The second invitation is given to the church, to those who have come to the God of creation by the ministry of Christ. **Oh come** (also Ps. 95:11: "enter") uses a verb effectively synonymous with the two verbs in 95:1–2. The verbs **worship**, **bow down**, and **kneel** are emphatic and possibly sequential, ending with a kneeling posture of humble attentiveness. When we come to God the Creator, through Christ, the firstborn of creation, we come also to God the **Maker** of the church, to belong to Christ the head of the church (Col. 1:15–20). **Our Maker** here means the Creator of his people, rather than the Creator of the world (cf. Deut. 32:6; Isa. 43:1).

> 7   For he is our God,
>   and we are the people of his pasture,
>   and the sheep of his hand.

Psalm 95:7 begins with **for** (as 95:3): here is the reason why the church should worship. The reason is covenantal and pastoral. The phrase **our God** and reference to his **people** echoes the tagline of the covenant: "I will be your God, and you will be my people" (cf. Ex. 6:7). If **he** (emphatic) **is our God**, then we must ask, says Augustine, "What are we? We need to know, if we are to fall down before him without fear."[21] The answer is that **we** (again emphatic) **are the people of his pasture / and the sheep of his hand** (i.e., under his care and authority; cf. Ps. 79:13). God is pastor for the journey to the promised land (cf. 74:1; 77:20; 79:13). The combination of God as pastor and God as Creator of his people is repeated in 100:3.

95:7d–11 Cleave to Christ and Be Faithful to God, Heeding the Warnings Given to the Untrue Church

> Today, if you hear his voice,

With the final line of Psalm 95:7, the music changes. After warm invitations, we are summoned to heed a sober warning, ultimately from the mouth

---

21 Augustine, *Psalms*, 4:419.

of Christ our prophet, for this is an "exhortation to his church visible, to believe and obey the voice of our great prophet Jesus Christ."[22]

Today echoes the appeals of Moses in Deuteronomy (e.g., Deut. 4:40).[23] Neither past obedience nor future intentions count for anything before the word of God; it is always "today," this present moment of choice (Deut. 5:2–3; 2 Cor. 6:1–2).

Some translators (e.g., CSB, ESV)[24] express the rest of the line as a simple conditional clause, the protasis "If you hear his voice" taking "[then] do not harden" as the apodosis. Others (e.g., NIV, NRSV, REB)[25] understand it as optative, "Oh [I wish] that you would listen to his voice!" The psalmist's desire is the same either way, that the voice of God should not only be heard with the ear but heeded in the heart.[26]

8   do not harden your hearts, as at Meribah,
       as on the day at Massah in the wilderness,
9   when your fathers put me to the test
       and put me to the proof, though they had seen my work.

The command **Do not harden** uses a verb applied to Pharaoh (e.g., Ex. 7:3), to Sihon king of Heshbon (Deut. 2:30), and to Israel ("Be no longer stubborn," Deut. 10:16), in each case with reference to a deliberate rejection of God in the face of clear evidence.[27] The **as . . . as . . . when . . .** that follows fleshes out what the hard **heart** looks like. **Meribah** (controversy, contention) and **Massah** (testing)[28] are used of the incident described in Exodus 17:1–7, which this verse seems to refer to.[29] Psalm 95:9 speaks of the agents (**your fathers**), the character of their actions (**put me to the test / and put me to the proof**) and the inexcusability of what they did (**though they had seen my work**). The designation **your fathers** raises the question

---

22 Dickson, *Psalms*, 2:171.
23 Of all the Old Testament occurrences of this word (הַיּוֹם), 17 percent (75/439) appear in Deuteronomy, often in significant contexts.
24 Goldingay, *Psalms*, 3:94; Hengstenberg, *Psalms*, 3:167.
25 Tate, *Psalms 51–100*, 497; Delitzsch, *Psalms*, 3:87.
26 Tucker and Grant, *Psalms*, 2:404.
27 The verb (hiphil of קשׁה) also appears in Neh. 9:16, 29, in the idiom of a stiff neck.
28 The same root (נסה) is used in Ps. 95:9, "put . . . to the test" (cf. Ex. 17:2, 7).
29 The names also appear together in Deut. 33:8. Meribah alone appears in connection with the later episode described in Num. 20:1–13 (cf. Ps. 81:7). Massah appears in Deut. 6:16; 9:22.

of the spiritual paternity of every "today" generation that hears the psalm: Are we the spiritual children of these **fathers** or not? The synonymous verbs **put to the test**[30] and **put to the proof**[31] describe the nature of Israel's actions, which was to doubt the word of God and insist that God prove himself; this is to live by sight rather than by faith. All this is despite what they had seen (**though they had seen my work**), the exodus and the crossing of the Red Sea, which gave more than adequate grounds for a reasonable faith. The church in the wilderness (Acts 7:38) was no better than hard-hearted Pharaoh in Egypt.

> [10]   For forty years I loathed that generation
>   and said, "They are a people who go astray in their heart,
>   and they have not known my ways."
> [11]   Therefore I swore in my wrath,
>   "They shall not enter my rest."

What God felt and said about **that generation** is terrifying. **Forty years** speaks of persistent unbelief (cf. Ex. 17:1–7; Num. 13–14; 20:2–13; 21:4–5; 25:1–9). The verb **loathed** conveys utter disgust and detestation;[32] this is the only time the verb is used in Scripture with God as subject.[33] The disgusted exclamations of Jesus with reference to his "generation" express the same horrified feeling (e.g., Matt. 11:16; 12:39–42; 16:4; 17:17). And yet he loves, warns, and appeals—just as God did in the wilderness.

Psalm 95:10 gives God's verdict, and 95:11 his sentence. The verdict is that **they** (emphatic) **go astray** (cf. 58:3; 107:4, 40; 119:110, 176), like errant sheep (cf. Isa. 53:6; Luke 15:3–7), and do so **in their heart**, from the core of their being. In parallel with this, **they** (again emphatic) **have not known**—that is, known in personal obedience and love—**my ways**—that is, the ways of God's good and perfect law (cf. the references to God's law in Pss. 93:5; 94:12).

---

30   Piel of נסה, often used of God testing people (e.g., Deut. 8:2; Ps. 26:2) rather than of people testing God.

31   בחן, also often used of God testing people (e.g., Pss. 26:2; 66:10; 81:7; 139:23). But note Mal. 3:10 (where God invites his people to do it).

32   BDB: "feel a loathing," s.v. קוט. *HALOT*: "feel disgust," s.v. קוט. The NIV translation, "I was angry," is perhaps a little weak.

33   Hossfeld and Zenger, *Psalms*, 2:461. In Pss. 119:158 and 139:21, it is used with a righteous believer as subject.

In Psalm 95:11 the verb **I swore** gives a deep seriousness to the verdict. God's **wrath** is his hot, settled righteous anger against sinners. The verdict is **They shall not enter my rest**. This solemn oath is given in Numbers 14:21–23 and 28–30, after the response to the unbelieving spies. The concept of **rest** is rich with nuance. In Genesis 2:15 God "put" (a cognate that could almost be rendered "made to rest") Adam in the garden; we lost this rest in the fall.[34] God gives this rest in the wilderness when the ark "rests" (Num. 10:33–36), as an anticipation of the promised land, where God "rests" among his people and they "rest" with him (cf. Deut. 12:9; 1 Kings 8:56; Ps. 132:8, 14). The verb **enter** is the same as "come" in Psalm 95:6, for to come into God's presence is to enter God's rest. Hebrews 3:7–4:13 makes it clear that the "rest" of the promised land (denied to the wilderness generation, as it was denied to the generation in exile) is a shadow of the final "Sabbath rest for the people of God," which is entered in Christ (Heb. 4:9).

REFLECTION AND RESPONSE

1. It is wonderful that Christ is the true Israel for whom Psalm 95 calls. Because he is the true Israel, he can be the representative substitute and federal head of his people. Before considering our response, we should meditate on the marvel of Christ's obedience, both to the calls to worship (95:1–7) and to the warning against unfaithfulness (95:8–11).

2. We hear the exhortations as those justified by faith, covered by Christ's righteousness. Psalm 95:1–5 stirs us to consider the unparalleled greatness of the only true God in creation. A joyful noise of delighted thanksgiving (what Augustine calls "a great banquet of joy")[35] and praise is the only proper response to this true God, who made, governs, and rules all things, visible and invisible. Christ takes us by the hand and brings us to this triune God. As David Dickson says, "Whatsoever evil or grief trouble us there is reason of joy, and praise, and thanks, when we look to Jesus Christ and his benefits."[36]

---

34 In Ps. 95:11 "rest" is the noun מְנוּחָה; in Gen. 2:15 the verb "put" is the hiphil of נוּחַ, lit., "caused him to rest" (cf. what God does for Lot when he saves him from Sodom: "set him," Gen. 19:16).

35 Augustine, *Psalms*, 4:409.

36 Dickson, *Psalms*, 2:168.

3. The invitation to come into the presence of God presupposes that, by nature, we are far from God. This is the call of the gospel of Christ: Come! Come to God! Come today!

4. Psalm 95:6–7 adds to this invitation the wonder of adoption and the joy of belonging to Christ's church, whom God "cherishes . . . with a peculiar and fatherly regard," and to ponder "the inestimable favour conferred upon them in their adoption, by virtue of which they were called to live under the faithful guardianship of God, and to the enjoyment of every species of blessing."[37] Christ takes us by the hand and brings us into the family of this wonderful triune God.

5. Franz Delitzsch says of the greatness of God, "He is exalted above all gods as King, above all things as Creator, and above His people as Shepherd and Leader."[38]

6. Psalm 95:8–11 warns us that it is possible to be in church but not in Christ, just as old covenant Israel could enjoy the outward blessings of the exodus without faith. The warning of Hebrews 3–4 drives us to cleave afresh to Christ and to cry to Christ that we may follow him all our days. Commenting on the kneeling of Psalm 95:6, Ernst Wilhelm Hengstenberg writes, "In the shell of the kneeling, there must be contained the kernel of unreserved *surrender*, which manifests itself in willing obedience."[39]

7. The terrible sentence of Psalm 95:11 should move us to cry to Christ for grace to persevere to the end. Nothing can be better than God's "rest." As Dickson observes,

> There is a rest of God ordained for believers who give up their hearts to the impression of God's voice in the obedience of faith; to wit, the rest of justification, reconciliation, and peace with God; the rest of begun sanctification, and ceasing from their own works; and the rest of everlasting refreshment, begun in this life, and perfected in the life to come.[40]

8. It is profitable to meditate on the mix of joyful exultation and sober warning in this psalm, for the life of faith must consist of both joy in

---

37 Calvin, *Psalms*, 4:35.
38 Delitzsch, *Psalms*, 3:85.
39 Hengstenberg, *Psalms*, 3:167.
40 Dickson, *Psalms*, 2:173–74.

Christ and serious self-examination. With only joy, we may slip into a false assurance; with a preoccupation with self-examination, we may lose the joy that is ours in Christ.

*Make the gospel known from day to day. . . . Preach
to all human beings in the whole world the grace
offered and given through Christ to believers.*

KONRAD PELLIKAN
Commentary on the Bible

[Psalm 96] is a grand missionary hymn.

CHARLES H. SPURGEON
The Treasury of David

PSALM 96

ORIENTATION

Psalm 96 is a resounding missionary appeal to "all the earth / . . . all the earth" (96:1, 9) to bow in worship before the one true God because that God is coming to set "the earth" (96:13) to rights. In the context of the Old Testament, this is a call with an astonishing reach and kindness; not only is the world summoned to surrender, they—who have caused such suffering to the people of God (e.g., Pss. 74; 79)—are invited to join with Israel in glad worship: "For God so loved *the world*, that he gave . . ." (John 3:16). Two questions await the New Testament for clear answers: Who makes the appeal? Who exactly is coming?

Who makes the appeal? Who calls the world to worship? The anonymous psalmist does, but he does so by the Spirit of Christ. His voice is fulfilled when Jesus Christ calls, "Come to me, all who labor" (Matt. 11:28); brings us to God (1 Pet. 3:18); breaks down the dividing wall of hostility (Eph. 2:14); throws the doors of the kingdom open to any and all who will believe. He it is who continues to make the Father known (John 17:26), who praises God's name among the Gentiles (Rom. 15:9, quoting from Ps. 18:49), and who leads his church in mission (cf. the implications of Acts 1:1 that mission is what Jesus continues to do and to teach). Psalm 96 is the worldwide gospel invitation and summons of Jesus Christ.

Who is coming to judge? The phrase "judge the world in righteousness" (96:13) is echoed in Acts 17:31 when Paul teaches that God "has fixed a day on which he will judge the world in righteousness by a man whom he has appointed" and guaranteed this to us by raising this man from the dead.[1]

---

1 Acts 17:31 includes, almost verbatim, the LXX of Pss. 96:1 and 98:1.

Jesus not only declares that there will be a judgment (e.g., Luke 18:1–8); he claims that he will be the Judge (Matt. 25:31–46; John 5:22, 27; cf. Rev. 19:11).[2]

Jesus Christ both speaks the psalm (he gives the missionary call) and fulfills its promise (he comes to judge the world). This is a psalm "of the final victory of God and of God's Messiah."[3] It is remarkable that such a confident invitation should be given from such weakness (of Israel, of Jesus, and of the New Testament church).

Psalm 96:1–6 is almost a musical variation of 95:1–5. In each there is a call to rejoice in the covenant Lord (95:1–2; 96:1–3), a praise of his "salvation" (95:1; 96:2), a reference to his being "great" and "above all gods" (95:3; 96:4), and a celebration that he is the Creator (95:4–5; 96:5). Other links include "the earth" (95:4; 96:1, 9, 13), "today" (95:7) with "from day to day" (96:2), and "the sea" (95:5; 96:11). The theme of judgment in Psalm 96 also echoes 94:1–7 and 15.

But the differences between Psalms 95 and 96 are perhaps as significant as the parallels. In Psalm 95 it is we, the church, who sing to the Lord ("Let us sing," 95:1), the salvation is "our salvation" (95:1), he is "our Maker" (the Maker of his people, 95:6), and it is "we" who are "the people of his pasture" (95:7). The psalm closes with a sober warning to be the true church in the wilderness of this world. By contrast, in Psalm 96 the appeal is to "all the earth" and to the "families of the peoples" (96:1, 7, 9). It is given "among the nations" and "among all the peoples" (96:3). And it closes with a longing for the day when the whole created order is glad that God has set things right. John Calvin, following older writers, is correct to argue that this must be a prophecy of the kingdom of Christ, both in his first coming, after which the missionary call is given throughout the world, and in his second coming, when he comes to judge the world.[4]

Echoing themes in Acts and in Romans 9–11, Charles Spurgeon perceptively notes that the unfaithfulness of Israel (the subject of the closing sec-

---

2   Justin Martyr argues that Ps. 96 speaks of Christ, to whom the Father has given authority over the world. See Justin Martyr, *Dialogue with Trypho*, 74, in *ACCS* 8:191–92.

3   Bonhoeffer, *Prayerbook of the Bible*, 176.

4   "This psalm contains an exhortation to praise God, an exhortation which is directed not only to the Jews, but to all nations. We must infer from this, that it has reference to the kingdom of Christ. . . . The Holy Spirit stirred up the saints who were under the Law to celebrate the Divine praises, till the period should arrive when Christ, by the spread of the Gospel, should fill the whole earth with his glory." Calvin, *Psalms*, 4:47.

tion of Ps. 95) leads, in the providence of God, to the spread of the gospel to the world (the subject of Ps. 96; cf. Acts 28:28 and the logic of Romans 11).[5]

Psalm 96 is associated with David bringing the ark to Jerusalem. Apart from 96:1a and 2a, it is very close to 1 Chronicles 16:23–33. (Other parts of the song are close to sections of Pss. 105 and 106.) First Chronicles does not explicitly say that David or his songwriters actually wrote this song,[6] and it is possible that the Chronicler includes this medley of anonymous psalms because it was so appropriate to help his readers grasp the significance of the occasion. But the most natural reading is that David did write the song and that either he or some later psalmists used parts of it in Psalms 96, 105, and 106.[7]

So Psalm 96 helps us look back on the bringing of the ark to Jerusalem. But its call for a "new song" draws our eyes forward to the first and second comings of Christ (rather as Ps. 68 prefigures the victory and ascension of Jesus Christ).[8] The significance of the "new song" will be discussed below (see on 96:1). In looking both backward and forward, this two-pronged approach is like the Lord's Supper, in which we "proclaim the Lord's death [looking back] until he comes [looking forward]" (1 Cor. 11:26).

The theme of Psalm 96 has been anticipated in the worldwide worship of Psalm 86:9 and Psalm 87. There are many links forward to Psalms 97–99 (esp. Ps. 98), and these will be noted in the treatment of those psalms. The triumphant conclusion to the work of the cross in Psalm 22:27–31 has several parallels with Psalm 96, confirming the connection between this missionary call and the work of Christ. Psalm 29:1–2 displays some similarities with 96:7–9. Isaiah 40–55 includes several themes shared with this psalm. These include polemics against idolatry (e.g., Isa. 40:18–31; 41:21–24; 44:6–8), the theme of creation (e.g., Isa. 40:22; 42:5; 44:24; 45:12), the response of elements of the created order to God's salvation (e.g., Isa. 44:23; 49:13; 55:12), and the prominence of "the nations" (e.g., Isa. 45:20; 49:7; 56:3–8; 60:9–12, 14, 16; 66:18). For the restoration of creation in Psalm 96:11–13, see also on Psalm 65.

5 Spurgeon, *Treasury*, 2.2:180.

6 *Pace* the NIV's interpretive addition "in this manner" in 1 Chron. 16:7.

7 Hamilton, *Psalms*, 2:189–90.

8 Combining the backward look to the ark and the forward look to Christ, Dickson notes that the meaning of the psalm is "in substance, and almost in words also, one and the same with [1 Chron. 16]; for as there, so here the prophet foreseeth in the Spirit the spreading of the kingdom of Christ among the nations." Dickson, *Psalms*, 2:174.

The worldwide blessing of the Abrahamic covenant (Gen. 12:1–3) lies behind much of the psalm. Galatians 3:10–14 shows that this reaches its fulfillment through the sin-bearing death of Christ and the gift of the Holy Spirit.

In terms of its style, the psalm is characterized by the technique of picking up a word or phrase from the end of one line at the start of the next.[9] This gives it a vibrantly enthusiastic feel.

THE TEXT

Structure

The psalm is punctuated by clear appeals in Psalm 96:1–3, 7–9, and 11–12. This suggests three sections: 96:1–6 (a call to worship in 96:1–3, followed by reasons for worship in 96:4–6); 96:7–10 (a call to worship in 96:7–9, followed by a reason for worship in 96:10); and 96:11–13 (a call to worship in 96:11–12, followed by a reason for worship in 96:13).[10]

96:1–6 Christ Calls the Whole World to Worship the One True God

1   Oh sing to the LORD a new song;
    sing to the LORD, all the earth!
2   Sing to the LORD, bless his name;
    tell of his salvation from day to day.
3   Declare his glory among the nations,
    his marvelous works among all the peoples!

The psalm opens with a threefold emphatic plural imperative (**sing . . . sing . . . sing**), followed by three more plural imperatives (**bless . . . tell . . . declare**). Each of the first three is followed by the covenant name (**the LORD**). Psalm 96:1 speaks of what is to be sung (**a new song**) and who is to sing it (**all the earth**). In the light of the rest of the Scriptures, three elements of newness are implied.[11] First, new people sing it: **all the earth**. Second, the

---

9 This staircase parallelism is diagrammed by Greidanus, *Preaching Christ from Psalms*, 159.

10 This structure is noted by, among others, Greidanus, *Preaching Christ from Psalms*, 163; Hossfeld and Zenger, *Psalms*, 2:464.

11 A "new song" appears in the Old Testament in Pss. 33:3; 40:3; 98:1; 144:9; 149:1; Isa. 42:10. While it sometimes celebrates a new victory, it can anticipate a promised victory. Tate, *Psalms 51–100*, 513–14. In the New Testament this appears in Rev. 5:9; 14:3—sung in praise of Christ by all the redeemed,

song responds to the promise of a new work of God, to be fulfilled in Christ (witness the new songs that surrounded the birth of Jesus in Luke 1–2).[12] Third, in the light of Christ and the new covenant, the people who sing it are renewed people with a new nature.[13]

Psalm 96:2 repeats **Sing to the Lord** and goes on to focus on what it is about the Lord that we are to make the subject of our song. We are to **bless his name**, his revealed nature, all that he is to us by covenant in the Scriptures, not singing of what we like to think God is like but glorying in who he has told us he is. And with a shift in focus from God to the world, we are to **tell** (an evangelism verb that speaks of proclaiming news)[14] **of his salvation**, his great work of rescue for his people and indeed for the whole created order. This we are to do **from day to day**, for the song has fresh mercies each day (cf. Lam. 3:23).

Psalm 96:3 continues with another verb of proclamation: **Declare his glory** (the visible manifestation of his being), which is made visible in **his marvelous works** (of creation and of redemption, leading to the new creation). All this is to be proclaimed **among the nations**—indeed, in case we were in any doubt about its extent, **among *all* the peoples!** Here is a joyful appeal and a call for the whole world to join with the people of God in a glad worldwide proclamation of the one true God. David Dickson observes, "As sadness and sorrow, misery and mourning, are the condition of all people, till Christ, the true ark of the covenant, come unto them, so Christ coming among them is the matter of the greatest joy that ever sinners heard of."[15]

4   For great is the Lord, and greatly to be praised;
             he is to be feared above all gods.
5   For all the gods of the peoples are worthless idols,
             but the Lord made the heavens.

---

focusing both on the subject (the person and work of Christ) and the singers (those redeemed by Christ).

12   Greidanus, *Preaching Christ from Psalms*, 165.

13   The newness of the new covenant is noted by several older writers, including Eusebius of Caesaria (ca. 260–ca. 340), *Proof of the Gospel*, 6.5, in *ACCS* 8:190; Augustine, *Psalms*, 4:424.

14   Piel of בשׂר, used of bringing news in, e.g., 1 Sam. 4:17; 31:9; 2 Sam. 1:20; 4:10; 18:19–20; Isa. 40:9; 41:27; 52:7; 60:6; 61:1. The last of these is especially relevant, echoed in the Nazareth sermon in Luke 4.

15   Dickson, *Psalms*, 2:174.

6   Splendor and majesty are before him;
     strength and beauty are in his sanctuary.

The word **for** that begins Psalm 96:4 and 96:5 introduces the reason why the church ought to tell the world about God and why the world ought to heed this call. This is stated positively in 96:4. Again, the covenant name, **the LORD**, is used. He is **great**, and he is **above all gods** (see on 95:3). Therefore, he and he alone is to be **praised** and **feared**, with reverent fear. The phrase **greatly to be praised** is literally "one praised exceedingly."[16]

Psalm 96:5, addressed to a world in which idolatry is endemic, introduces a necessary negative note: **For all the gods of the peoples**—and there are many—**are worthless idols** (cf. 97:7), a word that means nonentities, no-gods, worthless, useless, powerless, utterly pathetic.[17] This is true of **all** these so-called gods, whether they be the so-called gods of major world religions or the idols of secular culture. No matter how popular and influential they are, they are worth nothing.[18] By contrast, the covenant Lord **made the heavens**, which, by implication, means that since he created the very highest things, he created everything else (see on 95:4–5). There is one true God, the covenant Lord, made known to us by Christ.

Theodoret of Cyrus notes the cosmic miracles at the crucifixion in this connection:

> While the so-called gods were seen as wicked demons, ours appeared as maker of the heavens. At the time of his voluntary passion not only was the sun darkened, rocks split, and the veil of the Temple was torn asunder, but also the powers of the heavens were moved and, in short, the universe threatened destruction on seeing the one who carries all things fixed to the cross.[19]

---

16 The CSB translation, "highly praised," is literal. The ESV ("to be praised") and NIV ("most worthy of praise") interpret this language to mean that he ought to be praised, which is undoubtedly true.

17 The word (אֱלִילִים) is probably a disparaging pun on "God" (אֱלֹהִים). Alter suggests that it is a pun on עַל and אֵל, and he proposes the rendering "ungods." In Job 13:4 and Zech. 11:17, it is used as an adjective to mean "worthless." Examples of other uses include Lev. 19:4; 26:1; Isa. 2:8, 18, 20; 10:10–11.

18 There may be an echo of this theme in Rev. 9:20, where the finally impenitent do not heed the appeal of the psalm (the LXX translates the Hebrew as δαιμόνια, "demons"). See Hossfeld and Zenger, *Psalms*, 2:467.

19 Theodoret of Cyrus, *Psalms*, 2:128.

In **his sanctuary** are **splendor and majesty,**[20] **strength and beauty.**[21] These are not separable attributes, let alone attendants or companions of God, for God's attributes are inseparable from his being (the doctrine of the simplicity of God). In the **sanctuary** (and, by implication, in the signs and Scriptures of the covenant, fulfilled in Christ), we know God in all his glory. Christ not only calls the whole world to bow to the one true God; by making the Father known, he enables the world to do what he summons us to do.

96:7–10 Christ Invites the Whole World to Enter His Church

7   Ascribe to the LORD, O families of the peoples,
    ascribe to the LORD glory and strength!
8   Ascribe to the LORD the glory due his name;
    bring an offering, and come into his courts!
9   Worship the LORD in the splendor of holiness;
    tremble before him, all the earth!

Like Psalm 96:1–3, 96:7–9 begins with a threefold imperative, in each case addressed to the covenant Lord: **Ascribe to the LORD**. **Ascribe** means to acknowledge that these things are true and therefore to bow in worship before the covenant Lord (cf. Deut. 32:3; Ps. 29:1–2). The word translated **families**[22] means something larger than a nuclear family and (usually) smaller than a tribe or nation. Although it covers a spectrum of social or familial groupings, it reminds us that the appeal of the gospel comes to us not as isolated individuals but as members of cultures, societies, and ethnic groups; the similar phrase "all the families of the nations" comes in 22:27 in connection with the fruits of the Messiah's sin-bearing sufferings. The phrase **glory and strength**, together with **the glory due his name** (lit., "the glory of his name," that is, the outward shining of his inward being through his revelation of himself), links this section back to 96:6 with its focus on the revelation of God in Christ. That God's glory is "the glory of his name" includes the truth that, as Calvin puts it, "God

---

20 The words "splendor" and "majesty" are used in Pss. 21:5; 45:3; 104:1; 111:3.
21 The Hebrew words for "strength" and "beauty" are used in Ps. 78:61 (translated "power" and "glory" in the ESV) of the ark of the covenant, strengthening the link with 1 Chron. 16.
22 Plural of מִשְׁפָּחָה.

borrows nothing from without, but comprehends all that is worthy of praise in himself."[23]

Psalm 96:7–8 looks forward to the worldwide blessing promised to Abraham (Gen. 12:1–3), which is fulfilled in Christ (Gal. 3:10–14).

In the second line of Psalm 96:8, the world is called not simply to surrender but to worship: **Bring an offering** is language sometimes used of sacrificial offerings (here in **his courts**, i.e., in the sanctuary, as in 20:3; 76:11), but it can also refer to any gift or tribute (e.g., 72:10). The New Testament transposes this offering into a new covenant key by speaking of "a sacrifice of praise to God, that is, the fruit of lips that acknowledge his name" (Heb. 13:15), "your bodies as a living sacrifice" (Rom. 12:1), and "spiritual sacrifices acceptable to God through Jesus Christ" (1 Pet. 2:5). We **bring an offering** when we offer ourselves to God through Christ in whole-life worship.

Psalm 96:9 continues this invitation to enter God's people and belong. We are not certain how to translate the phrase rendered **the splendor of holiness** (also in 1 Chron. 16:29; 2 Chron. 20:21; Ps. 29:2).[24] Whose holiness? What splendor? If this refers to God's holiness,[25] it links with **his courts** and refers to his holiness as revealed in the signs of the covenant in his house. If it refers to the holiness given to the worshipers, it probably means in the first instance the "holy attire" (ESV mg.; cf. 2 Chron. 20:21 and the plural in Ps. 110:3) in which the priests had to be dressed to enter the presence of God; in a derivative sense, then, it means the beauty of the holiness given to us by grace. In the light of the Gentiles bringing offerings in Psalm 96:8, W. Dennis Tucker and Jamie Grant make the attractive suggestion that the phrase may refer to "the complete 'rebadging' of the gentile nations. They are reclothed in priestly clothing so that they too can enter the real presence of God."[26]

The verb **tremble** means to writhe, often in labor pains; here it conveys a deep sense of awe in the presence of the immeasurable power and searching holiness of God. The phrase **all the earth** takes us back to 96:1 and the

---

23 Calvin, *Psalms*, 4:54.

24 הַדְרַת־קֹדֶשׁ. See the helpful notes on this question in Tate, *Psalms 51–100*, 511; Tucker and Grant, *Psalms*, 2:418n14.

25 The LXX interprets it to mean "in his [i.e., God's] holy court"; the CSB, "in the splendor of his holiness"; the NIV, "in the splendor of his holiness."

26 Tucker and Grant, *Psalms*, 2:418n14.

grand theme of the psalm; no one is exempt from this invitation of grace, given by Christ.

10   Say among the nations, "The LORD reigns!
       Yes, the world is established; it shall never be moved;
       he will judge the peoples with equity."

The emphasis in Psalm 96:10 is not so much on the speaking (**say**) as the context (**among the nations**) and the content: **The LORD reigns!** (cf. 93:1; 97:1; 99:1). **Yes, the world is established; it shall never be moved** echoes 93:1. But this raises the question of what it can mean in a disordered world to speak of it as stable. The new note here is in the final line (anticipating 96:13): **He will judge**[27] **the peoples with equity**. To **judge** here means not simply to punish evildoers (although it includes that) but to set all that is wrong to rights (**equity**), and he will do this for **the peoples**, the whole world. This introduces the thought, implied though not explicit in Psalm 93, that the statement **The LORD reigns** is not a static philosophical assertion but a dynamic truth: the God who always has been, is, and always will be sovereign over the affairs of people is coming to bring in his kingdom, so that his will will be done on earth in the same manner as it is done in heaven. This happens in Christ.[28]

Dickson speaks of the "inexpressible joy which Christ bringeth to his people" because of the "putting of all things which are in disorder and confusion in the world by sin, into their own order again."[29]

The reign of God is established on earth through the cross of Christ. This was understood very early in the Christian church, as is evident from the Old Latin text, which reads, "The Lord will reign from a tree."[30] While this translation is textually inaccurate, it demonstrates how Christians interpreted the verse from an early date.[31]

This good news provides the great incentive to all people in the world to accept the gospel invitation to come and belong to Christ's church.

27 The verb "judge" here is דין. In Ps. 96:13 it is the more common word שׁפט. The meaning is the same in this context.
28 Calvin, *Psalms*, 4:57.
29 Dickson, *Psalms*, 2:178.
30 In Latin, *Dominus regnavit a ligno*. This is "quoted by many of the Latin Fathers from Tertullian onwards as a prophecy of Christ's triumph through death." Kirkpatrick, *Psalms*, 3:577–78.
31 Eveson, *Psalms*, 2:177.

96:11–13 Christ Leads His Church in Longing for the Day When He Will Come to Set All Creation to Rights

¹¹   Let the heavens be glad, and let the earth rejoice;
         let the sea roar, and all that fills it;[32]
¹²   let the field exult, and everything in it!
      Then shall all the trees of the forest sing for joy
¹³   before the LORD, . . .

We are to long that the whole created order will be glad in the presence of the covenant Lord (**before the LORD**). Seven elements highlight universality:[33] **the heavens** (the skies, the invisible world above), **the earth** (the visible world below), **the sea** (which is such a threat, e.g., in Ps. 93, but which belongs to God, 95:5), **all that fills it** (including Leviathan! [104:26]), **the field** (the cultivated and inhabited world of human beings), **everything in** the field, and finally **the trees of the forest** (cf. Isa. 44:23; 55:12). The whole creation, groaning in anticipation, will **be glad . . . rejoice . . . exult . . . sing for joy**. Even the sea, whose thunderous noise has been such a threat to the order of creation and the church of God, will now **roar** in glad acclamation of the God who made it: "Will not every billow soon flash forth the praises of him who once trod the sea?"[34] This is an intoxicating vision of the renewed created order in which righteousness dwells (2 Pet. 3:13). The jussive forms (**let the . . . let the . . . let the . . . let the**) stir us to groan and long for this day.[35] There may be an echo of the clause **Let the heavens be glad** in Revelation 18:20 ("Rejoice . . . , O heaven") in connection with the final defeat of evil.[36] If the children had not praised Jesus the Messiah, the very stones would have cried out with joy (Luke 19:40).[37]

---

32 Ps. 96:11b is repeated in 98:7a.

33 Tucker and Grant, *Psalms*, 2:419.

34 Spurgeon, *Treasury*, 2.2:184.

35 The jussive may be used rather than direct imperative because this section expresses a wish about what the (partly inanimate) creation will do; it makes more sense to wish that it will do it than to command it to do it. See Hossfeld and Zenger, *Psalms*, 2:464.

36 Compare the LXX, εὐφραινέσθωσαν οἱ οὐρανοί, and Rev. 18:20, Εὐφραίνου ἐπ' αὐτῇ, οὐρανὲ. This may also be echoed in Rev. 12:12. See Hossfeld and Zenger, *Psalms*, 2:467.

37 Kidner, *Psalms*, 2:349.

Psalm 96:11–12 answers the groaning of creation (Rom. 8:20–22). Calvin expresses it in this way: "As all elements in the creation groan and travail together with us [Rom. 8:22], they may reasonably be said to rejoice in the restoration of all things according to their earnest desire."[38]

13   . . . for he comes,
            for he comes to judge the earth.
        He will judge the world in righteousness,
            and the peoples in his faithfulness.

Psalm 96:13 is the climax. The repeated **for he comes, / for he comes** evokes a spine-tingling anticipation. He comes **to judge the earth. / He will judge the world**.[39] The repetition of **judge** ties what he will do to the anticipation that he comes (he comes to judge, he comes to judge). In his example sermon on this psalm, Sidney Greidanus catches the excitement of this expectation: "For he is coming. Jesus is coming. Jesus is coming to set things right, to make straight what is crooked, to restore justice."[40] Andrew Bonar speaks of this as "the happiest day our world has ever seen," the day that the cross guaranteed and the day that will be completed "by the total suppression of Satan's reign, and the removal of the curse."[41]

The three words **earth, world**, and **peoples** emphasize a glorious universality. The words **righteousness** and **faithfulness** are covenant words, for the new creation is the fulfillment of the covenant, all of whose promises are "Yes!" in Christ (2 Cor. 1:20).

REFLECTION AND RESPONSE

1. In meditating on this psalm, we do well to take the three sections (Ps. 96:1–6, 7–10, 11–13) in turn. The joyful call to worship in 96:1–3 reminds us that, as Dickson puts it, "we have need again and again to be stirred up to joy in Christ, to praise him; for we are dull, and the work excellent, and

---

38 Calvin, *Psalms*, 4:58.
39 On the fulfillment of this verse in Acts 17:31, see the *orientation* section of this psalm.
40 Greidanus, *Preaching Christ from Psalms*, 175.
41 Bonar, *Psalms*, 289.

no man dischargeth the duty sufficiently."[42] Indeed, commenting on 96:3, Calvin goes so far as to say, "The words teach us that we can never be said to have rightly apprehended the redemption wrought out by Christ, unless our minds have been raised to the discovery of something incomparably wonderful about it."[43]

2. The call to declare this gospel publicly among all the peoples of the world (Ps. 96:2–3) is a resounding missionary charge. We ought not to say this psalm without examining our hearts and the lives of our churches, to see if we are taking it seriously.

3. The phrase "all the gods of the peoples" in Psalm 96:5 reminds us that there are many so-called "gods" in the world and many "peoples"; idolatry pervades every culture. If religion were determined democratically, we should be swept this way and that in our beliefs. Derek Kidner expresses it well, speaking of 96:5: "Its robust challenge to the accepted ideas of the day invites the Christian to be equally unimpressed by currently revered nonsense, whatever its pedigree or patronage."[44]

4. We marvel at the grace evidenced in the invitation of Psalm 96:7–9, while remembering that we need a work of the Holy Spirit if the gospel is to penetrate the many groupings that come under the umbrella of "families of the peoples."

5. Psalm 96:10 prompts us to consider that this world will never be hell on earth but also that God's will will be done on earth as it is in heaven only when Jesus returns.

6. While the joyful creation language of Psalm 96:11–12 may indeed encourage us to be responsible stewards of creation, its main thrust is to make us long, with 96:13, for the glorious return of the Lord Jesus. Only then will all things, including the whole created order, be set finally and fully to rights.

---

42 Dickson, *Psalms*, 2:175.
43 Calvin, *Psalms*, 4:49.
44 Kidner, *Psalms*, 2:347.

*If we want to keep to the path of correct understanding we
must apply the whole psalm to Christ; let us not let go of
the cornerstone, lest our interpretation collapse in ruins.*

AUGUSTINE
Expositions of the Psalms

*The description which we have of the kingdom of God in this
psalm, does not apply to the state of it under the Law. We may
infer, accordingly, that it contains a prediction of that kingdom of
Christ, which was erected upon the introduction of the Gospel.*

JOHN CALVIN
Commentary on the Psalms

*He reigns! ye saints, exalt your strains;
Your God is King, your Father reigns;
And he is at the Father's side,
The Man of love, the Crucified.*

JOSIAH CONDER
"The Lord Is King! Lift Up Thy Voice"

PSALM 97

God demonstrates that he reigns over the world by making his presence felt (a "theophany") to bring judgment on his enemies and salvation for his people. Psalm 97 speaks of that appearing (97:1–6) and how to respond (97:7–12). The most important question for us is this: How did or does or will God make his presence felt? What does the poetry mean? It looks back to past appearings, most significantly at Sinai. But the New Testament teaches that such language looks forward, first to the appearing of God on earth in the incarnation of Christ and then, finally, to his return. In between, there is a sense in which the proclamation of the gospel can be an "appearing" of God on earth. I expound the psalm with this threefold fulfillment in view: the first coming of Christ, the proclamation of the gospel, and the second coming of Christ.

Augustine, citing Matthew 13:17, says that the psalmists enjoyed "a harvest of magnificent joy even in their own day, when they contemplated in spirit realities not yet present but guaranteed for the future."[1]

The clause "Let all God's angels worship [the Son]" (Heb. 1:6) may partly echo Psalm 97:7 ("Worship him, all you gods!"), although the primary source is probably the Septuagint of Deuteronomy 32:43, which says something similar.[2] Hebrews indicates that these Old Testament words find their fulfillment when all divine beings ("gods," "angels") bow down to Jesus Christ the Son. This identifies the God who appears in Psalm 97 with Jesus Christ; ultimately, the appearing of God comes with the return of Christ.[3]

---

1 Augustine, *Psalms*, 4:438–39.
2 See the clear discussion of the complex textual issues in Guthrie, "Hebrews," in *CNTOT* 931–32.
3 Hossfeld and Zenger, *Psalms*, 2:477.

The other possible echo is of 97:3 in Revelation 11:5, where the "fire" and the "adversaries/foes" are echoed in the Greek. The "two witnesses" who speak for Christ do what Psalm 97:3 says that God does when he appears in glory. The appearing of God is linked with Christ and his witnesses.

Psalms 93–99 are closely connected. The common theme of the reign of God is applied in different ways—for example, as a warning to the church (Ps. 95), as an invitation to the world (Ps. 96), and now as an exhortation to the church (97:10–12). Psalm 97 is tied to Psalm 96 most significantly by the word "worthless idols" (96:5; 97:7),[4] together with the "gods" (96:4–5; 97:7, 9). Other links include the theme of universality (note especially "all the earth" in 96:1, 9; 97:5), the significance of God's "righteousness" (96:13; 97:2, 6), and God's "glory" (96:7–8; 97:6). Where Psalm 93 speaks about the created order, Psalm 97 looks forward to the return of Christ.[5]

We do not know the date or circumstances that gave rise to the psalm. The Septuagint superscription[6] (none of which appears in the Hebrew) suggests that Psalm 97 may have been associated at an early date with the return from exile, although it does not mean it was written then.

THE TEXT

Structure

The clearest section is Psalm 97:10–12, bracketed by exhortations to the people of God. Psalm 97:8–9 is second-person address to God, and it makes sense to include 97:7 with these verses since 97:7–9 speaks entirely about response to God's appearing. Psalm 97:1–6 focuses on God's appearing. I consider 97:1–6 (the appearing of God) and then 97:7–12 (responses to God's appearing).

97:1–6 Christ Brings the Awesome Presence of God to Earth

1   The LORD reigns, let the earth rejoice;
         let the many coastlands be glad!

---

4   The only two uses of this word in the Psalms.
5   Hossfeld and Zenger, *Psalms*, 2:470.
6   Τῷ Δαυιδ, ὅτε ἡ γῆ αὐτοῦ καθίσταται ("Pertaining to David. [When his land is being brought to order.]" NETS).

2   Clouds and thick darkness are all around him;
            righteousness and justice are the foundation of his throne.
3   Fire goes before him
            and burns up his adversaries all around.
4   His lightnings light up the world;
            the earth sees and trembles.
5   The mountains melt like wax before the LORD,
            before the Lord of all the earth.
6   The heavens proclaim his righteousness,
            and all the peoples see his glory.

Psalm 97:1–6 begins and ends with a universal revelation (**the earth** and
the many coastlands, 97:1; **all the peoples,** 97:6), both veiled (**clouds and
thick darkness,** 97:2) and finally seen (**All the peoples see his glory,** 97:6).

In 97:1, **The LORD reigns** echoes 93:1 and 96:10 and anticipates 99:1.
Martin Luther perceptively connects it with the casting out of the "ruler
of this world" through the cross of Christ (John 12:31).[7] The Messiah who
proclaimed the kingdom of God brought that kingdom to earth, inaugurated
the reconquest of a rebellious world, nullified the power of the rebellious
"ruler of this world," and sits at the right hand of God waiting for his enemies
to be made a footstool for his feet. The appearing of God that follows in
Psalm 97:2–6 was manifested on earth by Jesus in his incarnation, continues
in the ministry of the gospel, and will reach its consummation when Jesus
returns. This theophany bears similarities with the makings of covenants
in Genesis 15 (Abraham) and Exodus 19–20 (Israel). The theophany of the
psalm looks forward to a new covenant, just as book 4 of the Psalms looks
forward to a new exodus out of exile.[8]

Coastlands translates a word that means both coasts and islands;[9] although in the first instance this may have been the Mediterranean coasts
(including southern Europe and northern Africa) and islands, it comes to
mean the most distant parts of the inhabited world. The word **many** (the
last word in Hebrew, literally, "Let them rejoice, the coastlands many") is
emphatic—many, many such remote places, indeed all of them (cf. Ps. 96).

7   Luther, *Luther's Works,* 11:267.
8   Hamilton, *Psalms,* 2:194.
9   See *HALOT,* s.v. אִי; Tate, *Psalms 51–100,* 516; Hossfeld and Zenger, *Psalms,* 2:472n7.

No inhabited place on earth is too remote for the revelation of God in Christ; the worldwide mission of the church reaches out until the farthest outpost of humanity becomes glad in Christ.

The appearing of God in 97:2–6 is the only valid source of true gladness.[10] John Calvin rightly deduces that "his inviting men to rejoice, is a proof that the reign of God is inseparably connected with the salvation and best happiness of mankind" and must therefore be the kingdom of Christ.[11] David Dickson robustly writes, "The psalmist proclaimeth Christ King among the Gentiles, and commendeth his kingdom to them, as full of joy, full of majesty, and full of righteousness."[12]

Psalm 97:2 is an enigmatic pair of lines. **Clouds and thick darkness** speaks of a frightening hiddenness that can engulf us and shroud us with fear (cf. Zeph. 1:15).[13] The phrase echoes that awesome day at Sinai when "the mountain burned with fire to the heart of heaven, wrapped in darkness, cloud, and gloom" (Deut. 4:11; cf. 5:22).[14] When the ark came to Zion, Sinai came to the sanctuary (Ps. 68:17); the same words "cloud" and "thick darkness" appear when Solomon's temple is dedicated (1 Kings 8:10–12). The phrase speaks both of our fear in the presence of God's holiness and of "the invisibility of the divine nature" to sinful human beings.[15] The second line (cf. Ps. 89:14a) links to the first through the significance of Sinai. **Righteousness and justice** have always been the moral **foundation** of God's government (his **throne**; cf. Gen. 18:19); the law given at Sinai is the expression of these qualities, as they are the basis of Messiah's reign (Ps. 72:1). The world would disintegrate without this righteousness and justice, and yet these terrify us because we are sinners. Only the atoning death of Christ (cf. the exposition of Sinai's terror and Zion's comfort in Heb. 12:18–29) can make this a source of gladness (Ps. 97:1).

---

10 The phrase "Let the earth rejoice" is repeated verbatim from Ps. 96:11. The root "be glad" (שׂמח) appears also in 96:11; 97:8, 11–12 ("joy," "rejoice" in 97:11–12).

11 Calvin, *Psalms*, 4:60.

12 Dickson, *Psalms*, 2:180–81.

13 The famous words *Dies irae, dies illa* (The day of wrath, that day) are taken from the first line of Zeph. 1:15 (Vg.), which uses similar imagery to Ps. 97:1.

14 In Deut. 4:11 "cloud, and gloom" is the same phrase "clouds and thick darkness" (עָנָן וַעֲרָפֶל). The other use of "thick darkness" in the Psalms is in 18:9, the vision of God coming in power to rescue his King.

15 Theodoret of Cyrus, *Psalms*, 2:133.

Psalm 97:3 continues with the Sinai imagery of the burning **fire** of God's holiness (cf. Ex. 19:18; 24:17; Pss. 18:8, 12–13; 50:3; Ezek. 1:4; Rev. 11:5). Throughout the age of the gospel, Jesus casts this fire on the earth (Luke 12:49) by the Holy Spirit, who burns with holiness (Matt. 3:10–12). When Jesus returns, that fire will cleanse the whole created order (2 Pet. 3:7, 11–13; cf. 2 Thess. 1:8; Heb. 10:27).

Psalm 97:4 (cf. 77:18) combines thunderstorm and earthquake, prominent at Sinai (Ex. 19:16–20; cf. Hab. 3:4–16). The **lightnings** bring a terrifying light from the darkness of the invisible God, making his presence known. The verb **trembles** is also used of the writhing of a woman in labor, for these are the birth pangs of the new age, the shaking so that only "the things that cannot be shaken may remain" (Heb. 12:27; cf. Hag. 2:6).[16] In Psalm 97:5 **the mountains**, the most solid and immovable parts of creation, **melt like wax** before the burning holiness of God, who is the covenant LORD and the sovereign **Lord of all the earth**. The repetition of **before**[17] adds to the feeling of terror. After the **lightnings light up**, **the earth . . . trembles**, and **the mountains melt**, the drama is completed as **the heavens proclaim**; the very skies themselves **proclaim his righteousness**, that God is putting the world to rights, that what 97:2b says is true: **righteousness and justice** really **are the foundation of his throne**. This is what the theophany means. Finally, in conclusion, **all the peoples**, the whole world (cf. "all the earth," 97:5), **see his glory**, the visible shining of his inward being, a glory that will be universally seen when Jesus returns. This **glory**, displayed in the incarnation (John 1:14), shines in the ministry of the gospel (cf. 2 Cor. 3:7–4:6).

97:7–12 Responses to Christ Deeply Divide the Human Race

7   All worshipers of images are put to shame,
        who make their boast in worthless idols;
        worship him, all you gods!
8   Zion hears and is glad,
        and the daughters of Judah rejoice,
        because of your judgments, O LORD.

---

16 Hamilton, *Psalms*, 2:194–95.
17 מִלִּפְנֵי probably has the sense of "before, and moving away from (in terror)."

9   For you, O LORD, are most high over all the earth;
       you are exalted far above all gods.

Psalm 97:7–9 is bracketed by reference to the **gods** (97:7, 9).

Psalm 97:7 (echoing and expanding 96:5) draws the first conclusion from the appearance of God in Christ. It piles up derogatory words in a threefold portrait of idolatry: **images** (objects of worship shaped by human imagination and design),[18] **worthless idols** (utterly useless objects of worship; cf. 96:5),[19] and **gods** (i.e., heavenly beings, or those who claim to be divine).[20] To be **put to shame** means final humiliation and visible failure.[21] Not only some but **all** of the **gods** must **worship** the one true God.[22] The incarnation makes this certain; the proclamation that Jesus Christ is Lord announces it; the return of Christ will bring it into irreversible effect.

Psalm 97:8 (cf. 48:11) shifts the focus from a warning for idolaters to the gladness of **Zion**, the people of God and ultimately the church of Christ. **Zion hears**, for it is the hearing of a message that brings gladness;[23] joy came from hearing that Jesus was born and from hearing that Jesus is the Christ. So today the hearing of the gospel is necessary before gladness in Christ can be experienced. The idiom **the daughters of** refers to towns and villages;[24] it is not just **Zion**, the capital, that rejoices but even the most insignificant part of Christ's church. The gladness is **because of your judgments**, your enacted decisions against impenitent evildoers and in favor of all who belong to Christ.

Psalm 97:9 gives the basis of (**for**) both 97:7 and 97:8. **For you** (emphatic), the covenant Lord, **are most high** (echoing the title "Most High" elsewhere)

---

18 This is the only use of the word (פֶּסֶל) in the Psalms. It refers to a so-called god carved or shaped by human beings in the image of some created thing.
19 Pss. 96:5 and 97:7 are the only two uses of the word (אֱלִילִים) in the Psalms. See on 96:5.
20 The LXX has "angels," possibly echoed in Heb. 1:6.
21 Tate, *Psalms 51–100*, 519.
22 Because the forms of the indicative and the imperative are the same in the Hebrew here, there is some difference in how the verbs "put to shame" and "worship" are translated, sometimes as jussives (e.g., REB: "May those who worship images / . . . be put to shame") and sometimes as imperatives. The overall sense is much the same.
23 There is an attractive consonance in Hebrew between "hears" (שָׁמְעָה) and "is glad" (וַתִּשְׂמַח).
24 For this idiom, see, e.g., Num. 32:42 (where "villages" is literally "daughters"); Josh. 15:45 (where "towns" is literally "daughters").

over all the earth (cf. "the Lord of all the earth," 97:5b; "the Most High over all the earth," 83:18), or, to express this in another way, **exalted far above all gods** (cf. 95:3; 96:4–5), where **far** gives emphasis. This exaltation finds its fulfillment when Jesus is given "all authority in heaven and on earth" (Matt. 28:18) and granted "the name that is above every name, so that at the name of Jesus every knee should bow" (Phil. 2:9–10).

> 10   O you who love the LORD, hate evil!
>   He preserves the lives of his saints;
>   he delivers them from the hand of the wicked.
> 11   Light is sown for the righteous,
>   and joy for the upright in heart.
> 12   Rejoice in the LORD, O you righteous,
>   and give thanks to his holy name!

Psalm 97:10–12 is bracketed by contrasting imperatives (**hate**, 97:10; **rejoice** and **give thanks**, 97:12), the latter pair echoing the joy of 97:1.

The first imperative is negative: **O you who love the LORD, hate evil!**[25] (cf. Ps. 34:14; Prov. 8:13; Amos 5:15) follows from the triumphant logic of the psalm. If all evildoers will be put to shame (Ps. 97:7), then those who **love the LORD** with passionate loyalty and warm affection (cf. Deut. 6:5; 10:12; 11:13, 22; 19:9; 30:6; Josh. 22:5; 23:11) will find hatred of wickedness rising in their hearts because they begin to grasp the terrible "wages of sin" (Rom. 6:23). So Paul declares, "Let everyone who names the name of the Lord depart from iniquity" (2 Tim. 2:19).

Psalm 97:10b–11 gives reasons to heed the imperatives. The first is that **he preserves the lives of his saints** (חֲסִידִים, *khasidim*, his loyal faithful ones, the recipients of his faithful love and then those who show that love in their lives); the next line develops this theme by focusing on the threat, **from the hand** (i.e., power) **of the wicked**, ever present, frightening, and strong. Believers need to remember that "the Lord knows how to rescue the godly from trials" (2 Pet. 2:9); the God who rescued Lot even from Sodom is well able to deliver his faithful ones from every threat.

---

25 The REB translation, "The LORD loves those who hate evil," results from an unnecessary emendation of the MT. For discussion, see Tate, *Psalms 51–100*, 517n10a.

If Psalm 97:10 is about preservation, 97:11 promises **light** and **joy** to
the righteous (those who are righteous by faith).[26] There is a vivid picture
of this celebration in Esther 8:16: "The Jews had light and gladness and
joy and honor" when God rescued them from the wicked.[27] The phrase
Light is sown is unusual but evocative.[28] It may suggest that light (as a
picture of hope and joy) is sown to illuminate the path of the righteous
or, perhaps more likely, that light grows in the lives of the righteous, who
look forward to a harvest of righteousness with joy (cf. the New Testament
parables of the coming kingdom).[29] Robert Alter writes, "The delicate
agricultural image of light sown—presumably, to bear refulgent fruit—
is an elegant counterpoint to the fierce fire that burns up God's enemies
and to the lightning that makes the earth quake."[30] Charles Spurgeon
writes colorfully, "Right leads to light. In the furrows of integrity lie the
seeds of happiness, which shall develop into a harvest of bliss. God has
lightning for sinners and light for saints."[31] The phrase **upright in heart**
reminds us that imputed righteousness is inseparable from a change of
heart and life.

Although we must hate evil (Ps. 97:10), the last word is joy. In 97:12 the
righteous (by faith) are to lead the whole renewed creation (97:1) in joyful thanksgiving. As Spurgeon puts it, "The Psalmist had bidden the earth
rejoice, and here he turns to the excellent of the earth and bids them lead
the song."[32]

REFLECTION AND RESPONSE

1. Perhaps the most natural way to appropriate the psalm is to begin
with meditation on God making his presence felt in Psalm 97:1–6 before
being guided in 97:7–12 about how to respond.

26 Although "the righteous" is singular in Hebrew, the meaning is clearly generic.
27 Bonar, *Psalms*, 291.
28 MT: אוֹר זָרֻעַ. The verb זרע (to sow) is often emended to זרח (to shine) to yield "Light dawns."
The emendation is problematic partly because it adopts the *lectio facilior* and partly because it
involves a consonantal emendation. Hossfeld and Zenger, *Psalms*, 2:479.
29 Hossfeld and Zenger, *Psalms*, 2:476.
30 Alter, *Psalms*, 343.
31 Spurgeon, *Treasury*, 2.2:197.
32 Spurgeon, *Treasury*, 2.2:197.

2. A faithful reading of Psalm 97:1–6 will hold together the echoes, especially from Sinai, and the fulfillments in the incarnation, the progress of the gospel in the world, and the consummation when Jesus returns.

3. Calvin writes of the "theophany" that it is "a representation of the formidable majesty attaching to God, that he may dash and humble vain confidence and carnal pride."[33]

4. Psalm 97:7 gives a robust warning against idolatry in all its forms. Our challenge is to discern the hidden ways in which idolatry worms its way into our hearts.

5. Psalm 97:8 causes a gentle gladness to rise in our hearts, and the idiom of the "daughters of Judah" encourages us, however insignificant we may feel in the church of Christ. The emphatic words of 97:9 hammer home the import of the coming of Christ.

6. We find the "raison d'être"[34] of the psalm in Psalm 97:10–12, for here the church is directly addressed. To "hate evil" goes deeper than simply resisting temptation and points to "the expulsive power of a new affection"—to borrow the phrase from Thomas Chalmers (1780–1847).[35] We cannot do this for ourselves but must cry to God to work this godly hatred in our hearts.

7. The promises of Psalm 97:10–11 repay a slow and glad meditation. For although we acknowledge it to be true in theory, we rarely feel its trustworthiness with a deep conviction. As Dickson puts it, "Whatever can be taken from the godly, their right and interest in Christ can never be taken from them, and so there is cause to give thanks for this gift for ever."[36]

---

33 Calvin, *Psalms*, 4:60.
34 Tate, *Psalms 51–100*, 520.
35 Thomas Chalmers, *The Expulsive Power of a New Affection*, CSC (Wheaton, IL: Crossway, 2020).
36 Dickson, *Psalms*, 2:185.

This psalm . . . prophesies both appearances of the Savior.

THEODORET OF CYRUS
Commentary on the Psalms

---

*This psalm is an exhortation to Jew and Gentile, to rejoice and bless
the Lord for Christ's coming to set up his kingdom in the world.*

DAVID DICKSON
A Commentary on the Psalms

Joy to the earth, the Savior reigns;
Let men their songs employ;
While fields and floods, rocks, hills, and plains
Repeat the sounding joy.

ISAAC WATTS
"Joy to the World"

PSALM 98

No praise or joy is too great for what God has done in Christ. Psalm 98 shares much with Psalms 96 and 97; I use the same framework to read Psalm 98 as I used with those psalms. As in those psalms, we may hear the voice of Christ. The major focus is on the work of Christ, both in his first appearing and when he returns. When Mary sings about her son that God "has helped his servant Israel, / in remembrance of his mercy" (Luke 1:54), she echoes Psalm 98:3.[1] What Psalm 98 celebrates approached its fulfillment when Jesus was born. The echo in Romans 1:16–17 of Psalm 98:2 suggests that the "salvation" and "righteousness" celebrated there are expressed today in the preaching of the gospel.[2] The echo of 98:9 in Acts 17:31 encourages us to look for the fulfillment of Christ's return (as in Pss. 9:8; 96:13; cf. Rev. 19:11). So all three of the foci we saw in Psalm 97—the first coming of Christ, the proclamation of the gospel, and the return of Christ—are celebrated in Psalm 98.

The most significant links with Psalm 96 are (1) the same line beginning both psalms (96:1a = 98:1a); (2) the words "Let the sea roar, and all that fills it" (96:11b; 98:7a); and (3) the very similar endings (compare 96:13 with 98:9 and indeed all of 96:11–13 with 98:7–9). Other links with nearby psalms include (1) "salvation" (95:1; 96:2; 98:1, 2, 3); (2) "marvelous works/things" (96:3; 98:1); (3) "righteousness" (96:13; 97:2, 6; 98:2); (4) the nations, peoples,

---

1 In Luke 1:54 the three Greek words for "Israel," "remembrance," and "mercy" echo "Israel," "remembered," and "steadfast love" in the LXX of Ps. 98:3; see Pao and Schnabel, "Luke," in *CNTOT* 262.

2 In Rom. 1:16–17 the three Greek words for "salvation," "revealed," and "righteousness" echo the LXX of Ps. 98:2. See Kraus, *Theology of the Psalms*, 199; Tucker and Grant, *Psalms*, 2:440.

and earth (96:1, 3, 5, 7–8, 10, 11, 13; 97:1, 4, 5, 9; 98:3, 4, 7, 9); (5) the call to "make a joyful noise" (95:1–2; 98:4, 6; 100:1); and (6) "holy" (97:12; 98:1).

Given these many overlaps, how is Psalm 98 distinctive? First, it consists entirely of praise, with no rebukes, warnings, or instruction: "All is joy and exhilaration."[3] Those who have been taught, warned, exhorted, and invited in previous psalms here unite in praise. A second distinction is the mention of "steadfast love and faithfulness / to the house of Israel" in 98:3a, leading to "all the ends of the earth" seeing "the salvation of our God" in 98:3b. Jesus, who comes first for "the lost sheep of the house of Israel" (Matt. 10:6; 15:24), expands the boundaries of his mission to fulfill the promise of worldwide blessing, given to Abraham in Genesis 12:1–3 (cf. "so that in Christ Jesus the blessing of Abraham might come to the Gentiles," Gal. 3:14; "men of Israel," Acts 13:16, leading to "We are turning to the Gentiles," Acts 13:46).

We know neither the original context of the psalm nor its date. Its canonical context within book 4 suggests its appropriateness for those in exile or for those returning from exile, and this is supported by the many parallels with prophecies in Isaiah 40–55 that relate to the same "new exodus" redemption. The psalm is both a glad remembrance of Jesus's first coming (his incarnation, atoning death, resurrection, and ascension) and a "rehearsal" or "prelude" to his return.[4] Charles Spurgeon suggests that while Psalm 97 "described the publication of the gospel," Psalm 98 "is a kind of Coronation Hymn, officially proclaiming the conquering Messiah as Monarch over the nations."[5]

THE TEXT

Structure
The psalm breaks naturally into three sections: Psalm 98:1–3, 4–6, and 7–9.[6]

Superscription

S   A Psalm.[7]

---

3   Kidner, *Psalms*, 2:352. Kidner also notes that Ps. 98 has been used as the canticle "Cantate Domino," an alternative to the Magnificat in the service of evening prayer in the Book of Common Prayer.
4   Kidner, *Psalms*, 2:353.
5   Spurgeon, *Treasury*, 2.2:210.
6   E.g., Hossfeld and Zenger, *Psalms*, 2:479–80; Hengstenberg, *Psalms*, 3:188–89.
7   In Hebrew this word is the beginning of verse 1.

This one-word superscription (in Hebrew) highlights the psalm's musical character. The same root appears in the word translated "sing praises" in Psalm 98:4–5 and in the cognate word for "melody" in 98:5.[8]

98:1–3 Christ Calls His Church to Sing of the Victory He Has Won for the World

1   Oh sing to the LORD a new song,
        for he has done marvelous things!
    His right hand and his holy arm
        have worked salvation for him.
2   The LORD has made known his salvation;
        he has revealed his righteousness in the sight of the nations.
3   He has remembered his steadfast love and faithfulness
        to the house of Israel.
    All the ends of the earth have seen
        the salvation of our God.

The mention of **our God** in parallel with **the house of Israel** suggests that the focus in Psalm 98:1–3 is the true Israel, fulfilled in Christ and his church. The psalm begins with an appeal: **Oh sing to the LORD a new song** (see on 96:1a; cf. Isa. 42:10, immediately after the first Servant Song, Isa. 42:1–9).

Writing of this **new song**, Dietrich Bonhoeffer traces the songs at creation (Job 38:7) and the song at the Red Sea (Ex. 15) right through to the Magnificat, to the songs of Paul and Silas in prison (Acts 16:25), and all the way to "the new song of the heavenly community" in Revelation 15:3–4. This song, he says, "is the Christ hymn, new every morning. . . . We are called to join in the singing of it. It is God who has prepared one great song of praise throughout eternity, and those who enter God's community join in this song." He goes on to observe, "This song has a different sound on earth than it does in heaven. On earth, it is the song of those who believe; in heaven, the song of those who see."[9]

The rest of Psalm 98:1–3 gives the reasons for this **new song** in six clauses. First, **he has done marvelous things**, a word that speaks of all God's acts of

8   The root is זמר.
9   Bonhoeffer, *Life Together*, 65.

rescue (e.g., as in 72:18; 96:3), looking back to the exodus (e.g., 106:7) and forward to all that God will do in Jesus Christ.

Second, **his right hand** (cf. Ex. 15:6, 12; Isa. 41:10) **and his holy arm** (cf. Isa. 52:10)[10] / **have worked salvation for him**. This means he has won a victory for himself,[11] both in defeating his enemies and redeeming his people. God did this in shadow in the exodus; he achieved it in substance in Christ, for "our Lord Jesus Christ is God's arm, and God's right hand."[12] As David Dickson notes,

> It is by battle against the enemies of our salvation that we are delivered: for Christ hath wrestled with the guiltiness, demerit, and punishment of our sin; wrestled with the curse of the law, with Satan, death, and hell, and whatsoever could hinder our redemption and salvation, and hath gotten unto himself the victory to our advantage.[13]

Third and fourth (in parallel), **the LORD has made known his salvation**—that is, he has achieved his victory and made it public—or, to put it another way, **he has revealed his righteousness in the sight of the nations**. When Simeon gazes at the infant Jesus and says, "My eyes have seen your salvation" (Luke 2:30), he grasps that this child is God's victory made known on earth, in fulfillment of Psalm 98:2. **Righteousness** here means God doing the right thing by fulfilling his covenant promises. The echo of 98:2 in Romans 1:16–17 (see above) expounds this idea in the righteousness of the gospel. As Philip Eveson says, Jesus

> revealed God's righteousness in his spotless life and ministry. His cross demonstrated God's righteousness in the condemnation of sin and Satan as Jesus experienced the judgment of God. The resurrection proclaimed God's righteousness in the vindication of his Son to the Father's side in glory. In the gospel the righteousness of God is revealed in all its won-

---

10 Ps. 98:1 is the only other use of the phrase "holy arm" in the Bible besides Isa. 52:10.
11 Miles Coverdale (1488–1569), from the Book of Common Prayer: "With his own right hand, and with his holy arm: hath he gotten himself the victory"; CSB: "have won him victory"; NASB: "have gained the victory."
12 Augustine, *Psalms*, 4:459.
13 Dickson, *Psalms*, 2:186.

der and power. All will see the kingdom of righteousness when the new creation dawns.[14]

All this is achieved **in the sight of the nations**, in an unboundedly public act in Jerusalem, made known in ever-widening circles of Christian mission, and reaching its climax when the Son of Man returns to be seen by all humankind (Matt. 24:27).

Fifth, **he has remembered his steadfast love and faithfulness / to the house of Israel**. Steadfast love and faithfulness are covenant words (e.g., Pss. 36:5; 88:11; 89:2, 24, 33; 92:2), fulfilled in Christ (cf. the equivalent "grace" [= steadfast love] and "truth" [= covenant faithfulness] in John 1:14, 17). Konrad Pellikan (1478–1556) states, "He remembered his promises so that he might fulfil them in Christ. . . . For the gospel of the kingdom is preached through Christ and his apostles to the whole earth."[15]

Finally, and climactically, **all the ends of the earth have seen / the salvation** (victory) **of our God**. The phrase **the ends of the earth** appears in various Old Testament contexts, including, significantly, 1 Samuel 2:10 and Psalms 2:8; 22:27; and 72:8 (all referring to the victory of God's messianic King); Isaiah 52:10 (see above for "holy arm"); Micah 5:4 (the Bethlehem Messiah prophecy); and Zechariah 9:10 (after the Palm Sunday prophecy in Zech. 9:9). These other uses reinforce the conviction that this is a prophecy of Christ.

98:4–6 Christ Calls the World to Praise the Triune God for All That Christ Has Won for Them

4   Make a joyful noise to the LORD, all the earth;
         break forth into joyous song and sing praises!
5   Sing praises to the LORD with the lyre,
         with the lyre and the sound of melody!
6   With trumpets and the sound of the horn
         make a joyful noise before the King, the LORD!

---

14 Eveson, *Psalms*, 2:185.
15 Konrad Pellikan, *Commentary on the Bible*, in *RCS* 8:147.

The address **all the earth** widens the call from the church to the world (which was a witness in Ps. 98:1–3 and becomes a participant in 98:4–6), for "when God should break down the middle wall of partition all would be gathered to the common faith, and one Church formed throughout the whole world."[16] The bounding exhilaration is partly conveyed by the repetitions of **sing praises** (98:4–5), **the lyre** (98:5 [2x]), and **the sound** (98:5–6). This section is bracketed by **Make a joyful noise** (98:4a, 6b; cf. 95:1–2; 100:1), which means here a triumphant shout of jubilation. Psalm 98:4a is similar to 66:1 (cf. Pss. 47:1; 95:1–2). The verb **break forth** always appears with the verb "sing joyfully" (here rendered **into joyous song**). Often in Isaiah this combination is used in connection with the prophesied return from exile (e.g., Isa. 44:23; 49:13; 52:9;[17] 54:1; 55:12). Psalm 98:5–6 is similar to 47:5–7. The **sound of melody** translates a word that indicates a song sung to music (CSB: "melodious song"). The string instruments (98:5) and loud wind instruments (98:6)[18] combine to make a great orchestra of joy, acclaiming **the LORD** as **King**, an acclamation very similar to "The LORD reigns" (93:1; 96:10; 97:1; 99:1; cf. "a great King above all gods," 95:3). This is, in the end, the victory of Christ.

98:7–9 Christ Calls Creation to Rejoice When He Comes to Judge the World in Righteousness

> 7　Let the sea roar, and all that fills it;
> 　　the world and those who dwell in it!
> 8　Let the rivers clap their hands;
> 　　let the hills sing for joy together
> 9　before the LORD, for he comes
> 　　to judge the earth.
> 　He will judge the world with righteousness,
> 　　and the peoples with equity.

Psalm 98:7–9 is very similar to 96:11–13. The call to praise—to the church in 98:1–3, expanded to all humankind in 98:4–6—now encompasses the

---

16　Calvin, *Psalms*, 4:72.
17　Note the parallels with Isa. 52:10 above.
18　The use of "trumpets" was sometimes associated either with the ark of the covenant (e.g., 1 Chron. 13:8; 15:24, 28; 16:6) or with acclamation of a king at a coronation (e.g., 2 Kings 11:14) but was also used in other contexts (e.g., Ezra 3:10).

whole created order. The four lines of 98:7–8 desire **the sea** to give its roaring praise (using the same words as 96:11b), **the** (inhabited) **world and those who dwell in it** to add their exaltation (using the same words in Hebrew as 24:1b), **the rivers** (cf. 93:3) to **clap their hands** (cf. Isa. 55:12, where the trees clap their hands in applause at what God does in bringing his people back from exile) in acclamation (as at a coronation; cf. 2 Kings 11:12), and **the hills** (or mountains) to **sing for joy together** (language used in Isa. 44:23; 49:13; 55:12).

Robert Alter comments,

> There is a concordance between the human orchestra—in all likelihood, an actual orchestra accompanying the singing of this psalm—with its lutes and rams' horns, and the orchestra of nature, both groups providing a grand fanfare for God the king. The thundering of the sea is a percussion section, joined by the clapping hands of the rivers, then the chorus of the mountains.[19]

Like Psalm 96:13, Psalm 98:9 is the climax (see on 96:13 and the fulfillment in Acts 17:31).[20]

REFLECTION AND RESPONSE

1. To join in this "new song," we first meditate on all the ways in which Psalm 98:1–3 is fulfilled in the incarnation, earthly ministry, atoning death, resurrection, and ascension of Christ, together with the outpouring of the Holy Spirit and the beginning of the worldwide mission of the church. These echoes of earlier victories (and especially the exodus) are here to direct our eyes to Christ. As Martin Luther expresses it, we have here "the voice of the prophet exhorting the people then present to faith and hope in the coming incarnation and advent of Christ, as if to say: 'Celebrate all your festivals and sing praise, since, behold, He will come to you, the Son of God is promised you for salvation.'"[21]

---

19 Alter, *Psalms*, 345.
20 The differences are that in Ps. 98 the words "he comes" are not repeated and "with faithfulness" is replaced by "with equity" (but "equity" appears in 96:10).
21 Luther, *Luther's Works*, 11:272.

2. Gentile believers especially need to heed the exhortation of Psalm 98:4–6 to exuberant praise of God in Christ: "Do not let your joy be dumb."[22] Indeed, as John Calvin says, "The most ardent attempts men might make to celebrate the great work of the world's redemption would fall short of the riches of the grace of God."[23]

3. As at the close of Psalm 96, the final three verses of this psalm whet our appetite for the day when creation's sorrowful groaning is replaced by joy (Rom. 8:18–25), for "the rule of Christ is the joy of nature."[24]

4. Even if the whole church throughout the ages praises with every breath in our bodies, we cannot sufficiently praise what God has done in Christ. As Dickson notes,

> If every drop of water in the sea, and in every river and flood, every fish in the sea, every fowl of the air, every living creature on the earth, and whatsoever else is in the world: if they all had reason and ability to express themselves; yea, and if all the hills were able by motion and gesticulation to communicate their joy one to another; there is work for them all to set out the praise of Christ.[25]

22 Augustine, *Psalms*, 4:461.
23 Calvin, *Psalms*, 4:73.
24 Spurgeon, *Treasury*, 2.2:213.
25 Dickson, *Psalms*, 2:188.

*Now that the shadowy dispensation has passed away
. . . God cannot otherwise be properly worshipped,
than when we come to him directly through Christ,
in whom all the fulness of the Godhead dwells.*

JOHN CALVIN
Commentary on the Psalms

*For the comfort of the church against a multitude of enemies
round about her, there is in this psalm a declaration of the
kingdom of Christ, reigning as God, one with the Father and
Holy Spirit in the church of Israel, before his incarnation. . . .
Christ was King in his church before his incarnation, and reigned
in the sight of his saints from the beginning of the world.*

DAVID DICKSON
A Commentary on the Psalms

PSALM 99

ORIENTATION

Psalm 99 makes God known as thrice holy. The voice summons us to worship (because we must) and invites us to worship (because we may); it declares God to be King and speaks of priestly intercession. Since Jesus is the prophet who makes the Father known (John 17:26), the King given the name above every name (Matt. 28:18; Phil. 2:9), the priestly intercessor (John 17), and the Holy One (Luke 4:34; John 6:69; Acts 2:27) whom God made our "sanctification" (1 Cor. 1:30), there is a plethora of rich fulfillments in Christ. As in Psalms 93, 96, and 97, which share the announcement that the Lord reigns, perhaps the strongest line of fulfillment is to Christ, the divine-human King. But in our consideration of the psalm, I endeavor to nuance this connection with the themes of Christ our prophet, Christ our priest, and Christ our holiness.

Psalm 99 has many links with Psalms 93–98, especially God's greatness; God's name; God's justice, equity, and righteousness; calls to worship; and memories of the wilderness wanderings. Close links with Psalm 93 suggest that these two psalms are intended to bracket Psalms 93–99. These links include (1) "power/strength" (עֹז, *oz*, 93:1; 99:4); (2) a "throne" or someone sitting enthroned with a footstool (93:2; 99:1, 5); (3) exaltation (93:4; 99:2); (4) God's law as a bulwark against disorder, using the same Hebrew word, עֵדֻת, *eduth* ("decrees," 93:5; "testimonies," 99:7);[1] (5) holiness (93:5; 99:3, 5, 9); and (6) "establish" (93:1; 99:4).[2]

Outside the Psalms, perhaps the most important Old Testament connection is with Isaiah 6:1–4, in which we hear the threefold "Holy!" in the

---

1   It is a pity that the CSB and ESV disguise this link.
2   The same root (כּוּן), niphal in Ps. 93:1, polel in 99:4.

context of God's exaltation in the temple and with a response of shaking.[3] Since John says that Isaiah here saw the glory of Jesus (John 12:41), we may reasonably expect to see the exalted Jesus also in the covenant Lord of Psalm 99.[4]

THE TEXT

Structure

The clearest structural markers are (1) the threefold ascription of holiness to God in Psalm 99:3, 5, and 9 (identical in 99:3, 5) and (2) the identical openings to 99:5 and 9 ("Exalt the LORD our God; worship at . . .").[5] It is most natural to take these as closing three sections: 99:1–3, 4–5, and 6–9. The covenant name, "the LORD," appears seven times.[6]

99:1–3 Praise the Holy God for the Reign of Christ

1   The LORD reigns; let the peoples tremble!
        He sits enthroned upon the cherubim; let the earth quake!
2   The LORD is great in Zion;
        he is exalted over all the peoples.
3   Let them praise your great and awesome name!
        Holy is he!

For the declaration **The LORD reigns,** see on Psalms 93:1; 96:10; and 97:1. Derek Kidner rightly notes that although this is "true eternally," in these contexts it is "primarily a proclamation, it seems, of God's final advent"[7] in the second coming of Christ. The reign of the triune God is established on earth by Christ (cf. Matt. 28:18; Phil. 2:9; Rev. 19:6). He reigns **over all the**

---

3   Hossfeld and Zenger, *Psalms,* 2:485.
4   Eveson, *Psalms,* 2:189.
5   There is perhaps a movement from "Holy is he" (Ps. 99:3, repeated in 99:5) to "Exalt the LORD our God" and "worship . . . at his footstool" (99:5, repeated in 99:9 with the change ". . . at his holy mountain"), carrying forward the thought with growing emphasis.
6   There are also seven occurrences of the emphatic personal pronoun for God: Ps. 99:2b ("he"), 3b ("he"), 4 ("you . . . you"), 5c ("he"), 6c ("he"), 8a ("you"). Harman, *Psalms,* 2:715.
7   Kidner, *Psalms,* 2:354.

peoples, and therefore **the peoples** are summoned to **tremble**[8]—indeed, the whole **earth** to **quake**[9]—before his majesty. In the context of all the Scriptures, this declaration embraces both the present reign of Jesus in heaven and the future fulfillment of that reign when he "delivers the kingdom to God the Father after destroying every rule and every authority and power" (1 Cor. 15:24).

The announcement emphasizes from where he reigns, with reference to **the cherubim** and **Zion**. The reign of Christ is foreshadowed in the types of the old covenant.

The phrase **sits enthroned upon** (or between) **the cherubim** refers to the "mercy seat" (Ex. 25:17–22), associated with atonement for sin. A cherub is a winged creature, fierce enough to wield a flaming sword (Gen. 3:24), fast enough to speed God to the rescue of his King (Ps. 18:10; cf. the appeal of Hezekiah in 2 Kings 19:15), strong enough to provide protection under its wings. It is associated with the ark of the covenant (1 Sam. 4:4; 2 Sam. 6:2; cf. Ps. 80:1) and carries with it all the connotations of God's salvation, fulfilled in Christ; the very creatures who barred the way to paradise are the creatures who stand by the mercy seat of atonement.

The covenant God **is great in Zion**, which finds its fulfillment when the church gathers to Jesus (Heb. 12:22–24). **He** (emphatic) **is exalted** (cf. Ps. 93:3; Isa. 6:1) **over all the peoples**, for the Christ who is head of his church is also the firstborn over all creation (Col. 1:15–20).

Christ therefore summons the world to **praise** God's **great**[10] **and awesome**[11] **name**, the name that is above every name, the name for which missionaries have gone out all over the world (3 John 7).

The acclamation **Holy is he!** is repeated verbatim in Psalm 99:5 and expanded in 99:9. The holiness of God, emphatic in the law (cf. Lev. 11:44), expresses both his moral perfection and his ontological difference from mortal human beings: he is pure, and he is "other." This attribute of God

---

8   The verb "tremble" (רגז) is used several times of the created order before God (e.g., Job 9:6; Pss. 18:7; 77:16, 18). Harman notes from Jer. 33:9 that trembling is not incompatible with receiving good news. Harman, *Psalms*, 2:716.

9   The verb (נוט) is an Old Testament hapax legomenon. Delitzsch describes it here as "not a trembling that is the absolute opposite of joy, but a trembling that leads to salvation." Delitzsch, *Psalms*, 3:99.

10   For the theme of God's greatness, see, e.g., Pss. 47:2; 48:1; 95:3; 96:4.

11   The word "awesome" means "to be feared."

is associated with the incarnation in the Magnificat ("Holy is his name," Luke 1:49). Jesus addresses the Father as "Holy Father" (John 17:11); in Psalm 22:3 the suffering Messiah acknowledges God's holiness in his passion ("Yet you are holy"). Jesus himself is the "Holy One" of God (Luke 4:34; John 6:69; Acts 2:27), a priest characterized by holiness (Heb. 7:26), who becomes holiness "to us" (1 Cor. 1:30).

99:4–5 Worship the Holy God for the Righteous Reign of Christ

> 4   The King in his might loves justice.
>   You have established equity;
>   you have executed justice
>   and righteousness in Jacob.
> 5   Exalt the LORD our God;
>   worship at his footstool!
>   Holy is he!

The verb **loves** controls Psalm 99:4. This **King**, unlike so many kings, **loves justice**; this is his settled affection, his creational decision, his action in history, and his work in salvation.[12] This love is demonstrated in the earthly ministry of Jesus, in which the proud are humbled, the oppressor rebuked, and the humble poor given hope and grace. The words **justice, equity** (fairness; cf. 9:8; 17:2; 58:1; 75:2; 96:10; 98:9), and **righteousness** are more or less synonymous in this verse and speak of the proper order of creation, everything fair and as it should be. In the phrase **You** (emphatic) **have established,** the verb **established** (cf. 24:2; 48:8; 65:6; 74:16; 87:5; 93:1; 96:10) indicates a moral order that no hostile power, human or demonic, can destroy; this righteous government, prophesied for centuries was announced by Jesus (Matt. 4:17) and will be consummated when he returns (1 Cor. 15:24–25).

Psalm 99:4b adds that **you** (emphatic) **have executed** (lit., "done"; CSB: "administered") / **justice and righteousness in Jacob,** that is, among the

---

12 In the line translated "The King in his might loves justice," it is not easy to be sure exactly how the "might" of the King relates to his love of justice. The most likely solutions are along these lines: (1) all the King's power is directed toward his love of justice, or (2) the strength of the King consists even in his love of justice, which is what ultimately makes him stronger than any other king. Cf. Tucker and Grant, *Psalms,* 2:445. For detailed discussion, see Tate, *Psalms 51–100,* 526–27; Hossfeld and Zenger, *Psalms,* 2:483.

people of God.[13] The worldwide reestablishment of moral order begins in the church. Christ will shape a church that will in the end be marked by "righteous deeds" (Rev. 19:8) and actions that will "adorn the doctrine of God our Savior" (Titus 2:10).

The declaration **Holy is he!** (see on Ps. 99:3) is now prefaced by a sustained call to worship (strengthening the call of 99:3a). Both the lowness of **footstool** and of **worship** (bow ourselves down low) contrast with the height of **exalt** (lift Christ high in our praises; cf. John 3:30). The **footstool** refers to the ark of the covenant (cf. 1 Chron. 28:2; Ps. 132:7), to the temple containing the ark, or to Jerusalem containing the temple—even ultimately to the whole earth, of which the temple is a microcosm (Isa. 66:1; Matt. 5:35), as the place where God's right order is reestablished on earth.[14]

99:6–9 Worship the Holy God by the Priestly Intercession of Christ, Which Makes Worship Possible

6   Moses and Aaron were among his priests,
        Samuel also was among those who called upon his name.
        They called to the LORD, and he answered them.
7   In the pillar of the cloud he spoke to them;
        they kept his testimonies
        and the statute that he gave them.
8   O LORD our God, you answered them;
        you were a forgiving God to them,
        but an avenger of their wrongdoings.
9   Exalt the LORD our God,
        and worship at his holy mountain;
        for the LORD our God is holy!

If Psalm 99:1–2 introduces the theme of Christ's reign, and 99:4 characterizes that rule by a love of justice, 99:6–8 develops that theme with a focus on the priestly intercession that makes worship possible. We are summoned to

13 Noting how these qualities described David's reign (at least partially) in 2 Sam. 8:15, Hengstenberg writes, "What was there said of Israel's visible king shall be performed in future times in all its truth by his invisible true King." Hengstenberg, *Psalms*, 3:103.
14 Hossfeld and Zenger, *Psalms*, 2:490.

worship God not simply because we ought but because we may. The focus shifts from the kingship of Christ to his priestly intercession.

The parallelism of 99:6 shows that the focus of the word **priests** is on their intercession (**those who called upon his name;**[15] **they called**[16] **to the LORD**). Although **Moses**[17] mostly fulfilled the role of a prophet rather than a priest (cf. Deut. 34:10–12), he sprinkled the blood of the covenant in Exodus 24:1–8 and consecrated **Aaron** and his sons as priests (Lev. 8), and perhaps these acts lie behind his designation here as a priest; more to the point, he was a great intercessor for God's people (e.g., Ex. 17:8–13; 32:11–14, 31–32; 33:12–23; Num. 11:2; 14:13–19; 21:7; Deut. 9:18–19; Ps. 106:23). **Aaron** interceded in Numbers 16:44–48, and intercession is inseparable from priestly ministry.[18] **Samuel** (associated with Moses and Aaron in 1 Sam. 12:6 and with Moses as intercessor in Jer. 15:1) interceded for the people repeatedly (e.g., 1 Sam. 7:7–9; 12:6–25). "The intercessory roles of Moses, Aaron, and Samuel are . . . perfectly fulfilled in the person of Christ."[19]

The repeated **he answered them** (Ps. 99:6c) and **you answered them** (99:8a) brackets 99:7. This repetition strongly suggests that what he gave in answer was the law (**his testimonies / and the statute that he gave them,** 99:7). He delivered this law to Moses (note Ex. 25:22); all prophetic ministry is a continued application of the law, both as it expresses the order of creation[20] and also as it displays dimensions of salvation, foreshadowing the atoning work of the Messiah. God led his people by **the pillar of the cloud** by day (Ex. 13:21; 14:24; Num. 12:5; 14:14; Deut. 31:15; Neh. 9:12), in which he hid his holy presence (cf. Ps. 97:2), just as the fire by night revealed his blazing purity.[21]

---

15 Calling on the "name" of God is standard terminology for prayer. See J. Gary Millar, *Calling on the Name of the Lord: A Biblical Theology of Prayer*, NSBT 38 (Downers Grove, IL: InterVarsity Press, 2016). It is especially appropriate when linked to the revelation of God's "name" in Ex. 33:19 and 34:5–7, in the context of Moses's intercession after the episode of the golden calf.

16 "They called" is a participle, suggesting that this is what they habitually did. See Tate, *Psalms 51–100*, 525.

17 For Moses in the Psalms, see on the superscription to Ps. 90.

18 Aaron is associated with Moses in Pss. 77:20; 105:26; 106:16. Hengstenberg notes that "what constitutes the essence of the ordinary priestly office" is "inward connection with God, free access to the throne of grace, and the gift and power of intercessory prayer." Hengstenberg, *Psalms*, 3:195.

19 Tucker and Grant, *Psalms*, 2:448.

20 Note the important echo of עֵדוּת ("decrees," Ps. 93:5; "testimonies," 99:7), tying the law to the order of creation.

21 The speaking here is "from" the pillar of cloud rather than "in" the pillar of cloud (this is the likely meaning of בְ here). Although we are not told of God speaking to Samuel from a pillar of

Psalm 99:8b–c answers the question raised by the declaration of God's holiness and the reminder of God's law: How may sinners worship? Will not their attempts at worship be rebuffed by a holy God? **You were a forgiving God to them** echoes Exodus 34:7 ("forgiving iniquity and transgression and sin") in the context of Moses's intercession. **Them** here is not so much Moses, Aaron, or Samuel but the people for whom they interceded. Through their priestly intercession, God decreed that he would forgive. This intercession prefigures the final priestly intercession of Jesus, who, by his atoning death, makes forgiveness possible, brings us to God, places his Holy Spirit within us, and enables us to walk with God (John 1:29; 1 Pet. 3:18; 1 John 2:2, 6).

The phrase **but an avenger of their** (i.e., the people's) **wrongdoings**[22] balances forgiveness with a reminder of the seriousness of sin, which— even when forgiven—has sad entailments in the life of the sinner. Psalm 95:8–11 has warned against hardness of heart, pictured in the generation that despaired and defied God when they heard the spies' report. Even those pardoned for their rebellion in that matter must be excluded from the land (Num. 14:20–23). Even forgiven sins have consequences.

The final exhortation (Ps. 99:9a–b) is the same as 99:5, with the substitution of **his holy mountain**, that is, Zion, the holy hill where Messiah rules (e.g., 2:6; 3:4; 15:1; 43:3; 48:1). The concluding affirmation—**For the LORD our God is holy!**—is emphatic, using the covenant name, **the LORD**, and the covenant designation **our God**. This God, who is thrice **holy**, can be worshiped only because of the covenant, fulfilled in Jesus Christ, in whom is forgiveness.

REFLECTION AND RESPONSE

1. The psalm exhorts us to "tremble," "quake," "praise," "exalt," and "wor-ship" God as he is known to us in Christ. Before we respond in any other way, we should do this—repeatedly, urgently, emphatically. We do so with hearts filled with gratitude for the priestly intercession of Jesus Christ, which makes worship possible.

---

cloud, he spoke to him first in the sanctuary at Shiloh (1 Sam. 3:1–14), and it may be that he did so from a pillar of cloud from the altar. Tate, *Psalms 51–100*, 530.

22 Many efforts have been made to change this line to make it positive, but none of these is persua-sive or necessary. For discussion, see Hossfeld and Zenger, *Psalms*, 2:484; Tate, *Psalms 51–100*, 527–28. There is assonance between "forgiving" (נֹשֵׂא) and "avenging" (וְנֹקֵם).

2. The threefold acclamation of God's holiness drives us to thank Christ, who has become for us sanctification (1 Cor. 1:30) and without whom the holiness of God would lead us to despair. But it then moves us to "strive for . . . the holiness without which no one will see the Lord" (Heb. 12:14; cf. Matt. 5:48; 1 Pet. 1:15).

3. In a world so tragically spoiled by injustice, Psalm 99:4 brings a deep comfort that at the heart of the universe is a God who loves justice and will establish it through the church in the whole created order when he creates the new heavens and new earth.

4. In Christ we are "a holy priesthood" (1 Pet. 2:5) praying in Jesus's name. The examples of Moses, Aaron, and Samuel are not simply prefigurings of the intercession of Christ; they are examples for us, that we too should devote our hearts to calling on the triune God in Jesus's name, interceding for his lost world.

All people that on earth do dwell,
Sing to the Lord with cheerful voice.
Serve him with joy, his praise forth tell,
Come ye before him and rejoice.

WILLIAM KETHE
Sung to "The Old Hundredth"

This is a prophecy of Christ and says that
the whole world should be joyful.

MARTIN LUTHER
Summaries

An exhortation, short, indeed, but joyful, to praise and celebrate
the name of Christ in the whole earth, and among all nations. For
he who conquers all by his majesty, and offers his beneficence to be
enjoyed by all, deserves to be worshipped and celebrated by all.

JOHANNES BRENZ
In Hengstenberg, *Psalms*

PSALM 100

Psalm 100 is a joyful invitation, given by Jesus Christ, to give thanks for all that God has done for the world. This reflects its canonical context in the light of a wider appreciation for biblical theology. Some of the many ways in which Psalm 100 concludes Psalms 93–99 (or even Pss. 91–99) are mentioned below; these encourage us to appropriate Psalm 100 along the same lines as the preceding psalms, with their joyful motif that the Lord God reigns in Christ. Specifically for Psalm 100, the invitation and call to come into the presence of God finds its fulfillment when Jesus Christ opens for us "the new and living way" (Heb. 10:20) into the presence of God and "bring[s] us to God" (1 Pet. 3:18); it is by Jesus, and only by Jesus, that men and women can accept the invitation of Psalm 100.

That the Lord God has "made us" (the church) and is for us a shepherd (100:3) finds its full meaning when we grasp that Jesus Christ is the head of the church (Col. 1:18), that it is by his atoning death that the Holy Spirit can give new birth (creating and growing the church), and that Jesus is the good shepherd (John 10), the chief shepherd (1 Pet. 5:4), the great shepherd of his people (Heb. 13:20).

The "steadfast love" and "faithfulness" of God (Ps. 100:5) are ours only in Christ (cf. John 1:14, 17) and are ours "forever" and "to all generations" (Ps. 100:5) because Jesus Christ is "the first and the last" (Rev. 1:17), "the same yesterday and today and forever" (Heb. 13:8); because nothing can separate us from his love (Rom. 8:38–39); and because we are chosen in him before the foundation of the world (Eph. 1:4).

When cleansing the temple in Mark 11:17, Jesus cites the prophecy of Isaiah 56:7 that the temple will be "a house of prayer / for all peoples." Alexander Francis Kirkpatrick rightly observes that "the invitation of this Psalm corresponds to the prediction of the prophet."[1] This is what Jesus comes to fulfill through the worldwide mission of his church.

I suggest therefore that we may boldly sing Psalm 100 as words given to us by Christ and in glad thanksgiving for all that God has done for us through Christ.

The clearest echoes from Psalms 93–99 are (1) 100:1, which repeats 98:4a; (2) the very close links between 100:3 and 95:6–7;[2] (3) coming into God's "courts" (96:8; 100:4); (4) "bless his name" (96:2; 100:4); (5) "all the earth" (96:1, 9; 97:5; 100:1); and (6) "steadfast love" with "faithfulness" (92:2; 98:3; 100:5). There may be a thematic echo from the endurance of God's covenant love in 100:5 back to the transience that is such a painful theme of Psalm 90.

THE TEXT

Structure
Both Psalm 100:1–3 and 100:4–5 comprise a call for thanksgiving (100:1–3a, 4–5a) and a reason that follows (100:3b, 5b). Another structural feature worth noting is that there are seven imperatives ("Make a joyful noise," "Serve," "Come," "Know," "Enter," "Give thanks," and "Bless").

Superscription

S   A Psalm for giving thanks.[3]

This unique superscription echoes "Give thanks to him" from Psalm 100:4 and gives us "the sum and scope" of the psalm, which is written "for stirring up the whole church to praise God cheerfully."[4] The verb **giving thanks** may be used for a "thank offering" but here designates thanksgiving and the public declaration of these truths about God in Christ.

---

1 Kirkpatrick, *Psalms*, 3:587.
2 God as Creator of his people, and his people as sheep of his pasture.
3 In Hebrew the superscription is the start of verse 1.
4 Dickson, *Psalms*, 2:194.

100:1–3 Give Thanks for Jesus Christ, the Head of the Church

1   Make a joyful noise to the LORD, all the earth!

2   Serve the LORD with gladness!
        Come into his presence with singing!

In Psalm 100:1–2 each line contains one imperative.[5] **Make a joyful noise** (Lat. *Jubilate*, the title of this psalm sung as a traditional canticle) indicates a loud, glad acclamation, suitable for a King (e.g., "shouted," 1 Sam. 10:24; "shout aloud," in a messianic acclamation, Zech. 9:9). The address to **all the earth** (cf. Pss. 96:1, 9; 97:5, 9; 98:4) is a bold invitation to the whole world to join the church of God; this invitation is given in the gospel of Christ: "The exhortation presupposes the arrival of those mighty events in which occasion is given to the nations of the earth to shout for joy to the Lord, and to salute him joyfully as their king."[6] With characteristic gospel confidence, Augustine writes,

> This command has indeed been heard by all the earth. Already the entire earth is shouting its joy to the Lord; or if any part is not shouting yet, it soon will be, for the blessing is extending to all peoples. The church began from Jerusalem, but as it spreads it overthrows impiety in every place and builds up godliness instead.[7]

In 100:2, **Serve the LORD with gladness!** is very similar to 2:11, with **gladness** qualifying the godly "fear" with which rebels surrender in Psalm 2 to God and his Christ. In the context of this collection of psalms, this verse contrasts with "all worshipers of images" (97:7, using the same Hebrew verb). The verb to **serve** embraces both the concrete obedience of our lives and our corporate worship (in the sense that a corporate worship "service" expresses our whole-life service). **Gladness** describes this service because Christ our King is the one "whose service is perfect freedom."[8] Quoting John 8:31–32 and Galatians 5:13, Augustine writes, "Do not be afraid of

---

5 The wording of Ps. 100:1 is identical to 98:4a and is very similar to 66:1; 95:1–2; 98:6b.

6 Hengstenberg, *Psalms*, 3:200.

7 Augustine, *Psalms*, 5:13–14.

8 Book of Common Prayer, "Collect for Peace."

slavery to this Lord of ours; there will be no complaining among his slaves, no grumbling, no resentment. No one begs to be emancipated from that service, because it is so delightful that all of us have been redeemed."[9]

Come into his presence completes the tricolon, with **singing** continuing the atmosphere of exuberance. We may come into the presence of this holy God (cf. Ps. 99:3, 5, 9) through Christ.

3   Know that the LORD, he is God!
        It is he who made us, and we are his;
        we are his people, and the sheep of his pasture.

Know is the fourth imperative (and perhaps the pivotal of the seven). It includes cognition but also acknowledgment and the response of submission. Some of the most important uses of this verb in similar contexts are Deuteronomy 7:9 ("Know therefore that the LORD your God is God"); Psalm 46:10 ("Be still, and know that I am God"); and the new covenant prophecy of Jeremiah 31:34, in which knowing the covenant Lord will be the birthright, by the Holy Spirit, of all God's people. The statement **that the LORD, he** (emphatic) **is God!** means that he, the covenant Lord, and he alone, is the true God (cf. 1 Kings 18:39). To grasp not simply that there is some kind of deity but that the revealed covenant Lord of the Scriptures is the true God is an integral part of true conversion. When God became incarnate, only the Holy Spirit enabled disciples to grasp this wonder.

The remainder of Psalm 100:3 gives the first motivation to accept the gracious invitation of Christ. **It is he** (emphatic) **who made us**—that is, he created his people (see on "our Maker" in 95:6), which he did in and through Christ. John Calvin writes of "that spiritual regeneration by which he created anew his image in his elect."[10] There is some uncertainty about the words **and we are his**; some translations have "and not we ourselves." Either is possible, although, in the light of the final line and the parallel with 95:6–7, the translation **and we are his** is perhaps more likely.[11] **We are his people,**

9   Augustine, *Psalms*, 5:18.
10   Calvin, *Psalms*, 4:84.
11   In the MT the kethib reads, "He made us and not we" (reading לֹא, "not"), while the kere suggests, "He made us and we are his" (reading לוֹ, "to him" or "his"). Both are true. For discussion and

and the sheep of his pasture is very similar to 95:7. In the combination of kingly possession and the pastoral image, Theodoret of Cyrus notes that "he indicated not only his lordship but also his care."[12]

Only in Christ is this invitation given to "all the earth" (100:1).

100:4–5 Give Thanks for Jesus Christ, Whose Love Endures Forever

4   Enter his gates with thanksgiving,
     and his courts with praise!
     Give thanks to him; bless his name!

Psalm 100:4 contains the remaining three imperatives. **Enter** uses the same verb translated "come" in 100:2. The **gates** (cf. 122:2) and **courts** (cf. 65:4; 84:10; 96:8) indicate the privilege of entering the old covenant temple. This is—astonishingly—offered to "all the earth." It should be no surprise that there is to be **thanksgiving, praise,** and the giving of **thanks,** for as Derek Kidner observes, "The simplicity of this invitation may conceal the wonder of it."[13] This old covenant promise is fulfilled in the new covenant as "a great multitude that no one could number, from every nation, from all tribes and peoples and languages," stands "before the throne and before the Lamb" (Rev. 7:9). These will **bless his name** (cf. Pss. 91:14; 92:1; 96:2, 8; 97:12; 99:3, 6), the covenantal revelation of himself that is fulfilled in Christ, lifting high the name of Jesus.

5   For the LORD is good;
     his steadfast love endures forever,
     and his faithfulness to all generations.

Psalm 100:5, beginning with **for,** and paralleling 100:3b, gives the second great motivation for all the earth to hear and accept this gracious invitation of Christ. The language is strongly covenantal (the name of the covenant **LORD,** the designation **good,** and the attributes of **steadfast**

---

differing opinions, see, e.g., Tate, *Psalms 51–100,* 533–34; Harman, *Psalms,* 2:720; Hengstenberg, *Psalms,* 3:201.

12   Theodoret of Cyrus, *Psalms,* 2:145.

13   Kidner, *Psalms,* 2:357.

love and **faithfulness**), all fulfilled in Jesus Christ. This language echoes the gracious aftermath to the episode of the golden calf, especially Exodus 34:6.[14] It is language that we hear much in later psalms (notably the refrain of Ps. 136).

The emphasis rests on the timeless endurance of such covenant love, in the word **forever** and the phrase **to all generations**, guaranteed to us in Jesus.

REFLECTION AND RESPONSE

1. Since this is a psalm for giving thanks, the clear and primary response ought to be that we give thanks—gladly, corporately, and exuberantly. Singing the psalm itself helps us do this. And as Augustine delightfully suggests, "Your songs of praise are like eating: the more you praise, the more strength you acquire, and the more delightful does he become whom you are praising."[15] In history the church of Christ has sung "The Old Hundredth" often and regularly. We must not lose it today.

2. Psalm 100:3 leads us to a deep and profitable meditation on Christ as the one through whom the triune God has created his people. The fact that Christ has made us means that we belong to him, that he is our good, chief, and great shepherd. "What a passionately loving shepherd we have!" exclaims Augustine. "He left the ninety-nine and came down to search for this one."[16] There is no limit to the comfort that flows from this truth.

3. In a similar vein, there is abundant comfort from a slow pondering of Psalm 100:5, not least in seeing how Christ makes the Father known to us as perfectly good and gives us a steadfast covenant love that is unchanging and unending.

4. Ernst Wilhelm Hengstenberg speaks of the sacred writers of old preparing "for themselves ladders out of the glorious deeds of God in times past, on which they ascended to joyful hope in regard to the future." They did this, for example, by starting with the exodus or the grace of God after the golden calf and looking forward to the coming of the Messiah. We have

---

14 In Ex. 33:19 the goodness of the covenant Lord is associated with the revelation of his "name" to Moses.

15 Augustine, *Psalms*, 5:28.

16 Augustine, *Psalms*, 5:27.

much deeper grounds than they do for hope, for we look back to the first coming of Christ, his incarnation, earthly ministry, atoning death, resurrection, and ascension. Our ladders of hope ought to be by far stronger than theirs. If we only followed their example, Hengstenberg continues, "we would not feel so often dispirited."[17]

---

17 Hengstenberg, *Psalms*, 3:200–201.

EPIGRAPH SOURCES

SOURCE INFORMATION FOR THE EPIGRAPHS is provided here in short-ened citations, listing out the sources in the order of quotations at the heads of each chapter. For the full bibliographic information for these sources, see the bibliography.

Psalm 51

Augustine, *Psalms*, 2:414.

Chalmers, in Spurgeon, *Treasury*, 1.2:408.

Delitzsch, *Psalms*, 2:134–35.

Psalm 52

Athanasius, *Marcellinus*, 20.

Longman, *Psalms*, 225.

Eveson, *Psalms*, 1:332.

Psalm 53

Athanasius, *Marcellinus*, 16.

Augustine, *Psalms*, 3:32.

Selnecker, *Whole Psalter*, in *RCS* 7:396.

Psalm 54

Athanasius, *Marcellinus*, 12.

William Hill Tucker (fl. 1890s), in Spurgeon, *Treasury*, 1.2:442.

Psalm 55

Theodoret of Cyrus, *Psalms*, 1:314.

Bonar, *Psalms*, 169.

Spurgeon, *Treasury*, 1.2:445.

Psalm 56

Athanasius, *Marcellinus*, 20.

Augustine, *Psalms*, 3:84.

Bonar, *Psalms*, 173.

Psalm 57

Cassiodorus, *Psalms*, 2:44.

The Venerable Bede, *Homilies on the Gospels*, 2.15, in *ACCS* 8:31–32.

Selnecker, *Whole Psalter*, in *RCS* 7:413.

Bonar, *Psalms*, 175.

Psalm 58

Augustine, *Psalms*, 3:123.

Bonar, *Psalms*, 179.

Psalm 59

Luther, *First Lectures on the Psalms*, in *Luther's Works*, 10:272.

Selnecker, *Whole Psalter*, in *RCS* 7:422.

Bonar, *Psalms*, 180.

Eveson, *Psalms*, 1:363.

Psalm 60

Dickson, *Psalms*, 1:355.

Hamilton, *Psalms*, 1:555.

Psalm 61

Dickson, *Psalms*, 1:361.

Eveson, *Psalms*, 1:376.

Psalm 62

Calvin, *Psalms*, 2:416–17.

Eveson, *Psalms*, 1:379.

Psalm 63

Athanasius, *Marcellinus*, 20.

John Chrysostom, quoted in Kirkpatrick, *Psalms*, 2:353.

Bonar, *Psalms*, 189.

Psalm 64

Augustine, *Psalms*, 3:247.

Jerome, in Neale and Littledale, *Psalms*, 2:298.
Cassiodorus, *Psalms*, 2:91.
Eveson, *Psalms*, 1:389.

Psalm 65
Bonar, *Psalms*, 194.

Psalm 66
Dickson, *Psalms*, 1:387.
Hamilton, *Psalms*, 1:588.

Psalm 67
Theodoret of Cyrus, *Psalms*, 1:377.
Cassiodorus, *Psalms*, 2:120–21.
Calvin, *Psalms*, 3:1–2.

Psalm 68
Justin Martyr, *Dialogue with Trypho*, 39.4 (cf. 87.6).
Calvin, *Psalms*, 3:4–5.

Psalm 69
Athanasius, *Marcellinus*, 26.
Luther, *First Lectures on the Psalms*, in *Luther's Works*, 10:351.
Spurgeon, *Treasury*, 2.1:175.

Psalm 70
Augustine, *Psalms*, 3:402.
Book of Common Prayer, "Order for Evening Prayer," mentioned by Eveson, *Psalms*, 1:428.
Spurgeon composed four verses of a metrical version of Ps. 70, of which the stanza at the chapter head is the first; see Spurgeon, *Treasury*, 2.1:204.

Psalm 71
Tertullian, *Against Praxeas*, 11, in *ACCS* 8:92. Tertullian writes in the context of opposition to modalist Monarchianism, which denies the distinct persons of the Holy Trinity.
Book of Common Prayer, "Order for the Visitation of the Sick."
Dickson, *Psalms*, 1:434–35.

Psalm 72
Watts, "Jesus Shall Reign" (1719), inspired by Ps. 72. Public domain.

James Montgomery (1771–1854), "Hail to the Lord's Anointed" (1821), inspired by Ps. 72. Public domain.

Dickson, *Psalms*, 1:437.

Psalm 73

Athanasius, *Marcellinus*, 21.

Calvin, *Psalms*, 3:121–22.

Dickson, *Psalms*, 1:445.

Psalm 74

Calvin, *Psalms*, 3:158.

Bonar, *Psalms*, 223.

Spurgeon, *Treasury*, 2.1:272.

Psalm 75

Augustine, *Psalms*, 4:38.

Cassiodorus, *Psalms*, 2:225.

Calvin, *Psalms*, 3:182.

Psalm 76

Dickson, *Psalms*, 1:477.

Jeremy Taylor (1613–1667), "Collect for Psalm 76," *Works*, 15:149–50, in *RCS* 8:26.

Psalm 77

Augustus M. Toplady (1740–1778), "A Sovereign Protector I Have" (1774), in Eveson, *Psalms*, 2:45. Public domain.

Bonar, *Psalms*, 229–30.

Spurgeon, *Treasury*, 2.1:312. With his own history of dark moods, Spurgeon understood well the deep feelings expressed in this psalm.

Psalm 78

Luther, *First Lectures on the Psalms*, in *Luther's Works*, 11:38. Luther says this when reflecting on the quotation of Ps. 78:2 in Matt. 13:35.

Bonar, *Psalms*, 235.

Psalm 79

Athanasius, *Marcellinus*, 21.

Dickson, *Psalms*, 2:29.

Psalm 80

Theodoret of Cyrus, *Psalms*, 2:45.

Eveson, *Psalms*, 2:70.

Psalm 81

Bonar, *Psalms*, 242.

Bonhoeffer, *Prayerbook of the Bible*, 167.

Psalm 82

Athanasius, *Marcellinus*, 8.

Hengstenberg, *Psalms*, 3:32.

Psalm 83

Calvin, *Psalms*, 3:337.

Psalm 84

Augustine, *Psalms*, 4:187.

Lancelot Andrewes (1555–1626), "Sermon on Luke 11:2," in *RCS* 8:82.

Bonar, *Psalms*, 249.

Psalm 85

Kirkpatrick, *Psalms*, 2:511.

Psalm 86

Luther, *Summaries*, in *RCS* 8:88.

Calvin, *Psalms*, 3:379.

Psalm 87

Augustine, *Psalms*, 4:246.

Calvin, *Psalms*, 3:393.

Bonhoeffer, *Prayerbook of the Bible*, 167.

John Newton (1725–1807), "Glorious Things of Thee Are Spoken" (1779).
   Public domain.

Psalm 88

Athanasius, *Marcellinus*, 7.

Augustine, *Psalms*, 4:258.

Book of Common Prayer, "Order for the Burial of the Dead."

Dickson, *Psalms*, 2:97.

Hamilton, *Psalms*, 2:124.

Psalm 89

Augustine, *Psalms*, 4:273.

Dickson, *Psalms*, 2:126.

S. J. Stone (1839–1900), "The Church's One Foundation" (1866). Public domain.

Psalm 90

Walter Chalmers Smith (1824–1908), "Immortal, Invisible, God Only Wise" (1867). Public domain.

Jerome, *Homilies on the Psalms*, 19, in *ACCS* 8:167.

Virgil (70–19 BC), *Georgics*, 3.66, quoted in Luther, *Luther's Works*, 13:103.

Augustine, "Sermon 359.9," in *ACCS* 8:167.

Psalm 91

Lyte, "There Is a Safe and Secret Place" (1834). Public domain.

Eveson, *Psalms*, 2:148.

Psalm 92

Calvin, *Psalms*, 3:492.

Eveson, *Psalms*, 2:154.

Psalm 93

Athanasius, *Marcellinus*, 23.

Bonar, *Psalms*, 283.

Psalm 94

Hieronymus Weller von Molsdorf (1499–1572), *Interpretation of Some Psalms*, in *RCS* 8:130.

Motyer, *Psalms*, 548.

Psalm 95

Luther, *Summaries*, in Luther, *Luther's Works*, 38:50, in *RCS* 8:134.

Watts, "Come, Let Our Voices Join to Raise" (1719), one of at least three hymns he wrote based on Ps. 95. Public domain.

Spurgeon, *Treasury*, 2.2:164.

Psalm 96

Pellikan, *Commentary on the Bible*, in *RCS* 8:139.

Spurgeon, *Treasury*, 2.2:180.

Psalm 97

Augustine, *Psalms*, 4:439.

Calvin, *Psalms*, 4:59.

Josiah Conder (1789–1855), "The Lord Is King! Lift Up Thy Voice" (1836). Public domain.

Psalm 98

Theodoret of Cyrus, *Psalms*, 2:136.

Dickson, *Psalms*, 2:185.

Watts, "Joy to the World" (1719), verse 2, based on Ps. 98. Public domain.

Psalm 99

Calvin, *Psalms*, 4:78.

Dickson, *Psalms*, 2:189.

Psalm 100

William Kethe (d. 1594), sung to "The Old Hundredth." The other well-known metrical version is Isaac Watts, "Before Jehovah's Aweful Throne."

Luther, *Summaries*, in *RCS* 8:152.

Johannes Brenz (1499–1570), quoted in Hengstenberg, *Psalms*, 3:199.

BIBLIOGRAPHY

Adams, James E. *War Psalms of the Prince of Peace: Lessons from the Imprecatory Psalms*. Phillipsburg, NJ: P&R, 1991.

Alter, Robert. *The Art of Biblical Poetry*. Rev. ed. New York: Basic Books, 2011.

Alter, Robert. *The Book of Psalms: A Translation with Commentary*. New York: Norton, 2007.

Anderson, A. A. *The Book of Psalms*. 2 vols. New Century Bible. London: Oliphants, 1972.

Ash, Christopher. *Bible Delight: Heartbeat of the Word of God; Psalm 119 for the Bible Teacher and Bible Hearer*. Fearn, Ross-shire, Scotland: Christian Focus, 2008.

Ash, Christopher. *Job: The Wisdom of the Cross*. Preaching the Word. Wheaton, IL: Crossway, 2014.

Ash, Christopher. *Psalms for You: How to Pray, How to Feel, and How to Sing*. Epsom, UK: Good Book, 2020.

Ash, Christopher. *Remaking a Broken World: The Heart of the Bible Story*. Rev. ed. [Epsom, UK]: Good Book, 2019.

Ash, Christopher. *Teaching Psalms: From Text to Message*. 2 vols. Fearn, Ross-shire, Scotland: Christian Focus, 2017–2018.

Ash, Christopher, and Steve Midgley. *The Heart of Anger: How the Bible Transforms Anger in Our Understanding and Experience*. Wheaton, IL: Crossway, 2021.

Athanasius. *The Life of Antony and the Letter to Marcellinus*. Translated by Robert C. Gregg. Classics of Western Spirituality. London: SPCK, 1980.

Augustine. *Expositions of the Psalms*. Translated by Maria Boulding. Edited by John E. Rotelle and Boniface Ramsey. 6 vols. New York: New City Press, 2000.

Beale, G. K. *The Book of Revelation: A Commentary on the Greek Text*. New International Greek Testament Commentary. Grand Rapids, MI: Eerdmans, 1999.

Beale, G. K. *The Temple and the Church's Mission: A Biblical Theology of the Dwelling Place of God*. New Studies in Biblical Theology 17. Downers Grove, IL: InterVarsity Press, 2004.

Beale, G. K., and D. A. Carson, eds. *Commentary on the New Testament Use of the Old Testament*. Grand Rapids, MI: Baker Academic, 2007.

Belcher, Richard P., Jr. *The Messiah and the Psalms: Preaching Christ from All the Psalms*. Fearn, Ross-Shire, Scotland: Mentor, 2006.

Berlin, Adele. *The Dynamics of Biblical Parallelism*. Rev. ed. Grand Rapids, MI: Eerdmans, 2008.

Blaising, Craig A., and Carmen S. Hardin, eds. *Psalms 1–50*. Old Testament vol. 7 of *Ancient Christian Commentary on Scripture*. Downers Grove, IL: IVP Academic, 2008.

Bonar, Andrew A. *Christ and His Church in the Book of Psalms*. London: J. Nisbet, 1859.

Bonhoeffer, Dietrich. *Life Together; Prayerbook of the Bible*. Edited by Geffrey B. Kelly. Translated by Daniel W. Bloesch and James H. Burtness. Vol. 5 of *Dietrich Bonhoeffer Works*. Minneapolis: Fortress, 2005.

Briggs, Charles Augustus, and Emilie Grace Briggs. *A Critical and Exegetical Commentary on the Book of Psalms*. 2 vols. International Critical Commentary. Edinburgh: T&T Clark, 1906.

Brueggemann, Walter. *Israel's Praise: Doxology against Idolatry and Ideology*. Philadelphia: Fortress, 1989.

Brueggemann, Walter. *The Message of the Psalms: A Theological Commentary*. Augsburg Old Testament Studies. Minneapolis: Augsburg, 1984.

Brueggemann, Walter. *Praying the Psalms*. A Pace Book. Winona, MN: Saint Mary's Press, 1982.

Brueggemann, Walter, and William H. Bellinger Jr. *Psalms*. New Cambridge Bible Commentary. Cambridge: Cambridge University Press, 2014.

Bunyan, John. *The Pilgrim's Progress*. Edinburgh: Banner of Truth, 1977.

Calvin, John. *Commentary on the Book of Psalms*. Translated by James Anderson. 5 vols. In *Calvin's Commentaries*. Grand Rapids, MI: Baker, 1993.

Cassiodorus. *Explanation of the Psalms*. Translated and edited by P. G. Walsh. 3 vols. Ancient Christian Writers 51–53. New York: Paulist, 1990–1991.

Chalmers, Thomas. *The Expulsive Power of a New Affection.* Crossway Short Classics. Wheaton, IL: Crossway, 2020.

Cole, Robert Luther. *The Shape and Message of Book III (Psalms 73–89).* Journal for the Study of the Old Testament Supplement Series 307. Sheffield: Sheffield Academic Press, 2000.

Dahood, Mitchell. *Psalms.* 3 vols. Anchor Bible. New York: Doubleday, 1965.

Davidson, Robert. *The Vitality of Worship: A Commentary on the Book of Psalms.* Grand Rapids, MI: Eerdmans, 1998.

DeClaissé-Walford, Nancy L., Rolf A. Jacobson, and Beth LaNeel Tanner. *The Book of Psalms.* New International Commentary on the Old Testament. Grand Rapids, MI: Eerdmans, 2014.

Delitzsch, F. *Biblical Commentary on the Psalms.* Translated by Francis Bolton. Clark's Foreign Theological Library, 4th ser., vols. 29–31. Edinburgh: T&T Clark, 1892.

Dickson, David. *A Commentary on the Psalms.* 2 vols. London: Banner of Truth, 1959.

Eaton, J. H. *Kingship and the Psalms.* Studies in Biblical Theology. 2nd ser., vol. 32. London: SCM, 1976.

Eveson, Philip. *Psalms: From Suffering to Glory.* 2 vols. Welwyn Commentary Series. Darlington, UK: EP Books, 2014–2015.

Ferguson, Sinclair B. "'Blessèd Assurance, Jesus Is Mine'? Definite Atonement and the Cure of Souls." In *From Heaven He Came and Sought Her: Definite Atonement in Historical, Biblical, Theological, and Pastoral Perspective*, edited by David Gibson and Jonathan Gibson, 607–31. Wheaton, IL: Crossway, 2013.

Ferguson, Sinclair B. *Deserted by God?* Edinburgh: Banner of Truth, 1993.

Gillingham, Susan. *Psalms through the Centuries.* 3 vols. Wiley-Blackwell Bible Commentaries. Malden, MA: Wiley-Blackwell, 2008–2022.

Goldingay, John. *Psalms.* 3 vols. Baker Commentary on the Old Testament Wisdom and Psalms. Grand Rapids, MI: Baker Academic, 2006–2008.

Greidanus, Sidney. *Preaching Christ from Psalms: Foundations for Expository Sermons in the Christian Year.* Grand Rapids, MI: Eerdmans, 2016.

Grogan, Geoffrey W. *Psalms.* Two Horizons Old Testament Commentary. Grand Rapids, MI: Eerdmans, 2008.

Gunkel, Hermann. *Introduction to Psalms: The Genres of the Religious Lyric of Israel.* Edited by Joachim Begrich. Translated by James D. Nogalski. Macon, GA: Mercer University Press, 1998.

Hamilton, James M., Jr. *Psalms*. 2 vols. Evangelical Biblical Theology Commentary. Bellingham, WA: Lexham, 2021.

Harman, Allan. *Psalms*. 2 vols. A Mentor Commentary. Fearn, Ross-Shire, Scotland: Mentor, 2011.

Hays, Richard B. *Echoes of Scripture in the Letters of Paul*. New Haven, CT: Yale University Press, 1989.

Hengstenberg, E. W. *Commentary on the Psalms*. Translated by P. Fairbairn and J. Thomson. 3 vols. Clark's Foreign Theological Library 1–2, 12. Edinburgh: T&T Clark, 1845.

Holladay, William L. *The Psalms through Three Thousand Years: Prayerbook of a Cloud of Witnesses*. Minneapolis: Fortress, 1993.

Horne, George. *A Commentary on the Book of Psalms*. London: Longman, Brown, 1843.

Hossfeld, Frank Lothar, and Erich Zenger. *Psalms*. Translated by Linda M. Maloney. Edited by Klaus Baltzer. 3 vols. Hermeneia. Minneapolis: Fortress, 2005–2011.

Justin Martyr. *The First Apology; Dialogue with Trypho*. Translated by Thomas B. Falls. Revised by Thomas P. Halton. Edited by Michael Slusser. Fathers of the Church 6. Washington, DC: Catholic University of America Press, 2003.

Keel, Othmar. *The Symbolism of the Biblical World: Ancient Near Eastern Iconography and the Book of Psalms*. Translated by Timothy J. Hallett. Winona Lake, IN: Eisenbrauns, 1997.

Ker, John. *The Psalms in History and Biography*. Leopold Classic Library. Edinburgh: Andrew Elliot, 1886.

Kidner, Derek. *Psalms*. 2 vols. Tyndale Old Testament Commentaries. London: Inter-Varsity Press, 1973.

Kirkpatrick, A. F. *The Book of Psalms: With Introduction and Notes*. 3 vols. Cambridge Bible for Schools and Colleges 20. Cambridge: Cambridge University Press, 1892.

Kraus, Hans-Joachim. *Psalms*. Translated by Hilton C. Oswald. 2 vols. Continental Commentaries. Minneapolis: Fortress, 1993.

Kraus, Hans-Joachim. *Theology of the Psalms*. Translated by Keith Crim. Minneapolis: Augsburg, 1986.

Lane, Eric. *Psalms 90–150: The Lord Reigns*. Focus on the Bible. Fearn, Ross-shire, Scotland: Christian Focus, 2006.

LeFebvre, Michael. *Singing the Songs of Jesus: Revisiting the Psalms*. Fearn, Ross-shire, Scotland: Christian Focus, 2010.

Lewis, C. S. *Reflections on the Psalms*. London: Fount, 1977.

Longman, Tremper, III. *Psalms*. Tyndale Old Testament Commentaries. Downers Grove, IL: InterVarsity Press, 2014.

Luther, Martin. *Luther's Works*. Edited by Jaroslav Pelikan. Vol. 10, *First Lectures on Psalms I (Pss. 1–75)*. Saint Louis, MO: Concordia, 1974.

Luther, Martin. *Luther's Works*. Edited by Jaroslav Pelikan. Vol. 11, *First Lectures on Psalms II (Pss. 76–150)*. Saint Louis, MO: Concordia, 1976.

Luther, Martin. *Luther's Works*. Edited by Jaroslav Pelikan. Vol. 12, *Selected Psalms I*. Saint Louis, MO: Concordia, 1955.

Luther, Martin. *Luther's Works*. Edited by Jaroslav Pelikan. Vol. 13, *Selected Psalms II*. Saint Louis, MO: Concordia, 1956.

Luther, Martin. *Luther's Works*. Edited by Jaroslav Pelikan. Vol. 14, *Selected Psalms III*. Saint Louis, MO: Concordia, 1958.

Mays, J. L. *Psalms*. Interpretation: A Bible Commentary for Teaching and Preaching. Louisville: John Knox, 1994.

Millar, J. Gary. *Calling on the Name of the Lord: A Biblical Theology of Prayer*. New Studies in Biblical Theology 38. Downers Grove, IL: InterVarsity Press, 2016.

Miller, Patrick D. *Interpreting the Psalms*. Philadelphia: Fortress, 1988.

Motyer, J. A. *The Psalms*. In *New Bible Commentary*, 21st century ed., edited by G. J. Wenham, J. A. Motyer, D. A. Carson, and R. T. France, 485–583. Leicester, UK: Inter-Varsity Press, 1994.

Mowinckel, Sigmund. *The Psalms in Israel's Worship*. Translated by D. R. Ap-Thomas. New York: Abingdon, 1967.

Naselli, Andrew David. *The Serpent and the Serpent Slayer*. SSBT. Wheaton, IL: Crossway, 2020.

Neale, J. M., and R. F. Littledale. *A Commentary on the Psalms from Primitive and Medieval Writers and from the Various Office-Books and Hymns of the Roman, Mozarabic, Ambrosian, Gallican, Greek, Coptic, Armenian, and Syriac Rites*. 2nd ed. 4 vols. London: Joseph Masters, 1869–1874.

Prinsloo, W. S. "Psalm 95: If Only You Will Listen to His Voice!" In *The Bible in Human Society*, edited by M. Daniel Carroll R., David J. A. Clines, and Philip R. Davies, 393–41. Sheffield: Sheffield Academic Press, 1995.

Robertson, O. Palmer. *The Flow of the Psalms: Discovering Their Structure and Theology*. Phillipsburg, NJ: P&R, 2015.

Ross, Allen P. *A Commentary on the Psalms*. 3 vols. Kregel Exegetical Library. Grand Rapids, MI: Kregel, 2011–2016.

Ross, Michael F. *The Light of the Psalms: Deepening Your Faith with Every Psalm*. Fearn, Ross-shire, Scotland: Christian Focus, 2006.

Schreiner, Thomas R. *Romans*. Baker Exegetical Commentary on the New Testament. Grand Rapids, MI: Baker Academic, 1998.

Selderhuis, Herman J., ed. *Psalms 1–72*. Old Testament vol. 7 of *Reformation Commentary on Scripture*. Downers Grove, IL: IVP Academic, 2015.

Selderhuis, Herman J., ed. *Psalms 73–150*. Old Testament vol. 8 of *Reformation Commentary on Scripture*. Downers Grove, IL: IVP Academic, 2018.

Shead, Andrew G., ed. *Stirred by a Noble Theme: The Book of Psalms in the Life of the Church*. Nottingham, UK: Apollos, 2013.

Spurgeon, Charles H. *The Treasury of David*. 3 vols. Peabody, MA: Hendrickson, 2016.

Tate, Marvin E. *Psalms 51–100*. Word Biblical Commentary 20. Grand Rapids, MI: Zondervan Academic, 2018.

Theodoret of Cyrus. *Commentary on the Psalms*. Translated by Robert C. Hill. 2 vols. Fathers of the Church 101–102. Washington, DC: Catholic University of America Press, 2000.

Tucker, W. Dennis, Jr., and Jamie A. Grant. *Psalms*. Vol. 2. NIV Application Commentary. Grand Rapids, MI: Zondervan, 2018.

VanGemeren, Willem A. *Psalms*. Vol. 5 of *The Expositor's Bible Commentary*, edited by Tremper Longman III and David E. Garland. Rev. ed. Grand Rapids, MI: Zondervan, 2008.

Waltke, Bruce K., and James M. Houston. *The Psalms as Christian Worship: A Historical Commentary*. With Erika Moore. Grand Rapids, MI: Eerdmans, 2010.

Waltke, Bruce K., James M. Houston, and Erika Moore. *The Psalms as Christian Lament: A Historical Commentary*. Grand Rapids, MI: Eerdmans, 2014.

Weiser, Artur. *The Psalms: A Commentary*. Old Testament Library. London: SCM, 1962.

Wesselschmidt, Quentin F., ed. *Psalms 51–150*. Old Testament vol. 8 of *Ancient Christian Commentary on Scripture*. Downers Grove, IL: IVP Academic, 2007.

Whitney, Donald S. *Praying the Bible*. Wheaton, IL: Crossway, 2015.

Wilcock, Michael. *The Message of the Psalms: Songs for the People of God*. 2 vols. Bible Speaks Today. Leicester, UK: Inter-Varsity Press, 2001.

Wilson, Gerald Henry. *The Editing of the Hebrew Psalter*. Society of Biblical Literature Dissertation Series 76. Chico, CA: Scholars Press, 1985.

Wilson, Gerald Henry. *Psalms*. Vol. 1. NIV Application Commentary. Grand Rapids, MI: Zondervan, 2002.

Witherington, Ben, III. *Psalms Old and New: Exegesis, Intertextuality, and Hermeneutics*. Minneapolis: Fortress, 2017.

Woodhouse, John. "Reading the Psalms as Christian Scripture." In *Stirred by a Noble Theme: The Book of Psalms in the Life of the Church*, edited by Andrew G. Shead, 46–73. Nottingham, UK: Apollos, 2013.

SUBJECT INDEX

Aaron, 336, 345
  as intercessor, 646
  priesthood of, 648
Aaronic blessing, 202, 205
Abaddon, 491, 497
"Abide with Me" (hymn), 538
abiding, 551
Abishai, 116
Abraham
  covenant with, 83
  seed of, 325
Abrahamic covenant blessing, 276, 610, 632
Absalom, rebellion of, 127, 129, 135, 139,
    149, 156, 170, 465n3
abundance, 10, 29, 178, 181–82, 188, 193,
    361, 494, 556
abusive pastors, 37n9
adder, 91
Adonai, 245
Adonijah, 254n3
adoption, 604
adversaries, 57, 68, 369. *See also* enemies
affliction, 287
  days of, 541
  prayer of, 501–2
Agag, 435
aging, 253, 254–55, 258, 260, 262, 538
"Aha!," 248
Ahab, 220
Ahimelech, 23–24, 31
Ahithophel, 49
all generations, 509, 533, 534, 651, 656
"all the earth," 189, 190, 430, 438, 607, 608,
    610, 614, 622, 625, 627, 636, 653, 655
"all the upright," 162, 170

Amalek, 434–35
Amalekites, 439
"Amen," 509n14, 524
Ammon, 430, 434–35
Ammonites, 380, 435
Ananias and Sapphira, 28
angels, 361, 554
  worshiping the Son, 621
angels of destruction, 366
anger of God, 302, 375, 394, 537, 539, 564
anguish, 52
anointed King, 447
another generation, 253, 260
anthropomorphism, 102–3, 364, 369, 575
antichrist, 24, 28
Antiochus IV Epiphanes, 299n1
Aram-naharaim, 115
Aram-zobah, 115
arise, 210
"Arise, O God," 424
ark of the covenant, 305, 636n18, 643, 645
  brought up to Mount Zion, 208, 210–11,
    217–18, 222, 368
  brought to Jerusalem, 609
  captured by the Philistines, 368
  resting of, 603
  in the wilderness, 214
arm of God, 513
arrogance, 584
arrows, 165, 326–27, 344
  blunted, 93
Asaph, 3, 137, 283, 350, 421, 493
  celebrates nearness with God, 292–93
  functions as a prophet, 403
  as man in Christ, 296

NAME INDEX

Alexander, Thomas, 19n73

Alter, Robert, 16n60, 25n14, 29n40, 51n15,
54n21, 77n8, 78n18, 89n9, 95n33,
106n25, 191n16, 246n3, 257n16,
269n18, 273nn27–28, 341n24,
362n43, 367n53, 396n18, 418n5, 466,
535n25, 537n32, 539n43, 542n52,
553n23, 574n3, 583n8, 612n17, 628,
637

Anderson, A. A., 26n18, 389n1, 418n5

Andrewes, Lancelot, 440

Ash, Christopher, 457n14, 491n8

Athanasius, 22, 38, 62, 146, 197, 226, 265,
416, 488, 572

Augustine, xviii, 4, 10–11n30, 15, 18, 20,
23n2, 26, 28, 29n35, 29n39, 31–32,
34, 39n1, 40–41, 46, 54n19, 56n28, 62,
63, 78, 79, 81, 83, 84, 85n38, 86, 91,
99n1, 101, 104, 109, 127n1, 130, 131,
132, 133, 140n24, 141, 144, 150n13,
151, 152n20, 155n28, 160, 167,
176, 177n24, 193, 195n32, 196, 197,
202n14, 205, 212, 218n31, 223, 231,
234, 244, 249n15, 250, 258, 262, 266,
269n19, 270, 290, 294n26, 295–96,
314, 321, 325n9, 326n11, 337n6,
354, 357, 361, 362n44, 363n46, 397,
409n19, 417n2, 422n18, 424, 431, 433,
438, 440, 448, 456, 458–59, 460, 465,
469n20, 469n22, 470, 472, 473n34,
475n40, 476, 478, 482n15, 483n18,
484, 486, 488, 490, 494n24, 495n30,
501, 504, 510n19, 516n33, 518n39,
520, 526nn60–61, 528, 541, 552, 553,
556, 564, 571, 575n8, 587, 591n33,
592, 598, 600, 603, 611n13, 620, 621,
634n12, 638n22, 653–54, 656

Basil the Great, 124n40

Beale, G. K., 30n42, 320n16, 472n30,
506n4, 559n1

Bede, the Venerable, 23n4, 74, 101n9

Belcher, Richard P., Jr., 6n7, 7n12, 218n27,
283n2, 284n4, 507n8, 547n2, 548n5,
549n9, 555n35

Bernard of Clairvaux, 147n2

Blomberg, Craig L., 351nn7–8

Bonar, Andrew A., 6n6, 19n72, 48, 62,
74, 86, 98, 146, 165n19, 172, 174n5,
183, 202n16, 218, 230n12, 231n19,
255n6, 257n12, 269n18, 286n12, 298,
334, 345–46, 348, 402, 440, 461n25,
471n26, 530n2, 561n4, 572, 593, 617,
628n27

Bonhoeffer, Dietrich, 150n13, 157, 158,
231n19, 402, 469n22, 478, 489–90,
608n3, 633

Brenz, Johannes, 650

Brueggemann, Walter, 467n13

Bucer, Martin, 569

Bugenhagen, Johannes, 483n20

Bunyan, John, 490

Calvin, John, 11n33, 12n42, 14, 15n56,
18, 20n76, 35, 44–46, 54n20, 67n18,
72–73, 83, 85, 90, 107, 116n12, 133,
134, 138, 139n21, 142, 157, 168,
176n20, 177n22, 187n2, 189, 198,
202n14, 202n20, 206, 207n2, 213n21,
218n32, 224, 231n18, 232n21,

SCRIPTURE INDEX

References to the book of Psalms as a whole have been omitted from the Scripture index, as have individual references to an entire psalm when they occur within a chapter treating that psalm (though an entry for the chapter is included). Also omitted are references in notes about versification differences in Hebrew (such as when the Hebrew begins verse numbering with the superscription). References here reflect English version numbering.